Development Centre Studies

Policy Coherence Towards East Asia

DEVELOPMENT CHALLENGES FOR OECD COUNTRIES

Edited by
Kiichiro Fukasaku, Masahiro Kawai, Michael G. Plummer, Alexandra Trzeciak-Duval

DEVELOPMENT CENTRE OF THE ORGANISATION FOR ECONOMIC CO-OPERATION AND DEVELOPMENT

ORGANISATION FOR ECONOMIC CO-OPERATION AND DEVELOPMENT

The OECD is a unique forum where the governments of 30 democracies work together to address the economic, social and environmental challenges of globalisation. The OECD is also at the forefront of efforts to understand and to help governments respond to new developments and concerns, such as corporate governance, the information economy and the challenges of an ageing population. The Organisation provides a setting where governments can compare policy experiences, seek answers to common problems, identify good practice and work to co-ordinate domestic and international policies.

The OECD member countries are: Australia, Austria, Belgium, Canada, the Czech Republic, Denmark, Finland, France, Germany, Greece, Hungary, Iceland, Ireland, Italy, Japan, Korea, Luxembourg, Mexico, the Netherlands, New Zealand, Norway, Poland, Portugal, the Slovak Republic, Spain, Sweden, Switzerland, Turkey, the United Kingdom and the United States. The Commission of the European Communities takes part in the work of the OECD.

OECD Publishing disseminates widely the results of the Organisation's statistics gathering and research on economic, social and environmental issues, as well as the conventions, guidelines and standards agreed by its members.

THE DEVELOPMENT CENTRE

The Development Centre of the Organisation for Economic Co-operation and Development was established by decision of the OECD Council on 23 October 1962 and comprises 20 member countries of the OECD: Austria, Belgium, the Czech Republic, Finland, France, Germany, Greece, Iceland, Ireland, Italy, Korea, Luxembourg, Mexico, the Netherlands, Norway, Portugal, Slovak Republic, Spain, Sweden, Switzerland, as well as Brazil since March 1994, Chile since November 1998, India since February 2001, Romania since October 2004 and Thailand since March 2005. The Commission of the European Communities also takes part in the Centre's Governing Board.

The purpose of the Centre is to bring together the knowledge and experience available in member countries of both economic development and the formulation and execution of general economic policies; to adapt such knowledge and experience to the actual needs of countries or regions in the process of development and to put the results at the disposal of the countries by appropriate means.

The Centre is part of the "Development Cluster" at the OECD and enjoys scientific independence in the execution of its task. As part of the Cluster, together with the Centre for Co-operation with Non-Members, the Development Co-operation Directorate, and the Sahel and West Africa Club, the Development Centre can draw upon the experience and knowledge available in the OECD in the development field.

ISBN 92-64-01442-X © OECD 2005

Foreword

The increasing interdependence between OECD and non-OECD economies has sharpened the recognition that mutual interests entail mutual responsibilities. This, together with the international development commitments taken at the highest levels of government, has prompted OECD's Council at Ministerial level to mandate the Secretariat to look at the dimensions of OECD countries' policies beyond aid alone, and to assess impacts, trade-offs and synergies across whole-of-government policies. This initiative by Ministers has taken shape in the programme on policy coherence for development, which has gradually been taking root in different parts of the OECD.

Clearly, all policy makers should strive for policy coherence. But this is not always politically acceptable to those who may lose out. To look at coherence in the abstract is not meaningful. In order to make policies more coherent – in order to muster the necessary political will – we need to make the issues at stake clear and concrete. Issues drawn from specific country and regional cases can provide the most meaningful information on the impacts and coherence of OECD-country policies. That was the reason for launching a joint research project between the Policy Research Institute of the Ministry of Finance in Japan and the OECD Secretariat to draw policy lessons from one of the greatest economic miracles of all time – East Asia. We are most appreciative to all participants in this project for taking up the complex challenge of addressing policy coherence for development in East Asia.

Much has been written and said about the domestic policies that contributed to the East Asian miracle, but our focus here is on how OECD policies helped or hindered in achieving it. The focus is on the impacts of OECD policies – negative and positive – on the region over the past 15-20 years. It is very difficult to isolate completely one set of policies from the other, and indeed complementarity is a key part of the story that unfolds in reading the various contributions. Secondly, our aim is to draw the policy-

ISBN 92-64-01442-X © OECD 2005

relevant implications not only for future development challenges in Asia, but also for other regions of the world. Policy relevance and lessons have been an important goal of this project.

Taking the East Asian experience as a concrete case study allows our discussions to cover a wide range of policy inter-linkages and interactions. The papers in this volume examine the trade-investment nexus, how aid has contributed, how developed country trade and agricultural policies have affected the region, how these policies interact on development. They look at impacts of macroeconomic and financial policies and regional co-operation, as well as emerging issues related to migration and the environment. They probe how OECD-country policies in several areas can help meet emerging economic and social challenges to ensure Asia's sustainable economic development.

The authors consider whether there are *sine qua non* factors that apply universally. Are there basic enabling conditions without which development and competitiveness cannot flourish? Are there behaviours and policy orientations that OECD countries should modify to help emerging countries to catch up? Can the same or similar behaviours and policies be applied to the least developed countries that tend to be much less integrated into the global economy? Do we need to think about alternatives to aid for emerging economies that have graduated? Do we have in place sufficient tools with which to track and monitor policy coherence? Could we improve the dialogue with non-OECD countries on coherence issues?

In all these respects, the study is an important contribution to the OECD's horizontal work on policy coherence for development. Its findings provide valuable insights to guide the Organisation's future work on policy coherence in specific sectors, as well as in new regions. This will certainly entail the recognition that full replication is impossible and that there is no single model for success. The basic political, economic, and socio-cultural conditions between regions and countries differ significantly. As macroeconomic and structural conditions are continuously evolving, all regions, including East Asia, need to adjust and adapt on an ongoing basis.

Kiyo Akasaka
Deputy Secretary General
OECD

Teruhisa Kanai
President
Policy Research Institute
Ministry of Finance
Japan

31 March 2005

ISBN 92-64-01442-X © OECD 2005

Acknowledgements

The editors are grateful to Colm Foy, Vanda Legrandgérard and the members of the Development Centre's Communication Unit for their dedication and able assistance, without which this book would never have appeared in its present form.

Financial support from the Government of Japan is gratefully acknowledged.

The views expressed in each chapter of this book are strictly personal and do not necessarily reflect those of the OECD, the Development Centre or their member countries.

ISBN 92-64-01442-X

Table of Contents

Preface *Louka Katseli* 9

Abbreviations and Acronyms 12

PART ONE
INTRODUCTION, OVERVIEW AND POLICY CONCLUSIONS

Chapter 1 Miracle, Crisis and Beyond
K. Fukasaku, M. Kawai, M.G. Plummer and A. Trzeciak-Duval 17

PART TWO
INTERACTIONS AND IMPACTS OF OECD-COUNTRY POLICIES

Chapter 2 Macroeconomic Management and Financial Stability: The Implications for East Asia
Menzie D. Chinn 89

Chapter 3 US and EU Trade Policies and East Asia
Peter Drysdale and Christopher Findlay 137

Chapter 4 Japan's Structural Reform, Liberalisation and Market Opening: Implications for East Asia
Fukunari Kimura 163

Chapter 5 Economic Development and Poverty Reduction in East Asia: The Impact of OECD-Country Agricultural Policies
Richard Barichello 193

Chapter 6 Sustaining East Asia's Economic Dynamism: The Role of Aid
Hadi Soesastro 219

Chapter 7 OECD-Country Economic and Environmental Policies: What Implications for East Asia?
David O'Connor 255

ISBN 92-64-01442-X

Part Three
The Regional Dimensions of Policy Linkages

Chapter 8 Regional Economic Integration and Co-operation in East Asia
Masahiro Kawai 289

Chapter 9 East Asia's Multi-Layered Development Process: The Trade-FDI Nexus
Shujiro Urata 347

Chapter 10 Korea's Experience as an Asian Developing Economy and as a Newly Industrialised Asian Economy
Soogil Young 411

Chapter 11 China's Miracle: How Have OECD-Country Policies Contributed?
Justin Yifu Lin and Zhiyun Li 459

Chapter 12 The Migration of Highly Skilled Asian Workers to OECD Member Countries and its Effects on Economic Development in East Asia
Yongyuth Chalamwong 487

Part Four
Development Lessons for Other Regions

Chapter 13 Integrating East Asia's Low-Income Countries into the Regional and Global Markets
Siow Yue Chia 527

Chapter 14 OECD-Country Policies towards Developing Economies: Learning from East Asia, Lessons for South Asia
Mustafizur Rahman 575

Chapter 15 The Impact of Coherence of OECD-Country Policies on Asian Developing Economies: Development Lessons for Central Asia
Richard Pomfret 591

Chapter 16 Latin America and the OECD: How Can Bilateral Support Help Improve Performance?
Barbara Stallings 601

List of Contributors 619

ISBN 92-64-01442-X © OECD 2005

Preface

The implementation of coherent policies is a precondition for effective development outcomes. Development is about change; it is about restructuring and extending the productive base; it is about deepening markets, building capacity and strengthening institutions; it is about expanding opportunities, most notably for employment and greater participation in economic and political life; it is about empowering individuals, mobilising societies and promoting human and social rights.

These changes cannot be achieved by market forces alone; they require the active engagement of all development stakeholders. In particular, they call on policy makers to adopt a strategic vision, to be committed to reform and to implement effective policies. No less importantly, they call on both OECD and developing countries systematically and continuously to promote mutually reinforcing policy actions, i.e. to work within a framework of "policy coherence for development".

The practical application of this framework consists in:

a) identifying and promoting the implementation of an appropriate set of integrated policies that will help relax the binding constraints currently hampering development;

b) identifying and promoting the positive dynamics of complementarities and synergies and locating and addressing cases of incoherence both across policy goals and between policy goals and policy instruments, most notably in macroeconomic management, trade, competition, investment, migration and ODA;

c) strengthening or creating institutional mechanisms as well as providing political incentives to facilitate the coordination of policies, both in their design and in their implementation;

d) ensuring credibility and predictability in national and global governance; and, finally,

e) monitoring and evaluating development outcomes with a view to understanding the impact of the various policies and their interdependence in shaping development dynamics and then acting upon the lessons learnt.

Addressing these issues effectively presents pressing challenges to both OECD and non-OECD countries alike. This is to a large extent a by-product of globalisation. The growth of trade, investment and migration – spurred by the liberalisation of goods, services and capital markets and underpinned by advances in information and communication technologies – have enhanced, for both developed and developing countries alike, the net gains that can be accrued from establishing global production and trade networks and ensuring the smooth functioning of well-integrated global markets. At the same time, the costs of remaining an "outsider" have increased; as a consequence, developing countries are faced with the urgent requirement to pursue policies that will provide the necessary impetus to capacity building and a restructuring of their productive bases.

Though the pursuit of greater policy coherence for development has indeed become a global priority, the scope and dimensions of the required policy changes vary across continents. They are shaped by the drivers of change together with regional and national specificities that affect development dynamics. It is therefore important for policy analysts to adopt a regional approach based on country case studies. The work on East Asia presented in this volume has focused on the interactions between foreign and domestic policies and their impact on development outcomes. Careful account has been taken of the institutional characteristics of the East Asian countries, the growth strategies they have adopted and the way in which they have responded to the risks and challenges posed by their progressive integration into global markets.

The so-called East Asian miracle has not been the outcome of a specific set of domestic policies. In fact, domestic policies have been quite diverse in approach, ranging from hands-off to highly interventionist. The striking feature of the East Asian experience has been the predominance of a common strategic vision for development supported by the implementation of proactive policies to promote sequential industrialisation and strategic trade liberalisation and to exploit regional trade-investment and migration inter-

ISBN 92-64-01442-X © OECD 2005

linkages. This common strategic vision has been the major driving force behind East Asia's sustained economic dynamism and has underpinned the coherence of the region's development policies.

The individual papers contained in this volume provide valuable insights regarding the ways in which various OECD-country policies, including those pertaining to trade, investment, development assistance and migration, have contributed, through their interactions, to influence this East Asian approach to development as well as their specific development trajectories. In so doing, these analyses fill an important gap in the existing literature and provide an important contribution to the ongoing policy debate.

Chapter 1 presents a synthesis of these findings with the object of drawing out the necessary policy implications for all the countries involved: for East Asian countries so that they can maintain their current growth trajectories, promote social cohesion and ensure political stability; for OECD countries so that they can create a stable and enabling economic environment and thereby maintain peace and security and promote a more democratic, transparent, accountable and inclusive global governance system; for low-income countries, so that they can seize the available opportunities and develop for themselves effective growth and development strategies.

The conclusions of this joint project will provide valuable inputs to the OECD work on development issues over the coming years, including the *Mutual Review of Development Effectiveness* undertaken in the context of NEPAD. As a follow-up to this East Asian project, the Development Centre will, as part of its 2005-06 Programme of Work, conduct a series of country case studies across Africa, Latin America, East and Central Asia, with the aim of identifying the impact of OECD-country policies on development and their interactions with the institutional characteristics and development strategies of these countries and regions.

It is only through a deeper understanding of these interactions that policy makers can prioritise the measures needed to deal with development bottlenecks and establish much-needed reform agendas.

Louka Katseli
Director
OECD Development Centre
2 June 2005

Abbreviations and Acronyms

ADB	Asian Development Bank
AFAS	ASEAN Framework Agreement on Services
AFTA	ASEAN Free Trade Area
AIA	ASEAN Investment Area
APEC	Asia-Pacific Economic Co-operation
ARF	ASEAN Regional Forum
ASEAN	Association of Southeast Asian Nations
ATC	Agreement on Textiles and Clothing
BIS	Bank for International Settlements
CEPT	Common Effective Preferential Tariff
CER	Australia-New Zealand Closer Economic Relations Trade Agreement
CLMV	Cambodia, Laos, Myanmar and Viet Nam
DAC	Development Assistance Committee
EBRD	European Bank for Reconstruction and Development
EFTA	European Free Trade Association
EPZs	Export-Processing Zones
EU	European Union
FAO	Food and Agriculture Organization
FDI	Foreign Direct Investment
FTA	Free Trade Area (or Agreement)
GATS	General Agreement on Trade in Services
GATT	General Agreement on Tariffs and Trade
GCC	Gulf Cooperation Council
GMS	Greater Mekong Sub-region
GSP	General System of Preferences
HRD	Human Resource Development
HS	Harmonised System
ICT	Information and Communication Technology
IFAD	International Fund for Agricultural Development
IFC	International Finance Corporation
IFIs	International Financial Institutions

ISBN 92-64-01442-X © OECD 2005

IMF	International Monetary Fund
ISIC	International Standard Industry Classification
JBIC	Japan Bank for International Cooperation
JETRO	Japan External Trade Organization
MCA	Millennium Challenge Account
MDGs	Millennium Development Goals
MENA	Middle East and North Africa
MERCOSUR	Southern Common Market
MFA	Multifibre Arrangement (formerly Arrangement regarding International Trade in Textiles)
MFN	Most Favoured Nation
MNEs	Multinational Enterprises
NEPAD	New Partnership for Africa's Development
NIEs	Newly Industrialising Economies
NTMs	Non-Tariff Measures
ODA	Official Development Assistance
OECD	Organisation for Economic Co-operation and Development
OEM	Original Equipment Manufacturing
OOF	Other Official Flows
PPP	Purchasing Power Parity
R&D	Research and Development
RTA	Regional Trade Arrangement
S&D	Special and Differential Treatment
SAARC	South Asian Association for Regional Cooperation
SACU	Southern African Customs Union
SITC	Standard International Trade Classification
SMEs	Small and Medium-Sized Enterprises
SPS	Sanitary and Phytosanitary Measures
SOEs	State-Owned Enterprises
TBT	Technical Barriers to Trade
TRIMs	Trade-Related Investment Measures
TRIPS	Trade-Related Intellectual Property Rights
UNCTAD	United Nations Conference on Trade and Development
WDI	World Development Indicators
WTO	World Trade Organization

ISBN 92-64-01442-X © OECD 2005

Part One

Introduction, Overview and Policy Conclusions

Chapter 1

Miracle, Crisis and Beyond[1]

K. Fukasaku, M. Kawai, M.G. Plummer and A. Trzeciak-Duval

Abstract

The East Asian growth experience is still not well understood, especially the region's clustered, sequential development and neighbourhood effects linking economies at different levels of industrial development. Moreover, the impact on it of OECD-member policies has never been subjected to systematic analysis. A central question involves how different policy vectors transmitted by OECD countries, notably in trade, investment and aid, may or may not have contributed to the region's progress. The intensity of such policy impacts has also depended critically on the capacity of East Asian economies to respond through their own public policies. This overview looks at what has happened to East Asia over past decades, particularly since the mid-1980s, through the lens of OECD members' "policy coherence for development". It discusses critical challenges facing both East Asian and OECD economies to help sustain the region's progress. It also draws lessons for many low-income economies in other parts of the world, including the message that policy coherence in OECD countries can bear fruit only when developing economies have the capacity to respond. Key challenges highlighted for OECD countries are:

— to ensure the fundamental enabling conditions of security and political stability;

— to pay greater attention to the impacts of macroeconomic policies on developing-country growth;

— to increase both market access and capacity building for developing economies;

— to assure governance structures that help maintain financial stability; and

— to improve aid effectiveness and its complementarity with host country strategies and policies.

Mutual reviews of their policies in these fundamental areas with partner countries would help to enhance OECD members' accountability in economic policy making for development.

ISBN 92-64-01442-X

Introduction

This chapter sketches out the main story lines of East Asian development, particularly since the mid-1980s. Subsequent chapters deal in greater detail with individual country and policy developments. The chapter opens by describing the background of this joint research project and the reasons for undertaking a regional approach with a focus on East Asia. It then highlights the main features of the region's development experience, discussing key policy challenges for East Asia and drawing developmental lessons for low-income countries in other parts of the world. Finally, it focuses on the policy coherence challenges for OECD countries to help sustain the region's progress.

Why Policy Coherence for Development?

While the reforms necessary to achieve development goals should be home grown, international initiatives can support them significantly and in some cases may define their political feasibility. The United Nations Declaration of the Millennium Development Goals in September 2000 prompted the international community to step up its efforts to build a global partnership for development. This led to the launching at Doha in November 2001 of a new trade round under the auspices of the WTO, followed in 2002 by the Monterrey Consensus on Financing for Development in March and the World Summit on Sustainable Development in Johannesburg in September. A key to success in these endeavours is to seek "greater coherence in global economic policy-making" (Paragraph 5 of the Doha Ministerial Declaration) in which OECD countries have an important stake.

Within this internationally shared perspective, the OECD Ministerial Meeting in 2002 issued a statement on development, calling upon the OECD to "*enhance understanding of the development dimensions of member country policies and their impact on developing countries*". The OECD responded to this ministerial mandate by launching a broad programme on policy coherence for development[2]. The term "policy coherence" encompasses policy interactions at several levels. Internationally, coherence is needed among policies applied by different institutions as well as in the positions that countries take in them. At the national level, coherence refers to the consistency between objectives and instruments applied by individual OECD countries in a given policy area, such as development co-operation, as well as between objectives

ISBN 92-64-01442-X © OECD 2005

in different areas, such as aid and trade, in light of their combined effects on developing countries. Thus, the problem of policy *in*coherence for development arises when the objective of a policy undertaken in a particular field — such as aid policy or transitional preferential arrangements — gets undermined or obstructed by actions of government in other policy fields — such as trade protection and agricultural subsidies. The OECD's programme focuses on identifying such mismatches in specific policy contexts and suggesting alternative actions to ensure that OECD countries' policies help promote or at least do not harm the economic interests of developing countries[3].

Furthermore, OECD work on this topic seeks to facilitate and support efforts of both OECD and developing countries to encourage the systematic promotion of mutually reinforcing policy actions, including aid but extending beyond it[4]. Indeed, the notion of policy coherence so defined may provide a useful framework for rethinking the co-operation of OECD member countries with non-member (developing and transition) economies (see Box 1.1). More than 35 years ago, Harry Johnson (1967) stated:

> "[T]he expansion of aid should be integrated with the expansion of trade opportunities, and … the two together should be used to provide the maximum inducements to the less developed countries to modify the policies of currency overvaluation and import substitution to which they are addicted and to concentrate their efforts instead on economic development through trade with the rest of the world" (p. 245).

Since then, as discussed below, several East Asian developing economies have displayed remarkable development records based on outward-oriented growth strategies advocated by Johnson and many others. Growing numbers of developing economies in other regions have also undertaken policy reforms to liberalise foreign trade, investment and exchange-rate regimes, albeit to varying degrees, and to attract foreign direct investment (FDI), thereby integrating their economies more closely into the world economy. As a consequence, the economic linkages between OECD and developing countries have strengthened and will continue to intensify (OECD, 1995 and 1997). This requires OECD member countries to formulate their economic policies to reflect properly their deepening economic relations with non-OECD countries.

ISBN 92-64-01442-X © OECD 2005

Box 1.1 **Towards Greater Coherence in Development Policy Making**

The issue of policy coherence for development is hardly new. It goes back to the mid-1960s (Johnson, 1967). Yet it has become increasingly important since the mid-1980s, as closer linkages between developed and developing countries through trade, investment and technology flows have become recognised as crucial to the success of developing countries in sustaining growth and catching up.

Langhammer (1995, p. 213) has stated that "[d]eveloping countries stand to gain if OECD countries fully exploit their growth potential to act as engines, refrain from protectionist measures, provide stable money, export private risk capital and aid to net borrowers, and create fresh human capital that cascades down to lower-income countries and thus keeps world-wide structural change moving". In this view, a top priority for OECD countries is to keep their own houses in order by maintaining macroeconomic stability, providing private and public funds for investment and increasing structural flexibility in their own economies.

From the developing-country perspective, the problem of incoherence may arise under a serious mismatch between policy objectives and instruments applied by OECD countries in light of their combined effects on development. For instance, OECD countries provide financial resources to developing countries in the form of official development assistance (ODA), the benefits of which might be offset by the adverse effects of their actions in other policy areas, such as trade. Examples are numerous at bilateral, regional and global levels.* James Michel (1997), a former OECD Development Assistance Committee (DAC) Chairman, has noted that while it is increasingly evident that a comprehensive approach employing coherent policies across a range of government activities is essential, officials in aid agencies and trade ministries often act independently of one another as if aid and trade are independent or even competing policy instruments. The DAC regularly conducts peer reviews of its member countries' aid policies, which now involve discussions on policy coherence. Closer co-operation between the DAC and other relevant Committees within the OECD would add weight to this review process. The first Mutual Review of Development Effectiveness discussed jointly in 2005 by OECD and NEPAD (New Partnership for Africa's Development) Heads of State and Ministers has provided an important occasion for both groups to evaluate policy-coherence issues that impact on African economies.

ISBN 92-64-01442-X © OECD 2005

Box 1.1 (contd.)

Seeking greater coherence in development co-operation has become even more important for the European Union. Article 130v of Title XVII of the Maastricht Treaty** is often referred to as the "coherence article" for development co-operation (Hoebink, 1999). Sweden has become the first nation in the world to pass into law an integrated global development policy (IDRC Press Release, 28/1/2004). The country's agriculture, environment, migration, trade and other policies must now, by law, align to fight poverty and promote sustainable development.

Policy coherence for development has an international dimension as well. Kindleberger (1986) has stated that in the absence of a world government, the rich countries have primary responsibility for providing international public goods, such as an open and stable international marketplace upon which the economic welfare of all countries depends. Some OECD countries now consider that stricter trade rules and obligations should be applied to several more advanced developing countries as they join the ranks of major players on world markets.

* See, for example, Grilli (1993) for the European Community, and Krueger (1993) for the United States. More generally, see Fukasaku *et al.* (1995), OECD (1995 and 1997) and Forster and Stokke (1999) for coherence issues related to North-South economic linkages.

** Article 178 of the Amsterdam Treaty as from 1 May 1999.

Why Focus on East Asia?

The East Asia region has particular interest for studying the impact of OECD countries' policies. The links between the region's developing and transition economies and major OECD countries are strong, not only through the international exchange of goods and services but also through international flows of capital, technology and labour. Several high-performing East Asian economies have maintained high economic growth by historical standards for a significant period. Their development in the 1970s and 1980s has often been called the "East Asian miracle" since the publication of a World Bank report in 1993. Explaining the miracle has stirred policy debate among academic researchers and policy makers. It has shown the possibility of growth, poverty reduction and even "graduation"[5] in the developing world, given the correct policies in an enabling international economic environment.

Not surprisingly, most of the "miracle" economies have rebounded strongly from the financial and currency crises that hit the region badly in 1997-98. Nonetheless, they face several new challenges that relate closely to the often-heard question whether East Asia's clustered and outward-oriented growth is sustainable. Moreover, the region still includes several least-developed, low-income countries as well as transition economies, with a significant number of the world's poorest people. Thus, it remains a huge challenge for these governments and peoples to sustain or repeat the "miracle" performance. One of the main objectives of this joint project is to draw major development lessons, based on the actual experiences of more advanced developing economies of East Asia, for low-income countries in the region, as well as for many developing countries in other regions.

Revisiting East Asia's "Miracle" Performance

One of the defining characteristics of world development during the second half of the 20th century was the emergence of East Asia as the third growth pole of the world economy (Table 1.1)[6].The region's real GDP grew at an average annual rate of 5.8 per cent, and East Asia's share of world GDP climbed to 27 per cent in 2001 from 11 per cent in 1950. Meanwhile, the East Asian population — a little over 2 billion at the beginning of the new millennium — remained at roughly the same one-third of the world population as five decades before. The growth of East Asia's per capita GDP thus became the most prominent among major regions. In 1950, the region's average per capita GDP was estimated at $685 (at 1990 international prices), lower than the corresponding figure for Africa ($894)[7]. By the turn of the century, it had risen more than sevenfold to over $5 000. With few exceptions, the region's rapid economic growth brought significant reductions in absolute poverty and noticeable improvements in social conditions, such as life expectancy, infant mortality and literacy (see Annex Tables 1-3).

ISBN 92-64-01442-X © OECD 2005

Table 1.1. **The Performance of Major Regions, 1950-2001**

Major Regions	Population (million)		GDP ($ billion 1990)		GDP per Head ($ 1990)	
	1950	2001	1950	2001	1950	2001
Western Europe (29)	305	392	1 396	7 550	4 579	19 256
Western offshoots (4)[a]	176	340	1 635	9 156	9 268	26 943
of which: United States	152	285	1 456	7 966	9 561	27 948
Eastern Europe (7)	88	121	185	729	2 111	6 027
Former USSR (15)	180	290	510	1 343	2 841	4 626
Asia (57)	1 382	3 654	984	14 106	712	3 861
of which: East Asia (16)	850	2 029	582	10 222	685	5 038
Japan	84	127	161	2 625	1 921	20 683
China	547	1 275	240	4 570	439	3 583
Others[b]	220	627	181	3 028	825	4 831
South Asia (5)	461	1 346	286	2 499	621	1 857
India	359	1 024	222	2 003	619	1 957
Others[c]	102	322	64	496	629	1 539
West Asia (15)	60	241	106	1 343	1 776	5 580
Africa (57)	227	821	203	1 223	894	1 489
Latin America (47)	166	531	416	3 087	2 506	5 811
World (216)	2 524	6 149	5 330	37 194	2 111	6 049
	Percentages				Relative to USA (100)	
Western Europe (29)	12	6	26	20	48	69
Western offshoots (4)[a]	7	6	31	25	97	96
of which: United States	6	5	27	21	100	100
Eastern Europe (7)	3	2	3	2	22	22
Former USSR (15)	7	5	10	4	30	17
Asia (57)	55	59	18	38	7	14
of which: East Asia (16)	34	33	11	27	7	18
Japan	3	2	3	7	20	74
China	22	21	5	12	5	13
Others[b]	9	10	3	8	9	17
South Asia (5)	18	22	5	7	6	7
India	14	17	4	5	6	7
Others[c]	4	5	1	1	7	6
West Asia (15)	2	4	2	4	19	20
Africa (57)	9	13	4	3	9	5
Latin America (47)	7	9	8	8	26	21
World (216)	100	100	100	100	22	22

Notes: a) Australia, Canada, New Zealand and United States; *b)* excluding Japan and China; *c)* excluding India.
Source: Calculated from Maddison (2003).

ISBN 92-64-01442-X

Explaining East Asia's Growth and Development

Throughout much of the post-war period, a number of economies in the region have managed sequentially to achieve historically high per capita GDP growth rates — typically 4 to 6 per cent per annum and sometimes even higher — for a significantly long time. Starting with Japan in the 1950s and 1960s, the region's dynamic growth has continued apace since the 1970s. The ascendancy of Asian newly industrialising economies (NIEs: Chinese Taipei; Hong Kong, China; Korea and Singapore) followed. Then came the turn of several economies in the Association of Southeast Asian Nations (ASEAN: Indonesia; Malaysia; the Philippines; Thailand; and most recently Viet Nam) as well as China. Although less spectacularly, India has moved closer to similar growth performance over the last decade.

Based on historical data provided by Maddison (2003), Figure 1.1 traces real per capita GDP ratios relative to the United States for nine East Asian economies from 1950 to 2001. It displays several interesting features of East Asia's multi-layered growth process:

- As Japan's super-growth performance came to an end in the early 1970s, both Hong Kong, China and Singapore managed high growth in the 1970s and again in the second half of the 1980s and the early 1990s. This momentum appears to have weakened substantially or at least become more volatile in the aftermath of the East Asian crisis.
- Chinese Taipei and Korea recorded the region's best growth throughout the entire post-war period. It even accelerated after 1973, in sharp contrast with Japan. Moreover, despite the very severe 1997-98 crises in the region, Korea has managed a V-shaped recovery.
- Growth in three countries rich in natural resources, Indonesia, Malaysia and Thailand, also began in the early 1970s and accelerated from the mid-1980s as manufactured exports became an engine of growth. The outbreak of the 1997-98 crises temporarily halted this process.
- China lifted growth rates substantially in the 1980s, owing to its "Reform and Opening-up" policy that began in late 1978. It has emerged as the best performer over the past decade, and the East Asian crisis did not arrest its momentum.

ISBN 92-64-01442-X © OECD 2005

Figure 1.1. **Real Per Capita GDP for Nine East Asian Economies Relative to United States, 1950-2001**
(percentages of US per capita income)

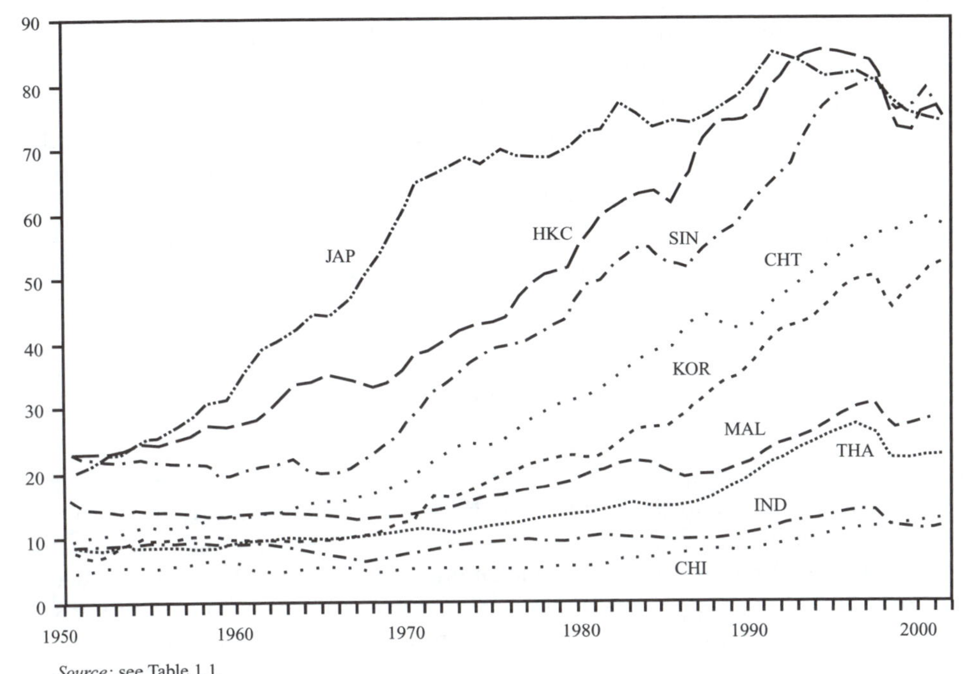

Source: see Table 1.1.

These economies are highly diverse in terms of population size, availability of natural resources, initial income levels and relative factor endowments as well as economic, political and social systems, religion and culture. Despite such diversity, East Asia's economic success through most of the post-war years has been remarkable by historical standards (Maddison, 1995 and 2001). Furthermore, the apparent success in adjustment and growth in several Asian NIEs during the turbulent period of the 1970s and 1980s has stimulated the academic and development-policy communities to probe the exact policy mixes that enabled such superior performance[8].

The World Bank's 1993 report, *The East Asian Miracle: Growth and Public Policy*, was one of the first major attempts in this direction (see Box 1.2). It focused on linking growth performance and domestic policy developments in eight East Asian economies[9]. In a nutshell, it argued that rapid growth in *each* economy arose primarily from the application of a set of common, market-friendly policies ("getting the fundamentals right"), which led to both higher accumulation and better allocation of resources. The report also stressed the

ISBN 92-64-01442-X © OECD 2005

importance of creating and securing a pro-business environment that led to very high levels of growth led by the private sector. The authors admitted that much remained to be studied about the role of selective intervention by governments in their attempts to accelerate growth. Nonetheless, they argued that the institutional context within which intervention policies are implemented is as important to their success or failure as the policies themselves. Debate about the role of government for development in general and the interaction between policy choices and institutional capability in particular has broadened to include issues related to public and corporate governance. Notwithstanding a large body of literature on the topic, rethinking the growth strategies and experiences of East Asia and other regions continues[10].

Box 1.2. The East Asian Miracle: What the World Bank's 1993 Report Tells Us

Most of East Asia's rapid growth stemmed from higher accumulation of physical and human capital, better allocation of resources to more productive investment and the capability to acquire, use and master technology. There is no single "East Asian model" of development. These eight economies applied different and changing sets of policies to achieve rapid growth and poverty reduction. These diverse policies ranged from hands-off to highly interventionist, depending on individual cases and particular periods. Nevertheless, the report concludes that the East Asian miracle depended on six key policy fundamentals (pp. 347-352):

1) ensuring low inflation and competitive exchange rates to support outward-oriented growth;
2) building human capital, which is critical to rapid growth with equity;
3) creating effective and secure financial systems to encourage financial savings and channel them into productive investment;
4) limiting price distortions, to draw resources into labour-intensive production in the early stages of development, then into capital-intensive and knowledge-intensive activities later;
5) absorbing foreign technology *via* licensing and/or foreign direct investment (FDI); and
6) limiting the bias against agriculture, which is key to reducing rural-urban income differentials in East Asia.

ISBN 92-64-01442-X © OECD 2005

Box 1.2 (contd.)

The report also highlights the importance of creatin based bureaucracy and public-private consultati policies and to establish a market-friendly environm investment. It is sceptical about the effectiveness of g in promoting specific industries or industrial sub-secto the high costs involved in the use of directed credit, e worked in certain situations.

The eventful experience of the 1990s and research work past decade have led to a series of reappraisals and cou including another World Bank study (Yusuf, 2001), regarding of growth in East Asia and the roles of public policy and form institutional arrangements. While it is not yet clear at this stage targeted industrial policies had positive, negative or little impac growth in East Asia, governments certainly can do more than m management in promoting and sustaining economic growth. Ind Asian phenomenon suggests that governments have played sign in many areas of particular importance to sustained growth, inclu and education, infrastructure development, technology transfer and building (Noland and Pack, 2003).

East Asia's Clustered, Sequential Development. East Asia's success re primarily from successful industrialisation, seen as a secular change i composition of GDP away from agriculture to industry (Table 1.2, Pane Furthermore, in recent years, Korea and other advanced economies of region, such as Hong Kong, China and Singapore, have increasingly orient their production towards services, like OECD countries (Chane-Kune *et al* 2003). More important in the current context, this has resulted in *clustered, sequential* industrialisation, accompanied by a rapid rise in the share in total merchandise exports of manufactures, notably machinery and transport equipment, as these economies have become more open (Table 1.2, Panel B).

Table 1

China
Panel A. S
- Agricu
- Indus
- Servi
Panel B.
- Trad
- Mar
- Ma
Indon
Panel
- A
- Ir
- S
Pan

ISBN 92-64-01442-X © OECD 2005

East Asia's development is a *sequential* industrialisation in two senses. First, it began in labour-intensive sectors with small capital requirements, then moved up to capital-intensive sectors, such as heavy industries and petrochemicals, and finally to technology-intensive sectors such as machinery and electronics industries. Such a sequence is often called the "flying-geese pattern" (Akamatsu, 1961 and Yamazawa, 1990). Ito (2001) presents some supporting evidence which shows a fall in the share of labour-intensive sectors in total value added and a corresponding rise in the share of technology-intensive sectors in several East Asian economies[11].

Second, the "flying-geese pattern" also implies that as the first economies upgraded their industries from labour-intensive to capital-intensive and then to technology-intensive activities, another group came to follow a similar pattern. As the forerunners achieved higher levels of industrialisation, the next tier of countries emerged to catch up with them. Japan achieved high levels of industrialisation by the 1970s. The Asian NIEs (Chinese Taipei; Hong Kong, China; Korea and Singapore) were the first to follow. The middle-income ASEAN countries came next, and China has been the last economy to catch up with — and even threaten — the ASEAN economies. In "flying geese" terms, Japan was the lead goose, followed by the NIEs, middle-income ASEAN and China. One can hope that the low-income ASEAN countries will be able to emerge next. While the "flying-geese" metaphor captures the regional patterns of industrial development quite nicely, it does *not* explain what made such clustered, sequential industrialisation possible.

Most of the literature on East Asian development has focused on how domestic policies and institutions in individual economies were growth-generating (as in the case of World Bank, 1993), but it has not paid adequate attention to how growth stimuli and incentives were generated and transmitted from more advanced to less advanced economies in a particular region. As Ozawa (2003, p. 710) states, the effectiveness of growth-promoting policies in individual economies depends critically on how well and how quickly each economy can respond to and exploit the external policy environment and opportunities by means of its own public policies[12]. From this perspective, it is important to take a close look at six external factors — including the influence of OECD-country policies — which have helped to shape the region's development process. They are *i)* the influence of geography and security; *ii)* multilateral trade liberalisation and "open regionalism"; *iii)* OECD-country macroeconomic and technological vectors; *iv)* the emergence of a trade-FDI nexus; *v)* labour migration as a complementary factor; and *vi)* the role of international aid.

ISBN 92-64-01442-X

Shaping East Asia's Development Process: The Role of External Factors

The Influence of Geography and Security. Geography and security influence development significantly[13]. There is wide recognition that natural and human geography affects the development of a particular country or region through factors such as climate, inherited health and proximity to markets[14]. For instance, countries that find themselves in the tropical zone (mostly developing countries) may have adverse growth prospects compared with those in the temperate zone. The reasons for this include, among others, the long-lasting, negative impact of tropical diseases on education and health and thus on labour productivity, the dominance of extractive industries in national economies and their potentially negative consequences for public institutions and governance, and low soil quality or plant diseases that may lead to low productivity in agriculture. A study by Gallup *et al.* (2003) examines the influence of geography on per capita GDP growth by estimating standard growth equations augmented by additional explanatory variables representing both natural and human geography[15]. Perhaps their most relevant finding is that geography can explain only a small fraction of the growth gap observed between Latin America and East Asia. Moreover, geographical factors would tend to make East Asia grow slightly less fast than Latin America. This would imply that good infrastructure, appropriate policies and well-functioning institutions can help developing countries overcome many of the obstacles imposed by geography.

Security has had a direct bearing on the development of East Asian economies. During the Cold War, maintaining regional security had the utmost importance for economies with strategic alliances with the Western bloc. East Asia has had no region-wide security arrangement in a traditional sense. It has had a combination of US-centred, bilateral security treaties — for Japan, Korea, the Philippines and Thailand — and loose regional forums for security co-operation (Kawai, 2004*a*). The US-centred security treaties are traditional arrangements that oblige signatories to defend their allies if adversaries attack or threaten them militarily. Forums for security co-operation have been developed around ASEAN[16], including the Treaty of Amity and Co-operation in Southeast Asia (1976), and, more recently, the ASEAN Regional Forum (1994). Security co-operation in East Asia entails multilateral dialogue and information exchange, not only among allies but also with potential adversaries, to deepen mutual understanding and build trust, thereby reducing the probability of military conflict. Domestic political stability, underpinned primarily by the US-centred security arrangements,

 ISBN 92-64-01442-X © OECD 2005

laid a critical foundation for development. Individual countries then undertook major policy initiatives to promote growth and poverty reduction within the general framework of the GATT/WTO.

Multilateral Trade Liberalisation and "Open Regionalism". Multilateral trade liberalisation under the auspices of the GATT/WTO can be regarded as an institutional foundation underlying East Asia's clustered, sequential development. One can argue that a gradual opening of OECD markets through the eight rounds of multilateral trade negotiations has been a *sine qua non* for the region's growth based on outward-oriented industrialisation (Table 1.3). China represents perhaps one of the most successful episodes to date. It embarked on the "Reform and Opening-up" policy in late 1978 and moved to embrace the coastal development strategy in the mid-1980s in order to promote trade and attract FDI. Indeed, China's reforms related closely to the long and often painful accession negotiations at the GATT/WTO, which began in 1986 (Fukasaku and Solignac Lecomte, 1998).

Table 1.3. **GATT/WTO Trade Negotiations 1947-2005**

Year/Period	Place/Name	Subjects Covered	Countries Participating
1947	Geneva	Tariffs	23
1949	Annecy	Tariffs	13
1951	Torquay	Tariffs	38
1956	Geneva	Tariffs	26
1960-1961	Geneva (Dillon Round)	Tariffs	26
1964-1967	Geneva (Kennedy Round)	Tariffs, anti-dumping measures.	62
1973-1979	Geneva (Tokyo Round)	Tariffs, non-tariff measures, "framework" agreements.	102
1986-1994	Geneva (Uruguay Round)	Tariffs, non-tariff measures, rules, agriculture, services, textiles, intellectual property, dispute settlements, creation of WTO, etc.	123
2002-2005 (planned)	Geneva (Doha Development Agenda)	Tariffs, non-tariff measures, rules, agriculture, services, special & differential treatment, etc.	148

Source: Based on WTO (1998) p. 9.

Until quite recently, East Asian economies have taken a route different from that of other regions, namely to accelerate trade liberalisation within a trans-regional framework as well as the global framework of the GATT/WTO. Asia-Pacific Economic Co-operation (APEC) was created in 1989 as the first broad intergovernmental forum aiming at closer economic co-operation and

ISBN 92-64-01442-X © OECD 2005

partnership involving both developed and developing countries across the Pacific[17]. It was a brainchild of Bob Hawke, then Australian Prime Minister, who coined the term "open regionalism".

APEC stands out as a unique case of trans-regional integration and co-operation agreements, based on three pillars. First, it has involved non-discriminatory confidence-building measures, such as enhanced exchange of economic information, increased transparency of trade policies among member economies, trade and investment facilitation, consultation, voluntary codes and networking. Second, APEC has sought to design and implement voluntary but common liberalisation programmes. At the Bogor Meeting in 1994, the APEC Economic Leaders announced their intention to pursue "free trade and investment" in the region by 2010 for developed economies and by 2020 for developing economies, based on the principle of *voluntary* unilateral liberalisation. Compared with the habitual incentives for trade negotiations, the APEC route towards free trade and investment among member economies has indeed been a novel approach. If traditional political economy is a guide, however, it would not be realistic to expect concerted unilateral liberalisation to succeed beyond marginal measures because of the free-rider problem under voluntarism and the non-binding nature of policy commitments (Pelkmans and Fukasaku, 1995). Third, APEC has also dedicated itself to technical and development co-operation under the rubric of "ECOTECH". This pillar began to receive special attention at the 1996 APEC Economic Leaders' meeting in the Philippines and continues to be a priority, though arguably progress made so far in this area has been less concrete than in other areas.

OECD-Country Macroeconomic and Technological Vectors. Figure 1.1 shows that the East Asian economies (except China) simultaneously experienced major economic transformations in the early 1970s and again in the mid-1980s. As Hsiao and Hsiao (2003) point out, it would be implausible to consider such coincidence either as random or as deliberate and co-ordinated on the part of governments[18]. The transformation resulted more from significant changes in the international economic environment and less as the consequence of any particular domestic economic policies.

Indeed, the 1970s saw sea changes in the international economic system, with the emergence of strong inflationary pressures in major OECD countries, a breakdown in the Bretton Woods fixed exchange-rate system and the first OPEC oil price shock. In retrospect, adjustment to these developments led to the end of a "golden age of unparalleled prosperity" for Western economies (Maddison, 1995). The Japanese economy had already reached the post-war peak after the "era of rapid economic growth" in the 1960s. Meanwhile, the

ISBN 92-64-01442-X © OECD 2005

country had also changed from a labour-surplus to a labour-shortage economy. A significant tightening of labour market conditions, together with successive rounds of the yen's real appreciation in the 1970s, propelled Japanese firms to invest abroad, and import more goods from other East Asian economies. This adjustment process accelerated further in the wake of the Plaza Accord under the dollar-yen currency realignment that took place in September 1985.

Furthermore, easy monetary policy among OECD countries in the 1970s led to low real interest rates, and the Asian NIEs found it convenient to finance their strong investment demand by borrowing petrodollars recycled through banks in London and New York (Frankel and Roubini, 2003). In the early 1990s, real interest rates in the United States and other OECD countries were once again low, so that international capital went to East Asian and other emerging economies to earn higher returns. Thus external macroeconomic factors exerted an important impact on the East Asian economies through trade and financial linkages.

The 1970s also marked the beginning of what is now called the "microelectronics revolution". This helped both to revitalise mature industries through the development of labour-saving and energy-saving technologies (e.g. numerically-controlled machine tools, robotics, compact cars) and to develop the electronics, computer and other high-tech industries. One of the major consequences of these technological and industrial developments is the growing importance of intra-product specialisation in manufactured trade. Trade in parts and components (as opposed to final products) is hardly new, but its share in total trade has risen significantly in East Asia (see Drysdale and Findlay, 2005, in this volume). If the stages of a production process are physically separable, its manufacture becomes amenable to fragmentation so that the various stages of production can be separated spatially and undertaken at different locations where the costs of production are lowest with the best mix of technologies. Although spatial dispersion of production across countries usually entails costs of communication, co-ordination and logistics as well as other trade costs due to restrictive trade policies and practices, advances in telecommunication and transportation technologies and reductions in trade and investment barriers substantially reduced the trade costs and thus stimulated fragmentation of production processes across national borders (Arndt and Kierzkowski, 2001).

These macroeconomic and technological developments emanating from OECD countries and their policies facilitated East Asian economies' entry into the network of global production sharing and establishment as viable

ISBN 92-64-01442-X © OECD 2005

competitors in world markets. The economic ascendancy of four Asian NIEs during the 1970s was seen as the harbinger of a promising growth model for other East Asian countries.

The Emergence of a Trade-FDI Nexus. It is interesting to note that opinions on the role of FDI for economic development diverged greatly in the 1970s. While the divergence appears to have narrowed considerably over the past three decades, the question still remains politically sensitive for certain developing and transition economies. The sensitivity persists because FDI is "not only owned and controlled by private groups in pursuit of private profits but also by private interests that are non-resident to boot" (Reuber *et al.*, 1973, p. 16). Much of the FDI flowing into many developing countries has been attracted by the availability of natural resources. Since the mid-1980s, however, East Asia has seen a rapid rise in a new kind of investment, namely export-oriented, manufacturing FDI, particularly of a production-fragmenting type (Kawai, 2004*c*). Many developing economies of the region have significantly, and in some cases dramatically (e.g. China), altered their attitudes and policies toward FDI — a change linked closely to a significant shift in growth strategies. FDI can play an important role in the development of new export bases in host economies, the restructuring of home economies, the expansion of trade flows, the transfer of technology and knowledge and hence the growing interdependence of national and regional economies. It also serves as long-term capital to finance current-account deficits. Among developing areas, the East Asia region has proved a highly attractive location for FDI, with foreign investors increasingly taking a differentiated approach between countries within the region.

While trade and FDI flows are closely linked through the procurement and sales activities of multinational corporations, the net impact of FDI can be either trade-creating or trade-replacing. In fact, the relationship between trade and FDI flows is very complex at both the macroeconomic and firm levels[19].Nonetheless, FDI flows in East Asia tended to be more trade-creating than trade-replacing because of the region's growing emphasis on export-oriented manufacturing. A study by Kawai and Urata (1998) on Japanese manufacturing FDI in East Asia found a strong complementarity between Japan's FDI and its exports in many sectors (e.g. food, textiles, chemical products, general machinery and electrical machinery), while at the same time reverse imports were promoted from FDI hosts.

The positive effects of trade and FDI on growth count among the most critical factors underlying the strong East Asian growth performance, although the relationship between openness to international trade and

ISBN 92-64-01442-X © OECD 2005

investment and growth has been the object of intensive discussion among academic researchers (Box 1.3). Liberalisation of trade and investment policy regimes undertaken unilaterally by many economies in the region has improved the policy environment, favouring the expansion of both trade and FDI flows. Conversely, strong trade and FDI performance has encouraged governments to sustain these outward-oriented policies, thereby integrating their economies more closely into the international market. This positive relationship between liberalisation initiatives and strong trade and FDI growth seems to have worked in East Asia's favour. The emergence of a "trade-FDI nexus" has thus been a key feature of the region's outward-oriented growth (Petri, 1995; and Katseli, 1997).

Box 1.3. **Openness and Growth**

Openness to trade and FDI can potentially bring many benefits to liberalising economies. First, imports are an important source of new ideas, new goods and new services essential to improve productivity and sustain growth (Romer, 1993, 1994). Import liberalisation also stimulates domestic competition and can act as a catalyst for greater efficiency and innovation. Second, exports are crucial to financing imports essential for development. In addition to this obvious role, exports of manufactures and non-traditional goods and services may provide a useful yardstick against which governments can design and implement the most effective policy mixes (World Bank, 1993). Third, FDI augments capital stock, stimulates inflows of technology and know-how from more advanced countries and enhances competition in domestic markets. Although a significant proportion of FDI flows into developing countries in the 1960s and 1970s went into natural resource extraction, FDI flows in the manufacturing and service sectors have become increasingly important since the 1980s. To attract sustained FDI, host governments must provide a favourable investment climate by ensuring stable macroeconomic conditions and reducing product-market distortions in their economies (Hiemenz *et al.*, 1991).

The positive relationship between openness and growth appears to be fairly robust (see, among others, Dollar, 1992; Sachs and Warner, 1995; Frankel and Romer, 1999; Dollar and Kraay, 2001; Baldwin, 2003; Wacziarg and Welch, 2003; and Winters, 2004). Still, it is difficult to establish the causation rigorously. Three points bear on this issue. First, several conventional measures of "openness" frequently applied in cross-country regression analysis (i.e. trade-GDP ratios, tariff rates, the extent of non-tariff barriers and the degree of distortion in foreign exchange markets) may not necessarily reflect the impact of trade policy *per se*.

ISBN 92-64-01442-X

Box 1.3 (contd.)

They may well capture the impact of good institutions and government policy in general (Pritchett, 1996; and Rodriguez and Rodrik, 1999). Second, the transmission mechanisms through which freer trade may cause higher growth in liberalising economies are not well specified in cross-country studies. Some argue that import liberalisation rather than export expansion may have a stronger impact on productivity and growth (Clerides *et al.*, 1998; and Lawrence and Weinstein, 2001). Causation might also run in the opposite direction: higher productivity in manufacturing industries leads to higher exports (Bradford, 1994). Third, empirical analysis needs to account more explicitly for the trade-FDI-growth dynamics in liberalising economies (Urata, 2001). Démurger (2000) makes a useful contribution to understanding the dynamics in China by investigating the effects of opening to foreign capital on the country's growth and on the evolution of inter-provincial disparities over the last two decades. This study also shows the added value of a country-specific approach to empirical research on openness and growth.

Table 1.4 presents major trends in inward and outward FDI stocks as a percentage of GDP in selected East Asian economies during the past two decades. The role of FDI for East Asia's clustered, sequential growth has been quite diverse among the economies of the region; some have relied more on FDI than others. For Hong Kong, China; Singapore; Malaysia and, more recently, China and three new members of ASEAN (Cambodia, Laos and Viet Nam), FDI inflows have become increasingly important. This contrasts sharply with Japan, Korea and Chinese Taipei in the 1970s and 1980s, which relied much less on FDI packages and more on licensing arrangements to import foreign technology. Only quite recently (particularly after the 1997-98 crisis) have FDI-stock/GDP ratios started to rise markedly in Chinese Taipei and Korea, as they have eased restrictions or taken measures to encourage FDI inflows[20]. The table also shows that not only Japan but also relatively advanced developing economies, especially the four Asian NIEs, have emerged as direct investors in the region, as their economies climb technological ladders in industrial development and relocate labour-intensive segments of production to less advanced developing economies. China has benefited enormously from this clustered, sequential development since the mid-1980s (see Box 1.4). More recently, similar forces appear to be driving the Vietnamese economy (Van Arkadie and Mallon, 2003).

ISBN 92-64-01442-X © OECD 2005

Table 1.4. **Inward and Outward FDI Stock as Percentage of GDP in Selected East Asian Economies, 1980-2003**

		1980	1985	1990	1995	2000	2003
Hong Kong, China							
	Inward	623.8	525.5	269.6	160.6	275.4	236.5
	Outward	0.5	6.7	15.9	55.6	234.9	211.9
Singapore							
	Inward	52.9	73.6	83.1	78.2	121.5	161.3
	Outward	31.7	24.8	21.3	41.8	61.3	99.5
Malaysia							
	Inward	20.7	23.3	23.4	32.3	58.5	57.2
	Outward	0.8	4.3	6.1	12.4	23.6	28.8
Viet Nam							
	Inward	0.2	1.1	4.0	27.8	48.2	50.6
	Outward	..	..	..	..	..	..
Cambodia							
	Inward	2.4	2.0	3.4	10.8	43.3	46.4
	Outward	..	..	..	4.2	5.4	5.7
China							
	Inward	0.5	2.0	5.8	19.3	32.2	35.6
	Outward	..	-	0.7	2.3	2.4	2.6
Laos							
	Inward	0.3	-	1.5	11.4	31.6	30.1
	Outward	..	..	..	-	9.7	14.9
Indonesia							
	Inward	13.2	28.2	34.0	25.0	40.4	27.5
	Outward	..	0.1	0.1	0.6	1.6	1.3
Thailand							
	Inward	3.0	5.1	9.7	10.5	24.5	25.8
	Outward	-	-	0.5	1.4	2.1	2.3
Philippines							
	Inward	3.9	8.5	7.4	8.1	17.1	14.5
	Outward	0.5	0.6	0.3	1.6	2.1	1.2
Chinese Taipei							
	Inward	5.8	4.7	6.1	5.9	9.0	11.9
	Outward	0.2	0.3	8.0	9.5	15.9	22.8
Korea							
	Inward	2.1	2.3	2.1	1.8	7.3	7.8
	Outward	0.2	0.5	0.9	2.0	5.2	5.7
Japan							
	Inward	0.3	0.3	0.3	0.7	1.1	2.1
	Outward	1.8	3.2	6.6	4.5	5.9	7.8

Notes: "..": not available; "- ": negligible.
Source: UNCTAD, *World Investment Report 2004* (Annex Table B.6).

Box 1.4. **The Trade-FDI Nexus, Chinese Style**

Outward orientation differs widely in degree from country to country and period to period. In China, one cannot easily tell precisely how actual policy and the extent of protection in the trade and FDI regimes have evolved. Yet it is safe to say that in the mid-1980s the authorities gave clear signals both at home and abroad that they intended to establish a trade regime in favour of export production. This period also saw China's *de facto* adoption of the coastal development strategy, an active encouragement of FDI inflows through various schemes of preferential treatment and the beginning of successive real effective devaluation of the Chinese currency (Fukasaku and Wall, 1994).

Perhaps the most dramatic turnaround of the "Reform and Opening-up" process was the shift away from prohibition of FDI inflows to their active encouragement. Given that the economy has a high domestic saving rate, this change aimed primarily to gain access to modern technology, both embodied and disembodied, packaged with capital, management skills and international business networking. A key aspect of this reform involves the enactment of politically crucial but unspecific "enabling laws" first, which allows the government to introduce more specific policy measures later, when political and economic conditions are ripe. The first measure taken after 1978 was the landmark 1979 Joint-Venture Law, followed by numerous laws and regulations in various areas directly relevant to both Chinese and foreign firms, including income tax, profit repatriation, labour management, land use, property rights and so on. The country's current FDI policies are well documented in OECD, 2002*c*, pp. 330-337.

For FDI, the Chinese authorities use the terms "foreign-invested" or "foreign-funded" enterprises which comprise three types: equity joint ventures, contractual (or co-operative) ventures and wholly foreign-owned ventures. As the table below shows, foreign-invested enterprises (FIEs) have rapidly become major exporters. Despite their fast export growth, their trade performance has resulted in net trade deficits in most years until quite recently. The major turnaround came in December 1996, when the renminbi became convertible on current account. This policy change has "not only assisted China's international traders but also greatly facilitated the business operations of foreign investors in China" (OECD, 2002*c*, p. 328).

ISBN 92-64-01442-X © OECD 2005

Box 1.4 (contd.)

Trade Performance of Foreign-Invested Enterprises in China

Year	1985	1990	1995	1997	1999	2000	2001	2002
Value of FIE trade ($ billion)								
Total trade	2.4	20.1	109.8	152.6	174.5	236.7	259.1	330.2
Exports	0.3	7.8	46.9	74.9	88.6	119.4	133.2	170.0
Imports	2.1	12.3	62.9	77.7	85.9	117.3	125.8	160.3
Balance	-1.8	-4.5	-16.0	-2.8	2.7	2.2	7.4	9.7
FIE trade relative to China's total trade (per cent)								
Total FIE trade	3.4	17.4	39.1	47.0	48.4	49.9	50.8	53.2
Exports	1.1	12.6	31.5	41.0	45.5	47.9	50.1	52.2
Imports	4.9	23.1	47.7	54.6	51.8	52.1	51.7	54.3

Source: OECD (2002c), Table 10.2, p.327 (for 1985-1999); *China Statistical Yearbook 2003* (for 2000-2002).

FDI inflows into China's manufacturing sector have concentrated heavily in the so-called "labour-intensive" industries. Such FDI, however, is not necessarily a poor source of transferable, useful technology and know-how and might help to enhance China's industrial efficiency. A recent study based on a firm survey of Hong Kong, China garment-sector investing in China has found that FIEs based in Hong Kong, China act as an effective channel for transferring advanced, market-focused managerial know-how and practices to the mainland (Thompson, 2003).

Labour Migration as a Complementary Factor. The pattern of labour migration seems to have complemented the emergence of a trade-FDI nexus in the region. China, Indonesia and the Philippines are predominantly migrant-sending economies, while Chinese Taipei, Japan and Korea are on the receiving side, although their stocks of foreign labour remain small in relative terms. Some middle-income economies, such as Thailand and Malaysia, have made a transition from net emigration to net immigration, reflecting the co-existence of unskilled immigrants and highly skilled emigrants. The basic policy approach taken by Japan and other receiving economies has been to promote job creation in less advanced economies in the region and relocate their uncompetitive manufacturing operations to them, in order to control the inflow of unskilled foreign workers (Chalamwong, 2005, in this volume).

Migrant remittances have played an important role in supporting the living standards of some East Asian sending countries, notably the Philippines where remittances accounted for over 9 per cent of GDP in 2002. The international business networks established by emigrants have also provided an additional source of capital flows into the home countries. For instance, investments from entrepreneurial emigrants, together with their diaspora networks, have played a critical role in the recent rapid growth of ICT-related industries and service sectors in China and India.

Highly skilled migrants within the region are mostly company transferees who are frequently shifted within multinational enterprises[21]. This type of labour migration tends to accompany FDI in the more advanced productive sectors, and it contributes to technology transfer and human resource development in host economies (Katseli, 2004). The notion of "brain exchange" or "brain circulation", as opposed to "brain drain", may better capture the real nature of the regional movement of high-skilled workers. Within the vision of an "East Asian Community" (see the next section), migration policy needs firmer embedding in a coherent policy of regional integration and development.

The Role of International Aid. International aid has supported East Asia's post-war development and the region's emerging trade-FDI nexus through concessionary financing for economic and social infrastructure and technical assistance for human and institutional capacity building. While its precise impact on development cannot be measured easily[22], East Asia has definitely benefited from the range of official development assistance (ODA) programmes offered by the donors (Soesastro, 2005, in this volume). Soesastro cites, for example, several successful cases of large infrastructure development projects in ASEAN countries, including the Brantas River Basin Management Project in East Java. International aid seems to have also helped recipient countries, through policy dialogue and consultation, to strengthen their capacity to formulate and implement their own development policies. Such impact is even more difficult to measure, but some anecdotal evidence regarding China's reform experience in the 1980s points to the usefulness of such policy dialogue and interaction between the donor community and the recipient country (Lin and Li, 2005, in this volume).

Annex Table 1.4 presents major trends in ODA commitments in East Asia by donor and by sector over the last three decades. Overall, economic infrastructure (transport, communications, energy, etc.) has been given the top priority. This certainly reflects Japan's long-term commitment to economic infrastructure building, but the table also shows the relative importance

ISBN 92-64-01442-X

attached by EU member countries to this category during the 1980s and 90s. Together with macroeconomic stability and complementary policy reforms aimed at improving local business conditions, the development of economic infrastructure can be seen as a critical requirement for promoting private investment — both domestic and foreign — in the region. ODA has provided an important source of foreign funds to finance it, with relatively stable net flows averaging on the order of 6 billion dollars at 2002 prices and exchange rates[23]. This contrasts sharply with fast-rising private flows (mostly direct investment and bank loans) after the mid-1980s (Figure 1.2)[24].

Figure 1.2 **Total Resource Flows to East Asia**
(Net disbursements at 2002 prices and exchange rates, $ billion)

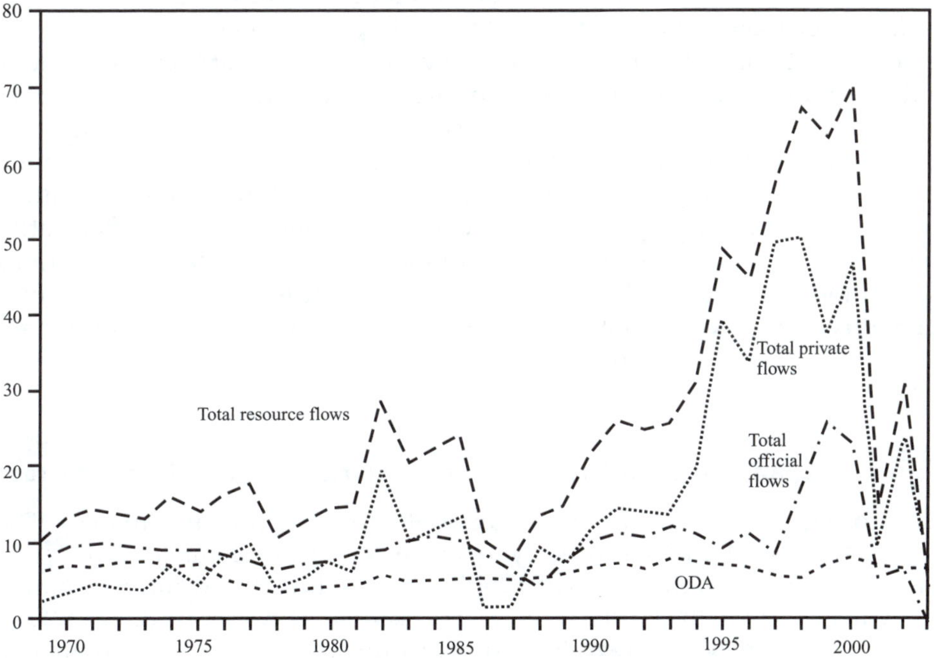

Source: OECD/DAC, International Development Statistics (on-line).

There is some evidence that government financing has helped promote Japanese FDI in the region, in line with the country's industrial restructuring and the corresponding need to relocate manufacturing industries losing comparative advantage *vis-à-vis* lower-wage countries. For FDI flows into Indonesia, Thee (1994) highlights an important role played by overseas investment credit — part of other official flows (OOF) — to facilitate Japanese direct investment in manufacturing in the early 1990s. Technical co-operation programmes, such as training local workers and technical consultation for private sector development, also assisted overseas investment activities by Japanese private companies. The Eastern Seaboard Development Plan in Thailand during the 1980s provides yet another example to support the view that the region-wide development of economic infrastructure assisted firms in improving productivity and promoting growth (see JBIC, 2000). More recently, the development community has increasingly recognised the importance of seeking the synergies between ODA and private investment, domestic and foreign. Nonetheless, the volume of net private flows to East Asia dropped abruptly with the onset of the 1997-98 East Asian crisis.

International aid in East Asia is not free from problems and criticism (McCawley, 1998). One source of such criticisms comes from the increased desire of recipient countries themselves to improve domestic governance in relation to international aid. Criticisms have been levelled at social dislocations and environmental damage caused by large-scale infrastructure projects in some recipient countries. Another concern relates to the changing needs for foreign aid as recipient economies develop. Many donor countries feel domestic pressures due to budgetary constraints on foreign aid. Although the squeeze to cut back aid money appears to have abated somewhat in the aftermath of the 1997-98 crisis, the fundamental question remains: What role should international aid play in East Asia in the future? It is particularly important for the reform of ODA policy and management in Japan, the top bilateral donor in the region (see Box 1.5).

Box 1.5. **Japan's ODA in East Asia: from "Hard" to "Soft" Infrastructure**

It is often stated that the dominance of infrastructure in Japan's ODA commitments in East Asia is deeply rooted in its own development experience, as the country developed itself rapidly by building "hard infrastructure" — with loans from the World Bank — in the early post-war years (OECD, 2004, pp. 31-32). Large government-led infrastructure projects have long dominated Japan's ODA loans, called yen loans, to East Asia. From a recipient countries' perspective, too, infrastructure development has had high priority — at least until quite recently — as a key ingredient of the region's development assistance menu, together with human resource development, institution building for industrialisation and promotion of SMEs. This overall situation did not change much in practice until the 1997-98 East Asia crisis (Annex Table 1.4).

ISBN 92-64-01442-X © OECD 2005

Box 1.5 (contd.)

During and after the crisis, interest in ODA revived in East Asia, with a major shift in priorities towards "social infrastructure" (education, health, water and other social services) by all donors, especially Australia, EU member countries and the United States. In value terms, Japan accounted for more than one-third of total ODA commitments for social infrastructure in the region in 1997-2002, although this sector still has relatively modest importance in Japan's ODA.

Meanwhile Japan's aid policy has come under strong domestic and international criticism. Domestic political support for maintaining the large aid budget has declined with rising fiscal deficits and debt as a result of stagnation of the Japanese economy. Internationally, Japan's aid policy has been criticised for excessive bias toward hard infrastructure projects, its preference for a bilateral approach to aid management and its hesitation to work as a partner within the multilateral framework (see, for example, Kawai and Takagi, 2004; and Soesastro, 2005, in this volume).

These developments led to a major change in Japan's aid policy and management, initiated in March 2000 by the establishment of the Inter-Ministerial Meeting on ODA. Following intensive consultations and public hearings under the leadership of the Ministry of Foreign Affairs, the Government of Japan adopted a new ODA Charter in August 2003, with emphasis on a more balanced approach to ODA. It states:

> "The most important philosophy of Japan's ODA is to support the self-help efforts of developing countries based on good governance, by extending cooperation for their human resource development, institution building including development of legal systems, and economic and social infrastructure building, which constitute the basis for these countries' development. Accordingly, Japan respects the ownership by developing countries, and places priorities on their own development strategies".

Looking to the future, Kawai and Takagi (2004) emphasise, among other points, the importance of adopting a strategic approach with a focus on economic development and poverty reduction in low-income countries. They argue that Japan must be more involved in providing "ideas" for institution building and policy reform, based on its own historical experience, in order to make aid more effective, even for hard infrastructure projects.

Soesastro (2005, in this volume) presents an insightful account of the changing landscape of policy issues related to international aid from the perspective of ASEAN countries as recipients. He takes Japan as a case study, because it has been the most important bilateral donor for East Asia. He highlights diverging views among donors themselves on how aid *should* work. From the East Asian economies' point of view, aid has served as a useful vehicle to facilitate human resource development, improve both hard and soft infrastructure, promote SME development and create various institutions for industrialisation. Emphasis among these priorities differs across recipients and over time. Over the last couple of years, it appears that the pendulum has swung back to place the role of economic infrastructure in a new perspective. Owing to the limited investment in it during the crisis and post-crisis period, many developing economies that have resumed growth have found their industrial overhead capital increasingly inadequate. Thus they have started to focus on economic infrastructure development once again, but this time by positioning its role within well-designed sectoral programmes and overall development policies, by paying full attention to the social and environmental implications and by maintaining the right balance with social infrastructure building. The donor community must therefore come up with a viable menu of modalities and areas of development assistance in which individual donors can specialise based on their comparative advantages. To make such a menu approach coherent, better and more effective co-ordination among donors becomes even more important.

Key Coherence Lessons from East Asia

As was discussed above, the emergence of a market-driven, trade-FDI nexus in the form of a positive relationship between liberalisation initiatives and strong trade and FDI performance was a critical factor underlying East Asia's development (Urata, 2005, in this volume). Japan and the Asian NIEs became major sources of FDI, as they climbed technological ladders in industrial development and began relocating labour-intensive activities to less advanced developing economies within the region. In other words, growth stimuli and incentives were generated and transmitted from more advanced to less advanced economies through continuous industrial restructuring and adjustment on the one hand and gradual reductions in trade and FDI barriers on the other. Unilateral tariff reductions for parts and components in machinery industries, together with the extensive use of a duty drawback system, played a pivotal role in the formation of international

ISBN 92-64-01442-X © OECD 2005

production and distribution systems, thereby stimulating intra-regional trade and investment in manufactured goods, especially electronic products (Kimura, 2005, in this volume).

International aid, largely in the form of concessional loans, supported the developing economies' growth by focusing on the importance of foreign trade and inward direct investment, through financing economic infrastructure and human resource development. International aid also helped to strengthen recipient countries' policy frameworks and institutional fundamentals, as in China's reforms (Lin and Li, 2005, in this volume). The East Asian economies were able to create a trade-FDI nexus with their market-friendly policy environments (good investment climate) and their institutional and human capability to absorb foreign capital. They used such opportunities to expand exports and imports for industrialisation and development. With manufactured trade, FDI and official development assistance (ODA), these economies were positioned to benefit from the positive impact of OECD-country policies. However, coherence was prominently weak in agricultural policy.

The impact of OECD-member agricultural policies on growth and poverty reduction appears to differ significantly across developing economies within the region (Barichello, 2005, in this volume). In the case of commodities, this depends on, among other things, the extent to which the policies in question affect world agricultural commodity prices, the extent to which the domestic agricultural sectors in East Asian economies are linked to those commodity markets and some other structural and institutional characteristics of the economies themselves. For example, the effects of rice and sugar policies in OECD countries on poverty reduction efforts in the East Asian economies are likely to be more substantial in Viet Nam than in Indonesia. In Indonesia, there is so much integration in the labour market that rural wage rates are largely exogenous to the rural and agricultural sector. It is less so in Viet Nam. Given that the rural labour market is less well integrated with the urban labour market, lower agricultural prices (caused by OECD-country agricultural policies) will likely have a depressing effect on agricultural wage rates, with a more direct impact on rural poverty. In the case of processed products, OECD-member policies, such as tariff escalation and non-tariff barriers, may be curbing the development of food industries that could become significant sources of employment, value added and scientific advance. During and after the 1997-98 crisis, several ASEAN countries, most notably Thailand, rediscovered that the agricultural sector played an important role in sustaining export earnings and rural household income and absorbing displaced workers, thereby contributing to economic recovery and political stability.

The East Asian Crisis and Beyond

The East Asian Crisis in 1997-98

The rapid growth of several East Asian economies since the mid-1980s, enhanced by their financial opening and exchange rate pegs, led to large inflows of private capital in the mid-1990s[25]. Fuelled by such capital inflows, private credit booms created pre-crisis vulnerabilities in the region. A greater availability of international private funds was considered a good thing for development, potentially welfare-enhancing for recipient countries. Yet greater financial integration made these economies more vulnerable to sudden changes in investor sentiment and the external economic environment, such as international interest-rate shocks. The experience of several East Asian economies in the early 1990s suggests that difficulty in managing large capital inflows was a critical policy issue for macroeconomic management at that time, as these economies were running near or at full capacity (IMF, 1995). Indeed, heavy capital inflows became disruptive for countries such as Thailand, as they induced a real appreciation of the currency, heightened inflationary pressures through increased money supply and widened current-account deficits to an unsustainable level[26].

Table 1.5 shows major trends in total capital inflows into 24 developing Asian countries, five crisis countries and China for 1994-2002. While the predominant type of capital inflow into China has been direct investment, the five crisis countries had become increasingly dependent on portfolio investment and other (short-term) capital to finance ever-increasing investment demand prior to the crisis. Domestic financial systems proved too weak as conduits for heavy capital inflows, which resulted in over-borrowing and declining credit quality, thereby increasing financial fragility (Montes, 1998; Reisen, 1999; and Milelli, 2003).

The World Bank (1998) summarised the major causes of the 1997-98 crisis. It pointed out three common forces that interacted to leave these economies vulnerable to external shocks: *i)* ready availability of private capital, especially short-term capital; *ii)* macroeconomic and exchange-rate policies that permitted capital inflows to fuel a credit boom; and *iii)* newly liberalised but insufficiently regulated financial systems[27].While the Thai stock market had already declined substantially during the first half of 1997, a trigger to the crisis came when the government yielded to the repeated attacks against the baht and abandoned the peg on 2 July. The Thai financial and currency crisis developed into a region-wide one as contagion spread to Indonesia, Malaysia, the Philippines, Korea and other economies by causing a sudden, huge outflow of capital and a simultaneous fall in asset prices.

ISBN 92-64-01442-X

In addition to the associated detrimental social effects, the 1997-98 crisis dealt a heavy blow to the economies of the region in the fiscal cost of bailing out and reconstructing the financial sector and the output forgone owing to the historically worst-ever recession that ensued (Figure 1.3). Moreover, some concern arose that the social impact of the crisis might have a lasting economic effect over the longer term (Box 1.6). Such concern has drawn greater attention to the question of social cohesion and domestic governance in East Asian societies.

Table 1.5. **Net Capital Inflows in Developing Asia**
($ billion)

	1994	1995	1996	1997	1998	1999	2000	2001	2002
Developing Asia[a]									
Total capital flows, net	94.9	152.5	176.5	7.0	-86.6	-46.4	-34.0	-9.9	-16.5
Direct investment, net	52.0	64.8	72.2	80.4	74.9	74.7	59.7	61.6	52.0
Portfolio investment, net	19.1	24.4	34.1	14.3	2.7	32.5	11.3	-64.4	-61.2
Other capital flows, net	23.8	63.3	70.2	-87.7	-164.2	-153.6	-104.9	-7.0	-7.2
Memorandum items									
ODA, net	15.4	14.2	12.1	10.1	12.3	12.9	11.7	11.8	n.a.
Changes in reserves[b]	-59.7	-50.7	-69.2	5.5	-67.5	-87.2	-61.6	-77.1	-131.4
Current Account	-27.0	-64.6	-78.4	-1.2	140.3	142.4	113.9	98.1	135.9
Crisis countries[c]									
Total capital flows, net	33.3	62.5	74.9	-13.1	-33.5	-12.5	-15.8	-12.1	-7.1
Direct investment, net	6.4	8.4	11.1	12.4	11.8	12.4	6.3	2.7	2.6
Portfolio investment, net	11.2	20.6	28.7	16.6	-3.4	13.1	7.2	6.2	0.0
Other capital flows, net	15.7	33.5	35.2	-42.1	-41.9	-38.0	-29.4	-21.0	-9.7
Memorandum items									
ODA, net	3.2	3.3	2.2	1.8	2.8	4.0	3.0	2.4	n.a.
Changes in reserves[b]	-8.5	-14.9	-14.6	33.4	-46.4	-39.5	-26.0	-9.0	-23.2
Current account	-22.2	-39.1	-53.8	-26.4	69.8	62.5	44.3	30.0	33.0
China									
Total capital flows, net	32.6	38.7	40.0	21.0	-6.3	5.2	2.0	34.8	32.3
Direct investment, net	31.8	33.8	38.1	41.7	41.1	37.0	37.5	37.4	46.8
Portfolio investment, net	3.5	0.8	1.7	6.9	-3.7	-11.2	-4.0	-19.4	-10.3
Other capital flows, net	-2.7	4.0	0.2	-27.6	-43.7	-20.5	-31.5	16.9	-4.1
Memorandum items									
ODA, net	3.2	3.5	2.6	2.1	2.4	2.4	1.7	1.5	n.a.
Changes in reserves[b]	-30.5	-22.5	-31.7	-35.9	-6.2	-8.7	-10.7	-47.4	-75.2
Current account	6.9	1.6	7.2	37.0	31.5	21.1	20.5	17.4	35.4

Notes: *a)* 24 economies in Asia and the Pacific, including Korea and Singapore but excluding Chinese Taipei. *b)* A minus sign indicates an increase. *c)* Indonesia, Korea, Malaysia, the Philippines and Thailand.

Sources: IMF, *International Financial Statistics* (CD-ROM) and OECD/DAC, *International Development Statistics*.

Figure 1.3. **Real GDP Growth Rates: Five Crisis Countries** (%)

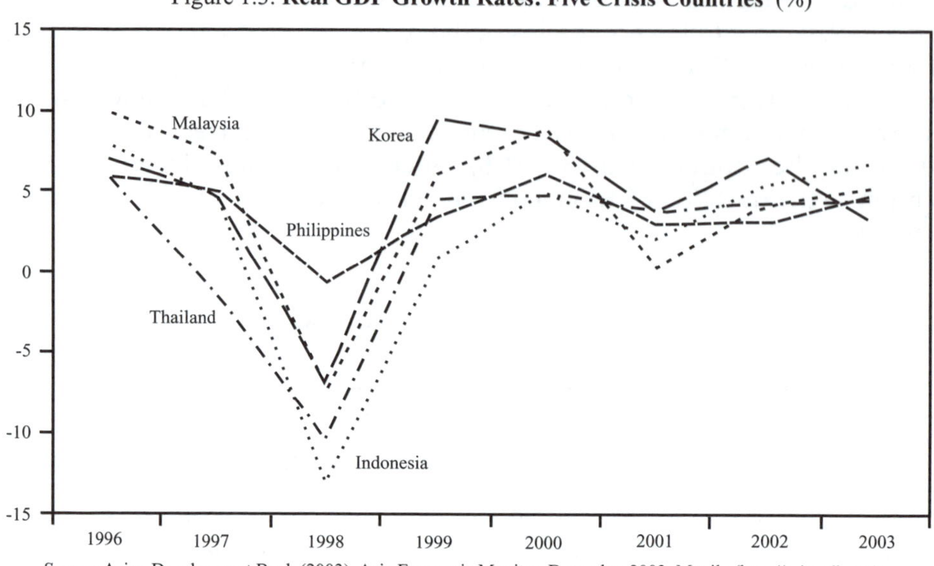

Source: Asian Development Bank (2003), Asia Economic Monitor, December 2003, Manila (http://aric.adb.org).

Box 1.6. **Social Impact of the Crisis**

The crisis negatively affected the wellbeing of individual households through four direct channels. First, a sharp contraction in production reduced the demand for labour, which resulted in a reduction in real wage rates and/or an increase in unemployment. Second, high inflation during the crisis and its aftermath dented real household expenditure. The annual rate of consumer price inflation in Indonesia shot up from 6.2 per cent in 1997 to 58.5 per cent in 1998 and stayed over 20 per cent in 1999. Third, higher import prices due to real currency devaluation reduced the purchasing power of household income. Fourth, a substantial loss of property incomes (dividends, capital gains and rents) reduced total household income. In addition, the welfare of poor households further deteriorated *indirectly* through the government's lower spending on education, health care and other social services. Such direct and indirect effects of the crisis are difficult to measure empirically, because hard figures are often lacking (Rol, 2003, p. 382).

 ISBN 92-64-01442-X © OECD 2005

Box 1.6 (contd.)

Despite these difficulties, national authorities in the crisis countries and multilateral financial institutions have attempted to assess the nature and extent of the social impact of the crisis.*Having reviewed the results of some earlier assessments, Booth (1999) concludes that the initial fear over theimmediate impact of the crisis on mass poverty and destitution was an exaggeration; poverty incidence increased substantially in all crisis-hit countriesbut more dramatically in some than in others. She also points out that the increase in the head-count incidence of poverty came largely from the effects of high inflation in Indonesia, while a surge in open unemployment was the main factor in Korea, Malaysia and Thailand.

The indicators at hand cannot fully capture the social consequences of the crisis, because poverty phenomena are dynamic. Many households that fell below the poverty line during the crisis may have moved up to non-poor status later on. Such cases of "transient poverty" are not well understood. More important, the financial damage incurred by poor households (e.g. lost educational opportunities) may be irreversible, affecting children negatively over their life spans.

* See, among others, Knowles *et.al.* (1999); Booth (1999); World Bank (1998, 2000); Rol (2003); and country case studies in OECD (2002*a*).

Lessons from the Financial Crisis

The three major lessons to draw from the financial crisis all relate to policy. They stress the importance of:

- managing financial globalisation;
- improving national economic structures and foundations; and
- strengthening social protection.

Managing Financial Globalisation. The successive financial and currency crises of the 1990s have led the international financial community to realise that they resulted not only from specific (and often idiosyncratic) factors in particular countries, but also from some common trends inherent in today's international financial system. The risks involved in large flows of short-term capital and their sudden reversals are now widely recognised. It is therefore necessary but not sufficient for host economies to put their own financial houses in order, so as to reap the benefits of financial globalisation without falling victim to its associated risks. Major reforms are required at all levels, global, regional and national.

At the global level, active discussions on policy initiatives to strengthen the international financial architecture had begun soon after the Mexican peso crisis in December 1994. The East Asian crises gave further impetus to them and to agenda setting (Eichengreen, 1999; Kenen, 2001). In June 1999, at the G7 Summit Meeting in Cologne, the Report of G7 Finance Ministers made a six-point, comprehensive set of recommendations to promote global financial stability through appropriate national actions and enhanced international co-operation[28]:

- strengthening and reforming the international financial institutions (notably the IMF) and arrangements;
- enhancing transparency and promoting best practices (in various areas, including disclosure of financial data, transparency in fiscal and monetary policies, corporate governance and so on);
- strengthening financial regulation in industrial countries (particularly for the operation of highly leveraged institutions and offshore financial centres);
- strengthening macroeconomic policies and financial systems in emerging economies;
- improving crisis prevention and management, and involving the private sector; and
- promoting social policies to protect the poor and most vulnerable.

Over the past five years a number of reform proposals have emerged to reduce the severity and frequency of future crises (see, for example, Chinn, 2005, in this volume). They are admittedly "modest and incrementalist, rather than sweeping and revolutionary — perhaps more like redoing the plumbing and electricity in the house than redesigning the architecture from the ground up" (Frankel and Roubini, 2003, p. 272). Yet the crisis has played a strong catalytic role in advancing reforms in all the countries it struck. To restore investor confidence and better manage financial globalisation, prudential supervision and regulation in the banking sector have been strengthened, together with restructuring of the financial and corporate sectors. Indonesia and Thailand, for example, have made significant legislative changes in their bankruptcy procedures. Another prominent area of reform has involved further liberalisation and deregulation of foreign investment in nearly all countries in the region.

Meanwhile, in three particular areas, efforts to promote regional monetary and financial co-operation have been substantial: enhancing information exchange and surveillance, improving resource provision and

ISBN 92-64-01442-X © OECD 2005

promotion of the Asian bond market. For the first, the Manila Framework Group established in November 1997 brings together deputies from the finance ministries and central banks of 14 countries within and outside East Asia, together with the IMF, World Bank, ADB and BIS. Furthermore, the ASEAN+3 (China, Japan and Korea) surveillance process was established in November 1999 and its first peer review meeting held in May 2000. In the second area, the Chiang Mai Initiative launched in May 2001 has two parts: an expanded ASEAN Swap Arrangement and a network of bilateral swap and repurchase agreements among ASEAN+3 countries (Kuroda and Kawai, 2002)[29]. The third area has received greater attention more recently, in the development of deeper and more liquid local currency-denominated bond markets, which can produce a more balanced regional financial system and facilitate more efficient allocation of the large pool of domestic savings, thus reducing the "double mismatch" problem. ASEAN countries are also exploring the possibility of improving cross-border bond issuance.

National Efforts to Strengthen Economic Policies and Institutions. As recommended in the Cologne Report of G7 Finance Ministers, individual developing economies have made efforts to strengthen policy and institutional frameworks with an emphasis on macroeconomic management capacity and financial-sector reform. Attention has focused particularly on the need to improve regulation and supervision in the financial sector, to strengthen corporate governance and to establish effective domestic insolvency procedures to deal with non-viable banks and corporations. With stronger domestic underpinnings in these areas, crises should become less likely to occur and, even if they do arise, their impact on the economy will tend to be limited.

One of the principal instruments for strengthening domestic policies and institutions is international best-practice information on macroeconomic policy making, financial regulation and supervision and capital-market infrastructure. Reports on the Observance of Standards and Codes (ROSCs) cover 12 issues in these three areas. Macroeconomic policy includes monetary and financial policy transparency, fiscal transparency and special data-dissemination standards in addition to the general data-dissemination system. Financial regulation and supervision include banking supervision, securities regulation, insurance supervision, payments systems and countering money laundering. Capital market infrastructure includes corporate governance, accounting standards, auditing standards and insolvency and creditor rights[30]. These processes are undoubtedly useful, but take time for effective implementation.

Five sets of corporate governance issues can serve to illustrate the linkages to public policy in East Asia. First, group affiliation is the most frequent organisational form, by which several firms, often family controlled, link through complex ownership structures. Some such groups may suffer from resource misallocation and mismanagement. Second, the high diversification of firms does not help them to weather turbulent times favourably, contrary to expectations. Third, financial disclosure and transparency tend to be low, although earnings information is better in foreign-held firms.Fourth, a review of issues related to the financial crisis indicates that relation-based financial systems may result in the misallocation of capital in the face of external shocks. Finally, firms' financing structures and relationship banking raise further corporate governance issues, such as high debt-asset ratios and less effective use of recourse to bankruptcy (Claessens and Fan, 2002). Links between corporate and public governance thus exist in terms not only of ownership patterns, but also of competition policy and the regulatory framework in which firms operate. The quality of public governance also affects corporate life through governments' and politicians' tolerance for collusion, rent seeking and corruption as well as the extent of rule enforcement.

Social Protection. East Asian countries have made great strides in alleviating extreme poverty (measured by the lower international poverty line) over the last ten years or so. The 1997-98 crisis arrested and temporarily reversed this overall trend and made one thing clear to every citizen in East Asia. Informal, family-based mechanisms on which traditional societies relied as the main form of social protection have been revealed as inadequate to cope with nation-wide shocks that could bring down large numbers of households simultaneously. Evidence thus far indicates that the social impact of the crisis was substantial, but more important, the impact on poverty was much less severe in some countries than in others. Some of the less affected economies could absorb workers displaced from the formal industrial sector in agricultural and (informal) service employment — in other words, much of the adjustment took the form of lower real wages. In Malaysia migrant workers bore the brunt of adjustment more than domestic ones did (World Bank, 2000, p. 117). In Thailand, agricultural exports received a positive boost from real currency devaluation, which contributed to supporting rural household income.

The crisis underscored an urgent need to establish more formal mechanisms for managing risk and protecting the poor and socially vulnerable. The decline of *relative* poverty (measured by the upper international poverty line) has been much slower than that of extreme poverty (see Annex Table 1.2).Four years after the crisis, the proportion of the "near-poor"

ISBN 92-64-01442-X © OECD 2005

remained very high in Indonesia (58 per cent) and the Philippines (43 per cent), followed by Thailand (27 per cent). All five crisis countries have undertaken initiatives to adapt existing institutions to evolving social conditions and to establish new ones (see OECD, 2002*a*).

A number of proposals have been put forward to improve the design and implementation of social protection — particularly for social assistance, social insurance, employment and community-based schemes. First, under-coverage is recognised as a serious drawback in social protection regimes. Workers in the informal sector as well as in rural areas, frequently women, constitute the majority of the workforce most vulnerable and often excluded from public social services. Second, the design and choice of targeting mechanisms require further study, taking into account individual countries' particular situations. Trade-offs are evident in terms of economic incentives, fiscal objectives and political acceptability. Third, involvement of civil society in programme implementation and monitoring is essential to enhance the efficiency and coverage of social protection policy.

Policy Implications and Challenges Ahead

Challenges for East Asia

There is a case for rethinking the basic approach to the sustainability of East Asia's economic growth and development from several fundamental perspectives. Many East Asian economies have in common longer-term policy challenges that deserve much more serious attention in coming years. To meet these post-crisis challenges, East Asian societies need to take forward-looking, more coherent approaches, several of which are discussed below.

Managing Regional Trading Arrangements. The only formal regional trade arrangement in East Asia used to be the ASEAN Free Trade Area (AFTA). Following its establishment in 1967, ASEAN countries began joint efforts to promote intra-regional trade and economic co-operation among themselves[31]. They established the AFTA in 1992. Despite the slow pace of trade liberalisation, AFTA has been in effect among the original five ASEAN members (Indonesia, Malaysia, the Philippines, Singapore and Thailand) and Brunei Darussalam since January 2002. Although the exclusion list is long and individual country circumstances vary, the bulk of goods traded between these countries now bear tariffs of only 0-5 per cent[32]. Viet Nam will comply with the same tariff

ISBN 92-64-01442-X

standards by 2006, Laos and Myanmar by 2008 and Cambodia by 2010. ASEAN as a whole is expected to become a tariff-free FTA by 2010 for the six members and by 2015 for the new members. At their Summit meeting in Bali on 7 October 2003, ASEAN leaders agreed to the creation by 2020 of an ASEAN Community, comprising three pillars, namely political and security co-operation (an ASEAN Security Community), economic co-operation (an ASEAN Economic Community) and socio-cultural co-operation (an ASEAN Socio-Cultural Community). These three pillars are mutually reinforcing to ensure security, shared prosperity and social stability in the region, within which there would be free flows of goods, services, investment and skilled labour.

Recently, East Asia has begun to embrace North-South FTAs as a means to accelerate market opening and structural reform to sustain growth momentum within the region. As many of the region's economies recover from the 1997-98 crisis, external pressures that FTAs would generate are considered necessary to liberalise trade and FDI further and to deepen structural reforms in pursuit of regained and sustained economic growth. The East Asian economies also consider FTAs as an integral component of broader economic partnership agreements that include, *inter alia,* trade and FDI facilitation, harmonisation of standards, rules and procedures and economic co-operation in many areas.

Table 1.6 presents a list of the FTAs involving East Asian economies that are already in action, concluded, under negotiation or under study. This FTA bandwagon may reflect a fundamental change in the attitude of many East Asian governments towards market-driven economic integration and the institutionalisation of such integration (Kawai, 2004*b*).

It is often pointed out that an East Asia-wide FTA would be economically desirable[33]. Yet current initiatives to establish FTAs involving China, Japan and Korea on the one hand and ASEAN, either as a group or individually, on the other might eventually produce an East Asia with competing trade arrangements. To avoid this "spaghetti bowl" effect and to maximise potential benefits, the regional economies need to draft a clear road map to establish a region-wide FTA in East Asia. Regional trade arrangements that ensure greater coherence of trade, FDI and aid policies need to be created to promote the region's growth and development[34].

 ISBN 92-64-01442-X © OECD 2005

Table 1.6. **FTAs and East Asian Economies** (as of August 2005)

In Effect	Under Official Negotiation	Under Consultation/Study
Bangkok Treaty (1976)	Singapore-Mexico (July 2000)	Japan-Australia
Laos-Thailand (1991)	Singapore-Canada (Jan. 2002)	Japan-Chile
ASEAN FTA (1992)	Singapore-Chile	Japan-India
Singapore-New Zealand (Jan. 2001)	Singapore-P3 (Aus, Chile, NZ)	Japan-Switzerland
Japan-Singapore (Nov. 2002)	Singapore-India	Japan-China-Korea
Singapore-Australia (July 2003)	Singapore-Jordan	China-Korea
Singapore-EFTA (Jan. 2003)	Hong Kong, China-New Zealand (Nov. 2000)	China-Singapore
Chinese Taipei-Panama (2004)	Japan-Philippines (a.c. Nov. 2004)	China-SACU
Singapore-USA (Jan. 2004)	Japan-Malaysia (a.c. May 2005)	China-GCC
China-Hong Kong, China (Jan. 2004)	Japan-Thailand (a.c. Aug. 2005)	Korea-Mexico
China-Macao (Jan. 2004)	Japan-Korea (Dec. 2003)	Korea-Malaysia
Korea-Chile (April 2004)	Japan-ASEAN (April 2005)	Korea-Thailand
Thailand-Australia (Jan. 2005)	Japan-Indonesia (July 2005)	Korea-New Zealand
China-ASEAN (Jan. 2005)	China-New Zealand (Dec. 2004)	Korea-MERCOSUR
Japan-Mexico (April 2005)	China-Chile (Jan. 2005)	Korea-USA
Singapore-India (Aug. 2005)	China-Australia (May 2005)	Korea-South Africa
	Chinese Taipei-Guatemala (concluded Mar. 2005)	
	Chinese Taipei-Nicaragua (Sept. 2004)	
	Korea-EFTA (concluded July 2005)	Korea-India
	Korea-Singapore (signed Aug. 2005)	Singapore-Chinese Taipei
	Korea-ASEAN (Feb. 2005)	ASEAN-EU
	Korea-Canada (July 2005)	ASEAN (bilateral)-USA
	Thailand-Bahrain (signed)	
	Thailand-India (signed)	
	Thailand-Peru (agreed April 2004)	
	Thailand-New Zealand (signed April 2005)	
	Thailand-USA (June 2004)	
	Malaysia-Australia (May 2005)	
	ASEAN-India (Jan. 2004)	
	ASEAN-CER (Feb. 2005)	

Notes: a) The shaded items are those within East Asia. *b)* "a.c." refers to "almost concluded."
Source: Official sources.

Developing Domestic Technological Capability. The increasing importance of technology as a factor in industrial competitiveness poses a pressing challenge to economies of the region. Through clustered, sequential industrialisation, the advanced Southeast Asian economies built similar industrial and export structures, particularly in electronics, thereby intensifying competition between them (Abe, 2003). As global competition increased, the financial crisis shed light on a number of structural weaknesses. This has augmented pressures for greater innovation and movement towards a knowledge-based economy. To enable this to happen, and in addition to assuring enabling macroeconomic, tax and competition policies, governments should provide information infrastructure, improve skill levels and education, upgrade research and development (R&D) and innovation systems, and implement institutional reforms.

Recent OECD work on the sources of economic growth (OECD, 2003*b*) confirms that fundamental macroeconomic and structural policy prescriptions for sustainable, long-term growth remain valid. Nonetheless, access to and effective use of information and communications technology (ICT) as well as the type and quality of education have driven growth in a number of countries. Not only does this imply the need for better youth education, including the integration of ICT into curricula, but also more adult, life-long learning, including an improved distribution of vocational training across different categories of workers. Pro-competitive regulations that facilitate the entry of innovative firms are also important growth drivers. Analysts of the current East Asian situation point to the need to tap better into knowledge and R&D and to upgrade human resources, as well as to increase competition between firms (Chen, 2003, Pai *et al.*, 2003 and Yusuf, 2003).

China's ascendancy and its impact on East Asia intensify the competitive pressures for industrial upgrading in these economies. Policy makers are concerned about the changing shares and composition of trade, as well as shifts in investment flows toward China and away from their economies. China's imports and China's FDI-induced trade are seen to benefit mainly developed countries (Chen, 2003), while areas of trade overlap are greatest with neighbouring economies. As labour costs increased in the Asian NIEs and ASEAN by the mid-1990s, Japanese investment gradually shifted to China (Abe, 2003). Thus, countries such as Malaysia will have to depend less on labour-intensive, low-wage manufacturing than before (Yusof, 2003). Simulations have shown that additional welfare losses in ASEAN-4 will occur only if they fail to improve their capacities to absorb new foreign technologies and to engage in home-grown technical innovations (McKibbin and Woo,

ISBN 92-64-01442-X © OECD 2005

2003). The sheer size and rapid rise of China imply that other East Asian economies will face major industrial adjustment and restructuring. At the same time, they will also see new opportunities in terms of growth stimuli and incentives, which might be comparable to those presented by the rise of Japan and the Asian NIEs during earlier decades (Reisen *et al. 2005).*

Improving Governance. Governance challenges for the further development of East Asia arise at the regional, national and firm levels. As the discussion of regional integration and competitive market pressures suggests, trade and investment considerations drive current efforts to strengthen and formalise co-operation among East Asian economies. To expect greater regional political and economic integration in the near future would be premature, in part owing to the prevailing diverse national governance structures.

Most facets of national public governance equate with institutional development. Good governance may be regarded as a package of "good institutions" that frequently includes democracy, a clean and efficient bureaucracy and judiciary, strong protection of private property rights, including intellectual property rights; good corporate governance frameworks, especially disclosure requirements and bankruptcy law; and well-functioning financial systems (Chang, 2002). Applying the analytical framework of a "relation-based" system of governance as practised in East Asia compared with the "rule-based" version predominant in the West reveals that the governance package is poorly developed or lacking in the *guanxi* (relations or connections)-based system (Li *et al.*, 2003). This gap in the institutional infrastructure of East Asia has received greater attention in the aftermath of the crisis; the previous sub-section discussed some of the changes underway. The question is whether attitudes and behaviours are changing in favour of implementing and not just creating a rule-based paradigm.

Movement towards better public governance requires the participation of citizens, including women, supported by strong civil-society institutions to hold government accountable and monitor performance. At the corporate level an analogous need arises to protect minority shareholders and investors. The technological means to facilitate the normal transition from relation-based to rule-based governance exist in information and communications technologies. East Asian countries can draw on good practice from other developed countries. The pressures of closer economic linkages with these countries and of globalisation more broadly will further encourage the transition, as the costs of maintaining the relation-based system become too high (Li *et al.*, 2003). Nonetheless, the necessary institutions take time to function properly, which calls for long-term commitment and investment.

The OECD countries' coherent, mutually reinforcing contribution to good governance consists in helping to strengthen policy frameworks and institutional fundamentals through policy consultation, promoting transparency and transferring good practices. Demonstration effects based on good governance standards and instruments, including regulatory and supervisory frameworks, can be useful points of reference. To minimise incoherent policies and practices, OECD countries should continuously strengthen their own application and enforcement of anti-bribery and anti-corruption measures, the international investment instruments, and the *Guidelines for Multinational Enterprises* (see Box 1.7), as well as widen the number of East Asian countries that adhere to these instruments. Peer review can maintain good standards of behaviour and exchanges of practices and experience.

Box 1.7. **International Investment Instruments**

Although no universal rules govern international investment, OECD member countries have committed themselves to provide non-discriminatory treatment to inward direct investment and related financial flows in the legally binding *OECD Codes of Liberalisation*. The 35 countries* that adhere to the *OECD Declaration on International Investment and Multinational Enterprises* have also undertaken a political commitment to accord national treatment to established foreign direct investors, to promote voluntary standards of corporate responsibility by multinational enterprises, to encourage restraint in the use of investment incentives and to avoid the imposition of conflicting regulatory requirements on multinational enterprises. These instruments have proved an effective framework for international co-operation and have served to underpin the liberalisation achieved in recent decades.

*All 30 OECD member countries plus Argentina, Brazil, Chile, Estonia and Lithuania. The OECD encourages non-members to adhere to this Declaration, which includes the *Guidelines for Multinational Enterprises*.

Improving Environment. Developed countries have been responsible for most of the environmental damage to the planet, and OECD countries have the most financial and institutional capacity to address the consequences. Yet environmental pressures will be generated to an increasing extent by developing countries, which also need to become more fully engaged in preventing and mitigating their impacts. The East Asia region currently faces a host of serious environmental problems and challenges. They include especially (Davis, 2003; ADB, 2001):

ISBN 92-64-01442-X © OECD 2005

- extensive land and soil degradation and severe deforestation, further menaced by more intensive agricultural practices;
- water shortages and pollution, air pollution, solid and hazardous waste generation that will increase with rapid and unplanned urbanisation and the growth of mega-cities;
- unsustainable use of non-renewable energy;
- over-fishing as well as marine and coastal pollution;
- acid rain, ozone-depleting chemical production and greenhouse gases; and
- threats to the biodiversity of one of the world's most richly endowed areas.

The combination of current and mounting problems threatens the health, wellbeing and security of the population, especially the poorest. Even if East Asian countries are aware of the increasing dangers to the environment created by their rapid industrialisation and economic growth, income levels will constrain the willingness and ability of their populations to address them. Provision of information, transparency, and participation of civil society in decision making will be necessary to generate political support for the actions required.

Because many of the environmental problems involve spillover effects and implicate more than one country, co-operation, governance and policy integration at the regional level must be part of future strategies. The importance of adopting integrated river-basin management not only for national but also for trans-boundary water resources provides one illustration. Other examples include air pollution and dwindling fisheries resources as well as issues of climate change and biodiversity, which are of even wider, global concern (OECD, 2002*d*). OECD countries — including Asian members — have made significant progress in addressing environmental problems, although much remains to be done. They have gained considerable experience in developing environmental policies, applying policy instruments and generating technological solutions for environmental problems. The efficient process of technology transfer that has contributed to East Asia's rapid growth could be part of the solution in addressing the serious environmental challenges that threaten sustainable development in the region.

Eradicating Rural Poverty. More than in any other part of the developing world, economies in East Asia have succeeded in combining high growth with significant poverty reduction (see Annex Tables 1.1 and 1.2). With the poorest people concentrated in rural areas, three sets of factors have

ISBN 92-64-01442-X

contributed to this remarkable achievement: agricultural productivity increases coupled with off-farm rural and urban employment generation; the provision of rural social and economic infrastructure; and a supporting institutional framework that includes participation of local communities. The resulting transition of agriculture in terms of its diminishing contribution to GDP that took about 100 years in many OECD countries happened in Korea, for example, in 26 years.

Despite the remarkable reduction in the numbers of poor people, poverty remains predominantly rural in East Asia and will continue to pose a difficult challenge. The disproportionate concentration of the poor in rural areas accounts for 80 per cent to 90 per cent of poverty in all the major countries of the region (IFAD, 2002). According to FAO projections, the number of undernourished people in East Asia will still amount to some 140 million in 2015, and poverty is likely to persist in parallel (Viatte, 2004). Among those most likely to suffer from rural poverty are the landless, marginal farmers and tenants, women and female-headed households, indigenous peoples, ethnic minorities and forest and upland dwellers, as well as internally displaced persons and victims of landmines. Rural poverty links closely with environmental problems, especially in areas at the margins of forest land (IFAD, 2002).

It is important to differentiate between patterns of rural and agricultural development in the Northeast Asian economies of Chinese Taipei, Korea and Japan and those in ASEAN countries. Owing to their differing stages in the sequential pattern of development, countries in Southeast Asia have created fewer productive non-agricultural employment opportunities in their rural areas. Agriculture is the primary source of employment for over 40 per cent of the labour force in all Southeast Asian countries (except Brunei, Malaysia and Singapore) and for more than 80 per cent in some, like Laos (Booth, 2002; World Bank, 2001). None of them has yet reached Korea's 1977 departure point, when agriculture's share of employment was at 40 per cent before dropping to 16 per cent within 14 years (Kim and Lee, 2003). The situation calls for a renewed focus on equitable land reform, productivity gains, off-farm employment and economic, social and institutional infrastructure adapted to today's conditions. Low and sometimes declining public expenditures in agriculture will need reversal.

For several economies in the region, including the Northeast, structural adjustment measures could help transform a lagging, traditional agricultural sector into a more competitive and economically viable one. Enhanced competitiveness implies economies of scale; higher standards, quality and

 ISBN 92-64-01442-X © OECD 2005

food safety; better packaging and delivery; developing brand names and niche products; removing restrictions and protection; and more research and development. Developing the food industry would generate employment, add value, increase exports and provide a gateway to new economic activities related to biology, life sciences, etc. It may also help reduce regional disparities, because the hubs for the food industry could be different from those of other industries and could provide employment opportunities to poor segments of the population (Viatte, 2004). Any strategy of exporting high value-added products, however, faces the two-pronged challenge of increasing competition from China and of tariff escalation and non-tariff measures in potential OECD importing countries. The OECD area needs greater attention to policy coherence by reducing escalating tariffs that discriminate against value-added products and by ensuring that non-tariff measures are not used to reduce developing-country access to OECD markets.

The Dynamics of Another Miracle

In retrospect, what was the East Asian crisis, when viewed from the perspective of the region's clustered, sequential development process? Was it a temporary aberration in the long-term growth trend or something more fundamental? Is the coherence of OECD policies a relevant issue for the future?

There are reasons to believe that East Asia will continue to lead as the world's most dynamic growth centre. East Asian economies generally have demonstrated remarkable resilience to multiple shocks, such as the bursting of the high-tech bubble and a recession in major OECD countries, high and volatile oil prices, jitters of terrorism and the Iraq War and the SARS epidemic. Part of the resilience is due to the support that came from OECD countries such as Japan, as well as the way that OECD countries kept their markets open to East Asian trade during times of crisis. Moreover, new growth dynamics are at work in the region. They include the ascendancy of China (and India in neighbouring South Asia) and the emergence of new players such as Viet Nam, the rapid growth in intra-regional trade and a coming of age of the Asian consumer with greater sophistication and purchasing power.

In considering whether East Asia can achieve another miracle of growth over a sustained period, at least three issues come to the fore. The first involves the design of necessary domestic policies and institutions to ensure that the benefits of economic growth become more broadly and equitably shared within society. Although many East Asian economies successfully alleviated extreme poverty over the past decades, it has proved more difficult to reduce

ISBN 92-64-01442-X © OECD 2005

income inequality. Designing effective social protection presents a major challenge for this purpose, and the experience of relatively advanced economies of the region (e.g. Chinese Taipei and Korea) may provide useful lessons.

Second, FDI flows into ASEAN have slowed in recent years relative to those into China. Middle-income ASEAN countries — Malaysia, Thailand, Indonesia and the Philippines — now face the major challenge of improving their attractiveness as hosts to FDI in a rapidly changing economic environment[35]. To remain attractive and competitive, the ASEAN economies must maintain FDI-friendly climates, continue to upgrade human capital and move on to a technological rather than a factor-intensive mode of production by shifting to knowledge-based economies. They also need to implement the AFTA by eliminating their often-long exclusion lists in order to enjoy a larger market and economies of scale.

Third, several low-income countries — such as Cambodia, Laos and Myanmar — have been left behind and less successful in participating in the region's multi-layered, sequential development process. Institution building for economic development and progressive poverty elimination in these countries should have the highest priority. An important policy question concerns how ODA programmes can be linked more directly to trade and FDI through their emphasis on promoting infrastructure development. One of the key lessons from East Asia's sequential development is that Japan and other advanced economies have regarded outward FDI to the less advanced economies of the region as part of the industrial restructuring necessary to move up technological ladders and shift domestic resources to more efficient uses. Now, the roles of not only these advanced economies but also middle-income countries are becoming increasingly important to keep this dynamic process moving.

More analytical work from the perspective of low-income countries is required to address how a dynamic trade-FDI nexus can be sustained in the less and least developed parts of East Asia and replicated in other developing regions. One important line of inquiry looks at the role of export-processing zones (EPZs) and other special zones as a transitional policy. Recent work by Schrank (2001) highlights contrasting experiences in the development of EPZs between the Dominican Republic and Korea and Mexico. This study provides an important reminder that the success of EPZs depends not so much on the attitudes and capacities of foreign investors as on those of local manufacturers. Subramanian and Roy (2001) attribute the success of EPZs in Mauritius to the quality of domestic institutions in managing both rent seeking and the inefficiency involved in selective intervention. These studies point more

ISBN 92-64-01442-X © OECD 2005

generally to building productive and institutional capacity in developing countries, especially least-developed ones. This topic has gathered increased attention since the late 1990s, particularly in the context of post-Doha development challenges[36].

Implications for Other Developing Regions

Drawing lessons from international development episodes is difficult, and the East Asian experience is no exception. All countries and regions are different in essential ways, e.g. in political, legal and economic institutions, economic fundamentals, macroeconomic policy formation and implementation, industrial organisation, characteristics of the factors of production, degree of outward orientation and so on. These characteristics can greatly influence how economic policy gets transmitted or filtered. The subjective historical context in which development takes place also has importance. As noted above, East Asian growth since the early 1970s and particularly the mid-1980s was a function of various positive developments in the international marketplace, such as favourable exchange-rate and interest-rate changes, copious capital flows in financial markets and technological change that facilitated globalisation and industrial restructuring. A "one-size-fits-all" approach to economic policy formation holds considerable risks. Hence, the first rule in applying lessons is to do so with considerable caution, bearing in mind country-specific circumstances.

Nevertheless, the East Asian experience, although somewhat varied from one country to another, does have some constant features that figure in the success of each country-specific case. After all, there should be reasons why East Asia could prosper over the past few decades, while Latin America and Africa have remained stagnant. Indeed, based on the East Asian experience and in fact that of the OECD area, one can argue that there does exist a vector of key economic policy variables underlying economic success:

- The first key variable would be political stability, enabled by functioning security arrangements and ensured through democracy or social consensus.
- Second, macroeconomic stability is key. Contrary to popular belief, the five crisis-affected countries had fairly strong macroeconomic fundamentals on the eve of the crisis. Distorted financial market incentives and insufficient institutional development were the main culprits in the crisis.

ISBN 92-64-01442-X © OECD 2005

- Third, in order to benefit from good policies and reforms pursued by OECD countries, such as trade liberalisation, FDI expansion, low interest rates and macroeconomic expansion, developing economies must have in place the policy frameworks and institutional and human capacity to respond.
- Fourth, outward-oriented trade and FDI policies are necessary at least in the medium run. While there is no consensus among economists regarding whether openness is a necessary or sufficient condition during the initial phase of industrialisation, there is consensus that it is necessary (though still not sufficient) in the medium-long term. This reality is clear in the East Asian case as well as from the negative examples of African, Middle Eastern and Latin American countries.
- Fifth, promoting high levels of domestic saving and investment is important in fostering development of efficient financial institutions and generating positive real interest rates.
- Sixth, financial development needs to play a prominent role in any successful economic reform package, but correct sequencing is extremely important, and reform of financial institutions can proceed effectively only if appropriate financial institutions, and particularly supervision and monitoring, are developed.
- Seventh, governments need to place a strong priority on human-capital development and embrace a clear, gender-neutral approach to education and training.
- Finally, effective governance policies at all levels are critically important to allow economic development to progress.

Challenges Ahead for Policy Coherence in OECD Countries

The East Asian experience has shown that the foregoing set of successful and indispensable policy variables must be both enabled and reinforced through OECD policy stimuli and support. OECD member countries play at least five essential roles in fostering policy coherence for development:

- help maintain security and political stability, which are fundamental to long-term growth, development and poverty reduction in developing economies;
- get the macroeconomic policy framework right, to avoid unintended policy shocks and create an enabling external environment conducive to private sector-led growth in developing economies;

ISBN 92-64-01442-X © OECD 2005

- promote an open and predictable international marketplace for goods and services on a multilateral and non-discriminatory basis, as well as orderly movement of people, complemented by trade-related assistance;
- strengthen the governance structure for international investment and finance to facilitate the flow of capital and technology in developing economies and help maintain financial stability; and
- increase the effectiveness of aid from both bilateral and multilateral donors through aid co-ordination and partnership and with a focus on economic growth and capacity building, both human and institutional.

There is no need to elaborate how fundamental security and political stability are to long-term growth and poverty reduction in developing economies. A key challenge is to find appropriate instruments to make significant contributions to efforts towards confidence building and conflict prevention in major developing regions. In East Asia, the role of OECD countries in promoting the region's political and security co-operation deserves particular emphasis. The ASEAN Regional Forum (ARF), currently including all ten ASEAN countries, seven OECD member countries (counting the European Union as one) and seven other countries[37], has also played an increasingly important part in fostering constructive dialogue and confidence building on political and security issues of common interest and concern.

It is impossible to consider policy coherence for development without paying due attention to macroeconomic linkages, which have become stronger during the past two decades. In current circumstances, particular attention must go to the challenge of correcting global current-account imbalances among North America, Europe and East Asia without inducing excessively large exchange-rate changes or economic disruptions. Developing countries stand to gain most if OECD countries can promote, over the medium term, policies designed to achieve the highest sustainable rates of economic growth and employment, while at the same time refraining from protectionist measures at the border.

Improving market access for the products and services of major interest to developing-country exporters must be complemented by necessary policy reforms and capacity-building efforts on the part of developing countries, notably the least developed. International assistance can and should play an important, facilitating role in helping them to strengthen domestic supply responses to emerging market opportunities and challenges in an increasingly open trading environment. Trade-related assistance constitutes a salient component of the coherence package OECD countries can offer to make trade work for development.

As this overview has shown, governance issues related to international investment and finance in East Asia have come into play at the national, regional and international levels. The OECD as a guardian and promoter of international investment instruments (see Box 1.7) can play a significant role at both national and regional levels. A key challenge is to strengthen existing channels and find new ones necessary to translate this important unfinished agenda into concrete policy actions.

It bears repeating that the reforms necessary to achieve development goals should be home grown and that such reform efforts can be supported by international aid. East Asia's development strongly supports this view. Many East Asian economies made *unilateral* efforts to strengthen productive and trade capacity so as to respond effectively to market opportunities and challenges. The economic ascendancy of the world's two most populous countries, China and India, makes this task even more urgent. Donors have been called upon to help them in this regard. On the other hand, East Asian economies have also learned from the events of 1997-98 that it is equally critical to manage financial risk and protect the poor and vulnerable more effectively. This requires governments to strengthen the banking and corporate sectors, while at the same time improving social safety nets and establishing a good working partnership with civil society. Once again, donors have been called upon to assist them. Donors will face a long list of priority sectors for development assistance. This is where aid co-ordination comes into the picture.

Despite the enormous progress of several East Asian economies and more recently China, the circumstances of the region's poorest countries, still highly dependent on a narrow range of commodity or manufactured exports, call for special OECD-country attention. Capacity-building efforts to position their supply side to benefit from globalisation and greater openness in the regional market have high priority. While regional and broader south-south co-operation will likely gain importance in coming years, their dependence on the OECD area for mutually reinforcing, coherent policies will remain significant. For example, a more strategic use of ODA to help them overcome their unfavourable conditions is warranted. There is an urgent need to strengthen human-resource development through greater investment in education and vocational training for skill upgrading. A focus on agriculture and rural development is also essential to reduce poverty and inequality. At the same time, OECD countries must make further efforts to bring down trade barriers and enhance market access to imports from these developing countries.

ISBN 92-64-01442-X © OECD 2005

As noted earlier (see Box 1.1), the DAC/OECD regularly conducts peer reviews of its member countries' aid policies, which involve discussions on policy coherence. Such peer reviews currently focus mainly on institutional aspects, including anecdotal illustrations of coherence issues. There are several ways in which this process could be constructively enhanced to obtain greater "buy-in" from policy communities other than development policy makers in national capitals. One approach would apply an analytical framework to the peer reviews on a systematic basis, drawing on key elements emphasised in this study and others. Second, a periodic comparative monitoring report involving several OECD Committees in its review could be launched. A third approach could build on experience with the joint Mutual Review of Development Effectiveness to be discussed in early 2005 by NEPAD and OECD Heads of State and Ministers as a model for similar dialogue with other partner countries. Analysis and case studies provided by partner countries should be an integral part of the process. A key challenge for OECD countries is to improve and broaden this peer and mutual review function with a view to enhancing whole-of-government accountability in economic policy making for development.

Building on technical work by the DAC/OECD and multilateral development banks, the international development community has committed itself to deliver and manage aid more effectively to increase development impact. The commitment is part of the Monterrey Consensus (2002) and is set out in the Rome Declaration on Harmonisation (February 2003), followed up and strengthened in the Paris Declaration on Aid Effectiveness (March 2005). Simplification and harmonisation of donor systems, procedures and requirements and reduction of their costs lie at the core of this undertaking. An ambitious programme of work agreed in Rome has a central focus on implementation at country level, emphasising country ownership and government leadership, capacity building and diverse aid modalities. Bilateral and multilateral donors and partner countries, including Cambodia and Viet Nam, co-operate in the DAC Working Party on Aid Effectiveness and Donor Practices to demonstrate that aid and expected increased volumes of aid can be managed effectively and coherently. The challenge is to turn examples of good practice into generalised practice on the ground. Indicators of progress were agreed in Paris, with measurable targets to be adopted by the time of the September 2005 UN Summit.

Notes

1. This is a revision based on an earlier draft presented by one of the authors at the Experts' Seminar held on 10-11 June 2004 at the OECD Headquarters. The authors are grateful to Louka Katseli, Richard Pomfret and other seminar participants as well as Shigeo Kashiwagi, Daisaku Kihara, Willi Leibfritz, and Charles Pigott, for their helpful comments and suggestions. Thanks are also extended to Federico Bonaglia, Orsetta Causa, Phyllis Flick, Mayrose Tucci and Hiroko Uchimura for their able assistance. The views expressed in this paper are strictly personal and do not necessarily reflect those of the OECD, the Development Centre or their member countries.

2. See the OECD website: http://www.oecd.org/development/policycoherence.

3. See House of Commons (2004) on this point.

4. The OECD Policy Brief on "*Policy Coherence: Vital for Global Development*" (OECD, 2003*c*) highlights the types of issues at stake and identifies the potential for seeking greater coherence between official development assistance (ODA) and other policies. These include, *inter alia*, such issues as agriculture, trade policy, investment, knowledge transfer, migration and global resources.

5. Two countries in the region have acceded to the OECD membership (Japan in 1964 and Korea in 1996).

6. The long-term statistical database on population and GDP (at 1990 international dollars) used for this chapter is available on-line from Maddison (2003). In this chapter "East Asia" is defined geographically as a region covering both Northeast and Southeast Asia. It stretches from the Korean peninsula to Myanmar and from Mongolia to Indonesia and the Pacific island countries. The paper does not consider Mongolia or the Pacific island countries. Note that Angus Maddison defines "East Asia" differently. His definition covers not only Northeast and Southeast Asia but also the Indian subcontinent and Afghanistan.

7. To convert currencies into a common unit on a multilateral basis, Maddison (2003) has applied the Geary-Khamis purchasing power parity (PPP) approach, which weights countries by the size of their GDP. For further discussion, see Maddison (1995, Appendix C).

ISBN 92-64-01442-X © OECD 2005

8. See, among early contributors, Amsden (1989), Wade (1990) and Young (1992 and 1995).

9. Chinese Taipei; Hong Kong, China; Indonesia; Japan; Korea; Malaysia; Singapore and Thailand.

10. See, for example, Amsden (2001), Stiglitz and Yusuf, eds. (2001), Subramanian and Roy (2001), Van Arkadie and Mallon (2003) and Rodrik (2003).

11. Labour-intensive sectors (ISIC 311-332) include food, beverages, tobacco, textiles, apparel, leather products, shoes, lumber and furniture, while technology-intensive sectors (ISIC 382-390) involve general, electronic, transport and precision machinery and equipment. The relative share of capital-intensive sectors (ISIC 341-381, including paper, printing and publishing, petrochemicals, rubber, plastics, non-metal minerals, steel and non-ferrous metals) in total value added expanded initially and then declined as income rose.

12. Rodrik, (2003) argues that the effectiveness of growth-promoting policies is context-specific. The experience of domestic policy reforms and development outcomes during the past five decades is indeed very diverse across developing countries and regions, and even within the group of high-performing East Asian economies, as discussed in Box 1.2. Thus, beyond several key policy fundamentals, reforming countries have substantial room for manoeuvre in packaging growth-promoting policies that are sensitive to local constraints and opportunities. For example, Young (2005, in this volume) emphasises that "Korea's rapid economic development has been achieved through an active and sustained pursuit of export-led growth and industrialisation *in the context of the international economic environment that has been supportive of this strategy*" (p. 2, italics added.)

13. We owe much to Richard Carey and Paul Isenman who brought up these issues at the preparatory meeting in November 2003 and at the Mid-Term Review Meeting in April 2004.

14. Note that the influence of geography on development has historical and cultural dimensions as well. Countries tend to interact closely with their neighbours both in history (alas, often in wars and conflicts) and through cultural exchanges, which has important ramifications for economic development.

15. Their results do lend support to the view that health conditions related to geography may be a major obstacle to long-term growth. Other things equal, countries at high risk of malaria tend to grow more slowly than countries free from malaria by 0.6 percentage points, which is large relative to other explanatory variables.

16. ASEAN itself was created in 1967 to deal mainly with political fears originating from instability in Indochina and in mainland China at the time.

17. The 12 original members of APEC are six ASEAN countries (Brunei Darussalam, Indonesia, Malaysia, Philippines, Singapore and Thailand), five OECD countries (Australia, Canada, Japan, New Zealand and the United States) and Korea (which became an OECD member in 1996). The current 21 member economies of APEC include, in addition to the original 12, Chile; China; Chinese Taipei; Hong Kong, China; Mexico; Papua New Guinea; Peru; Russia and Viet Nam.

18. Hsiao and Hsiao (2003) present an interesting comparative economic development analysis of Chinese Taipei and Korea, covering both the pre-war and post-war periods. East Asia's multi-layered catching-up process during the post-war period also involved other developing economies of the region, as Figure 1.1 shows.

19. See, for example, Katseli (1997), JBIC (2002, Chapter IV) and OECD (2002*b*, Chapter IV) for further discussions.

20. Note also that Japan's FDI stock-GDP ratio tripled between 1995 and 2003, although it started from a very low level.

21. A "highly-skilled" worker is generally defined in terms of educational background, official professional qualification, working experience or some combination of these factors. In practice, however, this definitional question poses a number of practical problems, which makes an international comparison very difficult, since there are many different types of "high-skilled" workers in different countries. See OECD (2003*a*) for further discussion.

22. More generally, the impact of aid on development has been hotly debated for a long time. The impact of some aid programmes, such as financing for social infrastructure, technical assistance to capacity and institution building, would be much more difficult to measure at the macro level compared with other programmes that are more short-term in nature (Clemens *et al.*, 2004).

23. In comparison with ODA, total official flows, including OOF, have been less stable in more recent years, because of large emergency loans to the crisis countries in 1997-98 and loan repayments in the subsequent years. In 2002, the total amount of official flows (ODA plus OOF) to East Asia turned negative, owing to large loan repayments.

24. The data used for this figure were extracted from OECD, *International Development Statistics Online*. The official flow data are expressed both at current prices and exchange rates and at 2002 constant prices and exchange rates. The deflators for official flows were used to convert private flows at current prices and exchange rates into the volume data. Private flows include direct investment and bank loans as well as grants by NGOs. Note that "East Asia" here excludes Myanmar.

ISBN 92-64-01442-X © OECD 2005

25. It has been argued that falling US interest rates in the early 1990s were an important "push" factor in driving private capital to emerging economies (Fernández-Arias and Montiel, 1996).

26. In Thailand, for example, the current-account deficit in 1996 amounted to -7.9 per cent of GDP. The size of a"sustainable" deficit is difficult to determine *a priori* and depends crucially on the perceptions of investors, which may be influenced by a country's stage of development, its government deficit, the way funds are spent and so on.

27. There is now a large body of literature on the causes of the East Asian crisis. Interested readers should see, among others, Montes (1998), Radelet and Sachs (1998) and Woo *et al.* (2000).

28. Before the Cologne Summit, the new Financial Stability Forum was created in April to enhance international co-operation and co-ordination in financial market supervision and surveillance (see http:/www.fsforum.org).

29. The total number of bilateral swap agreements has reached 16 and the total size of these arrangements amounts to $36.5 billion excluding the arrangements under the New Miyazawa Initiative, and $44 billion including the NMI (see Kawai, 2004*b*).

30. The most prominent among these is the Financial Sector Assessment Program (FSAP) supported jointly by the IMF and the World Bank.

31. These efforts included, among others, the ASEAN Industrial Project (1976), the ASEAN Preferential Trade Arrangement (1977), the ASEAN Industrial Complementation Scheme (1981), the ASEAN Industrial Joint Venture Scheme (1983) and the ASEAN Free Trade Area (AFTA). In AFTA, the Common Effective Preferential Tariff (CEPT) Scheme is used to reduce tariffs within the region to 0 to 5 per cent. The ASEAN Industrial Cooperation Scheme (AICO) applies the CEPT tariff rates (0 to 5 per cent) on approved AICO products to strengthen industrial co-operation within the region. AFTA is complemented by the Framework Agreement on the ASEAN Investment Area (AIA), which promotes free investment and movements of skilled workers, professionals and technologies within the region.

32. See *ASEAN Online* (http://www.aseansec.org).

33. See, for example, Scollay and Gilbert (2001, 2003), Cheong (2003) and Urata (2004).

34. How regionalism may or may not contribute to development has been under intensive discussion. See, for example, Kreinin and Plummer (2002) for a critical review of this topic.

35. A recent study by McKibbin and Woo (2003) regarding the global economic impact of China's accession to the WTO suggests the possibility of de-industrialisation in ASEAN-4 economies if they allow the drop in FDI inflows

to reduce the rate of technological diffusion to them. The authors argue that ASEAN-4 economies must give the highest priority to deepening and widening their pool of human capital by speeding up the diffusion of new knowledge to their scientists and managers and providing appropriate retraining programmes for displaced workers.

36. See the Policy Brief on "*Trade Capacity Building: Critical for Development*" (OECD, 2003*d*, August) for further discussion.

37. China, India, Korea DPR, Mongolia, Pakistan, Papua New Guinea and Russian Federation.

ISBN 92-64-01442-X © OECD 2005

ANNEX

Annex Table 1.1. **International Poverty Lines and Poverty Incidence by Region**

Region	Headcount Index (per cent living in households that consume less than the poverty line)					Number of Poor (millions)				
Panel A. International Poverty Line – $1.08 Per Day at 1993 PPP										
	1981	1990	1996	1999	2001	1981	1990	1996	1999	2001
East Asia & Pacific	57.7	29.6	16.6	15.7	14.9	795.6	472.2	286.7	281.7	271.3
China	63.8	33.0	17.4	17.8	16.6	633.7	374.8	211.6	222.8	211.6
Eastern Europe & Central Asia	0.7	0.5	4.2	6.3	3.7	3.1	2.3	19.8	29.8	17.6
Latin America & Caribbean	9.7	11.3	10.7	10.5	9.5	35.6	49.3	52.2	53.6	49.8
Middle East & North Africa	5.1	2.3	2.0	2.6	2.4	9.1	5.5	5.5	7.7	7.1
South Asia	51.5	41.3	36.6	32.2	31.3	474.8	462.3	428.5	431.1	428.4
India	54.5	42.1	42.2	35.3	34.7	382.4	357.4	399.5	352.4	358.6
Sub-Saharan Africa	41.6	44.6	45.6	45.7	46.9	163.6	226.8	271.4	294.0	315.8
Total	40.4	27.9	22.8	22.2	21.1	1481.8	1218.5	1096.9	1095.1	1092.7
Panel B. International Poverty Line – $2.15 Per Day at 1993 PPP										
Region	Headcount Index (per cent living in households that consume less than the poverty line)					Number of Poor (millions)				
	1981	1990	1996	1999	2001	1981	1990	1996	1999	2001
East Asia & Pacific	84.8	69.9	53.3	50.3	47.4	1169.8	1116.3	922.2	899.6	864.3
China	88.1	72.6	53.4	50.1	46.7	875.8	824.6	649.6	627.5	593.6
Eastern Europe & Central Asia	4.7	4.9	20.6	23.7	19.7	20.2	22.9	97.4	112.3	93.5
Latin America & Caribbean	26.9	28.4	24.1	25.1	24.5	98.9	124.6	117.2	127.4	128.2
Middle East & North Africa	28.9	21.4	22.3	24.3	23.2	51.9	50.9	60.9	70.4	69.8
South Asia	89.1	85.5	81.7	78.1	77.2	821.1	957.5	1029.1	1039.0	1063.7
India	89.6	86.1	85.2	80.6	79.9	630.0	731.4	805.7	804.4	826.0
Sub-Saharan Africa	73.3	75.0	75.1	76.0	76.6	287.9	381.6	446.8	489.1	516.0
Total	66.7	60.8	55.5	54.4	52.9	2450.0	2653.8	2673.7	2737.9	2735.6

Source: World Bank, Global Poverty Monitoring http://iresearch.worldbank.org/PovcalNet/jsp/index.jsp.

Annex Table 1.2. **Poverty Incidence in East Asia**

(Headcount Index: percentage of the population living in households that consume less than the international poverty lines described in Annex Table 1.1)

Year	Cambodia		Indonesia		Laos		Malaysia		Philippines		Thailand		Viet Nam	
	A	B	A	B	A	B	A	B	A	B	A	B	A	B
1990	48.3	83.7	20.8	71.1	53.0	89.6	0.5	22.7	19.1	53.5	12.5	47.0	50.8	87.0
1991	..	..	..	..	..	..	..	..	19.8	55.0	..	..	..	..
1992	..	..	..	..	48.8	88.1	..	16.2	..	..	6.0	37.5	..	..
1993	..	..	14.8	61.6	..	..	..	..	..	..	..	..	39.8	81.6
1994	..	..	..	..	..	..	..	..	18.4	53.1	..	..	..	..
1995	..	..	..	..	..	..	..	13.3	..	..	..	..	..	..
1996	36.7	76.9	7.8	50.5	41.3	83.1	..	11.5	14.8	46.5	2.2	28.2	18.8	67.9
1997	38.4	78.0	..	..	38.4	81.3	..	6.0	12.1	45.2	..	..	..	..
1998	36.9	77.4	..	..	39.5	81.8	..	9.3	14.5	47.4	3.9	33.2	18.8	67.9
1999	39.6	78.2	12.0	65.1	36.7	80.5	..	8.1	13.0	46.1	4.3	32.2	18.0	67.3
2000	39.7	77.2	10.5	63.3	35.1	79.7	..	6.1	12.0	44.8	3.7	30.8	15.2	84.7
2001	38.1	76.1	8.9	60.5	32.6	78.3	..	5.2	11.3	43.9	3.2	28.5	12.6	61.3
2002	37.2	75.2	7.5	57.8	31.0	77.0	..	4.0	11.0	43.2	2.6	26.7	10.4	57.6
2003	35.7	74.2	..	..	29.0	76.1	..	..	..	..	..	..	8.4	53.3

Notes: A = \$1.08 per day at \$ 1993 PPP. B = \$2.15 per day at \$ 1993 PPP. ".." = not available.

Source: Asia Recovery Information Centre (Poverty and social indicators available from http://www.aric.adb.org).

ISBN 92-64-01442-X © OECD 2005

Annex Table 1.3. **Social Indicators by Region and by Economy**

	Life Expectancy at Birth (total, years)					Mortality Rate, Under Five, per 1 000 Births					Literacy Rate, Adult Total (per cent of people aged 15 and above)			
	1960	1970	1980	1990	2002	1960	1970	1980	1990	2002	1970	1980	1990	2002
Region														
East Asia & Pacific	39	59	64	67	69	204	124	79	59	42	54	68	79	90[a]
Latin America & Caribbean	56	60	65	68	71	154	123	82	53	34	73	79	84	89[a]
Middle East & N. Africa	47	52	58	64	69	257	201	134	77	54	25	40	56	69[b]
South Asia	44	49	54	58	63	243	205	176	130	95	33	41	48	59[b]
Sub-Saharan Africa	40	44	48	50	48	275	239	197	187	174	..	..	..	65
Memo Item:														
Least Dev. Countries	39	43	47	50	51	278	243	208	183	159	25	31	38	54
Economy														
Cambodia	43	42	39	50	54	..	..	190	115	138	49	55	62	69
China	36	62	67	69	71	225	120	64	49	38	53	67	78	91[a]
Hong Kong, China	66	70	74	78	80	..	..	..	..	..	..	..	..	..
Indonesia	41	48	55	62	67	216	172	125	91	43	56	69	80	88
Japan	68	72	76	79	82	40	21	11	6	5	..	..	..	..
Korea, Dem. Rep.	54	60	67	66	62	120	70	43	55	55	..	..	..	..
Korea, Rep.	54	60	67	70	74	127	54	18	9	5	..	..	..	..
Laos	40	40	45	50	55	235	218	200	163	100	39	48	57	66
Malaysia	54	62	67	71	73	105	63	42	21	8	58	71	81	89[a]
Mongolia	47	53	58	63	65	..	..	140	107	71	95	97	98	98[a]
Myanmar	44	48	51	55	57	252	179	134	130	108	70	76	81	85
Philippines	53	57	61	66	70	110	90	81	63	37	82	88	92	93[a]
Singapore	64	68	71	74	78[b]	40	27	13	8	4	73	83	89	93[a]
Thailand	53	58	64	69	69	148	102	58	40	28	80	87	92	93[a]
Vietnam	44	51	60	65	70	112	87	66	53	26	83	87	90	..

Notes *a)* 2000; *b)* 2001. ".." = not available.

Source: World Bank, *World Development Indicators 2004*, online.

Annex Table 1.4. **Official Development Assistance to East Asia[a] by Donor and Sector, 1975-2002**

(ODA in each sector as per cent of total)

Three-Year Averages	Social Infrastructure and Services	Economic Infrastructure	Production Sectors	Multi-Sector	Commodity Aid and Programme Assistance	Emergency Assistance	Others	Total
	(A)	(B)	(C)	(D)	(E)	(F)	(G)	(H)
			All Donors, Total[b]					
1975-1977	10	30	20	6	28	1	5	100
1980-1982	11	45	24	3	15	1	1	100
1985-1987	18	39	22	4	14	0	3	100
1990-1992	14	40	23	9	10	1	3	100
1995-1997	19	56	11	11	6	2	7	100
2000-2002	25	37	11	11	6	2	7	100
			DAC Countries, Total					
1975-1977	11	30	20	4	28	1	5	100
1980-1982	11	49	20	1	16	1	1	100
1985-1987	15	43	19	2	16	0	4	100
1990-1992	13	45	19	6	12	1	4	100
1995-1997	17	60	10	8	3	1	2	100
2000-1002	23	39	11	11	6	2	9	100
			Australia					
1975-1977	11	52	5	0	30	2	0	100
1980-1982	19	9	35	11	18	9	0	100
1985-1987	34	8	44	10	1	3	0	100
1990-1992	31	18	14	37	1	0	0	100
1995-1997	57	25	7	5	1	3	1	100
			EU Members, Total					
1975-1977	16	17	31	2	25	2	8	100
1980-1982	7	48	28	2	14	3	2	100
1985-1987	13	44	26	3	8	1	4	100
1990-1992	12	52	28	5	1	1	1	100
1995-1997	20	49	13	7	6	1	3	100
2000-2002	41	17	11	12	2	3	14	100
			Japan					
1975-1977	9	53	21	8	8	0	1	100
1980-1982	9	57	18	1	15	0	0	100
1985-1987	14	54	17	0	10	0	4	100
1990-1992	10	46	16	4	18	1	5	100
1995-1997	13	68	9	7	2	0	1	100
2000-2002	14	52	10	10	6	0	8	100

ISBN 92-64-01442-X © OECD 2005

Annex Table 1.4. (contd.)

Three-Year Averages	Social Infrastructure and Services	Economic Infrastructure	Production Sectors	Multi-Sector	Commodity Aid and Programme Assistance	Emergency Assistance	Others	Total
	(A)	(B)	(C)	(D)	(E)	(F)	(G)	(H)
			United States					
1975-1977	7	4	11	2	68	0	9	100
1980-1982	33	10	15	4	30	0	8	100
1985-1987	14	6	13	6	58	0	2	100
1990-1992	30	27	8	13	16	2	4	100
1995-1997	46	5	1	18	4	0	26	100
2000-2002	42	12	4	7	24	10	2	100

Notes: *a)* "East Asia" in this table corresponds to the DAC definition "Far East Asia", which includes Myanmar.
b) "All Donors" include DAC countries, multilateral institutions and non-DAC donors.
(A) = Education, health, water and other social infrastructure and services. (B) = Transport, communications, energy, financial business and other services. (C) = Agriculture, industry, mining, construction, trade and tourism. (D) = General environmental protection, WID and other multi-sector services. (E) = Structural adjustment and other non-sector allocable support programmes and food aid (excluding relief food aid). (F) = Relief food aid and other emergency aid. (G) = "Others" include actions relating to debt relief or rescheduling, support to NGOs, etc.

Source: OECD, *International Development Statistics Online*, the Creditor Reporting System.

Bibliography

ABE, S. (2003), "Is 'China Fear' Warranted?: Perspectives from Japan's Trade and Investment Relationships with China", *Asian Economic Paper,* Vol. 2, No. 2, pp. 106-131.

AKAMATSU, K. (1961), "A Theory of Unbalanced Growth in the World Economy", *Weltwirtschaftliches Archiv,* Vol. 86, No. 2, pp. 196-217.

AMSDEN, A.H. (1989), *Asia's Next Giant: South Korea and Late Industrialization,* Oxford University Press, New York, NY.

AMSDEN, A.H. (2001), *The Rise of the 'Rest': Challenges to the West from Late-Industrialising Economies,* Oxford University Press, New York, NY.

ARNDT, S.W. and H. KIERZKOWSKI (2001), *Fragmentation: New Production Patterns in the World Economy,* Oxford University Press, Oxford.

ASIAN DEVELOPMENT BANK (2001), *Asian Environment Outlook 2001* (http://www.adb.org/Documents/Books/AEO/2001/aeo2020.asp)

BALDWIN, R.E. (2003), "Openness and Growth: What's the Empirical Relationship?", *NBER Working Paper* No. 9578, March.

BOOTH, A. (1999), "The Social Impact of the Asian Crisis: What Do We Know Two Years On?", *Asian-Pacific Economic Literature,* Vol. 13, pp.16-29.

BOOTH, A. (2002) "Rethinking the Role of Agriculture in the 'East Asian' Model: Why is Southeast Asia Different from Northeast Asia?", *ASEAN Economic Bulletin,* Vol. 19, No. 1, pp. 40-51.

BRADFORD, C.I. (1994), *From Trade-Driven Growth to Growth-Driven Trade: Reappraising the East Asian Development Experience,* OECD Development Centre, Paris.

CHANE-KUNE, B., K. FUKASAKU, J-C. MAUR and R.S. RAJAN (2003), "Liberalisation and Competition in the Service Sectors: Experiences from Europe and Asia", *in* BRAGA DE MACEDO, J. and T. CHINO, eds., *Asia and Europe: Services Liberalisation,* OECD Development Centre Seminars, OECD, Paris.

CHANG, H-J. (2002), *Kicking Away the Ladder: Development Strategy in Historical Perspective,* Anthem Press, London.

ISBN 92-64-01442-X © OECD 2005

CHEN, T-J. (2003) "Will Taiwan Be Marginalized by China?", *Asian Economic Paper,* Vol. 2, No.2, pp. 78-97.

CHEONG, I-K. (2003), "Regionalism and Free Trade Agreements in East Asia", *Asian Economic Paper*, Vol. 2, No. 2, pp. 145-180.

CLAESSENS, S and J.P.H. FAN (2002), "Corporate Governance in Asia: A Survey", paper prepared for *The International Review of Finance,* online at: http://www1.fee.uva.nl/fm/PAPERS/Claessens/Corporate%20Governance%20in%20Asia%20A%20Survey.htm in.pdf.

CLEMENS, M.A., S. RADELET and R. BHAVNAI (2004), "Counting Chickens when They Hatch: The Short-term Effect of Aid on Growth", Working Paper No. 44, Center for Global Development, Washington, D.C., July.

CLERIDES, S., S. LACH and J. TYBOUT (1998), "Is Learning by Exporting Important? Micro-Dynamic Evidence from Colombia, Mexico and Morocco", *Quarterly Journal of Economics*, Vol. 113, pp. 903-948.

DAVIS, J. (2003), "Regional Economic Integration, the Environment and Community", *International Review of Applied Economics*, Vol. 17, No. 1, pp. 69-83.

DÉMURGER, S. (2000), *Economic Opening and Growth in China,* OECD Development Centre Studies, OECD, Paris.

DOLLAR, D. (1992), "Outward-Oriented Developing Countries Really Do Grow More Rapidly: Evidence from 95 LDCs, 1976-85", *Economic Development and Cultural Change*, Vol. 40, pp. 523-44.

DOLLAR, D. and A. KRAAY (2001), "Trade, Growth and Poverty", Policy Research Working Paper, No. 2587, World Bank, Washington, D.C.

EICHENGREEN, B. (1999), *Toward a New International Financial Architecture: A Practical Post-Asia Agenda,* Institute for International Economics, Washington, D.C., February.

FERNÁNDEZ-ARIAS, E. and P.J. MONTIEL (1996), "The Surge in Capital Inflows in Developing Countries: An Analytical Overview", *World Bank Economic Review,* Vol. 10, No. 1, pp. 51-77.

FORSTER, J. and O. STOKKE (1999), *Policy Coherence in Developing Co-operation,* EADI Book Series 22, Frank Cass, London.

FRANKEL, J. and D. ROMER (1999), "Does Trade Cause Growth?", *American Economic Review,* Vol. 89, pp. 279-396.

FRANKEL, J. and N. ROUBINI (2003), "Industrial Country Policies", *in* FELDSTEIN, M. ed., *Economic and Financial Crises in Emerging Market Economies,* University of Chicago Press, Chicago.

FUKASAKU, K. and D. WALL (1994), *China's Long March to an Open Economy,* OECD Development Centre Studies, OECD, Paris.

FUKASAKU, K., M. PLUMMER and J. TAN, eds. (1995), *OECD and ASEAN Economies*, Institute of Southeast Asian Studies and OECD Development Centre, Paris.

FUKASAKU, K. and H.-B. SOLIGNAC LECOMTE (1998), "Economic Transition and Trade Policy Reform: Lessons from China", *in* O. BOUIN, F. CORICELLI and F. LEMOINE, eds., *Different Paths to a Market Economy: China and European Economies in Transition*, CEPII-CEPR-OECD Development Centre, Paris.

GALLUP, J.L., A. GAVIRIA and E. LORA (2003), *Is Geography Destiny?: Lessons from Latin America*, Inter-American Development Bank, Washington, D.C.

GRILLI, E.R. (1993), *The European Community and the Developing Countries*, Cambridge University Press, New York, NY.

HIEMENZ, U., J.P. AGARWAL and P. NUNNENKAMP (1991), *The International Competitiveness of Developing Countries for Risk Capital*, Kiel Institute for the World Economy, (Chapter 8), J.C.B. Moh, Tübingen.

HOEBINK, P. (1999), "Coherence and Development Policy: The Case of the European Union", *in* J. FORSTER and O. STOKKE, eds., *Policy Coherence in Developing Co-operation*, EADI Book Series 22, pp.323-345, Frank Cass, London.

HOUSE OF COMMONS (2004), *The Commission for Africa and Policy Coherence for Development: First Do No Harm*, First Report of Session 2004-05, International Development Committee, London.

HSIAO, F.S.T. and M-C.W. HSIAO (2003), "'Miracle Growth' in the Twentieth Century — International Comparisons of East Asian Development", *World Development*, Vol. 31, pp. 227-257.

IFAD (2002), *Assessment of Rural Poverty: Asia and the Pacific*, Palombi, Rome.

IMF (1995), *International Capital Markets: Developments, Prospects and Policy Issues*, Washington, D.C.

ITO, T. (2001), "Growth, Crisis and the Future of Economic Recovery in East Asia", *in* J.E. STIGLITZ and S. YUSUF, eds., *Rethinking the East Asian Miracle*, Oxford University Press, New York, pp.55-94.

JAPAN BANK FOR INTERNATIONAL COOPERATION (2000), "Thailand's Eastern Seaboard Development Plan: Comprehensive Impact Assessments" (in Japanese), available from: http://www.jbic.go.jp/japanese/oec/post/2000/index.php.

JAPAN BANK FOR INTERNATIONAL COOPERATION (2002), "Foreign Direct Investment and Development: Where Do We Stand?", JBIC Institute Research Paper No. 15, Tokyo.

JOHNSON, H. (1967), *Economic Policies Towards Less Developed Countries*, George Allen & Unwin, London.

KATSELI, L.T. (1997), "Investment, Trade and International Competitiveness", *in* J.H. DUNNING and K.A. HAMDANI, eds., *The New Globalism and Developing Countries*, United Nations University Press, Tokyo.

 ISBN 92-64-01442-X © OECD 2005

KATSELI, L.T. (2004), "Comments on Yongyuth Chalamwong's paper on The Migration of Highly Skilled Asian Workers in OECD Member Countries and its Effects on Economic Development in East Asia", prepared for the Experts' Seminar on *the Impact and Coherence of OECD-Country Policies on Asian Developing Economies*, 10-11 June 2004, Paris.

KAWAI, M. (2004*a*), "Regional Economic Integration, Peace and Security in East Asia", paper presented to the Economists Allied for Arms Reduction (ECAAR) Session on "Real Homeland Security," at the Allied Social Science Associations Annual Meetings, 3-5 January 2004, San Diego.

KAWAI, M. (2004*b*), "Regional Economic Integration and Cooperation in East Asia", paper prepared for the Experts' Seminar on *the Impact and Coherence of OECD-Country Policies on Asian Developing Economies*, 10-11 June 2004, Paris.

KAWAI, M. (2004*c*), "Trade and Investment Integration and Cooperation in East Asia: Empirical Evidence and Issues", paper presented to the High-Level Conference on "Asia's Economic Cooperation and Integration", organised by the Asian Development Bank, 1-2 July 2004, Manila.

KAWAI, M. and S. TAKAGI (2004), "Japan's Official Development Assistance: Recent Issues and Future Directions", *Journal of International Development*, Vol. 16, pp. 255-280.

KAWAI, M. and S. URATA (1998), "Are Trade and Direct Investment Substitutes or Complements? An Empirical Analysis of Japanese Manufacturing Industries", *in* H. LEE and D.W. ROLAND-HOLST, eds., *Economic Development and Co-operation in the Pacific Basin: Trade, Investment and Environmental Issues*, Cambridge University Press, Cambridge.

KENEN, P.B. (2001), *The International Financial Architecture: What's New? What's Missing?*, Institute for International Economics, Washington, D.C.

KIM, H. and Y. LEE (2003), "Agricultural Policy Reform and Structural Adjustment: Historical Evidence from Korean Experience", paper prepared for "Policy Reform and Adjustment Workshop", Wye College, 23-25 October 2003, United Kingdom.

KINDLEBERGER, C.P. (1986), "International Public Goods without International Government", *American Economic Review*, Vol. 76, No. 1, pp. 1-13.

KNOWLES, J.C., E.M. PERNIA and M. RACELIS (1999), "Social Consequences of the Financial Crisis in Asia", Economic Staff Paper No. 60, EDRC, Asian Development Bank, Manila.

KREININ, M.E. and M.G. PLUMMER (2002), *Economic Integration and Development: Has Regionalism Delivered for Developing Countries?*, Edward Elgar Publishing Limited, Cheltenham.

KRUEGER, A. (1993), *Economic Policies at Cross-Purposes: the United States and Developing Countries*, Brookings Institution, Washington, D.C.

KURODA, H. and M. KAWAI (2002), "Strengthening Regional Financial Cooperation in East Asia", *Pacific Economic Papers*, 51, October.

LANGHAMMER, R.J. (1995), "On the Coherence of EC Policies", *in* FUKASAKU, K. *et.al*, eds., *OECD and ASEAN Economies*, Institute of Southeast Asian Studies and OECD Development Centre, Paris, pp. 213-235.

LAWRENCE, R.Z. and D.E. WEINSTEIN (2001), "Trade and Growth: Import-Led or Export-Led? – Evidence from Japan and Korea", *in* J.E. STIGLITZ and S. YUSUF, eds., *Rethinking the East Asian Miracle*, Chapter 10, pp. 379-408, Oxford University Press, New York, NY.

LI, S., S.H. PARK and S. LI (2003), "The Great Leap Forward: The Transition from Relation-Based Governance to Rule-Based Governance", *Organizational Dynamics* Vol. 33, No. 1, 2004, pp. 63-78.

MADDISON, A. (1995), *Monitoring the World Economy 1820-1992*, OECD Development Centre Studies, OECD, Paris.

MADDISON, A. (2001), *The World Economy: A Millennial Perspective*, Development Centre Studies, OECD, Paris.

MADDISON, A. (2003), *The World Economy: Historical Statistics*, OECD Development Centre Studies, OECD, Paris.

MCCAWLEY, P. (1998), "Development Assistance in Asia in the 1990s", *Asian-Pacific Economic Literature*, Vol. 12, pp. 41-50.

MCKIBBIN, W. J. and W.T. WOO (2003), "The Consequences of China's WTO Accession for Its Neighbors", *Asian Economic Paper*, Vol. 2, No. 2, pp.1-38.

MICHEL, J. (1997), "A New Approach to Development", *The OECD Observer*, No. 204, February/March.

MILELLI, C. (2003), "Restructuration financière en Asie du Sud-Est" *in* J-M. BOUISSOU *et al.*, *Après la Crise: Les économies asiatiques face aux défis de la mondialisation*, pp. 71-92, Éditions Karthala, Paris.

MONTES, M.F. (1998), *The Currency Crisis in Southeast Asia*, Institute of Southeast Asian Studies, Singapore.

NATIONAL BUREAU OF STATISTICS (2003), *China Statistical Yearbook 2003*, China Statistics Press, Beijing.

NOLAND, M. and H. PACK (2003), *Industrial Policy in an Era of Globalization: Lessons from Asia*, Institute for International Economics, Washington, D.C.

OECD (1995), *Linkages: OECD and Major Developing Economies*, Paris.

ISBN 92-64-01442-X © OECD 2005

OECD (1997), *The World in 2020: Towards a New Global Age*, Paris.

OECD (2002*a*), *Towards Asia's Sustainable Development: the Role of Social Protection*, Paris.

OECD (2002*b*), *Foreign Direct Investment for Development: Maximising Benefits, Minimising Costs*, Paris.

OECD (2002*c*), *China in the World Economy: the Domestic Policy Challenges*, Paris.

OECD (2002*d*), *Promoting Environmentally Sustainable Development: Proceedings of a Workshop held on 22-23 November 2001*, Paris.

OECD (2003*a*), *Migration and the Labour Market in Asia: Recent Trends and Policies*, Paris.

OECD (2003*b*), *The Sources of Economic Growth in OECD Countries*, Paris.

OECD (2003*c*), *Policy Coherence: Vital for Global Development*, Policy Brief, Paris.

OECD (2003*d*), *Trade Capacity Building: Critical for Development*, Policy Brief, Paris.

OECD (2004), *Peer Review: Japan*, Development Assistance Committee, Paris.

Ozawa, T. (2003), "Pax Americana-led Macro-clustering and Flying-geese-style Catch-up in East Asia: Mechanisms of Regionalised Endogenous Growth", *Journal of Asian Economics*, Vol. 13, pp. 699-713.

Pai, K.S., K-H. Park, and S-I. Chang (2003) "Korea's Drive for a Knowledge-based Economy" *in* O.Y. Kwon, S-H. Jwa and K-T. Lee, eds., *Korea's New Economic Strategy in the Globalization Era*, pp. 215-230, Edward Elgar Publishing Limited, Cheltenham.

Pelkmans, J. and K. Fukasaku (1995), "Evolving Trade Links between Europe and Asia: Towards 'Open Continentalism'?", *in* K. Fukasaku (ed.)., *Regional Integration and Co-operation in Asia*, pp.137-174, Asian Development Bank and OECD Development Centre, Paris.

Petri, P. (1995), "The Interdependence of Trade and Investment in the Pacific", *in* E.K.Y. Chen and P. Drysdale, eds., *Corporate Links and Foreign Direct Investment in Asia and the Pacific*, Harper Educational Publishers, Canberra, ACT.

Pritchett, L. (1996), "Measuring Outward Orientation in LDCs: Can It Be Done?", *Journal of Development Economics*, Vol. 49, pp. 307-335.

Radelet, S. and J. Sachs (1998), "The Onset of the East Asian Financial Crisis", *Brookings Papers on Economic Activity*, Vol. 28, pp. 1-74.

Reisen, H. (1999), "After the Great Asian Slump: Towards a Coherent Approach to Global Capital Flows", OECD Development Centre Policy Brief No. 16, OECD, Paris.

Reisen, H., M. Grandes and N. Pinaud (2005), "Macroeconomic Policies: New Issues of Interdependence", *OECD Development Centre Working Paper* No. 241, OECD, Paris.

REUBER, G., H. CROOKELL, M. EMERSON and G. GALLAIS-HAMONNO (1973), *Private Foreign Investment in Development*, Clarendon Press, Oxford.

RODRIGUEZ, F. and D. RODRIK (1999), "Trade Policy and Economic Growth: A Skeptic's Guide to the Cross-National Evidence", NBER Working Paper, No. 7081, Cambridge, MA.

RODRIK, D. (2003), "Growth Strategies", *NBER Working Paper* No.10050, October.

ROL, S. (2003), "Les nouveaux défis de la protection sociale en Asie du Sud-Est" *in* J-M. BOUISSOU *et al., Après la crise: Les économies asiatiques face aux défis de la mondialisation*, pp. 373-397, Éditions Karthala, Paris.

ROMER, P.M. (1993), "Two Strategies for Economic Development: Using Ideas and Producing Ideas", Proceedings of the World Bank Annual Conference on Development Economics 1992, pp. 63-91.

ROMER, P.M. (1994), "New Goods, Old Theory and the Welfare Costs of Trade Restrictions", *Journal of Development Economics*, Vol. 43, pp. 5-38.

SACHS, J.D. and A.M. WARNER (1995), "Economic Reform and the Process of Global Integration", *Brookings Papers on Economic Activity*, Vol. 1, pp. 1-118.

SCOLLAY, R. and J. GILBERT (2001), *New Subregional Trading Arrangements in the Asia-Pacific*, Institute for International Economics, Washington, D.C.

SCOLLAY, R. and J. GILBERT, (2003), "Impact of East Asian Regional or Subregional FTAs." Report for the Australian Department of Foreign Affairs and Trade, Canberra, ACT, May.

SCHRANK, A. (2001), "Export Processing Zones: Free Market Islands or Bridges to Structural Transformation?", *Development Policy Review*, Vol. 19, pp. 223-242.

STIGLITZ, J.E. and S. YUSUF, eds. (2001), *Rethinking the East Asian Miracle*, Oxford University Press, New York, NY.

SUBRAMANIAN, A. and D. ROY (2001), "Who Can Explain the Mauritian Miracle: Meade, Romer, Sachs or Rodrik?", *IMF Working Paper*, WP/01/116, Washington, D.C.

THEE. K.W. (1994), "Interactions of Japanese Aid and Direct Investment in Indonesia", *ASEAN Economic Bulletin*, Vol. 11, pp. 25-35,.

THOMPSON, E.R. (2003), "Technology Transfer to China by Hong Kong's Cross-Border Garment Firms", *The Developing Economies*, Vol. XLI-1, March, pp. 88-111.

UNCTAD (2004), *World Investment Report 2004*, Geneva.

URATA, S. (2001), "Emergence of an FDI-Trade Nexus and Economic Growth in East Asia", *in* STIGLITZ, J.E. and S. YUSUF, eds., *Rethinking the East Asian Miracle*, pp.407-459, Oxford University Press, New York, NY.

URATA, S. (2004), "Towards an East Asia Free Trade Area", *Development Centre Policy Insights*, No.1, OECD, Paris.

ISBN 92-64-01442-X © OECD 2005

VAN ARKADIE, B. and R. MALLON (2003), *Viet Nam: A Transition Tiger?*, Asia Pacific Press, Australian National University.

VIATTE, G. (2004), "Comments on Rick Barichello's paper on Agricultural Development and Poverty Reduction in East Asia" prepared for the Experts' Seminar on the Impact and Coherence of OECD-Country Policies on Asian Developing Economies, 10-11 June 2004, Paris.

WACZIARG, R. and K.H. WELCH (2003), "Trade Liberalization and Growth: New Evidence", *NBER Working Paper* No. 10152, National Bureau of Economic Research, Cambridge MA.

WADE, R. (1990), *Governing the Market*, Princeton University Press, Princeton, N.J.

WINTERS, L.A. (2004), "Trade Liberalisation and Economic Performance: An Overview", *Economic Journal*, Vol. 114, No. 2, pp.4-21.

WOO, W.T., J. D. SACHS and K. SCHWAB (2000), *The Asian Financial Crisis: Lessons for a Resilient Asia*, MIT Press, Cambridge, MA.

WORLD BANK (1993), *The East Asian Miracle: Growth and Public Policy*, Washington, D.C.

WORLD BANK (1998), *East Asia: the Road to Recovery*, Washington, D.C.

WORLD BANK (2000), *East Asia: Recovery and Beyond*, Washington, D.C.

WORLD BANK (2001), *Reaching the Rural Poor in the East Asia and Pacific Region*, Inkwell Publishing Company, Inc., Philippines.

WORLD TRADE ORGANIZATION (1998), *Trading into the Future* (2nd Edition), Geneva.

YAMAZAWA, I. (1990), *Economic Development and International Trade: The Japanese Model*, East West Centre, Honolulu.

YOUNG, A. (1992), "A Tale of Two Cities: Factor Accumulation and Technological Change in Hong Kong and Singapore", *National Bureau of Economic Research Macroeconomics Annual 1992*, MIT Press, Cambridge MA.

YOUNG, A. (1995), "The Tyranny of Numbers: Confronting the Statistical Realities of the East Asian Growth Experience", *Quarterly Journal of Economics*, Vol. 110, pp. 641-80.

YUSOF, Z.A. (2003), "Malaysia's Responses to the China Challenge", *Asian Economic Paper*, Vol. 2, No. 2, pp.46-73.

YUSUF, S. (2001), "The East Asian Miracle at the Millennium", *in* STIGLITZ, J. E. and S. YUSUF, eds., *Rethinking the East Asian Miracle*, pp.1-53, Oxford University Press, New York, NY.

YUSUF, S. (2003), *Innovative East Asia: the Future of Growth*, World Bank, Washington, D.C.

Part Two

Interactions and Impacts of OECD-Country Policies

Chapter 2

Macroeconomic Management and Financial Stability: The Implications for East Asia[1]

Menzie D. Chinn

Abstract

This chapter looks at the determinants of economic and financial linkages between developed and developing countries, with a special focus on East Asia. The synchronisation of business cycles depends on trade flows, production structures and to a lesser extent capital-account openness, and the correlation of stock and bond returns in emerging markets depends on the trade flows. No statistically significant difference appears between the behaviour of East Asian economies and developing countries in other parts of the world. The analysis confirms that dollar movements have had a large effect on East Asian competitiveness, especially in the years leading up to the crises of 1997-98. The effect of dollar/euro movements appears larger than that of dollar/yen movements, contrary to expectations. In the post-crisis period, only the Chinese yuan conforms to the general presumption that dollar/yen fluctuations have a dominant impact on East Asian effective exchange rates. In light of these identified empirical relationships, the chapter moves on to discuss some recent suggestions for reform of the international financial architecture and concludes with thoughts on the prospects for adjustment.

ISBN 92-64-01442-X

Introduction

The ties that link the developed and developing economies seem ever strengthening — or binding, depending on one's perspective. Economic events that in previous decades would hardly elicit a nod from the policy community now provoke vigorous responses from average citizens and small and medium-sized firms. These statements apply with even greater force to interactions between the developed countries and the newly industrialising and developing economies of East Asia. Vast capital flows to the region set the stage for the boom and bust cycle of the 1990s. The rapid recovery from the resulting East Asian financial crises came partly from the very high share of electronics trade with the United States coincident with the US New Economy boom. More recently, economic policies set in the Asia-Pacific capitals have aided and abetted the insatiable American demand for capital.

Against this backdrop of heightened interdependence it is useful to step back and quantify the nature and extent of these economic linkages, especially because the course of macroeconomic adjustment will depend on them. This chapter examines data for the last quarter century with an eye to identifying the factors that determine the degree to which business cycles, asset returns and exchange rates co-vary between developed and developing economies, with special reference to East Asia[2].

The next section surveys some broad stylised facts about the macroeconomic linkages between developed and developing countries. The synchronisation of business cycles is then related to trade links, production-structure similarities, openness to capital flows and macroeconomic policy coherence. The concept of such coherence can have a multitude of differing interpretations. One might start with a particular typology that identifies coherence *i)* within macro policy (i.e. between monetary and fiscal policies); *ii)* between macro and other policies; *iii)* between OECD or G-7 countries; and *iv)* between OECD and non-OECD countries[3]. The focus lies on the correlation between business cycles — i.e. business cycle coherence — and identifies its determinants.

The analysis then examines the relationship between asset-price returns in major advanced economies and other economies. Asset-return correlation relates to trade links, bank lending and direct investment flows as well as openness to capital flows. Both this and the previous section thus identify trade flows as the central determinants of the synchronisation of economic and financial activity. The openness of economies to capital flows also has importance in certain instances.

 ISBN 92-64-01442-X

The following section discusses the implications for East Asian developing and newly industrialising economies of G-3 currency movements. While some evidence points to movements in the dollar/yen rate as important determinants of shifts in East Asian competitiveness, it is not conclusive. Indeed, changes in the dollar/euro rate appear as more important, especially in light of the relative substitutability of trade flows emanating from and going to the various East Asian countries.

The penultimate section recounts some of the major initiatives to reform the international financial architecture, with a focus on aspects of special concern to the East Asian economies. A final discussion provides some conjectures on macroeconomic adjustment in current circumstances, given the empirical relationships uncovered.

Macroeconomic Linkages

Previous Literature and Stylised Facts

Given the weight of the developed economies in the world economy, it would be surprising if macroeconomic conditions in them had little impact on the performance of developing economies. Business cycles in the developed economies have large effects on developing-country exports in terms of both quantities and prices. The link to aggregate demand in those countries is obvious. Moreover, in addition to private demand, monetary and fiscal polices affect asset prices in the industrial countries, and these price changes spread to the non-industrial countries. These interest rate changes also have an impact on the quantities and composition of capital flowing to the developing countries.

Some of these channels have undergone numerous examinations over the years. Dornbusch (1985) is an early example. As capital markets have grown in importance, the emphasis has changed to stress alternative linkages, but most of the points will still be familiar to the typical macroeconomist interested in developing economies. More recently Frankel and Roubini (2003) and Reinhart and Reinhart (2003) have reviewed some major linkages[4]. Instead of replicating their analyses, this study highlights some key stylised facts that provide a backdrop for analysis of the determinants of these linkages.

ISBN 92-64-01442-X © OECD 2005

Reinhart and Reinhart (2003) have developed a typology useful for setting the stage systematically. It differentiates (somewhat artificially) between business cycle and monetary policy shocks. Table 2.1 depicts it, as adapted from their table. Business cycle effects link developed to developing countries by way of both the volumes and the terms of trade.

Table 2.1. **Advanced and Developing Country Links**

Shock	Linkage	Developing Country "Amplifier"
Advanced country business cycle	(for booms)	
Income effects	Trade volumes (+)	High trade exposure; high income elasticity for exports
Relative price effects	Terms of trade (+)	Low price elasticity of demand (esp. commodities)
International capital flows	Capital flows to developing countries (-)	
Monetary policy cycle	(for expansionary policy)	
International capital flows	Portfolio capital flows (+)	Developed bond/equity markets and financial openness
Debt servicing	Lower financing costs (+)	High debt levels

Source: Adapted from Reinhart and Reinhart (2003).

Frankel and Roubini (2003) provide the simplest summary statistic regarding this growth linkage. They report that from 1977 to 1999 a one percentage point increase in the growth rate of GDP in the G-7 countries led to a 0.78 point GDP gain in emerging markets. This is hardly a structural parameter, but as a stylised fact it can serve as a departure point for more detailed analysis. Kose *et al.* (2003) conducted one such study. They calculated a G-7 aggregate GDP and consumption measure (evaluated in PPP terms) for 1960-99, then examined how correlations between the G-7 aggregate and developing country aggregates evolved. They found that the correlation of output did not increase monotonically over time, but rose during a period they define as one of "common shocks" (1973-86) and fell in the "globalisation" period (1987-99).

Simple scatter plots of series can illustrate some of the key aspects of the linkages between developed and developing economies, using data for several IMF aggregates over the past quarter century. The data cover the major advanced countries (the G-7), all developing countries, developing Asia and the newly industrialising Asian economies. Figure 2.1 plots developing country and developing Asia GDP growth rates against G-7 growth rates,

ISBN 92-64-01442-X © OECD 2005

along with a simple bivariate regression line relating developing-country growth to G-7 growth. It has a clear positive slope. The regression line for developing Asia is also included for comparison. No substantial difference in the strength of the relationship appears, although Asian countries grow more rapidly than the overall developing-country group[5]. As indicated by the regression lines in Figure 2.2, on the other hand, growth in the newly industrialising Asian economies[6] does appear to be more sensitive to growth in the G-7 countries than does that in the developing Asian countries. Hence, not unexpectedly, the responsiveness of developing countries to conditions in the advanced economies varies across groupings, even within Asia.

Figure 2.1. **Growth Rates: Developing Country and Developing Asia against Advanced Countries**

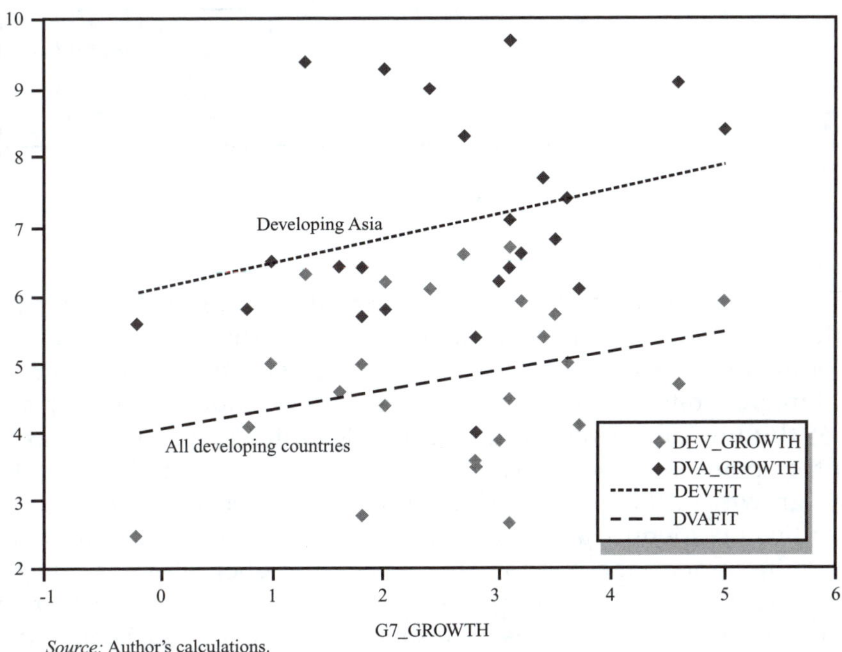

Source: Author's calculations.

Figure 2.2. **Growth Rates: Developing and Newly Industrialising Asia against Advanced Countries**

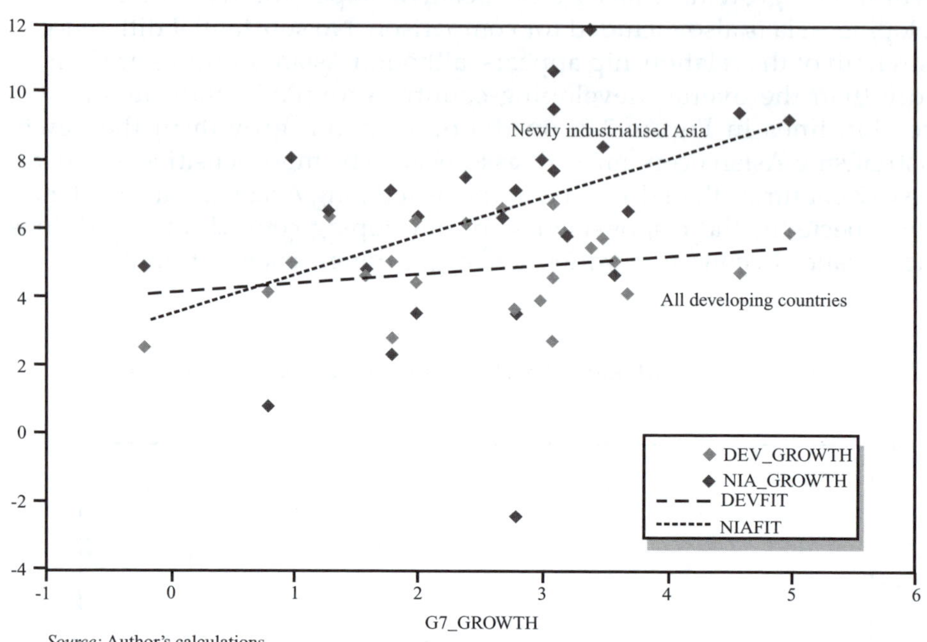

Source: Author's calculations.

This is not the place to examine exhaustively all of the other factors important to growth, but two of them merit some discussion. First, one can think of the real rate of interest in the advanced economies, for example the US real interest rate, as a crude proxy measure for monetary policy and the state of the business cycle. Frankel and Roubini (2003) find that a one percentage point increase in real G-7 rates leads to a 0.77 point reduction in income growth in the Western Hemisphere, but also find the effect much more difficult to identify in the full set of market borrowers. It is indeed hard to determine exactly the mechanisms whereby higher US rates affect these countries. In a more select group of seven emerging markets, Uribe and Yue (2003) determine that US interest rate shocks explain about 20 per cent of the variation in economic activity. About two-thirds of this effect is mediated through the country spread effect, i.e. country spreads on the US Treasury bill rate increase systematically with US interest rate shocks.

ISBN 92-64-01442-X © OECD 2005

A simple scatter plot of developing country growth on the *ex post* real rate confirms the lack of a simple bivariate pattern. After extracting the amount of the correlation associated with G-7 GDP growth[7], the correlation turns negative (Figure 2.3), reflecting the commonly held belief that developing country growth is sensitive to US credit-market conditions. This effect is manifested in the international capital flow entries in the business cycle and monetary policy panels of Table 2.1.

Figure 2.3. **Developing Countries Growth Residual on US Real Interest Rate**

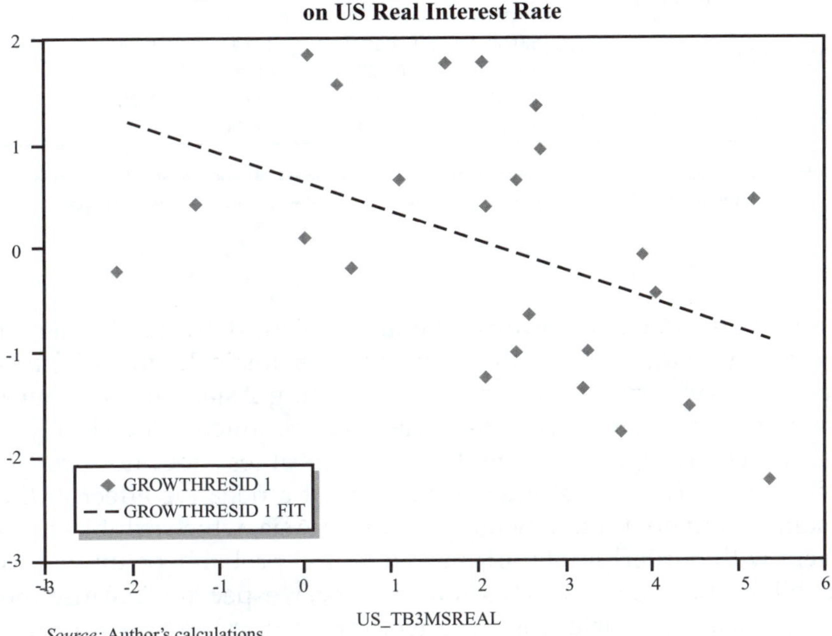

Source: Author's calculations.

Table 2.2 displays the correlations more explicitly. Growth rates for developing country groupings — all developing countries, developing Asia and newly-industrialising Asia — are regressed against the G-7 country growth rates and the real interest rate (Panel A). To check for robustness, the regressions are repeated using advanced-country growth rates in the place of G-7 growth (Panel B).

Table 2.2. **Advanced and Developing Country Growth, 1980-2003**

Dep.Var.	Constant	Δy	r^{US}	Adj. R^2	SER
		Panel A: G-7 Countries			
All developing countries	4.242***	0.506***	-0.341***	0.23	1.089
	(0.578)	(0.159)	(0.122)		
Developing Asia	6.189***	0.474***	-0.168	0.04	1.477
	(0.758)	(0.115)	(0.164)		
Newly industrialising Asia	3.343**	0.881**	0.366*	0.15	2.908
	(1.268)	(0.374)	(0.212)		
		Panel B: Advanced Countries			
All developing countries	4.025***	0.553***	-0.341***	0.26	1.067
	(0.605)	(0.172)	(0.117)		
Developing Asia	6.027***	0.499***	-0.164	0.04	1.471
	(0.793)	(0.127)	(0.164)		
Newly industrialising Asia	2.673*	1.093**	0.334	0.20	2.825
	(1.408)	(0.414)	(0.243)		

Notes: Variables expressed in percentage points. Newey-West robust standard errors are in parentheses. *, ** and *** indicate significance at the 10%, 5% and 1% levels respectively.

The regression results confirm the impressions delivered by the figures. The sensitivity to advanced-country growth is statistically indistinguishable between all developing countries and developing Asia. On the other hand, the newly industrialising Asian countries may be much more closely linked to the advanced countries, although the statistical test does not firmly reject the null of equality. US real interest rates exert a negative effect in the first two instances, but not for newly industrialising Asia, which exhibits a positive coefficient with borderline significance. It would probably be unwise to read too much into these simple regressions, however, especially because the only highly significant coefficient is negative, for all developing countries. This pattern is essentially reproduced in Panel B.

Through what channels might economic activity in the core countries get propagated to developing countries? Increased economic activity might work through changes in the terms of trade, a factor especially relevant for commodity exporters[8]. This is the "Relative Price Effect" in the business-cycle panel of Table 2.1. Figure 2.4 presents a scatter plot of the change in developing-country terms of trade and the advanced-country growth rate. The association is positive and statistically significant. Borensztein and Reinhart (1994) report that the elasticity of commodity prices with respect to developed-country industrial production lies between 1.4 and 1.6.

 ISBN 92-64-01442-X © OECD 2005

Figure 2.4. **Change in Terms of Trade against Advanced Country Growth Rate**

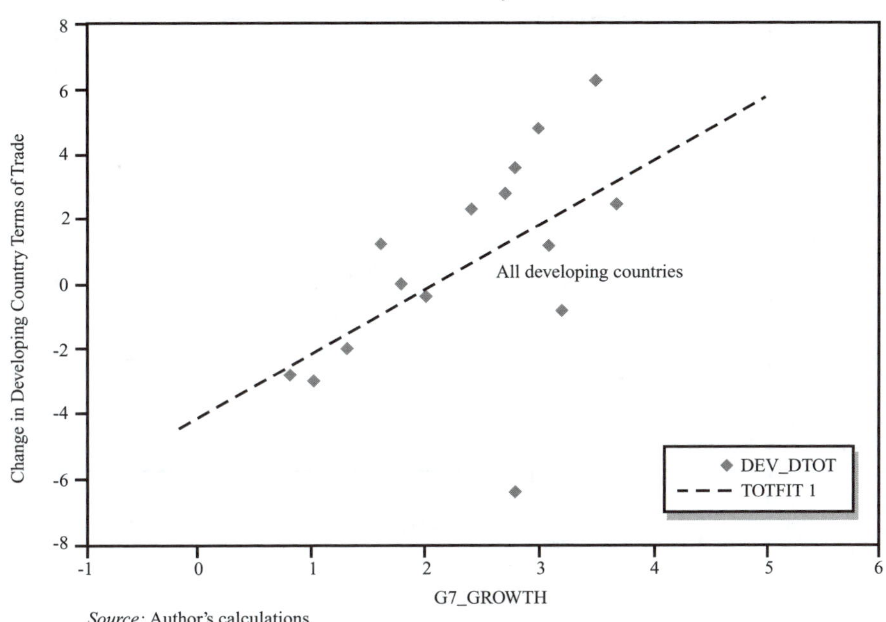

Source: Author's calculations.

Capital flows offer another channel; some observers have pointed to the "capital flow cycle" as the origin of the "unholy trinity of financial contagion" (Kaminsky *et al.*, 2003)[9]. Regardless of one's view on this, surges in capital flows to and from emerging markets clearly complicate the policy maker's task and influence developing-country economic activity, so it is important to consider how developed-country conditions affect these flows. One prominent view holds that capital flows respond primarily to the push of low interest rates in the developed countries[10]. Figure 2.5 illustrates, showing net private capital flows to emerging markets as a function of the US real interest rate. The clear negative relationship validates the "push", as opposed to the emerging-market "pull" hypothesis. The relationship is statistically significant (Table 2.3.) A one percentage point increase in the US real rate decreases capital flows in the subsequent year by about 20 billion 1995 US dollars. Of course, this effect is very imprecisely estimated, and disaggregating to components leads to even greater imprecision. Net direct investment and portfolio flows exhibit an even less tight relationship to real rates (Figures 2.6 and 2.7 and the corresponding rows of Table 2.3). Net other capital flows (essentially bank loans) link more reliably (Figure 2.7); a one percentage point increase in the US real rate decreases net flows by about 8 billion 1995 dollars[11].

Figure 2.5. **Net Private Capital Flows (1995$) to Emerging Markets against US Real Interest Rate**

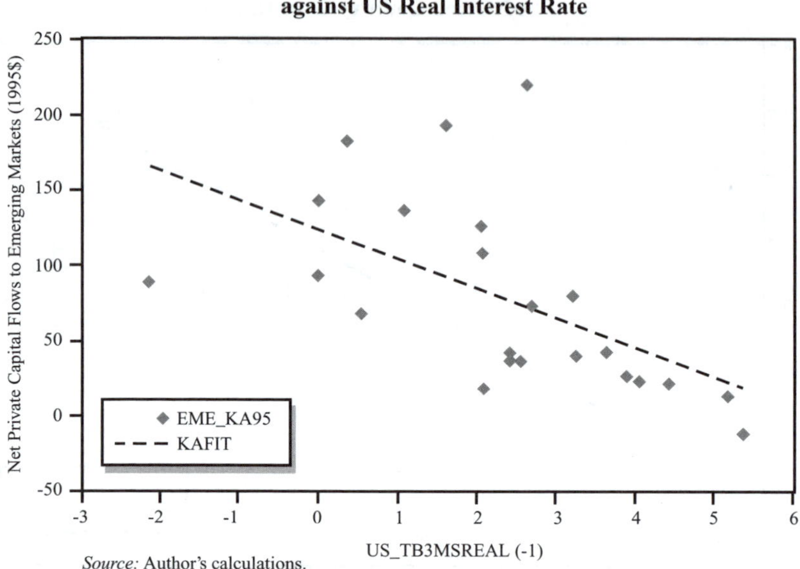

Source: Author's calculations.

Table 2.3. **Capital Flows to Emerging Markets, 1980-2003**

Dep.Variable	Const.	$r^{US}(t-1)$	Adj. R^2	SER
Net Private Capital Flows	123.81*** (26.76)	-19.49*** (6.63)	0.27	53.88
Net Direct Investment Flows	89.34*** (24.18)	-8.49 (7.03)	0.03	55.28
Net Portfolio Flows	26.96 (23.36)	-3.46 (5.57)	-0.02	37.27
Net Other Private Capital Flows	7.50 (14.38)	-7.54** (3.45)	0.03	47.48

Notes: Dependent variable in billions of constant 1995 US$. Newey-West robust standard errors are in parentheses. *, ** and *** indicate significance at the 10%, 5% and 1% levels respectively.

ISBN 92-64-01442-X © OECD 2005

Figure 2.6. **Net FDI Flows (1995$) to Emerging Markets against US Real Interest Rate**

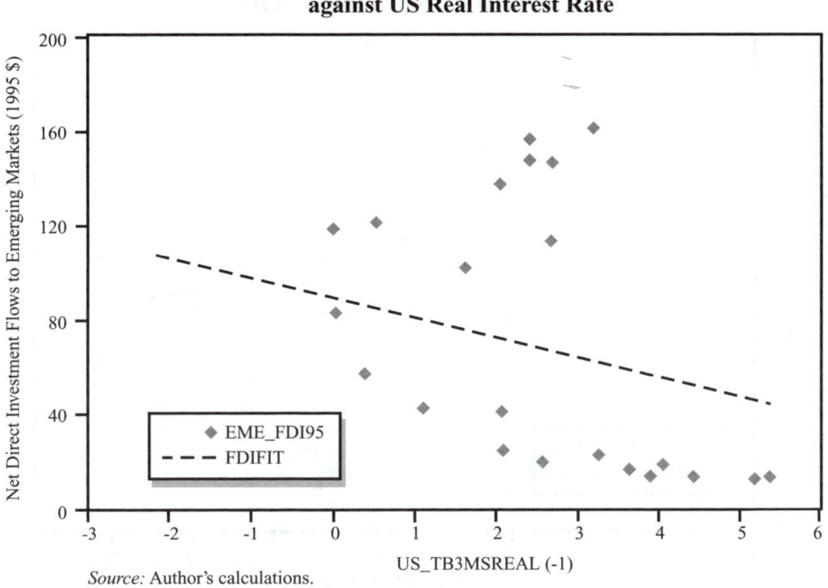

Source: Author's calculations.

Figure 2.7. **Net Portfolio Flows (1995$) to Emerging Markets against US Real Interest Rate**

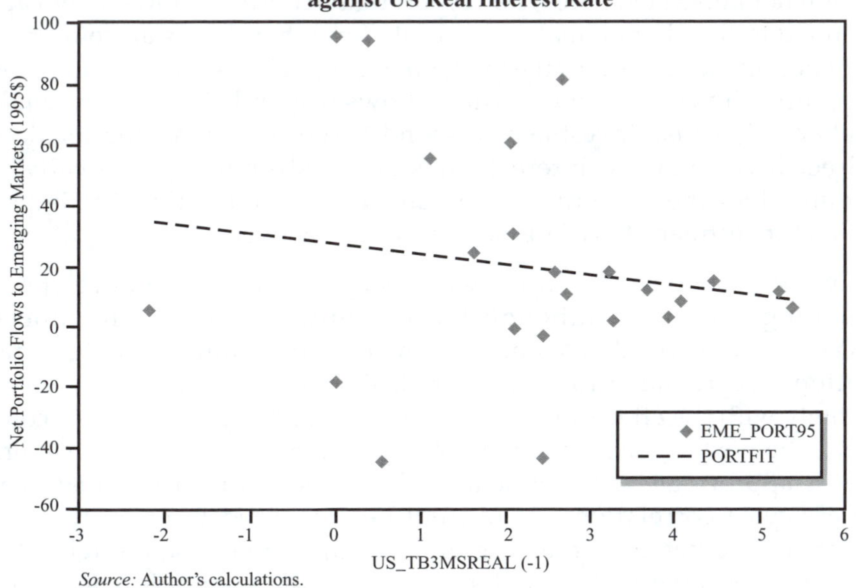

Source: Author's calculations.

Figure 2.8. **Net Other Private Flows (1995$) to Emerging Markets against US Real Interest Rate**

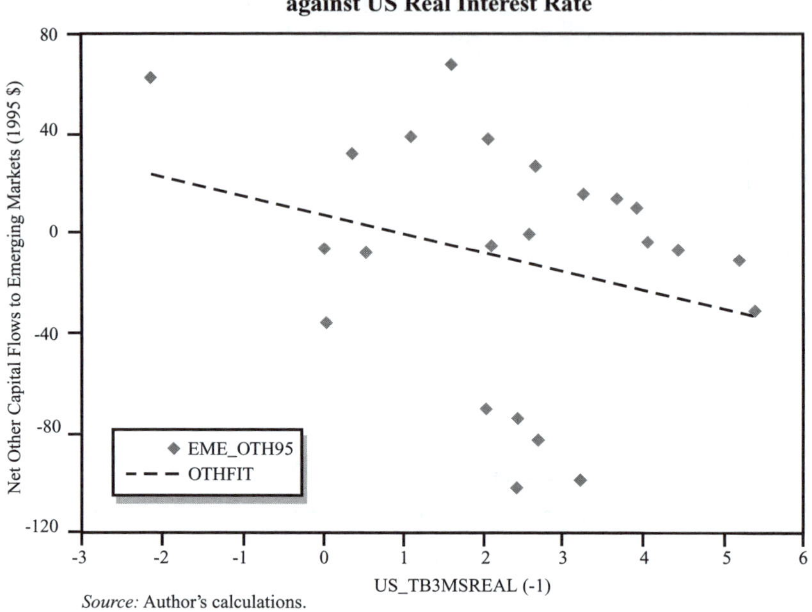

Source: Author's calculations.

Reinhart and Reinhart (2003) note some geographical and categorical variation not illustrated here. They report that net private flows do not appear to respond to the US nominal interest rate for either the Asian countries that experience financial crises or the other emerging Asian markets. For the former group, direct investment and portfolio flows respond significantly, while for the latter only direct investment responds. Across regions, the relationship of direct investment to interest rates is the strongest statistically, most pronounced for the Western Hemisphere and least for Africa. The impact on net direct investment to Asia is somewhere in between.

In sum, a series of well-known linkages connects the developed and developing countries, although the magnitudes are in some question, especially as the world economy has evolved over time. Some geographic variation also remains to be explored. Because this study is concerned ultimately with the effects of these linkages on developing-country economic activity, the next subsection extensively examines the business-cycle link. A caveat is appropriate at this juncture. The focus on the factors that increase business-cycle correlations should not be construed to mean that higher correlations are better. Rather, the exercise should best be thought of as in the nature of positive analysis: a characterisation of the empirical determinants of how output fluctuations are connected.

 ISBN 92-64-01442-X © OECD 2005

Identifying the Determinants of Business-Cycle Linkages[12]

To analyse systematically how various economic factors — including the strength of international economic linkages — influence the degree to which national economies co-vary, one must define the variable of interest. Two measures corresponding to two widely accepted definitions of the business cycle are used here: the correlation between quarterly growth rates in real GDP and the correlation between output gaps. Furthermore, what variables might have influence in determining the degree to which business cycles move together between countries? Several are considered, including trade flows[13] and the dissimilarity of economic structures (proxied by the absolute values of per capita income differentials), impediments to capital flows and dissimilarities in monetary policy.

Trade flows are themselves endogenous, reacting to other economic factors. Modelling them using the gravity model takes this into account[14]. Exchange-rate volatility might also be endogenous, especially long sweeps of low-frequency (say, annual) volatility. The volatility under consideration, however, involves high-frequency (monthly) nominal exchange-rate movements. Similarity or dissimilarity of macroeconomic policies could also affect business-cycle congruity. For monetary policy, the policy interest rate serves as a summary indicator of the policy stance. Because of the difficulty in sampling fiscal policies and their divergences at frequencies high enough to calculate measures of similarity, they are omitted[15]. Finally, as Kose *et al.* (2003) points out, common shocks could be a factor in raising business cycle correlations. Consequently, they are modelled here using time fixed effects.

Empirical Results

The sample covers data for 1980-2000 on 47 countries which include almost all OECD countries and the largest countries (by GDP) outside the OECD area, plus most East Asian emerging markets. Hence, the data set expands on the coverage of OECD-specific studies such as Imbs (2003), although at the cost of less sectoral detail (see the Appendix for more information). To address how developed-country economic conditions and policies affect developing-country conditions, one has to take a stand on what constitutes a developed economy. One possibility is to take the OECD countries as a grouping, but this set of countries has changed over time, and it is not clear whether Korea, Mexico and Turkey should be considered developed countries. Hence, this study defines the G-7 as the set of major advanced economies and categorises the non-OECD countries plus Korea, Mexico and Turkey as the set of emerging and developing economies.

Business-cycle correlations are calculated over three-year or five-year periods, although only results based upon the former are reported. The business-cycle variables are calculated using quarterly GDP data, while the exchange-rate and interest-rate volatility variables use monthly data. The GDP growth rate is easily calculated, but construction of the output gap is contentious. Many countries do not calculate such series, and one cannot rely on national sources for the measures of potential output necessary to calculate them. Furthermore, the unavailability of capital stock and labour stock figures for many countries renders unfeasible any attempt to calculate potential output using such data. In consequence, the Baxter-King band pass filter is used to extract low frequency variations in GDP and equate this measure with trend or potential output.

Figure 2.9 depicts average business cycle correlations (measured using output gaps)[16] between the G-7 countries and two other groups: all non-OECD countries in the sample and the East Asian sample countries ex-Japan. It illustrates how average correlations[17] for the developing countries have fluctuated over most of the last 20 years, with a marked upward surge in 1998-2000. Kim *et al.* (2003) also documents the increasing correlation between East Asian and G-7 output.

Figure 2.9. **Average Business Cycle Correlations, G-7 Countries with Selected Groups**

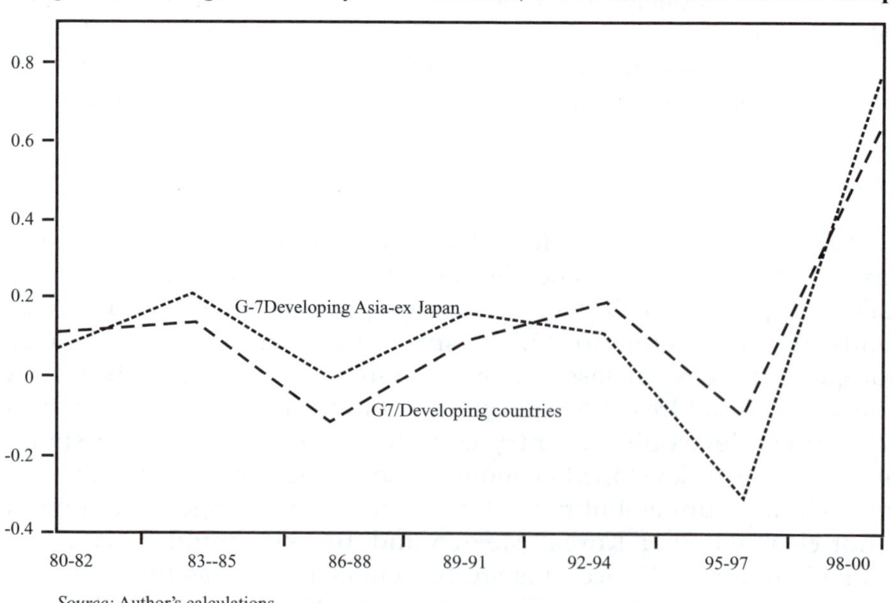

Source: Author's calculations.

ISBN 92-64-01442-X © OECD 2005

The trade and gravity variables are measured at annual frequencies, and the trade variables must somehow be normalised. One way is to normalise bilateral trade flows (the sum of exports and imports) by total trade flows. Another is to normalise by GDP, expressed either at official exchange rates or in purchasing-power parity (PPP) terms. Both methods have been used here.

As Table 2.4 on the following page shows, the relationship between business-cycle correlations and trade links is not statistically significant with growth rates as the dependent variable (first and second columns). This pattern is partially replicated even with the output gap as the measure of the business cycle. Only when trade flows are normalised by GDP does it appear that trade links determine business-cycle correlations, irrespective of whether the endogeneity of trade flows is accounted for (columns three through six). In other words, the results clearly are not robust[18].

The contrast between the results for the G-7 and emerging/developing country links and for the entire set of links suggests that other factors become important. One possibility is that differing economic structures mediate the business-cycle linkages. Imbs (2003) and Calderon *et al.* (2002) have measured the dissimilarity between economic structures of the OECD countries by differences in shares of output in individual sectors. This procedure is too cumbersome for the present analysis, which encompasses many emerging and developing countries[19]. Instead, structural dissimilarity is proxied as the absolute value of the percentage difference in per capita incomes (expressed in PPP terms). Augmenting the business cycle-trade regression with this proxy variable for specialisation yields a negative coefficient on it. Hence, countries more dissimilar in GDP have lower business-cycle correlations, after controlling for trade linkages (columns seven and eight, Table 2.4). This coefficient is never statistically significant in this sample, although it is in other samples (such as OECD *vs.* non-OECD).

At least two other factors could also influence business-cycle correlations. The first is similarity in monetary policies. It is difficult to measure, especially because indicators of monetary policy have varied over different periods and countries[20]. Including the standard deviation of interest differentials (expressed in decimal form) as a variable measuring monetary policy differences leads to insignificant coefficients in all cases. The variable exhibits extremely wide variations, however, because of several instances of hyperinflation during the 1980s. Censoring the sample to eliminate standard deviations of differentials in excess of 50 percentage points yields the results in columns 9 and 10 of Table 2.4.

Table 2.4. **Determinants of Business Cycle Correlations, G-7 – non-OECD links, 1980-2000**

	[1]	[2]	[3]	[4]	[5]	[6]	[7]	[8]	[9]	[10]	[11]	[12]
Est.	OLS	OLS	OLS	OLS	IV	IV	OLS	OLS	OLS	OLS	IV	IV
Dep. Var.	Growth	Growth	Gap	Gap	Gap	Gap	Gap	Gap	Gap	Gap	Gap	Gap
Trade Var.	Trade	GDP	Trade	GDP	Trade	GDP	Trade	GDP	Trade	GDP	Trade	GDP
Trade	-0.0132	-0.0071	0.0307	0.0473**	0.0422	0.0841***	0.0194	0.0450	0.0404*	0.0777**	0.0620**	0.1040***
	(0.0120)	(0.0125)	(0.0206)	(0.0214)	(0.0273)	(0.0283)	(0.0264)	(0.0317)	(0.0279)	(0.0062)	(0.0312)	(0.0355)
Specialisation							-0.0493	-0.0270	-0.0051	0.0374	-0.0278	0.0061
							(0.0357)	(0.0409)	(0.0380)	(0.0428)	(0.0413)	(0.0437)
Interest Rate Volatility									-0.0158***	-0.0150***	0.0440*	0.0523**
									(0.0039)	(0.0040)	(0.0248)	(0.0251)
Fin. Open.											0.0613**	0.0527*
											(0.0304)	(0.0309)
Year Effects	Yes	Yes	Yes	Yes	Yes	Yes	Yes	Yes	Yes	Yes	Yes	Yes
Adj. R2	0.026	0.025	0.173	0.185	0.163	0.162	0.164	0.165	0.223	0.218	0.207	0.198
N	637	637	637	637	630	630	630	630	511	511	393	393

Notes: The dependent variable represents business-cycle correlation. "Growth" indicates GDP growth rate correlations; "Gap" indicates output gap correlations. "Trade" in the Trade Var. row indicates bilateral trade linkages normalised by total trade. "GDP" in the Trade Var. row indicates bilateral trade linkages normalised by GDP (calculated using PPP exchange rates). Newey-West robust standard errors are in parentheses. *, ** and *** indicate significance at the 10 per cent, 5 per cent and 1 per cent levels respectively.

ISBN 92-64-01442-X © OECD 2005

In this specification, trade flows become significant once again and so does the variability of interest differentials. A ten percentage point increase in the standard deviation of interest-rate differentials (at monthly frequency) results in a decrease of the business-cycle correlation of 0.16, a rather substantial change. Such a shift in the standard deviation of the differentials is a big one, of course — the same as the difference between UK-Thailand volatility in 1998-2000 (2.6 percentage points) and UK-Turkey volatility in 1989-92 (12.2 percentage points)[21]. This finding merely characterises the effects of monetary policy convergence; it may in fact be desirable to have lower business-cycle correlations. If so, one can view the results as highlighting the possibility of using monetary policy to insulate economies from other countries' policies.

The second factor to consider is financial openness, namely the effect of capital controls. To the extent that such controls impede the movement of capital, fluctuations in the rate of return to capital may not be transmitted across borders as easily as otherwise. From among the many different measures of capital controls, this study uses the Chinn-Ito (2002) index, which maximises country coverage[22]. It is the first principal component of all four of the indicator variables the IMF compiles on exchange restrictions, restated so that higher values indicate greater financial openness. The simple average of two paired countries' financial openness is entered into the specification. Business cycle correlations do not seem robustly related to financial openness as measured by this index. Only after omitting countries with medium and high inflation by limiting admissible interest-differential volatilities to less than five percentage points does a statistically significant role emerge for financial openness. The interest-rate volatility variable then exhibits a perverse sign. Taking these estimates at face value, a one-unit increase in financial openness increases the business cycle correlation between a G-7 economy and a developing one by between 0.05 and 0.06. Because this index is in some ways "unitless" it helps to consider an example. The degree of openness between Brazil and Thailand over 1998-2000 and between Israel and Thailand during 1998-2000 differs by "one unit". Holding all else constant, the Brazil-Thailand and Israel-Thailand business cycle correlations should differ by about 0.05.

To sum up, business cycles in the less developed economies are indeed connected to those in the major industrialised economies. The strength of these connections depends upon a variety of factors, some of which, like the similarity of production structures, are not easily influenced by policy. On the other hand, policy, especially tariffs and non-tariff barriers, does to some extent affect the extent of bilateral trade flows. The regulatory dimension of financial openness is clearly policy-determined.

Can one draw some specific conclusions regarding the linkages of the East Asian developing economies? Unfortunately, restricting the sample to them reduces the sample size by over half, so that the precision of estimates falls considerably. A typical regression yields a statistically insignificant coefficient on the trade variable, with the sign equally likely to be positive or negative. The results improve somewhat when Singapore, an outlier in terms of trade, is excluded. The resulting estimates for the trade-variable coefficient are slightly lower than for the entire developing-country sample. While the monetary policy and specialisation variables are not statistically significant, that for financial openness does exhibit statistical significance in the specifications that include it. This suggests that the business-cycle linkages for East Asia have a stronger financial component than do those for the overall set[23].

Implications

The estimates suggest that for the developing countries as a group, the tight linkage in business cycle correlations means that rapid developed-country growth in the 1990s resulted in faster growth in the less developed economies. The results for East Asia are less definite. Trade does not appear as a statistically reliable determinant of business-cycle synchronisation, although the estimated economic magnitude of the effect is not that much smaller, at roughly two-thirds that for all links. Policy measures such as financial openness appear as the only statistically important factor. These results suggest that financial opening, combined with rapid economic growth in the G-7 economies, served to sustain economic growth in the region during the last decade and a half. The growth in trade links likely also supported this phenomenon, although the data do not strongly support this conclusion.

Financial Linkages

Literature Review

One can view financial linkages from two perspectives, namely stocks and flows on the one hand and asset prices on the other. The previous section recounted some of the evidence on flow-based linkages. Here, the focus is on asset-price linkages, broadly construed. A large portion of the voluminous literature on this subject deals with highly liquid debt instruments. It would

 ISBN 92-64-01442-X © OECD 2005

be impossible to do a survey of just the work on emerging markets, but a few key references would include Frankel and MacArthur (1988), Chinn and Frankel (1994) and Bansal and Dahlquist (2000). Another substantial literature deals with equity prices in emerging markets; Bekaert and Harvey (2002) contains a useful survey. The results of work by Frankel and Roubini (2003) provide some feeling for the magnitude of the effects, particularly how much developed country asset prices affect asset prices in developing countries. They find that the IFC Global index of equities declines by 17 percentage points for each one-point increase in the real G-7 interest rate. The Emerging Markets Bond Index (EMBI) drops by 34 per cent. Similar magnitudes emerge using the real US Fed Funds rate instead of the G-7 real rate. These effects are quite large, especially considering that the effect on the S&P500 drops only about 16 percentage points for a one-point increase in the real Fed Funds rate. Frankel and Roubini did not examine the impact of changes in US equity indices, but presumably there are high correlations there as well.

A Cross-Country Analysis

Forbes and Chinn (2003) examine whether real and financial stocks and flows between countries can explain why the world's biggest financial markets often appear to have large yet varying effects on other financial markets and how these cross-market linkages have changed over time. The paper estimates a factor model of market returns in different countries. It assumes that a country's market returns are a function of global factors (global interest rates, oil prices, gold prices and commodity prices), sectoral factors (stock returns for 14 sectoral indices), cross-country factors (returns in other large financial markets), and country-specific effects. It focuses on the estimated cross-country linkages between the five largest economies (France, Germany, Japan, the United Kingdom and the United States) and about 40 developed countries and emerging markets over 1985-2000[24]. The analysis relates these cross-country linkages to four specific bilateral ones, two of which are real (direct trade flows and competition in third markets[25]) and two of which are financial (bank lending and foreign direct investment). In addition, it augments the specifications with capital controls.

The most consistent finding (see Panel A, Table 2.5) is that the coefficient on import demand is positive and significant in determining the correlation of dollar-denominated stock returns. On average, direct trade may have been the most important bilateral linkage determining how shocks to the world's largest economies affected others' stock markets. The estimated coefficient on bank lending is positive but insignificant. The results for trade competition and foreign investment fluctuations are less robust, so definite conclusions are difficult to make regarding them. This pattern of results is repeated when returns are measured in local-currency terms.

Table 2.5. **Bilateral Linkage Regressions for Stock Returns in US Dollars**

Factor Model with Global, Sectoral and Cross-Country Factors							
Years	N	R^2	Import Demand	Trade Comp.	Bank Lending	Foreign Direct Investment	Capital Controls
Panel A: Full Period Average: 1986-2000							
1986-2000	161	0.07	1.715**	-0.439**	0.282	-0.064	-0.001
			(0.492)	(0.209)	(0.207)	(4.074)	(0.017)
Panel B: 5-Year Averages							
1986-1990	60	0.06	-2.074*	0.754	-0.075	2.342	-0.102**
			(1.193)	(0.564)	(0.390)	(36.788)	(0.047)
1991-1995	104	0.03	-2.909	0.413	0.120	8.314	-0.036
			(2.070)	(0.672)	(0.216)	(17.143)	(0.066)
1996-2000	149	0.18	1.932**	-1.065**	1.418**	0.088	0.022
			(0.677)	(0.232)	(0.372)	(2.656)	(0.017)

Notes: Standard errors in parentheses. *, ** and *** indicate significance at the 10 per cent, 5 per cent and 1 per cent levels respectively.

Source: Forbes and Chinn (2003).

To investigate whether the importance of factors changed between 1986 and 2000, the full sample period was divided into three sub-periods of equal length. Panel B of Table 2.5 reports the results for these five-year averages. The coefficient estimates indicate substantial changes in the importance of the bilateral linkage variables. In the two earlier periods (1986-90 and 1991-95), most of the coefficient estimates are insignificant, and of those that are significant none are robust across the specifications. Not only does the coefficient significance vary across specifications, but even the estimated signs show a remarkable lack of stability. Not surprisingly, the proportion of the variance explained by the models in both of these periods is very low. Estimates for 1996-2000, however, reflect very different patterns. A dramatic increase occurs in the model's explanatory power, with the proportion of the variance now explained increasing considerably. There is also a substantial increase in the consistency of some of the estimates across the different specifications. Most noteworthy, the coefficient on import demand is positive and significant.

ISBN 92-64-01442-X © OECD 2005

An effort to focus on global linkages in bond markets rather than stock markets confronts much more limited data availability, especially for local-currency bonds. These estimates thus cover a shorter period, from 1994 to 2000. The results, reported in Table 2.6 for both dollar denominated bonds (Panel A) and local-currency bonds (Panel B), indicate that import demand determines bond links, although trade competition also matters (negatively, as it turns out). Given the limited coverage of the data, it is more difficult to assess the evolution of the linkages over time. There is some evidence that the strength of the linkages is easier to detect in 1998-2000, suggesting that they are growing stronger over time for bond markets as well — but the short sample span of less than one business cycle makes it foolhardy to make inferences. Still, to the extent that East Asian economies are becoming increasingly linked with the G-5 economies through higher levels of trade, one should anticipate that the correlations in asset prices, after accounting for global and sectoral factors, will rise.

Table 2.6. **Bilateral Linkage Regressions for Bond Returns**

Factor Model with Global and Cross-Country Factors						
N	R^2	Import Demand	Trade Competition	Bank Lending	Foreign Investment	Capital Controls
Panel A: Full Period — Dollar-Denominated Bonds						
142	0.16	3.082**	-0.905**	1.364	6.428	0.046*
		(0.471)	(0.331)	(0.828)	(5.255)	(0.027)
Panel B: Full Period — Local Currency Bonds						
85	0.18	2.868**	0.595**	0.786	-1.410	0.052
		(0.515)	(0.255)	(0.797)	(3.115)	(0.065)

Notes: Standard errors in parentheses. ** and * indicate significance at the 5 per cent and 10 per cent levels respectively.

Source: Forbes and Chinn (2003).

Exchange-Rate Variability

G-3 Exchange-Rate/Interest-Rate Variability Tradeoffs

It seems intuitive that large swings in the values of the major currencies should be avoided for a number of reasons. For instance, shifts in currency values force changes in trade patterns that may incur large adjustment costs.

Yet when analysts argue for the stabilisation of currency values, they typically have in mind other arguments, related more to the problems that occur as incompletely hedged firms and governments confront radically different relative prices. In that sense, one can think of the volatility in major currency exchange rates as affecting the emerging markets mainly through the increase in uncertainty surrounding the terms of trade, the current account and capital flows. As a consequence, several authors have investigated the benefits of target zones for the major currencies[26], but it remains an open question whether the management of exchange rates can be achieved without a commensurate increase in volatility among other important macroeconomic variables[27].

Target zones have long been viewed as means of eliminating unwanted exchange-rate variability. Sometimes, the mere commitment to a target zone (if it is credible) is viewed as bringing stabilisation[28]. Older analyses suggested that sterilised intervention could influence exchange rates (see Dominguez and Frankel, 1993). In more recent studies (e.g. Flood and Rose, 1995; Jeanne and Rose, 2002), the existence of noise traders suggests that elimination of variability in exchange rates need not cause a transference of volatility to another market. The Flood and Rose argument applied with greatest persuasiveness to switches from managed floating to hard fixes. For the major currencies, it seems unlikely that the authorities will soon give up their monetary autonomy. Hence, one is left with the question whether it would make sense to stabilise exchange rates. This question cannot be answered without reference to what impacts on other conditions might occur as a consequence.

Reinhart and Reinhart (2003) make the trade-off explicit in the context of a small north-south model of the world. In the absence of noise-trader, portfolio-balance and signalling effects, exchange rate stabilisation can be achieved only at the cost of higher interest-rate variability. How to measure the resulting costs to the developing countries is contentious, but Reinhart and Reinhart evaluate this using net capital flows and developing-country growth. On the first, they conclude that the changes in capital flows resulting from stabilising exchange rates are sufficiently small to make the choice a toss-up. On the second, they obtain a slightly more ambiguous result — that higher G-3 exchange-rate volatility is indeed associated with a somewhat higher incidence of banking and currency crises. This result seems to keep open the question of G-3 exchange-rate stabilisation, although they reach a different conclusion.

ISBN 92-64-01442-X © OECD 2005

The Interaction of East Asian Dollar Targeting and Dollar Variability

The general issue of G-3 exchange-rate variability has particular resonance for East Asia. As several recent studies point out, the East Asian economies have largely — although not completely — restored their earlier policy, documented by Frankel and Wei (1994), of pegging largely against the US dollar[29]. The substantial accumulations of dollar assets by several East Asian central banks is testimony that management against the dollar has aimed explicitly at keeping their currencies at lower values than they would have had in the absence of intervention (see Hernandez and Montiel, 2001)[30]. To a large extent, this intervention made sense insofar as policy makers wished to avoid premature currency overvaluation that might have endangered economic recovery.

Attention focuses on this combination of dollar variability against the yen and euro (and prior to the euro's inception, the deutschemark) and pegging against the dollar. Two questions arise specifically in the context of East Asia. First, were the crises of 1997-98 attributable to the dollar's 40 per cent appreciation against the yen over the preceding two years? Second and more generally, does bilateral exchange-rate variation induce excessive variability in East Asian terms of trade?

On the first point, the critique of dollar overvaluation appears in a number of studies (Ito *et al.*, 1998; Ogawa and Ito, 2002; Kuroda and Kawai, 2003). In contrast, Frankel and Roubini (2003) cast doubt on this thesis. They point out that the dollar appreciation occurred in the context of a snapback from an unusually low value of the dollar against the yen. Hence, the overvaluation thesis is in dispute. In addition, while there were some competitiveness effects[31], the debt-denomination effects worked in the opposite direction to the extent that some of the developing-country liabilities were denominated in yen[32]. There is no *prima facie* case that dollar/yen appreciation was the core cause of the 1997-98 financial crises.

On the other hand, the rapid movement in the dollar/yen rate after 1995 may have increased risks for firms and consumers in the East Asian economies. This raises the second question, the policy issue of how sensitive East Asian exchange rates are to variations in G-3 bilateral exchange rates. To address it requires identification of the important variable. In the narrow case of competitiveness, the relevant variable is the real effective exchange rate, and the analysis here addresses the question by investigating the correlations between changes in bilateral dollar exchange rates and changes in the real effective exchange rates of several East Asian economies over 1990-2003. To set the stage, Figures 2.10 to 2.12 below display the effective exchange rates constructed by JP Morgan (in levels, re-scaled so that January 1990 = 100).

ISBN 92-64-01442-X © OECD 2005

Figure 2.10. **Trade Weighted Real Currency Values for Crisis Countries**

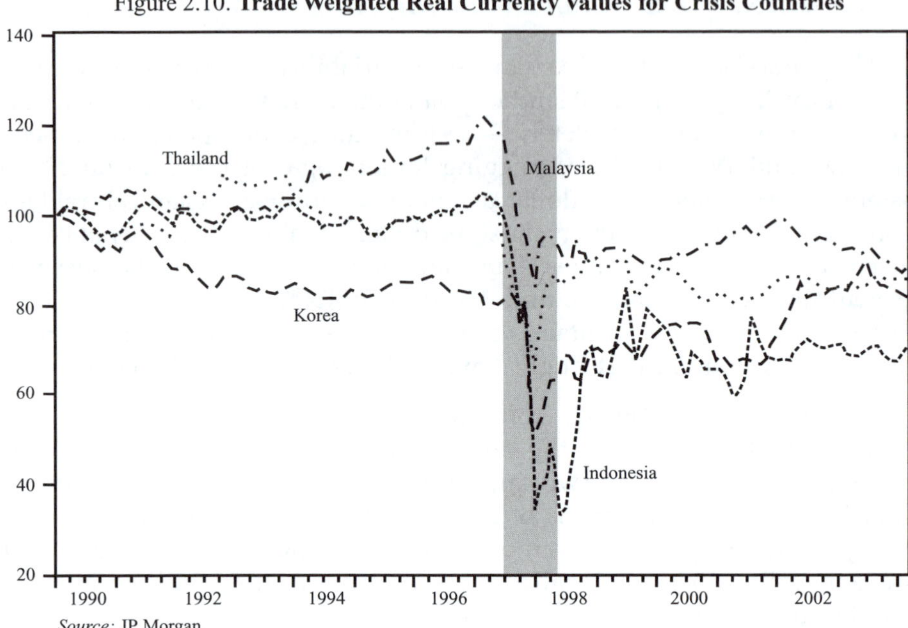

Source: JP Morgan.

Figure 2.11. **Trade Weighted Real Currency Values for Philippines and Singapore**

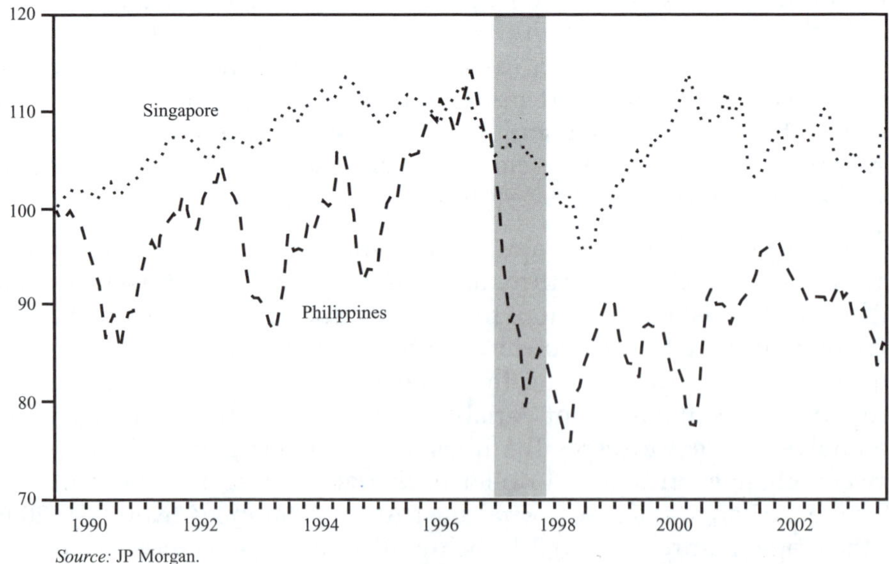

Source: JP Morgan.

ISBN 92-64-01442-X © OECD 2005

Figure 2.12. **Trade Weighted Real Currency Values for China; Hong Kong, China and Chinese Taipei**

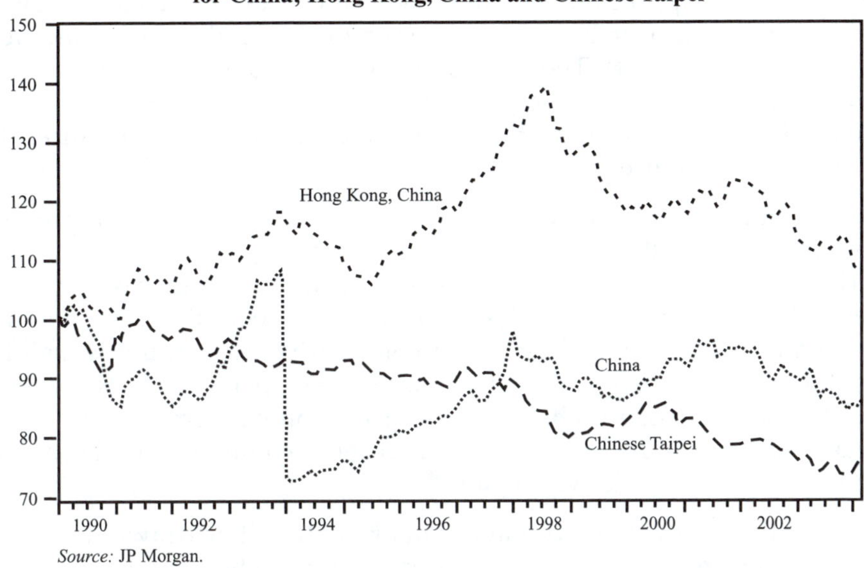

Source: JP Morgan.

Table 2.7 reports the correlation coefficients. Panel A shows the results for the 1997-98 crisis economies, Panel B for the other East Asian countries. Negative coefficients indicate that dollar depreciation against the yen or euro results in a weakening of the local currency. A caveat is necessary at this point. The regression coefficients clearly are not structural parameters. Rather they are quasi-reduced-form coefficients relating the real effective rates to the bilateral rates, assuming that the bilateral rates are exogenous (a point returned to below).

The Panel A results fail to validate for the full sample the view that dollar/yen movements dominate changes in local rates, but that is not the whole story. It is of course particularly hazardous to make inferences regarding non-structural parameters over such a long sample involving structural breaks. For the early period prior to June 1997, the results generally confirm the impression that before the currency crises, movements in the dollar had a large impact on trade-weighted exchange rates. In most cases, dollar depreciation is associated with a decline in the trade-weighted value of the local currency. Variations in the dollar-yen rate had a less pronounced effect than those in the dollar-euro rate. In Thailand, for a ten percentage-point increase in the rate of dollar appreciation against the euro, the rate of effective baht appreciation increases by 1.8 percentage points. A ten percentage-point increase in dollar appreciation against the yen causes an increase in the rate of baht appreciation of less than one percentage point (not statistically significant at 10 per cent). The results for Korea support somewhat more the view that dollar swings were important, with the dollar/yen rate now having a statistically significant impact, but the effect still is less pronounced than for shifts in the dollar/euro rate.

In general, the evidence fails to support the view that dollar appreciation against the yen resulted in a substantial worsening in competitiveness for the crisis countries. Dollar appreciation was indeed important, but such movements against the euro, rather than the yen, seem the more important determinant of changes in East Asian competitiveness. In the wake of the crises, these patterns appear, if anything, to have persisted[33]. These results will rather surprise many observers of East Asian economic events. Part of the reason for them is that some of the earlier series commonly used in analyses did not account for trade with China[34].

Regardless of the lessons that might or might not be drawn from events during the run-up to the East Asian crises, how did other East Asian effective exchange rates respond to dollar changes? Panel B of Table 2.7 reports analogous results for the non-crisis countries. There is even less evidence of a role for dollar/yen shifts. As a robustness test, the analysis was redone using the series calculated by Deutsche Bank[35]. These series differ from JP Morgan's in that the export weights do not account for third-market effects. The results reported in Table 2.8 provide even less evidence of a critical role for shifts in the dollar/yen rate in the years leading up to the East Asian crisis.

Naturally, a country on a hard, unadjustable peg would be most influenced by dollar exchange-rate variations, and the Hong Kong, China dollar's effective rate clearly responded to the US dollar/euro rate over the entire sample period. Nevertheless, its links to the dollar/yen rate still appear as much weaker. Overall, the dollar/yen rate has significance in very few instances, and they take an unanticipated direction in certain cases (e.g. the Singapore dollar). Prior to the East Asian crises, only the Philippine peso appreciated faster when the dollar appreciated more rapidly against the yen.

 ISBN 92-64-01442-X © OECD 2005

Table 2.7. **East Asian Effective Exchange Rates and Dollar Exchange Rates**

Panel A: Crisis Countries

	Indonesia		Korea		Malaysia		Thailand	
	$/€	$/¥	$/€	$/¥	$/€	$/¥	$/€	$/¥
Full	0.169	0.095	-0.243***	0.063	-0.170***	-0.051	-0.038	-0.035
Early	-0.251***	-0.191***	-0.244***	-0.113***	-0.187***	-0.119***	-0.178***	-0.075
Late	0.219	0.437	-0.334**	0.089	-0.158**	-0.063	-0.004	-0.058

Panel B: Non-Crisis Countries

	China		Hong Kong, China		Philippines		Singapore		Chinese Taipei	
	$/€	$/¥	$/€	$/¥	$/€	$/¥	$/€	$/¥	$/€	$/¥
Full	-0.229***	-0.114*	-0.198***	-0.139***	-0.203**	-0.342***	-0.079*	0.018	-0.206***	-0.064**
Early	-0.298***	-0.025	-0.267***	-0.075**	0.022	-0.213	-0.037	-0.046*	-0.209***	-0.080*
Late	-0.176***	-0.148***	-0.131**	-0.199***	-0.079*	0.018	-0.176***	0.140**	-0.188***	-0.045

Notes: The dependent variable is the real effective value of the local currency. The regressions use JP Morgan trade-weighted exchange-rate indices. OLS estimates. *,** and*** indicate significance at the 10 per cent, 5 per cent and 1 per cent levels respectively, using Newey-West robust standard errors. A negative sign indicates that dollar appreciation causes local-currency appreciation; a positive sign indicates that dollar appreciation causes local-currency depreciation. The samples in the left-hand column are: Full, 1990m02-2004m01; Early, 1990m02-1997m06; Late, 1998m07-2004m01.

Table 2.8. **East Asian Effective Exchange Rates and Dollar Exchange Rates (Alternative Data)**

Panel A: Crisis Countries

	Indonesia		Korea		Malaysia		Thailand	
	$/€	$/¥	$/€	$/¥	$/€	$/¥	$/€	$/¥
Full	0.100	0.250	-0.238***	0.195¶	-0.143***	0.120¶	0.017	0.130¶
Early	-0.115	0.093	-0.171***	0.028	-0.158*	-0.006	-0.136**	0.084*
Late	0.142	0.132	-0.228*	0.266***	-0.132*	0.116	0.057	0.063

Panel B: Non-Crisis Countries

	China		Hong Kong, China		Philippines		Singapore		Chinese Taipei	
	$/€	$/¥	$/€	$/¥	$/€	$/¥	$/€	$/¥	$/€	$/¥
Full	-0.147*	-0.140**	-0.163***	-0.054	-0.076	0.058	0.032	0.069**	-0.092**	0.057
Early	-0.095	-0.148	-0.200**	-0.012	-0.148	-0.192**	0.056	0.076**	-0.112**	0.073
Late	-0.188***	-0.122*	-0.124***	-0.067	-0.055	0.303	0.033	0.055	-0.043	0.026

Notes: The dependent variable is the real effective value of the local currency. The regressions use Deutsche Bank trade-elasticity weighted exchange rate indices. OLS estimates. *,** and *** indicate significance at the 10 per cent, 5 per cent and 1 per cent levels respectively, using Newey-West robust standard errors. ¶ indicates significance at the 11 per cent level. A negative sign indicates that an increase in dollar appreciation causes an increase in local-currency appreciation; a positive sign indicates that an increase in dollar appreciation causes an increase in local-currency depreciation. The samples described in the left-hand column are: Full, 1990m02-2004m02; Early, 1990m02-1997m06; and Late, 1998m07-2004m02.

ISBN 92-64-01442-X © OECD 2005

The Chinese yuan's effective rate does respond by depreciating faster when the dollar depreciates against either the euro or the yen. A ten percentage-point depreciation of the dollar against the euro (yen) has caused a two (one) percentage-point depreciation of the RMB in the period after the East Asian crises. The yuan thus best fits the view that movements in the dollar/yen rate have a large impact on the competitiveness of the local currency.

While the conventional effective exchange rate indices take into account the share of trade associated with each trading partner, they fail to allow for the possibility that trade flows associated with differing trade partners might have different price sensitivities. This factor might be important. Fernald *et al.* (1999), which examined whether China's 1994 exchange rate unification caused the East Asian currency crises three years later, suggested such importance. Spilembergo and Vamvakidis (2003) provide further evidence. They find that export equations fit better when different degrees of substitutability are allowed between intra-OECD and intra-non-OECD exports.

Would these conclusions hold up in an analysis using an exchange-rate index that does account for the degree of substitutability between flows of trade originating from different countries? Unfortunately, such indices do not exist to the author's knowledge, but attempts have been made to infer the appropriate weights using regression analysis. Estimates by Spencer and Wong (2002) suggest somewhat smaller weights on the Japanese yen than simple bilateral trade flows would indicate. For instance, in their simple trade weighted index for China, Japan has a weight of 0.22, while the weights based on bilateral competition and estimated elasticities suggest one no greater than 0.10. They conclude in consequence that movements in the Japanese yen/US$ exchange rate have much less impact than that implied by conventional measures.

Another question concerns whether the findings using monthly data frequencies are relevant. Most critiques of the implicit dollar pegs in effect before the 1997 crises centred on long-duration misalignments associated with long swings in dollar rates. Such effects may be difficult to discern using monthly changes. To see if the results are indeed sensitive to data frequencies, the above analysis was repeated using annual changes in the exchange rates. The results are broadly similar to those reported. Dollar/yen exchange rates do not typically have the anticipated effects on trade-weighted exchange rates.

Implications

The findings reported above do not serve as evidence that changes in dollar movements are unimportant. They do indicate that the impact on competitiveness is not always in the direction expected. Where dollar movements — against the euro or the yen — are important, alternative nominal anchors might still be considered. For example, Kawai and Takagi (2000) have recommended moving to a managed float with a G-3 currency-basket peg as the central rate. Williamson (1999, 2001) also suggests pegging to a basket, but with a crawling band. He emphasises that the nominal external anchor should be used in conjunction with a monetary policy of inflation targeting[36]. The need for such an adjunct to inflation targeting is probably higher if exchange rate pass-through is fairly high[37].

Finally, recall that the correlations reported here merely reflect an amalgam of current policies, shocks and trade weights. They are useful to validate the impact of past and current policies, but they obviously are not structural parameters and should not be construed as restricting policy choices. If countries so choose, they can simply de-link. Why they elect not to do so has been examined much more thoroughly elsewhere[38].

Regulatory Initiatives and Efforts to Reform the International Financial Architecture

Reforms of the International Financial Architecture

The plethora of initiatives to reform the international financial system ranges widely. Proposals include suggestions for more reliance on consultative groups such as the Group of 20, agreements to increase transparency in data provision by countries and in decision making by international financial institutions as well as a move to increase BIS capital adequacy standards. Renewed interest has arisen in "bailing-in" the private sector, so that it bears the costs and risks of investing in emerging markets. A comprehensive discussion of these topics is clearly beyond the scope of this chapter. For an excellent discussion of many of these issues, see Frankel and Roubini (2003).

The following discussion centres on initiatives and findings over the last five years under two headings. The first involves attempts to mitigate the high costs associated with "sudden stops", with the resulting financial

ISBN 92-64-01442-X © OECD 2005

crises and their attendant heavy financial costs[39], by modifying the terms under which sovereign debt is incurred. The second is an effort to implement new regulations to reduce the likelihood of financial crises.

One major initiative in regard to the first was the effort to establish an international bankruptcy system to accelerate an orderly workout of international debt when a developing country falls into an extreme indebtedness crisis. Debt relief often needs to be an integral component of "rescue" packages in order to encourage creditor-debtor bargains to stretch out loans, convert debts to equity and occasionally make permanent write-downs of claims. Private creditors should bear the major burden for renegotiating the timing and repayment terms on existing debts when a financial crisis emerges.

Such initiatives can fall into two broad categories: statutory and contractual. The first embraces proposals for a sovereign debt restructuring mechanism (SDRM), such as that forwarded by First Deputy Managing Director Anne Krueger (2002*a,b*). Her proposal would have established a US-style, court-based approach to restructuring sovereign debt, operating under the auspices of the IMF and enshrined in the IMF's Articles of Agreement. As early as mid-2003, however, it became clear that the proposal lacked the key support of the US government. Movement along this path thus appears to be at a standstill.By default, it appears that the second route will be the one adopted, namely the inclusion of "collective action clauses" (CACs), which lay out how defaults are to be handled. Eichengreen (2003) discusses some of the details of how such clauses could be incorporated into bonds. To the extent that there is a proposal for systematic implementation of "private sector involvement", the encouragement of CACs is its concrete manifestation. In contrast with the proposal for an SDRM, some empirical evidence already exists on CACs. Bonds issued in London already incorporate such clauses. One question, aside from whether welfare in borrowing countries would actually increase[40], concerns the distributional effect. Eichengreen and Mody (2001) found that when collective action clauses are included, low-risk countries face lower interest rates while high-risk countries face higher ones[41].

The implications — beyond those pertaining to all developing countries — are unclear for the newly industrialising and developing countries of Asia. To the extent that most East Asian economies are less risky than countries in Latin America, South Asia and Africa, these governments will tend to face lower interest rates, if the Eichengreen-Mody results are correct. Furthermore, East Asia stands apart from many other parts of the emerging world in one key sense. Liquidity does not currently seem to be an issue.

Outside China, investment remains depressed. This situation may of course change if another crisis should strike. Indeed, the Chiang Mai Initiative (CMI), a regional swap arrangement, aims to address just such a contingency[42]. Corresponding initiatives such as the Supplemental Reserve Facility (SRF) are not underway at the global level. The existing Contingent Credit Line (CCL) facility of the IMF is essentially moribund; no country has actually accessed it.

Regulatory Changes: The Basle II Standards

One imminent change in the international regulatory framework is the implementation of new capital adequacy standards for international banks[43]. Its objective is to reduce the tendency toward risky lending, a clear lesson from the East Asian crisis. Yet a myriad of concerns with it have emerged. A key one surrounds the additional procyclicality induced by the new standards. To understand it, note that in a static context it makes much sense to calibrate required capital reserves to the riskiness of a bank's total loan portfolio. What makes sense for an individual bank at a given time, however, may have unintended consequences over time. The riskiness of loan portfolios generally rises in times of economic stress, such as recession, and bank lending will tend to fall exactly at such times. For the overall economy, the implementation of the standards could make bank loans even more procyclical. Kashyap and Stein (2004) conclude from simulations that under certain assumptions the Basle II standards might induce just such a result. They argue that it might be useful to adjust the capital standards by some index of macroeconomic conditions.

Implications for Adjustment

The links between the developed and developing economies are strengthening in many ways. The causes of this phenomenon are unclear, although empirical analysis suggests that the increasing magnitude of trade flows is a key factor. To the extent that trade integration proceeds apace, one should anticipate a continuation of this process even if the mechanism through which it takes place is little understood. The analysis in this chapter indicates that movements in dollar exchange rates have strongly affected the trade competitiveness of the East Asian economies and will continue to do so. The

ISBN 92-64-01442-X © OECD 2005

ordering of the effects is not always as anticipated. Evidence that dollar/yen fluctuations have the largest impact on the region's terms of trade is not firmly established, either for the pre-1997 period or the post-crisis era. Consequently, the competitiveness-based arguments either for stabilising G-3 exchange rates or for East Asian countries to adopt currency baskets remain incomplete.

Efforts to reform the international financial architecture have made some progress over the last few years, especially in establishing consultative forums, but large, substantive changes have yet to be implemented. Other reforms, including the Basle II accord, may very well improve the microeconomic efficiency of international banks but may also have unintended macroeconomic effects.

What implications for adjustment can one draw from this analysis? One key aspect involves the sensitivity of the East Asian economies to developments in the G-7 economies, perhaps most importantly the United States. Any discussion must address the prospects for the US economy. With the US trade deficit in excess of 5 per cent of GDP, it is clear that at some juncture a decline of the deficit must occur. This long-awaited development has failed thus far to materialise, despite a substantial drop in the trade weighted value of the dollar since 2002. In part, this is due to the relative insensitivity of US trade flows to the real exchange rate (Chinn, 2003). In addition, the revival of American economic growth has served partly to offset the effects of dollar depreciation.

Given current views of likely trends in growth around the world, it is difficult to see how the adjustment will proceed[44]. Indeed, with US short-term interest rates likely to rise over the next year, adjustment may proceed even more slowly than anticipated, because higher real US rates will tend to increase inbound capital inflows and raise the value of the dollar. This prospect makes clear why it is ever more urgent for the United States to set forth on a path of fiscal consolidation in order to reduce the demand for world savings and mitigate the upward pressure on real interest rates[45]. If fiscal policy were returned to a more responsible mode, a relatively smooth adjustment could occur, as long as sustained growth resumes in the euro area and Japan. This confluence of events could result in a soft landing in current-account adjustment as both Europe and East Asia take up more of the burden of sustaining world consumption. If European growth also becomes driven by accelerated productivity, then the increased profitability of financial assets in the euro area could partly offset the tendency for world financial savings to flow to the United States, putting additional downward pressure on the dollar. One major auxiliary requirement is that Japan resumes its upward trajectory. Without a sustained Japanese recovery based on domestic consumption, East Asian trade will falter. Recent domestically based growth provides hope that the US current account adjustment will be accommodated.

The full realisation of this scenario requires, however, a willingness of East Asian governments to allow greater flexibility in their exchange rates *vis à vis* the US dollar. Increased flexibility on the part of East Asian central banks in terms of what currencies or baskets of currencies they target will prove essential. The urgency of the situation is highlighted by the dire circumstances associated with alternative scenarios. A more precipitous decline in private willingness to purchase US assets could lead to a more rapid and disruptive re-balancing of global current account balances[46]. The likelihood of financial crises is greatest during such events, which provides an even stronger argument for avoiding them.

Appendix

Data Sources, Description and Calculation

Note: The information below is organised according to the section and subsection headings under which the data and their applications appear.

Macroeconomic Linkages

Previous Literature and Stylised Facts

The data for GDP growth rates, terms of trade and capital flows are drawn from the IMF's *World Economic Outlook* (September 2003) database, which is available at:

http://www.imf.org/external/pubs/ft/weo/2003/02/data/index.htm.

These data are expressed in annual terms for the following aggregates: advanced developed countries, major advanced countries (G-7), developing countries, developing Asian countries[47] and newly industrialising Asian countries. These categories are described at:

http://www.imf.org/external/pubs/ft/weo/2003/02/data/groups.htm.

Growth rates of GDP are expressed in constant local currency terms.

The US real interest rate is the three-month Treasury bill rate (secondary market) adjusted by the annual CPI-U inflation rate over the previous year, using monthly data. These series are drawn from the Federal Reserve Bank of St. Louis FRED database, at:

http://research.stlouisfed.org/fred2/.

Capital flows are converted into constant 1995 dollars using the US CPI-U.

ISBN 92-64-01442-X

Empirical Results

This data set encompasses 47 countries and covers 1980-2000. These countries include almost all the OECD countries and the largest ones (by GDP) outside the OECD in addition to most East Asian emerging markets[48]. The annual nominal GDP data are drawn from the World Bank's *World Development Indicators* while the real GDP data come from the Penn World Tables. Bilateral and total trade data are from the IMF's *Direction of Trade Statistics*. The gravity variables (distance, adjacency, common linguistic ties, island, colonial links, and common colony) are drawn from Andrew Rose's website at:

http://faculty.haas.berkeley.edu/arose/RecRes.htm#Trade.

The Chinn and Ito (2002) measure of capital account openness in each country is calculated as a standardised principal component of four IMF dummy variables measuring different types of external account restrictions, with an adjustment for the length of time that the capital controls were in place. Higher value indicates greater capital-account openness. This data set is available at:

http://www.ssc.wisc.edu/~mchinn/KAOPEN.csv .

The quarterly real GDP data used to construct the business cycle variables are drawn from IMF's *International Financial Statistics* (*IFS*) as well as national data sources. The growth rates are calculated as log first differences, while output gaps are calculated as deviations from band-pass (Baxter-King) filtered data. Exchange-rate and interest-rate volatility variables are measured as standard deviations of monthly log-differences. The underlying data are drawn from IFS, with the exception of Chinese Taipei data, which come from national sources.

Financial Linkages

The data sources used in obtaining the results cited are described further in Forbes and Chinn (2003)[49]. The data used to estimate the factor model of returns where stock returns or weekly bond returns are measured in either US dollars or local currency are compiled by DataStream and weighted to be representative of all major markets in the given country. The bond data for developed countries is based on the total country return indices compiled by Morgan Stanley Capital International (MSCI) for 7-10 year bonds. The bond data for emerging markets are based on the EMBI Global total country return indices compiled by JP Morgan.

ISBN 92-64-01442-X © OECD 2005

The four global factors are global interest rates, oil prices, gold prices and commodity prices. The sectoral factors are weekly returns based on the MSCI Industrial Sector Indices. The cross-country factors are returns for France, Germany, Japan, the United Kingdom and the United States in the asset market corresponding to the left-hand variable.

The GDP data used as the denominator for many of these statistics are taken from the World Bank's *World Development Indicators* and reported in US dollars. The trade data used to calculate import demand and trade competition are from the Statistics Canada database. Trade competition is competition in third markets, evaluated at the four-digit SITC level; its construction is described in detail in Forbes and Chinn (2003). Bank lending is based on lending data reported by the Bank for International Settlements (BIS), measured as the total stock of bank lending from major country *c* in non-major country *i* as a share of country *i* GDP. Foreign investment is calculated on data from the OECD's *International Direct Investment Statistics Yearbook* and measured as the total stock of foreign investment from country *c* in country *i* as a share of country *i* GDP.

Exchange-Rate Variability

Data on trade-weighted PPI-deflated real exchange rate indices are drawn from JP Morgan and the Deutsche Bank. The JP Morgan series was downloaded from:

http://www2.jpmorgan.com/MarketDataInd/Forex/currIndex.html

for February 2002 (older series omitting China trade weights) and April 2004 (including China trade weights). The Deutsche Bank series was obtained *via* personal communication from Aileen Wong. Additional real exchange-rate indices and bilateral nominal exchange rates are drawn from the IMF's *International Financial Statistics* database, accessed 7 April 2004.

The interpretation of the regression results depends on the method by which trade weighting is implemented. The latest version of the JP Morgan series weights by both import and export flows, where the export weighting accounts for third-market effects. This methodology is described in Hargreaves and Strong (2003). In contrast, the Deutsche Bank series do not include third-country effects and merely use as trade weights the simple averages of exports and imports. The Deutsche Bank series do use a Chinese exchange rate that is adjusted for the importance of swap transactions prior to the 1994 exchange-rate unification (see Fernald *et al.*, 1999 for a discussion).

Notes

1. This paper was originally presented at the OECD Experts' Seminar on "The Impact and Coherence of OECD-Country Policies on Asian Developing Countries", Paris, 10-11 June 2004. The author thanks the discussant, Stijn Claessens, conference organisers Kiichiro Fukasaku, Masahiro Kawai and Michael Plummer and the seminar participants as well as Steve Kamin and Ramkishen Rajan for very useful comments. Thanks go also to Hiro Ito for assistance in compiling part of the data set. This research was supported by research funds of the University of California at Santa Cruz and the University of Wisconsin at Madison. The views contained herein are solely those of the author and do not necessarily represent those of the institutions or organisations with which the author is associated.

2. See Prasad *et al.* (2003) for an examination of the broader issues of globalisation and macroeconomic volatility. Cheung *et al.*, (2003) examine the links between the United States, Japan and the economies of China; Hong Kong, China; and Chinese Taipei from the perspective of parity conditions.

3. I owe this enumeration to a speech by Otto Genee of the Netherlands Ministry of Foreign Affairs.

4. This is a very large literature, so that it is difficult to enumerate all the relevant studies. In addition to the citations in the text, see also Agenor *et al.* (2000).

5. This result might appear counterintuitive, given East Asia's heavy dependence on electronics exports during 1998-2000. For instance, electronics and electronic components accounted for about 25 per cent of Thai exports in 2000 and grew by 20 per cent in the first half of 2000. This period represents more recent trends, however, and the correlation is higher for the newly industrialising countries that were also highly dependent upon electronics exports (19 per cent of Korean exports, with a 94 per cent growth rate in the first half of 2000) (Spencer, 2000).

6. This group comprises Hong Kong, China; Korea; Singapore and Chinese Taipei. These economies also appear in the "advanced countries" grouping.

ISBN 92-64-01442-X © OECD 2005

7. The residual from a regression of developing country growth on G-7 growth is used as the dependent variable.

8. See for instance Borensztein and Reinhart (1994) and Dornbusch (1985).

9. Defined as an abrupt reversal in capital inflows to emerging markets, or "sudden stop", surprise announcements and a leveraged common creditor (Kaminsky, Reinhart and Vegh, 2003: 54-55).

10. Some earlier analyses include Calvo, Leiderman and Reinhart (1993) and Fernandez-Arias (1996). The latter finds that the "push" factor is more important than "pull" factors in the early 1990 resumption of lending to emerging markets. Dooley *et al.* (1994) finds that bond prices depend primarily on developed country interest rates.

11. Reinhart and Reinhart (2003) estimate similar regressions for 1970-99 and find considerably smaller coefficients. For instance, regressing net private capital flows (in 1970 dollars) on the nominal US rate and real GDP growth leads to a coefficient of -2.32, which after adjusting for different units leads to about -9 billion 1995 US dollars per percentage point change. The difference may occur because the later period in this analysis includes more large magnitudes.

12. This section draws from results obtained in ongoing research conduced with Shang-Jin Wei.

13. This follows several other works, including most importantly Frankel and Rose (1998) and Calderon *et al.* (2002). Intuitively, it might seem that higher trade flows are associated with higher business cycle correlation, but theory suggests that the direction of effect depends on the nature of trade (inter-industry *vs* intra-industry trade).

14. Trade flows are modelled as a function of the GDPs of the trading countries, the distance between them and a number of other geographical variables (whether they share a common border, whether one of the countries is landlocked or is an island) as well as other institutional variables (whether the countries share a common language or one was a former colony of the other). In addition, exchange-rate volatility is allowed to enter into the determination of trade flows (and hence indirectly into the coherence of business cycles).

15. Kose *et al.* (2003) does not find that fiscal policy similarity measures have a significant role in determining business cycle correlations.

16. As the discussant, Stijn Claessens, noted, the use of correlations is problematic when variances increase, as in times of crises. See, for instance, the work of Forbes and Rigobon (2002).

17. Average correlations estimated by running a regression of relevant correlations on time dummies.

18. In fact, the statistical significance is probably lower than that suggested by the t-statistics, since it is possible that the observations are not independent across observations. Some of this cross-pair correlation is mitigated by the use of fixed time effects.

19. Imbs (2003) can rely on disaggregated data for the OECD countries, while Calderon *et al.* (2002) use only the sectoral shares at the beginning of the sample and so generate this sectoral difference variable only once for each country. As noted by the discussant, Stijn Claessens, the measure used in this paper would capture only indirectly the commodity orientation of an economy such as, for instance, Indonesia.

20. Another measure would be the fiscal impulse. It would be difficult to obtain a consistent measure across all the time periods and countries in this sample. Moreover, Kose *et al.* (2003) find that the budget surplus to GDP ratio fails to exhibit much explanatory power, so this measure was avoided.

21. Reverse causality is a plausible alternative interpretation of this correlation. It could be that country pairs with lower business-cycle correlations adopt more divergent monetary policies.

22. See Edison *et al.* (2002) for a description of other measures of capital controls.

23. For instance, in the specification corresponding to column 11 of Table 2.4, the coefficient on trade normalised is 0.04, versus 0.06. The coefficient on the financial openness variable is 0.07 (significant at the 10 per cent level) versus 0.06.

24. Note that since the linkages are measured as regression – not correlation – coefficients, the volatility of the right hand side variables does not affect the statistic of interest.

25. The competition variable takes into account product overlap at the four-digit SITC level. See Forbes and Chinn (2003) for details.

26. Clarida (2000) provides an extensive survey of the topic.

27. One could also argue on similar grounds for interest-rate stabilisation, but to the extent that interest-rate parity conditions hold, minimisation of interest-rate variability might require more variability in other asset prices.

28. The key references are Krugman (1991) and Froot and Obstfeld (1991).

29. See McKinnon and Schnabl (2003). Kawai (2004) argues that Thailand and Korea have moved toward a basket peg. The deterioration in Argentine competitiveness during the 1996-2001 dollar appreciation also highlighted the danger of being on a dollar peg when most of the trade flows are not with the United States.

ISBN 92-64-01442-X © OECD 2005

30. The motivation for these policies is a subject of debate. Indeed, there may be a multiplicity of rationales, varying in importance over time. In the immediate wake of the East Asian crises, the primary motivation probably was self-protection, while in more recent times the desire to maintain export demand was probably of greater importance.

31. There remains a real question whether there was a substantial degree of overvaluation. See for instance the estimates by Chinn (2000) and the arguments by Furman and Stiglitz (1998) that the overvaluations were not key to the currency crises. On the other hand, others have recently maintained the existence of large overvaluation; see Rajan *et al.* (2002).

32. Whether most of Japanese debt was denominated in dollars or yen remains an open question.

33. Note that these results pertaining to the impact of the dollar/yen rate are not sensitive to omission of the dollar/euro exchange rate.

34. Up until 2003, the indices used 1990 trade weights omitting China (see Hargreaves and Strong, 2003). Regressions using these earlier series find a greater role for shifts in the dollar/yen rate.

35. The characteristics of these indices are described in Spencer and Wong (2002). They do not take into account third-market export effects.

36. See also Bird and Rajan (2002). A general argument for "inflation targeting plus" is presented by Goldstein (2002). For critiques of currency basket arrangements, see DeBrouwer (2000) and Frankel (2003). Frankel proposes "pegging the export price" (PEP).

37. It does appear that pass-through is higher for emerging markets than for developed economies. However, the East Asian economies typically have lower pass-through coefficients than their Latin American counterparts. See Choudhri and Hakura (2001) as reported by Ho and McCauley (2003).

38. See Calvo and Reinhart (2000*a,b*) in particular. Hausmann *et al.* (2000, 2001) and Goldfajn and Olivares (2001) also discuss this issue.

39. "Sudden stops" are analysed by Calvo (2002). Hutchison and Noy (2002) assess empirically the cost of these crises.

40. While it would seem obvious that easier resolution of debt defaults and avoidance of the resulting financial crises would result in smaller welfare losses, some have argued that the costs associated with the defaults are part of the disciplining device which enables borrowing to occur. See Dooley (2000).

41. See Becker *et al.* (2001).

42. The Chiang Mai Initiative is a regional financing network introduced by the ASEAN countries plus China, Japan and Korea (often termed the ASEAN+3) in May 2002. Technically, the initiative is an expansion of the ASEAN swap arrangement to pool dollar reserves to include the three newcomers. The objective is to improve the countries' ability to guard against bouts of financial speculation. See Ito (2004) for a brief review. For a broader discussion of regional initiatives, see Kawai (2005) in this volume.

43. See Basel Committee on Banking Supervision (2003).

44. Although some have argued that the financing of the US current account deficit can continue for many years. See Dooley *et al.* (2003).

45. For a detailed analysis of the role of US fiscal policy in determining long-term real interest rates, see Chinn and Frankel (2003).

46. See BIS (2004), Chapter V, for three scenarios for US current account adjustment. For a slightly different perspective on how US and euro-area adjustment might proceed, see IMF (2004).

47. The data for the developing Asia group include Bangladesh, Bhutan, Cambodia, China, Fiji, India, Indonesia, Kiribati, Laos, Malaysia, Maldives, Myanmar, Nepal, Pakistan, Papua New Guinea, Philippines, Samoa, Solomon Islands, Sri Lanka, Thailand, Tonga, Vanuatu, and Viet Nam.

48. Argentina; Australia; Austria; Bangladesh; Belgium; Brazil; Canada; Chile; China; Colombia; Denmark; Egypt; Finland; France; Germany; Greece; Hong Kong, China; Hungary; India; Indonesia; Iran; Ireland; Israel; Italy; Japan; Korea; Malaysia; Mexico; Netherlands; New Zealand; Norway; Pakistan; Panama; Peru; Philippines; Poland; Portugal; Saudi Arabia; Singapore; South Africa; Spain; Sweden; Switzerland; Thailand; Turkey; United Kingdom and United States.

49. The countries covered include the five major countries: France; Germany; Japan; United Kingdom and United States, and the non-major countries: Argentina; Brazil; Canada; Chile; Colombia; Mexico; Venezuela; Australia; China; Hong Kong, China; India; Indonesia; Korea; Malaysia; New Zealand; Philippines; Singapore; Thailand; Austria; Belgium; Denmark; Finland; Greece; Hungary; Iceland; Ireland; Italy; Netherlands; Norway; Poland; Portugal; Spain; Sweden; Switzerland; Israel; Morocco; South Africa and Turkey.

 ISBN 92-64-01442-X © OECD 2005

Bibliography

AGENOR, P.-R., C.J. McDERMOTT and E. PRASAD (2000), "Macroeconomic Fluctuations in Developing Countries: Some Stylized Facts", *World Bank Economic Review*, 14(2), pp. 251-85.

BANK FOR INTERNATIONAL SETTLEMENTS (2004), *Annual Report*, BIS, Basel.

BANSAL, R. and M. DAHLQUIST (2000), "The Forward Premium Puzzle: Different Tales from Developed and Emerging Economies", *Journal of International Economics*, 41, pp. 115-144.

BASEL COMMITTEE ON BANKING SUPERVISION (2003), "An Overview of the New Basel Capital Accord", consultative document, BIS, Basel.

BECKER, T., A.J. RICHARDS and Y. THAICHAROEN (2001), "Bond Restructuring and Moral Hazard: Are Collective Action Clauses Costly?", IMF Working Paper No. 01/92, July.

BEKAERT, G. and C.R. HARVEY (2002), "Research in Emerging Markets Finance: Looking to the Future", paper presented at the conference "Valuation in Emerging Markets", U.VA, 28-30 May.

BIRD, G. and R. RAJAN (2002), "Optimal Currency Baskets and the Third Currency Phenomenon: Exchange Rate Policy in Southeast Asia", *Journal of International Development*, 14, pp. 1053-1073.

BORENSZTEIN, E. and C.M. REINHART (1994), "The Macroeconomic Determinants of Commodity Prices", *IMF Staff Papers*, 41(2), pp. 236-260.

CALDERON, C., A. CHONG and E. STEIN (2002), "Trade Intensity and Business Cycle Synchronization: Are Developing Countries any Different?", mimeo, Inter-American Development Bank, Washington, D.C., March.

CALVO, G. (2002), "Explaining Sudden Stop, Growth Collapse and BOP Crisis: The Case of Distortionary Output Taxes", paper presented at Third Annual IMF Research Conference.

CALVO, G., L. LEIDERMAN and C.M. REINHART (1993), "Capital Inflows and the Real Exchange Rate in Latin America: The Role of External Factors", *IMF Staff Papers*, 40(1), pp. 108-150.

CALVO, G. and C. REINHART (2000*a*), "Fear of Floating", NBER Working Paper No. 7993.

CALVO, G. and C. REINHART (2000*b*), "Fixing for Your Life", NBER Working Paper No. 8006.

CHEUNG, Y.-W., M. CHINN and E. FUJII (2003), "The Chinese Economies in Global Context: The Integration Process and Its Determinants", NBER Working Paper No. 10047, October.

CHINN, M. (2000), "Before the Fall: Were East Asian Currencies Overvalued?", *Emerging Markets Review*, 1(2), pp. 101-126.

CHINN, M. (2003), "Doomed to Deficits? Aggregate U.S. Trade Flows Revisited", NBER Working Paper No.9521, February.

CHINN, M. and J. FRANKEL (1994), "Financial Links Around the Pacific Rim: 1982-1992", *in* R. GLICK and M. HUTCHISON (eds.), *Exchange Rate Policy and Interdependence: Perspectives from the Pacific Basin*, Cambridge University Press, Cambridge, pp. 17-26.

CHINN, M. and J. FRANKEL (2003), "The Euro Area and World Interest Rates", paper presented for the CEPR/ESI conference on "The Euro Area as an Economic Entity", Eltville, Germany, 12-13 September.

CHINN, M. and H. ITO (2002), "Capital Liberalization, Institutions and Financial Development: Cross Country Evidence", NBER Working Paper No. 8967, June.

CHOUDHRI, E.U. and D.S. HAKURA (2001), "Exchange Rate Pass-Through to Domestic Prices: Does the Inflationary Environment Matter?", IMF Working Paper No. 01/194.

CLARIDA, R.H. (2000), "G3 Exchange Rate Relationships: A Recap of the Record and A Review of Proposals for Change", *Princeton Essays in International Economics*, No. 219, September.

DEBROUWER, G. (2000), "Does a Formal Common-Basket Peg in East Asia Make Economic Sense?", mimeo, Asian-Japan Research Centre, Australia National University.

DOMINGUEZ, K.M. and J.A. FRANKEL (1993), "Does Foreign Exchange Intervention Matter? The Portfolio Effect", *American Economic Review*, 83, pp. 1356-1359.

DOOLEY, M. (2000), "Can Output Losses Following International Financial Crises Be Avoided?", NBER Working Paper No. 7531, February.

DOOLEY, M., E. FERNANDEZ-ARIAS and K. KLETZER (1994), "Recent Private Capital Inflows to Developing Countries: Is the Debt Crisis History?", NBER Working Paper No. 4792, July.

 ISBN 92-64-01442-X

DOOLEY, M., D. FOLKERTS-LANDAU and P. GARBER (2003), "An Essay on the Revived Bretton Woods System", NBER Working Paper No. 9971, September.

DORNBUSCH, R. (1985), "Policy and Performance Links between LDC Debtors and Industrial Nations", *Brookings Papers on Economic Activity*, 1985:2, pp. 303-356.

EDISON, H.J., M.W. KLEIN, L. RICCI and T. SLØK (2002), "Capital Account Liberalization and Economic Performance: A Review of the Literature", mimeo, IMF, Washington, D.C., May.

EICHENGREEN, B. (2003), "Restructuring Sovereign Debt", *Journal of Economic Perspectives*, 17(4), pp. 75-98.

EICHENGREEN, B. and A. MODY (2001), "Bail-ins, Bailouts and Borrowing Costs", *IMF Staff Papers*, Special Issue 47, pp. 155-187.

FERNALD, J., H. EDISON and P. LOUNGANI (1999), "Was China the First Domino? Assessing Links between China and other Asian Economies", *Journal of International Money and Finance*, 18(4), pp. 515-535.

FERNANDEZ-ARIAS, E. (1996), "The New Wave of Private Capital Inflows: Push or Pull?", *Journal of Development Economics*, 48, pp. 389-418.

FLOOD, R. and A. ROSE (1995), "Fixing Exchange Rates: A Virtual Quest for Fundamentals", *Journal of Monetary Economics*, 36(1), pp. 3-37.

FORBES, K.J. and M. CHINN (2003), "A Decomposition of Global Linkages in Financial Markets over Time", NBER Working Paper No. 9393 and *Review of Economics and Statistics*, Vol. 83(3), August 2004.

FORBES, K.J. and R. RIGOBON (2002), "No Contagion, Only Interdependence: Measuring Stock Market Comovements", *The Journal of Finance*, 57, pp. 2223-2261.

FRANKEL, J. (2003), "Experiences and Lessons from Exchange Rate Regimes in Emerging Economies", NBER Working Paper No. 10032.

FRANKEL, J. and A. MACARTHUR (1988), "Political vs. Currency Premia in International Real Interest Differentials: A Study of Forward Rates for 24 Countries", *European Economic Review*, 32, pp. 1083-1121.

FRANKEL, J. and A. ROSE (1998), "The Endogeneity of the Optimum Currency Area Criteria", *The Economic Journal*, 108(449), pp. 1009-1025.

FRANKEL, J. and N. ROUBINI (2003), "The Role of Industrial Country Policies in Emerging Market Crises", *in* M. FELDSTEIN (ed.), *Economic and Financial Crises in Emerging Market Economies*, University of Chicago Press, Chicago, pp. 155-278.

FRANKEL, J. and S.-J. WEI (1994), "Yen Bloc or Dollar Bloc? Exchange Rate Policies of the East Asian Economies", *in* T. ITO and A. KRUEGER (eds.), *Macroeconomic Linkage: Savings, Exchange Rates, and Capital Flows*, University of Chicago Press, Chicago.

FROOT, K. and M. OBSTFELD (1991), "Exchange Rate Dynamics under Stochastic Regime Shifts: A Unified Approach", *Econometrica*, 59, pp. 241-50.

FURMAN, J. and J. STIGLITZ (1998), "Economic Crises: Evidence and Insights from East Asia", *Brookings Papers on Economic Activity*, 1998:2 pp. 1-136.

GOLDFAJN, I. and G. OLIVARES (2001), "Can Flexible Exchange Rates Still 'Work' in Financially Open Economies?", G-24 Discussion Paper No. 8, Intergovernmental Group of Twenty-Four on International Monetary Affairs, UNCTAD, Geneva, January.

GOLDSTEIN, M. (2002), *Managed Floating Plus, Policy Analysis in International Economics*, Institute for International Economics, Washington, D.C., March.

HARGREAVES, D. and C. STRONG (2003), "JP Morgan Effective Exchange Rates: Revised and Modernized", Economic Research Note, JP Morgan Chase Bank, New York, NY, May.

HAUSMANN, R., U. PANIZZA and E. STEIN (2000), "Why Do Countries Float the Way They Float?", Working Paper, Inter-American Development Bank, Washington, D.C., April.

HAUSMANN, R., U. PANIZZA and E. STEIN (2001), "Original Sin, Passthrough, and Fear of Floating", Working Paper, Kennedy School of Government, Harvard University, Cambridge, MA, June.

HERNANDEZ, L. and P. MONTIEL (2001), "Post-Crisis Exchange Rate Policy in Five Asian Countries: Filling in 'Hollow Middle'?", IMF Working Paper No. 01/170.

HO, C. and R.N. MCCAULEY (2003), "Living with Flexible Exchange Rates: Issues and Recent Experience in Inflation Targeting Emerging Market Economies", BIS Working Papers, No. 130, BIS, Basel, February.

HUTCHISON, M. and I. NOY (2002), "Sudden Stops and the Mexican Wave: Currency Crises, Capital Flow Reversals and Output Loss in Emerging Markets", mimeo, University of California, Santa Cruz, April.

IMBS, J. (2003), "Trade, Finance, Specialization and Synchronization", mimeo, London Business School, London.

INTERNATIONAL MONETARY FUND (2004), "The Euro Area: 2004 Article IV Consultation – selected issues", IMF, Washington, D.C.

ITO, T. (2004), "East Asian Economic Cooperation and Integration", paper presented at AEA session on "East Asian Economic Cooperation and Integration", San Diego, January.

ITO, T., E. OGAWA and Y. NAGATAKI SASAKI (1998), "How Did the Dollar Peg Fail in Asia?", *Journal of the Japanese and International Economies*, 12(4), pp. 256-304.

 ISBN 92-64-01442-X © OECD 2005

Jeanne, O. and A.K. Rose (2002), "Noise Trading and Exchange Rate Regimes", *Quarterly Journal of Economics*, Vol. 117(2), May.

Kaminsky, G., C. Reinhart and C. Vegh (2003), "The Unholy Trinity of Financial Contagion", *Journal of Economic Perspectives*, 17(4), pp. 51-74.

Kashyap, A. and J. Stein (2004), "Cyclical Implications of the Basel II Capital Standards", *Economic Perspectives*, 2004Q1, Federal Reserve Bank of Chicago, Chicago.

Kawai, M. (2004), "Regional Economic Integration and Cooperation in East Asia," paper presented at Experts' Seminar on the "Impact and Coherence of OECD-Country Policies on Asian Developing Economies", OECD, Paris, June 10-11 (see Chapter 8 in this volume).

Kawai, M. and S. Takagi (2000), "Proposed Strategy for a Regional Exchange Rate Arrangement in Post-Crisis East Asia", Policy Research Working Paper No. 2502, World Bank, Washington, D.C., December.

Kim, S.H., M.A. Kose and M.G. Plummer (2003), "Dynamics and Business Cycles in Asia: Differences and Similarities", *Review of Development Economics*, Vol. 7, No. 3, pp. 462-477.

Kose, M.A., E. Prasad and M. Terrones (2003), "Volatility and Comovement in a Globalized World Economy: An Empirical Exploration", IMF Working Paper No. 03/246, IMF, Washington, D.C., December.

Krueger, A.O. (2002*a*), *A New Approach to Sovereign Debt Restructuring*, IMF, Washington, D.C.

Krueger, A.O. (2002*b*), "New Approaches to Sovereign Debt Restructuring: An Update on Our Thinking", address at IIE conference on "Sovereign Debt Workouts", 1 April, Washington, D.C.

Krugman, P. (1991), "Target Zones and Exchange Rate Dynamics", *Quarterly Journal of Economics*, 106, pp. 669-82.

Kuroda, H. and M. Kawai (2003), "Strengthening Regional Cooperation in East Asia", PRI Discussion Paper Series No.03A10, Ministry of Finance, Tokyo, May.

McKinnon, R. and G. Schnabl (2003), "Synchronized Business Cycles in East Asia and Fluctuations in the Yen/Dollar Exchange Rate", mimeo. 22 January.

Ogawa, E. and T. Ito (2002), "On the Desirability of a Regional Basket Currency Arrangement", *Journal of the Japanese and International Economies* 16, pp. 317-334.

Prasad, E., K. Rogoff, S.-J. Wei and M.A. Kose (2003), "Effects of Financial Globalization on Developing Countries: Some Empirical Evidence", IMF Occasional Paper, IMF, Washington, D.C.

RAJAN, R., R. SEN and R. SIREGAR (2002), "Misalignment of the Baht, Trade Imbalances and the Crisis in Thailand", mimeo, May.

REINHART, C. and V. REINHART (2003), "What Hurts Most? G-3 Exchange Rate or Interest Rate Volatility", *in* M. FELDSTEIN (ed.), *Economic and Financial Crises in Emerging Market Economies*, University of Chicago Press, Chicago, pp. 133-166.

SPENCER, M. (2000), "Quantifying the Risks to Asia", Global Markets Research, Emerging Markets, Deutsche Bank, 29 September.

SPENCER, M. and A. WONG (2002), "Asian Export Competitiveness and the Yen", mimeo, Global Markets Research, Deutsche Bank, 25 February.

SPILEMBERGO, A. and A. VAMVAKIDIS (2003), "Real Effective Exchange Rate and the Constant Elasticity of Substitution Assumption", *Journal of International Economics*, Vol. 60(2), August.

URIBE, M. and V.Z. YUE (2003), "Country Spreads and Emerging Countries: Who Drives Whom?", NBER Working Papers No. 10018, October.

WILLIAMSON, J. (1999), "The Case for a Common Basket Peg for East Asian Countries", *in* S. COLLINGON, J. PISANI-FERRY and Y. CHUL PARK (eds.), *Exchange Rate Policies in Emerging Asian Countries*, Routledge, London, pp. 327-343.

WILLIAMSON, J. (2001), "The Case for A Basket, Band and Crawl (BBC) Regime for East Asia", *in* D. GRUEN and J. SIMON (eds.), *Future Directions for Monetary Policies in East Asia*, Reserve Bank of Australia, Sydney.

ISBN 92-64-01442-X © OECD 2005

Chapter 3

US and EU Trade Policies and East Asia

Peter Drysdale and Christopher Findlay

Abstract

This chapter identifies a number of examples of apparent lack of coherence in United States and European Union trade policies. They include the effect of preferential policies that lock in trade shares and inhibit growth-promoting structural adjustment, biases in tariff structures, policies that affect incentives of developing countries to make commitments in the WTO, the use of anti-dumping actions and the nature of tariff peaks and escalation. The origins of the lack of policy coherence lie within the domestic policy-making processes of the developed economies. An important question, then, is whether opportunity exists for East Asian economies to mobilise to induce an external shock sufficient to shift policy consensus in the United States and the European Union. The key elements of such a grand bargain on trade in manufactured goods would include an explicit East Asian commitment to bind more tariff lines, initiatives to resolve the problem of accelerating anti-dumping actions and a replacement for the programme of tariff preferences. A package of trade policy reforms of this type in East Asia would constitute a substantial offer and benefit to the United States and the European Union. It has the potential to trigger a response of equal benefit to East Asian economies.

ISBN 92-64-01442-X

Introduction

East Asia benefited hugely from the post-war multilateral trade regime and the establishment of a confident basis on which economies in the region could commit to specialisation in international trade. Although discrimination against Japan continued under Article XXXV of the GATT early in the period, and later the Multi-fibre Arrangement (MFA)[1] restricted access to most developed markets for exports of textiles and clothing, the regime provided the platform on which countries could successfully build outward-oriented development strategies. Japan; Korea; Chinese Taipei; Hong Kong, China and Singapore have more or less achieved economic parity with Western industrial economies, significantly because of the favourable international trading environment created through the GATT.

The United States and Europe were both key players in entrenching the GATT system. The United States was long the leading champion of the core GATT principles on non-discrimination and most favoured nation (MFN) treatment in international trade policy. These principles had crucial importance for new, developing country entrants to the international marketplace. Under the terms of the San Francisco Peace Treaty, the United States also never exercised its right as an original signatory of GATT to discriminate against Japan under Article XXXV. Europe, of course, through the establishment of the Common Market and the Common Agricultural Policy, discriminated against developing-country partners in East Asia. It joined fully, however, in the successive rounds of GATT liberalisation with the United States through the 1950s, 1960s and 1970s that saw industrial tariffs in the major industrial countries virtually eliminated. Both, however, participated actively in the MFA and have yet to eliminate the remaining vestiges of this system of protection against textile exports that was negotiated away under the Uruguay Round.

The United States and Europe remain key players in international trade policy through their impact on developing-country access to international markets for manufactured goods. Their markets occupy a large proportion of the international market. They also play the main role in shaping international trade diplomacy. Japan is also important. It and Australia were the only two industrial countries not to join the MFA restrictions on textile exports from developing countries, but in international trade diplomacy it now tends to play a less active role and to influence outcomes more by default than by the prosecution of proactive policy strategy.

 ISBN 92-64-01442-X

The impact on trading partners in East Asia of current trade policy choices in the United States and the EU and their implications for policy coherence are the subjects of this chapter. It limits its scope to manufactured products and excludes agricultural products[2]. Although the analysis might also apply to EU and US policy choices in the service sector, that topic also is beyond its scope. The interest lies in the coherence of policies in their international dimensions. A distinction is sometimes made between trade policy coherence at the national and international levels. The former refers to the adoption of complementary national policies that support a liberalisation programme, to the design of trade policies linked to national development strategies and to achieving consistent positions across the elements of government. The latter refers to the consistency of positions taken with respect to the various instruments of trade policy. Policy coherence at an international level is also sometimes defined to refer to the design and application of aid policy and could be extended to policy on foreign direct investment. Those matters, too, are left aside here.

The chapter first reviews briefly a framework that allows more careful specification of the set of international economic policies that matter for a consideration of coherence. It then discusses some aspects of current policy in both the EU and the United States and provides some examples of lack of coherence in that policy mix. It concludes with comments on how contradictions in policy choices might be tackled and focuses in that context on the core elements of an East Asian international trade policy response.

Framework

Previous work on trade patterns in East Asia has highlighted the transition in the export mix, the accumulation of capital and the shift in the combination of factor endowments during economic development (see, for example, Findlay, 2001). Manufactured-goods trade can include labour-intensive, capital-intensive and technology-intensive products. The decline in the importance of labour-intensive products in exports from Japan led the transition, followed by a similar shift for Hong Kong, China (data in the figures for Hong Kong, China are net of re-exports from China) and later for Korea and Chinese Taipei. Simultaneously, shares of these products in the exports of China, ASEAN and India have risen. The shares in exports of capital-intensive products of developing economies remain much lower than those of labour-intensive products, and the adjustment process in developed economies started more recently, but still with Japan leading the way. No sign has yet appeared of any significant adjustment in technology-intensive goods. Their shares in the exports of developing economies have started to rise, but this may reflect merely a change in the production processes of these items still classified as technology-intensive. This topic needs further study. The key lesson to take from this work on trade patterns concerns the significance of the transition with respect to labour-intensive and capital-intensive products.

This transition also plays out in more dramatic form in world markets. Labour-intensive products show a wider set of changes, with the economies experiencing rising shares of world markets on the left-hand side and those experiencing declining shares on the right. In capital-intensive products, Japan so far has made space for newcomer suppliers, and a similar story applies to technology-intensive products.

Some important drivers of this process of particular note in the East Asian region differentiate it from the rest of the world. First, the adjustment process and the gains from trade associated with it drive the accumulation of capital and the changes in factor endowments that in turn reinforce structural change. The origins of this process often lie in the initial, successful export of agricultural products. The changes just discussed are follow-on events, reinforced by the complementarity between the region's economies. Even before China's reform programme began, the value of this complementarity was evident. China has now become the main driver of structural change in the region.

A second driver is the growing sophistication of supply chains in the region. It interacts strongly with the emergence of China as a regional processing zone. The divisions in production processes are becoming finer. This is made possible by technological change linked to the standardisation of various parts of the production process of particular products, facilitating their relocation. Reductions in transport and communication costs also have important roles. A consequence is the growth in component trade, evident in Table 3.1. Component products accounted for over 40 per cent of East Asia's and 55 per cent of ASEAN's export growth in the 1990s. The contribution of these products to China's export performance remains relatively low, but their share in China's import growth is much larger. In other economies, components contribute to trade growth in both directions, indicating a new degree of developing complexity in regional trade patterns.

 ISBN 92-64-01442-X © OECD 2005

Table 3.1. **Share of Parts and Components in Manufactures Trade**
(percentage)

A. Exports					
Country/Region	Share of Parts and Components			Export Growth	Contribution of Parts and Components to Export Growth
	1992	1996	2000	1992-2000	1992-2000
East Asia	21.3	28.0	32.0	3.8	43.5
Developing East Asia	19.7	26.7	32.8	5.1	41.9
ASEAN	26.4	35.0	44.4	5.6	55.0
Japan	22.9	30.2	30.6	1.8	50.4
Indonesia	4.0	7.4	14.2	4.4	22.7
Malaysia	40.4	42.6	49.7	6.2	54.3
Philippines	23.9	52.5	64.0	9.0	74.3
Singapore	28.2	39.7	49.6	4.9	64.5
Thailand	21.2	23.4	35.9	4.8	46.7
Viet Nam	2.0	5.2	8.7	21.0	8.9
China	6.7	9.8	14.5	6.7	17.9
Hong Kong, China	21.5	26.7	25.8	-3.2	16.3
Korea	17.8	25.2	30.6	4.5	41.0
Chinese Taipei	20.1	28.8	37.8	5.8	47.4
South Asia	4.7	4.9	0.7	14.4	0.3
Oceania	6.4	18.9	15.2	12.6	16.3
NAFTA	26.2	27.2	28.1	4.1	30.0
USA	26.9	30.5	31.6	3.3	37.5
Canada	19.4	19.7	18.0	4.2	16.8
Mexico	21.5	19.4	21.1	8.1	21.0
Europe	13.9	16.2	17.5	3.6	21.4
EU	15.5	17.7	18.9	3.9	22.2
Latin America	8.6	11.7	10.2	11.6	10.5
Middle East	3.0	13.6	18.9	13.9	20.5
Africa	6.9	8.0	8.6	8.0	9.2
World	20.7	21.7	25.4	4.2	29.5

Table 3.1 (contd.)

B. Imports					
Country/Region	Share of Parts and Components			Import Growth	Contribution of Parts and Components to Import Growth
	1992	1996	2000	1992-2000	1992-2000
East Asia	22.8	27.9	35.4	4.4	45.9
East Asia – Japan	24.8	30.2	38.4	4.5	49.3
ASEAN	30.4	39.3	48.6	3.6	68.2
Japan	15.4	19.3	24.2	4.1	32.1
Indonesia	20.5	23.8	19.4	-0.1	63.6
Malaysia	37.9	47.5	58.8	4.2	77.5
Philippines	32.6	43.6	55.1	6.9	64.4
Singapore	32.0	42.8	51.7	3.9	70.7
Thailand	26.6	32.9	39.8	2.6	62.0
Viet Nam	4.2	11.1	19.1	10.1	22.1
China	19.5	21.1	33.5	5.4	42.0
Hong Kong, China	15.1	20.4	28.2	5.2	36.7
Korea	26.7	27.4	38.9	3.6	52.1
Chinese Taipei	29.6	35.0	37.3	5.1	42.5
South Asia	14.0	14.6	7.2	7.9	5.0
Oceania	10.4	15.2	15.6	12.9	16.2
NAFTA	20.4	23.6	22.8	4.8	24.6
USA	18.2	21.7	19.4	4.7	20.3
Canada	24.6	28.7	26.3	3.8	28.0
Mexico	19.1	30.6	30.7	7.3	35.1
Europe	15.2	16.6	18.7	3.4	22.8
EU	16.0	18.9	20.3	2.4	28.0
Latin America	14.4	14.6	15.1	12.6	15.2
Middle East	23.6	18.5	16.7	2.3	3.5
Africa	11.8	14.5	10.7	6.7	10.2
World	21.7	21.4	24.5	5.9	26.0

Note: Data not available.
Source: Table 4 in Athukorala (2003).

Rapid growth of regional trade might lead to the expectation that the region is becoming more self-reliant. Yet growth of intra-regional trade in finished goods does not necessarily accompany the growth of intra-regional

 ISBN 92-64-01442-X © OECD 2005

trade in components. Table 3.2 shows the destinations of final products, or total exports net of parts and components. The striking result is that the geographic structure of East Asian exports changed little over the 1990s — about 38 per cent of exports of final products stay in the region, with 28 per cent going to the United States and 18 per cent to the EU. That is, nearly half of the region's exports of final goods go to these two developed regions (the US share is a little lower when Japan is excluded)[3].

Table 3.2. **Direction of Manufactured Exports Net of Parts and Components**

(per cent of total; final column in $ billion)

Origin / Destination		EAS	JPN	DEA	ASEAN	NAFTA	USA	EU	Other	World
East Asia (EAS)	1992	37.5	4.8	32.8	10.1	29.7	27.6	18.4	14.4	511.5
	1996	43.2	7.7	35.5	13.1	25.9	23.1	16.4	14.5	715.7
	2000	38.4	7.6	30.8	9.9	29.9	27.6	17.5	14.2	881.9
Japan (JPN)	1992	29.0	0.0	29.0	9.8	31.5	28.2	21.8	17.7	241.1
	1996	38.0	0.0	38.0	14.7	29.8	27.9	17.0	15.2	261.7
	2000	33.9	0.0	33.9	10.4	35.0	32.5	17.8	13.3	302.1
East Asia excluding Japan	1992	45.1	9.1	36.3	10.3	28.1	26.9	15.3	11.4	270.3
	1996	46.1	12.1	34.1	12.2	23.6	20.3	16.1	14.1	454.0
	2000	40.8	11.5	29.3	9.7	27.2	25.0	17.3	14.7	579.7
ASEAN	1992	37.0	8.7	28.3	16.6	28.7	27.0	21.1	13.2	86.3
	1996	46.1	12.5	33.7	19.1	24.9	23.6	18.1	10.9	159.9
	2000	43.2	12.3	30.9	17.2	25.2	23.7	18.5	13.1	179.3
NAFTA	1992	18.2	6.6	11.6	3.7	44.8	23.1	20.2	16.9	316.8
	1996	18.5	6.6	11.9	4.2	50.4	29.1	15.3	15.8	468.4
	2000	13.7	4.7	9.0	2.6	58.3	34.9	15.7	12.2	641.2
USA	1992	23.7	8.6	15.1	4.8	29.2	0.0	25.7	21.4	231.9
	1996	26.3	9.5	16.8	5.9	31.5	0.0	21.2	21.0	311.3
	2000	21.4	7.4	14.0	4.1	37.3	0.0	23.6	17.7	394.4
European Union (EU)	1992	4.4	1.4	3.0	1.3	6.6	5.6	70.2	18.9	705.7
	1996	8.6	2.5	6.1	2.4	8.2	7.3	60.0	23.2	1283.3
	2000	6.4	2.1	4.3	1.3	11.6	10.2	60.1	21.9	1394.8
World	1992	21.4	4.2	17.2	5.4	27.1	19.8	32.9	18.6	1057.5
	1996	18.4	4.3	14.1	5.2	20.2	15.5	40.1	21.3	2632.0
	2000	15.1	3.7	11.4	3.6	26.0	20.3	39.4	19.5	3087.2

Note: DEA = developing East Asia.

Source: Extracted from Table 5 in Athukorala, 2003.

As a corollary of the growth of component trade and the impact of China in the region, one might expect China to take over from its regional trade partners some export markets in the United States and the EU. The integration of the supply chain means, however, that China's component suppliers retain a strong interest in the openness and coherence of US and EU trade policies, even though those economies may no longer be supplying those markets directly. Weiss (2005) in a study of these trends came to the following conclusion:

> "...[The] PRC's recent rapid growth has generated substantial opportunities for trade and investment in regional partner economies. This rapid growth has sucked in large volumes of imports of both primary and manufactured goods that have compensated its neighbours for their losses of market share in the US and Japan. Even the concern over FDI diversion, which appeared an obvious 'threat' a few years ago, can be set aside on the basis of substantial empirical evidence. Central to the growth of intra-industry trade in the region has been the spread of global production networks either between units of the same firm or with independent contract manufacturers, who provide goods to the buyer's specification. Hence final products made in PRC may contain parts and components from many different parts of the region with value-added at stages in a production chain that stretches across a number of countries. FDI has been a prime mover in this process in integrating PRC-based firms in these global networks and in developing the 'triangular trade' between PRC, the rest of East-Southeast Asia and the large markets in the US and Europe. In this emerging specialisation its regional neighbours provide the inputs for manufactures from PRC, which are then exported out of the region. Currently this is proving strongly mutually beneficial." (p. 19)

The rate at which "triangular trade" develops will be limited by policy applying in both the exporting countries and their trading partners. The former affects the ability of a country to shift its production mix and to locate itself at the right place in the supply chain. The main focus here, however, is the policy mix in developed-country export markets, in particular the United States and the EU.

Trade policy is not all that matters. As Weiss's conclusion implies, the capacity to undertake the adjustments necessary for trade and economic growth in East Asia is supported by large capital flows between economies

 ISBN 92-64-01442-X © OECD 2005

in the region, promoting the relocation of production and the upgrading of industrial structures. Capital flows from major industrial trading partners such as the EU and the United States are central to this process. Most of the policy questions with respect to FDI arise in the host rather than in the home countries, although recently out-sourcing has become a focus of interest in the United States and other countries. Therefore, consideration of FDI policies within the broad topic of coherence is not dealt with here (see Urata, 2005, in this volume).

The capacity to undertake adjustment relatively quickly in fast-growing economies depends on a range of domestic policies affecting human resource development, R&D and the acquisition of physical infrastructure. Those policies are often the focus of international aid and other programmes provided through the institutions of international cooperation. While important, their management and the contributions of the EU and United States to them also lie outside the scope of this chapter (see Soesastro, 2005, in this volume).

US and EU Trade Policies

Incidence of Protection

A number of aspects of US and EU trade policies impede the movement of the East Asian economies along the "ladder of development" evident in the framework just discussed. Table 3.3 shows US and EU applied and bound tariff rates compared with those in East Asia[4]. The United States and the EU have bound all their tariff rates, although the proportion of tariff lines that are actually duty-free is low relative to Japan, for example (but significantly higher than in Australia). A relatively high proportion of imports is duty-free and average applied tariff rates are low. The United States particularly, however, has a significant number of tariff lines with rates above 15 per cent ("international peaks"). Depending on the pattern of East Asian exports, these remaining peak tariffs could have a significant effect on trade growth. The impact of US or EU tariffs very much depends on the distribution of East Asian exports by tariff line. Data relevant to this question are available for East Asian exports to all industrial countries. In 1997, East Asia faced average tariffs of 5.1 per cent on all exports of non-agricultural products to the industrial countries[5]. This is relatively low compared with an average tariff of 8.2 per cent on exports of those products within the region, 15.1 per cent on exports to Latin America and 28.1 per cent on those to South Asia (Table 9 in Messerlin and Zedillo, 2004).

Table 3.3. **Bound and Applied Tariffs on Industrial Products**

(Tariff rates in per cent *ad valorem*, other measures as noted. Shares are shares of total tariff lines)

A. MFN Bound Tariffs

Import Markets	Binding Coverage (%)	Simple Average	Coefficient of Variation	Maximum *ad valorem*	Last Year of Implementation	Duty Free (%)	Non *ad valorem* (%)	International Peaks (%)
United States	100.0	3.2	1.3	48.0	2004	38.5	4.8	1.8
European Union	100.0	3.9	0.9	26.0	2004	23.9	0.7	0.8
Australia	96.5	11.0	1.0	55.0	2000	17.2	0.1	14.9
Japan	99.5	2.3	1.5	30.0	2004	57.1	3.6	0.6
Korea	93.7	10.2	0.8	80.0	2009	15.1	0.1	11.9
Hong Kong, China	37.4	0.0	0.0	0.0	2000	37.4	0.0	0.0
Chinese Taipei	100.0	4.8	1.2	90.0	2011	29.0	0.9	1.7
Singapore	64.5	6.3	0.7	10.0	2004	17.4	0.0	0.0
Malaysia	81.2	14.9	0.7	40.0	2005	4.1	0.1	38.5
Thailand	70.9	24.2	0.4	80.0	2005	2.5	14.9	47.2
Philippines	61.8	23.4	0.5	50.0	2005	2.2	0.0	50.2
Indonesia	96.1	35.6	0.2	150.0	2005	2.2	0.0	89.8

B. Applied Tariffs

Import Markets	Year	Total Number of Tariff Lines	Simple Average	Coefficient of Variation	Maximum	Duty Free (%)	Non *ad Valorem* (%)	International Peaks (%)
United States	2001	8 447	3.8	1.2	109.7	31.1	0.0	4.1
European Union	2002	8 305	4.2	0.9	26.0	17.1	0.7	0.9
Australia	2001	5 019	4.6	1.3	25.0	43.1	0.0	4.8
Japan	2001	7 243	2.7	1.4	33.8	47.7	3.9	0.7
Korea	2001	9 767	7.5	0.4	30.0	5.4	0.1	1.6
Hong Kong, China	2002	5 645	0.0	0.0	0.0	100.0	0.0	0.0
Chinese Taipei	2001	7 183	6.3	0.9	50.0	13.9	1.1	4.3
Singapore	2001	5 133	0.0	0.0	0.0	100.0	0.0	0.0
Malaysia	2001	9 215	8.1	1.3	300.0	51.4	0.2	23.3
Thailand	1999	5 866	15.5	0.9	80.0	1.2	18.0	31.2
Philippines	2002	4 852	5.2	0.9	30.0	2.4	0.0	0.4
Indonesia	2002	6 450	6.7	0.9	170.0	20.6	0.0	2.6

Source: WTO (2003), Appendix Tables of Most Favoured Nation (MFN) bound and applied tariffs.

ISBN 92-64-01442-X © OECD 2005

Table 3.3 also highlights two other features of the tariff structures in these economies. First, some East Asian economies, particularly in ASEAN but also Korea, have relatively high average tariff rates. Second, note the gap between applied and bound tariff rates for the East Asian economies (and Australia). These features of the structure of protection within and outside the region suggest elements of a strategy for designing an East Asian trade coalition in response to the problems and lack of coherence identified in the industrial countries, and the conclusion of this chapter returns to this question. The following subsection turns to other aspects of trade policy, including the impact of trade preferences, both reciprocal and non-reciprocal, of tariff escalation and of the use of anti-dumping.

Trade Discrimination

Consideration of preferential arrangements must include the impact of the sector-specific preferences in the MFA. The experience of East Asian economies in exporting to Japan and Australia compared with the United States and the EU illustrates the impact of the MFA. Japan and Australia were not members of the MFA while the US and the EU both were. Figure 3.1A shows the East Asian share of imports of clothing into these four markets. Japan is the benchmark. The East Asian share of imports of clothing into Japan, already high, grew steadily after 1990. Australia reveals a similar story. The share of imports in the United States has fallen steadily since 1980, however, and is now much lower than that of Japan and Australia. The EU's share was always much lower and changed little. The penetration of East Asia into textiles markets in Japan is more dramatic than that for clothing; a rising share is also evident in Australia (Figure 3.1B). Little change has occurred in the East Asian textile import share in the United States since 1990, and only a small change in East Asia's share in the EU.

More detailed information is needed to identify the determinants of these changing trade shares. The extent of the trade covered by quotas is one consideration but more important is whether the quotas are binding. Evans and Harrigan (2004) conclude that overall the shares of US imports under binding textile or clothing quotas remained steady during the 1990s. From this perspective no significant liberalisation of market access occurred over these years. They also report that the presence of binding quotas has a significant effect on US prices of the imported products (on average lifting prices 6.3 percentage points) and also has generated substantial quota rents (estimated at $6.71 billion between 1990 and 1998).

Figure 3.1A. **East Asian Shares of Imports of Clothing**

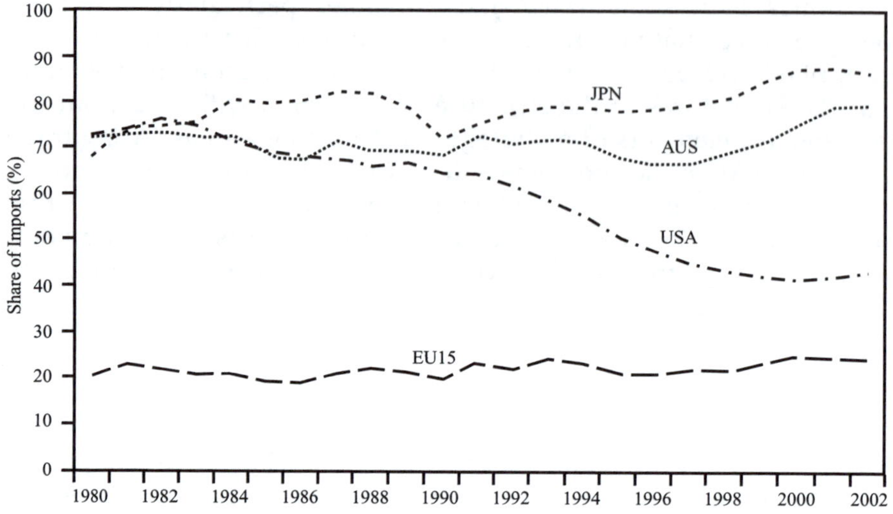

Source: International Economic Data Bank, The Australian National University.

Figure 3.1B. **East Asian Shares of Imports of Textiles**

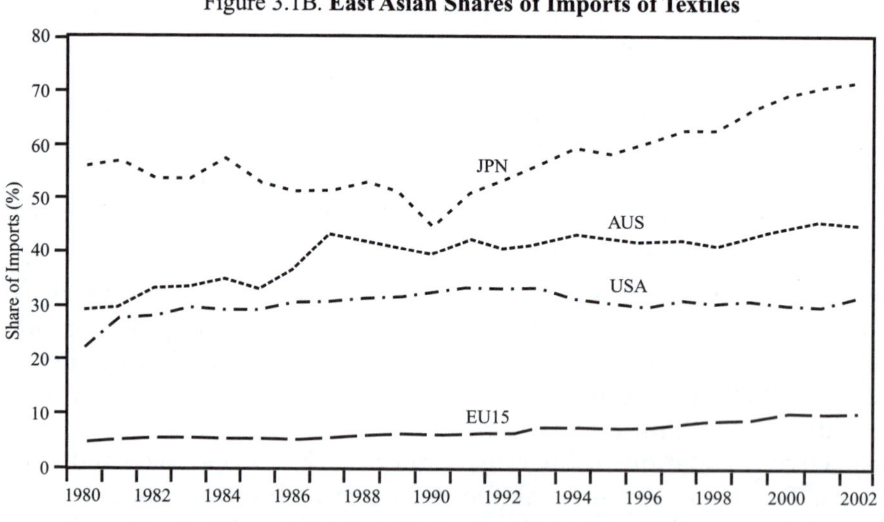

Source: International Economic Data Bank, The Australian National University.

ISBN 92-64-01442-X © OECD 2005

Evans and Harrigan also find that the degree to which various East Asian exporters faced binding quotas varied considerably given the differences in the export mixes of these economies. No clear pattern appears of effects related to stages of development. The share of US imports under binding quotas fell between 1991 and 1998 from 74 per cent to 57 per cent for China, from 73 per cent to 57 per cent for Hong Kong, China and from 83 per cent to 58 per cent for Chinese Taipei. For other countries, however, such as Thailand (59 per cent by 1998), Indonesia (99 per cent), Korea (65 per cent) and the Philippines (70 per cent), the coverage increased.

Evans and Harrigan (2004) note too that tariff liberalisation favouring Mexico and the Caribbean also favoured those countries as sources of imports, subject to the constraint that import quotas were also more likely to bind as tariffs were cut preferentially. In addition, they identify a significant contribution to trade growth from proximity, especially when demand is sensitive to delivery times and reliability.

Messerlin and Zedillo (2004) make the important point that the Agreement on Textiles and Clothing (ATC) under the Uruguay Round phases out quotas (see their Box 25), even though that process is subject to back-loading, but it does not remove tariffs. They stress that this sector will continue to provide examples of tariff peaks and tariff escalation and therefore high levels of effective protection. They remain concerned that the phase-in of the ATC will lead to an increase in anti-dumping actions. By way of assessment of the significance of the current policy mix, they report IMF/ World Bank estimates (p. 102) that every job saved by protection in this sector in a developed economy costs 35 jobs in developing countries.

The United States and the EU provide non-reciprocal preferences, and some East Asian economies benefit from them[6]. Hoekman (2005) concludes, however, that, "preferences do little good" (p. 27). He cites several factors that contribute to this result. They include: the difficulty of meeting the necessary rules of origin (which leads to low utilisation rates of preferential quotas); the lack of preferences offered for products in which developing countries have comparative advantage; the risk of unilateral change or withdrawal; and the imposition of other conditions unrelated to trade (for example, labour rights or environmental standards). He notes that a substantial share of the rents created by quotas is captured in the importing country and stresses that "preferences may impede own liberalization by recipient countries by reducing domestic political pressure to reduce anti-export bias" (p. 28). Hoekman also points out that not all developing countries are beneficiaries, and trade gets diverted away from those who have export patterns similar to those of the recipients of the preferences.

ISBN 92-64-01442-X © OECD 2005

The United States and the EU also apply reciprocal preferential policies. East Asian economies (apart from Singapore) have no preferential agreements with either economy, but US and EU preferential trade policies with other trading partners affect East Asia. An instance of this evidently occurs in the substitution already noted of textile and clothing imports into both the US and Europe from Mexico and other Latin American countries.

Tariff escalation distorts movements along the production chain. Flowers and Bosworth (2002) report average tariffs by sectors where these calculations can be made by stage of processing for the EU and the United States, including a comparison with Australia. Table 3.4 shows these data. The degree of escalation, significant for all the products shown, is especially striking for textiles, clothing and footwear. Not shown in the table is the pattern of protection for processed food, but Messerlin and Zedillo (2004) report high rates of escalation in that sector as well. They recount the story of the cocoa bean. The EU tariff on it is 0.5 per cent and its tariff on chocolate is over 30 per cent, so that while developing countries grow 90 per cent of the world's cocoa beans, they account for just 4 per cent of chocolate production.

Table 3.4. **Bound Tariffs on Industrial Products: Simple Average Tariff Rates by Stage of Processing in the United States, the EU and Australia**

	Import Markets								
	European Community			United States			Australia		
	Raw Materials	Semi-manufactures	Finished Products	Raw Materials	Semi-manufactures	Finished Products	Raw Materials	Semi-manufactures	Finished Products
Wood, pulp, paper and furniture	0	1	0.5	0	0.7	0.7	0.3	7	0.9
Textiles and clothing	2.6	6.6	9.7	2.8	9.1	9.1	1.5	22.9	35.7
Leather, rubber, footwear and travel goods	0.1	2.4	7	0	2.3	11.7	4.2	11.5	22
Metals	0	1.2	2.8	0.8	1.1	2.9	0.6	0.8	11.8
Chemicals and photographic supplies	--	5.2	3.4	--	4.1	2.3	--	9.8	7.6
Transport equipment	--	--	4.7	--	--	2.7	--	--	15.1
Non-electric machinery	--	--	1.8	--	--	1.2	--	--	9.1
Electrical machinery	--	--	3.3	--	--	2.1	--	--	13.3
Mineral products and precious stones and metals	0.4	2.4	3.7	0.6	1.3	5.3	2.4	6	11.1
Manufactured articles not elsewhere specified	--	--	2.7	--	--	3	--	--	7
Fish and fish products	11.2	13.3	14.1	0.7	1.7	4	0.4	0	3.2

Source: Flowers and Bosworth (2002).

ISBN 92-64-01442-X © OECD 2005

Anti-Dumping Measures

Developed countries have used anti-dumping measures extensively since 1981, but developing economies apply them increasingly as well (Figure 3.2). Zanardi (2004) finds that their traditional users, measured by the number of actions, were the United States, the EU, Australia and Canada. From 1981 to 2001, this group accounted for 64 per cent of all anti-dumping petitions (the United States and the EU accounted for 35 per cent, shared equally). The pattern shifted in the more recent years. Between 1995 and 2001, the seven largest users imposed 64 per cent of all anti-dumping actions, and they included the original four plus India, South Africa and Argentina, with the new users taking larger shares than Australia or Canada.

Figure 3.2. **Anti-dumping Measures in Force by Groups of Countries**

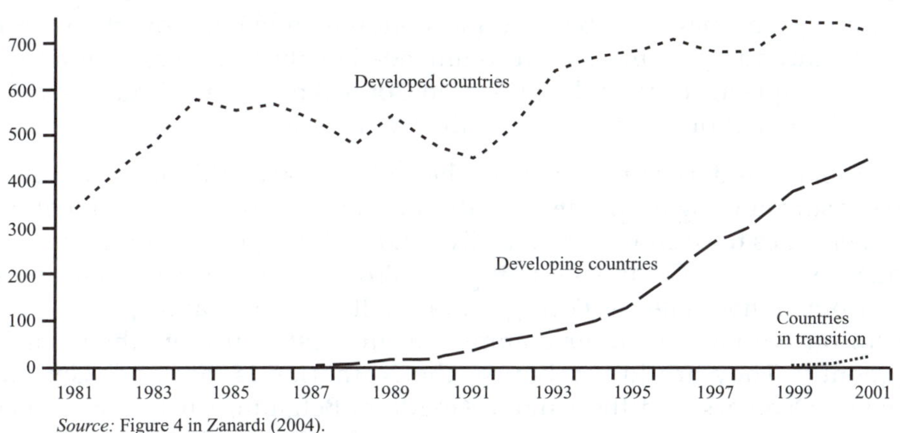

Source: Figure 4 in Zanardi (2004).

China was the most targeted country in all anti-dumping actions from 1995 to 2001[7]. Korea and Chinese Taipei have also moved up the ranks. Zanardi (2004) finds that nearly 70 per cent of the anti-dumping actions initiated by developed countries target developing economies or those in economic transition. Yet he stresses that developing countries and those in transition (which together account for about as many actions as developed countries) tend to target economies at the same stage of development, i.e. the distribution of actions is similar for both groups. He suggests, therefore, that analysis of options for restraining the use of anti-dumping actions should not be built on a perspective in which the conflict on this matter arises only between developed and developing countries.

Messerlin and Zedillo (2004) report anti-dumping actions per dollar of imports as a measure of the intensity of their use. While the United States initiated more cases than other countries between 1995 and 2002, other countries, such as Brazil, Australia, South Africa, India and Argentina showed much higher intensity of use by this measure[8]. Developing countries were the targets in 58 per cent of the anti-dumping actions in the period, compared with 28 per cent for developed economies and 14 per cent for transition economies[9].

Since 2001, the number of anti-dumping investigations in the EU declined from over 60 in 1999 to about 30 in 2000 and 2001 and fewer than ten in the first six months of 2003. Evenett and Vermulst (2004) attribute this fall in part but not necessarily completely to the "politicisation" of the process. The European Commission in response to a complaint will investigate the claim, establish "injury" and then determine a tariff that is "in the Community's interest" (p. 3). Until March 2004, before the duties were imposed, a majority in the European Council had to vote in favour of the Commission proposal. The initial steps may have been political but the voting was overtly so. Since then, an anti-dumping measure recommended by the Commission is adopted unless a simple majority of the European Council rejects it, within one month after submission of the proposal by the Commission.

Evenett and Vermulst inspect the publicly available material on the debates surrounding proposals for anti-dumping duties[10]. They find that some member states have shifted from a "live and let live" position on them to one of questioning each Commission proposal. Proposals are most often supported by a group of five states — Portugal, France, Italy, Greece and Spain. Another seven, on the basis of their commercial interests, support them far less frequently. They are Luxembourg, the Netherlands, Finland, Germany, Sweden, Denmark and the United Kingdom. Belgium, Austria and Ireland took a middle position. The expansion of the EU in 1995, when Austria, Finland and Sweden joined, therefore tended to strengthen the anti-duty block. Evenett and Vermulst also note that the usual prescription for reducing the risks of excessive use of anti-dumping actions is to hand the procedure to a technocratic system. As noted, such a system does operate in the EU, but it does not appear to have been driving the drop in actions. The diverse economic interests of member states play the more important role. A similar approach, bringing to bear the different interests of trading partners, might also be adopted within other regions like East Asia, to try to limit the application of anti-dumping duties. At the least, knowledge of the dynamics of anti-dumping decision making in the EU helps non-members build strategies of advocacy in the short term and of new rule making in the longer term, aimed at reducing the risks of EU anti-dumping duties[11].

 ISBN 92-64-01442-X © OECD 2005

Table 3.5 provides an indication of the orders of magnitude of the gains that might flow from policy reform to resolve some of these issues. The country aggregates used in this table (reported by Anderson, 2004) are wider than the immediate interest here, but they provide some indication of the priorities. The table shows estimates of the gains from removing goods-trade barriers following the Uruguay Round. It divides the effects between the liberalising group (high or low income as well as total) and the affected group of economies. Shown in the table are the percentage distributions of the gains. The total gain from full liberalisation for all economies was $254 billion, and the value to developing economies was $108 billion (in 1995 dollars). Policy change initiated by developed economies generates about 55 per cent of the total gain, of which about 30 per cent goes to developing countries. Reform of trade policy affecting manufactured goods accounts for about 72 per cent of the gains received by developing countries from all policy reform in developed countries[12].

Table 3.5. **Sectoral and Regional Contributions to Comparative Static Estimates of Economic Welfare Gains from Completely Removing Goods Trade Barriers Globally, Post-Uruguay-Round, 2005**

(per cent of total global gains[a])

Liberalising Region:	Benefiting Region	Agriculture and Food	Other Primary	Textiles & Clothing	Other Manufactures	Total
High income						
	high income	43.4	0.0	-2.3	-3.2	38.0
	low income	4.6	0.1	3.5	8.8	16.9
	total	48.0	0.0	1.3	5.6	54.9
Low income						
	high income	4.4	0.1	4.1	10.9	19.5
	low income	12.3	1.0	1.4	10.9	25.6
	total	16.7	1.1	5.5	21.7	45.1
All countries						
	high income	47.9	0.1	1.9	7.7	57.5
	low income	16.9	1.0	4.9	19.6	42.5
	total	64.8	1.1	6.8	27.3	100.0

Note: *a)* The total value of the welfare gain from full liberalisation for all economies in the study from which this decomposition is derived is $254 billion and the value to developing ("low-income") economies is $108 billion (1995 US dollars).

Source: Reported by Anderson (2004).

While developing countries gain from manufacturing-sector policy reform in developed economies, the latter do not gain from their own reform, at least in the aggregate. According to Table 3.5, reform in developed economies *alone* in the manufacturing sector leads to a welfare loss for those economies.

The removal of protection and the increase in imports shifts the terms of trade against these economies. Their reform leads to higher world prices for the previously protected products. To the extent that social evaluations of welfare drive policy choices, this result suggests that developed economies will be less willing to take the initiative in these areas.

Concluding Remarks

This review reveals a number of examples of incoherence in the application of trade policies in the United States and the EU, even within the scope of tariff policy as discussed here. Some of the more serious examples include the following.

1. Changes in market shares are important to successful development built on trade specialisation, a point well understood by footloose investors home-based in developed economies. Yet preferential trade policies try to lock in the market shares of particular suppliers, both through the ATC and in bilateral agreements.

2. Developed countries argue for mainstreaming trade into development strategies on the basis of the gains to exporting countries. Yet their tariff structures are biased against trade in products in which developing countries are likely to be more competitive, and their use of preferential policies helps transfer the rents created by restrictions to their own importers.

3. Developed economies urge developing ones to undertake reform through the WTO, for which they also provide capacity-building support, but the application of preferential policies reduces the incentives to make commitments in the WTO.

4. Developed economies laud China's reform programme, but reward it with anti-dumping actions that in turn encourage China and other developing economies to join in the protectionist anti-dumping "game".

5. The field of contradictions would be even larger if aid policy were included in this review. Aid policy is often designed to promote industrial upgrading, the scope for which is seriously limited by tariff escalation, a common feature of developed-country tariff structures. A look at policies affecting services trade would also increase the incidence of policy incoherence. The United States, for example, extols the virtues of

ISBN 92-64-01442-X © OECD 2005

participation in the world economy but inhibits the reform of the maritime and air transport sectors, setting a bad example for developing countries in the regulation of services industries.

6. There is an evident contradiction between protection in the United States and the European Union in aggregate or average terms and in the details of its application. In aggregate terms these economies are quite open, with low average applied rates, all tariffs bound and small gaps between bound and applied tariffs. The issues for developing East Asian economies, as illustrated in the examples just presented, arise in the instruments applied to "tailor make" policy for the sensitive sectors. These instruments include the remaining tariff peaks and tariff escalation. They arise in measures designed to deal with the interests of favoured trading partners, i.e. the use of preferential tariffs (reciprocal or not) and the threat of anti-dumping actions. The policy instruments necessarily involve more discretion in their implementation and it is more difficult to establish rules on their application, not just politically but also in technical terms. These aspects of policy all tend to be biased against East Asian exporters.

East Asian economies (at least the developing ones) might reasonably complain about these examples of incoherence in the trade policies of their developed-country partners. They might insist that something be done, appealing perhaps to notions of leadership or duty. Yet the origins of the lack of policy coherence lie within the domestic policy-making processes of the developed economies. The positions they take result from interaction between political constituencies, and any policy change requires some external shock to upset the consensus that the political "markets" in those countries have produced. An important question, then, is whether there is opportunity for East Asian economies to mobilise with the objective of inducing an external shock sufficient to shift policy consensus in the United States and the European Union.

At one level, success in removing some of the contradictions in US and EU policies requires engaging the domestic political constituencies within each economy. The current WTO negotiations provide an opportunity to work on this, and given the complexity of the policies the negotiations also provide an opportunity to achieve more consistency in the development of new rules and procedures.

At a higher level, shifting policy positions in the United States requires leadership in trade diplomacy, not by the United States and the European Union but by East Asia itself. In the past a coalition of developing and

ISBN 92-64-01442-X © OECD 2005

developed economies within East Asia (the Western Pacific trade ministers' group) played an effective role in shaping the agenda for the Uruguay Round. The issues in US and EU trade policies that confront East Asian developing countries are not likely to be dealt with unless East Asia can re-group in this way. A foundation for an East Asian trade policy coalition exists in the structure of the trade policy problems outlined in this chapter. The structure of tariff protection (set out in Table 3.3) and the modelling results (described in Table 3.5) provide the rationale for working together in East Asia to deal with these problems in the US and EU markets.

What are the elements of a grand bargain on trade in manufactured goods?

- The first would be an explicit East Asian commitment to bind more tariff lines, to narrow the gap between bound and applied rates and to bind more tariff lines at zero. The East Asian coalition could also commit to reduce bound tariffs under a formula designed to deal with tariff peaks, and it could agree to schedule further reductions in the remaining tariffs, consistent with stated regional objectives. Credit for previous liberalisation could be allowed, for example, for commitments documented in the APEC process. Messerlin and Zedillo (2004) suggest (p. 106) that focusing on bindings offers credit to developing countries for previous reductions in applied tariffs, while rewarding further coverage of bound rates.

- Next, East Asian economies and China in particular have an interest in resolving the problem of accelerating anti-dumping actions. At a minimum, accepting China's status as a "market economy" could bolster China's interest in the regional coalition and its value to China in the current round of negotiations. That commitment could be accompanied by another one among all East Asian economies (analogous to the outcome of the more formal process in the European Union) to tighten and harmonise their own rules on the application of anti-dumping measures. This involves a clear understanding of their own interests in the contribution of that measure to their own competitiveness and to their full participation in regional supply chains. Potential interlocutors on these matters among EU members were noted earlier[13].

- The coalition might also propose to abandon the application of preferences to developing countries. Hoekman (2005) suggests complementing this initiative with various capacity-building programmes (perhaps valued up to an estimate of the value of the preferences).

 ISBN 92-64-01442-X

A coalition based on these elements could attract wide participation. Not only do the developing and middle-income countries of East Asia have an interest in these proposals, but so also does Japan. It would be in the interests of Australia and New Zealand to support this agenda. These commitments would require a good deal of policy dialogue and interaction on each element, especially on anti-dumping policies. This process would help to cement a co-operative strategy and the coalition. Action by East Asia along these lines would also attract attention from other developing countries for which the East Asian region is a major market (Messerlin and Zedillo, 2004, p. 103).

This package of trade policy reforms in East Asia would constitute a substantial offer and benefit to the United States and the European Union. It has the potential to trigger a response of equal benefit to East Asian economies. The response would have to deal with the problems facing East Asia set out in this paper, including tariff peaks, preferences of various types, and anti-dumping measures. A response of that kind would help to resolve some of the contradictions and incoherence in US and EU trade policy.

ISBN 92-64-01442-X

Notes

1. This is formally called "the Arrangement Regarding International Trade in Textiles".
2. See Barichello (2005) in this volume for detailed discussions on OECD agricultural policies.
3. It is acknowledged that the shares of trade directed to East Asia are lower than they might otherwise have been following the financial crisis, but that observation also makes the point of the value of attention to US and EU trade policies.
4. Average applied tariffs are calculated at an earlier year than bound tariffs, which refer to the year of implementation. For that reason average applied tariffs can be higher than bound rates, especially for low tariff rate countries.
5. Detail for the USA and the EU is not available from this source.
6. Details of preferential access offered by the EU to East Asian economies are available from http://europa.eu.int/comm/taxation_customs/customs/customs_duties/rules_origin/article_403_en.htm. Details of US programmes are at http://www.ustr.gov/Trade_Development/Preference_Programs/Section_Index.html. Bora (2003) provides a summary of product exclusions and of data showing the significance of the preferential access available for East Asian economies.
7. China's is also treated as a non-market economy in anti-dumping actions. This means that cost data from a substitute country are used to calculate a normal value against which actual prices can be compared. For market economies, actual prices and costs are used. China argues that this situation is open to abuse because the criteria for the selection of substitute countries are not well specified. This adds to the likelihood of success in the case and therefore the incentives to take anti-dumping action.
8. Another important parameter in assessing the bias in the effects of anti-dumping actions is the duty applied. Messerlin and Zedillo (2004) suggest (p. 109) that perhaps because of differences in capacity to defend themselves, developing countries are more likely to be confronted with higher anti-dumping duties.

ISBN 92-64-01442-X © OECD 2005

9. The definition of developing countries in this case includes China but excludes economies in transition, while the EU15, Iceland, Japan, Australia, Canada, New Zealand, Norway, Switzerland and the US are the group of developed economies.

10. The target countries in these cases are concentrated in Asia. Of the cases they examine, the most often mentioned trading partners are China, Japan, Thailand and Korea in that order, followed by India, Chinese Taipei and Malaysia.

11. This experience also raises the question of why the same political constraints on anti-dumping have not emerged in the United States.

12. Developing economies receive larger gains from reform initiated by other developing economies but agricultural reform makes a larger contribution to those gains than does reform to manufacturing sector policies.

13. Messerlin and Zedillo (2004, p. 110) make suggestions, which this coalition could explore and rank, for specific initiatives to discipline anti-dumping measures.

Bibliography

ANDERSON, K. (2004), "Subsidies and Trade Barriers", paper prepared for the Copenhagen Consensus Project and forthcoming in B. LOMBORG (ed.), *Global Crisis, Global Solutions*, Cambridge University Press, Cambridge and New York, NY. Available from: www.copenhagenconsensus.com/Files/Filer/CC/Papers/Subsidies_and_Trade_Barriers_140504.pdf.

ATHUKORALA, P.-C. (2003), "Product Fragmentation and Trade Patterns in East Asia", *Asian Economic Papers, forthcoming*. Available from: rspas.anu.edu.au/economics/publish/papers/wp2003/wp-econ-2003-21.pdf.

BORA, B. (2003), "Appendix to Chapter 4: Market Access Barriers and Poverty in Developing East Asia", *in* K. KRUMM and H. KHARAS (eds.), *East Asia Integrates: A Trade Policy Agenda for Shared Growth*, World Bank, Washington, D.C.

EVANS, C. and J. HARRIGAN (2004), "Tight Clothing: How the MFA Affects Asian Apparel Exports", revision of a paper presented at the Fourteenth Annual East Asian Seminar on Economics, 5-7 September 2003, Taipei.

EVENETT, S. and E. VERMULST (2004), "The Politicisation of EC Anti-Dumping Policy: Member States, their Votes and the European Commission", paper presented to the Symposium on a Centennial of Anti-Dumping Legislation and Implementation, University of Michigan, March.

FINDLAY, C. (2001), "China's Admittance to the WTO and Industrial Structural Adjustment in the World Economy", *Pacific Economic Papers*, No. 315, May, Australia-Japan Research Centre, Australian National University.

FLOWERS, K. and M. BOSWORTH (2002), "WTO Market Access Negotiations for Non-Agricultural Products, Doha Round: Implications for East Asia", *Pacific Economic Papers* No. 334, December, Australia-Japan Research Centre, Australian National University. Available from: apseg.anu.edu.au/publish/pub_papers.php.

HOEKMAN, B. (2005), "The International Trade Order: Cooperation for Economic Development", Chapter 3 *in* H. SOESASTRO and C. FINDLAY (eds), Reshaping the Asia Pacific Economic Order, Routledge, London.

 ISBN 92-64-01442-X © OECD 2005

Messerlin, P. and E. Zedillo (2004), *Interim Report: Trade, Development and the WTO, An Action Agenda Beyond the Cancun Ministerial* (20 April). Available from: www.unmillenniumproject.org/html/tf9docs.shtm.

Weiss, J. (2005), "People's Republic of China and Its Neighbours: Partners or Competitors for Trade and Investment?", Research Paper No. 59, ADBI, Tokyo. Available from: www.adbi.org/research-paper/2005/01/21/882.prc.neighbors.trade/

World Trade Organization (2003), *World Trade Report 2003*. Available from: www.wto.org/english/news_e/pres03_e/pr348_e.htm

Zanardi, M. (2004), "Anti-dumping: What are the Numbers to Discuss at Doha?", *The World Economy*, 27, pp. 403-433.

ISBN 92-64-01442-X

Chapter 4

Japan's Structural Reform, Liberalisation and Market Opening: Implications for East Asia

Fukunari Kimura

Abstract

This chapter reviews policy coherence in Japan with particular focus on trade-related policies, assuming that economic co-operation policy for East Asia has been conducted purely to promote development. It finds various policies not at all designed to maintain coherence. Deliberately or by happenstance, they are sometimes coherent and sometimes inconsistent. Rice and some other agricultural products exemplify serious deficiencies in policy coherence, but it is misleading to characterise the whole agricultural sector as dominated by protectionists. For some products, such as vegetables and fishery products, freer trade encourages desirable domestic reform with increasing foreign trade. The most important positive contribution to East Asia by Japanese multinational enterprises and the Japanese government has been the formation of international production and distribution networks since the latter half of the 1980s. In the machinery industries, freer trade with Japan accelerates the formation of such networks. Explicit Japanese efforts further to promote overall policy coherence are obviously necessary.

ISBN 92-64-01442-X

Introduction

While naïve economists often assume the existence of a single social-welfare function dictating the whole scope of government policies, the reality is far more complicated. A government is not a single, unified economic agent that behaves consistently. Each part of it has peculiar interfaces with different interest groups and often makes decisions under politico-economic influences. A political leader typically has neither sufficient political/analytical capability nor egalitarian intentions to keep all policies consistent with a single objective. As a result, policies constructed by different governmental entities often cannot maintain coherence to achieve a given set of policy objectives. Japanese trade-related policies are not exceptions.

Japanese foreign aid for East Asian economies started as a form of reparations as well as a vehicle for export promotion in the 1950s and 1960s. Since the 1970s, however, the government has claimed consistently that the primary purpose of its ODA programme is to support the economic development of recipient countries. Although this intention is of course debatable, this chapter accepts it as valid and points out that trade policy has not necessarily or always stayed consistent with it.

Until the early 1980s, vertical inter-industry trade dominated exchanges between Japan and other East Asian economies. Developing East Asian economies exported resource-based products and goods made by unskilled labour to Japan while it exported the whole range of manufactures. Japanese policies on trade and outward foreign direct investment (FDI) generally supported this trade pattern. Imports of raw materials were always regarded as a lifeline for industrial development and economic growth. Trade policies also supported the later structural transition from labour-intensive industries to industries intensive in physical and human capital, allowing imports of labour-intensive products such as textiles and clothing from developing East Asian economies. Policy permitted and even encouraged outward FDI, particularly in sectors where domestic production was losing its competitive edge. Trade and FDI in East Asia therefore presented a dynamic "flying-geese pattern", which certainly contributed to the industrialisation of developing East Asia[1].

Yet some sectors in Japan, represented by agriculture and some limited branches of manufacturing and services, delayed necessary domestic structural reform by political means. Although the GATT negotiating rounds as well as bilateral talks with the United States resulted in substantial trade liberalisation and domestic de-regulation, some sectors got left behind or

ISBN 92-64-01442-X © OECD 2005

had reforms biased toward requests from politically strong countries. This lack of policy coherence presumably had some negative impact on East Asian economic development.

The East Asian economies started forming international production and distribution networks in the latter half of the 1980s, particularly in the machinery industries. Both their exports and imports of machinery, parts and components increased explosively, and their industrial structures have been transformed by the globalisation of corporate activities. Although traditional comparative advantage based on factor endowments and technological capability can still partially explain East Asian production and trade patterns, a full understanding of the mechanics of East Asian production and distribution networks requires new economic explanations such as fragmentation, agglomeration, and internalisation[2]. The commodity composition of Japanese imports drastically changed in the 1990s, from one-way trade based on comparative advantage to vertical intra-industry trade or production networking. International production and distribution networks in East Asia consist not only of transactions within and among Japanese firms but also of arm's-length transactions with firms of different nationalities.

The Japanese government continuously supported the overseas activities of Japanese multinational enterprises (MNEs). The drastic appreciation of the yen in the second half of the 1980s following the Plaza Accord triggered an outward FDI boom, and the commitment to overseas operations, particularly in East Asia, strengthened even after the financial bubble collapsed in the early 1990s. Although domestic reform aimed at demand expansion and de-regulation went only slowly, Japanese firms steadily constructed production and distribution networks in East Asia. The government provides both physical and moral support, particularly for small and medium-sized enterprises (SMEs); it includes some mild financial help but, more significantly, information dissemination. A free-trade policy on machinery products effectively minimised domestic fears of possible de-industrialisation due to outward FDI by increasing possibilities for firms to avoid all-or-nothing decisions in relocation of production sites. Some industries lagged behind, however, including petrochemicals and leather products. For them, slow domestic structural reform delayed trade liberalisation.

Because domestic structural-reform policies and associated trade policies are not wholly directed by unified intentions, they sometimes support and sometimes obstruct the development of East Asian economies. This chapter reviews the evolution of Japanese trade patterns since the latter half of the

1960s and broadly evaluates the multiple channels of trade-related policies. It finds that Japanese trade policy should not be regarded as wholly protective, although some specific industries still enjoy extremely high and complicated trade protection. More details follow on specific industries, particularly agriculture and machinery. They show the role of Japan in forming international production and distribution networks in East Asia. Structural reform in Japan, initiated by the *Maekawa Report* in the latter half of the 1980s, did not seem to affect Japanese firms' globalisation directly, but industrial and structural adjustment probably accelerated their outward FDI.

Evolution of Japan's Trade Patterns with East Asia

Japan has long been regarded as poor in natural resources relative to its population, forced to import raw materials and energy in exchange for exports of manufactures. This characterisation still applies to the current pattern of Japanese trade, but some important qualitative changes have occurred. Tables 4.1 and 4.2 present the commodity composition of Japanese exports and imports from 1965 to 2002. Until the 1980s, the pattern of vertical inter-industry trade dominated. Japan imported raw materials, fuels and some labour-intensive products such as textiles and garments while exporting a wide range of manufactured goods. For most commodities, one-way trade prevailed, and intra-industry trade (IIT) remained limited[3].

Table 4.1. **Japanese Exports by Commodity Groups, 1965-2002**

	1965	1970	1975	1980	1985	1990	1995	2000	2002
Value (billions of yen)	3 043	6 954	16 545	29 382	41 956	41 547	41 531	51 654	52 109
Composition (% of total)									
Foodstuffs	4.1	3.4	1.4	1.2	0.8	0.6	0.5	0.4	0.5
Textiles and textile products	18.7	12.5	6.7	4.8	3.6	2.5	2.0	1.8	1.8
Chemicals	6.5	6.4	7.0	5.3	4.4	5.5	6.8	7.4	8.0
Non-metallic mineral products	3.1	1.9	1.3	1.4	1.2	1.1	1.2	1.2	1.1
Metals and metal products	20.3	19.7	22.4	16.5	10.6	6.8	6.5	5.5	6.2
General machinery	7.4	10.4	12.1	13.9	16.8	22.1	24.1	21.5	20.3
Electric machinery	9.2	12.3	11.0	14.4	16.9	23.0	25.6	26.5	22.9
Transport equipment	14.7	17.8	26.1	26.5	28.0	25.0	20.3	21.0	24.9
Precision machinery	3.9	5.7	4.7	7.9	10.1	4.8	4.7	5.4	3.9
Others	12.1	9.9	7.4	8.1	7.7	8.5	8.2	9.5	10.4

Source: MCA (various years).

ISBN 92-64-01442-X © OECD 2005

Table 4.2. **Japanese Imports by Commodity Groups, 1965-2002**

	1965	1970	1975	1980	1985	1990	1995	2000	2002
Value (billions of yen)	2 941	6 797	17 170	31 995	31 085	33 855	31 549	40 938	42 228
Composition (% of total)									
Foodstuffs	18.0	13.6	15.2	10.4	12.0	13.5	15.2	12.1	12.5
Mineral fuels	19.9	20.7	44.3	49.8	43.1	23.9	15.9	20.3	19.4
Chemicals	5.0	5.3	3.6	4.4	6.2	6.9	7.3	7.0	7.7
Machinery and equipment	9.3	12.2	7.4	7.0	9.6	17.4	25.3	31.6	31.8
Others	47.8	48.2	29.5	38.4	29.2	38.3	36.2	29.0	28.7

Source: MCA (various years).

A salient structural break occurred in the 1980s. The share of machinery in exports exploded to almost 70 per cent in the 1990s. At the same time, machinery imports also expanded to over 30 per cent of the total by 2000. Japan thus has become not a simple exporter of capital goods and finished manufactures but an important participant in international production and distribution networks, both exporting and importing parts and components. Recent study confirms a steady increase in vertical IIT, particularly in machinery, throughout the 1990s[4].

The composition of trade counterparts has also changed. Tables 4.3 and 4.4 show shares of Japanese exports and imports by destination and origin. Although North America has continued as an important trading partner, the share of East Asia, including Asian NIEs (Korea; Chinese Taipei; Hong Kong, China; and Singapore), ASEAN4 (Malaysia, Thailand, the Philippines and Indonesia) and China has increased (with some fluctuation) to about 40 per cent of both exports and imports.

These tables confirm that the trade patterns in East Asia until the 1980s were dictated by the traditional logic of comparative advantage, whereby natural-resource endowments, capital-labour ratios and technological capabilities mostly determine industrial location and trade patterns. Since the 1990s, however, a vertical intra-industry division of labour has become important, particularly in the machinery industries. This and the resulting trade patterns have been realised by active FDI and the formation of international production and distribution networks with both intra-firm and arm's-length transactions.

Table 4.3. **Japanese Exports by Destination, 1965-2002**

	1965	1970	1975	1980	1985	1990	1995	2000	2002
Values (billions of yen)									
Total	3 043	6 954	16 545	29 382	41 956	41 547	41 531	51 654	52 109
Asia	985	2 172	6 078	11 192	13 658	14 143	18 911	22 319	23 881
Asian NIEs4	292	951	2 069	4 356	5 389	8 187	10 398	12 357	11 804
ASEAN4	266	499	1 305	2 062	1 755	3 195	5 025	4 890	4 865
China	88	205	670	1 141	2 991	884	2 062	3 274	4 980
Other Asia	339	517	2 034	3 633	3 523	1 877	1 428	1 798	2 232
North America	1 056	2 554	4 365	8 610	18 152	15 065	13 107	17 809	17 295
Europe	471	1 211	3 069	5 704	6 829	9 683	7 214	9 254	8 508
Rest of the World	531	1 017	3 033	3 876	3 317	2 566	2 299	2 272	2 425
Composition (% of total)									
Total	100.0	100.0	100.0	100.0	100.0	100.0	100.0	100.0	100.0
Asia	32.4	31.2	36.7	38.1	32.6	34.1	45.5	43.2	45.8
Asian NIEs4	9.6	13.7	12.5	14.8	12.8	19.7	25.0	23.9	22.7
ASEAN4	8.7	7.2	7.9	7.0	4.2	7.7	12.1	9.5	9.3
China	2.9	2.9	4.0	3.9	7.1	2.1	5.0	6.3	9.6
Other Asia	11.1	7.4	12.3	12.4	8.4	4.5	3.4	3.5	4.3
North America	34.7	36.7	26.4	29.3	43.3	36.3	31.6	34.5	33.2
Europe	15.5	17.4	18.5	19.4	16.3	23.4	17.4	17.9	16.3
Rest of the World	17.4	14.6	18.3	13.2	7.9	6.2	5.5	4.4	4.7

Table 4.4. **Japanese Imports by Origin, 1965-2002**

	1965	1970	1975	1980	1985	1990	1995	2000	2002
Values (billions of yen)									
Total	2 941	6 797	17 170	31 995	31 085	33 855	31 549	40 938	42 228
Asia	982	1 999	8 414	18 282	15 907	14 157	14 551	22 392	23 477
Asian NIEs4	97	236	822	1 677	2 352	3 749	3 870	5 009	4 441
ASEAN4	287	640	1 769	4 498	4 012	3 513	3 603	5 247	5 308
China	81	91	455	978	1 552	1 730	3 381	5 941	7 728
Other Asia	517	1 032	5 368	11 129	7 991	5 165	3 697	6 195	6 000
North America	1 094	2 479	4 426	6 969	7 950	9 233	8 344	9 094	8 542
Europe	362	920	1 734	2 853	3 370	6 744	5 608	6 172	6 627
Rest of the world	503	1 399	2 616	3 891	3 858	3 721	3 046	3 280	3 582
Composition (% of total)									
Total	100.0	100.0	100.0	100.0	100.0	100.0	100.0	100.0	100.0
Asia	33.4	29.4	49.0	57.1	51.2	41.8	46.1	54.7	55.6
Asian NIEs4	3.3	3.5	4.8	5.2	7.6	11.1	12.3	12.2	10.5
ASEAN4	9.8	9.4	110.3	14.1	12.9	10.4	11.4	12.8	12.6
China	2.8	1.3	2.6	3.1	5.0	5.1	10.7	14.5	18.3
Other Asia	17.6	15.2	31.3	34.8	25.7	15.3	11.7	15.1	14.2
North America	37.2	36.5	25.8	21.8	25.6	27.3	26.4	22.2	20.2
Europe	12.3	13.5	10.0	8.9	10.8	19.9	17.8	15.1	15.7
Rest of the world	17.1	20.6	15.2	12.2	12.4	11.0	9.7	8.0	8.5

Source: MCA (various years).

ISBN 92-64-01442-X © OECD 2005

An evaluation of the impact of Japanese trade or trade-related policies on East Asia's development must cover both dark-side and bright-side stories. On the dark side, while most industries with comparative disadvantage or declining international competitiveness have restructured or even faded out, others effectively lobby the government and obtain protection at the expense of domestic consumers and exporting countries. On the bright side, many industries actively extend international production and distribution networks through trade and FDI, thus accelerating the growth of East Asian economies. Although market forces basically direct the formation of such networks, a set of policies lies importantly in the background.

Overview of Trade-Related Policies in Japan

Because Japanese agricultural protection is so infamous, some may have an impression that Japanese trade policy is generally protective — but the data do not fully warrant such a view. Table 4.5 presents ratios of customs duties to imports from 1965 to 2002. High until 1970, they dropped to between 2 and 3 per cent by the mid-1970s. A small bump in 1995 arose from the tarification of non-tariff barriers on quantitatively protected products following the Uruguay Round. Tariffs at these levels do not represent high protection by any standard; they roughly equal the figures for the United States and the EU. Japan had already completed its overall trade liberalisation by the mid-1970s.

Table 4.5. **Customs Duty Import Ratios, 1965-2002**
(percentages)

	1965	1970	1975	1980	1985	1990	1995	2000	2002
Ratio A	7.5	7.0	3.0	2.5	2.4	2.7	3.3	2.1	2.1
Ratio B	7.5	5.6	2.2	2.0	2.0	2.4	3.0	2.0	2.0

Notes: Ratio A is measured as the sum of customs duties and crude oil and similar taxes divided by the c.i.f. value of imports. Ratio B is the ratio of customs duties to imports (CIF). The figures for 2002 are planned/forecast figures.
Source: MCA (various years).

These ratios, however, reflect only the tariffs imposed on traded commodities. They do not reflect levies on commodities with very high protection and small imports. Table 4.6 shows Japan's GATT-bound *ad valorem* tariff rates in 2000. Tariff rates are originally assigned for commodities at the HS (harmonised system) nine-digit level. Table 4.6 gives arithmetic averages and standard deviations of these tariff rates under each HS two-digit category. They indicate high-tariff spikes here and there, particularly in food products (HS 1-24), textiles (HS 50-63) and footwear (HS 64-67)[5]. In contrast, machinery (HS 84-92) now bears almost no tariffs.

ISBN 92-64-01442-X

Table 4.6. **GATT-Bound *Ad Valorem* Tariff Rates in Japan, 2000**

(percentages)

HS	Average	Standard Deviation	HS	Average	Standard Deviation	HS	Average	Standard Deviation	HS	Average	Standard Deviation
01	1.0	2.8	25	0.2	0.6	49	0.3	0.6	73	1.1	1.1
02	10.4	15.7	26	0.0	0.0	50	6.9	4.4	74	1.7	1.4
03	4.5	2.4	27	0.8	1.4	51	3.2	3.3	75	1.9	1.3
04	25.4	7.8	28	2.6	1.6	52	5.1	1.5	76	3.7	2.9
05	0.2	0.5	29	2.9	2.1	53	4.3	5.7	78	2.4	1.0
06	0.8	1.4	30	0.0	0.0	54	7.3	1.4	79	1.8	1.5
07	5.4	2.9	31	0.0	0.0	55	7.8	1.6	80	2.0	1.3
08	7.0	5.2	32	3.2	1.2	56	4.5	2.0	81	1.4	1.4
09	4.1	4.7	33	1.4	1.9	57	9.3	1.4	82	0.8	1.6
10	3.5	8.8	34	0.7	1.5	58	7.8	3.7	83	2.0	1.4
11	20.0	4.8	35	6.4	5.3	59	4.8	0.8	84	0.0	0.0
12	1.4	3.2	36	4.8	1.4	60	9.9	1.9	85	0.1	0.7
13	1.6	2.3	37	0.0	0.0	61	11.1	1.8	86	0.0	0.0
14	1.7	3.0	38	2.5	2.8	62	11.7	1.8	87	0.1	1.0
15	3.7	5.2	39	3.8	0.8	63	7.1	2.7	88	0.0	0.0
16	10.6	5.1	40	0.3	0,7	64	18.1	9,8	89	0.0	0.0
17	23.6	19.8	41	7.2	9.4	65	4.5	0.9	90	0.2	0.8
18	11.9	9.9	42	9.9	3.9	66	4.1	0.5	91	0.4	1.6
19	17.5	5.3	43	8.4	7.7	67	1.8	2.6	92	0.0	0.0
20	16.8	5.8	44	3.2	2.3	68	1.0	1.3	93	6.6	1.3
21	13.1	6.5	45	0.0	0.0	69	1.3	1.2	94	0.7	1.4
22	15.4	8.6	46	3.8	1.3	70	1.1	1.9	95	1.6	1.5
23	0.1	0.4	47	0.7	0.4	71	1.0	2.0	96	3.2	2.0
24	4.7	7.3	48	1.6	0.8	72	1.7	0.9	97	0.0	0.0

HS 01-24: Food Products
HS 25-27: Mineral Products
HS 28-38: Chemical Products
HS 39-40: Plastics and Rubber
HS 41-43: Hides and Skins
HS 44-46: Wood and Wood Products
HS 47-49: Wood Pulp Products
HS 50-63: Textiles and Textile Articles
HS 64-67: Footwear, Headgear
HS 68-70: Articles of Stone, Plaster, Cement, Asbestos
HS 71: Pearls, Precious or Semi-Precious Stones, Metals
HS 72-83: Base Metals and Articles thereof
HS 84-85: Machinery, Mechanical Appliances
HS 86-89: Transportation Equipment
HS 90-92: Instruments (measuring, musical)
HS 93-97: Others (HS 99 not included)

Source: Drawn from Kimura and Ando (2003). Original data source: UNCTAD (TRAINS).

ISBN 92-64-01442-X © OECD 2005

Table 4.7 summarises data on non-tariff measures (NTMs) compiled by UNCTAD for 1996. They follow an inventory approach; the figures and percentages in the table indicate the numbers of tariff lines with NTMs and their proportion of the total. Thus, high numbers may indicate that an administrative NTM machinery is in place and at least suggest its use for protection, but they do not measure the severity of the measures and hence do not prove directly that unduly severe NTM trade barriers exist. The table reveals heavy and extensive usage of NTMs in agriculture-related commodities. Technical measures particularly, including SPS (sanitary and phytosanitary measures) are in force for most of the tariff lines related to agriculture.

Japan introduced its generalised system of preferences (GSP) scheme in 1971 to offer preferential tariffs for commodities imported from developing countries. The current system covers 221 of about 1 600 agricultural/fishery products with tariffs and 3 284 of 4 400 mining and manufacturing products with tariffs. Potential recipients include 149 countries and 15 economies. Table 4.8 shows the proportion of Japanese imports covered by GSP in fiscal years 1991, 1996 and 2001. GSP is applied to only about 10 per cent of imports from developing countries. In 2001, for example, 41.9 per cent of total imports came from potential recipients, with 3.6 per cent of the total from all sources imported under the GSP. Note that GSP covers only a part of transactions even if the commodities fall under the GSP scheme. In 2001, 11.1 per cent of total imports were imports of commodities eligible for GSP, but only 3.6 per cent of the total actually received GSP tariff rates. This suggests that GSP quotas are sometimes binding and/or the bureaucratic procedure to obtain preferential status is sufficiently complicated that quotas cannot be fully used. Table 4.9 indicates the top 20 exporters that use GSP. Korea and Chinese Taipei, once major users, became excluded from the potential-recipients list in FY2000 because of their income levels. Nevertheless, East Asian countries maintained large shares throughout the period covered by the table. Considering the distortive nature of the GSP system, one might evaluate it either positively or negatively, but the East Asian economies do gain from it while developing countries in other regions do not gain much.

ISBN 92-64-01442-X

Table 4.7. **Frequency Ratios of Japanese NTMs, by Type and Sector, 1996**

(Numbers of tariff lines subject to NTMs in each sector and percentages indicating frequency ratios.)

Sectors	Number of Total Tariff Lines in Sectors	1: Price-Control Measures			3: Automatic Licensing Measures		4: Quantity-Control Measures			5: Monopolistic Measures		6: Technical Measures	
			1-(3) Variable Charges	1-(4) A-D Measures		3-(1) Automatic Licence		4-(1) Non-Automatic Licensing	4-(2) Import Quotas		5-(1): Single Channel for Imports		6-(1): Technical Regulations
Live animals and	549	**28**	28		**18**	18	**273**	271	47	**99**	99	**532**	532
products		**5.1%**	5.1%		**3.3%**	3.3%	**49.7%**	49.4%	8.6%	**18.0%**	18.0%	**96.9%**	96.9%
Vegetable products	561	**2**	2		23	23	**27**	10	17	**26**	26	**506**	506
		0.4%	0.4%		**4.1%**	4.1%	**4.8%**	1.8%	3.0%	**4.6%**	4.6%	**90.2%**	90.2%
Animal and vegetable	82						**6**	6				**74**	74
oils and fats							**7.3%**	7.3%				**90.2%**	90.2%
Food industry	762												
products													
Mineral products	207				**9**	9	**3**		3	**1**	1	**66**	66
					4.3%	4.3%	**1.4%**		1.4%	**0.5%**	0.5%	**31.9%**	31.9%
Chemicals	1 025	**1**	1				**93**	3	90	**22**	22	**827**	827
		0.1%	0.1%				**9.1%**	0.3%	8.8%	**2.1%**	2.1%	**80.7%**	80.7%
Plastic and plastic	283						**4**		4			**34**	34
materials							**1.4%**		1.4%			**12.0%**	12.0%
Skins (raw material)	173						**38**	38				**64**	64
							22.0%	22.0%				**37.0%**	37.0%
Wood and wood	213						**34**	34				**67**	67
products							**16.0%**	16.0%				**31.5%**	31.5%
Pulp and paper	174											**27**	27
												15.5%	15.%
Textiles	2 087						**902**	902		**10**	10		
							43.2%	43.2%		**0.5%**	0.5%		

ISBN 92-64-01442-X © OECD 2005

Table 4.7 (contd.)

Sectors	Number of Total Tariff Lines in Sectors	1: Price-Control Measures			3:Automatic Licensing Measures		4:Quantity-Control Measures			5:Monopolistic Measures		6: Technical Measures	
			1-(3) Variable Charges	1-(4) A-D Measures		3-(1) Automatic Licence		4-(1) Non-Automatic Licensing	4-(2) Import Quotas		5-(1): Single Channel for Imports		6-(1): Technical Regulations
Footwear, umbrellas	145						**1** **0.7%**	1 0.7%					
Cement, ceramics *et al.*	173											**15** **8.7%**	15 8.7%
Precious stones	78											**3** **3.8%**	3 3.8%
Base metals and their products	835	**35** **4.2%**	34 4.1%	1 0.1%			**302** **36.2%**	301 36.0%	1 0.1%			**39** **4.7%**	39 4.7%
Ordinary machinery	991						**18** **1.8%**		18 1.8%	**1** **0.1%**	1 0.1%	**30** **3.0%**	30 3.0%
Transport equipment	152						**8** **5.3%**		8 5.3%			**9** **5.9%**	9 5.9%
Precision machinery	308						**2** **0.6%**		2 0.6%			**61** **19.8%**	61 19.8%
Firearms	21						**21** **100.0%**		21 100.0%			**9** **42.9%**	9 42.9%
Various manufactured goods												**38** **18.4%**	38 18.4%
Art, antiques *et al.*	7						**1** **14.3%**		1 14.3%				

Note: Percentages indicate frequency ratios by type and sector. The figures above them show the numbers of tariff lines subject to NTMs in each sector.
Source: Drawn from calculations in Ando (2004), based on data from UNCTAD (TRAINS).

Table 4.8. **Japanese Imports under the GSP Scheme**
(values in millions of yen; shares in per cent)

	FY 1991		FY 1996		FY 2001	
	Value	Share	Value	Share	Value	Share
Total imports	30 501 255	100.0	39 130 278	100.0	40 781 355	100.0
Imports from GSP-eligible sources						
Total	14 781 066	48.5	20 771 501	53.1	17 105 594	41.9
Commodities with GSP	3 392 976	11.1	4 770 290	12.2	4 543 499	11.1
Imports under GSP	1 621 913	5.3	1 981 866	5.1	1 458 293	3.6
Agriculture, forestry, fishery products	2 210 895	7.2	2 737 828	7.0	2 111 438	5.2
Commodities with GSP	419 240	1.4	571 078	1.5	523 980	1.3
Imports under GSP	378 850	1.2	535 448	1,4	332 937	0.8
Mining and manufacturing products	12 570 171	41.2	18 033 674	46.1	14 994 156	36.8
Commodities with GSP	2 973 836	9.7	4 199 212	10.7	4 019 519	9.9
Imports under GSP	1 243 063	4.1	1 446 212	3.7	1 126 356	2.8

Source: MOF.

Table 4.9. **Usage of Japanese GSP**
(shares in per cent)

FY 1991		FY 1996		FY 2001	
Country	Share	Country	Share	Country	Share
Korea	23.0	China	30.8	China	55.5
Chinese Taipei	17.4	Korea	18.3	Thailand	9.2
China	13.5	Chinese Taipei	12.8	Indonesia	8.5
Brazil	7.3	Thailand	7.0	Malaysia	6.6
Thailand	4.3	Malaysia	5.2	Philippines	5.2
Philippines	4.3	Indonesia	4.3	Viet Nam	1.8
Malaysia	3.7	Philippines	3.7	India	1.6
Indonesia	3.5	Brazil	2.2	Brazil	1.3
Venezuela	2.2	Morocco	1.7	Chile	1.1
Singapore	1.9	Singapore	1.3	Morocco	0.8
Morocco	1.6	India	1.3	South Africa	0.8
India	1.4	Chile	1.2	Cambodia	0.5
Chile	1.4	South Africa	0.9	Mexico	0.7
UAE	1.0	Mexico	0.8	Saudi Arabia	0.7
Argentina	1.0	Mauritania	0.8	Cambodia	0.5
Mauritania	1.0	Saudi Arabia	0.8	Bangladesh	0.5
Saudi Arabia	0.9	Viet Nam	0.7	Mauritania	0.4
Hong Kong, China	0.9	Hong Kong, China	0.5	Sri Lanka	0.4
Peru	0.9	Canary Islands	0.5	Czech Republic	0.3
Canary Islands	0.8	Peru	0.4	Turkey	0.3
East Asia Total	72.5		84.6		87.3

Source: MOF.

ISBN 92-64-01442-X © OECD 2005

Although the GATT/WTO framework allows administered protection including countervailing duties, antidumping duties and safeguard measures, Japan has never used them heavily. Table 4.10 lists major government investigations to decide whether to implement such measures. In no case were countervailing duties actually imposed, and antidumping duties were levied in only a few. Provisional safeguard protection was provided once, in 2001. The author believes this case to have been strongly motivated by protectionist pressure arising in local politics to force the exporting country, namely China, to bear the cost of protection. China's retaliatory action complicated the situation[6].

Table 4.10. **Major Investigations for Administered Protection in Japan**

Countervailing Duties (CVDs)	Cotton yarn from Pakistan	Filed in December 1982 and withdrawn in February 1984 owing to the abolition of the subsidy at issue.
	Ferrosilicone from Brazil	Filed in March 1984 and withdrawn in June 1984 owing to the announcement of the abolition of the subsidy at issue as well as the recovery of the market.
Antidumping Duties (AD)	Cotton yarn from Korea	Filed in December 1982 and withdrawn in July 1983 owing to Korean announcement of voluntary export restraint.
	Ferrosilicone from Norway and France	Filed in March 1984 and withdrawn in June 1984 owing to announcements of voluntary export restraints and to market recovery.
	Sweaters from Korea	Filed in October 1988 and withdrawn in March 1989 owing to Korean announcement of voluntary export restraint.
	Ferrosilicomanganese from China, Norway and South Africa	Filed in October 1991. AD imposed only on imports from China in January 1993. AD terminated in January 1998.
	Cotton yarn from Pakistan	Filed in December 1993, with decision of AD imposition in August 1995 followed by partial removal and termination in July 2000.
	Polyester short fibre from Korea and Chinese Taipei	Filed in February 2001, with survey period extended by three months in April 2002.
Safeguards	Stone leeks, fresh *shiitake* mushrooms and rushes used to weave *tatami* mats, from China	Filed in November 2000. Provisional imposition of safeguard measures on April 2001. China retaliated with measures on some key manufactured goods. No impositions were finally agreed after bilateral consultation.

Source: MOF (2002).

Kataoka and Kuno (2003) apply the partial equilibrium approach proposed by Hufbauer and Elliot (1994) to estimate the cost of protection in Japan for 1999. They obtain numerical measures of trade barriers, including both tariffs and non-tariff barriers (NTBs), from differentials between c.i.f. import prices and domestic producer prices, as suggested by Sazanami *et al.* (1995). The model for each commodity treats imported and domestically produced goods as imperfect substitutes. The commodities selected from the seven-digit industry classification of input-output tables have imports of more than 1 billion yen and show price differences of more than 5 per cent between imported and domestically produced goods. The final sample has six commodities in agriculture, two in mining, nine in food processing, one in textiles, 16 in chemicals, six in petrochemicals, six in iron and steel and one in non-ferrous metals. The removal of all tariffs and NTBs for all of them enhances consumer surplus by an estimated 6.57 trillion yen or 20.7 per cent of domestic demand for these goods, equivalent to 1.3 per cent of the 1999 GDP. Of the 6.57 trillion yen, 3.45 trillion yen arise from the liberalisation of agricultural goods and processed food products. A large part of the consumer surplus gain is a transfer from producer surplus, and pure efficiency gains total 0.34 trillion yen. The liberalisation requires job replacement for 549 000 persons. This means that with the protection in place, consumers paid a job-preservation cost of 12 million yen (about $10 000) per worker.

In summary, Japan does not seem to be a protective country as a whole, but some specific products still have very high trade protection with complicated combinations of multiple protective measures. One may suppose this to have negative effects on East Asia's development and to suggest a lack of coherence in Japanese policies. On the other hand, trade in machinery and related products is almost completely free of protection, which allows international fragmentation of production processes and the formation of international production and distribution networks.

Agriculture

Agriculture is no longer a quantitatively important economic sector in Japan. The share of agriculture, forestry and fisheries in GDP has declined steadily to as low as 1.37 per cent by 2001[7]. Yet it remains disproportionately important in Japanese politics. It typically presents serious policy

 ISBN 92-64-01442-X © OECD 2005

inconsistencies and possibly provides negative impacts on developing economies. Rice offers a notorious example. Japan has long maintained virtually an import ban on rice, but it is one of the largest, most active importers of agricultural products in the world.

Table 4.11 shows the import patterns for the sector's products in 2002. The broadly defined product categories account for from 17 per cent to 20 per cent of total Japanese imports[8]. The imports range widely. Grain accounted for 8 per cent of the total in 2002. Fruits, vegetables, vegetable-based fats, tobacco and processed food and beverages each have about 5 per cent shares. Processed meat and fishery products take 14 per cent and 18 per cent respectively. By origin, the United States dominates with a share of 26 per cent. China had increased its share to 13 per cent by 2002, and one-fifth of the total originated in East Asian countries other than China.

Table 4.12 presents estimated self-sufficiency ratios for major food items. These figures reflect both the international competitiveness of domestic producers as determined by market forces and deliberately designed trade and other policies. Rice is an extreme example of "forced" self-sufficiency maintained by strict import restrictions. On the other hand, a number of food items do not have much protection and show substantial import penetration. They include vegetables, fruits, meat, diary products and fishery products. Most of them underwent substantial reduction of trade barriers through GATT negotiating rounds. Simple average tariff rates for agricultural products are reported as 12 per cent (OECD 1999). Vegetables and fishery products in particular now have very low tariffs. Most fresh vegetables have levies of only 3 per cent to 4.3 per cent, most fishery products only 3.5 per cent and shrimp and prawn only 1 per cent. Low self-sufficiency ratios are often used politically to justify prolonged protection. The number of food items with relatively low trade barriers suggests proof that efficient and stable supply networks can be constructed in co-operation with foreign suppliers.

Table 4.11. **Japanese Imports of Agriculture-Related Products, 2002**
(values in millions of yen; shares in per cent)

Product Categories	Value	Share	Countries of Origin	Value	Share
Total Imports	42 227 506	-----	Total Imports	42 227 506	-----
Imports of agriculture-related products	7 208 498	100.0	Imports of agriculture-related products	7 208 498	100.0
Agricultural products	4 301 128	59.7			
Farm and plantation products	3 043 047	42.2	United States	1 835 808	25.5
Grain and grain products	562 790	7.8	China	949 984	13.2
Fruits and fruit products	365 630	5.1	European Union	735 897	10.2
Vegetables and vegetable products	246 415	4.8	Denmark	172 546	2.4
Sugar and related products	47 774	0.7	France	148 874	2.1
Confectionery products	201 067	2.8	Italy	72 239	1.0
Other processed foods & beverages	408 533	5.7	Netherlands	58 821	0.8
Vegetable-based fats	334 655	4.6	Germany	54 131	0.8
Tobacco	320 842	4.5	United Kingdom	52 424	0.7
Natural rubber	70 121	1.0	Canada	502 208	7.0
Cotton	33 272	0.5	Australia	465 606	6.5
Animal husbandry	1 251 963	17.4	Thailand	373 633	5.2
Animals	24 618	0.3	Indonesia	310 541	4.3
Processed meats	971 562	13.5	Korea	181 392	2.5
Dairy products and eggs	138 685	1.9	Malaysia	179 233	2.5
Animal-based fats	6 182	0.1	Russia	178 768	2.5
Leather and wool	52 606	0.7	Chinese Taipei	151 406	2.1
Other animal husbandry products	58 312	0.8	Chile	149 445	2.1
Silk yarn	6 118	0.1	New Zealand	149 349	2.1
Forestry products	1 145 174	15.9	Brazil	138 769	1.9
Lumber	200 091	2.8	Philippines	111 289	1.5
Processed wood	332 962	4.6	Viet Nam	89 860	1.2
Veneer and plywood	226 348	3.1	Norway	75 175	1.0
Other wood	156 385	2.2	India	67 386	0.9
Other forestry products	229 388	3.2	South Africa	63 133	0.9
Fishery products	1 762 196	24.4	Mexico	53 507	0.7
Live fish	39 791	0.6			
Fish products (raw, chilled, frozen. salted, dried)	1 289 356	17.9			
Other fish products	286 637	4.0			
Fish-based fats	5 460	0.1			
Pearl	31 145	0.4			
Other fishery products	46 998	0.7			

Source: MAFF (2003*a*).

ISBN 92-64-01442-X © OECD 2005

Table 4.12. **Self-Sufficiency Ratios by Food Items, 1965-2001**
(percentages)

	1965	1970	1975	1980	1985	1990	1995	2000	2001
Rice	95	106	110	100	107	100	104	95	95
For staple food								100	100
Wheat	28	9	4	10	14	15	7	11	11
Barley	57	28	8	13	14	12	8	7	7
Starch	67	41	24	21	19	13	12	9	10
Peas and beans	25	13	9	7	8	8	5	7	7
Soybeans	11	4	4	4	5	5	2	5	5
Other peas and beans	70	65	45	30	40	41	36	28	26
Vegetables	100	99	99	97	95	91	85	82	82
Fruits	90	84	84	81	77	63	49	44	44
Mandarin oranges	109	105	102	103	106	102	102	94	96
Apples	102	102	100	97	97	84	62	59	58
Meat	93	89	76	80	81	70	57	52	53
Meat (except whale meat)	90	89	77	81	81	70	57	52	53
Beef	95	90	81	72	72	51	39	34	36
Pork	100	98	86	87	86	74	62	57	55
Chicken	97	98	97	94	92	82	69	64	64
Other meat	21	8	2	2	3	3	6	10	10
Whale meat	107	100	72	46	47	67	100	100	100
Eggs	100	97	97	98	98	98	96	95	96
Milk and dairy products	86	89	81	82	85	78	72	68	68
Fishery products	100	102	99	97	93	79	57	53	49
Fishery products for food	110	108	100	97	86	72	59	53	53
Seaweed	88	91	86	74	74	72	68	63	62
Sugar	19	15							
Sugar (including okinawa)	31	22	15	27	33	32	31	29	32
Oils and fats	31	22	23	29	32	28	15	14	13
Vegetable-based	19	11	8	7	5	4	3	3	3
Animal-based	55	46	69	94	124	113	68	70	65
Mushrooms	115	111	110	109	102	92	78	74	75

Note: The self-sufficiency ratio is calculated (in terms of weights) as [domestic production / domestic production + imports – exports – increases in stocks)]

Source: MAFF (2003*b*).

Very high trade protection affects some products. For rice, Japan negotiated exceptional treatment in the Uruguay Round to avoid tariffication temporarily with minimum access. Tariffication was implemented in April 1999, however, but with constant minimum access maintained. The current — prohibitive — tariff rate is 341 yen per kilogram or about 490 per cent *ad-valorem* equivalent. Other examples of extreme protection include:

ISBN 92-64-01442-X

- 55 yen per kilogram (210 per cent equivalent) for wheat;
- 90 yen per kilogram (90 per cent equivalent) for wheat flour;
- 39 yen per kilogram (190 per cent equivalent) for barley;
- 21.3 per cent plus 396 yen per kilogram (200 per cent equivalent) for powdered milk;
- 29.8 per cent plus 985 yen per kilogram (330 per cent equivalent) for butter;
- 119 yen per kilogram (290 per cent equivalent) for starch;
- 354 yen per kilogram (460 per cent equivalent) for peas and beans;
- 617 yen per kilogram (500 per cent equivalent) for ground nuts;
- 2 796 yen per kilogram (990 per cent equivalent) for tubers of *konnyaku*;
- 6 978 yen per kilogram (190 per cent equivalent) for silk;
- 103.1 yen per kilogram (270 per cent equivalent) for sugar; and
- 50 per cent for beef[9].

Table 4.13 shows the OECD's producer support equivalents (PSEs) for major developed countries[10]. PSE is an estimated transfer from consumers or taxpayers to producers through policy measures supporting agricultural production or farmers' incomes. The figures presented in the table are the ratios of PSEs to agricultural production evaluated at international prices. Japan obviously is not the only country that protects its agricultural sector. Despite its relatively light protection for some products, however, its overall protection is as high as 169 per cent, i.e. the Japanese government directly or indirectly pays subsidies of a sort that reach 1.7 times internationally competitive prices. Because most of such policy support takes the forms of border measures and price-maintenance policies rather than direct subsidies to producers, domestic consumers and potential foreign producers bear the costs of protection.

Table 4.13. **Producer Support Estimates, 1996-1998 Average**

(per cent of the value of domestic production)

	Japan	EU15	Australia	Canada	United States
Total, all products	169	65	7	18	20
Rice	434	37	6	n.a.	13
Wheat	622	88	5	12	41
Beef	50	120	5	6	3
Chicken	13	24	3	5	3
Eggs	20	5	7	36	4
Milk	350	112	37	111	105
Sugar	52	62	5	n.a.	69

Source: Japan Economic Research Center (2001). Originally from OECD.

 ISBN 92-64-01442-X © OECD 2005

In the current WTO agricultural negotiations, Japan has had difficulty in leading the discussion and has not taken an active stance on the modalities of liberalisation. Nevertheless, some signs of change in the agricultural lobby have appeared. Policy switching from border measures to direct subsidies is now openly discussed in places. The Ministry of Agriculture, Forestry, and Fisheries (MAFF) is now documenting the new *Basic Law on Food, Agriculture, and Rural Areas* that would emphasise the enhancement of productivity and international competitiveness. Japan's position in the WTO once stressed the so-called multi-functionality of the agricultural sector, but some now realise that the concept may work against their attempt to promote productivity enhancement through direct subsidies. Moreover, on-going negotiations over bilateral free trade agreements (FTAs) with Korea, Thailand, Malaysia and the Philippines provide many opportunities for the agricultural lobby to rethink its medium-term and long-run strategies, although substantial reform may not be initiated through FTA negotiations. Judging from these signs, one can now hope for reasonably fast agricultural policy reform.

Machinery Industries

One of the most important recent changes in East Asia has involved the formation of international production and distribution networks centred on the machinery industries. Because its influence penetrates deeply into the fundamental structures of the East Asian economies, it is almost impossible to generate counterfactuals to evaluate its impact quantitatively. One cannot doubt, however, that network formation has acted as one of the most important determinants of East Asia's superb growth performance. Japanese trade-related policies play an essential role in the development of such networks.

The East Asian networks consist of the vertical division of labour in production processes across countries with widely different income levels. Similar networks are developing between the United States and Mexico and between Germany and the Czech Republic, Hungary and Poland, but those in East Asia have advanced the most, with distinctive characteristics. These include their significance in the regional economy, their geographical extensiveness involving a large number of countries and the sophistication of both intra-firm and arm's-length relationships across different firm nationalities.

To understand the mechanics of these networks, one needs to add new analytical tools to the traditional comparative-advantage argument. The theory of comparative advantage based on relative advantages in autarky (i.e. before trade occurs) remains valid in a number of circumstances; technological gaps and factor-price differences explain the location patterns of industries to some extent. Yet the traditional theory does not explain why the division of labour in production processes, rather than inter-industry division of labour, becomes crucially important in East Asia. The semiconductor-related electronics industry provides a typical example of the division of labour in processes. This industry as a whole is intensive in capital (or human capital), but its production activities have become finely segmented and widely dispersed in both developed and developing countries.

The recently developed fragmentation theory neatly presents the economic logic behind such a location pattern[11]. Deardorff (2001) defines fragmentation as "the splitting of a product process into two or more steps that can be undertaken in different locations but that lead to the same final product." Suppose, for example, that initially a big factory in Japan takes care of all the production activities from upstream to downstream. A careful look at individual production blocks may reveal that some require close watch by technicians, while others are purely labour-intensive. In such a case, the location of the production blocks separately in Japan, Malaysia and China, for instance, may contribute to saving some production costs.

Fragmentation becomes economical when the cost of service links (SL) connecting production blocks (PB) is sufficiently low. SL costs include trade barriers, transport costs, telecommunication costs and various co-ordination costs between PBs. They depend heavily on the nature of technology in each industry. For example, a full-scale steel mill cannot be fragmented economically because of its energy efficiency. Globalisation reduces SL costs and enables firms in many industries to fragment their PBs and locate them not only within a country but also across countries to reduce total production costs. As SL tend to carry strong external economies of scale, globalisation may accelerate concentration and fragmentation at the same time.

Figure 4.1 indicates how significant machinery trade, particularly in parts and components, has become for the East Asian countries including Japan. Machinery is here defined as HS 84-92; i.e. to include general machinery, electric machinery, transport equipment and precision machinery. The figure plots countries from left to right in descending order of machinery parts and components export shares. The shares of machinery in each East Asian country's total exports and imports run as high as 40 per cent or even up to around 70 per cent, with few exceptions. Moreover, the shares of parts and components in machinery trade are very high, indicating active reciprocal transactions in parts and components (intermediate goods) among countries in the region.

 ISBN 92-64-01442-X © OECD 2005

Figure 4.1. **Trade in Machinery Goods and Machinery Parts and Components: Shares in Total Exports and Imports in 2000**

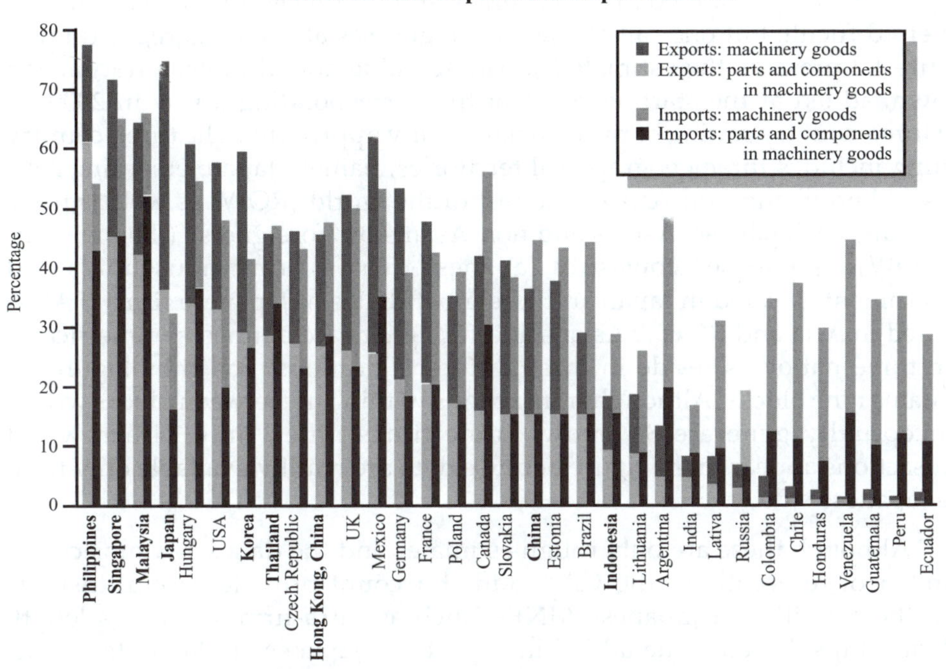

Source: Drawn from Ando and Kimura (2003). Original data source: authors' calculation based on PC-TAS (UN Comtrade only for exports of Hong Kong, China and exports and imports of Russia and Slovakia).

One of the important characteristics of the networks in East Asia lies in their sophisticated intra-firm and arm's-length relationships across different firm nationalities. A firm typically does not do everything from upstream to downstream. It sets its upstream boundary by purchasing materials or parts from other firms and determines its downstream boundary by selling products to other firms or consumers. A firm makes this "internalisation" decision and location decisions at the same time, considering its own firm-specific assets such as technology and managerial know-how. Such decision making is particularly important in East Asia, as various internalisation patterns with innovative inter-firm relationships emerge from efforts to concentrate on core competence. The proliferation of original equipment manufacturing (OEM) contracts and the growth of electronics manufacturing service (EMS) firms exemplify such organisational innovation. All these sophisticated arrangements are particularly salient in the machinery, textiles and garment industries. Technological progress in developing production and distribution "modules" accelerates the formation of sophisticated inter-firm relationships.

As parts and components trade increases, one would like to know the magnitude of value added in each country and trading entity. Such estimation is very difficult, but one can at least make guesses at some aggregated level. Figure 4.2 presents the estimated Japanese value added of each transaction shown, added at the starting point of the corresponding arrow in 2000, in the three-country setting of the firm nationality approach[12]. The three-country setting includes three geographical territories, namely Japan, emerging Asia ("Asia" here)[13] and non-Asia or the rest of the world (ROW) as well as three nationals, i.e. Japanese, Asians and non-Asians or "foreigners" (the nationals of ROW). "Japanese" consist of Japanese-owned firms, households and governments located in Japan and foreign affiliates of Japanese firms (FAJFs) located in Asia and ROW[14]. Asians and foreigners are defined symmetrically. The three nationals reside in three different locations, and thus Figure 4.2 contains nine blocks. Although transactions within and between blocks would conceptually generate 81 arrows (nine times nine), only 14 arrows of transactions appear in the figure because data are readily available only from the Japanese side.

Although these are only rough estimates and the data set is subject to a number of reservations, the value added account provides useful insights into the activities of Japanese MNEs, such as intra-firm and arm's length relationships. When value added in exports by Japanese in Japan to Asians and foreigners in Asia is compared with that to Japanese in Asia, the former is larger. Also, value added in sales by Japanese affiliates in Asia to Asians and foreigners in Asia is larger than that in sales to Japanese-owned firms in Japan. Thus, activities by Japanese firms are not based solely on subcontracting relationships or intra-firm relationships between Japanese parent firms and their affiliates in East Asia. Rather, the activities do include transactions with indigenous firms and MNEs in Asia. In other words, strong intra-regional production networks in East Asia consist not only of Japanese firms but also of a mixture of firms of different nationalities.

What background conditions affected Japanese FDI to East Asia? The Plaza Accord and subsequent yen appreciation triggered drastic expansion of outward FDI from Japan, but the characteristics of FDI to developed and developing countries differed. FDI to the United States and Europe aimed primarily at avoiding actual or expected trade disputes by substituting foreign production for exports. FDI to East Asia went to reorganise production systems to adjust to changes in comparative advantage. The government at that time had confidence in the international competitiveness of Japanese firms and Japan's location advantages. It provided support or at least remained neutral towards globalising corporate activities and did not fear possible industrial dislocation.

 ISBN 92-64-01442-X

Figure 4.2. **Japanese Value Added Embodied in Sales to Asians and Foreigners by Japanese: Three-country Setting (2000)**
(Unit: millon JPY)

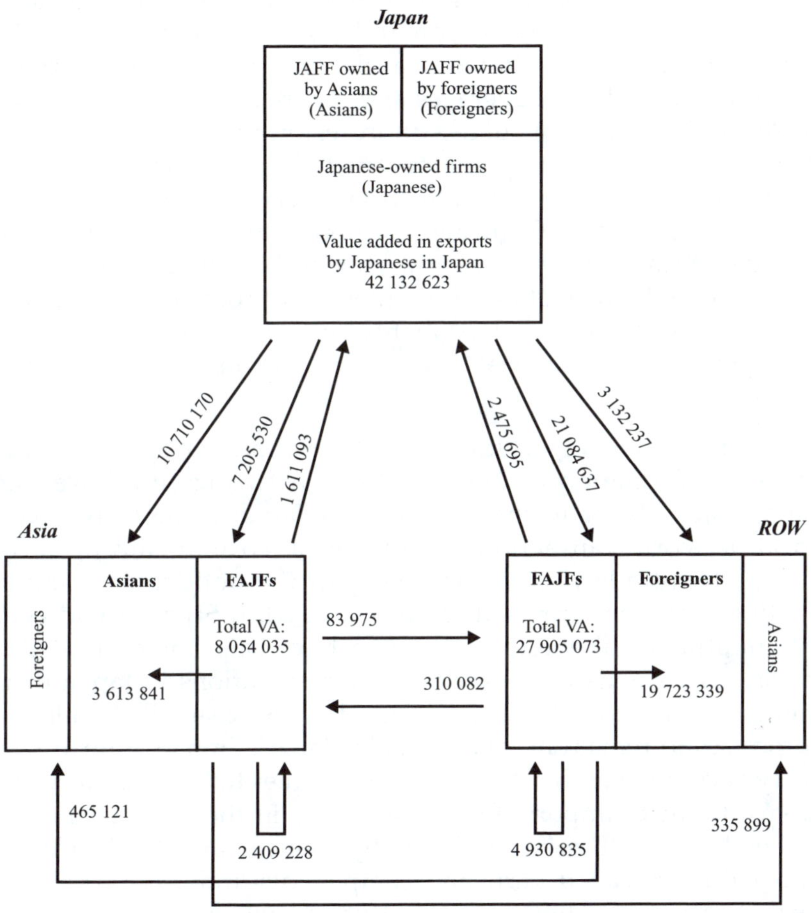

Source: Drawn from Ando and Kimura (2003). Original data sources: METI (2001), *White Paper on International Trade 2001* for exports of Japan; METI (2002) *The 35th Survey of Japanese Affiliates of Foreign Firms* for exports of JAFF; MITI (2002) *The 31st Survey of Overseas Business Activities of Japanese Companies* for sales and purchases of FAJF; Management and Coordination Agency (1999); 1995 *Input-Output Tables: Explanatory Report* for the import inducement coefficient of export in Japan for 1995.

Responding to an accumulating current-account surplus and changes in the international economic environment, the policy recommendations of the famous *Maekawa Report* appeared in 1986. The Report strongly advocated drastic expansion of domestic demand and deregulation, and it had a connection with the Japan-US talks on deregulation in retail services, rice, pharmaceuticals, alcoholic beverages and other sectors in the late 1980s and early 1990s. It did not seem successful in restoring macroeconomic balance, but it became a good starting point for structural reform in Japan. The central focus of structural reform actually affected the services rather than the tradable goods sector, notably manufacturing. The Report did not claim the importance of free trade, at least not persuasively. Thus it did not seem to play a direct, important role in the formation of international production and distribution networks in East Asia, but it probably did encourage FDI outflows by advocating the necessity of establishing a more competitive environment for private business.

Japan's free-trade regime for the machinery industries served as a crucial element in the formation of the East Asian networks. It allowed Japan to become a major player in the process. For Japan to be fully involved in reciprocal network transactions, reducing SL costs including tariffs was crucial. The free-trade regime also reduced the politico-economic risk of exacerbating sentiment opposed to outward FDI. If SL costs had been high, Japanese multinational enterprises would have been forced to make knife-edge decisions on whether to keep all their operations in Japan or relocate everything to other East Asian countries. Low SL costs likely allow at least some processes to remain in Japan. Finally, Japan's initiative for free trade in machinery encouraged other East Asian economies to liberalise as well. Ratios of customs duties to imports fell substantially in the East Asian economies throughout the 1990s. This happened partly owing to unilateral tariff reduction for semiconductor-related parts and components under the APEC initiative and partly because of extensive use of duty drawbacks, i.e. tariff rebates for intermediate goods imported to produce exported manufactured goods.

Concluding Remarks

This chapter reviews policy coherence in Japan with particular focus on trade-related policies. It finds that various channels of policies are not at all designed to maintain coherence. Near-sighted political economy has

ISBN 92-64-01442-X © OECD 2005

obviously directed policy decision making in Japan. Policies are sometimes inconsistent and sometimes consistent. Rice policy exemplifies a serious lack of coherence, but fishery products represent cases in which freer trade encourages desirable domestic reform with increasing foreign trade. In the machinery industries, Japan's free-trade stance accelerates the formation of international production and distribution networks. The overall effort to accelerate structural reform initiated by the *Maekawa Report* did not seem directly to restore policy coherence in the external sector, but it did result in a favourable environment for efficient industrial adjustment and accelerated outward FDI. Further explicit efforts to maintain overall policy coherence remain necessary.

ISBN 92-64-01442-X © OECD 2005

Notes

1. Kojima (2002) summarises his view on the flying-geese pattern and pro-trade-oriented FDI.
2. See Ando and Kimura (2003) for details.
3. On IIT in Japan and other Asia-Pacific countries in the 1970s and 1980s, see Fukasaku (1992).
4. See Fukao *et al.* (2003) and Kimura and Ando (2004).
5. These sectors also have specific tariffs and other complicated trade barriers. The APEC homepage provides tables.
6. For the author's view on the safeguard case, see Kimura (2001). Note also that the Japanese government used special safeguard measures for agricultural products in tens of cases. Article V of the Agreement on Agriculture in the Marrakech Agreement allows member countries to impose special safeguards for commodities with tarification under the Uruguay Round negotiations. At least some of the cases, such as beef in 2003, seemed to be motivated by the clear intention of protectionism.
7. According to MAFF (2003*a*, p. 56).
8. Japanese exports of these products are minimal; they account for less than 1 per cent of the total. Discussions on Fats with East Asian countries, particularly Korea, are investigating possibilities for exporting some agricultural products such as high-quality fruits.
9. The figures are GATT-based bound rates in 2000. The data are from JETRO (2003) and material provided by the MAFF. The tariff system is complicated for some products; see the original sources for details.
10. The details for PSE are available in OECD (2001) and on the OECD homepage.
11. On the fragmentation theory, see Jones and Kierzkowski (1990), Deardorff (2001) and Cheng and Kierzkowski (2001).

ISBN 92-64-01442-X © OECD 2005

12. Baldwin and Kimura (1998) and Kimura and Baldwin (1998) first proposed the firm nationality approach in a two-country setting. See Ando and Kimura (2003) for a detailed explanation of how these figures are estimated in the three-country setting.

13. "Asia" stands for the Asian countries east of Pakistan, excluding Japan.

14. Note that "Japanese" in this definition differs from both a residency basis and the sense of productive factor holders; FAJF are treated as Japanese-controlled and all their activities are regarded as Japanese.

ISBN 92-64-01442-X

Bibliography

ANDO, M. (2004), "Estimating Tariff Equivalents of Non-tariff Measures in APEC Member Economies", forthcoming in the conference volume entitled *APEC Capacity-Building Workshop on Quantitative Methods for Assessing NTMs and Trade Facilitation.*

ANDO, M. and F. KIMURA (2003), "The Formation of International Production and Distribution Networks in East Asia", *NBER Working Paper 10167*, forthcoming in T. ITO and A. ROSE (eds.), *International Trade (NBER-East Asia Seminar on Economics, Volume 14)*, University of Chicago Press, Chicago.

BALDWIN, R.E. and F. KIMURA (1998), "Measuring U.S. International Goods and Services Transactions", *in* R.E. BALDWIN, R.E. LIPSEY and J.D. RICHARDSON (eds.), *Geography and Ownership as Bases for Economic Accounting*, University of Chicago Press, Chicago.

CHENG, L.K. and H. KIERZKOWSKI (2001), *Global Production and Trade in East Asia*, Kluwer Academic Publishers, Boston.

DEARDORFF, A.V. (2001), "Fragmentation in Simple Trade Models." *North American Journal of Economics and Finance*, 12: 121-137.

FUKAO, K., H. ISHIDO and K. ITO (2003), "Vertical Intra-industry Trade and Foreign Direct Investment in East Asia", RIETI Discussion Paper Series 03-E-001, forthcoming in T. ITO and A. ROSE (eds.), *International Trade (NBER-East Asia Seminar on Economics, Volume 14)*, University of Chicago Press, Chicago.

FUKASAKU, K. (1992), "Economic Regionalisation and Intra-industry Trade: Pacific Asian Perspective", Working Paper No. 53, OECD Development Centre, Paris.

HUFBAUER, G.C. and K.A. ELLIOT (1994) *Measuring the Costs of Protection in the United States*, Institute for International Economics, Washington, D.C.

JAPAN ECONOMIC RESEARCH CENTER (JERC) (2001), *Kakudai suru Jiyuu Boueki Kyoutei to Nihon no Sentaku (Expanding Free Trade Agreements and the Choice of Japan)*, Tokyo, JERC (in Japanese).

JETRO (2003), *JETRO Agro-trade Handbook 2003*. Tokyo, JETRO (in Japanese).

ISBN 92-64-01442-X © OECD 2005

JONES, R.W. and H. KIERZKOWSKI (1990), "The Role of Services in Production and International Trade: A Theoretical Framework", *in* R.W. JONES and A.O. KRUEGER (eds.), *The Political Economy of International Trade: Essays in Honor of Robert E. Baldwin*, Basil Blackwell, Oxford.

KATAOKA, T. and A. KUNO (2003), "Boueki Hogo no Kosuto Keisan (Cost Estimates of Trade Protection)", *UFJ Institute Report*, 8, No. 2.

KIMURA, F. (2001), "The Dangers of Local Protectionism", *Journal of Japanese Trade and Industry*, 20, No. 6 (November/December): 8-11.

KIMURA, F. and M. ANDO (2003), "Intra-regional Trade among China, Japan and Korea: Intra-industry Trade of Major Industries", *in* Y. KIM and C.J. LEE (eds.), *Northeast Asian Integration: Prospects for a Northeast Asian FTA*, 245-279, KIEP, Seoul.

KIMURA, F. and M. ANDO (2004), "Fragmentation and Networking in East Asia: From One-way Trade to Vertical Intra-industry Trade and from Intra-firm to Arm's Length", mimeo.

KIMURA, F. and R.E. BALDWIN (1998), "Application of a Nationality-Adjusted Net Sales and Value Added Framework: The Case of Japan", *in* R.E. BALDWIN, R.E. LIPSEY and J.D. RICHARDSON (eds.), *Geography and Ownership as Bases for Economic Accounting*, University of Chicago Press, Chicago.

KOJIMA, K. (2002), "Asian Economic Integration for the 21st Century", *ICSEAD East Asian Economic Perspectives*, 13, 1-38, March.

MANAGEMENT AND COORDINATION AGENCY, GOVERNMENT OF JAPAN (MCA, currently the Ministry of Public Management, Home Affairs, Posts and Telecommunications) (various years), *Japan Statistical Yearbook*, Tokyo, MCA (in Japanese).

MINISTRY OF AGRICULTURE, FORESTRY AND FISHERIES, GOVERNMENT OF JAPAN (MAFF) (2003*a*), *Poketto Norin Suisan Toukei (Concise Agricultural and Fishery Statistics)*, Tokyo, Zaidan Houjin Nourin Toukei Kyoukai (in Japanese).

MINISTRY OF AGRICULTURE, FORESTRY AND FISHERIES, GOVERNMENT OF JAPAN (MAFF) (2003*b*), *Shokuryou Jukyuu Hyou (Tables of Self-Sufficiency in Food)*, Tokyo, MAFF (in Japanese).

MINISTRY OF FINANCE (MOF) (various years), *Kanzei Nenpou (Annual Report on Tariffs)*, Tokyo, MOF (in Japanese).

OECD (1999), *Agricultural Policies in OECD Countries: Monitoring and Evaluation 1999*, Paris.

OECD (2001), *Agricultural Policies in OECD Countries: Monitoring and Evaluation 2001*, Paris.

SAZANAMI, Y. S. URATA and H. KAWAI (1995), *Measuring the Costs of Protection in Japan*, Institute for International Economics, Washington, D.C.

Chapter 5

Economic Development and Poverty Reduction in East Asia: The Impact of OECD-Country Agricultural Policies

*Richard Barichello**

Abstract

This chapter asks whether OECD-country agricultural policies may have hampered poverty alleviation in East Asia, using Indonesia and Viet Nam as specific cases. The effects depend on country-specific circumstances, which may limit generalisations. In Indonesia low agricultural growth since the mid-1980s has done little to reduce poverty. Because its rural and urban labour markets are highly integrated, however, rapid, sustained non-agricultural growth has done much to raise incomes and reduce poverty, even if many people remain not far above it. On the other hand, Viet Nam's considerably higher agricultural growth in the 1990s helped greatly to raise rural incomes. Non-agricultural growth, though rapid, has done little to reduce rural poverty owing to the more limited integration of rural and urban labour markets. A key message of this chapter is that although OECD-country agricultural policies may have damaged some parts of Asian agriculture, notably rice and sugar, East Asia has other important tools to alleviate poverty, and some countries have used them to offset the negative effects to achieve very good poverty-reduction outcomes.

Introduction

Unusually rapid economic growth has been a striking and well-known feature in the countries of East Asia over the past three or more decades[1]. Possibly less well known, this growth also ushered in a substantial reduction in poverty. The bulk of the poverty in most developing countries occurs in rural areas. This raises questions about the structures of these economies, specifically the relative size and importance of their agricultural sectors. If countries make progress in reducing poverty and have sizeable rural components in their economies, then much of this progress should occur through improvements of various sorts in agriculture. This could come through a strengthening of world market prices for agricultural exports or improvements in productivity and efficiency in domestic agriculture.

This raises another question. To what extent do these favourable developments in income growth and poverty reduction result from domestic factors and to what extent are they due to external developments? This has particular importance for the agricultural sector, where both domestic agricultural policies and the functioning of world markets play known, important roles. This chapter focuses on the external factors. Not only are many agricultural products important as exports for developing countries, but world agricultural markets have a reputation for instability and sometimes-difficult terms of trade. These difficulties, in turn, are often laid at the feet of the OECD countries. They are criticised, for example, for the use of agricultural subsidies, export and domestic, known often to result in reduced world market prices. Their agricultural policies often get blamed for undesirable effects on developing countries such as exacerbating poverty. The impasse of the current WTO trade negotiations in Cancun in late 2003 was blamed specifically on these policies.

OECD-country agricultural policies affect developing countries including those in East Asia in many ways[2]. The most egregious policies pertain to export subsidies and market access for various commodities protected in the rich countries. These "commodity" policies have the well-known negative effects not only of limiting exports from developing countries, but also more broadly of lowering world market prices, with well-documented disincentive and distortive effects on East Asian agricultural production.

The commodity policies of OECD countries are not the only measures that hurt East Asian agriculture. Similar effects can stem from related trade policies, such as the rigid application of sanitary and phytosanitary measures and other standards that, with intent or not, keep out developing-country

ISBN 92-64-01442-X © OECD 2005

fruit exports, for example. Tariff escalation hampers development of the food and related value-added industries. International research programmes, such as the CGIAR (Consultative Group on International Agricultural Research) system, and foreign aid measures may provide some positive offsets. Yet aid-financed project funding is not always as beneficial as it may appear, as is seen in some projects that expand commodity plantings across countries and result in price declines for those commodities. Collectively, these negative effects on East Asian countries will lower economic growth more broadly (although less significantly in Indonesia), and this itself will have a secondary effect by lowering wage rates. They may have some importance in Viet Nam.

Have OECD countries' agricultural policies exacerbated poverty in East Asia? This claim is very much worth examining, especially in light of such clear progress on raising incomes and reducing poverty in the region, including poverty in rural areas. This chapter tries to explore the evidence from East Asia on this empirical question, on which country evidence is needed. It centres on two countries, Indonesia and Viet Nam, whose agricultural sectors are important and which are relatively poor. This choice has the added aspect of illustrating different economic models. Indonesia has followed a fairly common path for more than 35 years by relying more or less on a market economy. Viet Nam, on the other hand, is a transition economy. It started with a centrally planned system in the north in the 1950s but has moved in the direction of a market economy since the mid to late 1980s. Although this two-country focus does not allow generalisations for the whole region, it has the substantial advantage of greater detail, including moderately detailed knowledge of their agricultural policies, the structures of their agriculture sectors and their patterns of income growth. The chapter starts by outlining the mechanisms by which OECD-country policies could affect poverty in these countries. After reviewing their accomplishments in poverty reduction, it attempts to explain how they were achieved and the linkages with OECD-country agricultural policies. It closes by drawing some lessons from these cases.

Mechanisms by which Poverty is Affected by OECD-Country Agricultural Policies

Given that most of the poor in developing countries own little or no capital or land, they rely on labour markets for the dominant share of their incomes. Village or urban labour markets serve those who work off the farm

ISBN 92-64-01442-X © OECD 2005

in industry or services; landless labourers and farmers use the agricultural labour market. The key variable for rural poverty reduction is the rural or agricultural wage rate, and the analysis here will examine the effect on rural wage rates of different OECD-country agricultural policies. Employment levels in agriculture also are important, but more for determining whether people work in or outside the agricultural sector and whether migration is necessary to find a job, not for the remuneration they will receive. Employment levels are important for regions and industries, because it makes a difference whether they lose or gain jobs. For landless individuals, however, net incomes will not vary unless wage rates change, for either those who migrate or those who do not, as long as the two labour markets are well integrated.

Another important distributional effect of rich-country policies on rural people in poor countries is what happens to land prices. Policies that lower a crop's world market price will usually lower agricultural land prices where that crop is grown, as long as there is some integration between the domestic and world markets. As important as this is for rural households, this direct effect is unlikely to affect the poorest farmers and landless labourers for the simple reason that the poor are usually landless.

The effect may well touch a second tier of poor with higher incomes. Many relatively poor rural people, including middle-income farmers, own some land and rely on the rents from it to augment their otherwise modest wage incomes. Rich-country agricultural policies that reduce prices can lower their property income, possibly worsening their poverty, whether they farm the land directly or rent it to others. Moreover, an additional "multiplier effect" can affect the rural poor indirectly through lower regional incomes. If rich-country policies lower world market prices, in turn lowering land prices, this will have an income or wealth effect on rural landowners, who will spend less. This will likely reduce employment in rural areas even if major effects on the wage rate do not appear. In consequence, more individuals will end up migrating out of the region to take up industrial or urban jobs temporarily or more permanently, even if their net incomes have not fallen.

Another important group, namely consumers, also can feel distributional effects. OECD-country agricultural policies that lower world market prices actually have a *positive* effect on consumers worldwide. One segment of the rural poor, those who do not produce enough to be net sellers of the commodities at issue, typically includes the very poorest farmers. They are net food buyers. Their wellbeing is helped by lower food prices. This effect may be smaller than that on net sellers, who in Asia usually are more numerous, but it is worth flagging[3].

ISBN 92-64-01442-X © OECD 2005

Four conditions must be met for an OECD country's agricultural policy to have an effect on poverty alleviation in developing countries. First, the OECD country must have some market power in the commodity market in question. "Small" OECD countries by definition have no effect on world market prices by themselves. If they belong to larger economic groups that do affect world market prices, such as the EU, then of course policies taken collectively affect the developing countries.

Second, there must be an OECD-country policy that affects the developing-country commodity at issue, and it must affect that commodity's world price. In other words, commodity overlap must exist between what the OECD country grows and subsidises and what the developing country grows. This needs assessment with the realisation that commodity production is partly endogenous; there may be no current production of a crop in a developing country *because of* the existence of an OECD-country subsidy programme. For example, EU and US sugar programmes may have depressed prices sufficiently that Indonesian sugar production is very small, smaller than it otherwise would be, giving the appearance of little overlap in production of that commodity. Further, the OECD-country policies must affect world markets (i.e. there must be a "coupled" policy or one that is in the "amber box" under the WTO Agreement on Agriculture), typically by increasing production and exports of the commodity in question.

Third, the developing country must have a policy framework that allows world markets to affect local market prices. If its domestic market for a commodity is sufficiently separated from the world market (such as through some form of quantitative restriction on imports) so that domestic prices are unaffected by world prices, no OECD-country policy effect on that country would occur.

Fourth, wage rates in the developing country must be affected by local or world market prices for that commodity before the OECD-country policy can damage poverty alleviation efforts. This is a key issue for the poorest farmers, who are net sellers of the commodity but landless, the group that is the primary focus here. Furthermore, even if agricultural prices have no effect on rural wage rates, another poor group could suffer. If one considers middle-income farmers as poor, those who are the poorer among them and who own some land may feel a negative effect through lower land prices. Moreover, in addition to direct impacts on poverty levels themselves and the poorest segment of rural areas, other distributional effects may disturb the regional location and sectoral distribution of jobs available to the poor.

ISBN 92-64-01442-X © OECD 2005

A Picture of Agricultural Development and Poverty Reduction in East Asia

Income growth in East Asia has been dramatic both by historical standards and in comparison with other regions around the world (Table 5.1). While average GDP growth for all low and middle-income developing countries held at 3.2 per cent and 3.4 per cent per year in the 1980s and 1990s respectively, East Asian countries grew by 7.5 per cent a year in each of those decades, more than twice as fast. South Asia also grew quickly, at 5.5 per cent per year. No other region on the globe grew as quickly as the *average* rates for all developing countries. The next fastest growers over those 22 years, Latin America and the Middle East/North Africa (MENA), grew at about 2.5 per cent per year on average, one-third the rate of the East Asia and Pacific economies.

Table 5.1. **Growth Rates in GDP and Agriculture**

Country	GDP		Agriculture	
	1980-1990	1990-2001	1980-1990	1990-2001
East Asia/Pacific	7.5	7.5	4.6	3.2
Indonesia	6.1	3.8	3.6	1.9
Malaysia	5.3	6.5	3.4	0.3
Philippines	1.0	3.3	1.0	1.8
Thailand	7.6	3.8	3.9	1.7
Viet Nam	4.6	7.7	2.8	4.2
China	10.3	10.0	5.9	4.0
South Asia	5.6	5.5	3.2	3.1
India	5.7	5.9	3.1	3.0
Europe/Central Asia	2.1	-1.0	--	-1.9
Latin America	1.7	3.2	2.3	2.4
MENA	2.0	3.0	4.0	3.0
Sub-Saharan Africa	1.6	2.6	2.2	2.8
All dev. countries	3.2	3.4	3.3	2.2

Source: www.worldbank.org/data/wdi2003/tables/table4-1.pdf.

Part of this dramatic record came from China in East Asia and India in South Asia. Yet even after removing China from the East Asia data, the average growth of the five ASEAN countries included in Table 5.1 still reached 5 per cent per year. India showed only slightly higher growth than the average for South Asia. Thus, even after stripping these two large and rapidly growing

ISBN 92-64-01442-X © OECD 2005

economies from the data, the economies of East and South Asia expanded twice as fast as the next most rapidly growing regions anywhere on the planet. Significantly, these data include the sharp recession caused by the Asian financial crisis, which explains why countries such as Indonesia, Thailand and to a lesser extent the Philippines show relatively slow growth by Asian standards in the most recent decade. Yet East Asia still outperformed the other aggregate regions.

The right-hand columns of Table 5.1 show growth rates in the agricultural sector. They give some indication of the extent to which agriculture expands along with the rest of the economy. Given the close ties between a developing country's poverty and this sector, strong performance here will contribute to poverty reduction. This is not a necessary condition for poverty reduction, however. Sufficiently rapid growth in the non-agricultural component of the economy will also contribute, as long as the linkages between the two sectors are strong.

In agriculture, East Asia again performed well. In each period it had the highest agricultural growth rate of any of the regions listed, 4.6 per cent per year in the 1980s and 3.2 per cent in the 1990s. Nevertheless, agricultural growth's margin of superiority is considerably less than that for GDP. East Asian agriculture grew only half as fast again as the aggregate of all developing countries. South Asia had the third strongest regional performance. For East (and South) Asia and for virtually all the Asian countries listed in the table, growth in agriculture was only about half the GDP growth rate. The same was true in most regions outside Asia in the 1990s, but in the 1980s growth rates for agriculture and GDP were quite similar on average across all developing countries.

Poverty

Looking only at GDP or agricultural sector growth rates does not give a measure of success in reducing poverty. That requires more direct measures, such as the percentage of the population below some poverty level. Table 5.2 gives data from Asian countries on two such measures, the percentage of the population with incomes below nationally defined poverty lines and the percentage with incomes of less than $1 per day. The first is not so clearly comparable across countries, given that each country defines its own poverty line. The second, although arbitrary in its level, is at least comparable across countries.

ISBN 92-64-01442-X

Table 5.2. **Poverty Indicators across Asian Countries**

Country	Per Cent of Population below National Poverty Line	Per Cent of Population at <US$1/day (year)
South East Asia		
Indonesia	18.2	7.2 (2000)
Lao PDR	38.6	26.3 (1997)
Malaysia	8.1	<2.0 (1997)
Philippines	34.2	14.6 (2000)
Thailand	13.1	<2.0 (2000)
Viet Nam	37.4	17.7 (1998)
East Asia		
China	n.a.	16.1 (2000)
Korea	3.6	<2.0 (1998)
South Asia		
India	26.1	34.7 (1999)

Source: http://www.adb.org/Documents/Books/Key_Indicators/2003/xls/rt01.xls

Using the first measure, Korea has the lowest incidence of poverty (3.6 per cent). Within ASEAN, both Malaysia (8 per cent) and Thailand (13 per cent) have relatively low rates. Poverty is a little higher in Indonesia at 18.2 per cent, but the other countries (Philippines, Viet Nam and Laos) have double this level. Under the second measure, the pattern is very similar. Korea, Malaysia and Thailand all have less than 2 per cent of their population in poverty, Indonesia has 7 per cent, and the others all have more than twice the percentage in poverty as Indonesia. They range from the Philippines and China at 15 per cent and 16 per cent to India at 35 per cent. The Vietnamese data show a poverty rate of 18 per cent, but for 1998, two years earlier than for its closest comparators, China, Indonesia and the Philippines. Using data more comparable in time would almost certainly show a smaller number for Viet Nam.

A quite different measure of poverty comes from FAO data on food consumption, showing the percentage of the population that is undernourished (Table 5.3). These data cover two periods, 1990-92 and 1999-2001, and five major regions plus Indonesia and Viet Nam. Three regions have the lowest levels of under-nourishment in both periods: MENA, East Asia and Latin America. By the second period, only 10 to 11 per cent of the population in these three regions was undernourished. By contrast, the average across all developing countries was 17 per cent, and the levels for South Asia and sub-Saharan Africa were 22 per cent and 33 per cent respectively. Indonesia was below all regional averages at 6 per cent, while Viet Nam was just above the average for all developing countries. The average

ISBN 92-64-01442-X © OECD 2005

reduction in under-nourishment across all developing countries was 15 per cent, but East Asia recorded 31 per cent. Latin America had the second best regional performance, but sub-Saharan Africa performed poorly. East Asia won its impressive accomplishment despite the difficult crisis-induced recession period (1997-98). By 2000, it had achieved a level of under-nourishment as low as in any other developing region. Both Indonesia and Viet Nam also made excellent progress, reducing under-nourishment by 33 per cent and 30 per cent respectively.

Table 5.3. **Poverty Indicators across Regions: Under-nourishment**

Region/Country	Percentage Undernourished in Total Population		Percentage Change 1999/90
	1990-92	1999-2001	
MENA	8	10	+25%
East Asia/Pacific	16	11	-31%
Indonesia	9	6	-33%
Viet Nam	27	19	-30%
Latin America	13	10	-23%
South Asia	26	22	-15%
Sub-Saharan Africa	35	33	-6%
Total developing countries	20	17	-15%

Source: FAO, *The State of Food Insecurity in the World*, 2003.

Other data corroborate this success of East Asia and of Indonesia and Viet Nam specifically (Table 5.4). These data measure the percentage of the population in poverty in two ways, namely those with incomes of less than $1/day and those with incomes less than $2/day. They also indicate the incidence of child malnutrition. They cover two periods, 1990 and 2001. East Asia shows not only sharp reductions in poverty, but also a performance better than those of all other regions, although it has higher levels of poverty than do MENA, Europe and Central Asia and Latin America. Based on the poverty line of $1/day, East Asia reduced poverty by half. South Asia reduced it by almost a third, but down only to 37 per cent. In all other regions the percentage either stayed roughly constant or increased. Measuring poverty at $2/day, the number in poverty fell by 10 per cent across all developing countries during the 1990s. Only East Asia showed a large decrease. The percentage in poverty in MENA and Europe/Central Asia actually increased on this definition. The data on child malnutrition are less complete but show the same general pattern. East Asia was again the most successful region and within it Indonesia and Viet Nam did somewhat better than the regional average.

Table 5.4. **Changes in Poverty Indicators by Region**

Region	Per Cent of Population at <US$1/day		Per Cent of Population at <US$2/day		Child Malnutrition Incidence		GNI per capita	
	1990	2001	1990	1999	1990	2001	1990	2001
MENA	2.1	2.2	21.0	23.3	n.a.	n.a.	1 700	2 230
Europe/C. Asia	1.4	5.1	6.8	20.3	n.a.	n.a.	2 530	1970
E. Asia/Pacific	30.5	15.6	69.7	50.1	18.7	14.8	430	900
Indonesia	n.a.	7.2	n.a.	n.a.	34.0[a]	25.0	620	680
Viet Nam	n.a.	17.7[b]	n.a.	n.a.	45.0	34.0	130	410
Latin America	11.0	11.1	27.6	26.0	n.a.	n.a.	3 280	3 550
South Asia	45.0	36.6	89.8	84.8	64.1	53.0[a]	380	450
Sub-Saharan Africa	47.4	49.0	76.0	74.7	31.6	32.8	550	460
Developing countries	29.6	23.2	62.1	55.6	n.a.	n.a.	1 000	1 160

Notes *a)* for 1995. *b)* for 1998.
Source: World Development Indicators database, April 2002 http://www.developmentgoals.org/Goal1.xls http://www.developmentgoals.org/Poverty.htm

By all the measures of poverty examined here, East Asia clearly has the best record of all regions in reducing poverty over the last two decades. It does not have the lowest levels of income poverty, although it has as good a record as other regions in terms of malnutrition. Its income growth rates and rates of poverty reduction are routinely superior by a wide margin. Much the same can be said of Indonesia. It does not have the lowest level of poverty, consistent with its relatively low income level, but its success in poverty reduction is as good as almost any other country for which data are available. Viet Nam also has a strong poverty-reduction record, with two caveats. First, it started in 1980 as one of the poorest countries in all Asia, which made percentage improvements at this stage somewhat easier. Even by 1998, 45 per cent of its rural population and 37 per cent of its overall population still lived in poverty[4]. Second, although it has succeeded in lifting many people from poverty, it has experienced a significant widening of income differentials, particularly between rural and urban areas.

Explaining Success in Poverty Reduction

Any attempt to explain successes in reducing poverty must examine the government policies applied. Owing to the heterogeneity of country policies in East Asia and to limited data on those policies, this is possible for only two countries, Indonesia and Viet Nam. The attraction of using data

ISBN 92-64-01442-X © OECD 2005

from these two countries is that both countries have relatively large agricultural sectors and have had some successes in agricultural exports. Further, both have had success in alleviating poverty, especially Indonesia. Its record is one of the best of all countries in poverty alleviation, at least until the Asian financial crisis hit in 1997/98. Even more interesting, this country was considered almost beyond hope in its development prospects in the late 1960s and early 1970s, when its income levels were among the lowest in the world. It also had the benefit of petroleum resources, but only China has matched its record of alleviating poverty since 1970. It is still not a rich country, and it falls near the World Bank's dividing line between "low-income" and "middle-income" countries. It derived 17.5 per cent of its GDP from agriculture in 2002.

Viet Nam has interest because it is a transition economy shifting from central planning to a market economy from the later 1980s through the 1990s. Both its overall and its agricultural economic growth rates were excellent in the 1990s. Its performance in the 1980s was hampered by the stagnation that accompanied central planning in that decade and that led to its desire to shift towards a market economy. Despite growth in agricultural productivity in the 1990s, circumstances that led to a widening of the gap between rural and urban incomes may have hampered its poverty-alleviation performance. The widening occurred not from a lack of growth in rural incomes but because urban incomes rose twice as fast (60 per cent *vs.* 30 per cent between 1993 and 1998), and restricted internal migration flows did not permit equalisation of these quite different income levels. Income per capita is estimated at $400 in 2000. Agriculture accounted for about 25 per cent of GDP in 1999.

Agricultural Policies

Indonesia

Because poverty tends to concentrate in rural areas, one should start by examining policies that focus on agriculture. That sector has grown in East Asia at rates among the fastest in all developing regions — but the same cannot be said for Indonesia. Its farm sector has expanded at little more than half the growth rate of the whole economy over the last two decades, and at only 1.9 per cent per year in the 1990s it lagged behind growth in the 1980s both absolutely and relative to GDP growth. It also lagged behind agricultural growth in most other East Asian countries, as Table 5.1 showed. All this suggests that agricultural policies have not been very successful in increasing productivity growth, maintaining jobs in this sector or reducing poverty.

ISBN 92-64-01442-X

A closer examination of agricultural policies in Indonesia over the past two decades[5] supports this claim. In general, government has not devoted particularly large budget allocations to the agricultural sector, especially beyond a fairly costly fertiliser subsidy (Barichello, 2003). Although the fertiliser subsidy itself helped to increase productivity by appearing to speed adoption of the high-yielding rice varieties of the 1970s, this effect was pretty much exhausted by the middle to late 1980s. Agricultural research and extension represents one budget area where one would like to see high and growing expenditure to achieve increases in productivity. One does not find this, however. Such expenditure has not been relatively large for some years. No evident research results have given segments of agriculture a strong boost in yields, cost savings or other elements of productivity gain since the mid-1980s. Similarly, no large new expenditures on agricultural infrastructure, such as new irrigation investments, have acted to stimulate agricultural growth, especially in the 1990s. Finally, there is no real agricultural commodity policy in Indonesia. This means no sustained taxpayer-financed subsidies to purchase crops or give deficiency payments to farmers for particular crop production levels, aside from the combination of the fertiliser subsidy and rice prices somewhat higher than world market prices (by an average of 19 per cent in 1985-2000).

The other important side of agricultural policy concerns foreign trade. Indonesia has tended towards protectionism for import-competing products and *laissez-faire* for export crops. The most significant current protection covers rice, the most important crop, and sugar, a crop of doubtful comparative advantage but with considerable border protection, an average of 37 per cent over 1989-2000[6]. Soybeans have enjoyed very high rates of border protection, although it declined from 97 per cent in 1990-94 to a still sizeable 37 per cent in 1996-2000. On the export side, Indonesia's major crops are rubber, palm oil, coffee, tea, cocoa, pepper and most spices. These crops have had little support aside from some research expenditures. Indeed, periodic export taxes (notably on palm oil) have hurt them. Finally, protection in some parts of the industrial sector has the effect of increasing the value of the rupiah, taxing those crops that are export-competitive or import-competitive. On balance, then, Indonesia has done little to enhance productivity of its agricultural crops and commodities, particularly in the 1990s. Aside from periodic, short-term increases in world commodity prices, Indonesian agriculture has not had strong incentives to expand output and raise productivity, except for tree crops such as oil palm and rubber, in which Indonesia has maintained or increased its comparative advantage. Taken together, these factors are consistent with the slow growth in agricultural GDP outlined in Table 5.1, if not a major cause of it.

ISBN 92-64-01442-X © OECD 2005

Viet Nam

As noted in Table 5.1, this economy has registered relatively rapid growth in agricultural GDP. Its modest performance in 1980-90, 2.8 per cent, reflects the stagnation of the last years of central planning and the early years of reform before most of the policy and institutional changes that accompanied the shift to a market economy had time to take effect. When the take-off came, however, average agricultural growth in the 1990s became the highest of all countries in Table 5.1, including China.

Part of this rapid growth stemmed from the newly adopted institutions affecting agriculture, notably changes in property rights and land-tenure arrangements. One outcome of the Vietnamese land reform was a notable increase in land investment, in irrigation and drainage for example. The shift in decision making and land tenure from state and co-operative farms to individual family farms that began in the latter part of the 1980s resulted not only in higher yields but also in experimentation with crops relatively new to commercial production in Viet Nam. Viet Nam spent between 5 and 7 per cent of the state budget on agriculture in the 1990s (Government of Viet Nam, 2000). In the late 1990s, this went mainly into irrigation (50 per cent), land reclamation and a mix of reforestation and other forestry services (another 25 per cent). Agricultural research received only 1.7 per cent of agricultural budget expenditures, and agricultural extension another 0.6 per cent. Rural credit institutions have received considerable attention, mostly through expanding lending to agriculture through a state-owned bank.

Agricultural trade policy in Viet Nam has generally been more open than in Indonesia. This may only reflect that exports take a much larger proportion of total agricultural production than in Indonesia. Whereas Indonesia has protective border measures in place on a number of import-competing commodities, this has not been very important in Viet Nam owing to the large share of production that is exported. Heavily export-oriented rice and industrial (mostly tree) crops account for two-thirds of domestic production, not counting horticulture, cashew nuts or black pepper, where exports also are important.

These various measures resulted not only in more rapid growth in agricultural GDP over the 1990s than in all other Asian countries, but also a dramatic increase in agricultural exports. In that decade, Viet Nam became the second to fourth largest coffee and rice exporter in the world, depending on the year. It also became a major factor in the world rubber market, and exports of pork, aquaculture seafood products and some horticultural products increased substantially. With large increases in non-agricultural incomes, domestic demand expanded for many agricultural commodities, such as horticultural crops and meat. These developments involved large increases in agricultural production, better production methods and improved institutions, which collectively drove the rapid 4.2 per cent per year growth in agricultural value-added.

Industrial Growth and its Sources

In Indonesia or Viet Nam (as in most countries) rural people, even farmers, derive a sizeable portion of their household incomes from non-agricultural activities. This is striking in Indonesia but also true to an important extent in Viet Nam. Its importance lies in understanding that rural poverty depends increasingly on non-agricultural factors when non-farm incomes gain prominence in household income. How much rural households depend on non-farm income sources depends heavily on how well rural and urban labour markets are integrated. When they are highly integrated, as for most of the population of Indonesia (Naylor, 1991), growth in the industrial sector will push up its wages, which signals to people in rural areas that income prospects are more attractive in industry. If they have the education and skills necessary to take such jobs and if there are no regulatory or other barriers to migration, then labour will move from rural areas to the urban or industrial areas where economic growth is most rapid.

Such migration flows will not only tend to equalise wage rates between the two areas, subject to cost of living differences, but will also allow people in the slower-growing sectors to share in the economic gains derived from the faster-growing ones. This has immediate implications for poverty reduction in rural areas in Indonesia. With rapid industrial growth, workers will migrate from rural areas, enjoy the higher wage rates in the industrial sector and thereby pull themselves into higher income groups. This will also raise incomes in the rural regions from the normal competitive increase in rural wages (as rural employers must compete with urban industrial wage rates to hold labour) and from remittances from migrants back to rural family members. All these elements combine to provide income growth and poverty reduction in rural areas independent of the income growth in agriculture *per se*. If, however, there also is growth in the agricultural sector, this will help raise rural wage rates more directly and will succeed in holding larger quantities of labour in the farm sector.

 ISBN 92-64-01442-X © OECD 2005

Such labour-market integration can also be seen in terms of the labour supply curve in agriculture. It creates a highly elastic supply of labour to agriculture, making that sector virtually a price taker in the labour market. This has the implication that agricultural policies, in addition to world agricultural commodity markets, will not raise wage rates in agriculture. Both factors will only raise land prices and create more (or fewer) jobs, as mentioned above.

This appears to be exactly what happened in Indonesia in the two-plus decades from the early-1970s to the later 1990s, when the Asian financial crisis put a temporary end to growth rates above 6 per cent. The labour market became increasingly highly integrated over this period, as Naylor (1991) documents clearly. Not only did rural family members work at off-farm jobs in rural towns and villages, but migration flows from all rural areas to larger urban centres were common within Java, Sumatra and Bali and could be casually observed there at any time in the 1980s or 1990s. These large migration flows did not happen fortuitously. Many factors contributed, including improved education in rural areas, substantial population density, reasonable infrastructure development across much of the non-mountainous parts of the country and the absence of regulations prohibiting migration. These factors constitute the primary legacy of the Suharto regime in the rural sector.

Perhaps most important, the industrial economy expanded rapidly over much of this period. Aggregate GDP grew at approximately 7 per cent annually in 1970-96, and the industrial component usually grew even faster. This industrial growth was not restricted to the capital but occurred in many cities throughout Java and Sumatra. Its causes are more complex and difficult to assess (Barichello and Flatters, 1991). Clearly many factors were at work, beginning with appropriate macroeconomic policy, especially exchange rate policy. A relatively open trade environment was also a major contributor, especially after 1985, although protectionist policy characterised a number of sectors as well as some parts of agriculture. Protection most commonly affected industries dominated by state-owned enterprises or certain large and politically well-connected firms. Access for non-agricultural exports to open markets in the rest of the world, including the OECD countries, also contributed very positively to the exports that clearly fuelled Indonesian growth after 1985. Longer-run investment policies in education, health and infrastructure, including attention to building up rural areas and financing local government, were also at work.

Indonesia thus had presented a number of non-agricultural factors especially conducive to reducing poverty. They included rapid industrial growth as well as integrated rural-urban labour markets and the ability of large numbers of rural residents to move to urban work in higher-paying jobs. As a result and even with agricultural policies not consistently supporting increased productivity and broad income growth in agriculture, the country reduced poverty dramatically.

Contrasts in Viet Nam

Despite its quite good record in poverty reduction, Viet Nam has not seen the same proportionate reduction in poverty as has Indonesia, and its poverty levels remain quite high. At the end of the 1990s, 45 per cent of the rural population still lived below the poverty line and 18 per cent earned less than $1/day. In 2001, 19 per cent were undernourished and malnutrition affected 34 per cent of the child population.

Rapid economic growth (7.7 per cent per year) in the 1990s has continued through the Asian financial crisis to the present. In 2000 and 2001, overall economic growth was about 7 per cent per year. The industrial sector grew at an annual rate of 10 per cent over these two years and the agricultural sector at 3 to 4 per cent. Thus, unlike Indonesia, where agricultural growth has been relatively sluggish and most of the economy's growth has come from the industrial sector, Viet Nam has had enough agricultural growth to offer some help in reducing rural poverty.

Employment and wage rates also rose very quickly during the 1990s, particularly in urban areas. While this would seem sufficient to reduce rural poverty substantially, very large, startling premiums emerged for urban wages, particularly in Hanoi and Ho Chi Minh City — 50 per cent for overall wage rates and 75 per cent for skilled employment (Gallup, 2002). Nothing like such wage differentials exist across the major islands of Indonesia, and the premiums suggest that something inhibits the movement of labour to equalise wage rates. This is in fact true. Regulations control the movement of labour within Viet Nam, even if their enforcement may have been somewhat more relaxed in recent years. Required residency permits effectively tie people to the areas of their birth. However they may be enforced within smaller towns, the two largest cities use them to keep out people not born there. The regulations do not prevent migration, but migrant workers from outside Hanoi and Ho Chi Minh City operate in a grey market with the lowest wage rates within those cities. While this feature of Viet Nam's labour markets may

ISBN 92-64-01442-X © OECD 2005

distinguish it from Indonesia, it parallels a situation prevalent in China, where residency registration procedures limit access to government housing, health care and education for children.

Data on rural households' annual incomes for 1998 indicate that Vietnamese households do access off-farm income to a moderate extent. In an average rural household's income of about $700, 47 per cent came from agriculture, 19 per cent from non-farm enterprises and 34 per cent from wage and other income. The off-farm income, however, comes mostly from work in smaller cities and within a farm family's region. Wage rates have increased here also but not as quickly or as dramatically as they have in Hanoi and Ho Chi Minh City.

Thus, labour markets in Viet Nam are not as open or as integrated between rural and urban areas as they are in Indonesia, and judging by the wage premiums in the largest cities, this limits the success of poverty-alleviation efforts. The rural poor do enjoy more jobs, improved wages and better economic prospects from high growth in the agricultural sector and from the portion of overall economic growth arising in the small and medium-sized towns. Yet they find largely inaccessible the most rapidly growing wages and the large number of new big-city jobs that represent a good part of the country's 10 per cent industrial growth. Furthermore, the competitive effect on rural wages from arbitrage with the big urban labour markets is mostly lost. Yet the future does not look dim for poverty reduction. The labour-market regulations show signs of changing to a more relaxed stance on rural-urban migration. One can expect that poverty reduction will become more successful with better integration of the rural and urban labour markets.

Linkages with OECD-Country Agricultural Policies

What are the linkages between poverty-reduction efforts within Indonesia and Viet Nam and OECD-country agricultural policies? One would suspect that this connection is relatively weak in Indonesia, because its poverty-reduction successes are tied most directly to a variety of domestic non-agricultural policies. Agriculture also has not grown fast enough to be a primary vehicle for poverty reduction, although negative effects from OECD-country policies might influence this slower growth. In Viet Nam the situation is less clear because there have been weaker linkages between poverty in the rural sector and other domestic policies. Viet Nam has relatively robust agricultural growth, despite possible negative effects from OECD-country policies.

ISBN 92-64-01442-X © OECD 2005

The common argument claims that OECD countries hurt developing countries' agriculture and food sectors through domestic support policies for agriculture, through agricultural export subsidies and by limiting market access to foreign agricultural imports. That harm limits poverty alleviation or actually makes poverty worse. Trade is the main channel for this linkage, and its effects can be felt in either of two ways. OECD-country policies may affect an East Asian country's exports or imports directly, or, more likely, they may affect the markets, particularly the prices, into which the East Asian country may be selling or from which it is buying[7].

Indonesia

The agricultural sector (including aquaculture) in Indonesia has a large export component in absolute terms, averaging some $5 billion per year over the seven years from 1996 to 2002, but it accounts for only about 12 per cent of non-oil exports. The major exports aside from fish products are tree crops. The top five export commodities ranked by value for recent years are palm oil, rubber, coffee, tea and pepper. Foodstuffs (aggregated) would rank about third in such a list, as would aquaculture products (e.g. shrimp, lobster). Most food crops are not exported, although rice has been shipped periodically in the last two decades. In a typical year, rice, sugar, soybeans, corn and wheat are imported. Cotton, dairy products, meats, tobacco and cloves are also important imports. Wheat and cotton are not grown in any quantity in Indonesia and dairy production is quite modest.

In fact, Indonesia exports mostly tropical crops or products not grown in the OECD countries, so their domestic support, export subsidies and restricted market access for the traditional temperate-climate farm commodities have little effect on Indonesia's exports. Only one export crop may feel some impact, namely palm oil, because some limited substitution in consumption between palm and soybean oils may result in some price linkage between those two markets. US export subsidies and domestic support of soybeans, for example, could depress world soybean prices and result in some lowering of world palm-oil prices. This is not likely, however, given the size of US soybean support, the US share of the world soybean market and apparent concerns about the health effects of palm oils. The long-run price effects in the world soybean market would usually be small, and the onward price effects in the palm oil market would be smaller still.

ISBN 92-64-01442-X © OECD 2005

There would likely be some effects on import substitutes. Indonesia imports four product groups that OECD agricultural policies support, namely cotton, dairy products, sugar and rice. Indonesia has so little domestic cotton production that the effect is nil. It does have moderate domestic dairy output, equal to 25 to 30 per cent of consumption, and domestic policy leaves the sector completely open to world prices. Therefore, OECD-country policies have a distinct, negative effect on a relatively (for Indonesia) small number of farmers (about 100 000). For sugar, policy reforms have reduced domestic subsidies and regulations so that production is falling and imports are becoming more important. This industry also benefits from policies that insulate domestic producers from world prices to some extent, so the effect of OECD-country policies is present but it does not affect many farmers. Nevertheless, the price-depressing effects of OECD-country policies may have caused both the sugar and dairy industries to be smaller than they otherwise would be. Thus, negative effects on them are possible, and although the production affected may be relatively small the number of affected producers may be moderately substantial.

The rice sector saw some major policy changes after the financial crisis, and although the domestic policy environment remains protective, world prices have had an impact due to a shift from non-tariff barriers (NTBs) to primary use of a tariff for protection. OECD policies, particularly the Japanese, US and EU rice programmes, negatively affect world market prices and thus hurt Indonesian rice producers, who face more price sensitivity with tariffs than with NTBs in a less insulated domestic market. Policy changed again in 2004 with the introduction of a rice import ban to apply during the main harvest (January to June). If applied as written, this policy will mean higher and insulated domestic prices in the first half of the year followed by world prices plus the tariff in the second half.

Three factors govern the extent of this possible damage. First, what degree of subsidy or market-price distortion occurs owing to OECD-country programmes? Second, the US and EU shares in world rice production may be too small to have a significant effect, notwithstanding the much larger shares they hold of the world export market. Japanese rice policy is quantitatively important as well, although how much it affects Asian markets is debatable. There is no debate that it is among the most protective in the world. It closes off the Japanese market to otherwise potentially substantial imports. Its effect on Asian rice prices, at least in the short run, was illustrated in 1993/94 when imports allowed to compensate for a very poor Japanese rice crop caused Bangkok rice prices almost to double. Third, Indonesia enjoys

ISBN 92-64-01442-X © OECD 2005

some insulation at least from US policies because US farmers produce largely *japonica* rice whereas the bulk of Indonesia's output is *indica,* and these are not perfect substitutes.

To sum up, agricultural policies of the OECD countries have generally limited effects on Indonesian production and prices owing to the low level of commodity overlap. The likely effects are more substantial for sugar and dairy products, larger than the current numbers of producers or levels of production would indicate. Rice probably is most heavily affected. Unlike sugar and dairy products, any impacts in this market touch many producers and a high level of production. All these negative effects on sugar, dairy and rice production occur *via* distorted land-use decisions, limitations on potential comparative advantage and lower land rents or land prices. OECD agricultural policies help sugar, dairy and rice consumers, of course. Yet seen from the poverty-reduction perspective, they cannot have much impact on wage rates or the poorest farmers. They do lower land prices and hurt those middle-income farmers who own some land. They also reduce jobs in the sugar, dairy and rice industries and possibly dampen local economic activity, but migration to other jobs offsets the potential losses and holds wage rates steady.

Viet Nam

Viet Nam's export-intensive agriculture contributes significantly to the country's total exports. In 2000, agriculture and fish exports totalled $3.4 billion (for the seven largest agricultural commodities plus marine products) or 31 per cent of total non-oil exports. Rice, the largest export, accounted for between 4 and 5 per cent of all exports in the last three years. Coffee, fruits and vegetables, cashew nuts, rubber, black pepper and tea followed in order of export value in 2000. The three largest import categories in 2000 were cotton, sugar and wheat, with smaller amounts of soybeans imported as well. As in Indonesia, Viet Nam grows only minor amounts of cotton, but in contrast to Indonesia, sugar cane is a relatively important domestic crop (300 000 hectares).

In general, the comments made for Indonesia concerning the impact of OECD-country agricultural policies apply also to Viet Nam. It exports tropical crops, with the partial exception of vegetables, so there is little commodity overlap and hence little impact on Viet Nam's export prices. Rice represents the important exception. Most of the discussion on rice for Indonesia applies here as well. World prices often directly affect Vietnamese farmers, but policy is not as simple as in the case of an import tariff. Viet Nam has a *de facto* state-

ISBN 92-64-01442-X © OECD 2005

owned enterprise (SOE) that effectively monopolises the rice export trade, plus a quantitative export restriction that has sometimes been imposed. The exporter SOE effectively taxes export prices on the world market in varying degrees. The rice export restriction has in some periods broken the link between world and domestic prices, usually taxing domestic farmers to keep rice prices low for consumers. Thus Vietnamese rice farmers get hurt both externally through lower world rice prices and internally through the actions of a rice export monopolist.

The main import-competing crop is sugar, but the domestic sugar policy regime and its enforcement machinery are unknown. It may have mechanisms to soften or alter the impact of world market prices on domestic sugarcane prices. If not, and if world prices do prevail domestically, OECD-country agricultural policies would very likely hurt domestic sugar production by their acknowledged lowering of world prices.

The impacts that rice and sugar policies in OECD countries have on Vietnamese production, land prices and jobs will resemble those described for Indonesia[8]. The negative impact on poverty reduction is likely to be considerably more substantial. Indonesia's labour markets are so integrated that rural wage rates are largely exogenous to the rural and agricultural sector. Events that depress agricultural prices affect only land markets by lowering land prices. This will not affect the wages of landless farmers and labourers in agriculture and thus will leave poverty reduction efforts and processes largely untouched. This is much less likely in Viet Nam. With its rural and urban labour markets less well integrated, agricultural market conditions and lower prices in particular will likely depress agricultural wage rates and directly increase poverty. Other, more profitable crops may hold up rural wages and offset these effects at least partially, but rice and sugar (to a lesser extent) are crops sufficiently important as to influence rural wage rates measurably. Consequently there are valid reasons to worry that OECD-country agricultural policies damage poverty-reduction efforts in Viet Nam.

Summary and Concluding Remarks

Depending on the measure of poverty used, East Asian developing countries have poverty levels somewhat higher than in other, richer regions, partly reflecting relatively lower average income levels. Yet by any measure of poverty, no other region has reduced it as successfully as East Asia has

ISBN 92-64-01442-X © OECD 2005

done over the last two decades. This chapter considers two countries, Indonesia and Viet Nam, for which detailed information is available. The two are similar in having achieved rapid income growth and roughly similar in incomes per capita and success in poverty reduction. They show many intriguing differences as well.

Growth in both the non-agricultural and agricultural economies has contributed to poverty reduction in both countries, but with pointed differences. Indonesia enjoyed fast non-agricultural expansion over almost three decades, from 1970 to the Asian financial crisis of 1997-98. Its agriculture grew rapidly in the earlier part of this period but slowed considerably in the 1990s relative to both the rest of the economy and Viet Nam. Indonesia's considerable successes in poverty reduction in the 1990s did not arise in the agricultural sector. Instead, they arose from the tight integration of the country's urban and rural labour markets, which caused rural and urban wage rates to rise more or less together and thus spread poverty alleviation throughout the country.

In Viet Nam, industrial growth is not tied so closely with rural wages. Urban wages, particularly in Hanoi and Ho Chi Minh City, have increased much more than agricultural wages, reflecting the importance of residency permits in limiting access to urban employment. This has produced weaker links between the overall growth of the economy and rural poverty reduction. Fortunately, strong agricultural growth has raised rural wages. Thus, Viet Nam's moderately successful poverty-reduction efforts could have been much more substantial if labour-market integration like Indonesia's had been permitted.

OECD-country agricultural policies work largely through commodity markets in their impact on East Asian poverty. The developed countries' well known mechanisms for domestic support, export subsidies or inhibited market access result in lower world market prices under certain circumstances, namely:

- if the developed exporting country has world market power in a given commodity;
- if the policy (or combination of policies) in question will shift aggregate excess demand or excess supply and affect world market prices; and
- if the developing country's agricultural sector is linked to those world markets.

Such OECD-country agricultural policies will hurt the poorest farm and rural populations in developing countries if their rural wage rates are at least partially determined by agricultural-sector conditions. A variety of other

ISBN 92-64-01442-X © OECD 2005

distributional effects can occur through damage to agricultural production, jobs and land rents or prices, regardless of how rural wages are determined, although they will hurt farmers in an upper tier of rural poverty who own some land.

In Indonesia, the latter two conditions listed above are not often met. Most of its export markets involve commodities not produced or subject to trade distorting policies in OECD countries. One possible exception is palm oil, to the extent that it and soybean oil are substitutes. In the three main cases where the listed conditions are met — rice, sugar and dairy products — Indonesia has domestic policies that allow world prices to be largely transmitted to domestic markets. Here, OECD-country policies are likely to have damaged Indonesian profitability, production, jobs and land prices. Because rural wage rates in most populated areas in Indonesia are largely determined outside the agricultural sector, however, these effects are almost certainly minimal on efforts to reduce poverty of the poorest rural households, which depend on wages. On the other hand, by lowering land prices and rents, they hurt the next higher income tier of rural households, those who own small parcels of land.

Viet Nam has very similar commodity overlaps with OECD-country policies, specifically in rice and sugar. For rice, the linkage between domestic and world prices is similar to that in Indonesia, but it sometimes gets less directly transmitted due to actions of the monopoly (SOE) rice exporter. The policy details for sugar are not known, although it is not grown throughout the country. In both cases, some effects of world prices on domestic prices are likely. Unlike in Indonesia the effects on rural wage rates probably are more pronounced owing to the much lower degree of integration between the industrial and agricultural labour markets. This opens the clear possibility that OECD-country policies in these two commodity areas have negative effects on Vietnamese poverty reduction, including poverty of the lowest-income rural poor.

These two case studies can only illustrate what could be happening throughout East Asia. They do not point to general conclusions but rather to more local conclusions that follow from the situation in each country. Of greater fundamental importance, judgements on this subject require detailed knowledge of policy and economic structure in each country. Developing countries are so heterogeneous in their policies and circumstances that the effects of OECD-country agricultural policies are highly variable, as these two case studies reveal.

Notes

* The author would like to acknowledge the very helpful comments received from Gerard Viatte, Wayne Jones, Louka Katseli, Alexandra Trzeciak-Duval, Timothy Beatty and participants at the April and June OECD Workshops. None of them, however, is responsible for remaining errors or omissions.

1. The classic reference here is The World Bank, *East Asian Miracle* (1993).

2. These policies also have large budgetary costs to the OECD countries themselves.

3. This highlights the importance of defining "the rural poor". One can identify three groups: first, the very poorest, who are net consumers of rice; second, labourers and farmers who own virtually no land; and third, middle income farmers who are still poor but do own land. Although all three are important, the second group is the primary focus here, on the grounds that it has significantly lower income than those who own land and is quite large relative to the first group.

4. In both countries, poverty-alleviation successes may be somewhat tenuous because poverty levels are still moderately high and income levels are still fairly low. Large numbers of people may have been lifted above various poverty lines but for many their income situations are precarious enough that they are vulnerable to falling back into poverty in a recession. This became clear in Indonesia during the Asian financial crisis of 1997/98.

5. Prior to the mid-1980s, Indonesia had a number of public policies, often outside agricultural policy *per se*, which supported agricultural growth and employment. They included not only research and extension efforts, particularly on rice, but also investments in rural infrastructure such as irrigation, roads, communications and electrification as well as rural health and education investment. Laws on rural government finance also contributed.

6. Data on nominal rates of protection from 1985 to 2000 are provided for the four major import crops (rice, sugar, soybeans, and corn) in Barichello (2003).

7. Trade effects may arise not only from OECD-country agricultural commodity policies but also possibly through foreign aid programmes or rural development programmes.

ISBN 92-64-01442-X © OECD 2005

8. One difference worth noting is that land-use rights in Viet Nam are very widely distributed among farmers, possibly more so than is land ownership among Indonesian farmers. Thus Vietnamese farmers, including relatively poor ones, are more likely to own some land (use rights) and will be hurt both by wage-rate declines and land (use right) price declines due to OECD-country policies. This makes for a doubly negative effect from those policies.

ISBN 92-64-01442-X

Bibliography

BARICHELLO, R.R. (2003), "Taxation, Expenditure and Policy Situation Facing the Indonesian Agricultural Sector", paper prepared for International Food Policy Research Institute, mimeo, June.

BARICHELLO, R.R. and F.R. FLATTERS (1991), "Trade Policy Reform in Indonesia", reprinted in H. HILL (ed.) (2002), *The Economic Development of Southeast Asia*, Edward Elgar, Cheltenham, UK.

GALLUP, J.L. (2002), "The Wage Labor Market and Inequality in the 1990s", World Bank Working Paper #2896, Oct 2, 2002 [full text at: http://econ.worldbank.org/files/18863_wps2896.pdf]

GOVERNMENT OF VIETNAM: DONOR WORKING GROUP (2000), *Vietnam: Managing Public Resources Better*, Joint Report, Public Expenditure Review, Vol. 2: Annex D "Agricultural Sector", December.

NAYLOR, R. (1991), "The Rural Labour Market in Indonesia", *in* S. PEARSON, W. FALCON, P. HEYTENS, E. MONKE and R. NAYLOR (eds.), *Rice Policy in Indonesia*, Cornell University Press, Ithaca, NY, pp. 58-98.

WORLD BANK (1993), *East Asian Miracle*, World Bank, Washington, D.C.

Websites:

www.worldbank.org/data/wdi2003/tables/table4-1.pdf

http://www.adb.org/Documents/Books/Key_Indicators/2003/xls/rt01.xls

http://www.developmentgoals.org/Goal1.xls

http://www.developmentgoals.org/Poverty.htm

ISBN 92-64-01442-X © OECD 2005

Chapter 6

Sustaining East Asia's Economic Dynamism: The Role of Aid

Hadi Soesastro

Abstract

Foreign aid has played one of the key roles in East Asia's economic development since the early 1970s. Aid has flowed across a changing landscape with contours defined by shifting resource constraints within donor countries and evolving ideas in both donors and recipients about the main objectives of aid. East Asia is second only to Africa among the world's major regional aid destinations, so it is sensitive both to these shifts and movements in aid policies and to the coherence and incoherence that creep into them. This chapter focuses on three of the major donors to the region. Their varied approaches have brought rich and useful policy diversity. Although East Asia is not a principal destination for US development assistance, the United States exerts considerable policy influence. Australia, although not a large donor, has a visible policy influence as well. Of the three, Japan, by far the major donor, receives the most attention. It has had the difficult task of responding to internal pressures to reduce aid resources and external ones to redirect its aid objectives and co-operate more fully in international aid co-ordination. The resulting reforms include a more decentralised aid administration coupled with efforts to increase local participation in Japanese aid programmes. The chapter generally lauds Japanese aid for its accomplishments in East Asia. It argues that, while Japan should continue increasing its capacity to direct its aid towards social development, the international donor community should not expect Japan to reduce its "hard" aid for infrastructure, which has contributed so much to East Asia's development. It concludes by pointing out a nascent incoherence between aid policies designed to assist regional economic integration and Japanese policies to promote bilateral free trade agreements with key countries in the region.

Introduction

Foreign aid in East Asia has a history of over half a century. It became an important feature of the region's economic development in about the early 1970s when countries in Southeast Asia began to step up their development efforts. They drew inspiration from the achievements of Japan; Korea; Chinese Taipei and Hong Kong, China; many of which made use of international aid in their development. Japan, for instance, drew on funding from the World Bank from 1953 to 1966. Korea and Chinese Taipei received substantial sums of aid from the United States during the Cold War. All benefited from the development of large economic infrastructures, such as roads, ports, power generation and irrigation, financed largely by foreign aid. This helped to create the foundation for economic take-off as the infrastructure stimulated and facilitated large investments in resource extraction, industrial production and exports. Since 1951, Western countries have given developing countries more than $1 trillion in development assistance, including humanitarian aid.

Many other factors had equal if not more importance. Both recipients and donors understood that foreign aid should be seen as only a supplement to recipients' own efforts. Political stability and social integration were critical. Good infrastructure, especially in large countries such as Indonesia, also contributes to social and political cohesion. A certain level of human capacity development through formal or informal education had to be achieved. The right economic policies had to be adopted. To some extent foreign aid also played a role here, but governments in East Asia themselves brought these factors under an overarching framework employed as an instrument to manage development. In most cases, the framework took the form of five-year (or longer) development plans. They were of different scope and quality, and their implementation proceeded under a variety of political systems, including hard or soft authoritarian rule. Whatever their political systems, economies that adopted market-oriented regimes became attractive recipients of foreign aid from Western countries, especially during the Cold War.

East Asia's dramatic, historic change is still unfolding. The development of Korea has been used (and misused) to illustrate what a nation can achieve within one generation. Yet success itself calls for further changes. East Asia's *authoritarian developmentalism*, or authoritarianism with capacity (Ohno, 2002), sooner or later has to give way to more democratic systems. Some countries were ill prepared for this eventuality. Indonesia is a case in point, but there are encouraging signs that the foundation for a democratic polity and society

 ISBN 92-64-01442-X © OECD 2005

is slowly taking shape. Governments in the region face a host of new challenges, for which they often are less prepared and poorly equipped. That of globalisation alone cannot be underestimated. Successful introduction of new rules for a globalised national economy and the creation of new economic institutions to manage it require a change in mindset and new capacity in the state bureaucracy as well as private corporations. These things cannot happen overnight, but globalisation also will not wait. Sustaining East Asia's economic dynamism in the years to come hinges on the success of the region's economies in undertaking this transformation in the shortest time possible. Is there a role for development assistance? The world of aid, the aid "industry", itself is going through major changes. Can they effectively respond to East Asia's changing needs?

This chapter attempts to address these issues. It is not an historical account or an empirical study of the role of aid in East Asia's development. The first section discusses the changing landscape of development assistance and examines the place of East Asia in it. The second focuses on the recent evolution of development assistance policy. It briefly examines the recent policies and practices of aid disbursement of three major sources of official development assistance (ODA) to East Asia, namely Japan, the United States and Australia[1]. The third section focuses on Japan's efforts to reform its ODA policy, because Japan is the most important donor for the region and is likely to remain so for many years. The fourth section looks at Japan's ODA from the perspective of selected East Asian countries and highlights the issues, lessons and recommendations that have emerged on how aid could work to help meet the challenges faced by the region. A concluding section follows.

The Changing Landscape of Development Assistance: Implications for East Asia

In his survey of development assistance in Asia, Peter McCawley (1998) proposed that it has revolved around two main issues in recent years, namely resources and ideas. The donor community both is under constant pressure at home to reduce the resources allocated to foreign aid and has a preferred set of ideas to promote. On the other hand, the recipient community wants to see the volume of aid maintained and has its own ideas about development and the role that aid can play. It is probably correct to say that these issues still characterise the current development-assistance landscape in general.

Pressures to reform the aid-giving process have mounted since the early 1990s, possibly triggered by a widespread sense of frustration that the billions of dollars spent on aid have had only meagre results in eradicating poverty world-wide. This may have caused the stagnation in the volume of aid throughout the 1990s (Table 6.1). It certainly led to the development of new ideas about aid. McCawley was rather suspicious, however, that some of these ideas may simply seek consistency with the resource constraint.

Table 6.1. **Net ODA from Selected OECD Countries, 1993-2002**
($ million)

Country	1993	1997	1998	1999	2000	2001	2002
Australia	953	1 061	960	982	987	873	989
Canada	2 400	2 045	1 707	1 706	1 744	1 533	2 006
France	7 915	6 307	5 742	5 639	4 105	4 198	5 486
Germany	6 954	5 857	5 581	5 515	5 030	4 990	5 324
Japan	11 259	9 358	10 640	12 162	12 508	9 846	9 328
Netherlands	3 525	2 947	3 042	3 314	3 135	3 172	3 338
New Zealand	98	154	130	134	113	112	122
United Kingdom	2 920	3 433	3 864	3 426	4 501	4 579	4 924
United States	10 123	6 878	8 786	9 145	9 955	11 420	13 290
Other DAC (13)	11 001	10 425	11 635	10 389	10 671	11 602	13 467
Total DAC (22)	56 148	48 465	52 087	52 233	53 749	52 335	58 274

Note: Figures in parentheses denote number of countries.
Source: OECD Development Assistance Committee (DAC) updated January 2004.

The volume of ODA provided by OECD countries tripled in the 1970s, from less than $7 billion in 1970 to a little over $21 billion in 1979. In the 1980s, it fell short of doubling, from $26 billion in 1980 to $46 billion in 1989. In the 1990s, it increased from about $52 billion (including debt forgiveness) in 1990 to $59 billion in 1994 and 1995, but then declined to $53 billion in 1999. Japan's ODA rose until 1995, then experienced a major drop in 1996. It increased temporarily from 1998 to 2000, largely to provide increased assistance to countries hit by the Asian financial crisis. In 1997, Japanese Prime Minister Ryutaro Hashimoto had already announced that Japan's ODA budget would fall by 10 per cent a year for three years as part of his administrative and fiscal reform agenda.

Discussions about paring ODA led to serious a re-examination and re-evaluation of ODA in Japan. While many aspects of Japan's ODA needed rectification, the general opinion held that on the whole ODA had a meaningful place in the nation's post-war policy (Iokibe, 2003). Nonetheless,

ISBN 92-64-01442-X © OECD 2005

Japan's ODA renewed its decline in 2001. In 2003, the Japanese government issued a new ODA Charter meant to arrest this decline and if possible to give ODA a renewed push.

This is especially important for Japan because development assistance from the United States began to increase in 1998. By 2001, the volume of US ODA surpassed that of Japan, which had led the donor community by this measure since 1989. Various developments since 2000 appeared to have given a new push to increasing aid to the developing world. In September 2000 the UN Millennium Summit was held, following a meeting between the leaders of developing countries and the G-8 countries. The Millennium Summit adopted the Millennium Declaration. Integrated with the International Development Goals (IDGs) proposed earlier by the OECD DAC, this provided a common framework for the international community called the Millennium Development Goals (MDGs). In May 2001, the third UN Conference on the Least Developed Countries was held. Moreover, the 11 September terrorist attack could have been a decisive factor in President Bush's decision to increase aid.

An International Conference on Financing for Development held in Monterey, Mexico in March 2002 produced the Monterey Consensus. It urged developed countries to make efforts towards an ODA target of 0.7 per cent of GDP. Before this conference the United States and the EU had announced initiatives to increase their ODA. The Bush Administration has found a new purpose. It created a new medium, the Millennium Challenge Account (MCA) to channel its own increased funding. This new initiative has a significant governance component. The MCA will be administered through a new agency, the Millennium Challenge Corporation, and will disburse an additional $5 billion annually over current levels from 2006 onwards. It will be made available to "nations that root out corruption, respect human rights, and adhere to the rule of law ... invest in better health care, better schools and broader immunisation ... [and] have more open markets and sustainable budget policies, nations where people can start and operate a small business without running the gauntlets of bureaucracy and bribery" (Bush, 2002). In December 2002, US Secretary of State Colin Powell announced a second US initiative, the US-Middle East Partnership. Aimed at promoting democracy in the Muslim world, it has three pillars: education, economic reform and private-sector development, and strengthening civil society.

Amidst the great deal of rhetoric about aid for the poor, McCawley (1998) observed that the picture is much more complex, because foreign aid is generally the outcome of a rough-and-tumble internal bureaucratic and political process. The process is certainly complex in the United States, but also the most transparent. McCawley (*Ibid.*, p. 42) cited a survey of US foreign-aid policy by the Congressional Budget Office stating that:

> "The aid resources of bilateral donors, including the United States, tend to follow the donor's political and strategic priorities, not those of the countries that have the greatest need from a development perspective .... [F]oreign aid has been used primarily as a foreign policy tool .... Promoting economic development and human welfare has been an objective of US foreign aid but, overall, a secondary one".

Nevertheless, Table 6.1 shows that by 2002 total ODA from the DAC countries increased to $58.3 billion. Except for Japan, Spain and Austria, all other countries increased their assistance to developing countries. Japan further reduced its ODA budget by 5.8 per cent in FY 2003 (in yen), and another cut of 4.8 per cent (also in yen) was expected for FY 2004. Japan's financial situation is perhaps the major constraint. It remains unclear how these further reductions will affect the East Asian countries, the main destination of Japan's ODA.

McCawley noted that a recent, widely held perception in Western countries that Asia no longer needs foreign aid could affect aid flows to East Asia. He further noted two lines of argument — first, that the so-called Asian tigers and "near tigers" are doing well and do not seem to need foreign assistance; and second, that most obstacles to development are self-inflicted by a refusal to adopt good economic policies. Countries in East Asia that adopted sensible, pro-growth strategies are doing well and thus do not need aid. Countries that failed to take proper steps to tackle their own problems will only waste scarce aid. Indeed, Southeast Asian economies such as Malaysia and Thailand that have performed well have either already graduated from international assistance programmes or will soon do so. Malaysia has taken steps to become an ODA donor. Nevertheless, these countries continue to value development assistance that could come in different forms. They continue to seek assistance in areas of so-called "soft power", namely technology and knowledge. It is not difficult to see that East Asia is a very diverse region. The poorer part of the region definitely needs continued foreign assistance to be able to take off economically.

The least developed countries in East Asia, such as Cambodia and Laos, received the highest ODA per capita, $45 and $33 respectively in 2001 (Table 6.2). Malaysia received only $1.00 and also the least in absolute terms.

 ISBN 92-64-01442-X © OECD 2005

Thailand received $5.00 per capita, Indonesia and the Philippines $7.00 each, and Viet Nam $18. These amounts correlate with levels of economic development. Cambodia and Laos still depend on foreign aid for 60 to 70 per cent of their investment (gross capital formation). Foreign aid met about 18 per cent of the Viet Nam central government's budget in 2001. Overall, ODA to East Asia (and the Pacific) amounted to $4.00 per capita. South Asia received the same, which was much lower than ODA per capita to all other parts of the developing world.

Table 6.2. **ODA Indicators by Recipient, 2001**

	Total ($ million)	Per Capita ($)	Per Cent of GNI	Per Cent of Investment	Per Cent of Government Budget
Cambodia	409	33	12.4	66.9	--
China	1 460	1	0.1	0.3	2.2
Indonesia	1 501	7	1.1	4.9	4.3
Laos	243	45	14.6	62.9	--
Malaysia	27	1	0	0.1	--
Myanmar	127	3	--	--	0.3
Philippines	577	7	0.8	4.6	4.2
Thailand	281	5	0.2	1.0	1.2
Viet Nam	1 433	18	4.4	14.1	18.0
Total, East Asia and Pacific	7 394	4	0.5	1.3	--
Memo items:					
South Asia	5 871	4	1.0	4.3	--
Sub-Saharan Africa	11 933	21	4.6	24.6	--
Europe and Central Asia	9 783	21	1.0	4.3	--
Latin America and Caribbean	5 985	12	0.3	1.6	--

Note: -- = not available.
Source: World Bank, *World Development Report* 2004.

Will the less developed countries in East Asia be able to secure the amount and kind of funding they need? As McCawley observed, the East Asian countries have been wary of the implications of the new development agenda vigorously promoted since the early 1990s. Oriented towards "softer" and more people-oriented approaches, it has merit in drawing more serious attention to issues of poverty and human security. In 1996, DAC members reaffirmed poverty reduction as the ultimate goal of development. This is certainly to be applauded, but the swings of the pendulum in ideas about development and development assistance could become disruptive to these countries' development efforts.

Akiyama *et al.* (2003) describe the evolution of development assistance as influenced closely by that of ideas on development. They distinguish three periods. In the first, from the end of World War II to the mid-1970s, people believed in the effectiveness of government-led development and large infrastructure projects. Akiyama *et al.* call this the era of the engineers. When this approach failed to produce trickle-down effects, belief in the power of open markets championed by neo-classicists replaced it. This era of the economists, from the mid-1970s to the late 1980s, culminated in the Washington Consensus. International financial institutions (IFIs) made loans conditional on market-liberalising policy changes. Then the neo-classicists came under attack in turn and yielded to the emphasis on poverty reduction through targeted policies and to new, more people-centred views. Poverty reduction became the focus in this era of the social scientists. Despite a lot of preaching about the new paradigm of poverty reduction through sustainable development, the dynamics of this relationship remain unclear.

The competition of ideas unfolds not only between the developed countries as donors and the developing countries as recipients, but also within each group. On the receiving end and often not able to do things right, the developing countries have asserted their views rather weakly. They welcome calls for greater "ownership" of developing countries in the development process but feel that in the end the donors will put their own priorities ahead of the needs of recipients. Donors also have diverging views on the role of aid and how it should work. It is not at all clear why all donors must have the same, uniform view and should adopt the same approach to development and development assistance. Development is a complex process and no single approach would fit all. Elements in each of the schools of thought described above could be incorporated into tailor-made strategies that respond to the needs of recipients. If they are serious about ownership, donors must adopt a humble, non-doctrinaire attitude on development assistance, even if, for bureaucratic and political reasons, development agencies often cannot be flexible.

Better co-ordination among donors, not uniformity of ideas and approaches, should be strengthened. Some donor governments and agencies have come up with new, innovative ideas that have enriched the development assistance menu. The Department for International Development (DFID) of the United Kingdom led in fully untying its aid in the effort to help realise the MDGs. It further suggested that donors could do best by providing aid

ISBN 92-64-01442-X © OECD 2005

money directly to recipient governments (programme aid), to be used at their discretion. Because money, including aid money, is fungible, the DFID argued that this approach has several advantages. It could reduce donors' project costs for design, appraisal, monitoring and evaluation. It also would more effectively accommodate basic development needs that require long-term, recurrent funding, such as education and health care. Moreover, it would provide recipient government officials themselves the opportunity to take the lead in designing, implementing and evaluating projects (Lowcock, 2002).

The Scandinavian countries have joined the United Kingdom at the forefront in proposing that programme-based assistance should replace project-based assistance. Aid should be given for each economic and social sector, and funds from donors and international organisations should be pooled. They also propose to introduce common, standard procedures for aid implementation by donor countries to increase efficiency of aid disbursement. Japan, because its government needs accountability to Japanese taxpayers, has raised concerns about the excessive promotion of aid co-ordination and of standardising everything by "bringing the flag down" (Iimura, 2001).

Japan appears on the conservative side of the debate in arguing that sustained economic growth can greatly assist poverty reduction. It maintains that East Asian experience has substantiated the validity of this approach. It holds the view that assistance towards poverty reduction should focus not only on social-sector support, such as education and health and medical care, but also on economic support, including improvements in economic infrastructures and legal systems and human resource development. These can spur economic growth in recipient countries through expansion of trade and investment, fostering the private sector and promotion of technology transfer (Ministry of Foreign Affairs, Japan, 2004). East Asian countries basically subscribe to such an approach, but they would like to ensure the right balance in its implementation. Japan itself has not been a forceful voice in setting international development assistance policy. Compared with other DAC members, it has allocated a much larger share of its ODA to economic infrastructure development and a smaller share to social and administrative infrastructure (Table 6.3).

Table 6.3. **Commitments of Bilateral ODA by Major Purposes, Selected OECD Countries, 2002**
(per cent of total)

	DAC Total	Australia	France	Germany	Japan	United Kingdom	United States
Social and admin. infrastructure	33.8	35.5	33.5	33.5	23.8	34.9	42.3
Economic infrastructure	12.3	1.6	3.4	11.1	37.7	6.4	12.3
Production	6.8	9.3	4.1	4.1	11.6	7.9	6.8
Emergency aid	7.8	14.9	5.9	4.8	1.4	12.0	7.8
Other	39.3	38.7	53.1	46.5	25.5	38.8	30.8

Source: OECD (2004), Table 19.

Beyond debate on resources and ideas, the issue of policy coherence has also re-emerged. The Monterey Consensus appealed for enhanced policy coherence in addition to confirming that financing for development needs to be secured through all possible means. The 1992 DAC Report had already recognised the need for more coherent approaches to development co-operation, and in 2002 OECD Ministers reiterated it. Apart from its impact on the effectiveness of aid, policy coherence of OECD members becomes more important for developing countries as they become more integrated into the world economy. Aid is no longer the main economic policy instrument that developed countries apply towards developing countries. Economic relations have become more diversified and have deepened.

Policy coherence is certainly relevant for East Asia. As early as the late 1970s, ASEAN began to develop dialogues with its main economic partners (the USA, Japan, the EU, etc.), and the ASEAN side called for the developed countries to take a holistic view of aid, trade, and investment to avoid policy incoherence. ASEAN repeatedly expressed its appreciation for the aid given to the members, but appealed for better access to developed-country markets and for increased investment from them. The United States rejected the ASEAN proposal for a STABEX arrangement to cover ASEAN commodity exports, similar to that between the EC and the ACP countries, but Japan received it more favourably. An ASEAN-Japan STABEX arrangement failed to emerge, however, because the United States opposed Japan's involvement in it (Soesastro, 1980). As is further discussed later, Japan has had an interest in promoting regional co-operation in Southeast Asia and has seen it as beneficial to Japan. It has used some of its economic policy instruments to forge greater co-operation amongst ASEAN members. In 1977 at the ASEAN Summit in

ISBN 92-64-01442-X © OECD 2005

Kuala Lumpur, Japan firmly tied a $1 billion aid package to the five scheduled ASEAN industrial projects, provided that "each is established as an ASEAN project". In trade, in addition to several improvements of the Japanese generalised systems of preferences (GSP) and at the request of ASEAN, Japan agreed to introduce ASEAN cumulative rules of origin (CRO). Examples of policy incoherence abound, however. Fukasaku *et al.* (1995) describe some of them involving Japan, the United States and the EU in relation to the ASEAN countries. Efforts to further policy coherence may bear fruit under a peer review mechanism. The OECD has one and indeed uses it. Yet developing countries cannot take part in it, although they are on the receiving end. Aid policy, if seen within the framework of enhancing policy coherence, will have to maintain flexibility.

A final issue concerns channelling ODA directly through civil society organisations. They have emerged in East Asia. Their numbers have multiplied rapidly and many deliver services to people, especially the poor. In East Asia they demand increasingly to become a major force in the aid industry. In question is how this demand can be accommodated meaningfully in the changing landscape of development assistance in East Asia and elsewhere.

ODA Policies of Major Donors towards East Asia

DAC countries direct ODA mainly towards Africa, where the needs are greatest. In 2001-02, of total bilateral ODA, about 36 per cent went to Africa. East Asia came next with 19.5 per cent, followed by South and Central Asia with 16.6 per cent. Africa and Asia thus are the largest recipients of aid. In comparison, Latin America received only 7.5 per cent and the Middle East 3.9 per cent (OECD, 2004). Table 6.4 suggests that East Asia has become somewhat more important over the years, as its share in total ODA from DAC members increased from 14.4 per cent in 1981-82 to 17.2 per cent in 1991-92 and 19.5 per cent in 2001-02. This may seem rather surprising. Japan allocated almost half its ODA to East Asia, and Australia about 40 per cent. East Asia's share in Portugal's ODA also was high (38 per cent), perhaps largely because of aid directed to Timor Leste. The other figures are less surprising. Many studies have already examined this issue, and it needs no further examination here.

Table 6.4. **Gross Disbursement of ODA by DAC Members to East Asia**
(percentages of total)

	1981-82	1991-92	2001-02
Australia	17.1	34.5	42.0
Austria	16.5	22.1	11.4
Belgium	10.6	12.7	7.5
Canada	6.3	15.2	12.1
Finland	16.8	10.6	14.7
France	3.2	7.8	9.1
Germany	12.5	12.0	16.5
Greece	--	--	0.2
Ireland	0.5	2.8	2.4
Italy	4.1	9.0	3.3
Japan	51.0	49.5	48.0
Luxembourg	--	2.9	13.2
Netherlands	12.7	11.5	11.5
New Zealand	15.7	12.0	20.5
Norway	4.8	6.2	6.3
Portugal	--	0.0	37.7
Spain	--	17.9	9.3
Sweden	17.5	10.8	11.1
Switzerland	4.4	9.6	8.3
United Kingdom	3.3	8.6	6.0
United States	5.3	3.2	6.3
Total DAC	14.4	17.2	19.5

Source: As for Table 6.3.

To illustrate the range of ODA policies that East Asian countries can tap, the following subsections examine in succession the overall ODA policies of three DAC countries, the United States, Japan and Australia. This variety of policies has enriched the development-assistance landscape in East Asia.

United States

East Asia is not a major destination of US ODA, but the United States is a major donor because it exerts an important policy influence in recipient countries. It has regained and held its position as the world's largest ODA donor since 2001 and has argued that, based on a "full measure", its total assistance to developing countries is significantly larger than its ODA. In 2000, for example, ODA was estimated at only 18 per cent of US total international assistance to developing countries, which reached approximately

ISBN 92-64-01442-X © OECD 2005

$56.2 billion, slightly more than the combined ODA of all DAC countries ($53.7 billion). An additional 22 per cent consisted of all other US government assistance (including security assistance). The remaining 60 per cent came from US private sources — foundations, corporations, private voluntary organisations, universities and colleges, religious congregations and individuals. A US government report argued that "[O]fficial development assistance is a limited and outdated way of measuring a country's giving, and donors should re-evaluate it, given the enormous growth in the private sector around the world" (USAID, 2002).

As mentioned earlier, the United States has also pledged to provide additional resources of $5 billion a year in 2006 and thereafter to help realise the MDGs through its Millennium Challenge Account. This funding will be made available "to support reformers and reward good performance". Two principles will guide overall US ODA: first, to promote the participation of beneficiaries in programme design and implementation; and second, to broaden development partnerships by including more private firms, universities, foundations and private and voluntary organisations.

In assessing the role of US foreign aid, USAID (2002) concluded that the different types of US foreign aid have had varying success. Disaster relief and humanitarian aid have been regarded as successful and have received the strongest support from the American public. In fact, the US prided itself as being a leader in the field. Security assistance has contributed mainly to stronger alliances and agreements. The Report noted however, that since the 11 September terrorist attack, the focus has concentrated on the effectiveness of foreign aid in influencing developing-country policies. For economic assistance, the United States agrees with what it regards as an emerging consensus in the development community that aid reduces poverty only when economic policies support sustained economic growth and when the benefits of growth are widely shared.

The United States has outlined a progressive and rich agenda for its aid to support growth in developing countries. First, it should provide direct financial support for policies, programmes and projects through bilateral assistance, to improve agricultural productivity, implement competitiveness strategies, build infrastructure and provide scholarships and technical training. Second, it should engage developing countries in policy dialogue, often with the explicit or implicit promise of delivering more aid if policy actions are taken. Third, it should produce and disseminate new knowledge about development through economic research or project activities funded by USAID and other US government agencies. Fourth, it should involve the

ISBN 92-64-01442-X © OECD 2005

US in broader, often multilateral, discussions during diplomatic and trade negotiations, to help open up the door to the $10 trillion US economy. Fifth, it should help connect with the US economy through trade and investment, which will provide a vital engine of growth for developing countries. Sixth, it should help countries build the capacity to trade and to take part in multilateral trade negotiations.

In its economic growth policies towards East Asia, USAID has defined its assistance as efforts to increase competition, transparency and accountability in capital markets and other financial sector institutions. Its programmes mean to liberalise international trade, increase the degree of competition within domestic economies, eliminate restraints on foreign and domestic investment and privatise infrastructure. The programmes in East Asia also are designed to encourage sound natural-resource management, energy-sector reform, biodiversity conservation and clean urban and industrial development. The other main areas of support are in health, democracy, conflict resolution and humanitarian assistance.

USAID has stated that it seeks to continue to work with other donors and United Nations agencies to reach a consensus on development priorities and to co-ordinate programmes in every USAID-assisted country in the region. In particular, it seeks new opportunities to co-operate with Japan on parallel programmes in the region (www.usaid.gov/pubs/cbj2003/ane/).

US ODA to East Asia amounted to $298 million in 2002. It consisted of Development Assistance, the Economic Support Fund, PL 480 (Title II), and the Child Survival and Health Programs Fund. Indonesia received the largest share (43 per cent), followed by the Philippines (23.8 per cent), Cambodia (11.7 per cent) and Timor Leste (8.4 per cent). Other countries received much smaller amounts.

Australia

Although not a large donor, Australia has a visible presence in East Asia. It believes its international development co-operation programme helpful in advancing Australia's national interest by assisting developing countries to reduce poverty and achieve sustainable development. Its programme in East Asia aims to help build a secure, prosperous and democratic region and to contribute to global efforts to reduce poverty. Five guiding themes (www.ausaid.gov.au/keyaid/default.cfm) shape Australia's efforts:

ISBN 92-64-01442-X © OECD 2005

- *Governance:* promoting democratic and accountable government and effective administration.
- *Globalisation:* assisting developing countries to access and maximise the benefits from trade and new information technologies.
- *Human capital:* improving basic service to support stability and government legitimacy.
- *Security:* strengthening regional security by enhancing partner governments' capacity to prevent conflict, enhance stability and manage trans-boundary challenges.
- *Sustainable resource management:* promoting sustainable approaches to the management of the environment and the use of scarce resources.

Australia's ODA to East Asia amounted to A$484.6 million in 2002-03. Indonesia was the largest recipient (27.2 per cent), followed by Viet Nam (14.6 per cent), the Philippines (13.1 per cent), China (12.5 per cent) and Timor Leste (11.6 per cent). Other recipients are Cambodia and Laos. ODA to Thailand has dropped significantly as Thailand graduates from ODA requirements.

Country strategy papers help Australia to manage its ODA. Its bilateral development co-operation programme with Indonesia aims at strengthening economic and financial management, helping build the institutions of democracy, promoting stability and security and improving the quality and accessibility of government service delivery, particularly in the eastern part of Indonesia. Its programme with Viet Nam focuses on strengthening the institutional governance required for a competitive market economy and improving productivity and links to markets for the rural poor in the Mekong Delta and Central Coast region. The strategy for the Philippines has three key objectives: first, to improve economic governance in key ministries to create the environment for broad-based growth; second, to strengthen security and stability through counter-terrorism capacity building and support for the Mindanao peace process; and third, to raise living standards of the rural poor in the south of the country. In China, the programme also stresses improved governance and policy reforms, including capacity building to enhance regional trade and investment.

Japan

Japan is the most important source of ODA to East Asia. Its share of total ODA flows to some ASEAN countries (Indonesia, Philippines and Viet Nam) has been on the order of 50 per cent to 80 per cent (Table 6.5). About 60 per cent of its ODA goes to Asia as a whole. In 2002, China, Indonesia, Thailand, the Philippines and Viet Nam belonged to the ten top recipients. Aid relationships between Japan and East Asia, particularly ASEAN countries, quite intensive since the late 1960s, have also evolved greatly.

Table 6.5. **The Top Five DAC Countries' ODA Disbursements to Selected East Asian Countries, 2000**

	First	Second	Third	Fourth	Fifth
Cambodia	Japan (40.0)	Australia (10.4)	France (8.7)	United States (8.7)	Germany (7.8)
China	Japan (61.2)	Germany (16.9)	United Kingdom (6.6)	France (3.7)	Spain (2.5)
Indonesia	Japan (60.1)	United States (10.8)	Netherlands (8.9)	Austria (5.0)	Australia (4.5)
Laos	Japan (59.0)	Sweden (7.5)	Germany (6.8)	France (6.6)	Australia (6.1)
Malaysia	Japan (55.2)	Denmark (31.2)	Germany (12.7)	Australia (6.7)	Canada (5.1)
Myanmar	Japan (76.1)	United States (5.1)	Norway (4.3)	Australia (3.5)	Netherlands (2.3)
Philippines	Japan (60.6)	United States (15.1)	Australia (7.1)	Germany (4.6)	Netherlands (2.0)
Thailand*	Japan (88.5)	Germany (5.8)	Denmark (3.0)	Australia (1.3)	Finland (0.05)
Viet Nam	Japan (74.1)	France (4.2)	Denmark (3.3)	Belgium (3.0)	Sweden (3.0)

Notes * 1999. Figures in parentheses indicate shares of recipient country's total ODA.
Source: Ministry of Foreign Affairs, Japan (2004).

The following section discusses Japan's overall ODA policies. Here, the focus rests on its policies towards ASEAN, which have seen dramatic shifts (Hirono, 2001). They stemmed from changes in the Japanese economy, major industrial restructuring in Japan and the economic expansion of ASEAN and other East Asian economies. Hirono examined this evolution within three periods of Japan's relations with East Asia, namely those of fast trade expansion (1951-70), of rapid FDI expansion reinforced by increased foreign aid and trade (1971-90) and of hopes, crises and uncertainties (1991 to the present).

ISBN 92-64-01442-X © OECD 2005

Much has been written about the early period of Japan's aid policy towards Southeast Asia, which began with war reparations in the early 1950s. In 1959, Japan established a Fund for the Economic Development of Southeast Asia in the Eximbank of Japan to assist Southeast Asian countries to accelerate their economic development. In 1963, it organised a Ministerial Conference for the Economic Development of Southeast Asian Countries.

The following period saw major changes not only in Japan's ODA towards Asia (including ASEAN), but also in its trade and investment policies towards Asia. Japan began to open its market and promoted the expansion of FDI. The anti-Japanese riots in Southeast Asia led to a desire to develop "heart-to-heart" relations (Fukuda's 1977 Doctrine). Japan announced that it would double its ODA every three to five years beginning in 1978. Most importantly, it enshrined the basic philosophy of its ODA as a supplement to recipients' own efforts for raising domestic savings and development capacity, with ODA going preferably to sectors that would constitute a basic foundation and contribute most to national economic development.

The ongoing industrial restructuring of Japan in the 1980s led to the initiative of MITI Minister Tamura in 1987 to harmonise ASEAN's industrial development with Japan's restructuring. The proposed New Asian Industries Development Plan (New AID Plan) did not receive support in Southeast Asia because it was seen as a scheme to be controlled largely by Japan (Thee, 1994). Nonetheless, Japan-Asian economic partnership improved significantly during this period and continued to do so later in the wider framework of Asia-Pacific co-operation.

Japan played a significant role during the financial crisis in 1997/98, despite its own financial difficulties and deep recession. It was the first and largest bilateral donor to assist the crisis-hit countries. It made available $19 billion ($4 billion to Thailand, $5 billion to Indonesia and $10 billion to Korea) as part of the international rescue package organised by the IMF. In addition, it announced the New Miyazawa Plan to offer $30 billion for economic reforms to help the crisis-hit countries regain the confidence of international investors.

Japan's relations with East Asia, particularly with ASEAN, have expanded rapidly and have become deeper and more diversified. ODA has played an important role, especially in increasing trade and investment relations. In his survey, Hirono (2001) proposed that Japan's ODA to ASEAN should be re-directed in numerous ways towards:

ISBN 92-64-01442-X © OECD 2005

- the new ASEAN members;
- the social, environmental and humanitarian sectors;
- grassroots co-operation;
- promoting trade and investment;
- NGOs;
- policy-based technical co-operation;
- sector- or programme-based technical and financial co-operation;
- the creation and reinforcement of the environment conducive to adoption and application of new technologies;
- enhancing regional and sub-regional co-operation;
- more efficient and effective monitoring and evaluation of ODA and ODA-related projects;
- complementing ODA from the more advanced ASEAN members to less developed countries within and outside the region; and
- more diversified ODA to meet the diverse needs and requirements of each country in the region.

Summary

East Asia has clearly benefited from the range of ODA programmes offered by the donors, even if their precise impact on development cannot easily be measured. The United States and Australia help strengthen capacity for policy development and institution building as well as improving governance. The amounts involved may not be large, but the impact can be significant if the programmes are designed in the right way. Most of the criticisms that these countries are trying to impose their economic and political agenda on the recipient countries come from groups with nationalist traditions or those that resist change. One can sense an increased will within the recipient countries themselves, however, to promote improved economic governance and democratic political systems. Countries in the region have also made use of the large funding provided by Japan for economic infrastructure development. Criticisms have arisen about the funding of large projects and the social dislocations and environmental damage that they have caused,

ISBN 92-64-01442-X © OECD 2005

and efforts are ongoing to minimise these impacts. No other donor currently supplies ODA in sufficient quantities to meet the infrastructure requirements for further growth in the region.

Recipient countries do believe that greater co-ordination among donors would be beneficial, but they do not support uniformity in policy. They have clear views on the comparative advantages of different donors, and they want to be able to optimise the policy mix. Japan, for instance, has a clear advantage in economic infrastructure development. Nonetheless, it may have to adjust its ODA policies to changing conditions and needs in East Asia.

Reform of Japan's ODA

Since the beginning of the 1990s Japan has felt pressure for changes in its ODA policy, to adapt it to changing international aid strategies and to secure domestic support for ODA. Kawai and Takagi (2004) give an excellent account of the challenges facing Japan's ODA policy. On the domestic front, the Japanese economy stagnated for over a decade, the business community expressed growing opposition to now largely untied ODA and the public demanded greater visibility and accountability. Feeling increased that ODA did not yield returns commensurate with its costs, even considering it merely as a diplomatic tool. International criticism focused on Japan's tendency to lend for infrastructure-related projects and its hesitation to participate more openly in the multilateral framework. Kawai and Takagi summarise the specific criticisms as follows:

- It has no coherent national strategy.
- It lacks transparency and efficiency and is wasteful.
- The principles embodied in the ODA Charter of 1992 have not been strictly followed. In particular, ODA should not go to countries like China with large military spending and weapons of mass destruction.
- ODA is biased excessively towards hard infrastructure and places insufficient emphasis on soft infrastructure and social development.
- It is not participatory and does not promote partnership with other stakeholders in the international development community, including other bilateral donors and civil society.
- It is "faceless" and does not benefit Japanese taxpayers commercially, diplomatically or otherwise.

Kawai and Takagi recommend changes in seven main features of Japan's ODA.

— First, loans have a much larger share than for other DAC members. In 2001, they accounted for 27.6 per cent, grants for 48.2 per cent (of which 19.3 per cent was for technical assistance) and contributions to multilateral organisations for 23.3 per cent. The high share of loans reflects the institutional structure of Japan's aid administration, namely the importance of off-budget funding from the Fiscal Investment and Loan Program (FILP), which allowed Japan to expand its ODA rapidly over the years. The justification for ODA loans, called yen loans, argues that development assistance supports self-help efforts by developing countries. This essentially good feature of the programme requires governance structures in place to ensure that the loans are properly used. Loans also risk an impact on recipients' sovereign debt, especially in an era of volatile exchange-rate movements.

— Second, untying loans has resulted in the dominance of untied aid. The share of Japanese firms in ODA-related procurement declined from 70 per cent in the 1980s to about 20 per cent in 2000, leading many in the Japanese business community to view ODA as no longer serving Japan's economic interest.

— Third, a high although much reduced proportion of ODA continues to go to Asia. In 1970, the Asian share was 98 per cent; by 2001, it had dropped to 57 per cent. This characteristic relates both to the larger share of loans in Japan's ODA and to the special place that Japan has given Asia in its political and economic relations and diplomacy.

— Fourth, Japan provides development assistance on the basis of requests from recipient countries. Also based on the self-help philosophy, this will work well only if recipients have sufficient capacity to formulate and design their own projects or programmes. Short of that, it creates an opportunity for Japanese firms to suggest projects that they will formulate for the recipients.

— Fifth, hard-infrastructure assistance dominates. Japan has emphasised its importance for economic development and growth, based on its own development experience. East Asia has benefited from it, but the policy has encountered controversy, especially within the donor community.

ISBN 92-64-01442-X © OECD 2005

— Sixth, predominantly government-led ODA has rendered the participatory approach weak. Civil society and NGOs have limited involvement, and the share of Japanese grants with NGO participation is significantly lower than for other DAC members. This issue receives increased attention in some East Asian recipient countries.

— Seventh, Japan prefers a bilateral approach, in part because of its need to "fly the flag". The view is that Japan tends to work only with the governments of recipient countries. Japan does not support the idea of a "common fund" from pooled resources.

All these criticisms have been heard loudly and clearly in Japan and apparently heeded in reforming Japan's ODA. After the announcement of a Medium-Term ODA Policy in 1999, reform efforts have gathered steam since 2000. Changes took place in the Japan International Co-operation Agency's (JICA) organisation. A series of country assistance programmes (CAPs) has been formulated to identify assistance goals and priority themes for major recipient countries, based on an earlier recommendation by a Council on ODA Reforms for the Twenty-first Century established by the Ministry of Foreign Affairs (MOFA) in 1998.

Japan's ODA system is very complex. Its management involves the Cabinet Office, ten ministries (MOFA, Ministry of Finance, METI and other ministries) plus two agencies, JICA and the Japan Bank for International Co-operation (JBIC). MOFA is the *de jure* co-ordinator. JICA and JBIC are the implementing agencies, JICA for technical assistance, and JBIC for yen loans and some grants, but grant aid is managed and disbursed by MOFA. In its peer review of December 2003, the DAC questioned whether MOFA should end its operational role (OECD/DAC 2003). MOFA has taken the forefront in ODA reform. In March 2000, it and other relevant Ministries established the Inter-Ministerial Meeting on ODA as a forum discussing major ODA-related issues. The following year an Inter-Ministerial Liaison Meeting on ODA Evaluation was established to refine the ODA evaluation system. Also in 2001, the Second Consultative Committee on ODA Reform was established to advise the Foreign Minister and make recommendations on the directions for Japan's ODA. Its final report in March 2002 proposed building ODA reform on three major pillars: ODA to engage totally the mind, intellect and vitality of the Japanese people; a strategy to prioritise and enhance the effectiveness of ODA; and drastic improvement of the ODA implementing system. These pillars highlight the key reform concepts: transparency, efficiency and public participation.

Based on these proposals, June 2002 saw the launch of the Board on Comprehensive ODA Strategy. Chaired by the Foreign Minister, its members include officials from MOFA, former members of international organisations, NGO representatives, business leaders and journalists. It has examined basic ODA policies, including the revision of the ODA Charter and the formulation and revision of CAPs. In July 2002, MOFA announced that it would implement 15 specific measures in five areas: auditing, evaluation, partnership with NGOs, exploring, fostering and employing human resources and information disclosure and publicity. In December 2002, MOFA announced an agenda for "ODA Reform: Implementation of Three Measures", consisting of a review of the ODA Charter, changes in debt relief methods, and the establishment of the Committee for Grant Aid under the Director General of MOFA's Economic Co-operation Bureau. MOFA (2004) describes this reform in greater detail.

Other efforts of some significance accompanied the MOFA-led reforms. A Task Force on Foreign Relations chaired by the Special Advisor to the cabinet, Yukio Okamoto, has submitted a report entitled "Japan's ODA Strategy" to Prime Minister Junichiro Koizumi. This very strategic report could lead to the adoption of a dual track approach in Japan's ODA. It argues that even in light of Japan's severe fiscal conditions it is not desirable to cut ODA, and it proposes that Japan's ODA be divided into two categories. The first, assistance directly linked to Japan's national interest, should be prioritised by regions and sectors. The priority regions should be ASEAN, other developing countries in East Asia, the Indian subcontinent, the Middle East, Central Asia and the coastal countries of the Caspian Sea. The priority sectors should be infrastructure for economic integration and growth in East Asia, assistance in the fields of energy and the environment, poverty reduction, peace building and the promotion of understanding of Japan. The second category involves assistance not directly linked to the national interest, which Japan should continue providing as a contributing member of the international community. It certainly includes reducing poverty and enhancing human security in sub-Saharan Africa.

Another initiative came from the Liberal Democratic Party (LDP). In September 2002, it established an ODA Reform Working Team. Its report, entitled "Special Measures for ODA Reform: Toward ODA that is Understood by the Public" proposed many specific measures. They included:

- revising the ODA Charter;
- strengthening the functions of drafting an ODA strategy;
- increasing co-operation among ODA-related ministries and agencies;

 ISBN 92-64-01442-X © OECD 2005

- strengthening the ODA implementation functions of MOFA;
- giving local aid offices a greater role in policy making;
- strengthening co-operation with implementing organisations;
- fostering human resources with a high degree of specialised knowledge in the field of assistance; and
- the establishment of local ODA Task Forces. Perhaps one of the most important suggestions, this has since been implemented in important recipient countries.

A new ODA Charter issued in August 2003 states that "the objectives of Japan's ODA are to contribute to the peace and development of the international community, and thereby to help ensure Japan's own security and prosperity". This explicit statement of aid as a foreign policy tool is not new to Japan's neighbours in Asia and is certainly not dissimilar from the objective of US aid, for instance. Yet, Japan may have packaged it rather poorly. The *DAC Peer Review on Japan* recommended that "Japan should highlight that the primary objective of ODA is for the development of the recipient country and should ensure that narrower national interests do not over-ride this objective". (OECD/DAC, 2003). Under the new Charter, Japan adheres to the following basic policies:

- supporting self-help efforts by developing countries;
- promoting human security, *inter alia* by strengthening the capacity of local communities;
- assuring fairness, including attention to socially vulnerable groups;
- using Japan's experience and expertise; and
- partnership and collaboration with the international community.

Asia continues as the priority region, and the priority areas are:

- poverty reduction,
- sustainable growth,
- addressing global issues, and
- building peace.

Other parts of the Charter stipulate a new system for formulating and implementing ODA policy. They pledge:

- greater policy coherence;
- strengthening collaboration between ODA-related ministries and agencies;
- strengthening policy consultation with recipient countries;
- strengthening the functions of field missions in both policy making and implementation; and
- collaboration with aid-related entities including Japanese NGOs, universities, local governments, economic organisations, labour organisations, Japanese private companies and similar groups overseas.

It is perhaps too early to assess the overall impacts of the reforms. The Kawai and Tagaki recommendations were more far-reaching than those currently contemplated. They proposed stronger leadership from the Prime Minister to consolidate aid administration and perhaps even the creation of a single development assistance agency. They suggested that Japan should develop a coherent national strategy for ODA that focuses on poverty reduction and environmental improvements. They argued that Japan must respond to pressures to shift ODA away from hard infrastructure and to improve aid quality through collaboration with the wider developmental community, including other donors and civil society.

The DAC peer review of December 2003 made additional recommendations. First, Japan should increase ODA and build broad-based public support for it. Second, future lending policies should take into account the lessons learned from the provision of loans to indebted poor countries that resulted in heavy debt relief. Third, grant aid should be untied. Fourth, membership of the local ODA Task Forces should broaden to include non-Japanese. Fifth, the more decentralised operational system should be properly staffed. On this last point, JICA, which became an independent administrative institution in October 2003, began to decentralise its operations on 1 April 2004. It will put more workers in the field, going from the current 30 per cent of its employees there now to about half. Eight overseas JICA offices, including that in Viet Nam, will be upgraded as test cases.

Under current plans for ODA field operations in each country, an ODA task force led by the Japanese Ambassador and made up of staff of the Embassy and representatives of JICA and JBIC will formulate a Country Assistance Strategy. Regular consultations will be held with recipient-government agencies. A dialogue-based approach will in practice replace the request-based approach for project formulation and selection. An Advisory Group of local

ISBN 92-64-01442-X © OECD 2005

opinion leaders in various fields could be established (as in Indonesia) to exchange views on Japan's ODA and ways and means to improve bilateral economic co-operation. Poverty Reduction Strategy Papers (PRSPs) formulated by the recipient country, perhaps with the assistance of Japan and other donors, will be used to formulate and implement a Country Assistance Strategy. To assist field operations in the more decentralised system, JICA and JBIC have prepared guidelines on social and environmental impact assessment. JICA's Environmental Guidelines cover more than 20 sectors. The JBIC guidelines emphasise participation of stakeholders and require their involvement in project implementation starting at the planning stage. Because Japan's ODA helps recipient countries promote trade and attract foreign direct investment, JICA has also developed guidelines on "Effective Approaches for Trade and Investment Promotion".

Only time will tell whether this more decentralised system will enhance "partnership" and "ownership" in the recipient countries. Both the intentions and the efforts go in that direction, but bureaucracies often hamper change. In the final analysis, success requires work by both the donor and the recipients.

East Asian Perspectives on Japan's ODA

Malaysia

Malaysia is graduating from the international development assistance programme after many years in which Japanese ODA has been a steady and stable financial source. In 1994 Malaysia began requesting no ODA loans, and by 1997 it was making net repayments (Table 6.6). In 1998 as a result of the crisis, however, it went back to Japan and received JBIC loans of about 114 billion yen for seven projects. Additional loans came in 1999, whence ODA borrowing from Japan again dropped significantly (Ariff and Abubakar, 2001). As Ariff and Abubakar suggest, Japanese ODA flows to Malaysia have been influenced by the transition from one industrialisation phase to another and channelled mainly into infrastructure development. They characterise the programme as generally quite successful. The most important lesson from it lies in the predictability of the aid relationship over the years, which helped Malaysia in its long-term development planning. This also helped to enhance the use of aid. Malaysia offers a good example of a country that adopted a clear policy to use ODA in support of specific

ISBN 92-64-01442-X © OECD 2005

strategies. With graduation, Malaysia will need different types of development assistance that feature enhanced policy dialogue, knowledge, increased local participation in design and implementation, a focus on new areas such as information and communication technology (ICT) and attention to social and environmental concerns.

Table 6.6. **Japan's ODA to Selected East Asian Countries**
(net flows, in $ million)

Country	1997	1998	1999	2000	2001
Cambodia	62	81	51	99	120
China	577	1 158	1 226	769	686
Indonesia	497	828	1 606	970	860
Laos	79	86	133	115	75
Malaysia	-259	179	123	24	13
Myanmar	15	16	34	52	70
Philippines	319	298	413	304	298
Viet Nam	232	389	680	924	460
Other East Asia (2)	78	94	94	136	90
Total	2 068	3 687	5 240	4 028	2 792

Source: Ministry of Foreign Affairs, Japan (2004).

Thailand

Thailand's case highlights some key points (Chiasakul, 2001). Japan is Thailand's biggest aid donor, with cumulative flows of $1.6 billion over 30 years. Japan began providing technical assistance in 1950. ODA loans started in 1965, for rural development and other sectors. Much criticism of its implementation occurred in the early stages, as Japan set the terms and conditions with little flexibility in meeting Thai expectations. General criticism of bilateral aid in Thailand stresses an "aid dependency syndrome" in government agencies, which lack initiatives and capacity to formulate projects. This led to a situation in which Japanese firms designed projects for the government, resulting in inflated costs. Critics have suggested that "multilateral aid is better", because the multilateral agencies help their Thai counterparts with project design. Other negative aspects relate to the social and environmental impacts of mega-projects such as dams. Corruption is another important issue.

Japan's aid strategy in infrastructure building has conformed to Thailand's national development plan, but local participation and "ownership" remain problems. Chiasakul proposed improved policy dialogue

ISBN 92-64-01442-X © OECD 2005

and an ODA focus on human and institutional capacity building. Overall, however, Thailand has benefited from Japan's ODA projects. Currently, JBIC places priority on developing Thailand's urban infrastructure in view of the serious deterioration in urban conditions, on regional development to reduce growing regional income disparities and on human-resource development (JBIC, 2003*a*).

Philippines

Overwhelmingly the most important donor, Japan accounted for 82 per cent of total ODA in 1998, compared with 1.5 per cent from the United States. Loans averaged 87 per cent of its ODA in 1992-2000. A low share of social-development funding stemmed from the government's reluctance to use yen loans to fund human-development projects, largely because of recurrent balance of payments problems (Tecson, 2001). In 1996, however, the Filipino government raised the priority of the social sector in the Social Reform Agenda (SRA) of the Ramos Administration. ODA began to flow into it. Mapalad (2000) found that Japan's ODA had exerted a positive impact on the Filipino economy. Tecson (2001) suggested that the distribution of ODA partly reinforced regional income disparities, a main concern. Another major issue, an absorptive capacity gap, must be overcome, and ODA should be able to contribute to this. JBIC provides ODA loans to the Philippines today in four priority areas: strengthening the economic structure and overcoming bottlenecks in sustainable economic growth, reducing poverty and regional disparities, environmental protection and disaster prevention and human-resource development. These priorities conform to those stipulated in the 1999-2004 Medium-Term Philippine Development Plan. (JBIC, Manila)

Indonesia

Japan is also Indonesia's largest bilateral ODA donor, and Indonesia has belonged to Japan's top ten recipients throughout the history of Japanese ODA. For several years, it was the top recipient. In 2002 it ranked fourth. Aid to Indonesia has declined recently, in major part owing to a lack of absorptive capacity, a problem also encountered in the Philippines and Viet Nam. Indonesia's macroeconomic conditions have largely determined Japanese ODA flows (Center for Japanese Studies, University of Indonesia, 2000), in the sense that they have been structured as an integral part of Indonesia's development financing (Soesastro, 1991). Japan may not have viewed its ODA to Indonesia that way, however.

From Indonesia's perspective, Japan's ODA has played a critical role in the aid consortium for Indonesia, one of the success stories in development assistance. It is in Indonesia's interest to have a balanced overall programme, which makes aid co-ordination important, especially given donors' diverse priorities for the country (Table 6.7). The consortium has worked through the aid co-ordination forum for Indonesia, the Inter-Governmental Group on Indonesia (IGGI) and currently the Consultative Group for Indonesia (CGI). The CGI, an important instrument for the Indonesian government, helps to mobilise external resources (Soesastro, 2003*a*). A major issue for the government is to transform aid co-ordination from donor-driven to Indonesia-led (Bappenas, 2003). For donor members of the consortium, it provides a framework for justifying the assistance to their own publics at home. Japan may not have used it that way, however, although it has had concerns about "visibility". Nonetheless, Japan has been most forthcoming in providing programme aid to Indonesia in times of crisis — in the mid-1980s and again during the 1997-98 financial crisis, when it was in fact the largest contributor. In the mid-1980s it launched a government-sponsored debt rollover initiative, disbursing special assistance that aimed to avoid formal debt rescheduling, ease balance of payments pressures and maintain the momentum of economic development by funding the rupiah costs of several World Bank projects.

Table 6.7. **Priority Areas of Bilateral and Multilateral ODA Donors to Indonesia, 2003**

Donors	Priority Areas
Australia	Good governance, legal reform, empowerment of civil society, human resources development, basic human needs for vulnerable groups.
Canada	Good governance, SMEs, sustainable resource management.
Germany	Basic health and family planning, economic reform, sea transport and railways, decentralisation.
Japan	Balanced social and regional development, human resources development, environmental control and conservation, industrial restructuring, economic infrastructure.
United Kingdom	Good governance, forestry, poverty reduction.
United States	Democratic and decentralised governance, decentralised basic education, basic human services, economic governance including trade and investment and employment issues.
ADB	Good governance, regional development, human resources development, sustainable use of natural resources, long-term growth potential (infrastructure investment, corporate governance, promoting private sector).
World Bank	Economic recovery and economic growth, good governance, public services for the poor.

Source: Bappenas (2003) and other sources.

ISBN 92-64-01442-X © OECD 2005

Japanese ODA projects have not met criticism in Indonesia as they have in some neighbouring countries including Thailand. They have been less scrutinised, unlike some of the large projects financed by the World Bank, because Japan's ODA is seen mainly as meeting the country's need for development financing and to overcome financial crises. No major scandals, like in the Philippines under Marcos, have been reported in connection with Japanese ODA. Moreover, a few major success stories have gained notice, such as the integrated Brantas River project in East Java, which has received wide coverage and applause. Most of the loans have been directed towards economic infrastructure projects. "This is exactly the area that appears to the Indonesian government as well as to the public at large as most appropriate for Japan's participation in Indonesia's development" (Soesastro, 1991). Yet there have been some problems with the effectiveness of ODA projects. In March 1989, for example, *Mainichi Shimbun* reported that 80 per cent of the medical equipment provided under Japan's ODA since 1979 to Indonesian hospitals had not been used because the projects did not take insufficient electrical power supplies into account.

CGI loans constitute a major part of JBIC yen loans to Indonesia. Non-CGI lending, which is pledged after *ad hoc* consultations between Japan and Indonesia, has funded relatively large projects such as energy development and industrial development. During the crisis in the late 1990s, JBIC provided special commodity and sector-programme loans to provide local-cost financing for ongoing projects and programme-type lending. The programme loans were to improve Indonesia's balance of payments as well as to assist socially vulnerable groups (JBIC, 2003*b*). In 2005, JBIC plans to provide loans for big infrastructure projects in agriculture and irrigation.

Japan's huge ODA loans to Indonesia made the debt burden a major sticking point (Roesad, 2001). During the mid-1980s crisis, the government proposed to Japan a number of options to overcome these financial problems. They included conversion of the outstanding loan portfolio from debt to grants, a progressive shift in future commitments from loans to outright grants and a currency repayment option. None of them was acceptable to Japan, which instead offered assistance by committing to a continuation of high loan levels (Soesastro, 1991). To this day Indonesia still struggles to overcome its high debt burden.

Viet Nam

Viet Nam is a relative newcomer on the scene. Japanese ODA has increased steadily since its full-scale resumption in 1992. Japan has been the top donor since 1995. Total aid to Viet Nam surpassed $1 billion in 1997, and in 2000 Japan accounted for 57 per cent of total disbursements made by the ten top donors. In 2002, about 86 per cent of Japan's ODA to Viet Nam took the form of loans. Japan published its first assistance policy for Viet Nam in 1994. In 2000, it formulated a Country Assistance Program (CAP). The CAP gives priority to achieving balanced economic growth. Its two clear goals are to create the basic conditions for sustained growth to support poverty reduction. In a new CAP currently being drafted, priority will go on promoting sustainable economic growth and poverty reduction, improving living and social conditions and institutional development. Institutional improvements have priority because Viet Nam faces serious problems of absorptive capacity, including capacity for policy making. As part of a project to develop road infrastructure, Japan provides assistance for policy development, such as on user policy as well as funding for operations and maintenance. GRIPS (2002) contains a comprehensive survey of Japan's ODA to Viet Nam.

Japan's efforts to co-ordinate with other donors are most visible in Viet Nam, for example in efforts to upgrade the procurement system. In co-operation with the World Bank and the ADB and with the involvement of the government, Japan tries to overcome implementation weaknesses reflected in low and slow disbursements. Japan is also trying to work more closely with NGOs to promote community-driven projects. In addition, JBIC co-operates with the World Bank, the ADB, AFD (France), and KfW (Germany) to harmonise aid procedures for procurement, financial management, environmental consideration, resettlement and portfolio management (*Japan News*, 1 December 2003).

Viet Nam was the first East Asian country to adopt the PRSP approach in the effort to reduce poverty, which is the focus of aid donors there. During the drafting process frictions arose between the Vietnamese government, which considered the PRSP subordinate to the national development plans, and some donors who tried to elevate it as the central instrument for budgeting and policy making. With Japan's assistance, Viet Nam has expanded its PRSP to include economic infrastructure development, re-naming it the Comprehensive Poverty Reduction and Growth Strategy (CPRGS). In the end, the World Bank evaluated Viet Nam's strong ownership highly positively and lauded the document as "best practice" (Ohno, 2002). The PRSP approach

ISBN 92-64-01442-X © OECD 2005

cannot be applied uniformly across countries. It must have sufficient flexibility to reflect the different conditions of each poor country. Japan co-operates with the World Bank in co-financing some PRSP projects, for which they jointly develop the terms and conditions.

Despite their different views on priorities and modalities in aid giving, Japan and the United Kingdom have conducted a dialogue and strengthened co-operation in Viet Nam in five areas. They include the CPRGS and the role of large-scale infrastructure, linkage between the CPRGS and the resource-allocation mechanism, aid effectiveness, rural transport and the foreign investment environment and private-sector development. On the final item, Japan and Viet Nam launched in 2003 an initiative to improve the business environment. Japan will use its ODA to support the policy and institutional reforms incorporated in it. The establishment of a committee for evaluation and monitoring will follow.

It is too soon to assess the results of Viet Nam's efforts to reduce poverty with the assistance of the donor community. Owing to limited data, Le and Winters (2001) could not base their study on outcomes but relied on analysis of the pattern of aid allocation. They identified an imbalance between aid that promotes economic growth and aid that directly targets the poor, evident in disbursements both by sector and by approach to poverty. They also noted that aid is urban biased and thus not directed regionally in a manner conducive to poverty alleviation.

Concluding Remarks

The foregoing survey simply confirms the diversity of problems and challenges. It underlines the donor community's need for a menu of assistance options in terms of modalities and areas of assistance. In East Asia the emphasis has centred on human-resource development, infrastructure development, promoting SMEs and creating institutions for industrialisation. These overlap with the priority areas of Japan's ODA. Yet new challenges have brought new areas of great concern to the East Asian developing countries as they continue to integrate into the world economy and participate in globalisation. Japan cannot meet all of these needs, which makes co-operation and aid co-ordination necessary even as Japan preserves the areas of assistance in which it has a comparative advantage.

Nonetheless, Japan needs to begin to develop capacity to deliver more in the area of social development. Further reforms may be required for the growing "soft" component of its ODA policy to gain prominence. At the same time, the international community should not expect Japan to abandon the "hard" component of its development assistance. Japan is perhaps the only donor left still offering this opportunity. The region, especially Mainland Southeast Asia (Myanmar, Laos, Cambodia and Viet Nam), has a great need to improve the physical infrastructure that can help these economies to catch up and integrate with the rest of the region.

Japan has a long history of supporting regional co-operation in Southeast Asia. Its first major initiative was the 1963 Ministerial Conference for Southeast Asian Development. It has supported various ASEAN co-operation projects, including the Initiative for ASEAN Integration (IAI) to develop infrastructure in Mainland Southeast Asia for the new members of ASEAN. This project has yet to take off and depends on the willingness of ASEAN to establish the institutional structures necessary to manage it. Outside the IAI framework, JBIC has undertaken a number of infrastructure projects with regional reach. Moreover, wider East Asian regional co-operation is important, perhaps even imperative, for the region to sustain its economic dynamism. Many parallel efforts are under way to promote East Asian economic co-operation (Soesastro, 2003*b*). ASEAN +3, involving China, Japan and Korea, is the most important.

During his visit to Southeast Asia in January 2002, Prime Minister Koizumi proposed in a policy statement in Singapore that Japan build a closer economic partnership with ASEAN members and deepen regional co-operation, and stated that Japan's future East Asian ODA strategy would be based on this policy. Japan has taken this forward in its Initiative for Development in East Asia (IDEA). In August 2002, it organised the first IDEA Ministerial Meeting in Tokyo. The Joint Ministerial Statement contains the following points:

— The importance of development as a national agenda through self-help efforts. Human resources development is key to spearheading development and to enhancing government capacity.

— It is important to promote a comprehensive, growth-oriented approach to development, linking ODA, trade and investment and finance.

— Greater consideration should be given to vulnerable members of society to counter the negative effects of globalisation.

ISBN 92-64-01442-X © OECD 2005

- Support should go to countries in accordance with their respective capacities.
- The combination of official and private flows has worked to promote development in East Asia, as ODA-financed economic infrastructure improvements have attracted trade and investment.

To become operational, these points must be given prominence and be introduced into existing schemes, such as ASEAN+3 and the ASEAN-Japan Framework Agreement on Comprehensive Economic Partnership (CEP). In fact, a serious lack of coherence has appeared among the countries in the region in promoting East Asian economic integration through an East Asian Economic Community, as proposed by the ASEAN+3 Vision Group and endorsed by the ASEAN+3 leaders. Japan, in particular, should provide better justification for giving priority to bilateral free trade agreements (FTAs) with individual ASEAN countries rather than promoting and giving real substance to the ASEAN-Japan CEP. FTAs tend to weaken ASEAN as the new members feel pushed further back because they are not positioned to form FTAs. Even Indonesia is unlikely to have an FTA with Japan in the near future. Japan and other East Asians forming bilateral FTAs have yet to convince others that they will provide the building blocks for region-wide economic integration and a sense of regional community. ASEAN itself should perhaps also be blamed for inability to act as a group, but Japan's failure to adopt a coherent policy on East Asian regional co-operation is clear. It could negate Japan's IDEA effort to sustain East Asian economic dynamism through ODA co-operation.

Note

1. This review does not include assistance from multilateral agencies such as the World Bank and the Asian Development Bank, which have also played a very important role in East Asia.

Bibliography

AKIYAMA, T., S. AKIYAMA and N. MINATO (2003), *International Development Assistance: Evolution and Prospects,* Foundation for Advanced Studies on International Development, Tokyo.

ARIFF, M. and S.Y. ABUBAKAR (2001), "Overseas Development Assistance: Perspectives from Malaysia", Research paper for a project on Japan's Role in ASEAN-10 under Globalization, Center for Asia Pacific Studies, Japan Institute of International Affairs, Tokyo.

BAPPENAS (2003), *Existence and Role of the Consultative Group for Indonesia (CGI)* (in Indonesia), Government of Indonesia, Jakarta.

BUSH, G.W. (2002), "President Proposes $5 Billion Plan to Help Developing Nations", speech at the Inter-American Development Bank, March 14, http://www.whitehouse.gov/newsreleases/2002/03/20020314-7.html.

CENTER FOR JAPANESE STUDIES, UNIVERSITY OF INDONESIA (2000), *Japan's Official Development Assistance to Indonesia,* Research Report.

CHIASAKUL, S. (2001), "Official Development Assistance – ASEAN Perspectives: A Case Study of Thailand", Research paper for a project on Japan's Role in ASEAN-10 under Globalization, Center for Asia Pacific Studies, Japan Institute of International Affairs, Jakarta.

FUKASAKU, K., M. PLUMMER and J. TAN (eds.) (1995), *OECD and ASEAN Economies – The Challenge of Policy Coherence,* OECD, Paris.

GRIPS (2002), *Japan's Development Cooperation in Viet Nam,* GRIPS Development Forum, May.

HIRONO, R. (2001), "Changing Japanese Development Cooperation Policy Towards ASEAN in the Postwar Period", Research paper for a project on Japan's Role in ASEAN-10 under Globalization, Center for Asia Pacific Studies, Japan Institute of International Affairs, Tokyo.

IIMURA, Y. (2001), "Rethinking Japan's ODA: Flying the Flag or Not", *Gaiko Forum,* Winter, pp. 44-55.

ISBN 92-64-01442-X © OECD 2005

IOKIBE, M. (2003), "ODA as a Foreign Policy Tool", *Japan Review of International Affairs*, Vol. 17 No. 2, Summer, pp. 105-127.

Japan News (2003), "Japanese Assistance to Viet Nam", 1 December.

JBIC (2003*a*), *Annual Report 2003*, Tokyo.

JBIC (2003*b*), *Development Challenges in Indonesia*, Tokyo, Development Assistance Department I, JBIC, October.

JBIC MANILA (no year), *Creating a World of Opportunities.*

KAWAI, M. and S. TAKAGI (2004), "Japan's Official Development Assistance: Recent Issues and Future Directions", *Journal of International Development*, Vol. 16, pp. 255-280.

LE, T.H. and P. WINTERS (2001), "Aid Policies and Poverty Alleviation: The Case of Viet Nam", *Asia Pacific Development Journal*, Vol. 8 No. 2, December, pp. 27-44.

LOWCOCK, M. (2002), "New Approaches to Development", *Developments*, http://www.dfid.gov.uk/

MAPALAD, M.C.M. (2000), "Japan's ODA and Philippine Saving and Growth" *in The Philippine Review of Economics*, Vol. 37, No. 2, pp. 1-25.

MCCAWLEY, P.M. (1998), "Development Assistance in Asia in the 1990s", *Asian-Pacific Economic Literature*, Vol. 12, No. 1, May, pp. 41-50.

MINISTRY OF FOREIGN AFFAIRS, JAPAN (2004), *Japan's Official Development Assistance White Paper 2002*, Tokyo, Economic Cooperation Bureau, Ministry of Foreign Affairs.

OECD/DAC (2003), *DAC Peer Review on Japan* (December), http://www.oecd.org/ (published in *The DAC Journal*, Vol. 5, No. 2, 2004, pp.91-188).

OECD (2004), "Development Co-operation 2003 Report", *The DAC Journal*, Vol.5, No.1.

OHNO, K. (2002), "The East Asian Experience of Economic Development and Cooperation", GRIPS Development Forum, Policy Note No. 3, December.

ROESAD, K. (2001), "ODA in Indonesia: A Preliminary Assessment", Research paper for a project on Japan's Role in ASEAN-10 under Globalization, Center for Asia Pacific Studies, Japan Institute of International Affairs, Tokyo.

SOESASTRO, H. (1980), "Future ASEAN-US Economic Relations: Perspectives on Strategic Planning", in *ASEAN External Economic Relations*, Proceedings of the Fifth Conference of the Federation of ASEAN Economic Associations, Singapore, Chopmen Publishers for the Economic Society of Singapore), pp. 33-76.

SOESASTRO, H. (1991), *Japan's ODA and Indonesia: Resource Security Aid?*, CSIS Mimeograph, M60/91, April.

SOESASTRO, H. (2003*a*), "The Real Issue is not To End CGI" (in Indonesian), *Kompas*, 27 January.

SOESASTRO, H. (2003*b*), "ASEAN-Japan Cooperation towards East Asian Integration", *in* RYOKICHI H. (ed.), *Regional Co-operation in Asia*, Japan Institute of International Affairs, Tokyo, pp.24-49.

TECSON, G.R. (2001), "ODA for Development: Perspectives from the Philippines", Research paper for a project on Japan's Role in ASEAN-10 under Globalization, Center for Asia Pacific Studies, Japan Institute of International Affairs, Tokyo.

THEE, K.W. (1994), "Interactions of Japanese Aid and Direct Investment in Indonesia", *ASEAN Economic Bulletin*, Vol. 11, No. 1, July, pp.25-35.

USAID (2002), *Foreign Aid in the National Interest – Promoting Freedom, Security, and Opportunity*, USAID, Washington, D.C.

WORLD BANK (2004), *World Development Report*, Washington, D.C.

ISBN 92-64-01442-X © OECD 2005

Chapter 7

OECD-Country Economic and Environmental Policies: What Implications for East Asia?

David O'Connor[1]
UN-DESA

Abstract

Both environmental and economic policies of OECD countries can have impacts on environmental quality in non-member countries, including those in developing Asia. Some are more direct and easier to trace than others are. OECD environmental policies may have both a direct demonstration effect, leading to imitation or adaptation, and an indirect effect *via* induced technical change and international technology diffusion. The hypothesised effect through shifting comparative advantage has generally not been confirmed as empirically important. OECD economic policy impacts on the Asian environment usually are more indirect, working through a broad stimulus to economic growth and what one might loosely call the "quality of growth". Greater integration of developing Asia with OECD countries, for example, has generally accelerated technology diffusion through both trade and foreign direct investment. Thus, one can detect a certain coherence between OECD environmental policies and their economic policies *vis-à-vis* the Asian environment. The former induce pollution-reducing technical change in member countries, and the latter — particularly policies that foster international trade and investment — facilitate the transfer of the resultant cleaner technologies to relatively open Asian developing economies.

ISBN 92-64-01442-X

Introduction

This chapter focuses on how the panoply of OECD-country environmental and economic policies affects environmental quality in developing Asia. While there are a number of hypothetical transmission channels, environmental outcomes arise from a complex admixture of domestic and international influences, and firmly ascribing causality to any single influence or set of influences is a sizeable research challenge. The current analysis is merely suggestive of likely influences and their importance.

Environmental policies of OECD countries can affect Asian developing countries in several ways. First, the latter may study those policies to learn what works and try to replicate successes. Second, OECD business enterprises have spawned a variety of technological innovations in their efforts to comply with environmental regulations. Those innovations are available in turn to developing Asia, normally through trade and investment channels and possibly at a fraction of their original cost. Third, environmental policies of OECD countries may affect their comparative advantage and thereby alter global production and trade patterns. If OECD countries come to specialise in relatively clean industries, their Asian and/or other trading partners may specialise in relatively dirty ones, and *vice versa*. Fourth, consumer, shareholder and advocacy group preferences in OECD countries can have important effects on both products produced and the manner of their production in supplier countries.

Economic policies of OECD countries can also indirectly affect environmental quality in developing Asia, but these effects have to be seen in relation to environmental policies in both groups of countries because they condition how economic forces impact on the environment. For instance, expansionary macroeconomic policies of OECD countries can stimulate growth in developing Asia, but whether that growth results in environmental degradation depends heavily on the efficacy of environmental policies designed to promote investment in cleaner technologies and/or pollution abatement. It also depends importantly on how comparative advantage and economic policies of developing Asia may shape the pattern of export-led growth, i.e. whether the industries expanding to meet growing OECD-country demand are more or less polluting.

The next section briefly reviews economic and environmental trends in developing Asia over the past quarter century, with a particular focus on the period since 1990. Section three considers briefly each of the channels

 ISBN 92-64-01442-X © OECD 2005

mentioned above by which OECD environmental policies may affect environmental outcomes in developing Asia, providing a rough assessment of how they have contributed to the observed trends. The following section then considers economic policies of OECD countries insofar as they could be expected to have perceptible impacts on the environment and sustainable development in developing Asia. It focuses on agricultural, trade and financial policies, with a brief reference to development assistance policies. While it is difficult to quantify all these effects, some broad indication can be given of the likely more important ones and their directions. The final section reflects on the implications for OECD-country policies if they are to support the sustainable development of developing Asia, bearing in mind that those policies are designed first and foremost for the welfare of their own citizens.

Review of Economic and Environmental Trends in Developing Asia

The primary focus of discussion here lies on those developing countries of Asia that have close trade and investment links to OECD countries. On this criterion, most of East and Southeast Asia are included with the exception of Laos, Mongolia, Myanmar and North Korea. On the other hand, South Asia is largely excluded, given its relatively weak external trade and investment linkages, although links between India and certain OECD countries are growing stronger. Given its population size and potential future economic importance, reference to the subcontinent will be made as appropriate. What follows is a brief review of economic and environmental trends in major countries of developing Asia over the past quarter century and especially since 1990[2]. It is not meant to be exhaustive but attempts to capture the most important influences on and indicators of environmental performance.

Economic Trends in Developing Asia

The outstanding Asian economic event of the past quarter century has been the emergence of China as a major economic power. From 1991 to 2001, per capita income in China grew by roughly 9 per cent per annum. Outstanding though this performance has been, it is not exceptional in the region: Viet Nam witnessed per capita income growth of 6 per cent per year during this period, Korea 4.5 per cent and both India and Singapore 4 per cent. Bangladesh, Laos, Malaysia and Sri Lanka all registered per capita income growth of over 3 per cent per annum.

ISBN 92-64-01442-X © OECD 2005

While agricultural dynamism following de-collectivisation was an important early contributor to overall GDP growth in China and Viet Nam, the industrial sector has been the main driver of growth across the East Asian region. Its contribution has been less in South Asia, but then so too has the subcontinent's growth lagged behind much of East Asia's. The past quarter century has witnessed industrial growth in East Asia of roughly 9 per cent per annum. In China, from 1991 to 2001, industry's share of GDP rose from 42 per cent to 51 per cent; in Viet Nam the rise was from 24 per cent to 38 per cent and in Indonesia from 28 per cent to 47 per cent (World Bank, 2003). In India, by contrast, industry's share remained constant at 26 per cent.

Historically, serious environmental degradation accompanied rapid industrialisation until rising incomes and public concern caused effective remedial measures to be taken. There is little evidence to suggest that the experience of the late industrialisers of the latter half of the 20th century was significantly different in this regard from that of the earlier ones. In one important difference, however, the latecomers enjoyed greater availability of cleaner, more efficient technologies.

East Asia has followed a heavily trade-dependent industrialisation path. Over the decade of the 1990s, exports grew much faster than GDP in many countries. In China, the ratio of exports to GDP rose from 19 per cent to 26 per cent from 1991 to 2001, in Viet Nam it went from 31 per cent to 55 per cent and in the Philippines from 30 per cent to 49 per cent. Even India saw exports rise as a share of GDP from 9 per cent to 14 per cent. Manufactures — which already accounted for more than half of merchandise exports in most countries by the early 1990s — became even more dominant by 2001.

Whether trade-dependent or not, industrial and, more broadly, economic development will have environmental impacts *via* an increase in the sheer scale of economic activities and hence in the scale of materials and energy consumption, waste and emissions. At the same time, rising per capita incomes may engender a stronger preference for environmental quality, which gets manifested in a policy response, often beginning at the local level. Trade-oriented industrialisation, however, may exhibit significantly different factor intensity from inward-oriented industrialisation, and may rely to a significantly different degree on innovation and technological change. These differences may in turn have important environmental implications.

For a panel of 64 countries, Stern (2002) decomposes the change in sulphur dioxide (SO_2) emissions from 1973 to 1990 into scale effects, technical change and changes in input and output mix (or structural change). He

ISBN 92-64-01442-X © OECD 2005

finds that the first and second are by far the dominant influences on emissions, with technical change offsetting more than half of the effect on emissions of increased economic scale. Copeland and Taylor (2003) use a sample of some 100 major cities across the globe to examine the effects of trade liberalisation on SO_2 pollution, decomposing scale effects and "technique" effects. They find that for every 1 per cent increase in economic activity caused by liberalisation pollution, concentrations increase by 0.25 per cent to 0.5 per cent as a result of the scale effect. On the other hand, the induced policy response from rising per capita incomes combined with efficiency gains from heightened competition cause concentrations to decline by 1.25 per cent to 1.5 per cent. Thus, the net effect of liberalisation is to reduce pollution, at least in the case of SO_2.

To the extent that developing countries are labour-abundant, liberalisation should favour labour-intensive development, which in turn generally means less energy-intensive and less polluting sectors (notably with respect to air pollution). A capital-intensive path of industrialisation, by contrast, is apt to be a relatively dirty one. On various measures of pollution intensity, heavy industries like metals processing, non-metallic minerals, oil refining and petrochemicals and power generation consistently rank at the top. Across different Asian economies, the degree of capital-intensive industrial development varies markedly.

Environmental Trends in Developing Asia

Countries of the region face two sorts of environmental challenge, those associated with urban and industrial development and those associated with natural resource exploitation and management. Jha and Whalley (1999) refer to the first sort as pollution and the second sort as degradation, arguing that the severity of the two can differ markedly, as can their interaction with economic processes. Based on a review of estimates of the economic costs of environmental externalities in developing countries, they conclude that resource degradation rather than pollution dominates those costs. On the other hand, rising incomes may worsen one sort of problem while ameliorating the other. For instance, rapid industrialisation may relieve pressures on the land, as population moves to cities in search of higher-paying jobs. Soil degradation and deforestation would tend to slow, while industrial pollution and urban congestion would accelerate at first. Where government policy promotes resource-based industrialisation, however, degradation and pollution may rise simultaneously — as for instance with the Indonesian government's past promotion of wood-based industries.

ISBN 92-64-01442-X © OECD 2005

Demographic trends also need consideration in relation to the environment. Asia's total population is projected to grow by a little over a third between 2000 and 2030, but its urban population is projected to double, to 2.7 billion people (UN, 2002). This will pose major challenges to urban planners and managers to ensure adequate provision of water, sanitation, wastewater treatment and solid and hazardous waste treatment and disposal, and to avert ever-worsening problems of traffic congestion and air pollution.

Pollution

Air quality remains a serious problem throughout developing Asia. Airborne lead levels have been dramatically reduced over the past two decades, but particulate concentrations are persistently high in a number of major cities. A much smaller number suffer serious SO_2 pollution and, in many, levels of nitrogen oxides (NO_x) and other by-products of motor vehicle fuels have been growing rapidly, giving rise to photochemical smog problems in some cities. Carbon dioxide (CO_2) emissions are rising apace with energy consumption that fuels the region's rapid economic growth.

Air quality in Asia is not solely a national concern. There are also serious transboundary pollution problems. Five in particular deserve mention. First and perhaps best known is the regional haze in Southeast Asia caused by Indonesian plantation owners' practice of burning to clear land for planting, causing widespread forest fires. Second, the Asian brown cloud first identified in 1999 is a massive formation of particulates, sulphur aerosols and other pollutants caused by a combination of fossil fuel combustion by motor vehicles, power plants and industrial processes, and natural sources like sand and dust storms[3]. Third, sandstorms in northwest China are increasingly implicated in poor air quality in Chinese Taipei. Fourth, particulate pollution originating largely in China's Pearl River Delta is implicated in the worsening visibility problems plaguing Hong Kong, China. Finally, wind-borne SO_2 emissions from China's power plants are blown over Korea and Japan, where they seriously exacerbate the problem of acid rain. The last is perhaps the most tractable in that its source is a moderate-income developing country, while the aggrieved are two relatively wealthy OECD countries that can afford to compensate China for much of the cost of lowering sulphur emissions. In the case of the Southeast Asian haze, ASEAN has provided some support to devising and implementing a regional solution in the form of the Regional Haze Action Plan (UNEP, 2000).

 ISBN 92-64-01442-X © OECD 2005

While Asia has arid regions where water availability is a perennial problem, and seasonal shortages occur elsewhere, the problem in much of the region involves more *water quality* than availability *per se*. Also, in the rapidly growing urban centres of East and Southeast Asia, supplying safe drinking water to large numbers of new migrants from the countryside, many living in informal settlements, poses a major challenge. For example, in Southeast Asia from 1990 to 2000, the number of urban dwellers unserved by an improved water source[4] actually rose by six million, even as the number not served in rural areas declined by ten million (WHO/UNICEF, 2004). Similarly, in developing East Asia the number of urban dwellers unserved by improved drinking water sources rose steeply, from four million in 1990 to 29 million in 2000; the rural unserved, meanwhile, fell from 344 million to 282 million. Only in South Asia, where urbanisation was far less rapid over that period, did the numbers not served decline in both urban and rural areas, in the former by ten million and in the latter by 100 million.

Korea offers a picture of divergent trends in water quality, depending on measures used. On the one hand, biological oxygen demand (BOD) in the lower Han River fell by almost half between 1987 and 1993. Of the four major rivers, only the Keum has shown some sign of deteriorating quality on this measure. On the other hand, the accumulation of organic pollutants in lakes and reservoirs — in no small measure from input-intensive agriculture — presents a serious problem, with 46 out of a total of 207 being affected by eutrophication[5]. The 1997 target of 42 per cent of rivers meeting class I or II standards was missed (OECD, 2000*b*). Progress is being made, however, in guaranteeing minimum flows in rivers to meet the needs of aquatic ecosystems.

In other countries in the region, water pollution problems originate from a combination of industrial and agricultural sources, with domestic sewage generally less problematic. In Thailand, standards for such pollutants as lead, chromium, ammoniacal nitrogen and nitrates were all exceeded between Bangkok and the mouth of the Chao Phraya River, although not in the stretch of the river from which the city's water supply originates. In Malaysia, river pollution has increased. The Department of Environment calculates a composite pollution index based on several parameters, including BOD, suspended solids (SS) and ammoniacal nitrogen. In 2000, the number of slightly polluted rivers stood at 74, more than double the number in 1990, while the number of heavily polluted rivers stood at 12, also almost double the seven of 1990[6].

ISBN 92-64-01442-X © OECD 2005

Indonesia has adopted two innovative water-quality management programmes in the past two decades. The water-quality data, however, give a murky picture of how effective they have been. On the one hand, a report on water samples at various river-monitoring stations suggests a decline since 1989 in the proportion meeting standards. On the other hand, data on BOD and SS loadings in major rivers during the first two years after the onset of the PROKASIH (or "Clean Rivers") programme in 1989 show a significant decline — i.e. an improvement in water quality (Wood *et al.*, 1992). Inspired by if not modelled on the US "Community Right to Know" legislation, the PROPER programme was established in 1995 to require information disclosure as a means of encouraging firms to improve environmental performance. During its short life, it resulted in significant reductions in BOD and COD loads, but it is not known how enduring those improvements have been since the programme's phase-out in 1998 (Lopez *et al.*, 2004).

Levels of *solid waste* have generally risen in the dynamic Asian economies along with per capita income, although technology and input switching have partially severed the waste-income link. In Korea, for example, the volume of solid waste increased an average 8.3 per cent per year from 1988 to 1991 before declining rather steeply thereafter, in part as a result of substitution away from coal briquettes to cleaner fuels such as LNG and LPG. Also, Korea recycles a growing proportion of its solid waste. As of 1998, its per capita municipal waste generation stood at 350 kg (the OECD average for municipal waste was 520 kg) (OECD, 2002). Chinese Taipei's total and per capita municipal waste volumes have both risen steadily, with the latter reaching about 365 kg per year by 1991, roughly on a par with Germany (whose PPP per capita income was roughly twice as high in that year). Kuala Lumpur has one of the highest rates of per capita solid waste generation of any Asian city, much higher than Taipei's and lower only than Seoul's and Beijing's.

Resource Degradation

While the pollution trends just described can be linked only indirectly and somewhat loosely to developing Asia's evolving links with OECD countries and the global economy, certain trends in resource degradation would appear to have closer linkages. For instance, certain resource-abundant countries — mostly in Southeast Asia — have seen a rapid expansion of resource-intensive exports over the past few decades. Seafood, particularly prawns, has become a major export of countries like Thailand, Indonesia,

ISBN 92-64-01442-X © OECD 2005

Bangladesh and Viet Nam. The expansion of area devoted to prawn farming has in many cases placed stress on ecosystems, both aquatic and terrestrial. In Thailand, a strong demand for saltwater shrimp raised in freshwater areas led to a rapid expansion in the use of freshwater agricultural lands for aquaculture, resulting in introduction of significant amounts of brine into freshwater ecosystems and contamination of water supplies (UNEP, 2000). The conversion of rice fields to shrimp ponds can also leave soils saline and infertile once the ponds are abandoned. Expansion of prawn farming and other aquaculture in coastal areas has often occurred at the expense of mangrove forests, whose clearing has in turn caused coastal fishery yields to decline and increased vulnerability to tidal surges.

Primary terrestrial forests have also been subjected to pressures partly as a result of expanding exports of timber and timber products. In the case of plywood from tropical hardwood, for instance, OECD markets account for a sizeable share of total imports, led by Japan, the United States and Korea (UN-DESA Statistics Division Comtrade database). Indonesia is the largest exporter by a very wide margin, with its exports roughly equal in value to the combined imports of Japan and the United States. Even with its enormous wood-based exports, however, Indonesia is not one of the most seriously deforested Asian countries, although its rate of deforestation has been rapid in the past decade, as has Malaysia's. Although both countries have forest cover amounting to just under 60 per cent of their land area, both saw forest cover decline by a little more than 10 per cent over the decade 1990-2000. Meanwhile, the loss of forests and woodlands has been even steeper — albeit over a longer time span — in Thailand and Viet Nam. Thailand lost 33 per cent of its forests between 1970 and 1990, and Viet Nam lost 32 per cent, although in the past decade its forested area has recovered slightly (UNEP, 2000 and World Bank, 2003).

OECD-Country Environmental Policies and their Impact on Developing Asia

Learning from Predecessors and Peers

The preceding discussion identified several transmission mechanisms through which environmental policies of OECD countries may affect environmental quality in developing Asia. Here each is considered in turn. The first is simply to learn from OECD environmental policy experience what

ISBN 92-64-01442-X © OECD 2005

works and what does not. Much such learning has occurred in developing Asia, based on OECD countries' early experience with so-called "command-and-control" measures. Only fairly recently have OECD countries begun to reform their environmental policies for greater cost-effectiveness, making more extensive use of economic instruments. A few OECD countries – notably Japan – have relied extensively on voluntary agreements between government and polluters as part of their policy arsenal, and some Asian developing countries have experimented with that approach as well. In some instances Asian developing countries have pioneered cost-effective environmental policies, teaching OECD countries rather than learning from them. Singapore's early experiments with permit auctions for ozone-depleting substances and private vehicle ownership, and also with road congestion pricing, are cases in point.

Korea presents perhaps the clearest example of an Asian country that has benefited from OECD experience with environmental policy, having taken advantage of its admission to membership in the Organisation to subject its environmental policy regime to peer review. In the conclusions to its first Environmental Performance Review of Korea, OECD (2000*b*) notes four points. First, Korea invests in environmental infrastructure. Environmental expenditures constitute 1.5 per cent of GDP, on a par with other OECD countries. Second, it uses both regulatory and economic instruments. Third, local government plays an increasing role in implementing policies. Fourth, environmental information and public participation are increasingly called upon. The same report notes Korea's creativity in developing an array of economic instruments of environmental policy, including emission charges, traffic congestion charges, energy taxes, a deposit-refund system and a waste management charge, but remarks that it generally sets charge and tax rates too low to alter behaviour significantly.

China too benefits from its close co-operation with the OECD, mostly through joint workshops on topics of mutual interest. A number of such workshops have been held over the past decade on various aspects of environmental policy. The Chinese government as well as various provincial and municipal governments have shown keen interest in applying economic instruments to environmental policy. China has long had a national system of industrial effluent charges. More recently, local governments have undertaken experiments with emission trading schemes, notably in an effort to control stationary-source emissions of sulphur dioxide[7]. At its 2004 Environmental Ministerial meeting and at the request of the Chinese government the OECD announced plans to undertake its first Environmental Performance Review of China.

 ISBN 92-64-01442-X © OECD 2005

One highly successful instance of know-how transfer from OECD countries to developing Asia concerns measures to phase out the use of lead in petrol. Scientific evidence of lead's damaging effects on neurological development of children as well as other adverse health effects caused forceful action in OECD countries to phase out leaded petrol, beginning in the 1970s. Since the early 1990s at least, a number of Asian developing countries have taken decisive measures to phase out leaded petrol, including the introduction of technology-based standards — e.g. mandatory installation of catalytic converters on new vehicles — and economic instruments — e.g. differential taxation of leaded and unleaded petrol. As a result, air quality in this dimension has shown marked improvement in many Asian cities over the past decade.

In a similar vein, a number of governments in developing Asia have instituted regulations reducing allowable sulphur content of diesel and bunker fuel. In Singapore, for instance, the sulphur content of industrial fuel cannot exceed 2 per cent by weight, while the permissible level of sulphur in diesel fuel was reduced from 0.3 per cent by weight to 0.05 per cent by weight from March 1999[8]. Since 1 January 2001, all petrol- and diesel-driven vehicles in Singapore have been required to comply with the EURO II exhaust emission standard.

Technology Transfer and Diffusion

OECD policies can also affect the environment in developing Asia *via* the transfer of environmental technologies developed in response to OECD-country regulations. The existence of the technologies does not itself ensure their widespread adoption, even in OECD countries. Stringent pollution standards there have encouraged widespread diffusion of abatement technologies, and this has generally resulted in price reductions through learning-by-doing and to some degree economies of scale. Even with falling OECD prices for environmental goods and services, two further conditions are necessary for accelerated diffusion to developing Asia: adoption and enforcement there of relatively stringent environmental standards and liberalisation of their environmental goods and services markets. OECD (2000*a*) examines the extent of import protection of this sector in various countries and estimates the benefits of reducing levels of protection. The average level of applied MFN tariffs on environmental goods and services in so-called emerging economies is estimated at 18 per cent. Malaysia and

Indonesia rank lowest with applied rates of 6 to 7 per cent, while India ranks highest at 61 per cent. As a type of capital good, pollution-abatement equipment is generally subject to lower tariffs than are consumer goods.

As the focus of environmental management efforts within enterprises – encouraged to a degree by a changed policy emphasis – shifts from end-of-pipe treatment towards cleaner production methods, improved environmental performance increasingly gets built into new capital equipment and managerial processes. Thus, liberalisation only of environmental capital goods imports might not prove particularly effective in encouraging adoption of state-of-the-art environmental control technologies. Vaughan (2003*b*) argues that limiting coverage of Doha Round negotiations on early liberalisation to traditional end-of-pipe technologies and narrowly defined environmental services would both favour traditional environmental engineering firms from developed countries and bias technology choices against the new generation of integrated cleaner production technologies and methods. A broader question concerns whether the definition of "environmental goods and services" should encompass so-called "green consumer goods", such as organically grown produce, in which developing countries could well enjoy a comparative advantage.

Another sort of technology diffusion from OECD countries to developing Asia has occurred as the result of motor vehicle sales. While motor vehicles are among the major sources of air pollution in Asia's cities, the situation could be much worse in cities such as Bangkok, Jakarta and Kuala Lumpur were it not that relatively fuel-efficient, low-emission vehicles make up a significant percentage of new private vehicle purchases. For the middle classes, this means for the most part Japanese compact cars or minivans; for the upper classes, corporate managers and government officials, it means luxury cars from Germany and Sweden that meet strict European fuel-efficiency and emission standards. The commercial vehicle stock tends to be far more polluting, especially with respect to particulates, partly because diesel engines dominate and partly because commercial vehicles are often older and less well maintained than private vehicles. In Bangkok in 2000, passenger cars contributed only 1 per cent of fine particulate compared with 89 per cent for trucks and buses, even though cars make up 44 per cent of the vehicle stock (WB Thailand, 2002).

Motorcycles embody an even more important transport-technology import by developing Asia from OECD countries, overwhelmingly from Japan. Over the past two decades, the numbers of motorcycles in use have ballooned across the region. Thailand, for example, has three motorcycles for every

 ISBN 92-64-01442-X © OECD 2005

private car; in the Philippines, the ratio is roughly two to one. Two-stroke motorcycles are major sources of hydrocarbon emissions and contribute significantly to fine particle and CO emissions. In the Philippines, two-stroke engines still power more than three-quarters of motorcycles and tricycles (WB Philippines, 2002); in Thailand the proportion with two-stroke engines is also very high. Even if the vehicle stock is two-stroke heavy, the new motorcycles on the market throughout the region are mostly of the four-stroke variety, which is far less polluting. In Thailand, for example, four-stroke sales overtook two-stroke sales in 1999 and the latter represented less than 20 per cent of new motorcycle sales in 2001. The new engines have been developed in response to regulatory pressure in exporting countries like Japan, but importing countries are also imposing stricter controls on two-stroke engines — even outright bans. To address the pollution problems from in-use vehicles, waiting for the turnover of the existing stock could take many years, so a number of motorcycle upgrade efforts have been launched across the region.

The transfer of cleaner vehicles is by no means solely from OECD countries to developing Asia. There has also been transfer within the region. In 2002, for example, Bangkok's LPG-powered three-wheelers (or *tuktuks*) began replacing Dhaka's petrol-fuelled "baby taxis", a major source of the city's air pollution[9]. The Thai manufacturer is setting up a joint venture to make the vehicles in Bangladesh for the local market.

Alongside trade, foreign direct investment (FDI) is another important channel of technology transfer. Historically, some countries in developing Asia have been far more open to FDI than others. At present, China is by a wide margin the largest net recipient of FDI. Some evidence suggests that this has had a strong positive impact on the environmental performance of certain industries. In the electricity sector, for example, Blackman and Wu (1998) find that wholly foreign-owned or joint-venture power plants are significantly more energy efficient than existing domestically owned ones, as measured by coal consumption per kWh of electricity generated. The main contributing factor is the use of advanced technologies such as combined-cycle gas turbines and circulating fluidised bed boilers. The authors note that, even for conventional power plants, the foreign-invested ones rely more heavily on imported equipment than domestic ones, suggesting that this factor may also contribute to the higher energy efficiency of the former.

Not all evidence points to a significant positive effect of FDI on environmental performance of industry in developing countries, however. In their examination of Mexican manufacturing, for example, Dasgupta *et al.* (2001)

find little evidence that either investment or trade links with OECD countries significantly influence firms' environmental compliance; on the other hand, firm size, public listing and internal environmental management systems of the ISO14001 type do. The finding of no significant effect from foreign ownership on pollution intensity is corroborated by a study of water pollution in Indonesia (Pargal and Wheeler, 1995).

The Pollution-Haven Hypothesis

Perhaps the most widely studied and debated transmission mechanism operates through changing comparative advantage, as environmental regulations in OECD countries raise the relative costs of certain industries and their products. Generally, studies look at the interaction between pre-existing environmental regulations in OECD countries and trade liberalisation *vis-à-vis* countries with more lax regulations. The "pollution-haven" hypothesis is the simplest formulation of the relationship between asymmetric environmental regulation and industrial location. In practice, one seldom observes clear-cut instances of a polluting factory shutting down in OECD country *x* and reopening in developing country *y*. What one can observe, however, is a much more rapid growth of industrial activity in general, including many polluting industries, in developing countries than in OECD countries. This is almost guaranteed, given the high GDP growth rates of countries such as China and India. Two further empirical questions need answers in order to shed light on the hypothesis: *i)* are polluting industries growing faster in developing countries than other industries? and *ii)* are they growing faster in more open economies than in more closed ones?

One piece of evidence — relating to the energy intensity of the economy — is suggestive. Over the past 20 years, few other Asian developing countries have integrated into the global economy more rapidly than China. Nor have any grown more rapidly. Yet the energy intensity of the Chinese economy has steadily and steeply declined; from 1991 to 2000 it was cut in half (World Bank, 2003). The Chinese story is complicated by the transition from a centrally planned economy, in which energy was used very inefficiently and the industrial structure was biased towards heavy industry. Thus, even in 2000, the energy intensity of China's GDP was still very high by comparison with other Asian countries, although on a par with India's.

Copeland and Taylor (2003) examine the evidence for a pollution-haven effect in international trade and find little to support it. Other factors than differential environmental regulation have a far greater effect on patterns of

ISBN 92-64-01442-X © OECD 2005

specialisation and trade. Indeed, they find that OECD countries have a comparative advantage in dirty industries by virtue of their greater capital, skill and technology endowments. If this is true, then with dirty industries tending to concentrate in countries with relatively stringent environmental regulations global pollution would tend to be lower than with less specialisation and trade.

Cole and Elliott (2003) follow a similar research strategy but postulate three productive factors: land, capital and the environment. They hypothesise that poorer countries will generally have more lax environmental regulations, and, if the pollution-haven hypothesis is valid, those lax regulations would tend to attract polluting industries. On the other hand, if one examines relative endowments of labour and capital, then with free trade developed countries would tend to specialise in capital-intensive sectors. Yet because these also are relatively polluting sectors, this implies that developed countries would specialise in polluting industries. The two sorts of effect, then, work in opposite directions and can even cancel each other out. The authors find that, for SO_2 emissions, a trade-induced income increase of 1 per cent would tend to lower per capita emissions by 1.7 per cent *via* a combined scale and technique effect. Since the trade-intensity elasticity is positive, however — i.e. the composition effect for the median country favours polluting industries — the net effect of trade liberalisation on these emissions is ambiguous. In the case of BOD, moreover, trade liberalisation will tend to reduce per capita emissions, while it is likely to increase both NO_x and CO_2 emissions. When measured in terms of pollution intensity — emissions per unit of output — the effect of trade liberalisation is to lower intensity for all the pollutants studied.

Frankel and Rose (2002) estimate econometrically the impact of trade openness on three measures of air pollution, accounting for the simultaneous determination of trade, per capita income and environmental quality. They find that for all three measures openness is negatively associated with pollution levels[10], with the relationship highly significant for SO_2, moderately so for NO_2 and insignificant for particulates.

One can observe a different sort of relationship between openness and environmental performance in the rate of ISO14001 certifications across countries. While the author is aware of no econometric estimation of the impact of openness on the propensity of enterprises to seek such environmental management certification, the ISO14001 rankings are suggestive. The latest available set is for June 2002, and it shows China, Chinese Taipei, Korea, Brazil, Thailand and India ranking among the top 20, with Malaysia 21st; all the others at the top of the league are OECD countries[11].

Green and Not-So-Green Consumerism

Some environmental requirements, government-mandated or otherwise, may have effects on ease of access to OECD markets. These include product standards (e.g. energy efficiency standards), labelling requirements, packaging regulations and certain sanitary and phytosanitary measures. Even if these are non-discriminatory, the technical requirements of meeting them can prove especially burdensome for low-income developing countries and especially for the multitude of small and medium-scale enterprises that operate in those countries. To the extent that such measures restrict commerce with or divert commerce from such countries, they are likely to consign them to lower incomes than otherwise.

Changing consumer preferences in OECD countries can also have important implications for what gets produced and how in developing Asia. Eco-labelling schemes are an increasingly common means by which OECD consumers can seek to influence not just the environmental characteristics of products but those of production processes — e.g. through forest certification schemes that identify timber products as coming from sustainably managed forests. Sustainably grown coffee offers another example. While there is no internationally agreed definition of such coffee, the numerous labelling and certification schemes cover a range of criteria, including — in "fair-trade" schemes — the prices paid to small growers. These schemes are generally voluntary and as such do not contravene international trade rules. They offer to those who can qualify the prospect of a potentially sizeable price premium — between 52 and 62 cents per pound of coffee in early 2003 (Vaughan, 2003*b*). They also raise the question of the responsibility of OECD governments and/or business and consumer groups to provide technical assistance to small-scale developing country producers to enable them to qualify for a given eco-label. Otherwise, there is the risk of demand diversion to larger producers in developing countries and/or to countries already possessing the capacity to supply according to eco-label specifications. Indeed, a number of OECD countries provide technical assistance to developing-country exporters to help them comply with eco-labelling requirements[12].

In some instances, the demand for certification of production methods on criteria of environmental sustainability may be driven by large OECD buyers rather than directly by final consumers. For instance, UK supermarket chains require producers of fresh fruits and vegetables to abide by detailed integrated crop management standards and controls on genetically modified

 ISBN 92-64-01442-X © OECD 2005

organisms. Large automakers have begun to require suppliers to achieve compliance with an environmental management system based on ISO14001, with third-party certification (Najam and Robins, 2000). The motivations of such companies probably have more to do with trying to avoid costly boycotts by activist NGOs or lawsuits for alleged environmental damages than they do with satisfying the preferences of the majority of consumers. Another example is the decision by supermarket chains, under pressure from European consumer groups, to label fresh flowers as "grown without the use of methyl bromide", a potent ozone-depleting substance. This has forced Kenyan flower growers, the second largest source of cut flowers on the Dutch auction market, to alter their production methods, abandoning the use of this soil fumigant even though a close substitute does not yet exist (Barrett *et al.*, 2001). In any event, this trend suggests that, even as governments seek to resist encroachment on national sovereignty in the matter of dictating process and production methods (PPMs), the private sector is extending its control over such methods transnationally as part of the process of globalisation. As that happens, OECD-based multinationals have become increasingly active in managing their global supply chains to ensure that the environmental and social practices of their suppliers in developing countries do not pose liabilities to their own brand images. Asian manufacturers have been particularly affected by this trend, as they have evolved strong links to such supply chains.

Not all aspects of consumer demand in OECD markets are environmentally benign. In fresh foods, for example, a concern for aesthetics — how uniform and flawless fresh fruit and vegetables appear on supermarket shelves — has induced farmers to use chemical fungicides, insecticides and pesticides in large volumes. Dasgupta *et al.* (2001) find that in Brazil pesticide use concentrates in areas heavily dependent on export-oriented cash cropping, with more than one-third of water samples in those areas excessively contaminated. Conflicting evidence comes from Brazil on trade liberalisation's environmental impacts. In the soya, corn, millet and sorghum sectors there has been a shift to conservation tillage and non-tillage systems, which have allowed reduced use of herbicides and consequent conservation of biodiversity (UNCTAD, 2000). Nutrient-rich waste from the burgeoning export-oriented, large-scale livestock industry is also a major source of water pollution in a number of developing Asian countries, from China's and Chinese Taipei's piggeries to Thailand's and Viet Nam's poultry farms.

ISBN 92-64-01442-X © OECD 2005

OECD-Country Economic Policies and Developing Asia's Environment

As noted at the outset, the concern from the perspective of OECD countries' policy coherence *vis-à-vis* the environmental conditions of developing Asia is not just their environmental policies but the full range of policies that impact on the Asian environment, directly or indirectly. Moreover, one would like to be able to assess the net environmental effects of the application of the full policy suite, taking into account possible interactions and interdependencies among them. For instance, trade policies of OECD countries may well have important implications for the environment in developing Asia, not to mention other parts of the developing world. Supposing those effects in a given instance are adverse, one would like to know whether other policies — e.g. in the area of development co-operation — are designed to offset them.

Agricultural Policies

OECD agricultural policies clearly exemplify economic policies with significant environmental implications for developing countries, including those in Asia. How would anticipated OECD-country agricultural subsidy reforms under the Doha Development Round be expected to impact on the developing Asian environment? Substantial reductions of levels of protection in the rice markets of Japan and Korea would undoubtedly cause rice exports from countries like India, Thailand and Viet Nam to surge. Intensification of cultivation seems a more likely response than extending areas under cultivation, as population and competing economic pressures on scarce land resources are already acute, especially in India and Viet Nam. The effect could be higher nutrient loads and pesticide concentration in agricultural runoff and possibly chemical contamination of soils. On the other hand, agriculture in Japan and Korea is already among the most chemical-intensive in the world, so the environment in those countries could benefit from reduced agricultural activity[13]. In a similar vein, Abler and Shortle (1992) examine the impact on agricultural chemical use of the bilateral elimination of farm support programmes in the EU and the United States, predicting a shift of production and chemical use from the former to the latter.

ISBN 92-64-01442-X © OECD 2005

The exact environmental impacts of agricultural subsidies and, by implication, of subsidy removal are complex. Besides agricultural chemical use, agricultural practices can impact on the environment in a number of other ways. OECD (2002) reports several agriculture-specific environmental indicators: nitrogen efficiency in agriculture; methane (CH_4) and nitrous oxide (N_2O) emissions per unit of agricultural output; and water use per unit of agricultural output. By altering price signals, subsidies can induce substitution of polluting inputs for non-polluting ones and/or substitution of high-emission activities (e.g. dairy cows) for low-emission ones (e.g. cereals and sheep) (Lingard, 2002).

Using panel data for 22 OECD countries, Lewandrowski *et al.* (1997) find the size of the producer subsidy equivalent (PSE) positively and significantly related to fertiliser use per hectare. On the other hand, the amount of land cultivated tends to be negatively associated with the level of support, since a reduction in support makes land cheaper and stimulates its use. Using a computable general equilibrium model of the global economy, the OECD's *Environmental Outlook* estimates the impact of agricultural subsidy removal in OECD countries on irrigation water use in both member and non-member countries. In the former, it is projected to drop by 10 per cent, while in the latter it would rise by about 4 per cent (see Ruffing, 2003). Similar impacts are projected for livestock BOD loadings (with member countries experiencing a 2.5 per cent decline and non-members a 4 per cent increase) and nitrogen water pollution (6 per cent and 4 per cent respectively). These numbers are highly speculative, but they strike one by their relatively small size. The largest percentage increase in any of the impact measures in non-member countries is below 5 per cent, and it would follow a rather marked policy shift, namely the total elimination of OECD agricultural subsidies.

Another apparent impact of OECD production-linked agricultural subsidies and price support has been to discourage farmers from crop rotation, encouraging instead monoculture in the subsidised crop. This is one of the main causes of soil erosion and overuse of fertilisers and pesticides (UNCTAD, 2000).

One difficulty in assessing the environmental effects of changes in agricultural method — whether policy-induced or not — is the possibly long lag between such changes and any measurable environmental impacts. For instance, the delay between implementation of a measure to control nitrate pollution and a lowering of groundwater nitrate concentrations can be measured in decades (Brouwer, 2001).

Trade Policies

Trade policies more generally can have an important environmental dimension. Both regional and multilateral trade liberalisation could be expected to reorient production structures across countries and to have effects on income levels and possibly on technology choices. All three sorts of effect would tend to have environmental implications, as discussed above in connection with the pollution-haven hypothesis.

Vaughan (2003*a*) examines the environmental effects of the North American Free Trade Agreement (NAFTA), focusing in particular on US-Mexico agricultural trade. From analysis of the wheat, maize and fresh vegetables and fruits markets he concludes that the environmental safeguards in NAFTA have not directly improved environmental quality in the farm sector. He also finds that liberalisation of maize trade was too rapid and disruptive, causing price and employment shocks in Mexico and increasing ecological risk from the importation of genetically modified maize. Also, reduced maize prices have contributed to a structural change in the sector by way of deeper vertical integration with livestock operations based on large-scale confined-animal feedlots. These environmental pressures in turn cause others. Increased US maize exports to Mexico are estimated to have raised nitrogen, phosphorus, and potassium-based loadings in waterways by some 77 000 tons, with a concentration in the heavily polluted Mississippi River Delta. Also, the absence from NAFTA of any disciplines constraining subsidies has meant that both the United States and Mexico have raised subsidies, leading to overproduction of some crops as well as excessive application of fertiliser and other inputs. The distribution of subsidy payments has tended to favour large-scale, export-oriented farms, which also happen to use especially large quantities of agrochemicals and irrigation water per hectare. This finding is consistent with that of Dasgupta *et al.* (2001) for Brazilian agriculture.

Vaughan also finds that the expansion of large-scale, intensive agriculture does not seem to have yielded even those environmental benefits expected of it through a reduction in area under cultivation. He suggests that this is attributable to downward price pressure on maize from cheap US imports, which has impoverished marginal farmers in southern Mexico, leading to an expansion of cultivation into previously forested areas. Small-scale, rain-fed maize production has expanded by 18 per cent in marginal areas. Because Mexico is a leading centre of "megadiversity" — home to 10 per cent of all known species, of which 30 to 50 per cent are endemic — deforestation comes at a potentially high cost.

 ISBN 92-64-01442-X © OECD 2005

No comparable regional free trade agreement links Asian developing countries to developed ones, so the analysis of NAFTA has no direct applicability to the region. Most major countries in the region are, however, members of the WTO and those that are not soon will be. Thus, how the environmentally relevant provisions of the WTO are applied by OECD countries to their trade with developing countries of Asia is an issue. The main provisions are as follows. Article XX on "General Exceptions" permits unilateral trade restrictions under certain circumstances (including environmental protection), so long as the restrictions are non-discriminatory across countries. The Agreement on Technical Barriers to Trade (TBT) deals with technical standards such as packaging and labelling requirements. The Agreement on the Application of Sanitary and Phytosanitary Measures (SPS) deals with human, animal and plant health standards. The last two both aim to harmonise product standards and to avoid their use as disguised protectionism (Brack and Branczik, 2004).

Within the WTO, environment-related notifications under the TBT have been increasing, from 10 per cent of all such notifications in the early 1990s to 15 to 16 per cent in recent years (UNCTAD, 2004). Within the environmental category, product performance standards for energy efficiency represent the largest subcategory. As Asian developing countries are among the world's largest exporters of electrical appliances and electronic goods, these standards have clear relevance to their own market access. The mention of "sustainable development" in the preamble of the Agreement establishing the WTO was initially thought to be merely *pro forma*. Yet the WTO Appellate Body cited it as an acceptable justification for particular trade measures in the 1998 shrimp-turtle dispute between the United States and some Southeast Asian countries. In that case, the measure was a US embargo on imports of shrimp from countries which did not require the fitting to their trawlers of turtle-excluder devices designed to avoid incidental catches of endangered sea turtles (Brack and Branczik, 2004).

With increasing globalisation of agricultural and livestock product markets, sanitary standards are becoming a visible concern in international trade, as evidenced by the recent, highly publicised cases of livestock disease, from mad cow disease to avian flu. The latter has had an especially large impact on the poultry industries of several developing Asian countries, notably Thailand, which is one of the largest exporters of broiler chickens in the world, but also Viet Nam.

ISBN 92-64-01442-X

The question of whether goods and services should be distinguished in international trade — and associated customs codes — according to their environmental characteristics remains politically sensitive and technically complex. Nevertheless, the World Customs Organisation in January 2002 set a potentially significant precedent by including in its revised Harmonized System (HS) codes stand-alone criteria covering environmental and social issues (Vaughan, 2003*b*), in this case for wastes and chemicals specified under the Basel Convention and the Montreal Protocol.

Investment Policies

The large international capital flows of the past few decades have the potential to drive convergence towards governance practices based on certain shared social, political and environmental standards. The rapid growth of so-called "socially responsible investment" (SRI) funds is one important influence towards convergence, although not the only one. Approximately one in eight dollars of investment under professional management in the United States is subjected to social and/or environmental screening of some kind (Vaughan, 2003*b*). While the amount of such screened investment in Asian markets is still small (around $2 billion compared to $2 trillion in the United States), it is expected to grow rapidly[14]. In any event, to the extent that SRI funds influence practices of publicly listed companies in OECD countries, they will likely influence their global practices, not just their domestic ones. In an age of cheap and rapid global communications, highly abusive labour or environmental practices of high-visibility companies in developing countries stand little chance of going unnoticed and unpublicised for long. The threat of consumer boycotts is another influence on brand-conscious companies favouring adherence to certain widely recognised social and environmental standards.

Fund managers are bound by the "prudent man" rule not to take undue risks with their clients' money, but to seek always the highest possible return consistent with a given risk exposure. This has generally meant ignoring any investment criteria considered extraneous to the pursuit of financial performance. Interestingly, while the evidence is inconclusive on whether SRI funds outperform comparable non-screened funds, there is little evidence to suggest that SRI funds under-perform. Thus, it would appear that socially responsible investors do not pay a significant price for their portfolio choices.

ISBN 92-64-01442-X © OECD 2005

Multinational companies have increasingly applied corporate codes of conduct beyond the boundaries of their firms, to encompass their suppliers as well. Perhaps the most celebrated case involves Nike, the sports shoe manufacturer, which under pressure of adverse publicity over workers' treatment at a Korean-owned supplier in Viet Nam, has instituted an extensive programme to train and certify suppliers to meet company-mandated labour standards. Nike and many other reputation-sensitive multinationals have aligned themselves with one or another international code of good practice in an effort to pre-empt similar adverse publicity in future. The OECD Guidelines for Multinational Enterprises seek to reinforce and to complement the various private corporate-standard and reporting initiatives by providing a common frame of reference and an institutional home for international efforts to encourage progress towards good corporate governance in a broad sense[15]. By virtue of its association with the United Nations, the Global Compact has assumed a particularly prominent place among voluntary initiatives to promote corporate responsibility, involving the adherence by corporate members to ten basic principles in the areas of human rights, labour standards, the environment and anti-corruption[16]. The network of Global Compact affiliates spans the globe, encompassing local networks in a number of developing countries as well as most OECD countries.

O'Connor (2000) examines a range of international capital flows and their environmental characteristics, including public credits as well as private bank lending, capital markets and foreign direct investment. Export credit agencies of OECD governments have traditionally been important financiers of capital equipment exports to developing countries, including equipment for basic infrastructure such as power plants. Environmental and other NGOs have critically examined their loan portfolios, and they have faced some of the same pressures as multinational corporations to adhere to codes of good practice. In general, this has meant that bilateral export credit agencies have aligned their policies with those of the Bretton Woods institutions, which have become the *de facto* standard bearers in this regard. Those institutions, notably the World Bank, face difficult decisions. They must seek to reconcile the demands of their developing-country clients, including demands to finance power plants, with the recommendation of an independent review panel (headed by Indonesia's former Environment Minister, Emil Salim) against financing any project that would generate net greenhouse gas emissions.

Towards Policy Coherence in Support of Sustainable Development

This chapter has sought to evaluate — mostly in qualitative terms but with reference to the quantitative literature as well — the impacts of OECD member countries' environmental and economic policies on the environment of developing Asia. Those external impacts are mediated through the domestic policy environments in Asian countries. Where strong policies and practices encourage sustainable harvesting or extraction of natural resources, trade opening need not have an adverse environmental impact. Moreover, those policies and practices often themselves result from learning and know-how transfers from OECD countries.

Policy coherence implies not that individual OECD policies but rather combinations of policies — in the limit, the entire suite of policies, environmental and economic — have positive effects on the environment in developing Asia (or at minimum not negative ones). Demonstrating this systematically has not been possible, but a few broad patterns do emerge. First, while different environmental indicators show different patterns of change over the past few decades, the general tendency has been towards environmental improvement, especially in the more prosperous countries of the region. This may be attributable in part to the familiar relationship between rising incomes and increased demand for environmental quality, but arguably a number of other factors contribute, not least the growing interdependencies between developing Asia and OECD countries.

OECD-country environmental policies would appear generally to have had a positive demonstration effect on developing Asia. (One exception may be climate-change policy, where the incomplete OECD-wide ratification of the Kyoto Protocol may complicate efforts to persuade large greenhouse gas emitters in developing Asia to adopt measures to control their own emissions.) Environmental standards and policy instruments of OECD countries have often served as a point of reference if not always an explicit model as developing Asian countries have grappled with many of the same environmental challenges faced by their OECD predecessors. Moreover, the technologies and management techniques developed in response to OECD regulations have been available and frequently diffused to developing Asian countries, largely through trade and foreign investment. Development assistance has also been an important means of accessing good environmental practices, as the multilateral and regional development banks as well as bilateral donors have become increasingly conscious of the need to adopt such practices in their development projects.

ISBN 92-64-01442-X

OECD economic policies paint a mixed picture. OECD-country agricultural policies are generally harmful to developing-country agricultural exporters, including several major ones in developing Asia (India, Indonesia, Thailand and Viet Nam). While liberalisation of OECD agricultural markets might have some modest adverse effects on the environment in developing countries (e.g. through expansion of cultivated area at the expense of forest area), there could also be positive income effects on demand for environmental quality. Most exports from developing Asia are and will continue to be manufactures and services. OECD-country markets are already relatively open to them. To the extent, then, that trade openness is associated with environmental impacts, positive or negative, we should already be witnessing them to a significant extent. Two countries, however, offer by virtue of recent membership in the WTO (China) or prospective membership (Viet Nam) real-world experiments in the impact of trade liberalisation on the domestic environment. These cases commend themselves to study.

China should also provide fertile ground for the study of the impacts of FDI on the environment, as the developing country that has attracted by far the greatest amount of such investment in recent years. Similarly, both China and Viet Nam are among the largest borrowers from the World Bank, and Viet Nam is the largest IDA client. They are also among the largest recipients of bilateral assistance from certain major OECD donors. Once again, a meticulous study of ODA from all major sources and its environmental effects in these countries could prove enlightening.

With globalisation, consumers in OECD countries and the multinational enterprises that satisfy their demands play an increasingly prominent role in shaping the environmental practices of productive enterprises in developing Asia. Multinationals themselves may find it in their self-interest to transfer know-how on environmental management and labour standards to developing-country enterprises closely linked to their supply chains. In some cases, the environmental requirements of OECD markets are not mediated along supply chains. Rather, developing-country producers must themselves take measures to comply, e.g. with eco-labelling requirements or phytosanitary standards. In those cases, technical assistance supported by development co-operation funds may be an important means of ensuring that those requirements do not discriminate against small-scale and poor producers in the developing world. Also, associations of importers in OECD markets — e.g. major carpet importers or fresh-produce importers — could be offered

ISBN 92-64-01442-X © OECD 2005

some fiscal incentives to assist developing-country suppliers that are too small and/or too poor to adapt on their own, rather than switch to more technically adept and better capitalised ones.

In the final analysis, policy coherence is a matter of degree, not an absolute. On net, the judgement here based on the preceding analysis is that there has been progress towards greater coherence of OECD policies *vis-à-vis* the environment of developing Asia over the past few decades. This arises from a combination of:

— greater recognition in developing Asia of the value of stronger environmental safeguards;

— a tendency for those countries to look to OECD countries for guidance when crafting environmental regulations and policies;

— the profuse flow of technologies from OECD countries to developing Asia that has accompanied the two groups' closer economic integration; and

— a stronger appreciation by many OECD-based multinational enterprises of the value of greater corporate social responsibility and environmental stewardship.

There are exceptions to these generalisations, e.g. in the domain of climate change, but even here some OECD-based enterprises have seized the initiative from reluctant governments to promote development of low-carbon energy technologies and tighter controls on greenhouse gas emissions.

ISBN 92-64-01442-X © OECD 2005

Notes

1. The author would like to thank Tom Jones, Alexandra Trzeciak-Duval and Kiichiro Fukasaku, all of the OECD, as well as other participants in a seminar held at the OECD in Paris, June 2004, for valuable comments on an earlier draft. The views expressed here are the author's alone and do not necessarily reflect those of his affiliated institution.

2. For a discussion of environmental trends in the dynamic Asian economies through the early 1990s, see Appendix A of O'Connor (1996).

3. While originally identified over South Asia, it is now thought that a belt of such atmospheric pollution spans the globe from Los Angeles to Cairo to Mumbai and Delhi to Beijing; hence the change of name to "atmospheric brown cloud"; http://www.cnn.com/2004/TECH/science/02/25/asia.cloud.reut/.

4. An "improved" source is one that is likely to provide "safe" water, such as a household connection, a public standpipe, a borehole, a protected dug well or spring, or rainwater harvesting.

5. Korea's per hectare fertiliser use is 40 per cent higher than Japan's and over 60 per cent higher than China's.

6. Presentation by Z.A. Rahman, Department of Environment, Malaysia, on "Water Quality Management in Malaysia"; http://www.iges.or.jp/jp/ltp/pdf/fr2.pdf.

7. For instance, the ADB has signed an agreement with officials in Taiyuan, Shanxi province, to operate a sulphur dioxide trading system in an attempt to cut emissions by 50 per cent within five years. See Morgenstern *et al.* (2004) for an analysis of the experimental design.

8. http://app.nea.gov.sg/cms/htdocs/article.asp?pid=1528#air.

9. http://www.planetark.com/dailynewsstory.cfm?newsid=17066&newsdate=29-Jul-2002.

10. They also confirm the environmental Kuznets curve hypothesis for all three pollutants – most strongly for SO_2 and HO_2.

11. http://www.inem.org/htdocs/iso/speedometer/speedo-06_2002.html#Anchor-Top-49575. It is likely more than coincidence that all but one of the developing countries listed in the top 20 are Asian export-oriented economies, although they clearly vary in their degree of openness.

12. One recent example is Finnish technical assistance to Nepalese industry – including carpet and garment manufacturers – to comply with international eco-labelling schemes: http://www.fncci.org/ecolabelproject/about.html.

13. For example, pesticide application rates in Korea and Japan are 11.8 kg/ha and 19.4 kg/ha respectively, compared to around 1.0 kg/ha for Viet Nam. Application rates in Chinese Taipei are even higher than in Japan (see: http://www.fftc.agnet.org/library/article/ac1998e.html). In all three industrialised countries, however, pesticide use has been declining in recent years.

14. See http://www.asria.org/sri/asia/sriasia.

15. http://www.oecd.org/document/58/0,2340,en_2649_34889_2349370_1_1_1_37439,00.html.

16. www.unglobalcompact.org/Portal/?NavigationTarget=/roles/portal_user/aboutTheGC/nf/nf/theNinePrinciples.

ISBN 92-64-01442-X © OECD 2005

Bibliography

ABLER, D.G. and J.S. SHORTLE (1992), "Environmental and Farm Commodity Policy Linkages in the US and the EC", *European Review of Agricultural Economics*, 19, pp. 197-217.

BARRETT, C.B., E.B. BARBIER and T. REARDON (2001), "Agroindustrialization, Globalization, and International Development: the Environmental Implications", *Environment and Development Economics*, 6(4), 419-433.

BLACKMAN, A. and X. WU (1998), "Foreign Direct Investment in China's Power Sector: Trends, Benefits and Barriers", Resources for the Future Discussion Paper 98-50, Washington, D.C., September.

BRACK, D. and T. BRANCZIK (2004), "Trade and Environment in the WTO: after Cancun", Briefing Paper No. 9, The Royal Institute of International Affairs, London, February.

BROUWER, F. (2001), "Effects of Agricultural Policies and Practices on the Environment: Review of Empirical Work in OECD Countries", OECD Directorate for Food, Agriculture and Fisheries, available at: COM/AGR/CA/ENV/EPOC(2001)60/FINAL, 17 July, Paris.

COLE, M.A. and R.J.R. ELLIOTT (2003), "Determining the Trade-Environment Composition Effect: The Role of Capital, Labor and Environmental Regulations", *Journal of Environmental Economics and Management*, 46, pp. 363-383.

COPELAND, B.R. and M.S. TAYLOR (2003), *Trade and the Environment: Theory and Evidence*, Princeton University Press, Princeton, N.J.

DASGUPTA, S., N. MAMINGI and C. MEISNER (2001), "Pesticide Use in Brazil in the Era of Agroindustrialization and Globalization", *Environment and Development Economics*, 6(4), pp. 459-482.

FRANKEL, J.A. and A. K. ROSE (2002), "Is Trade Good or Bad for the Environment? Sorting Out the Causality", NBER Working Paper No. 9201, National Bureau of Economic Research, Cambridge, MA.

HEI (2004), *Health Effects of Outdoor Air Pollution in Developing Countries of Asia*, Health Effects Institute, Special Report 15, April.

JHA, R. and J. WHALLEY (1999), "The Environmental Regime in Developing Countries", NBER Working Paper No. 7305, Cambridge, MA, August.

LEWANDROWSKI, J., J. TOBEY and Z. COOK (1997), "The Interface between Agricultural Assistance and the Environment: Chemical Fertilizer Consumption and Area Expansion", *Land Economics*, 73(3), pp. 404-427.

LINGARD, J. (2002), "Agricultural Subsidies and Environmental Change", *Encyclopedia of Global Environmental Change*, John Wiley & Sons, Ltd., New York.

LOPEZ, J. G., T. STERNER and S. AFSAH (2004), "Public Disclosure of Industrial Pollution: The PROPER Approach for Indonesia?", Resources for the Future, Discussion Paper 04-34, Washington, D.C., October.

MORGENSTERN, R., P. ABEYGUNAWARDENA, R. ANDERSON, R. GREENSPAN BELL, A. KRUPNICK, J. SCHREIFELS, CAO D., WANG J., WANG J. and S. LARSEN (2004), "Emissions Trading to Improve Air Quality in an Industrial City in the People's Republic of China", Resources for the Future Discussion paper 04-16, Washington, D.C., April.

NAJAM, A. and N. ROBINS (2000), "Seizing the Future: the South, Sustainable Development and International Trade", *International Affairs*, 77(1), pp. 49-67.

O'CONNOR, D. (1996), "Grow Now/Clean Later, or Pursuit of Sustainable Development?", Working Paper No. 111, OECD Development Centre, Paris, March.

O'CONNOR, D. (2000), "Global Capital Flows and the Environment in the 21st Century", Working Paper No. 161, OECD Development Centre, Paris, July.

OECD (2000*a*), *Environmental Goods and Services: An Examination of the Environmental, Economic and Development Benefits of Further Global Trade Liberalisation*, Joint Working Party on Trade and Environment, COM/TD/ENV(2000)86/FINAL, Paris, 5 October.

OECD (2000*b*), *Environmental Performance Reviews (1st Cycle). Conclusions and Recommendations: 32 Countries (1993-2000)*, Paris, November.

OECD (2002), *Indicators to Measure Decoupling of Environmental Pressure from Economic Growth*, General Secretariat, SG/SD(2002)1/FINAL, Paris, 16 May.

PARGAL, S. and D. WHEELER (1995), "Informal Regulation of Industrial Pollution in Developing Countries: Evidence from Indonesia", Policy Research Department, World Bank, Washington, D.C., February.

RUFFING, K. (2003), "OECD Environmental Outlook: Main Features and Policy Implications", presentation to Workshop on Environmental Outlook/Future Scenarios, World Bank, Washington, D.C., 18 December.

 ISBN 92-64-01442-X © OECD 2005

STERN, D.I. (2002), "Explaining Changes in Global Sulphur Emissions: An Econometric Decomposition Approach", *Ecological Economics*, 42, pp. 201-220.

UNITED NATIONS (2002), *World Urbanization Prospects: The 2001 Revision*, New York, NY.

UNCTAD (2000), *Havana Workshop on Trade and Environment, 31 May-2 June 2000. Draft Workshop Report*, Geneva.

UNCTAD (2004), "Environmental Requirements and Market Access for Developing Countries", Note by the UNCTAD Secretariat, TD/(XI)/BP/1, Geneva, 20 April.

UNEP (2000), *Second ASEAN State of the Environment Report*, downloaded from:

http://www.rrcap.unep.org/sub-region/aseansoe/Chapter8%20.pdf.

VAUGHAN, S. (2003*a*), "The Greenest Trade Agreement Ever? Measuring the Environmental Impacts of Agricultural Liberalization", Chapter 3 of *NAFTA's Promise and Reality: Lessons from Mexico for the Hemisphere*, Carnegie Endowment for International Peace, Washington, D.C.

VAUGHAN, S. (2003*b*), "Trade Preferences and Environmental Goods", Trade, Equity and Development Series, No. 5, Carnegie Endowment for International Peace, Washington, D.C., February.

WOOD, S.M., H.H. AMIR and M. BORDT (1992), "Environmental Management in Indonesia: Challenge and Response", report prepared for the OECD Development Centre, Paris.

WORLD BANK (2003), *World Development Indicators 2003*, database on CD-ROM.

WB PHILIPPINES (2002), *Philippines Environment Monitor 2002*, Manila, November.

WB THAILAND (2001), *Thailand Environment Monitor 2000*, Bangkok, June.

WB THAILAND (2002), *Thailand Environment Monitor 2002*, Bangkok, November.

WHO/UNICEF (2004), Joint Monitoring Programme for Water and Sanitation website: http://www.wssinfo.org/en/236_wat_asiaSE_en.html (visited 10 May 2004).

Part Three

The Regional Dimensions of Policy Linkages

Chapter 8

Regional Economic Integration and Co-operation in East Asia

Masahiro Kawai

Abstract

This chapter examines the extent to which the East Asian economies are integrated through trade, FDI and finance and are interdependent in macroeconomic co-movements. It next explores the factors behind recent economic regionalism in East Asia, in trade and investment on the one hand and money and finance on the other, and identifies the important features. Finally, it discusses the role of OECD-country policies in further assisting economic integration and co-operation in East Asia. The main message is that OECD countries — notably Japan, Korea, the United States, Australia and those in Europe — have played critical roles in promoting regional economic integration in East Asia. They have maintained stable macroeconomic and financial environments, a liberal trading system and stable flows of private risk capital, particularly FDI, and they have set effective ODA policies. The chapter also argues that the emerging East Asian economies have achieved sustained economic development and poverty reduction through external liberalisation, domestic structural, institutional and governance reforms and market-driven integration with the global and regional markets. Although the Asian financial crisis in 1997-98 temporarily interrupted this process, these economies have pursued further liberalisation and reforms, deepened economic integration through trade, FDI and finance and regained dynamic growth. One lesson from the East Asian experience is that developing economies must strengthen domestic policy, institutional and governance underpinnings so that they can benefit from good policies pursued by OECD countries.

ISBN 92-64-01442-X

Introduction

Over the last two decades, the East Asian economies have achieved substantial liberalisation of foreign trade and direct investment (FDI) regimes within the frameworks of GATT/WTO and APEC. The resulting expansion of both trade and FDI has become the engine of economic growth and development in East Asia. Trade and FDI openness has encouraged domestic institutional and governance reforms, which have further promoted trade and investment. Since the early 1990s, emerging East Asia has also pursued increasing financial openness. This has contributed to rapid economic growth by attracting both long-term and short-term capital and, together with trade and FDI openness, has deepened market-driven economic interdependence in East Asia. Yet it added financial vulnerabilities, culminating in a financial crisis in 1997-98.

Since the crisis, the East Asian economies have embarked on regional economic co-operation in both trade/investment and money/finance. The crisis prompted them to realise the importance of closer economic co-operation among themselves because they were increasingly interdependent, and to undertake various initiatives for the institutionalisation of such interdependence. For example, Japan and Singapore concluded an economic partnership agreement (EPA), and many official discussions and negotiations for bilateral and sub-regional free trade agreements (FTAs) — such as a Japan-Korea EPA, a China-ASEAN FTA, a Japan-ASEAN EPA and a Korea-ASEAN FTA — are currently underway. In money and finance, the ASEAN+3 members — ASEAN, China, Japan and Korea — have begun the Chiang Mai Initiative, economic surveillance, policy dialogue and Asian bond-market development initiatives.

This chapter has three objectives. First, it examines the extent to which the regional economies are integrated through trade, FDI and finance and are interdependent in macroeconomic co-movements. Second, it explores the factors behind recent economic regionalism in East Asia, in trade and investment on the one hand and money and finance on the other, and identifies its important features. Finally, it discusses the role of OECD-country policies in further assisting economic integration and co-operation in East Asia. The main message is that OECD countries — notably Japan, Korea, the United States, Australia and those in Europe — have played critical roles in promoting regional economic integration in East Asia. They have maintained stable macroeconomic and financial environments, a liberal trading system and stable flows of private risk capital, particularly FDI, and they have set effective ODA policies. One lesson from the East Asian experience is that

ISBN 92-64-01442-X

developing economies must strengthen domestic policy, institutional and governance underpinnings so that they can benefit from good policies pursued by OECD countries.

The organisation of the chapter is as follows. The next section summarises the impact of the crisis on economic regionalism in East Asia. The following one discusses the logic of regional economic co-operation, emphasising the importance of increasing economic interdependence among the regional economies and the lack of regional institutions and mechanisms to match such interdependence. A fourth section reviews the current states of regional trade arrangements and examines the challenges for further institutionalisation of trade and investment integration. Section five turns to regional financial co-operation and investigates the challenges for greater institutionalisation of regional financial integration. Section six examines the role of OECD-country policies in promoting further economic integration and co-operation in East Asia. The concluding remarks argue that deeper economic integration in trade, investment and finance can induce market-based reforms in all countries involved and that OECD countries can assist such regional efforts.

Impact of the Asian Financial Crisis

Causes and Lessons of the 1997-98 Crisis

There is now a consensus that the East Asian financial crisis of 1997-98 resulted from interactions between the forces of financial globalisation and domestic structural weaknesses (World Bank, 1998, 2000)[1]. Financial globalisation induced massive reversals of capital flows and triggered currency crises and contagion. Although the deeper, structural causes of crises vary, there was a common factor across countries: imprudently managed domestic financial institutions over-extended loans to corporations that in turn invested the borrowed funds in unproductive projects. Furthermore, an initially benign-looking currency crisis evolved into a full-blown economic crisis due to the mutually reinforcing impacts of currency depreciation, financial-sector deterioration, and corporate distress.

Forces of Financial Globalisation

The crisis-affected countries that had liberalised international capital flows had been integrated with the international capital markets before the crisis. Many emerging East Asian economies clearly benefited from the

ISBN 92-64-01442-X

liberalisation and globalisation of financial markets. From the mid-1980s to the mid-1990s, large inflows of capital, particularly long-term capital such as FDI, helped finance the region's rapid economic development and growth. In the several years leading up to the crisis, however, countries had received large inflows of short-term capital in the financial and corporate sectors, particularly in the form of unhedged, foreign-currency denominated capital, owing to relatively high domestic interest rates with *de facto* US dollar-pegged exchange rates. As a result, the ratios of short-term external debt to foreign exchange reserves had risen to levels greater than one. The potential risk due to the "double mismatch" problem had become serious[2]. When market perceptions changed rapidly in 1997, these economies saw sudden outflows of capital and consequent large downward pressures on their currencies. The currency crisis was triggered by the sudden reversal of capital flows, which is why the crisis is often called the "capital account crisis" (Yoshitomi and Shirai, 2000; Kawai *et al.*, 2003).

The regional contagion of the crisis was spectacular. The Thai baht distress spread to Malaysia, Indonesia, the Philippines and eventually Korea within a few months, resulting in acute crises. At a later stage Hong Kong, China was also affected; here the authorities managed successfully to contain its impact using unconventional policy measures.

Domestic Structural Weaknesses

The affected countries also had domestic structural weaknesses. Some foreign capital was intermediated by domestic financial institutions that over-extended loans to domestic sectors including non-tradable real estate and construction; some found its way directly into domestic corporations. Over-investment in real estate and other assets contributed to the generation of asset-price bubbles, which left financial institutions with serious problems of non-performing loans when the bubbles ultimately burst. In this way, financial institutions that intermediated foreign capital to domestic sectors became exposed to currency and maturity mismatches. Highly leveraged domestic corporations were also exposed to interest and exchange rate shocks. Inadequate regulatory and supervisory frameworks had left banks and corporations with imprudent financial management and, more generally, weak corporate governance. Steep exchange rate depreciation, high interest rates and tight budgets, induced by the eruption of a currency crisis in 1997, aggravated financial and corporate distress and led to a sharp contraction of overall economic activity in 1998.

ISBN 92-64-01442-X © OECD 2005

The five crisis countries fell into severe recession (see Figure 1.3, p. 48, in Chapter 1 of this volume). Although the currency crisis was initially seen as benign, its adverse impact on real economic activity proved much more severe than first anticipated. Indeed, the currency crisis evolved into a full-blown economic crisis within months; it hit Indonesia, Korea, Malaysia and Thailand the most severely. For example, Indonesia's real GDP contracted by 13 per cent, Thailand's by 10.5 per cent and Malaysia's and Korea's both by 7 per cent. These economies underwent such rapid economic contraction because both their financial and corporate sectors became virtually paralysed by steep exchange-rate depreciation, interest-rate hikes and domestic demand shrinkage. Steep exchange rate depreciation as well as interest rate hikes adversely affected the balance sheets of banks and highly indebted corporations by inflating the value of their external debt measured in local currency, and increased their external debt-servicing obligations. High domestic interest rates also raised domestic debt-servicing obligations of corporations with large domestic debt, mainly loans from commercial banks and non-bank financial institutions. Clearly, the potential demand-stimulating effect of currency depreciation, working through a rise in the relative price of tradable goods, was completely swamped by the negative balance-sheet effects of the large-scale currency depreciation.

Major Lessons of the Crisis

The crisis episode taught at least three major lessons. First, policy makers in both developed and emerging market economies need to pay greater attention to managing the forces of financial globalisation, particularly in a world of rapid short-term capital flows. Until the crisis, the implications of the scope and magnitude of short-term capital flows were not fully understood by international investors, policy makers of the lending and borrowing countries or international financial institutions. More fundamentally, there was a lack of concern over the volatile nature of rapid capital flows and the need for monitoring and managing them. The management of financial globalisation requires global frameworks, including macroeconomic and exchange-rate policy making, that reduce capital-flow volatility and enhance borrower countries' capacity to mitigate the undesirable impacts of globalisation.

Second, emerging market economies need to strengthen domestic economic systems, in particular their financial and corporate sectors. This task requires effective regulatory and supervisory frameworks for enhancing management and governance of financial institutions and corporations.

Specifically, economies need to strengthen banks' asset-liability management capacity so as to avoid over-extension of loans and excessive currency and maturity mismatches; improve corporations' financial management capacity so as to maintain sound financial discipline; and develop deep capital markets so as to provide alternative financing sources for corporations. If the domestic economic system becomes robust and resilient, a crisis could be prevented or its impact on the economy mitigated even if a crisis occurred.

Third, the East Asian economies need to put greater emphasis on competitiveness, productivity and public-sector governance, although weaknesses in these areas were not the immediate causes of the crisis. The crisis-hit economies were in a sense complacent in this regard because they registered high growth and export performance in the pre-crisis period. In fact, with greater competitiveness, higher productivity and better governance, the negative impact of the currency crisis on the financial and real sectors of the economy would have been limited. There is a strong case for reforms in these areas because their rewards are high.

International Financial Architecture

Reflection on these lessons produced a recognition that putting effective mechanisms in place to manage the forces of globalisation and to strengthen the underpinnings of national economic systems was key to crisis prevention, management and resolution. Global efforts to reform the functioning of international financial markets and national efforts to strengthen country economic underpinnings have been made under the rubric of the "international financial architecture"[3].

Global Efforts to Reform the International Financial System

At the global level, various reforms for crisis prevention, management and resolution have been proposed and some have been put in place. First, the IMF has introduced new lending facilities to meet the greater financial needs of member countries at times of crises or as preventive measures. The Supplemental Reserve Facility was established in December 1997 and has been used in Korea, Brazil, Argentina and Turkey. It provides large financial assistance, without access limits, to members facing exceptional balance of payments difficulties resulting from a sudden and disruptive loss of market confidence. The Contingent Credit Line (CCL) was created in 1999 as a precautionary line of defence to help protect member countries in the event of an exceptional balance of payments need arising from the spread of financial

ISBN 92-64-01442-X © OECD 2005

crises, provided that the countries have pursued strong policies. The CCL, however, was virtually abolished in November 2003 because no country had been willing to use it[4].

Second, the IMF has improved the transparency of its operations and policy deliberations. It has also decided to streamline its conditionality, particularly structural conditionality, in order to enhance ownership and effectiveness of its programme[5]. The new approach is to formulate IMF programmes on the presumption that structural conditionality will be limited to a core set of essential features that are macro-relevant and in the IMF's core area of responsibility[6], with a broader approach requiring justification based upon the specific country situation. Hence, IMF structural conditionality is expected to cover only those reforms that are relevant for a programme's macroeconomic objectives. If structural reforms critical for the achievement of the programme's macroeconomic objectives lie outside the IMF's core areas of responsibility, the IMF should seek assistance from relevant international organisations — such as the World Bank and regional development banks — to provide inputs in designing and monitoring the reform measures.

Third, private-sector involvement (PSI) has been an important focus of reform. Given that the volume of private resources far exceeds that of official ones, private-sector involvement is vital for crisis prevention and resolution. Official intervention to bail out private investors without making them pay for their bad investment decisions would create serious moral hazard. While private financial institutions decided to share the burden in helping crisis-affected countries in several cases such as Korea and Brazil, a definitive framework has yet to be developed. This is particularly the case for the restructuring of emerging-economy bonds because of the large number and dispersion of bondholders involved[7]. Some modest progress has been made in this regard as several international issues of emerging-market sovereign bonds have introduced collective action clauses in their contracts.

National Efforts to Strengthen Domestic Underpinnings

At the national level, developing economies have made efforts to step up "self-help" mechanisms for crisis prevention and management. They include measures such as the accumulation of adequate foreign exchange reserves, appropriately sequenced capital-account liberalisation, prudential regulation of capital inflows as a financial safeguard and upgrading of regulatory capacity to monitor capital flows and to impose official standstills if necessary. Countries also have made efforts to strengthen policy and institutional frameworks with an emphasis on macroeconomic management capacity and financial-sector reform. Attention has focused particularly on the need to improve regulatory and supervisory frameworks in the financial system, to strengthen corporate governance and to establish effective domestic insolvency procedures to deal with non-viable banks and corporations. The expectation is that with stronger domestic underpinnings in these areas, crises are less likely to occur, and even if they do their economic impact will tend to be limited.

One of the principal instruments to strengthen domestic policies and institutions is the adoption of international best practices in macroeconomic policy making, financial-sector regulation and supervision and capital market infrastructure. Reports on the Observance of Standards and Codes (ROSCs), supported by various international organisations and agencies and adopted by the IMF in September 1999, cover 12 issues in three main areas. The macroeconomic policy area includes monetary and financial policy transparency, fiscal transparency and special data-dissemination standards in addition to the general data-dissemination system. The financial sector regulation and supervision area includes banking supervision, securities regulation, insurance supervision, payments systems and anti-money-laundering. The capital market infrastructure area includes corporate governance, accounting standards, auditing standards and insolvency and creditor rights[8]. These undoubtedly useful processes take time for effective implementation, and even if ROSCs are fully in place, crises may still occur.

Emergence of a New Regional Financial Architecture

While the international community and emerging market economies have focused on global and national policy reforms, a well-designed regional framework can also contribute to the stability of the international financial system, for three reasons[9]. First, global efforts are still inadequate and national efforts take more time to become effective. Although the global initiative has delivered certain results, they are far less than satisfactory — particularly in the areas of IMF facilities, including the CCL, and PSI. Second, as regional integration deepens through trade, FDI and financial flows — as is explained in more detail below — an effective framework for regional financial co-operation becomes essential to manage it. Third, as economic contagion tends to begin with a geographic focus, a regional framework for financial co-operation to address crisis prevention, management and resolution is a logical way to proceed[10]. From these perspectives, the regional economies have jointly embarked on initiatives to strengthen the regional financial architecture (see Table 8.1).

ISBN 92-64-01442-X © OECD 2005

Table 8.1. **Summary of Policy Lessons from the Asian Financial Crisis**

Objective	National Measures	Global Measures	Regional Measures
	Improve mechanisms for crisis prevention, management and resolution at the national level.	*Improve mechanisms for crisis prevention, management and resolution at the global level.*	*Improve mechanisms for crisis prevention, management and resolution at the regional level.*
Preventing or reducing the risk of crises	*Avoid large current account deficits financed through short-term, unhedged capital inflows.*		
	• Secure adequate foreign exchange reserves. • Maintain sound fiscal and monetary policy. • Adopt a viable exchange rate regime. • Establish orderly capital account liberalisation.	• Improve transparency and disclosure by IFIs. • Strengthen IMF surveillance and policy advice. • Remove regulatory biases to short-term and excessive international lending.	• Strengthen regional policy dialogue and surveillance. • Maintain intra-regional exchange rate stability. • Develop a regional early warning system. • Reduce "double mismatch".
	Aggressively regulate and supervise financial systems to ensure that financial institutions manage risks prudently.		
	• Strengthen regulatory and supervisory frameworks over financial institutions. • Allow prudential regulation as financial safeguards and cushions. • Improve information transparency. • Introduce limited deposit insurance.	• Tighten regulations over financial institutions that lend to highly leveraged institutions. • Support implementation of international standards and codes.	• Establish regional initiatives to improve regional regulatory and supervisory frameworks.
	Erect an incentive structure for sound corporate finance to avoid high leverage and excessive reliance on foreign borrowing.		
	• Establish good corporate governance. • Introduce greater competition to product, factor and financial markets. • Develop capital market-based finance. • Better information disclosure.	• Identify best-practice corporate governance and its implementation tailored to specific country conditions.	• Develop regional capital markets for mobilisation of regional savings. • Undertake regional initiatives for better corporate governance.

Table 8.1 (contd.)

Managing crises	***Mobilise timely external liquidity of sufficient magnitude.***		
	• Restore market confidence through coherent policy packages. • Reduce moral hazard problems.	• Strengthen IMF liquidity support, including CCL.	• Establish a regional liquidity support facility to contain crises and contagion.
	Adopt appropriate macro and structural policies to reflect the specific conditions and reality of the economy.		
	• Adopt appropriate monetary and fiscal policy contingent on the specific conditions of the economy.	• Streamline IMF conditionality on macroeconomic and structural policies.	• Strengthen regional capacity to formulate needed adjustment policies.
	Bail-in private international investors.		
	• Impose official stand-stills. • In extreme cases, allow involuntary private sector involvement (PSI).	• Establish international rules of the game through private sector involvement (PSI).	• Involve international creditors from outside the region.
Resolving the systemic effects of crises	***Move swiftly to establish resolution mechanisms for impaired assets and liabilities of banks and corporations.***		
	• Establish procedures for bank exits, recapitalisation and rehabilitation. • Establish legal procedures and formal frameworks for corporate insolvencies and workouts.	• Establish international frameworks for PSI in external debt resolution. • Strengthen capacity for official budgetary support.	• Finance regional programmes to help accelerate bank and corporate restructuring through regional MDBs and bilateral donors.
	Cushion the effects of crises on low-income groups through social policies to ameliorate the inevitable social tensions.		
	• Strengthen social safety nets to mitigate social consequences of crises.	• Finance the activity through the World Bank and other international organisations.	• Finance regional programmes to help mitigate social impact through regional assistance.

Source: Revision of Table 8 in Kawai (2002*a*) and Table 1 in Kawai *et al.* (2003).

ISBN 92-64-01442-X

Crisis Prevention

Regional information sharing, policy dialogue, economic surveillance and monitoring are instrumental to crisis prevention at the regional level. The process should focus on both macroeconomic and structural issues, such as monetary and exchange rate policies, fiscal positions and debt management, capital flows and external debts, financial system conditions and corporate-sector developments. Developing a reliable early warning system is useful to detect macroeconomic, external and financial sector vulnerabilities. With effective surveillance mechanisms in place, each economy in the region would come under peer pressure to pursue disciplined macroeconomic and structural policies conducive to stable external accounts and currencies. Regional economies also need to ensure intra-regional exchange-rate stability as well as reconstruct the banking sector and develop capital — particularly bond — markets to mobilise regional savings for regional investment, thereby reducing the "double mismatch" problem.

Crisis Management

Once an economy is hit by a currency crisis, appropriate policy responses and timely provision of international liquidity are needed to prevent it from slipping into a serious contraction of systemic proportions. The pace of liquidity disbursement at the global level may be slow in times of crisis or contagion because of cumbersome processes and disagreements over policy conditionality. To avoid long delays and to augment globally available resources, a regional financing facility can help close the gap. A financing facility that can rapidly mobilise a large amount of liquidity to head off a speculative attack is an obvious benefit if the attack is the result of irrational herd behaviour. To be effective, such financing must be accompanied by appropriate adjustment policy measures, and hence the region must develop analytical capacity to formulate appropriate conditionality. This approach must be consistent with and complementary to the global framework governed by the IMF, in order to exploit the synergy between the two and to involve private creditors from outside the region.

Crisis Resolution

To resolve a crisis requires international efforts to ensure that a crisis-affected economy returns to a sustainable growth path. In the face of a systemic crisis in the banking, corporate and social sectors, fiscal resource mobilisation

ISBN 92-64-01442-X

is essential for the quick resolution of the crisis. Fiscal resources needed to recapitalise weak banks, facilitate corporate debt restructuring and strengthen social safety nets may be limited by the lack of fiscal headroom or constraints on external financing on market terms in times of crisis. International mobilisation of such resources is important to mitigate the economic and social costs of the crisis[11].

The Logic of Regional Economic Co-operation in East Asia

Deepening of Economic Interdependence

The most fundamental rationale behind the emergence of regional economic co-operation is the deepening of regional economic interdependence in East Asia. Economic co-operation can resolve the "collective action" problem by internalising the externalities and spillover effects that arise from interdependence.

Trade Integration

East Asia has long enjoyed a market-driven expansion of trade and FDI and the resulting *de facto* integration of the regional economies within a multilateral liberalisation framework under the GATT/ WTO and open regionalism through APEC. Several GATT liberalisation rounds have reduced tariffs and non-tariff barriers to trade on a sustained basis. The region has avoided discriminatory trade practices. The APEC process successfully encouraged China as well as Chinese Taipei to pursue trade and FDI liberalisation outside the WTO framework. FDI flows to the East Asian economies, driven initially by Japanese multinational corporations after the Plaza Accord in the mid-1980s, have generated intra-industry trade within the region and have contributed to deeper economic integration. More recently, Asian NIEs – Hong Kong, China; Korea; Chinese Taipei and Singapore – have become active as investors, particularly in China, whose rise as a large trading nation has also strengthened the trade – particularly intra-industry trade – linkages among the East Asian economies, many of which are generated by multinationals. In this sense, regional economic integration has resulted naturally from market-based expansion of trade and FDI.

 ISBN 92-64-01442-X © OECD 2005

Regional economic integration through trade in East Asia has risen fast over the last 20 years. Table 8.2A summarises changes in the shares of intra-regional trade for various groupings in the world in 1980-2003. Intra-regional trade as a share of East Asia's total trade rose from 35 per cent in 1980 to 54 per cent in 2003 (including Japan) or from 22 to 44 per cent (excluding Japan). Now about 55 per cent of East Asia's trade is with itself. The share of intra-regional trade within East Asia is still lower than that in the European Union-15 (64 per cent), but exceeded that of the North American Free Trade Area (46 per cent) in 2003.

Table 8.2A. **Intra-Regional Trade Shares**[a]
(percentages)

Regions	1980	1985	1990	1995	2000	2001	2002	2003
East Asia-15, including Japan[(c)]	34.7	40.2	45.6	55.5	54.0	55.4	57.3	54.0
Emerging East Asia-14[(c)]	21.6	29.1	36.4	43.7	43.4	45.6	47.5	44.1
NIEs-4	7.7	10.7	14.3	18.1	16.4	17.5	17.1	16.1
ASEAN-10[(c)]	18.0	20.3	18.9	24.1	25.7	24.1	24.4	24.0
NAFTA	33.8	38.7	37.9	43.2	48.7	49.0	48.3	46.0
European Union-15	52.4	52.5	58.6	56.8	62.2	62.1	62.4	64.4

Table 8.2B. **Intra-Regional Trade-Intensity Index**[b]

Regions	1980	1985	1990	1995	2000	2001	2002	2003
East Asia-15, including Japan[(c)]	2.5	2.4	2.5	2.3	2.2	2.5	2.5	2.2
Emerging East Asia-14[(c)]	2.9	3.2	3.2	2.7	2.4	2.8	2.8	2.3
NIEs-4	2.0	2.1	2.1	2.0	1.7	2.1	2.1	2.0
ASEAN-10[(c)]	4.8	5.7	4.4	3.7	4.1	4.1	4.2	4.1
NAFTA	2.1	2.0	2.1	2.4	2.2	2.3	2.4	2.5
European Union-15	1.4	1.5	1.5	1.6	1.7	1.7	1.7	1.7

Notes: *a)* The intra-regional trade share is defined as: $X_{ii}/\{(X_{i.} + X_{.i})/2\}$ where X_{ii} represents exports of region *i* to region *i*, $X_{i.}$ represents total exports of region *i* to the world, and $X_{.i}$ represents total exports of the world to region *i*.

b) The trade intensity index is defined as: $[X_{ii}/\{(X_{i.}+X_{.i})/2\}]/[\{(X_{i.}+X_{.i})/2\}/X_{..}]$ where $X_{..}$ represents total world exports.

c) East Asia-15 includes Emerging East Asia-14 and Japan. Emerging East Asia-14 includes the Asian NIEs (Hong Kong, China, Korea, Singapore and Chinese Taipei), nine ASEAN members (Brunei, Cambodia, Indonesia, Laos, Malaysia, Myanmar, Philippines, Thailand and Viet Nam) and China. ASEAN-10 includes Singapore.

d) Computation is based on exporting countries' export data, except for Chinese Taipei where importers' import data are used when necessary.

Source: Computed from IMF, *Direction of Trade Statistics*. Adapted from Table 1 in Kawai (2005).

Table 8.2B summarises changes in the intra-regional trade-intensity indexes for the same groupings over the same period[12]. The table demonstrates that within East Asia, whether including Japan or not, the trade-intensity index at around 2.2 in 2003 was higher than that for the EU (1.7) although lower than that for NAFTA (2.5). This confirms that regional economic integration through trade in East Asia is quite high and comparable to levels seen in NAFTA or the EU. Intra-East Asia trade has expanded rapidly but not at the expense of extra-regional trade. This suggests that East Asia continues to maintain export competitiveness *vis-à-vis* countries outside the region.

FDI Integration

FDI inflows into East Asia have contributed to regional economic integration. Table 8.3 indicates that firms in the major industrialised countries are the main investors in emerging East Asia. Firms in the United States, Japan and the European Union accounted for 16 per cent, 12 per cent and 11 per cent, respectively, of emerging East Asia's cumulative FDI inflows in 1990-2002. The largest investors in the Asian NIEs, particularly in Singapore and Chinese Taipei, come from the United States. In contrast, Japan is the largest developed-country investor in ASEAN (excluding Singapore), particularly in Thailand and Indonesia. Hong Kong, China is the largest investor in China, however, and no major industrial country dominates in terms of FDI. Note also the rising importance of FDI by Asian NIE firms, which accounted for 48 per cent of total FDI inflows to ASEAN — particularly in Indonesia, Malaysia and Viet Nam — and to China[13]. All in all, Japan, the United States and the European Union are equally important foreign direct investors in East Asia, with Japan the most significant in ASEAN[14].

As a result of FDI activities and FDI-driven trade, East Asia has seen the formation of an "FDI-trade nexus" — mutual reinforcement between FDI and trade. An underlying determinant of the nexus is the establishment of regional production networks and supply chains by multinational corporations. These networks have promoted intra-regional division of labour in East Asia through fragmentation of the production process into different sub-processes located in different countries based on comparative advantage — relative factor proportions and technological capabilities. This strategy has stimulated vertical intra-industry trade in parts, components, semi-finished products and finished goods[15]. Its important implication is that large inflows of FDI to emerging East Asia have stimulated the region's engagement with trade in a way that reflects the individual economies' stages of industrial development. More recently China has also begun to participate in such activities in an explosive way.

 ISBN 92-64-01442-X

Table 8.3. **Emerging East Asia's FDI Inflows, 1990-2002**
($ million)

(a) Asian NIEs															
	1990	1991	1992	1993	1994	1995	1996	1997	1998	1999	2000	2001	2002	Total (1990-2002)	
FDI inflows from														$ million	%
USA	3 299	2 612	1 410	2 512	5 311	4 364	4 630	4 845	5 139	9 350	13 705	10 797	2 651	70 625	23.5
Japan	2 496	1 990	1 072	1 521	2 403	2 404	3 642	3 313	2 337	3 533	8 765	4 939	3 654	42 070	14.0
EU	1 391	2 081	772	1 499	2 187	2 822	2 781	2 979	5 483	8 425	2 805	6 639	4 323	44 185	14.7
Asian NIEs	200	165	254	225	441	242	568	419	847	1 642	9 112	2 117	876	17 109	5.7
Total	7 693	7 338	3 812	6 192	10 735	10 541	13 174	13 177	25 897	42 312	92 656	46 605	19 798	299 930	100.0

(b) ASEAN-9															
	1990	1991	1992	1993	1994	1995	1996	1997	1998	1999	2000	2001	2002	Total (1990-2002)	
FDI inflows from:														$ million	%
USA	359	758	1 633	1 923	865	1 494	1 782	2 187	3 546	1 872	2 349	422	614	19 805	16.3
Japan	2 061	1 784	1 440	1 999	1 069	2 389	4 052	3 548	2 853	959	1 156	1 644	1 889	26 843	22.0
EU	494	777	2 375	1 505	1 889	1 638	1 653	3 006	2 066	2 852	745	807	1 481	21 288	17.5
Asian NIEs	2 183	2 629	1 804	2 334	3 709	2 956	3 681	3 352	2 033	677	1 467	807	1 442	29 074	23.9
Total	6 399	8 038	9 301	10 052	9 408	12 070	15 125	14 930	13 109	7 078	5 222	3 672	7 408	121 814	100.0

(c) China															
	1990	1991	1992	1993	1994	1995	1996	1997	1998	1999	2000	2001	2002	Total (1990-2002)	
FDI inflows from:														$ million	%
USA	189	200	599	1 682	2 456	2 934	3 792	4 282	5 445	5 656	5 222	5 091	5 198	42 746	10.1
Japan	242	296	417	731	1 815	2 982	2 813	2 950	2 308	2 436	2 402	3 572	3 376	26 340	6.2
EU	119	277	185	786	2 301	2 914	3 706	3 668	4 988	3 850	5 780	3 491	2 872	34 937	8.3
Asian NIEs	2 081	2 687	9 021	21 831	23 681	22 978	23 959	24 014	21 192	19 220	16 591	22 405	25 496	235 156	55.5
Total	3 487	4 366	11 156	27 515	33 787	35 849	40 180	44 237	43 751	38 753	40 715	46 878	52 743	423 417	100.0

Note: FDI recipient data (compiled by IITI) are proportionally adjusted so that they are made consistent with BOP figures. Asian NIEs include Singapore and ASEAN-9 excludes Singapore.

Source: Institute for International Trade and Investment; UNCTAD, *World Investment Report 2004*.

Financial and Macroeconomic Interdependence

Market-driven financial integration has also been underway as a result of the increased deregulation of the financial system, opening of financial services to foreign institutions and liberalisation of the capital account in the East Asian economies. Commercial banks have extended cross-border loans to banks and corporations throughout the region, contributing to a closely connected banking sector within East Asia. The opening of securities markets, particularly equity markets, has attracted foreign portfolio capital inflows. Active commercial bank loans and portfolio flows have linked the economies in the region financially, creating positive correlations of asset price movements within the region. At least part of the contagion of currency crises in the region in 1997 was a reflection of such financial linkages.

Macroeconomic interdependence within the region has recently become stronger, as evidenced by a simultaneous contraction of economic activity throughout East Asia in 1998 and a simultaneous expansion in 1999-2000. Although some common global factors such as US economic cycles and information technology (IT) stock price movements may have affected the regional economies, many of the recent, synchronised economic activities in the region can be attributed to strong macroeconomic interdependence.

Cross-country correlation analyses of major macroeconomic variables — such as real GDP growth, real private consumption, real fixed investment, real stock prices and price inflation rates — over the last 20 years indicate that macroeconomic activities of the East Asian economies are generally highly correlated with each other, with the exception of China. Table 8.4 presents a summary of correlation coefficients between the first principal components of East Asian economies' variables and individual economy variables[16]. It indicates that Japan's real activity variables are more highly correlated with those of emerging East Asia than are US activity variables. On the other hand, inflation rates in the United States and Japan are equally highly correlated with those of emerging East Asia. This suggests that the degree of emerging East Asia's real economic interdependence with Japan is greater than with the United States, while the degrees of its nominal interdependence with Japan and the United States are equally strong. An important reason for this is that the United States is subject to supply shocks different from those affecting East Asia, while it has traditionally provided a nominal anchor for East Asia through currency pegging to the US dollar[17].

ISBN 92-64-01442-X © OECD 2005

Table 8.4. **Correlation Coefficients[a] between the First Principal Component Scores for East Asia[b] and the Individual Economy Data, 1980-2002**

Countries/Regions	Real GDP	Real Consumption	Real Investment	Real Money Supply	Real Effective Exchange Rate	GDP Deflator	CPI	WPI
USA	0.01	-0.32	-0.41	-0.39	0.48	0.17	0.85	0.30
EU-15	0.01	-0.18	-0.14	-0.15	-0.33	0.10	0.78	-0.01
Australia	-0.16	-0.15	-0.20	0.02	0.67	-0.02	0.31	0.00
New Zealand	0.27	-0.04	0.19	0.04	0.27	-0.07	0.40	0.22
India	0.09	0.01	-0.03	-0.31	0.40	0.06	0.63	0.34
Japan	0.58	0.39	0.41	0.14	-0.26	0.15	0.90	0.46
Korea	0.71	0.78	0.67	-0.10	0.70	0.27	0.89	0.48
China	0.07	-0.14	-0.26	-0.22	0.43	-0.40	0.15	--
Chinese Taipei	0.51	0.28	0.28	0.28	0.72	0.35	0.85	0.50
Hong Kong, China	0.74	0.63	0.58	0.41	0.48	-0.06	0.80	--
Singapore	0.77	0.76	0.59	0.04	0.77	0.08	0.87	0.45
Malaysia	0.90	0.87	0.95	0.53	0.81	0.40	0.79	0.68
Thailand	0.89	0.92	0.88	0.69	0.80	0.54	0.87	0.70
Philippines	0.33	0.31	0.55	0.77	0.81	-0.06	0.57	0.27
Indonesia	0.89	0.65	0.89	0.61	0.86	0.99	0.21	0.92

Notes: *a)* The figures are correlation coefficients between the first principal component scores for East Asia and the original log first-differenced data for individual economies.

b) In this analysis, East Asia includes Japan; Korea; China; Chinese Taipei; Hong Kong, China; Singapore; Malaysia; Thailand; Philippines and Indonesia.

Source: Adapted from Table 5 in Kawai and Motonishi (2004).

Institutionalisation of Economic Integration

Rising trade and FDI integration in East Asia generate a growing need for more formal institutional mechanisms for trade and investment facilitation, harmonisation of rules, standards and procedures and dispute settlement. Deepening macroeconomic and financial interdependence also suggests a need for concerted efforts to internalise externalities and spillover effects, because macroeconomic and financial developments and policies of one country can easily affect other countries' performance and developments. It makes sense for such interdependent regional economies to institutionalise *de facto* integration through the establishment of regional co-operative frameworks, such as trade and investment agreements and macroeconomic and financial co-operation mechanisms. Given that one country's turbulence, shocks and crises could be easily transmitted to other economies within the same region, it is critical to establish financial safety nets. Co-operation among such economies would be easier because they are small in number — so the transactions cost for co-ordination is small — and tend to face similar shocks and similar policy challenges.

Response to the Financial Crisis

Several motivations lie behind the recent move toward closer regional co-operation in money and finance. Some of them are defensive responses to the Asian financial crisis, while others are more pro-active:

- the hard lesson learned from the Asian financial crisis of 1997-98 — a need to establish regional "self-help" mechanisms for effective prevention, management and resolution of regional financial crises;
- dissatisfaction with the existing global financial architecture governed by the IMF; and
- desire to increase the Asian voice for, and in, global financial management.

First, as has been discussed earlier, the Asian financial crisis taught the important lesson that there is a clear need for effective prevention, management and resolution of financial crises and contagion. The global initiative for the new international financial architecture has been less than satisfactory and national efforts to strengthen domestic economic fundamentals take time to bear fruit. A clearly defined regional financial architecture can close the gap.

ISBN 92-64-01442-X © OECD 2005

Second, the East Asian economies have been dissatisfied with the way the IMF handled the crisis, particularly in Thailand and Indonesia. Hence, the general sentiment in East Asia has been that the regional economies must establish their own "self-help" mechanism through systematic monetary and financial co-operation for prevention and management of possible crises in the future. Given that regional financial stability is a basis for global financial stability, effective regional financial co-operation is an obvious benefit not only for individual economies in the region but also for the global community. In this sense the East Asian regional financial architecture is consistent with and even strengthens the IMF's global role.

Third, given the perceived imbalance and unfairness of the current distribution of IMF quotas, which is unrealistically skewed against East Asia, the regional economies have the desire to increase their voice in global financial management. Indeed they believe they can better achieve a greater voice by joining forces.

Response to European and North American Economic Regionalism

The regional economies have initiated efforts toward greater institutionalisation of trade and FDI integration for essentially three reasons:

— defensive response to the proliferation of regional trade arrangements elsewhere — particularly in Europe and the Western Hemisphere;

— dissatisfaction with the slow progress on trade and investment liberalisation at the global and trans-regional levels; and

— desire to enhance productivity and international competitiveness through exploitation of scale economies and dynamic efficiency.

Regionalism elsewhere — including the formation of an economic and monetary union in Europe and the EU's expansion to the east as well as the success of NAFTA and its move to the Free Trade Area of the Americas (FTAA) in the Western Hemisphere — is the first factor that has motivated the East Asian economies to pursue regional trade arrangements. Some 184 FTAs had been reported to the WTO for the whole world by 2003. Governments in East Asia fear that unless they strengthen their own regional trade arrangements they will be disadvantaged in global competition and multilateral negotiations. They have increasingly realised the importance of uniting to gain bargaining power *vis-à-vis* the EU, the United States and other groupings. The slow progress of the WTO/Doha liberalisation process and the perceived ineffectiveness of the APEC process have stoked these fears.

Policy makers in East Asia increasingly take the view that they need to secure a bigger market within their own region so that scale economies and dynamic efficiency gains can be exploited. They believe East Asia's FTAs can help raise both productivity and international competitiveness. This effort is basically one of institution building for further deepening of trade and investment integration. These FTAs are perceived as:

— facilitating trade and investment;

— promoting harmonisation of rule-making, standard-setting and procedures; and

— providing dispute-resolution mechanisms, particularly in services, labour mobility, investment, competition policy, intellectual property rights, contingency protection and rules of origin — areas in which it is difficult to make substantial progress in a multilateral framework (OECD, 2003*b*).

Initiatives for Regional Trade Arrangements

Early Attempts

ASEAN

Until recently, the only formal, regional trade arrangement in East Asia was the ASEAN Free Trade Area (AFTA) introduced in 1992[18]. Despite the slow pace of trade liberalisation, the AFTA has been in effect among the original five ASEAN members — Indonesia, Malaysia, Singapore, Thailand and the Philippines — since January 2002. Although the exclusion list is long and individual country circumstances vary, the bulk of goods traded between these countries are now subject to tariffs of only zero to 5 per cent. Viet Nam was to comply with the same tariff standards by 2003, Laos and Myanmar by 2005 and Cambodia by 2007. Advanced ASEAN members are expected to eliminate tariffs by 2010 and less advanced ASEAN members by 2015. By then ASEAN as a whole is expected to become a tariff-free FTA.

At the ASEAN Summit in October 2003, ASEAN leaders adopted the Declaration of ASEAN Concord II, whereby they declared the creation of three ASEAN Communities, one of which was an "ASEAN Economic Community" (AEC)[19]. According to the Declaration, the AEC is expected to realise a free flow of goods, services, investment and freer flow of capital,

 ISBN 92-64-01442-X © OECD 2005

with equitable economic development and reduced poverty and socio-economic disparities by 2020. It remains to be seen how ASEAN can implement the core elements of the AEC over time[20].

EAEG/EAEC Proposal

Following the unsatisfactory progress of the Uruguay Round Ministerial meeting in December 1990, Malaysian Prime Minister Mohamad Mahathir proposed the formation of a regional trade grouping comprised of the ASEAN countries, Japan, China, Korea and Hong Kong, China[21]. This group of economies was called the "East Asian Economic Group" (EAEG). The objectives behind the proposal were to establish a regional trade arrangement in response to the emergence of preferential regional trade arrangements elsewhere, including in North America, and to exercise a global impact on trade issues like that of the Cairns Group. In October 1991, ASEAN Economic Ministers considered Mahathir's proposal as useful and renamed the grouping as the "East Asian Economic Caucus" (EAEC) which would facilitate discussions on regional economic issues.

The United States objected to the EAEG/EAEC initiative on the grounds that it could divide the Asia-Pacific region by excluding the United States and reduce the effectiveness of the trade/investment liberalisation process within an emerging APEC. Japan hesitated to support the initiative because of its consideration of US opposition — Japan had many trade conflicts with the United States and did not wish to make the bilateral relationship any worse — and because of the strategic priority it placed on the APEC process. China did not show much interest in the idea. The momentum of the EAEG/EAEC initiative waned rapidly in the absence of support from these key countries in Northeast Asia[22]. Yet when the leaders of Japan, China and Korea were invited to the informal ASEAN Leaders' Meeting in December 1997 in the midst of the Asian financial crisis, the *de facto* ASEAN+3 process began. The EAEG/EAEC initiative can be considered a precursor to it because the memberships overlap.

APEC as a Trans-Regional Forum

Asia-Pacific Economic Co-operation (APEC), established in 1989, played a useful role in encouraging trade and investment liberalisation on a voluntary and unilateral basis within an Asia-Pacific context including the United States,

Canada and Australia as members. Australia played a major role in promoting APEC as a trans-regional forum with the basic principle of "open regionalism". One of APEC's most important achievements was to induce unilateral, voluntary trade liberalisation by non-WTO members such as China and Chinese Taipei. The Bogor Declaration (1994) set the goal of zero tariffs by 2010 for developed countries and by 2020 for developing countries. The so-called Osaka Action Agenda clarified the modalities of achieving the Bogor goals.

Although APEC's basic principles still prevail, its prominence appears to have diminished since the Asian financial crisis because of its inability to respond effectively to the crisis. In addition, the recent proliferation of bilateral and sub-regional FTAs pursued by the member economies has reduced the significance and role of APEC. This does not necessarily mean that APEC's basic principle of "open regionalism" has been abandoned. On the contrary, recent FTAs in East Asia take basic APEC — and WTO — principles as a liberalisation infrastructure and attempt to go beyond them. In response to the proliferation of various FTAs in the Asia-Pacific region, APEC agreed to encourage its members to pursue a best-practice FTA model.

Moves for Regional and Bilateral FTAs

Many governments in East Asia have recently promoted bilateral and regional trade arrangements. Notably, Japan implemented a bilateral economic partnership agreement (EPA) with Singapore in November 2002[23] and has concluded another one with Mexico. In response to the Japan-Singapore negotiation, China and ASEAN began official negotiations to complete an FTA by 2010 with advanced ASEAN members and by 2015 with less advanced members. They have already implemented the "early harvest" measures since January 2004[24]. Japan and ASEAN agreed to begin negotiations in 2005 on an EPA with a view to achieving free trade by 2012. Korea has agreed on a similar negotiation with ASEAN to be completed by 2009. Japan has begun bilateral negotiations for EPAs with Korea, Malaysia, Thailand and the Philippines; it may also begin negotiations with Indonesia. All this suggests domino and bandwagon effects among Japan, China and Korea in their drive for regional FTAs/EPAs with ASEAN. China has also proposed an FTA among China, Japan and Korea. A region-wide FTA for ASEAN+3, including China, Japan and Korea, has also been proposed[25]. Table 1.7 in the Overview Chapter summarises these and other recent initiatives for FTAs and EPAs pursued by the East Asian economies.

ISBN 92-64-01442-X © OECD 2005

An interesting feature of the East Asian move toward FTAs/EPAs is that these economies have also concluded deals or negotiated with countries or groups outside of East Asia. For example, Korea has already implemented an FTA with Chile, and Japan has concluded its negotiation with Mexico. Singapore has implemented a closer economic partnership agreement (CEPA) with New Zealand and FTAs with EFTA and the United States, has concluded its negotiation with Australia and is currently negotiating with Mexico and Canada. Thailand is negotiating FTAs with the United States and Australia. ASEAN as a group is also considering similar negotiations with India, the United States and the EU. These attempts suggest that the economies in the region wish to maintain open trading relations with other parts of the world.

Japan's conclusion of a bilateral FTA/EPA with Singapore symbolises a change in its long-standing policy of pursuing trade liberalisation only in a multilateral framework based on the WTO and APEC. Japan has decided to shift its trade policy to a three-track approach based on global (WTO-based) *cum* trans-regional (APEC-based), regional (within ASEAN+3) and bilateral liberalisation. For Japan, regional and bilateral liberalisation attempts to achieve deeper integration with its trading partners on a formal basis, going beyond reductions in border restrictions to pursue investment liberalisation, promote greater competition in the domestic market and harmonise standards and procedures. The challenge is to maintain not only consistency with but also to promote the WTO liberalisation framework, which remains an important element of Japanese trade policy.

Challenges for Further Institutionalisation of Trade Integration

An East Asia-wide FTA

An important next step for the East Asian economies is to form a single East-Asia-wide FTA through consolidation of a web of bilateral and sub-regional FTAs/EPAs. This is not an easy task given the proliferation of FTAs/EPAs in the region, each of which may have different external tariffs, exclusion lists, rules of origin and standards and procedures. To make this task easier, each FTA/EPA should have transparent, simple provisions with regard to these issues by ensuring consistency across different arrangements and thus avoid the so-called "spaghetti bowl" effect from the outset. Convergence towards common tariff rates, similar exclusion lists and identical rules of origin and other provisions would be highly desirable.

Impediments to a Region-Wide Trade Arrangement

There are three possible impediments to forming an East Asia-wide FTA:

— East Asia's global orientation in trade and FDI — i.e. trade and FDI openness to North America and Europe — and the consequent concern about possible conflict with global liberalisation governed by the WTO or trans-regional liberalisation under APEC;

— hesitation to induce further domestic sectoral adjustments due to trade liberalisation, particularly in the face of intensified competition from the rising economic powerhouse, China; and

— heterogeneity and diversity of economic and social developments within East Asia — differences in per capita incomes, industrial structures and domestic institutional capacities.

First, sceptics might argue that forming an East Asia-wide FTA without the United States and Europe is not a commendable idea because they are still important markets for the region's final products. The belief is that the expansion of intra-regional trade in East Asia, supported by FDI, has been made possible by open markets in the United States and Europe that have absorbed East Asian finished products. The sceptics would suggest, therefore, that trade and investment liberalisation within the WTO, or at least within APEC, would be more desirable than through regional FTAs. Hence, the global or trans-regional process should be pursued in East Asia. This argument tends to be supported by those who refuse East Asian trade regionalism because it might undermine the WTO principle of maintaining a liberal, non-discriminatory and multilateral trading system[26].

Second, it is politically difficult to convince those affected negatively by further trade liberalisation to accept the adjustment costs in certain non-competitive, sensitive sectors in each economy, such as agriculture in Japan and Korea, automobiles in Malaysia and petrochemicals in Thailand. Such costs could be high for ASEAN members in the shadow of China's exploding export performance. Since the Asian financial crisis, the ASEAN countries have lost large amounts of FDI, much of which has flowed into China because of its favourable growth prospects. This trend is likely to continue for some time, because many ASEAN countries are direct competitors of China in labour-intensive products in third markets. They are likely to be severely affected by China's competitiveness[27].

 ISBN 92-64-01442-X © OECD 2005

Third, the East Asian economies are quite diverse and varied in their economic systems and stages of economic and social development — such as per capita income levels, industrial structures, trade openness and patterns, human resource developments, institutional capacities and social conditions[28]. Diversity and heterogeneity imply that low-income countries — where private firms are insufficiently developed — will go slowly in trade liberalisation and market opening, and hence will find it difficult to integrate themselves quickly with the rest of East Asia. This constitutes an obvious impediment to trade and investment co-operation.

Assessments of the Impediments

Some of these impediments are not so serious. The United States is no longer the most dominant economic partner for many East Asian economies, and regional markets for final products are expanding fast. A large part of inward FDI flows now originates from within the region. Moreover, East Asia is in no way inward-looking, as evidenced by the many negotiations on FTAs with countries outside the region and the simultaneous focus on domestic structural reforms, higher productivity and economic growth, both of which would minimise trade diversion effects. The East Asian approach regards the WTO principle — as well as APEC principles — as the basic infrastructure for international trade rules, and it seeks to achieve greater liberalisation beyond the commitments of the WTO and APEC. It is called the "WTO-plus" or "APEC-plus" approach.

With or without China's aggressive export behaviour in regional and global markets, trade and FDI liberalisation and the required domestic reforms are in any case indispensable to increase each economy's international competitiveness. With China's emergence as an industrial power, it is even more important for neighbouring economies — particularly ASEAN members — to pursue further structural reforms, improve their investment climates and continue to attract or at least not to lose FDI.

Despite heterogeneity and differences in economic, political and social systems among the countries in the region, they have increasingly come to realise that the economic logic for establishing frameworks for regional trade and investment liberalisation is overriding. They have found the benefits of economic integration and its institutionalisation to outweigh the costs of eschewing them. It is extremely important to raise the economic basis of poor members within East Asia to encourage them to grow. For the time being, the only realistic approach to advise would be multi-track. Countries ready for liberalisation and deeper integration would negotiate FTAs/EPAs, while those not ready would pursue structural, institutional and governance reforms to enable them to participate in and benefit from trade and FDI expansion.

Initiatives for Regional Financial Co-operation

Early Attempts

ASEAN

In August 1977 the original five ASEAN central banks and monetary authorities — Indonesia, Malaysia, the Philippines, Singapore and Thailand — signed the first memorandum of understanding on the ASEAN Swap Arrangement (ASA) with a total facility of $100 million. The objective was to provide immediate, short-term swap facilities to any member facing a temporary liquidity shortage or a balance of payments problem. In 1978, the total was increased to $200 million, with each member contributing $40 million. In 2000 when the Chiang Mai Initiative was implemented, ASA membership was extended to include all ASEAN members and the facility was augmented to $1 billion.

ASEAN established a Surveillance Process in October 1998 to strengthen policy dialogue and policy making capacity in the monetary, fiscal and financial areas through information exchanges, peer reviews and recommendations for regional and national action. The Surveillance Process has two components: a monitoring mechanism that allows early detection of any irregular movement in key economic and financial variables; and a peer-review mechanism that induces appropriate policy responses to issues emerging from the monitoring exercise. The process is the first concrete attempt by a group of developing countries to establish mechanisms for regional policy dialogue.

Asian Monetary Fund (AMF) Proposal

Following the success of the August 1997 meeting in Tokyo to agree on a much-needed financial support package for crisis-affected Thailand[29], Japan, with support from Korea and the ASEAN countries that participated in the

ISBN 92-64-01442-X © OECD 2005

Thai package, proposed in September to establish an Asian Monetary Fund (AMF). Its objective was to supplement IMF resources for crisis prevention, management and resolution. It envisaged mobilising some $100 billion as a pool of foreign exchange reserves. The United States and the IMF opposed it on the grounds of moral hazard and duplication. They argued that an East Asian country hit by a currency crisis would bypass the IMF's tough conditionality and receive easy money from the AMF, thereby creating a potential for moral hazard, and that an AMF would be redundant in the presence of an effective global crisis manager, the IMF. Without China's support, the idea had to be aborted.

In November 1997 the East Asian economies, together with the United States, Canada, Australia and New Zealand, agreed to establish the so-called "Manila Framework Group" (MFG). Many but not all of the MFG member economies participated in the Thai financial package. The objective was to develop a concerted framework for Asia-Pacific financial co-operation in order to restore and enhance the prospects for financial stability in the region. MFG initiatives included the establishment of a new mechanism for regional surveillance to complement IMF surveillance; enhancement of economic and technical co-operation, particularly in strengthening domestic financial systems and regulatory capacities; strengthening the IMF's capacity to respond to financial crises; and development of a co-operative financing arrangement for the region to complement IMF resources. The MFG was terminated in December 2004, however, after seven years of meetings.

The New Miyazawa Initiative

Another, highly successful effort, the so-called "New Miyazawa Initiative", assisted the resolution of the Asian financial crisis. In October 1998, Japan pledged $30 billion to support the economic recovery of the crisis-affected countries. Half of the pledged amount was dedicated to short-term financial needs during the implementation of economic restructuring and reform, while the rest was earmarked for medium-term and long-term reforms. Part of the short-term financial support was dedicated to currency swap arrangements with Korea ($5.0 billion) and Malaysia ($2.5 billion). The initiative provided major assistance for restructuring corporate debt, reforming financial sectors, strengthening social safety nets, generating employment and addressing the credit crunch. The commitment to provide large resources helped stabilise the regional markets and economies, thereby facilitating the recovery process.

The short-term financial support provided to Korea and Malaysia became a model for bilateral currency swap arrangements under the Chiang Mai Initiative introduced later.

Asia Growth and Recovery Initiative

With the announcement of the New Miyazawa Initiative, the United States decided to take its own initiatives within a multilateral framework in order to assist the economic recovery of the crisis-affected countries. In November 1998, it and Japan jointly announced the Asia Growth and Recovery Initiative (AGRI), a multilateral effort to stimulate economic growth in Asia. With support from the World Bank and the Asian Development Bank (ADB), AGRI was intended initially to target the mobilisation of $5 billion in bilateral and multilateral support for further corporate restructuring and to restore market access to private capital, including for small and medium firms. Although it did not generate additional resources for East Asia's restructuring process or yield visible results, it established or strengthened the bond guarantee functions of the World Bank and the ADB.

Current State of Regional Financial Co-operation

The East Asian economies have embarked on initiatives for regional financial arrangements, founded on three major pillars:

- creation of a regional liquidity support facility through the Chiang Mai Initiative;
- establishment of economic surveillance, particularly through the ASEAN+3 Economic Review and Policy Dialogue process; and
- development of Asian bond markets.

The Chiang Mai Initiative

This is the hallmark financing arrangement in East Asia, designed to manage regional currency attacks, contagion and crises[30]. The Asian financial crisis highlighted the importance of establishing an effective financing facility so that the economies in the region can respond more effectively to the needs of their peers in a world of increased financial globalisation. The finance

ISBN 92-64-01442-X © OECD 2005

ministers of ASEAN+3 met in Chiang Mai in May 2000 and agreed to establish a regional network of bilateral swap arrangements (BSAs) for members, thus embarking on the so-called Chiang Mai Initiative (CMI)[31]. The CMI has two elements — the expansion of the existing ASA in both size and membership and the creation of a new network of swap arrangements among ASEAN+3 members. By the end of December 2003, 16 BSAs had been concluded in line with the main principles, reaching a total of $36.5 billion excluding the commitments made under the New Miyazawa Initiative and $44 billion including them (Table 8.5)[32]. This concluded all conceivable BSAs for the time being; no further BSA negotiation is currently underway.

Table 8.5. **Progress on BSAs under the Chiang Mai Initiative (as of end-December 2003)**

BSAs	Currencies	Conclusion Dates	Size
Japan-Korea	US$-won	4 July 2001	$7.0 billion[(a)] (1-way)
Japan-Thailand	US$-baht	30 July 2001	$3.0 billion (1-way)
Japan-Philippines	US$-peso	27 August 2001	$3.0 billion (1-way)
Japan-Malaysia	US$-ringgit	5 October 2001	$3.5 billion[(b)] (1-way)
China-Thailand	US$-baht	6 December 2001	$2.0 billion (1-way)
Japan-China	yen-renminbi	28 March 2002	$3.0 billion[(c)] (2-way)
China-Korea	renminbi-won	24 June 2002	$2.0 billion[(c)] (2-way)
Korea-Thailand	US$-won or US$-baht	25 June 2002	$1.0 billion (2-way)
Korea-Malaysia	US$-won or US$-ringgit	26 July 2002	$1.0 billion (2-way)
Korea-Philippines	US$-won or US$-peso	9 August 2002	$1.0 billion (2-way)
China-Malaysia	US$-ringgit	9 October 2002	$1.5 billion (1-way)
Japan-Indonesia	US$-rupiah	17 February 2003	$3.0 billion (1-way)
China-Philippines	renminbi-peso	29 August 2003	$1.0 billion[(c)] (1-way)
Japan-Singapore	US$-Singapore dollar	10 November 2003	$1.0 billion (1-way)
Korea-Indonesia	US$-won or US$-rupiah	24 December 2003	$1.0 billion (1-way)
China-Indonesia	US$-rupiah	30 December 2003	$1.0 billion (2-way)

Notes: *a)* The amount includes $5 billion committed (on 17 June 1999) under the New Miyazawa Initiative.
b) The amount includes $2.5 billion committed (on 18 August 1999) under the New Miyazawa Initiative.
c) The amounts are US dollar equivalents.

Source: Adapted from Table 5 in Kawai (2005).

One of the most important features of CMI BSAs is that members requesting liquidity support under the CMI can immediately obtain short-term financial assistance for the first 10 per cent of the BSA facility. The remaining 90 per cent is provided under IMF programmes. This means that up to 10 per cent of BSA drawings under the CMI can be provided for limited periods without IMF programmes, while subsequent additional disbursements have to be linked to IMF programmes and therefore their conditionality. Linking CMI liquidity support to IMF conditionality is designed to address two concerns. First, balance of payments difficulties may be due to fundamental problems rather than mere panic and herd behaviour by investors. Second, the potential moral hazard problem could be non-negligible in the absence of an effective adjustment programme. The majority view among the ASEAN+3 members is that, owing to the region's limited capacity to produce and enforce effective adjustment policies, they will have to rely on the IMF at least until appropriate conditions are met.

Surveillance Mechanism

Establishing processes for regional economic surveillance and policy dialogue is an obvious first step for meaningful financial co-operation. Economic surveillance involves not only analyses of macroeconomic and financial conditions and policies of member economies but also identification of vulnerable aspects of the economy and finance as well as appropriate policy responses. This process requires frank and candid exchanges of views and policy dialogue among member economies and should induce good policies through peer pressure.

There are several mechanisms for regional information sharing, policy dialogue and economic surveillance (Table 8.6). The most important is the ASEAN+3 Economic Review and Policy Dialogue (ERPD) process introduced in May 2000 by ASEAN+3 finance ministers[33]. Its purpose is to strengthen policy dialogue, co-ordination and collaboration on financial, monetary and fiscal issues of common interest. Its major focus lies on issues related to macroeconomic risk management, monitoring regional capital flows, strengthening banking and financial systems, reform of the international financial architecture and enhancement of self-help and support mechanisms in East Asia. Steps have been taken for co-operation in monitoring short-term capital flows and developing a regional early warning system to assess regional financial vulnerabilities, with a view to preventing financial crises in the future. This process has not yet become as effective as it should be, however. No independent, professional organisation prepares comprehensive analyses or assessments or identifies issues for discussion[34].

ISBN 92-64-01442-X © OECD 2005

Table 8.6. **Regional Forums for Finance Ministries and Central Banks**[a]

	Finance Ministries and/or Central Banks					Central Banks		
Groups (No. countries)	ASEAN (10)	ASEAN+3 (13)	MFG[b] (14)	APEC (21)	ASEM[c] (25)	SEANZA (20)	SEACEN (11)	EMEAP (11)
Year Established	1967.8	1999.4	1997.11	1994.3	1997. 9	1956	1966.2	1991.2
Japan		o	o	o	o	o		o
China		o	o	o	o	o		o
Korea		o	o	o	o	o	o	o
Hong Kong, China			o	o		o		o
Chinese Taipei				o			o	
Singapore	o	o	o	o	o	o	o	o
Brunei	o	o	o	o	o			
Cambodia	o	o						
Indonesia	o	o	o	o	o	o	o	o
Laos	o	o						
Malaysia	o	o	o	o	o	o	o	o
Myanmar	o	o					o	
Philippines	o	o	o	o	o	o	o	o
Thailand	o	o	o	o	o	o	o	o
Vietnam	o	o		o	o			
Mongolia						o	o	
Macao						o		
Papua New Guinea				o		o		
Australia, New Zealand			o	o		o		o
Nepal, Sri Lanka						o	o	
Bangalore, India, Iran, Pakistan						o		
USA, Canada			o	o				
Chile, Mexico, Peru				o				
Russia				o				
EU-15					o			

Notes: *a)* APEC = Asia-Pacific Economic Co-operation; ASEAN = Association of Southeast Asian Nations; EMEAP = Executives Meeting of East Asia-Pacific Central Banks; MFG = Manila Framework Group; SEACEN = South East Asian Central Banks; SEANZA = South East Asia, New Zealand, Australia.

b) MFG includes the International Monetary Fund, the World Bank, the Asian Development Bank and the Bank for International Settlements.

c) ASEM includes the European Commission.

Source: Kuroda and Kawai (2002).

Asian Bond Market Development

Initiatives have been undertaken to develop Asian bond markets in view of the need to channel a vast pool of savings to long-term investment for growth and development within the region. This effort reflects the recognition that the financial system in East Asia has been too dependent on bank financing domestically and on foreign-currency financing externally and hence needs strengthening through the development of local capital markets, in particular bond markets. The hope is that developing local-currency denominated bond markets will reduce the "double mismatch" problem of international capital flows, i.e. currency and maturity mismatches.

The EMEAP-led central bank process established an Asian Bond Fund (ABF) in June 2003 to facilitate bond issuance. Its idea is to help expand the bond market through the purchase of bonds using foreign exchange reserves. So far, only US dollar-denominated bonds have been purchased. Given the recognition that local currency bonds need promotion in order to address the "double mismatch" issue, EMEAP introduced ABF-2 in December 2004, which involves purchases of Asian-currency denominated bonds. The ASEAN+3 Finance Minister process has undertaken the Asian Bond Market Initiative (ABMI) to develop local currency denominated bonds. One of its aims is to establish a market infrastructure for bond market development — including the establishment of a regional bond guarantee agency, the strengthening of regional rating agencies and the promotion of secondary markets — and to encourage bond issues denominated in a basket of Asian currencies.

Next Steps for Closer Financial Co-operation

The ASEAN+3 countries have begun to review the CMI, focusing on the amount, modalities and IMF linkages. The total amount covered by the CMI may be limited in view of the potential size of speculative capital flows; hence it may be increased substantially, perhaps by as much as ten times the current commitment. Its bilateral nature may be modified to become multilateral and centrally administered in order to make its joint activation easier and prompt in the event of a crisis[35]. The decision-making process on its activation may be clarified. As the effectiveness and quality of surveillance improves, the CMI's linkage to IMF programmes may be reduced or even eliminated. The central issue is how to make the surveillance process effective

 ISBN 92-64-01442-X © OECD 2005

and how a good surveillance culture should be created within ASEAN+3. This should occur along the lines of the G-7 (IMF), the EU (Monetary Committee and ECOFIN) and OECD (Economic Policy Committee, Economic Development and Review Committee, and Working Party No. 3)[36]. One way to strengthen regional surveillance would be to set up a competent Secretariat, whose primary role would be to assist the ASEAN+3 surveillance process by providing high-quality and in-depth economic reviews and assessments, timely identification of emerging issues and vulnerabilities affecting the region and effective policy advice[37].

Once the CMI becomes a centrally administered institution with substantially larger stocks of resources than are presently available and its own secretariat for surveillance and financing, the ASEAN+3 countries will have effectively established an Asian Monetary Fund (AMF)[38]. The group would then be in position to address the earlier concern that an AMF which could lend too generously with too little conditionality might create a moral hazard for the government at the receiving end as well as for investors with stakes in the countries in question. It is essential to develop an effective surveillance culture, improve regional capacity to formulate an independent adjustment policy in the event of a liquidity crisis and, to the extent necessary, enforce effective private-sector involvement so that the potential for moral hazard is minimised.

To develop Asian-currency denominated bond markets, sufficient incentives must be created for both investors and issuers. Corporate governance of potential issuers needs to be enhanced, and a well-designed national and regional market infrastructure needs to be developed — including disclosure requirements, accounting and auditing standards, rating agencies, depository and clearance systems and insolvency procedures for bond defaults.

Exchange-Rate Policy Co-ordination

So far no concrete initiative has been undertaken for exchange-rate policy co-ordination. This presents a serious problem because intra-regional exchange-rate stability is essential to economic growth and stability in this region with rising economic interdependence through trade, investment and financial flows. One country's exchange-rate adjustment can have serious, competitive implications for neighbouring economies — hence the need for co-ordination on exchange-rate policies[39].

ISBN 92-64-01442-X

East Asia's exchange-rate policy co-ordination may evolve in three stages:

— loose policy co-ordination — i.e. information, initial institutional and resource co-ordination;

— tight policy co-ordination — macroeconomic and exchange-rate policy co-ordination for intra-regional exchange-rate stabilisation; and

— complete policy co-ordination — economic and monetary union with a single currency.

First, regional policy makers have already begun information co-ordination through such forums as ASEAN+ERPD and EMEAP and resource co-ordination through the establishment of the CMI. They need to strengthen these arrangements. They need to work harder for further institutional co-ordination, including the creation of a regional common unit of account — or the Asian Currency Unit (ACU) — and the adoption of a G-3 currency-basket system. The ACU can be created by constructing a basket of regional currencies that includes 13 currencies for ASEAN+3 or a subset of them, at least initially. Just like the European Currency Unit (ECU) under the EMS (1979-98), the weights of the regional currencies would reflect the relative importance of the countries in the region. The ACU could be used to measure the degree of each currency's exchange-rate deviation from the regional average. In addition, the emerging economies in East Asia might adopt a common basket of G-3 currencies — the US dollar, the euro and the yen — as a reference for exchange-rate stabilisation. This should enable them to achieve a certain degree of both intra-regional and extra-regional exchange-rate stability[40]. At least initially, the degree of exchange-rate stability or flexibility can be left to each economy's specific conditions and preferences[41].

Second, as the region becomes more integrated, exhibits greater economic and political convergence and hence is better prepared to make a more permanent commitment to economic policy co-ordination, more formal institutions capable of supporting intra-regional exchange-rate stability need to be built. In the second stage of exchange-rate policy co-ordination, a realistic approach is a multi-track one. Several groups of economies in East Asia that are close enough — for example Japan and Korea, or Singapore, Malaysia and Brunei — might initiate sub-regional currency stabilisation schemes *à la* European Snake or Exchange Rate Mechanism (ERM). Under this approach, economies that are ready can go ahead with closer monetary and exchange-rate policy co-ordination, and latecomers will gradually catch up with the forerunners. To help sustain this approach, systematic macroeconomic policy co-ordination is essential — particularly monetary and fiscal policy rules — to make the stabilisation system credible.

ISBN 92-64-01442-X © OECD 2005

Finally, in the last stage the region may establish an economic and monetary union with a common currency, like the euro regime. A common currency arrangement, however, can be expected only in the very distant future because of the lack of political commitments, of social, political and economic convergence, and of deeper complementary institutions[42]. Such an arrangement would require member economies' readiness to accept complete co-ordination of monetary policy — and closer co-ordination of other economic policies — long before its implementation.

Challenges for Further Institutionalisation of Financial Integration

Impediments to Closer Financial Regionalism

There are three possible impediments to further regional financial co-operation:

— East Asia's global orientation in finance — financial integration with the OECD countries and dependence on the US dollar — and the concern about possible conflict with the global financial system governed by the IMF;

— differences in stages of financial market development, capital-account liberalisation and regulatory capacities, and the consequent hesitation on further policy co-ordination owing to the fear of loss of national sovereignty; and

— the lack of political commitment to economic integration.

First, some might argue that East Asia is more closely integrated financially with the United States and Europe than with regional economies and that the region can gain more from further integration with the global market than with the regional economies in terms of risk sharing for smooth consumption. The East Asian economies are also still highly dependent on the US dollar for exchange-rate stabilisation, trade invoicing, external asset holding, foreign-exchange reserve holdings and external liabilities. This dependence means that it will not be easy to reduce the role of the US dollar and increase the use of Asian currencies for regional cross-border transactions. The region's global orientation in finance leads to the view that the global financial system governed by the IMF could be more important than an alternative, regional financial system.

ISBN 92-64-01442-X © OECD 2005

Second, wide differences in stages of financial development within East Asia – in financial market infrastructures, in scope and extent of exchange and capital controls and regulatory and institutional capacities – can constitute a serious impediment to greater policy co-ordination. Such differences imply that low-income countries whose financial systems are insufficiently developed will go slowly in capital-account liberalisation and financial opening and hence in integrating financially with the rest of East Asia. As a result, economies in the region have different policy objectives and priorities and desire to maintain national sovereignty over economic policies, including fiscal, monetary, exchange rate, financial and structural policies. This preference for national policy sovereignty would make it difficult to conduct closer economic policy co-ordination.

Third, sceptics might argue that there is no political consensus or commitment to economic integration owing to differences in political systems and the lack of mutual trust. No single economic power plays a dominant role in East Asia similar to that of the United States in the Western Hemisphere, nor does any bipolar relationship exist similar to the Franco-German alliance in Western Europe. Japan has been mired in economic stagnation over the last decade and China, while recently emerging as an economic power, has yet to achieve capital-account liberalisation and, more fundamentally, both economic and political transitions. It will take time for any bipolar alliance to emerge in East Asia, which will make it difficult to pursue closer economic policy co-ordination.

Assessments of the Impediments

Some of these impediments are real, but they are not insurmountable. It is true that financial integration tends to be global and the role of the US dollar remains predominant in East Asia. Yet regional policy makers have found it absolutely necessary to manage financial globalisation through various measures, including the strengthening of a regional financial architecture. Financial regionalism is not a substitute for but a complement to global efforts to strengthen the international financial architecture governed by the IMF as well as national efforts to strengthen the fundamental underpinnings of individual domestic economies. The region's governments have also found the cost of excessive reliance on the US dollar very high, so that they have embarked on measures including Asian bond-market development to increase the use of regional currencies.

ISBN 92-64-01442-X © OECD 2005

Cross-country differences in financial market development are not the ultimate impediments to regional policy co-ordination, but a lack of political will could be. On the issue of economic sovereignty, the regional economies realise increasingly that their economies are highly interdependent, which makes closer economic policy co-operation inevitable. A multi-track approach of strengthening policy co-ordination among countries that have enough convergence is a realistic option. At the same time, with assistance from Japan, Korea, advanced ASEAN members and multilateral development banks (MDBs), low-income countries can make efforts to upgrade their institutions and market infrastructures. As they catch up with their more advanced peers, they can start participating in closer economic policy co-ordination.

On political consensus and commitment, the East Asian Leaders agreed in Vientiane in November 2004 that they would make efforts to establish an "East Asian Community", the major component of which is an "East Asian Economic Community" (EAEC), and to hold an "East Asian Summit" for this purpose[43]. Japan and China are the most important drivers and they must form a solid bipolar alliance. The two giants in the region need to resolve the issues impeding deeper economic co-operation between them and to re-establish mutual trust. Japan has exercised its leadership role through: proposing an AMF, even if it failed; providing financial support to Thailand, Indonesia, Malaysia, the Philippines and Korea — jointly with the IMF programme or *via* the New Miyazawa Initiative; and guiding the ASEAN+3 process, particularly the CMI. China also is changing its approach rapidly. Its FTA initiative with ASEAN is one important sign of willingness to deepen its economic and political relationship with its Southeast Asian neighbours. Its active engagement with the CMI and surveillance is another sign. China's economic reform is expected eventually to lead to capital account liberalisation in a well-sequenced way, and its economic transition will lead ultimately to transition to a new political system needed for the formation of an "East Asian Community".

The Role of OECD-Country Policies

OECD countries affect developing economies directly through their individual or collective policies or indirectly through the international organisations in which they participate. This section draws development lessons from East Asia and then discusses the role of OECD-country policies further to assist economic integration and co-operation in East Asia.

Lessons from the East Asian Development Experience

East Asia's historic developmental experience reveals that three essential elements contributed to their successes[44]:

— political stability, sound policies, right institutions and national ownership;

— outward orientation with a focus on private-sector development and the investment-trade nexus; and

— effective development assistance.

Stability, Policies, Institutions and Ownership

Political stability, sound policies and right institutions played an essential role in the economic development of East Asia for two to three decades leading up to the financial crisis in 1997-98. Needless to say, the crisis revealed inadequacies and weaknesses in economic governance systems, particularly in the financial and corporate sectors across crisis-affected East Asia. They should have been strengthened through appropriate regulatory and supervisory frameworks in a way commensurate with the pace of globalisation. Nonetheless, the East Asian economies until the age of financial globalisation did have institutional capabilities that facilitated sustained growth, rapid development and poverty reduction. Sound policies, workable institutions and stable and predictable policy regimes were all important.

In addition, the East Asian states had clear national ownership over long-term economic development programmes, liberalisation, deregulation and structural reforms. Rigorous implementation of policy and institutional reforms backed by national ownership was an important driver of successful economic development. Strong institutional capacities and sufficient human resources were indispensable in their efforts to enhance national ownership.

Outward Orientation with Private Sector-Led Growth

The East Asian economies adopted outward-oriented policies with emphasis on private sector-led development and investment-trade linkages. Many of them initially focused on import substitution and then shifted to export promotion. A major mechanism for export growth was through the expansion of domestic markets and sales in international markets. They

 ISBN 92-64-01442-X © OECD 2005

achieved domestic market expansion through the emergence of clusters of firms, supplier networks and distribution systems, which later became a basis for successful export expansion. Export expansion in turn helped each economy overcome the limits of the domestic markets and the foreign-exchange constraints, and promoted learning, technology upgrading and economies of scale. The liberalisation of imports, FDI and the use of foreign technologies and ideas accompanied it. Formation of the regional trade-FDI nexus has been a natural consequence of their market-based, outward-orientated policies.

These East Asian economies emphasised the role of private investment — in capital equipment, human resources and market knowledge — and its nexus with trade as a basis for sustained economic development. Their governments focused on the creation of a favourable investment climate, reduction of the risks and uncertainty of investment activity and ensuring the availability of finance for productive investment opportunities. Their pro-growth development strategies were supported by the mutually reinforcing interactions between investment and trade: investment, by both domestic firms and foreign multinationals, and trade stimulated each other, thereby contributing to economic growth, which in turn stimulated further investment and trade.

Effective ODA

External development assistance was used effectively in East Asia. The number of people living in extreme poverty — below $1.05 per day at 1993 PPP — declined substantially from 470 million in 1990 to 270 million in 2001. The amount of official development assistance (ODA) that East Asia received during this period totalled $113 billion, or less than $10 billion per year on the average. This ODA performance in East Asia has been outstanding — in achieving rapid economic growth and poverty reduction — in comparison with any other part of the developing world. For example, a total of $192 billion was disbursed as ODA in sub-Saharan Africa during 1990-2001, but the number of poor rose (from 230 million to 320 million) rather than declined.

The reason behind the successful ODA performance in East Asia was that it was used as a catalyst to support broad, nationally owned development programmes. These programmes focused on overcoming the unfavourable initial conditions of the recipient countries — particularly low levels of industrial and social infrastructure such as power, telecommunications, transport, water, health and education — providing them with a basis for pursuing private sector-driven, outward-oriented, pro-growth strategies. The East Asian economies had sufficiently high absorptive capacity to use ODA for such purposes. Essentially, ODA in East Asia helped create a favourable investment climate and interacted positively with the recipient countries' political stability, stable macroeconomic policies, predictable business environments and right institutions.

Lessons for Other Developing Countries

There are three lessons for low-income countries in East Asia and elsewhere. First, trade and investment openness is key to success. Second, developing economies need to enhance domestic institutional and entrepreneurial capacities to respond proactively to favourable external environments. Third, ODA can effectively support this process if combined with efforts to improve domestic policies, institutions, governance, human resources and capacities and industrial and social infrastructure.

These lessons from the East Asian experience may not be readily transferable to other developing countries because of East Asia's favourable geography and some initial conditions. What matters is not the amount of money disbursed, but how external aid helps the country's own development programmes in building government capacities and institutions for development.

Impact through Individual OECD-Country/Area Policies

Macro, Financial, Trade and FDI Conditions

OECD-member economic conditions — particularly those in Japan, Korea, the United States, Australia and Europe — have affected prospects for growth, development and poverty reduction in emerging East Asia through their impact on trade and capital flows. First, OECD members' stable macroeconomic and financial conditions have greatly helped emerging East Asian economies to benefit from trade and investment openness. Although volatile short-term capital flows interacted with weak domestic fundamentals and prompted the Asian financial crisis in 1997-98, the East Asian economies have been able to improve their financial resilience since then. It is important for OECD members to maintain stable macroeconomic and financial conditions to stem volatile capital flows *vis-à-vis* developing economies.

ISBN 92-64-01442-X © OECD 2005

Second, OECD members' liberal trade and investment regimes and their provision of market access — through reductions of industrial tariffs and non-tariff barriers — to developing East Asian economies' exports of labour-intensive manufactured products have encouraged the latter's industrialisation. For this purpose, the OECD countries have accepted industrial adjustment on their part by increasing imports from East Asia of those manufactured products which would be costly to produce domestically, by sending abroad the industries that had lost their comparative advantage and by making their labour markets flexible.

Third, OECD countries' steady supply of long-term risk capital — such as FDI — to developing East Asia has been crucial. It has directly provided long-term funding, facilitated transfers of production technology, management know-how and organisational skills, and it has enabled firms to participate in global and regional production chains and in the innovation process.

The Role of OECD Countries' Aid

OECD members, both directly through their aid agencies and indirectly through the MDBs, provided relatively effective ODA to East Asia, as mentioned earlier. ODA has essentially three roles: concessionary financing, particularly for building "hard infrastructure"; policy advice for better policy making in institution building; and capacity building for policy implementation. OECD donors fulfilled all three roles by helping build industrial infrastructure and human resources, by encouraging recipient countries to strengthen their policy frameworks and institutional fundamentals through policy dialogue and consultation and by providing technical assistance for capacity building in a wide variety of areas. ODA loans provided by Japan, the World Bank and the ADB provided a certain degree of predictability in official resource flows for recipient countries. Because the number of donors was relatively small, the recipients' administrative burden in handling them was limited.

Challenges Ahead

An important challenge ahead for OECD members involves how to integrate the low-income countries in East Asia — such as Cambodia, Laos, Myanmar, Mongolia and Pacific Island countries — or elsewhere into regional and global markets. The OECD countries, together with the regional middle-income countries, can help this process by maintaining stable macroeconomic and financial environments, a liberal trading system, stable flows of private risk capital — particularly FDI — and setting effective ODA policies targeted at low-income countries. A realistic approach would be to encourage these countries to pursue structural, institutional and governance reforms so that they can participate in trade and FDI and eventually benefit from liberalisation and globalisation.

Given that low-income economies have adversary problems in their initial conditions, the OECD countries need to assist them in overcoming these unfavourable conditions and pursuing private sector-led development in the context of globalisation. As the East Asian experience demonstrates, ODA can have greater positive impact on recipient economies in terms of economic development and poverty reduction if it stimulates private investment, trade and FDI through provision of basic industrial infrastructure, human-capital development and institutional capacity building. OECD members can help low-income economies through development aid under the following conditions:

— The right policy environment in the recipient countries. Recipient countries must commit themselves both to political stability and to sound macroeconomic, structural and social policies, good governance and the rule of law. The resulting enabling environment would attract private capital, particularly foreign direct investment, which complements official aid.

— Recipient country ownership of development. Strong ownership by a country of its own development strategy is instrumental because without it policy and institutional reforms for economic development and poverty reduction cannot be achieved.

— Donor co-ordination of assistance efforts. The donor community needs to pursue harmonisation of policies and procedures in order to reduce transaction costs and focus assistance efforts on countries with sound economic management and good governance (OECD, 2003*a*).

— Donor-recipient partnership. The donor community and recipient countries must work together by involving other stakeholders in achieving the common goals of economic development and poverty reduction as the only objectives. This reflects past experience that aid effectiveness is reduced when aid is tied to other, often politically motivated objectives of donors.

 ISBN 92-64-01442-X © OECD 2005

Impact through Better Global Governance

The OECD member countries can contribute to development and poverty reduction in developing economies through their collective action. Co-ordination of economic policies at the global and regional levels — such as the G7 process and the European Commission — is essential to ensure a stable global or regional economy. OECD countries have indeed affected and will continue to affect regional economic integration and co-operation in East Asia directly through their individual actions or indirectly through international organisations because of their influence on them.

First, one of the major objectives of the IMF is to help maintain stable global finance, and in this context the IMF has focused on the international financial architecture in recent years. In this discussion, the roles to be played by various international organisations including the IMF are generally well established. Emerging market economies must make efforts to reduce risks of crisis through strengthening domestic policy and institutional frameworks, particularly through ROSCs. Industrial countries must regulate and monitor their financial institutions to reduce their bias toward short-term lending and to improve their risk management. The IMF must make efforts to strengthen Article IV surveillance, to provide international liquidity, to establish effective conditionality and to involve private creditors. The role of regional institutions also needs recognition. It is natural for a group of interdependent regional economies to take concerted action for financial stability at the regional level. A clearly focused regional approach designed to reduce vulnerabilities and crisis risks and to cope with the eruption of crises, can contribute to global financial stability. The IMF as a global crisis co-ordinator can benefit greatly from such regional initiatives[45].

The IMF needs to rectify the imbalance and unfairness of the current distribution of IMF quotas, which is heavily skewed against East Asia. The East Asian quotas are unrealistically small in relation to their actual weights in the world economy (see Buira, 2003 and Griffith-Jones, 2003). Greater allocation of quotas to East Asia would undoubtedly make its representation on the IMF Executive Board consistent with the changing world reality and restore fairness and integrity in its decision making.

Second, the World Bank has assisted poor countries to pursue structural reforms, strengthen policy and institutional underpinnings, improve their investment climates and integrate them with the global trading system. It needs to re-emphasise the importance of broadly based economic growth and development as a means of achieving poverty reduction and improving social conditions. The World Bank appears to have extended its businesses beyond its competency – into the areas of religion and culture – and it needs to take a more focused approach to development. It is also often criticised for its slow response in crisis situations. It needs to change its business culture and mode of operation by creating a system that enables quick mobilisation of its experts and resources in times of crisis.

Third, the WTO needs to accelerate the Doha process. Putting the Doha round back on track must be the highest priority for OECD countries, which must lead the process by showing good examples. They need to eliminate completely tariffs on manufactured products and subsidies for agricultural exports, decouple completely all domestic subsidies from production, reduce tariffs on agricultural products and commit to ensure free cross-border trade in services. In addition, the WTO needs to monitor regional trade arrangements continuously so that they do not go against the WTO principles of ensuring a liberal, non-discriminatory and multilateral trading system.

Fourth, the OECD is a unique organisation, which oversees both developed-country policies and official development assistance. It monitors progress on structural reforms of member economies, ODA flows and policies of members and development issues for non-member developing economies. Hence, its comparative advantage naturally lies in assessing policy coherence for development. It can apply peer pressure to its member countries to improve their structural policies in a way that can positively affect both the members themselves and non-members. From this perspective, the OECD has undertaken several recent initiatives. A "horizontal programme" on policy coherence for development looks at the impact of a broad range of OECD-country policies on developing economies. The Development Assistance Committee (DAC) peer reviews place greater emphasis on issues of policy coherence among members. The OECD Development Centre also has greater involvement in policy coherence. The OECD is advised to continue to strengthen its analytical capacity on policy coherence, particularly on the actual, quantitative impact of OECD-country policies on developing economies as well as on case studies of policy coherence for development.

Finally, it is important to ensure that international organisations reduce incoherence among themselves so that they can work jointly for economic development and poverty reduction in developing countries. Incoherence may arise between the IMF and the WTO, or between the IMF and the World Bank (and regional MDBs). The major focus of the IMF tends to be on "adjustment" – including fiscal improvements – while that of the WTO is

ISBN 92-64-01442-X © OECD 2005

on "trade liberalisation" — including reductions in tariffs and hence tariff revenues — and that of the Bank is often on fiscal support and growth. An IMF policy recommendation to restore fiscal balance can clash with a WTO recommendation to reduce tariffs. In a crisis situation, the IMF and the World Bank need to work closely with each other on programmes to strike the right balance between "adjustment" and "growth". In the Asian crisis, the IMF often went to crisis countries alone or with minimal involvement of the World Bank (and the ADB), notwithstanding that the MDBs' contribution to crisis resolution turned out to be substantial. When the IMF has no comparative advantage in formulating and monitoring structural reforms, it must involve the World Bank, other MDBs and other relevant institutions from the outset.

Concluding Remarks

This chapter has argued that the emerging East Asian economies have achieved sustained economic development and poverty reduction through external liberalisation, domestic structural, institutional and governance reforms and market-driven integration with the global and regional markets. Although the Asian financial crisis in 1997-98 temporarily interrupted this progress, these economies have pursued further liberalisation and reforms, deepened economic integration through trade, FDI and finance and regained dynamic growth.

OECD-country policies — particularly those in Japan, Korea, the United States, Australia and Europe — have helped the East Asian economies to grow, develop and reduce poverty in at least six ways. First, they have helped maintain peace and security, which has been critical to sustained economic growth. Second, they have maintained a relatively stable macroeconomic and financial environment ensuring stable flows of capital, except at times of crisis. Third, they have maintained an increasingly open trading system with no reversal or backtracking. Fourth, they have enacted pro-FDI policies through industrial restructuring and adjustment, including the expansion of imports, the encouragement of exit of inefficient industries and the migration of domestically non-competitive firms to emerging East Asia. Fifth, they have facilitated transfers of production technology and organisational skills and access to global distribution networks. Sixth, they have provided ODA to help build industrial infrastructure and human resources and to supplement social spending, through concessionary financing, policy

ISBN 92-64-01442-X © OECD 2005

dialogue and capacity building. They have also helped, partly through the international financial institutions, to strengthen recipient countries' policy frameworks and institutional underpinnings.

Regional economic co-operation in East Asia — through the institutionalisation of deepening economic interdependence — is still in its infancy. Nonetheless, some important progress has occurred in trade and finance for regional institution building. There is a mutually reinforcing interaction between economic integration and its formal institutionalisation. Joint co-operative action for such endeavours at the regional level also nurtures a sense of identity and community as well as building trust. All of these factors are critical to maintaining regional growth and economic stability and reducing security concerns in the region. Japan, China and ASEAN must move more aggressively to achieve deeper, real integration, which will contribute to the growth of the regional and world economies. The OECD community needs to embrace East Asian regionalism as a building block for a more liberal and stable international economic system.

The region faces several challenges. First, the regional economies should accelerate negotiations on bilateral and sub-regional FTAs/EPAs by avoiding the counterproductive "spaghetti bowl" effect and maintaining WTO consistency. This requires both substantial structural reforms in all economies, including their manufacturing and agricultural sectors, and common standard-setting and rule-making. ASEAN's middle-income member states must reform their economies to cope with greater international competition, particularly *vis-à-vis* China, while its low-income members must pursue institutional and governance reforms to enable them to benefit from trade and FDI openness.

Second, the regional economies need to make further progress on the Chiang Mai Initiative (CMI), the policy dialogue and economic surveillance process and Asian bond market development. It is crucial to enhance the functioning of the CMI through its substantial enlargement, multilateralisation and central administration of currency swap arrangements, a clearer decision-making process for its joint activation and the reduction of its IMF linkage. To achieve such reforms, the region must make the surveillance process effective, improve regional capacity to formulate independent adjustment policy in the event of liquidity crises and, to the extent necessary, enforce effective private-sector involvement. Once these efforts are made, East Asia will have effectively established an Asian Monetary Fund (AMF) that can contribute to regional financial stability without creating fears of moral hazard.

ISBN 92-64-01442-X © OECD 2005

Third, it is time to initiate exchange-rate policy co-ordination. The first step would be for the regional economies to discuss exchange-rate issues as part of an enhanced surveillance process. Next, it would be an attractive option for the emerging economies in the region to adopt a G-3 currency-basket system based on the Japanese yen, the US dollar and the euro. The following step would introduce a common regional unit of account — an Asian Currency Unit (ACU) — in which the weights of the regional currencies would reflect the relative economic importance of the countries. ASEAN+3 finance ministers may discuss member countries' exchange-rate deviations from the regional average in reference to the ACU.

Finally, it is important to overcome various impediments to closer regional economic co-operation. Some of the impediments will become less serious as economic interdependence deepens, while others require fundamental efforts such as integrating ASEAN latecomers with the regional and global markets. The region must nurture the sense of mutual trust and community by articulating the concept of an "East Asian Community", a long-term vision for the political and economic future of East Asia, and by having such a vision shared by the general public in the region. A core component of this "Community" is an East Asia-wide FTA, to evolve into a region-wide customs union, which may eventually lead to East Asian economic and monetary union with a single currency like the euro zone.

Notes

1. IMF (1998*a*, 1998*b*) and Summers (2000) emphasised the importance of domestic structural weaknesses, while Radelet and Sachs (1998, 2000) and Furman and Stiglitz (1998) emphasised the importance of financial globalisation.

2. When an emerging market economy borrows short-term, foreign-currency denominated funds from abroad, it faces both maturity and currency mismatches — hence the "double mismatch" — because the borrowed funds tend to be invested at home with long-term maturities in domestic currency. As a result, the economy is exposed to both "maturity risk" — unanticipated rejection of rollover of short-term liabilities — and "currency risk" — unanticipated currency depreciation.

3. See Eichengreen (1999) and Kenen (2001) for a discussion of reforms of the international financial architecture.

4. There were several reasons for this: (a) a prevailing perception that even without CCL, the IMF would step in anyway in the event of a crisis; (b) a CCL agreement with the IMF may send a wrong signal to the market that the country in question is in need of IMF financing; (c) a possible cancellation of CCL status can send a signal that the country's macroeconomic and financial conditions have deteriorated considerably, thereby triggering a crisis; and (d) the commitment fee was too high.

5. When the IMF intervened in crisis-affected countries in East Asia to contain the crisis, many viewed at least part of the IMF policies as not only inappropriate in some key areas but also exacerbating the severity of the crisis. A case in point is the initial Indonesian programme (November 1997), where the IMF insisted on the closure of 16 commercial banks without adequate protection of bank deposits, thereby exacerbating systemic bank runs (Sachs, 1998). In the January 1998 programme, the IMF added a long list of structural reforms, specifying in minute detail such things as the clove monopoly and selling plywood (Feldstein, 1998), which were largely irrelevant to the currency crisis. Misguided or excessively broad and detailed structural conditions undermined the country's "ownership" of the programme and damaged its successful implementation. Some of these are documented in the report released by the IMF Independent Evaluation Office (2003). The IMF programmes should have focused on the immediate need to stem capital outflows and restore currency market stability.

ISBN 92-64-01442-X © OECD 2005

6. The IMF's core areas of responsibility include: macroeconomic stabilisation; monetary, fiscal and exchange-rate policy, including the underlying institutional arrangements and closely related structural measures; and financial-sector issues including the functioning of both domestic and international financial markets.

7. The international community began to explore possible mechanisms for the debt restructuring of international sovereign bonds in the recognition that, at a time of liquidity crisis, holders of sovereign bonds along with other creditors would need to contribute to the resolution of such crises. Two methods were recommended: a contractual approach and a statutory approach. A contractual approach considers collective action clauses in sovereign bond contracts as a useful device for orderly resolution of crises; their explicit inclusion in bond documentation would provide a degree of predictability to the restructuring process. A statutory approach (Krueger, 2002) attempts to create the legal basis — through a universal treaty rather than through a set of national laws in a limited number of jurisdictions — for establishing adequate incentives for debtors and creditors to agree upon a prompt, orderly and predictable restructuring of unsustainable debt. Similar approaches might be needed for private debt instruments as well, because of the surge in private-to-private capital flows, as was the case in East Asia.

8. The most prominent among these is the Financial Sector Assessment Program (FSAP) supported jointly by the IMF and the World Bank. The FSAP is intended to strengthen the monitoring and assessment of financial systems, given that financial-sector weaknesses have played an important role in damaging a country's overall economic health.

9. See also Bird and Rajan (2002), Kawai (2002*a*, 2005) and Kuroda and Kawai (2002).

10. See Kawai *et al.* (2003).

11. A good example is the New Miyazawa Initiative of 1998, which supported the fiscal needs of crisis-affected countries in East Asia for restructuring and social spending. See below.

12. The advantage of using trade-intensity indexes over trade shares is that the former control for a region's relative size in world trade and hence present a better measure of closeness of the economies within a region. However, a small regional group tends to have a high trade-intensity index.

13. The large volume of Hong Kong, China's FDI flows to China, however, may contain "round tripping" from China, which aims to take advantage of tax and other favourable advantages given to "foreign" direct investment by the Chinese authorities.

14. If data for the 1980s are included, the importance of Japan as a major investor in ASEAN would become more significant.

15. See Kawai (1997, 2004), Kawai and Urata (1998, 2004), Urata (2001), Athukorala (2003), and Fukao *et al.* (2003).

16. See Kawai and Motonishi (2004) for details.

17. Earlier studies by Eichengreen and Bayoumi (1999) found that, in terms of supply shocks, some East Asian nations were just as closely connected with one another as European countries were. In terms of demand shocks, ASEAN countries were also reasonably connected. See also Goto and Hamada (1994), Bayoumi and Eichengreen (1994) and Bayoumi *et al.* (2000). Using more recent data, Kawai and Motonishi (2004) confirm that many East Asian economies are subject to largely symmetric supply shocks.

18. In AFTA, the Common Effective Preferential Tariff (CEPT) scheme is used to reduce the tariffs within the region to 0 from 5 per cent. The ASEAN Industrial Co-operation Scheme (AICO) applies the CEPT rate of tariffs (0 to 5 per cent) on approved AICO products to strengthen industrial co-operation within the region. AFTA is also complemented by the Framework Agreement on the ASEAN Investment Area (AIA), which promotes free movements of investments, skilled workers, professionals and technologies within the region.

19. Two other pillars were an "ASEAN Security Community" and an "ASEAN Socio-cultural Community".

20. See Hew and Soesastro (2003) for a number of ideas on deepening ASEAN economic integration.

21. Note that in the early 1990s ASEAN had only six members and in the latter half of the 1990s admitted five additional members — Viet Nam (1995), Laos and Myanmar (1997) and Cambodia (1999).

22. Nonetheless, this initiative was not completely forgotten. When the Asia-Europe Meeting (ASEM) was created in 1996, the Asian participants were essentially EAEG/EAEC economies.

23. More precisely, the Japan-Singapore agreement is called the "Agreement between Japan and the Republic of Singapore for a New-Age Economic Partnership (JSEPA)" and goes beyond a conventional free-trade agreement.

24. "Early harvest" refers to provisions of the "Framework Agreement on China-ASEAN Comprehensive Economic Co-operation", intended to liberalise, before the full completion of the FTA, tariffs in priority sectors of interest and to implement other trade and investment facilitation deemed to generate immediate benefits to ASEAN and China.

25. No timeframe is set for negotiations, however. Japan is indeed cautious about such an arrangement with China at this point. Its official view is that, before negotiating an FTA/EPA, China must clearly show its compliance with all the commitments made in WTO accession negotiations.

ISBN 92-64-01442-X © OECD 2005

26. Lloyd (2002) argues that bilateralism/FTAs will likely lead toward and not impede multilateralism, while Brown *et al.* (2003) believe in the superiority of multilateralism.

27. Wong and Chan (2003) emphasise that China is an economic threat to ASEAN countries, which must reform.

28. Ravenhill (2001) argues that diversity of membership and conflicts of power and interest sharply limit potential for co-operation in East Asia, while Terada (2003) provides a constructive and relatively optimistic account of the regional grouping.

29. Economies that participated in the Thai financial package were called the "Friends of Thailand" — Japan; Australia; China; Hong Kong, China; Malaysia; Singapore; Brunei; Indonesia and Korea.

30. There was another arrangement under the Manila Framework Group — called the MFG Co-operative Financing Arrangement — which was intended to be only a second line of defence. This arrangement was abolished when the MFG process itself was terminated.

31. ASEAN+3 was formed in April 1999. Stubbs (2002) takes the view that it will rise as a major regional and international player. See Kawai (2002*a*) and Kuroda and Kawai (2002).

32. This is the sum of all BSAs, including the amount that Japan committed under the New Miyazawa Initiative — a total of $7.5 billion, or $5 billion with Korea and $2.5 billion with Malaysia — except that two-way BSAs are doubled for calculation purposes. Excluding the amount committed under the New Miyazawa Initiative, the total sum is $36.5 billion. The Japan-Thailand BSA is expected to become a two-way arrangement; then the total amount of CMI BSAs will be $47 billion including the New Miyazawa Initiative commitments.

33. Other major mechanisms include the ASEAN Surveillance Process, EMEAP (Executives Meeting of East Asia-Pacific Central Banks), and trans-regional forums such as APEC and Asia-Europe Meeting (ASEM).

34. The Asian Development Bank provides some data on developing member economies. The IMF played a secretariat function for the MFG.

35. Rajan and Siregar (2004) propose to establish a centralised reserve pooling system.

36. See Girardin (2004) for issues on information exchange and surveillance.

37. This secretariat must have adequate human resources to monitor regional capital flows and financial and exchange market developments, update early warning indicators, and analyse regional and country economic conditions.

38. Nonetheless, Rapkin (2001) takes a pessimistic view of an AMF.

39. See Montiel (2004) for an excellent review.

40. In the post-crisis period, Korea and Thailand appear to be shifting to a *de facto* currency basket system, *à la* Singapore. (Kawai, 2002*b*). McKinnon (2000, 2004), however, takes the view that the East Asian economies have resurrected the US dollar-standard system. See Kawai (2004) and Kawai and Takagi (2005) who argue for the adoption of a G-3 currency-basket system. Several papers in Asian Development Bank (2004), including Eichengreen (2004), advocate floating exchange rates.

41. This approach is consistent with what Goldstein (2002) calls "managed floating plus". A "managed float" is a system with occasional intervention to limit excessive short-term fluctuations in exchange rates without a publicly announced exchange-rate target, and a "plus" is inflation targeting and aggressive measures to reduce currency mismatches. The approach here is to adopt a G-3 currency basket as an exchange-rate reference in the context of "managed floating plus," *à la* Williamson (1999, 2000, 2001). See also Hernandez and Montiel (2003). Even when a G-3 currency-basket system is desirable for the region as a whole, however, it may not be easy for any single economy to move unilaterally away from the current, US dollar-centred exchange-rate arrangement to a new arrangement in which the relative weight of the dollar is smaller and those of the yen and euro larger. When neighbouring countries stabilise their exchange rates primarily against the US dollar, there may not be much incentive for any one country unilaterally to alter its exchange-rate policy, which demonstrates a potential "collective action" problem associated with a move to a G-3 currency-basket arrangement (Ogawa and Ito, 2002). Overcoming this problem requires a concerted move among the economies concerned.

42. See Wyploz (2004) for the importance of institutional integration for a currency union.

43. East Asia Vision Group (2001) had put forward the idea of an "East Asian Community" and East Asia Study Group (2002), comprising government officials, supported the idea but the political action was delayed for two years.

44. Some of these elements, but not all, and others have been analysed by the World Bank (1993). This section draws on Kawai (2005).

45. Because crisis management and resolution can require involvement of international creditors from outside the region, a regional approach needs to be linked with a global framework.

ISBN 92-64-01442-X © OECD 2005

Bibliography

Asian Development Bank (ed.) (2004), *Monetary and Financial Integration in East Asia: The Way Ahead* (Vols. 1-2), Palgrave, MacMillan, Houndmills, New York, NY.

Athukorala, P.-c. (2003), "Product Fragmentation and Trade Patterns in East Asia", Working Paper No. 2003/21, Research School of Pacific and Asian Studies, Australian National University, Canberra.

Bayoumi, T. and B. Eichengreen (1994), "One Money or Many? Analyzing the Prospects for Monetary Unification in Various Parts of the World", *Princeton Studies in International Finance*, No. 76, International Finance Section, Princeton University, Princeton, NJ.

Bayoumi, T., B. Eichengreen and P. Mauro (2000), "On Regional Monetary Arrangements for ASEAN", *Journal of the Japanese and International Economies*, 14 (June), pp. 121-148.

Bird, G. and R.S. Rajan (2002), "The Evolving Asian Financial Architecture," *Essays in International Economics*, 226, February, International Economics Section, Princeton University, Princeton, NJ.

Brown, D.K., A.V. Deardorff and R.M. Stern (2003), "Multilateral, Regional and Bilateral Trade-Policy Options for the United States and Japan", *World Economy*, 26:6 (June), pp. 803-828.

Buira, A. (2003), "The Governance of the International Monetary Fund", *in* I. Kaul, P. Conceicao, K. Le Goulven and R.U. Mendoza (eds.), *Providing Global Public Goods: Managing Globalization*, pp. 225-244, Oxford University Press, New York, NY.

East Asia Study Group (2002), "Final Report of the East Asia Study Group", ASEAN+3 Summit, 4 November, Phnom Penh, Cambodia.

East Asia Vision Group (2001), "Toward an East Asian Community: Region of Peace, Prosperity and Progress", *East Asia Vision Group Report*.

EICHENGREEN, B. (1999), *Toward a New International Financial Architecture: A Practical Post-Asia Agenda*, Institute for International Economics, Washington, D.C., February.

EICHENGREEN, B. (2004), "The Case for Floating Exchange Rates in Asia", *in* ASIAN DEVELOPMENT BANK, (ed.) (2004), Vol. 2, pp.49-89.

EICHENGREEN, B. and T. BAYOUMI (1999), "Is Asia an Optimum Currency Area? Can It Become One? Regional, Global and Historical Perspectives on Asian Monetary Relations", *in* S. COLLIGNON, J. PISANI-FERRY and Y.C. PARK (eds.), *Exchange Rate Policies in Emerging Asian Countries*, London, Routledge, pp. 347-366.

FELDSTEIN, M. (1998), "Refocusing the IMF." *Foreign Affairs*, 77, March/April, pp. 20-33.

FUKAO, K., H. ISHIDO and K. ITO (2003), "Vertical Intra-industry Trade and Foreign Direct Investment in East Asia", *Journal of the Japanese and International Economies*, Vol. 17, pp. 468-506.

FURMAN, J. and J.E. STIGLITZ (1998), "Economic Crises: Evidence and Insights from East Asia", *Brookings Papers on Economic Activity*, 2: 1998, pp. 1-135.

GIRARDIN, E. (2004), "Information Exchange, Surveillance Systems and Regional Institutions in East Asia ", *in* ASIAN DEVELOPMENT BANK, (ed.) (2004), Vol. 1, pp. 53-95.

GOLDSTEIN, M. (2002), "Managed Floating Plus", *Policy Analyses in International Economics*, No. 66, Institute for International Economics, Washington, D.C.

GOTO, J. and K. HAMADA (1994), "Economic Preconditions for Asian Regional Integration", *in* T. ITO and A.O. KRUEGER (eds.), *Macroeconomic Linkage: Savings, Exchange Rates, and Capital Flows*, University of Chicago Press, Chicago, pp. 359-385.

GRIFFITH-JONES, S. (2003), "International Financial Stability and Market Efficiency as a Global Public Good", *in* I. KAUL, P. CONCEICAO, K. LE GOULVEN and R.U. MENDOZA (eds.), *Providing Global Public Goods: Managing Globalization*, Oxford University Press, New York, NY, pp. 435-454.

HERNANDEZ, L. and P.J. MONTIEL (2003), "Post-crisis Exchange Rate Policy in Five Asian Countries: Filling in the 'Hollow Middle'?", *Journal of the Japanese and International Economies*, 17:3, pp. 336-369, September.

HEW, D. and H. SOESASTRO (2003), "Realizing the ASEAN Economic Community by 2020 – ISEAS and ASEAN-ISIS Approaches", *ASEAN Economic Bulletin*, 20:3, pp. 292-296, December.

INTERNATIONAL MONETARY FUND (1998*a*), *International Capital Markets: Development, Prospects, and Key Policy Issues*, IMF, Washington, D.C.

 ISBN 92-64-01442-X © OECD 2005

INTERNATIONAL MONETARY FUND (1998*b*), *World Economic Outlook*, Washington, DC, IMF.

INTERNATIONAL MONETARY FUND (IMF) (2003), "The IMF and Recent Capital Account Crises: Indonesia, Korea, Brazil", Evaluation Report, IMF Independent Evaluation Office, IMF, Washington, D.C.

KAWAI, M. (1997), "Japan's Trade and Investment in East Asia", *in* D. ROBERTSON, (ed.), *East Asian Trade after the Uruguay Round*, pp. 209-226, Cambridge University Press, Cambridge.

KAWAI, M. (2002*a*), "Global, Regional and National Approaches to the International Financial Architecture: Lessons from the East Asian Crisis", *International Economy* (Japan Society of International Economics), Vol. 7, pp. 65-108.

KAWAI, M. (2002*b*), "Exchange Rate Arrangements in East Asia: Lessons from the 1997-98 Currency Crisis", *Monetary and Economic Studies, Special Edition*, 20, pp. 167-204, December, Institute for Monetary and Economic Studies, Bank of Japan.

KAWAI, M. (2004), "Trade and Investment Integration and Cooperation in East Asia: Empirical Evidence and Issues", revised version of a paper presented to the High-Level Conference on "Asia's Economic Cooperation and Integration", 1-2 July, organised by the Asian Development Bank, Manila.

KAWAI, M. (2005), "East Asian Economic Regionalism: Progress and Challenges", *Journal of Asian Economics*, Vol. 16, pp.29-55, February.

KAWAI, M. and T. MOTONISHI (2004), "Macroeconomic Interdependence in East Asia: Empirical Evidence and Issues", revised version of a paper presented to the High-Level Conference on "Asia's Economic Cooperation and Integration" 1-2 July, organised by the Asian Development Bank, Manila.

KAWAI, M., R. NEWFARMER and S. SCHMUKLER (2003), "Crisis and Contagion in East Asia: Nine Lessons", *Eastern Economic Journal* (forthcoming), *Policy Research Working Paper* No. 2610, June, World Bank, Washington, D.C.

KAWAI, M. and S. TAKAGI (2005), "Proposed Strategy for a Regional Exchange Rate Arrangement in Post-Crisis East Asia: Analysis, Review and Proposal", *Global Economic Review* (forthcoming).

KAWAI. M. and S. URATA (1998), "Are Trade and Direct Investment Substitutes or Complements? An Empirical Analysis of Japanese Manufacturing Industries, *in* H. LEE and D.W. ROLAND-HOLST, (eds.), *Economic Development and Co-operation in the Pacific Basin: Trade, Investment and Environmental Issues*, pp.251-293, Cambridge University Press, Cambridge.

KAWAI, M and S. URATA (2004), "Trade and Foreign Direct Investment in East Asia", *in* G. de BROUWER and M. KAWAI (eds.), *Economic Linkages and Implications for Exchange Rate Regimes in East Asia* , pp.12-102, Routledge Curzon, London and New York.

KENEN, P.B. (2001), *The International Financial Architecture: What's New? What's Missing?*, Institute for International Economics, Washington, D.C.

KRUEGER, A. (2002), "New Approaches to Sovereign Debt Restructuring: An Update on Our Thinking", paper presented to a conference on "Sovereign Debt Workouts: Hopes and Hazards", 1 April, Institute for International Economics, Washington, D.C.

KURODA, H. and M. KAWAI (2002), "Strengthening Regional Financial Cooperation in East Asia", *Pacific Economic Papers*, 51, October.

LLOYD, P. (2002), "New Bilateralism in the Asia Pacific." *World Economy*, 25 (9), September 2002, pp. 1279-1296.

MCKINNON, R.I. (2000), "The East Asian Dollar Standard: Life after Death?", *Economic Notes*, Vol. 29, pp. 31-82.

MCKINNON, R. I. (2004), "The East Asian Exchange Rate Dilemma and the World Dollar Standard", *in* C. SUTHIPAHND, E-M. CLAASSEN and J. SCHROEDER (eds.), *East Asia's Monetary Future: Integration in the Global Economy*, pp. 103-128, Edward Elgar, Cheltenham and Northampton.

MONTIEL, P.J. (2004), "An Overview of Monetary and Financial Integration in East Asia", *in* ASIAN DEVELOPMENT BANK,(ed). (2004), Vol. 1, pp. 1-52.

OGAWA, E. and T. ITO (2002), "On the Desirability of a Regional Basket Currency Arrangement", *Journal of the Japanese and International Economies*, Vol. 16, pp. 317-334.

ORGANISATION FOR ECONOMIC CO-OPERATION AND DEVELOPMENT (2003*a*), *Harmonising Donor Practices for Effective Aid Delivery, DAC Guidelines and Reference Series*, Development Assistance Committee, Paris.

ORGANISATION FOR ECONOMIC CO-OPERATION AND DEVELOPMENT (2003*b*), *Regionalism and the Multilateral Trading System*, Paris.

RADELET, S. and J.D. SACHS (1998), "The East Asian Financial Crisis: Diagnosis, Remedies, Prospects", *Brookings Papers on Economic Activity*, 1: 1998, pp. 1-90.

RADELET, S. and J.D. SACHS (2000), "The Onset of the East Asian Financial Crises", *in* P. Krugman (ed.), *Currency Crises*, pp. 105-153, University of Chicago, Chicago.

RAJAN, R. and R. SIREGAR (2004), "Centralized Reserve Pooling for the ASEAN + 3 Countries", *in* ASIAN DEVELOPMENT BANK, (ed.) (2004), Vol. 2, pp. 285-329.

RAPKIN, D.P (2001), "The United States, Japan, and the Power to Block: the APEC and AMF Cases", *Pacific Review*, 14:3, pp. 373-410, August.

RAVENHILL, J. (2001), *Asia Pacific Economic Cooperation: The Construction of Pacific Rim Regionalism*, Cambridge University Press, Cambridge.

SACHS, J. (1998), "The IMF and the Asian Flu", *American Prospect*, 37, pp. 16-21, March-April.

 ISBN 92-64-01442-X © OECD 2005

STUBBS, R. (2002), "ASEAN Plus Three: Emerging East Asian Regionalism?", *Asian Survey*, 42:3, pp. 440-455, May/June.

SUMMERS, L.H. (2000), "International Financial Crises: Causes, Prevention, and Cures", *American Economic Review (AEA Papers and Proceedings)*, 90:2, pp. 1-16, May.

TERADA, T. (2003), "Constructing an 'East Asian Concept' and Growing Regional Identity: From EAEC to ASEAN+3", *Pacific Review*, 16:2, pp. 251-277.

UNCTAD (2004), *World Investment Report*, UNCTAD, Geneva.

URATA, S. (2001), "Emergence of an FDI-Trade Nexus and Economic Growth in East Asia", *in* J. STIGLITZ and S. YUSUF, (eds.), *Rethinking the East Asian Miracle*, pp.407-459, Oxford University Press, New York, NY.

WILLIAMSON, J. (1999), The Case for a Common Basket Peg for East Asian Currencies", *in* S. COLLIGNON, J. PISANI-FERRY and Y.C. PARK, (eds.), *Exchange Rate Policies in Emerging Asian Countries*, pp.327-343, Routledge, London and New York, NY.

WILLIAMSON, J. (2000), *Exchange Rate Regimes for Emerging Markets: Reviving the Intermediate Option* (Policy Analyses in International Economics, 60), Institute for International Economics, Washington, D.C.

WILLIAMSON, J. (2001), "The Case for a Basket, Band and Crawl (BBC) Regime for East Asia", D. GRUEN and J. SIMON, (eds.), *Future Directions for Monetary Policies in East Asia*, pp.96-111, Reserve Bank of Australia, Sydney.

WONG, J. and S. CHAN (2003), "China-ASEAN Free Trade Agreement: Shaping Future Economic Relations", *Asian Survey*, 43:3, pp. 507-526, May/June.

WORLD BANK (1993), *The East Asian Miracle: Growth and Public Policy*, Washington, D.C.

WORLD BANK (1998), *East Asia: The Road to Recovery*, Washington, D.C.

WORLD BANK (2000), *East Asia: Recovery and Beyond*, Washington, D.C.

WYPLOZ, C. (2004), "Regional Exchange Rate Arrangements: Lessons from Europe for East Asia", *in* ASIAN DEVELOPMENT BANK, (ed.) (2004), Vol. 2, pp.241-284.

YOSHITOMI, M. and S. SHIRAI (2000), "Policy Recommendations for Preventing Another Capital Account Crisis", Technical Background Paper (July 7), Asian Development Bank Institute, Tokyo.

Chapter 9

East Asia's Multi-Layered Development Process: The Trade-FDI Nexus

Shujiro Urata[1]

Abstract

This chapter analyses foreign trade and FDI in East Asia since the 1980s and describes the formation of the trade-FDI nexus that initiated the region's multi-layered development. The region's remarkable sequential growth pattern became the basis of such development, as the trade-FDI nexus involved the NIEs, the ASEAN countries and China. The electronics industry has played a central role in the formation of the nexus, because it has special features, including production sub-processes that can be divided and situated in different locations *via* FDI to exploit opportunities for specialisation and international trade. The region has indeed become a major global production site for electronics products during the period concerned. OECD countries have played important roles in the formation of the trade-FDI nexus. They have been major sources of FDI, although FDI from East Asia's more advanced developing economies has increased notably in recent years. Many OECD countries have adopted measures to promote FDI to developing economies, such as provision of information on FDI environments and of FDI insurance. They have also contributed to the promotion of trade and FDI by providing ODA for infrastructure development in East Asia. The chapter concludes by discussing major challenges to the region's future growth based on the trade-FDI nexus.

ISBN 92-64-01442-X

Introduction

Global foreign direct investment (FDI) surged to 25 times its 1980 level in current US dollars in 2000[2]. World trade and GDP climbed by multiples of 3.3 and 2.9 respectively during the same period, so the importance of FDI in the world economy increased dramatically during these two decades. Although a large part of world FDI flows went to developed countries, FDI into developing countries increased notably in absolute terms. Among developing countries, those in East Asia very successfully attracted large amounts of it.

FDI recipients gain benefits that contribute to economic growth. FDI brings resources, such as funds for fixed investment, technology and management know-how, which are in acute shortage in many developing countries. It also enables recipient countries to use the sales and procurement networks of multinational corporations (MNCs) to expand trade. Export expansion promotes economic growth as it earns foreign exchange that can be used to import technology, intermediate goods, capital goods and other items. Successful export performance in turn attracts export-motivated FDI. This forms a trade-FDI nexus, a type of development that indeed has emerged in East Asia, in a remarkable sequential process. Formation of the regional trade-FDI nexus began in the early 1980s in two Asian Newly Industrialising Economies (NIEs), Singapore and Hong Kong, China. Four members of the Association of Southeast Asian Nations (ASEAN4), Indonesia, Malaysia, the Philippines and Thailand, followed in the latter half of the 1980s. China joined in the 1990s.

This sequential evolution of the trade-FDI nexus in East Asia has resulted in multi-layered development. This chapter analyses that process. It examines the patterns and characteristics of the trade-FDI nexus and identifies the factors that contributed to its establishment. It also tries to discern the impacts of policies in both developed and developing countries on the formation of the nexus, in order to draw lessons for developing countries interested in promoting economic growth in the same way. The analysis begins with a look at recent developments in foreign trade and FDI in East Asia. This sets the stage for the subsequent study of the emergence and characteristics of the trade-FDI nexus from several aspects, including the export-FDI relationship, the behaviour of MNCs and the regional production system. Some concluding remarks follow.

Expansion of Foreign Trade and Foreign Direct Investment in East Asia

East Asia saw rapid expansion of foreign trade and FDI in the 1980s and particularly the 1990s, indicating the increasing importance of international economic activities in its economies. FDI inflows expanded especially fast relative

 ISBN 92-64-01442-X © OECD 2005

to trade during the 1990s. Figure 9.1 shows exports, FDI inflows and GDP for East Asia. From 1980 to 2002, GDP increased five-fold, exports approximately eight-fold and FDI inflows a remarkable 40-fold until 2000, after which they declined.

Figure 9.1. **FDI, Exports and GDP in East Asia (1980=100)**

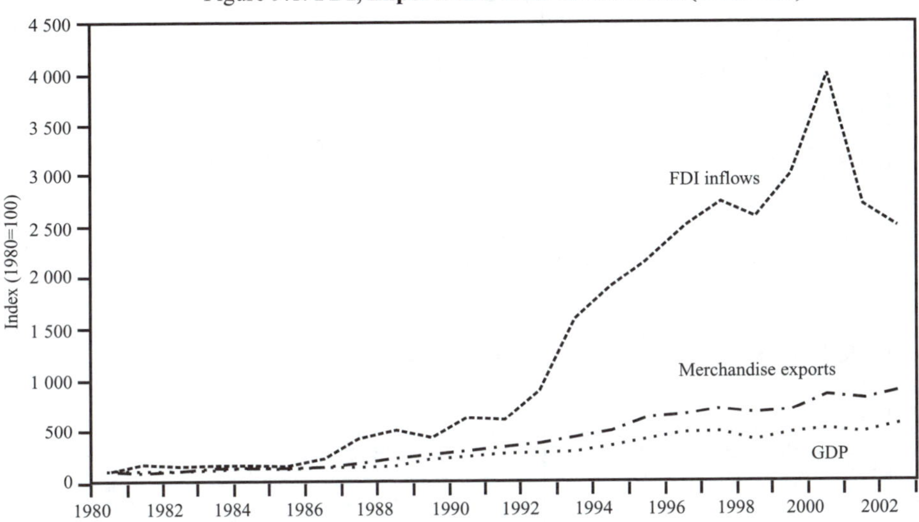

Source: GDP and Merchandise exports: World Bank (2004), *World Development Indicators*, CD-ROM; FDI Inflows: UNIDO, *Foreign Direct Investment Database* (on-line).

Foreign Trade

Rapid Expansion

East Asian foreign trade increased rapidly and continuously in the 1980s and 1990s with a decline in 1998 as a result of the financial crisis (Table 9.1). In the 22 years between 1980 and 2002 merchandise exports and imports increased 8.7-fold and 7.6-fold, or at annual average growth rates of 10.4 per cent and 9.7 per cent, respectively. The pattern of annual changes in trade reveals substantial fluctuations, with remarkable expansions in three different sub-periods, 1987-88, 1994-95, and 2000, when annual growth rates exceeded 20 per cent. As one would expect, these periods more or less corresponded to high growth of the world economy. Some other factors also contributed in 1987-88 and 2000. In the first period, substantial depreciation of the East Asian currencies *vis-à-vis* the Japanese yen increased the competitiveness of East Asian products against Japanese products. Behind the export gains in 2000 lay the strong recovery of the East Asian economies from the financial crisis and the emergence of an "information technology (IT) bubble" in the world economy, both of which increased demand for East Asian products.

ISBN 92-64-01442-X

Table 9.1. **East Asian Merchandise Trade, 1980-2002**

($ million)

Exports	1980	1981	1982	1983	1984	1985	1986	1987	1988	1989	1990	1991
World	1 985.0	1 955.2	1 816.3	1 773.5	1 884.9	1 894.5	2 072.0	2 445.9	2 802.9	3 039.2	3 452.5	3 531.3
East Asia	122.5	132.7	132.1	137.4	157.7	156.3	167.8	216.5	274.6	308.0	348.5	402.1
China	18.2	22.0	21.9	22.2	24.9	27.3	31.1	39.5	47.5	52.5	62.1	71.9
Hong Kong, China	20.3	21.8	21.3	22.5	28.3	30.1	36.1	48.7	63.5	73.3	82.4	98.7
Indonesia	21.9	22.3	22.3	21.2	21.9	18.6	16.1	17.1	19.5	22.2	25.7	29.1
Korea	17.5	21.3	21.9	24.4	29.2	30.3	34.7	47.3	60.7	62.4	65.0	71.9
Malaysia	13.0	11.8	12.0	14.1	16.6	15.4	13.8	17.9	21.1	25.1	29.5	34.3
Philippines	5.7	5.7	5.0	4.9	5.3	4.6	4.8	5.6	7.0	7.8	8.1	8.8
Singapore	19.4	21.0	20.8	21.8	24.1	22.8	22.5	28.7	39.3	44.7	52.7	59.0
Thailand	6.5	7.0	6.9	6.4	7.4	7.1	8.9	11.7	16.0	20.1	23.1	28.4
Exports (cont.)	1992	1993	1994	1995	1996	1997	1998	1999	2000	2001	2002	
World	3 780.7	3 790.2	4 324.8	5 160.5	5 391.0	5 577.0	5 495.7	5 707.3	6 444.5	6 191.1	6 454.9	–
East Asia	461.6	515.4	622.8	759.2	791.0	846.6	806.8	855.8	1 031.2	971.6	1 069.9	–
China	84.9	91.7	121.0	148.8	151.0	182.8	183.7	194.9	249.2	266.1	325.6	–
Hong Kong, China	119.6	135.4	151.5	173.9	180.9	188.2	174.9	174.4	202.7	191.1	201.2	–
Indonesia	34.0	36.8	40.1	45.4	49.8	53.4	48.8	48.7	62.1	56.4	57.1	–
Korea	76.6	82.2	96.0	125.1	129.7	136.2	132.3	143.7	172.3	150.4	162.5	–
Malaysia	40.8	47.1	58.8	73.9	78.3	78.7	73.3	84.5	98.2	88.0	93.3	–
Philippines	9.8	11.1	13.3	17.5	20.4	24.9	29.4	36.6	39.8	32.7	36.3	–
Singapore	63.5	74.0	96.8	118.3	125.0	125.0	109.9	114.7	137.8	121.8	125.2	–
Thailand	32.5	37.0	45.3	56.4	55.7	57.4	54.5	58.4	69.1	65.1	68.9	–

ISBN 92-64-01442-X © OECD 2005

Table 9.1. (contd.)

Imports	1980	1981	1982	1983	1984	1985	1986	1987	1988	1989	1990	1991
World	2 024.0	2 010.1	1 877.9	1 823.4	1 949.2	1 955.7	2 142.8	2 517.7	2 895.7	3 129.9	3 532.9	3 643.7
East Asia	128.5	145.1	142.3	147.9	160.7	168.4	172.3	213.2	280.1	323.8	365.9	428.2
China	20.0	22.0	18.9	21.3	26.2	42.5	43.2	43.2	55.3	59.1	53.3	63.8
Hong Kong, China	23.0	26.1	24.9	24.4	30.4	31.2	35.9	50.7	70.3	77.7	84.7	103.9
Indonesia	10.8	13.3	16.9	16.4	13.9	10.3	10.7	12.9	13.2	16.4	21.8	25.9
Korea	22.3	26.1	24.3	26.2	30.6	31.1	31.6	41.0	51.8	61.5	69.8	81.5
Malaysia	10.8	11.6	12.4	13.2	14.1	12.3	10.8	12.7	16.6	22.5	29.3	36.6
Philippines	8.3	8.5	8.3	8.0	6.4	5.5	5.4	7.1	8.7	11.2	13.0	12.9
Singapore	24.0	27.6	28.2	28.2	28.7	26.3	25.5	32.6	43.9	49.7	60.8	66.1
Thailand	9.2	10.0	8.5	10.3	10.4	9.2	9.2	13.0	20.3	25.8	33.0	37.6
Imports (cont.)	1992	1993	1994	1995	1996	1997	1998	1999	2000	2001	2002	
World	3 895.2	3 842.8	4 376.9	5 207.2	5 472.5	5 658.6	5 601.0	5 825.6	6 621.5	6 362.4	6 590.3	–
East Asia	485.2	553.1	655.2	805.2	849.6	854.9	682.1	749.1	945.4	901.0	982.0	–
China	80.6	104.0	115.6	132.1	138.8	142.4	140.2	165.7	225.1	243.6	295.2	–
Hong Kong, China	127.3	141.3	165.9	196.1	201.3	213.3	186.8	180.7	214.0	202.0	207.2	–
Indonesia	27.3	28.3	32.0	40.6	42.9	41.7	27.3	24.0	33.5	31.0	31.3	–
Korea	81.8	83.8	102.3	135.1	150.3	144.6	93.3	119.8	160.5	141.1	152.1	–
Malaysia	39.9	45.7	59.6	77.7	78.4	79.0	58.3	65.0	82.0	73.9	79.9	–
Philippines	15.5	18.8	22.6	28.3	34.1	38.6	31.5	32.6	33.8	31.4	35.2	–
Singapore	72.2	85.2	102.7	124.5	131.3	132.4	101.7	111.1	134.5	116.0	116.4	–
Thailand	40.7	46.1	54.5	70.8	72.3	62.9	43.0	50.3	61.9	62.1	64.7	–

Source: World Bank (2004), *World Development Indicators*, CD-ROM.

ISBN 92-64-01442-X

Since world exports and imports each increased only 3.3-fold during 1980-2002, or at an annual average rate of 5.5 per cent, the shares of East Asia in world exports and imports rose from 6.2 per cent and 6.4 per cent to 16.6 per cent and 14.9 per cent respectively. The region's exports grew faster than its imports, indicating that increased global linkages through foreign trade contributed to its gains in GDP and foreign exchange earnings. Indeed, foreign trade of all the East Asian countries in Table 9.1 except Indonesia recorded faster growth than that of world trade. China registered the best performance; its exports and imports increased by factors of 18 and 15 respectively over the period. Thailand; Hong Kong, China; Korea and others followed.

For many East Asian countries foreign trade grew faster than GDP, resulting in increased linkages to the global economy. The export/GDP and import/GDP ratios for East Asian countries increased from 27 per cent and 28 per cent respectively in 1980 to 43 per cent and 40 per cent in 2002 (Table 9.2). All the East Asian countries listed in Table 9.2 had export/GDP and import/GDP ratios higher than the world averages in 2002. The ratios increased most notably in the same three periods of fastest trade growth, 1987-88, 1994-95 and 2000.

Singapore and Hong Kong, China both showed extremely high trade-GDP ratios throughout the period, which is a structural phenomenon attributable to their active engagement in *entrepôt* trade. More remarkable are the increases in the ratios for other East Asian countries. Malaysia, the Philippines, Thailand and China more or less doubled their ratios from 1980 to 2002, although they show substantial differences in absolute levels. Indonesia and Korea, in contrast, experienced rather limited increases. China presents an exceptional case. Its ratios more than doubled to about 49 per cent in 2002, despite the empirical observation found in earlier studies that economies large in terms either of population or of economic activity itself tend to depend less on foreign trade[3].

Changing Structures of Foreign Trade

Table 9.3 shows the East Asian countries' export destinations and import sources. Note especially their increased importance to each other as both export destinations and import sources, which indicates expanded intra-regional trade[4]. For these countries as a group the share of total exports destined elsewhere in the region increased from 22.1 per cent in 1980 to 40.1 per

ISBN 92-64-01442-X © OECD 2005

cent in 2002. The intra-regional export share also rose for most of them individually as well — with the notable exception of China, for which East Asia lost its importance from 1990 to 2002 after a substantial increase from 1980 to 1990. For China the North American Free Trade Agreement (NAFTA) countries became increasingly important export markets from 1990 to 2002. Japan's importance as a regional export destination declined substantially over the whole period, whereas the positions of NAFTA and the EU remained more or less unchanged. On the import side, the patterns are similar in that intra-regional sourcing also rose. For East Asia as a whole, the share of imports from the region itself increased from 22.2 per cent in 1980 to 45.9 per cent in 2002. Nevertheless, comparison of the export and import patterns shows that intra-regional trade has more importance as an import source rather than as an export destination. This reflects patterns of trade and production, in which East Asian countries procure parts and components from other East Asian economies to make final products for export to non-East Asian economies such as the United States and the EU.

The commodity composition of East Asian foreign trade changed dramatically (Table 9.4). One particularly notable development was the rapid increase in the share of manufactures in total exports for the ASEAN4 countries (Indonesia, Malaysia, the Philippines and Thailand). The ASEAN4 countries can be grouped as two pairs in this respect. Malaysia and Thailand increased their shares of manufactured exports very fast, from 19 per cent and 25 per cent respectively in 1980 to 80 per cent and 74 per cent in 1999. As a result they joined China and the NIEs (Hong Kong, China; Korea; Singapore and Chinese Taipei) as countries with very high shares. Indonesia and the Philippines also registered huge share increases, but their levels remain below those of other East Asian countries. Among manufactures, office machines and telecommunications equipment, or electronic products, show interesting developments. The NIEs already had relatively high shares of electronics in total exports in the 1980s, and they increased in subsequent years. Malaysia and Thailand boosted these shares in the 1980s, while the Philippines and China did so in the 1990s. These sequential developments represent the essence of the multi-layered development process resulting from the formation of the trade-FDI nexus.

Table 9.2. **Trade in the East Asian Economies: Ratios of Exports and Imports to GDP, 1980-2002**

(percentages)

Exports/GDP	1980	1981	1982	1983	1984	1985	1986	1987	1988	1989	1990	1991
World	18.2	17.5	16.5	15.7	16.1	15.4	14.2	14.7	15.1	15.7	15.9	15.5
East Asia	26.7	26.8	25.4	25.2	26.6	24.4	26.1	32.5	34.5	33.6	34.6	35.8
China	9.7	11.4	10.8	9.7	9.7	9.0	10.5	14.7	15.5	15.3	17.5	19.1
Hong Kong, China	71.1	71.1	67.1	76.4	86.0	85.9	89.7	98.3	108.4	108.5	109.2	113.2
Indonesia	28.1	24.1	23.5	24.8	25.0	21.3	20.1	22.6	21.9	21.8	22.4	22.7
Korea	28.1	30.6	29.4	29.7	32.3	32.4	32.3	35.0	33.6	28.3	25.7	24.3
Malaysia	52.0	46.2	44.1	46.1	48.0	48.6	48.7	55.7	59.8	64.5	66.9	69.9
Philippines	17.7	15.9	13.3	14.7	16.8	15.0	16.0	17.0	18.6	18.2	18.3	19.4
Singapore	165.4	151.0	136.2	125.6	128.2	128.9	125.3	139.6	155.2	148.3	142.9	136.5
Thailand	20.1	20.2	19.0	15.9	17.7	18.3	20.6	23.1	25.9	27.8	27.0	28.9
Exports/GDP (cont.)	1992	1993	1994	1995	1996	1997	1998	1999	2000	2001	2002	
World	15.6	15.4	16.3	17.6	18.0	18.7	18.5	18.6	20.5	19.8	20.0	
East Asia	37.0	38.0	38.7	39.0	36.3	38.6	43.5	41.6	46.1	42.8	43.4	
China	20.3	21.2	22.3	21.2	18.5	20.3	19.4	19.7	23.1	22.6	25.7	
Hong Kong, China	117.0	114.7	113.7	122.7	115.6	108.4	105.8	108.6	122.6	117.3	124.5	
Indonesia	24.4	23.3	22.6	22.5	21.9	24.8	51.2	34.8	41.4	40.0	33.0	
Korea	24.3	23.8	23.9	25.6	24.9	28.6	41.7	35.4	37.3	35.2	34.1	
Malaysia	68.9	70.5	79.0	83.2	77.7	78.6	101.6	106.7	108.9	100.0	98.3	
Philippines	18.4	20.5	20.8	23.6	24.6	30.2	45.1	48.0	52.4	45.3	46.5	
Singapore	127.3	126.8	137.1	140.9	135.6	131.0	134.2	140.9	150.6	143.5	143.9	
Thailand	29.1	29.6	31.3	33.6	30.7	38.0	48.7	47.8	56.3	56.4	54.3	
Imports/GDP	1980	1981	1982	1983	1984	1985	1986	1987	1988	1989	1990	1991
World	18.6	18.0	17.0	16.1	16.6	15.9	14.7	15.2	15.6	16.1	16.3	16.0
East Asia	28.0	29.3	27.4	27.1	27.1	26.3	26.8	32.1	35.2	35.4	36.3	38.1
China	10.7	11.4	9.4	9.4	10.2	13.9	14.6	16.1	18.0	17.3	15.0	16.9
Hong Kong, China	80.5	85.3	78.2	83.1	92.4	89.1	89.3	102.3	120.1	114.9	112.3	119.2
Indonesia	13.9	14.4	17.8	19.2	15.8	11.7	13.4	17.0	14.9	16.2	19.1	20.2
Korea	35.8	37.6	32.6	31.8	33.8	33.3	29.3	30.3	28.7	27.8	27.6	27.6
Malaysia	43.4	45.5	45.4	43.0	40.7	38.7	38.3	39.5	46.,9	57.9	66.5	74.6
Philippines	25.5	23.8	22.1	24.0	20.5	17.8	18.1	21.6	23.0	26.2	29.4	28.3
Singapore	204.9	198.5	184.5	162.0	152.7	148.6	142.1	158.5	173.2	164.9	164.7	153.0
Thailand	28.5	28.6	23.4	25.7	24.9	23.8	21.3	25.8	32.9	35.7	38.7	38.2

ISBN 92-64-01442-X © OECD 2005

Table 9.2. (contd.)

Imports/GDP (cont.)	1992	1993	1994	1995	1996	1997	1998	1999	2000	2001	2002	
World	16.0	15.6	16.5	17.8	18.3	19.0	18.9	19.0	21.0	20.4	20.4	
East Asia	38.9	40.7	40.7	41.3	39.0	39.0	36.8	36.4	42.2	39.7	39.9	
China	19.3	24.1	21.3	18.9	17.0	15.8	14.8	16.7	20.8	20.7	23.3	
Hong Kong, China	124.6	119.8	124.5	138.4	128.6	122.8	113.0	112.5	129.4	124.1	128.3	
Indonesia	19.6	17.9	18.1	20.1	18.9	19.3	28.6	17.1	22.3	22.0	18.1	
Korea	26.0	24.2	25.4	27.6	28.9	30.4	29.4	29.5	34.8	33.0	31.9	
Malaysia	67.4	68.2	80.0	87.5	77.8	78.9	80.8	82.1	90.9	84.0	84.2	
Philippines	29.2	34.5	35.3	38.2	41.2	46.9	48.3	42.8	44.5	43.5	45.2	
Singapore	144.7	146.1	145.4	148.3	142.4	138.8	124.2	136.5	147.1	136.7	133.9	
Thailand	36.5	36.9	37.7	42.2	39.8	41.7	38.4	41.1	50.5	53.7	51.0	
(Exports + Imports)/GDP	1980	1981	1982	1983	1984	1985	1986	1987	1988	1989	1990	1991
World	36.8	35.5	33.5	31.8	32.7	31.3	29.0	29.9	30.7	31.8	32.2	31.5
East Asia	54.7	56.1	52.8	52.3	53.6	50.7	52.9	64.6	69.7	69.0	70.9	73.9
China	20.3	22.8	20.2	19.1	19.9	22.9	25.1	30.8	33.5	32.6	32.5	36.0
Hong Kong, China	151.6	156.4	145.3	159.5	178.5	174.9	179.0	200.6	228.5	223.5	221.5	232.4
Indonesia	42.0	38.4	41.3	43.9	40.8	33.0	33.5	39.5	36.8	38.1	41.5	42.9
Korea	64.0	68.1	61.9	61.5	66.1	65.7	61.6	65.3	62.3	56.1	53.4	52.0
Malaysia	95.4	91.7	89.5	89.1	88.7	87.3	87.0	95.2	106.8	122.4	133.4	144.5
Philippines	43.2	39.7	35.5	38.7	37.3	32.7	34.1	38.6	41.6	44.4	47.7	47.7
Singapore	370.2	349.5	320.7	287.6	280.9	277.5	267.3	298.1	328.3	313.2	307.6	289.6
Thailand	48.6	48.7	42.3	41.6	42.6	42.1	41.9	48.8	58.8	63.5	65.7	67.2
(Exports + Imports)/GDP (cont.)	1992	1003	1994	1995	1996	1997	1998	1999	2000	2001	2002	
World	31.6	30.9	32.8	35.4	36.3	37.7	37.4	37.6	41.5	40.2	40.4	
East Asia	75.9	78.7	79.4	80.3	75.3	77.6	80.3	78.0	88.3	82.6	83.3	
China	39.6	45.3	43.6	40.1	35.5	36.2	34.2	36.4	43.9	43.3	49.0	
Hong Kong, China	241.6	234.5	238.2	261.1	244.1	231.2	218.8	221.1	252.0	241.4	252.8	
Indonesia	44.0	41.2	40.7	42.6	40.8	44.1	79.8	51.9	63.7	61.9	51.1	
Korea	50.3	48.0	49.3	53.2	53.8	58.9	71.1	64.9	72.1	68.2	66.0	
Malaysia	136.3	138.7	159.0	170.7	155.4	157.5	182.4	188.8	199.9	184.0	182.4	
Philippines	47.6	55.0	56.1	61.8	65.8	77.1	93.5	90.8	96.9	88.9	91.7	
Singapore	272.0	272.9	282.5	289.3	278.0	269.9	258.4	277.4	297.7	280.1	277.8	
Thailand	65.6	66.4	69.0	75.8	70.5	79.7	87.1	88.9	106.7	110.1	105.3	

Source: World Bank (2004), *World Development Indicators*, CD-ROM.

Table 9.3. **East Asian Export Destinations and Import Sources, 1980-2003**

(per cent of total exports and imports)

	East Asia			Japan			NAFTA			EU		
	1980	1990	2003	1980	1990	2003	1980	1990	2003	1980	1990	2003
	Export Destinations											
China	30.6	50.0	30.3	22.2	14.6	13.6	6.3	9.3	23.2	13.7	10.0	16.5
Hong Kong, China	19.6	36.0	50.8	4.6	5.7	5.4	28.3	26.3	20.4	24.7	18.5	13.3
Korea	12.2	16.0	38.5	17.4	19.4	8.8	28.8	33.4	21.0	16.8	15.4	12.2
Singapore	32.2	36.3	48.6	8.1	8.8	6.7	13.4	22.3	15.1	13.2	15.0	13.4
Chinese Taipei	17.1	24.6	47.7	11.0	12.4	8.3	36.8	35.2	19.6	14.9	17.2	12.9
Indonesia	16.7	24.3	35.5	49.3	42.5	20.8	19.8	13.8	14.2	6.6	12.0	13.8
Malaysia	30.5	42.3	44.3	22.8	15.3	9.9	16.9	17.9	21.6	17.9	15.4	12.2
Philippines	15.4	17.6	44.2	26.6	19.8	14.3	28.9	39.5	22.7	18.0	18.5	14.3
Thailand	25.1	20.5	34.1	15.1	17.2	14.2	13.0	24.4	18.7	26.5	22.7	14.7
East Asia	22.1	31.7	40.1	19.8	14.5	10.6	21.7	24.6	20.5	15.8	15.7	14.1
	Import Sources											
China	10.3	47.2	46.1	27.0	12.5	14.9	24.2	12.6	7.9	14.4	15.0	10.9
Hong Kong, China	41.2	56.3	69.6	21.6	16.1	13.2	12.9	9.2	7.0	142	10.9	9.7
Korea	8.1	13.6	28.4	27.4	29.6	20.5	25.7	26.6	15.4	7.3	14.0	10.9
Singapore	29.2	34.6	45.7	14.9	19.3	11.6	12.2	15.1	13.6	10.4	13.6	12.2
Chinese Taipei	9.7	12.4	30.1	30.9	29.2	25.6	23.9	24.8	14.3	10.6	14.7	10.3
Indonesia	16.6	30.0	49.2	31.1	28.5	18.1	15.1	12.2	7.4	16.9	21.6	12.5
Malaysia	37.3	41.7	53.1	19.0	21.8	13.7	13.0	14.4	12.9	15.2	13.8	10.8
Philippines	19.1	28.5	40.2	20.1	19.0	20.6	24.9	20.0	18.1	11.0	12.5	8.0
Thailand	22.9	30.5	35.5	22.0	30.3	23.5	15.8	11.4	9.2	13.3	16.0	10.2
East Asia	22.2	34.1	45.9	23.3	22.2	16.7	18.3	16.4	10.6	12.2	13.9	10.7

Source: JETRO trade database.

ISBN 92-64-01442-X © OECD 2005

These observations suggest that many East Asian countries are large exporters of high-tech products such as office machines and telecommunications equipment. Note, however, that many of them engage in labour-intensive production such as assembly of high-tech products, rather than in technology-intensive production processes such as development of new products. One thus may argue that East Asian countries have a comparative advantage in the labour-intensive but not in the technology-intensive processes involved in making high-tech products. The discussion returns to this point later. Note also that light manufactures such as textiles, clothing and other consumer goods continue to account for a relatively large share of exports from many countries, including China and Hong Kong, China. This reflects continued comparative advantage in the production of these products.

Compared with these changes in export patterns, those of imports were less pronounced. The shares of manufactures in total imports for many East Asian countries remained at between about 60 per cent and 80 per cent throughout the period. A marked change in the compositional shares of imports among different manufactures did occur, however. Office machines and telecommunications equipment increased their shares for many economies, similarly to the pattern observed for exports. Increasingly high shares of office machines and telecommunication equipment in both exports and imports suggest the expansion of intra-industry trade in these products. Fukao *et al.* (2003) found that intra-industry trade grew rapidly in East Asia and that the pattern of intra-industry trade is largely vertical. Products of different quality are traded, unlike in the EU where much intra-industry trade is horizontal, i.e. trade in differentiated products of similar types[5].

ISBN 92-64-01442-X © OECD 2005

Table 9.4. **The Commodity Composition of East Asian Trade, 1980, 1990, 1999**

Part A: Exports

(per cent of total exports)

	China			Hong Kong, China			Korea			Singapore			Chinese Taipei		
	1980	1990	1999	1980	1990	1999	1980	1990	1999	1980	1990	1999	1980	1990	1999
Agricultural products	n.a.	16.2	7.3	1.9	2.8	1.9	8.8	4.6	2.9	18.4	7.8	3.4	10.1	5.5	2.4
Food	n.a.	12.7	6.0	1.4	2.6	1.7	7.4	3.3	2.0	8.1	5.2	2.8	8.6	4.0	1.4
Raw materials	n.a.	3.5	1.3	0.5	0.3	0.2	1.4	1.3	1.0	10.3	2.6	0.6	1.5	1.5	1.1
Mining products	n.a.	10.6	4.4	1.6	1.4	2.2	1.3	1.9	5.4	31.3	19.7	9.2	2.0	1.8	2.1
Ores and other minerals	n.a.	1.2	0.6	1.1	0.7	0.6	0.5	0.3	0.1	0.8	0.4	0.2	0.2	0.2	0.1
Fuels	n.a.	8.4	2.4	0.1	0.4	0.4	0.3	1.1	4.1	28.9	18.2	8.0	1.5	0.6	0.9
Non-ferrous metals	n.a.	1.0	1.4	0.4	0.3	1.2	0.5	0.6	1.3	1.6	1.1	1.0	0.3	1.0	1.1
Manufactures	n.a.	71.4	88.3	95.7	94.5	93.3	89.5	93.2	89.6	43.1	71.2	85.9	87.9	92.6	95.3
Iron and steel	n.a.	2.1	1.6	0.1	0.1	0.1	9.5	5.7	4.2	1.1	0.8	0.5	1.7	1.5	3.1
Chemicals	n.a.	6.0	5.3	0.8	2.9	3.2	4.3	3.8	7.4	3.4	6.2	7.8	2.5	4.0	5.6
Other semi-manufactures	n.a.	6.0	7.6	4.3	3.9	2.3	13.1	6.7	6.2	3.7	3.3	2.2	12.0	11.4	8.6
Machinery and transport equipt.	n.a.	17.5	30.1	18.2	24.9	22.9	20.3	39.3	54.2	26.8	50.1	66.3	24.7	39.1	55.8
Power generating machinery	n.a.	0.3	1.0	0.1	0.4	0.4	0.4	0.9	0.6	0.5	0.9	0.8	0.7	0.6	0.5
Other non-electrical machinery	n.a.	3.7	2.7	0.7	2.1	1.7	1.2	2.8	4..6	4.5	5.2	4.6	3.5	6.4	6.4
Office machines/telecom. equipt.	n.a.	5.0	15.5	12.6	16.5	16.1	9.7	22.1	29.9	14.0	36.5	52.8	13.6	21.0	36.4
Electrical machinery and appl.	n.a.	1.8	7.6	4.4	5.8	4.5	2.3	3.5	4.0	2.8	4.3	6.1	3.7	6.2	8.1
Automotive products	n.a.	5.6	0.5	0.0	0.0	0.0	0.7	3.3	8.9	1.1	0.6	0.5	0.5	1.1	1.3
Other transport equipment	n.a.	1.1	3.0	0.3	0.2	0.2	6.0	6.7	6.2	3.8	2.6	1.4	2.7	3.7	3.0
Textiles	n.a.	11.6	6.8	6.7	7.5	5.5	12.7	9.4	8.1	1.9	1.7	0.7	9.0	9.3	9.2
Clothing	n.a.	15.6	15.5	34.1	32.0	42.8	16.9	12.3	3.4	2.2	3.0	1.4	12.3	6.0	2.4
Other consumer goods	n.a.	12.7	21.5	31.6	23.3	16.7	12.8	16.0	6.1	4.0	6.0	7.1	25.7	21.4	10.7
Others	n.a.	1.9	0.1	0.8	1.3	2.6	0.4	0.3	2.1	7.2	1.3	1.5	0.1	0.1	0.2
Total	n.a.	100.0	100.0	100.0	100.0	100.0	100.0	100.0	100.0	100.0	100.0	100.0	100.0	100.0	100.0

ISBN 92-64-01442-X © OECD 2005

Table 9.4. Part A (contd.)

	Indonesia			Malaysia			Philippines			Thailand		
	1980	1990	1999	1980	1990	1999	1980	1990	1999	1980	1990	1999
Agricultural products	21.8	16.2	15.5	46.0	25.3	10.9	41.9	20.8	5.1	58.3	33.8	20.0
Food	7.6	11.1	11.7	15.0	11.7	8.0	35.9	18.9	4.5	47.0	28.7	17.0
Raw materials	14.1	5.1	3.8	30.9	13.7	2.9	6.1	1.9	0.5	11.2	5.1	3.0
Mining products	75.8	48.1	27.7	34.9	20.4	8.0	21.2	10.4	2.1	13.7	1.9	2.8
Ores and other minerals	2.0	2.6	3.2	1.2	0.5	0.2	18.1	4.6	0.6	3.1	0.5	0.6
Fuels	71.9	43.8	23.0	24.7	18.3	6.8	0.7	2.2	0.6	0.1	0.8	1.8
Non-ferrous metals	1.9	1.8	1.5	9.0	1.5	1.0	2.5	3.6	0.9	10.5	0.5	0.5
Manufactures	2.3	35.2	53.9	18.8	53.9	80.3	21.1	37.9	41.2	25.2	63.1	73.9
Iron and steel	0.1	0.9	1.0	0.1	0.8	0.6	0.8	1.0	0.1	0.8	0.6	1.0
Chemicals	0.4	2.4	4.8	0.6	1.6	3.2	1.5	3.2	0.8	0.7	2.0	5.0
Other semi-manufactures	0.6	14.5	14.2	2.6	4.5	4.6	4.6	3.8	1.4	5.7	8.6	7.2
Machinery and transport equipt.	0.5	1.4	10.8	11.5	35.7	62.3	2.1	12.2	31.7	5.9	21.9	41.9
Power generating machinery	0.0	0.0	0.5	0.0	0.2	0.7	0.0	0.0	0.1	0.0	0.4	1.4
Other non-electrical machinery	0.0	0.2	0.8	0.7	1.8	2.1	0.2	0.3	0.4	0.4	2.1	3.5
Office machines/telecom. equipt.	0.4	0.5	6.1	8.9	27.9	52.4	1.1	8.2	25.6	0.2	15.3	26.1
Electrical machinery and appl.	0.0	0.3	2.2	1.0	3.1	5.3	0.2	3.0	3.9	5.1	3.1	7.1
Automotive products	0.0	0.1	0.5	0.0	0.3	0.3	0.5	0.3	1.2	0.2	0.3	2.8
Other transport equipment	0.0	0.4	0.8	0.8	2.4	1.5	0.0	0.5	0.4	0.1	0.8	1.1
Textiles	0.2	4.9	6.2	1.4	1.3	1.3	1.3	1.2	0.7	5.2	4.0	3.1
Clothing	0.4	6.5	8.0	1.2	4.5	2.7	4.9	8.4	3.4	4.2	12.3	6.0
Other consumer goods	0.1	4.6	8.8	1.5	5.5	5.5	5.8	8.1	3.2	2.8	13.8	9.6
Others	0.1	0.5	3.0	0.3	0.4	0.9	15.7	30.9	51.7	2.9	1.2	3.3
Total	100.0	100.0	100.0	100.0	100.0	100.0	100.0	100.0	100.0	100.0	100.0	100.0

Table 9.4. **The Commodity Composition of East Asian Trade, 1980, 1990, 1999**

Part B: Imports

(per cent of total imports)

	China			Hong Kong, China			Korea			Singapore			Chinese Taipei		
	1980	1990	1999	1980	1990	1999	1980	1990	1999	1980	1990	1999	1980	1990	1999
Agricultural products	31.8	14.5	8.2	11.0	9.8	6.2	25.8	13.5	9.2	17.3	7.7	4.5	19.5	11.3	7.0
Food	18.4	8.7	4.0	7.4	7.7	4.9	12.8	5.6	5.6	9.1	6.1	4.0	10.1	6.4	4.5
Raw materials	13.4	5.8	4.2	3.7	2.1	1.3	13.1	7.9	3.6	8.2	1.7	0.5	9.5	4.9	2.5
Mining products	2.7	5.3	10.7	8.4	3.9	3.7	10.1	22.5	25.5	16.0	17.9	10.6	9.9	16.8	12.2
Ores and other minerals	1.0	1.8	2.5	0.2	0.3	0.2	4.6	3.9	3.0	0.5	0.3	0.3	3.3	2.1	1.3
Fuels	0.2	2.4	5.4	6.4	2.4	2.1	3.6	15.9	19.2	13.6	15.9	9.1	3.1	11.0	7.5
Non-ferrous metals	1.5	1.1	2.9	1.8	1.3	1.4	1.9	2.7	3.2	1.9	1.7	1.3	3.5	3.7	3.4
Manufactures	64.7	79.7	80.2	78.9	83.3	89.1	60.3	63.2	62.1	64.7	73.0	83.2	68.5	67.2	78.5
Iron and steel	13.4	5.4	4.6	3.3	1.8	1.7	6.6	4.7	3.4	4.3	2.9	1.5	8.2	5.3	3.9
Chemicals	11.3	12.5	14.3	7.4	7.2	6.3	11.3	10.5	9.1	5.7	7.5	5.8	11.2	12.5	11.1
Other semi-manufactures	5.9	5.1	6.8	12.4	8.9	8.0	4.5	5.1	3.7	6.4	5.4	4.2	4.3	4.7	4.1
Machinery and transport equipt.	27.1	40.3	41.9	29.2	27.2	38.5	31.2	34.3	36.4	38.2	44.7	60.1	37.7	37.0	48.9
Power generating machinery	1.2	2.8	2.1	1.3	0.8	1.4	2.6	1.7	1.3	0.9	1.9	1.6	3.7	1.5	0.9
Other non-electrical machinery	14.1	15.9	10.8	5.0	3.9	3.5	10.4	13.8	7.0	10.2	8.2	7.6	12.5	9.6	12.1
Office machines/telecom. equipt.	2.8	7.6	18.4	11.7	14.6	24.1	8.1	11.1	20.7	10.9	22.0	38.1	8.4	13.6	26.3
Electrical machinery and appl.	2.2	2.4	6.3	5.2	5.3	7.5	3.6	3.1	4.7	4.9	5.8	7.5	5.1	4.8	5.6
Automotive products	1.4	7.9	1.3	2.7	1.1	0.9	1.5	1.2	0.9	2.9	2.1	1.3	3.0	4.4	1.9
Other transport equipment	4.1	3.7	3.0	3.3	1.5	1.1	4.8	3.4	1.8	8.4	4.6	4.1	4.9	3.1	2.2
Textiles	3.7	10.2	6.8	11.7	12.1	7.0	2.6	3.0	2.6	3.6	2.9	1.0	2.2	1.9	1.4
Clothing	0.1	0.1	0.7	1.2	8.2	8.2	0.1	0.2	0.7	0.6	1.5	1.5	0.0	0.5	0.8
Other consumer goods	3.1	6.1	5.2	13.6	18.0	19.5	4.0	5.5	6.3	5.9	8.1	9.0	4.8	5.4	8.4
Others	0.8	0.5	0.9	1.7	3.1	1.0	3.8	0.8	3.3	2.0	1.3	1.7	2.0	4.7	2.3
Total	100.0	100.0	100.0	100.0	100.0	100.0	100.0	100.0	100.0	100.0	100.0	100.0	100.0	100.0	100.0

ISBN 92-64-01442-X © OECD 2005

Table 9.4. Part B (contd.)

	Indonesia			Malaysia			Philippines			Thailand		
	1980	1990	1999	1980	1990	1999	1980	1990	1999	1980	1990	1999
Agricultural products	15.8	9.7	n.a.	12.8	8.2	6.9	11.4	12.8	9.8	9.2	9.7	7.9
Food	12.5	5.1	n.a.	10.9	6.9	5.4	8.7	10.3	8.2	5.8	5.0	5.0
Raw materials	3.3	4.7	n.a.	1.9	1.3	1.4	2.6	2.4	1.6	3.5	4.7	2.9
Mining products	4.1	14.0	n.a.	11.8	8.6	6.4	9.1	18.3	10.6	14.3	12.9	12.6
Ores and other minerals	0.6	3.1	n.a.	1.8	1.5	0.8	0.8	2.0	1.5	0.6	1.5	0.7
Fuels	1.9	9.0	n.a.	8.3	5.1	3.1	7.0	14.9	7.9	11.3	9.3	9.7
Non-ferrous metals	1.6	1,9	n.a.	1.6	2.0	2.5	1.4	1.4	1.2	2.4	2.1	2.2
Manufactures	77.6	76.1	n.a.	72.1	78.2	83.6	78.1	53.1	59.5	72.1	74.4	77.2
Iron and steel	9.1	6.1	n.a.	6.0	5.0	3.4	5.9	4.8	3.2	8.8	8.1	5.4
Chemicals	12.1	15.3	n.a.	7.9	8.3	7.3	10.7	11.3	8.0	13.6	10.2	10.8
Other semi-manufactures	6.2	5.2	n.a.	6.3	5.6	4.3	6.8	4.3	3.6	5.7	8.2	9.2
Machinery and transport equipt.	44.8	42.6	n.a.	45.1	50.2	61.7	45.7	25.9	38.1	37.6	41.0	43.1
Power generating machinery	2.1	1.5	n.a.	1.0	0.7	1.3	2.4	1.6	1.0	1.4	2.6	1.3
Other non-electrical machinery	13.2	21.7	n.a.	12.5	12.7	7.9	14.1	8.1	6.3	11.4	13.1	7.3
Office machines/telecom. equipt.	3.6	4.1	n.a.	14.3	19.6	38.9	11.5	6.1	22.4	8.1	10.3	19.4
Electrical machinery and appl.	4.0	3.1	n.a.	4.3	6.3	8.4	3.0	2.8	4.7	3.2	4.1	7.6
Automotive products	8.6	5.6	n.a.	8.6	4.1	1.9	5.1	3.8	2.2	5.9	6.5	2.5
Other transport equipment	13.1	6.8	n.a.	4.5	6.7	3.4	9.7	3.5	1.6	6.8	4.5	5.1
Textiles	2.4	3.6	n.a.	2.8	3.3	1.6	4.4	4.3	2.7	2.7	2.7	2.7
Clothing	0.1	0.1	n.a.	0.3	0.3	0.2	0.1	0.1	0.2	0.1	0.1	0.2
Other consumer goods	2.9	3.2	n.a.	3.8	5.5	5.2	4.4	2.4	3.6	3.6	4.1	5.8
Others	2.5	0.2	n.a.	3.3	5.0	3.2	1.4	15.8	20.1	4.3	3.1	2.3
Total	100.0	100.0	n.a.	100.0	100.0	100.0	100.0	100.0	100.0	100.0	100.0	100.0

Note: n.a. = not available.
Source: Computed from World Bank database on foreign trade.

Foreign Direct Investment

Expansion of FDI Inflows

FDI inflows to East Asia started to increase in the latter half of the 1980s (Table 9.5). After a short period of stagnation in the late 1980s and early 1990s largely because of the world recession, they started to rise again in the mid-1990s as the world economy recovered from the recession. The rate of increase accelerated before reaching a peak in 1997. FDI inflows declined in 1998 because of the financial crisis, but they recovered quickly to reach a record high in 2000. They then dropped sharply again in 2001, largely because of the decline in the world economy, which in turn was attributable to the bursting of the IT bubble and the terrorist attacks.

A sequential pattern marked the expansion of FDI inflows to the NIEs, ASEAN4 and China from the mid-1980s to the early 2000s. Figure 9.2 reveals the longer-term trend by suppressing yearly fluctuations with three-year moving averages. It clearly shows a sequential pattern, in which FDI inflows to NIEs expanded rapidly in the latter half of the 1980s, before those to ASEAN4 or China. Toward the end of 1980s FDI inflows to ASEAN4 began to increase notably. Finally, China saw a sharp increase in the early 1990s and surpassed ASEAN4 and the NIEs. Divergent trends started to show toward the end of the 1990s, as FDI inflows to the NIEs and China continued to increase while FDI inflows to ASEAN4 started to decline.

China has attracted FDI successfully since the early 1990s (Table 9.5). Indeed, it has been the largest recipient of FDI among developing countries since the early 1990s, and it surpassed the United States to become the world's largest recipient in 2002. Even so, FDI inflows to China are likely to be overstated, because some actually originate in China to take advantage of preferential treatment for foreign investors, such as tax exemption. Some of the factors that make China an attractive host to FDI include its large market and the availability of low-wage workers. On the policy side, trade and FDI liberalisation, and especially China's accession to the WTO, contributed substantially to the recent increase in FDI inflows.

Among the ASEAN4 countries, Thailand, Malaysia and Indonesia recorded notable increases in FDI inflows before the crisis in the late 1990s. The crisis changed the situation dramatically, and FDI inflows to Malaysia and Indonesia dropped significantly. Those to Indonesia turned negative in 1998, i.e. to disinvestment, which continued through 2002. Political instability

 ISBN 92-64-01442-X © OECD 2005

resulting from change in the political regime is an important factor behind the decline[6]. In contrast, FDI inflows to Thailand increased after the crisis and remained relatively high through 2001. The Thai government promoted them by liberalising FDI policies in order to deal with the crisis. FDI inflows to the Philippines remained constant in the 1990s after increasing in the 1980s.

Among the Asian NIEs, Hong Kong, China exhibited substantial growth in FDI inflows in 1999 and 2000. Although they declined sharply in 2001, they remained substantially higher than the levels achieved by other NIEs. FDI inflows to Hong Kong, China are overvalued because a substantial portion of them has been reinvested in China. The jump in 2000 arose from a single large investment in telecommunications, worth $23 billion[7]. Singapore kept pace with Hong Kong, China until the outbreak of the crisis, and although FDI inflows dropped in the aftermath of the crisis, it quickly and successfully regained attractiveness. Korea, which received limited amounts of FDI throughout the post-WWII period, recorded a substantial increase after the crisis in 1998. This resulted largely from a drastic liberalisation of FDI policies that the Korean government adopted to deal with the negative impacts of the crisis. Similarly, FDI inflows to Chinese Taipei also increased after the crisis, although by substantially less than for Korea.

Expanded FDI inflows to East Asia resulted in the increased importance of MNCs in these economies. Several indicators confirm this. Table 9.6 shows two types of information, the importance of MNCs in employment, sales and value added, and the ratio of FDI inflows to domestic capital formation in selected East Asian countries. The first set of data reveals that the MNCs' importance varies widely among the countries. MNCs have a sizeable presence in Singapore; Malaysia and Hong Kong, China with shares in manufacturing employment and/or sales as high as 40 per cent to 80 per cent. Although significant, the MNCs' presence is smaller in Chinese Taipei and China. For many countries, increased FDI inflows resulted in the mid-1990s in increased weight of the MNCs in domestic capital formation[8]. The economies with high FDI/domestic capital formation ratios of 30 per cent to 50 per cent include Singapore and Hong Kong, China. Those with ratios of 10 per cent to 20 per cent are China, Malaysia and Thailand, while Chinese Taipei, Indonesia and Korea show very low figures of less than 10 per cent.

ISBN 92-64-01442-X © OECD 2005

Table 9.5. **East Asia: FDI Inflows and Outflows, 1980-2002**
Part A: Inflows
($ million)

	1980	1981	1982	1983	1984	1985	1986	1987
World	54 956.7	69 456.4	59 301.8	51 453.1	60 213.9	57 631.8	86 458.3	139 848.9
Developed countries	46 529.7	45 848.1	32 030.5	33 636.1	41 792.0	42 693.0	70 044.4	116 582.5
Developing countries	8 392.3	23 575.7	27 256.9	17 783.1	18 402.0	14 908.8	16 420.0	23 245.4
China	57.0	265.0	430.0	636.0	1 258.0	1 659.0	1 875.0	2 314.0
Hong Kong, China	710.2	2 062.8	1 236.9	1 144.1	1 287.7	-267.2	1 888.3	6 249.8
Korea	6.0	102.0	69.0	68.5	110.2	233.5	459.6	616.3
Singapore	1 235.8	1 660.0	1 601.9	1 133.9	1 301.9	1 046.8	1 710.3	2 836.2
Chinese Taipei	166.0	151.0	104.0	149.0	199.0	342.0	326.0	715.0
Indonesia	180.0	133.0	225.0	292.0	222.0	310.0	258.0	385.0
Malaysia	933.9	1 264.7	1 397.2	1 260.5	797.5	694.7	488.9	422.7
Philippines	-106.0	172.0	16.0	105.0	9.0	12.0	127.0	307.0
Thailand	189.4	294.0	188.3	357.6	408.0	163.6	262.7	351.6
East Asia total	3 372.3	6 104.4	5 268.2	5 146.7	5 593.2	4 194.3	7 395.7	14 197.6

	1988	1989	1990	1991	1992	1993	1994	1995
World	163 775.9	192 526.7	208 674.4	158 821.3	166 967.0	225 495.3	255 900.5	333 811.5
Developed countries	133 297.7	162 702.2	171 075.6	112 897.1	106 985.3	136 921.1	145 303.1	204 116.1
Developing countries	30 426.8	29 357.3	36 958.5	43 287.3	55 301.1	81 487.7	104 293.7	114 884.6
China	3 194.0	3 393.0	3 487.0	4 366.0	11 156.0	27 515.0	33 787.0	35 849.2
Hong Kong, China	4 979.0	2 041.1	3 275.1	1 020.9	3 887.5	6 929.6	7 827.9	6 213.4
Korea	1 014.1	1 117.8	788.5	1 179.8	728.3	588.1	809.0	1 775.8
Singapore	3 654.8	2 886.6	5 574.8	4 887.1	2 204.3	4 686.3	8 550.2	11 502.7
Chinese Taipei	961.0	1 604.0	1 330.0	1 271.0	879.0	917.0	1 375.0	1 559.0
Indonesia	576.0	682.0	1 092.0	1 482.0	1 777.0	2 003.0	2 108.0	4 346.0
Malaysia	719.4	1 667.9	2 611.0	4 043.0	5 138.0	5 741.0	4 581.0	5 815.0
Philippines	936.0	563.0	550.0	556.0	776.0	1 238.0	1 591.0	1 577.0
Thailand	1 105.6	1 778.0	2 575.0	2 049.0	2 151.0	1 807.0	1 369.0	2 070.0
East Asia total	17 139.8	15 733.3	21 283.3	20 854.8	28 697.1	51 425.0	61 998.1	70 708.1

ISBN 92-64-01442-X © OECD 2005

Table 9.5. Part A (contd.)

	1996	1997	1998	1999	2000	2001	2002
World	384 959.7	481 911.0	686 028.3	1079 082.8	1392 957.4	823 824.8	651 188.5
Developed countries	221 624.4	269 654.2	472 265.1	824 642.3	1120 527.8	589 379.0	460 334.4
Developing countries	149 758.8	193 223.7	191 283.9	229 295.2	246 056.6	209 431.2	162 145.1
China	40 180.0	44 237.0	43 751.0	40 319.0	40 772.0	46 846.0	52 700.0
Hong Kong, China	10 460.2	11 368.2	14 765.6	24 579.7	61 939.3	23 775.3	13 717.9
Korea	2 325.4	2 844.2	5 412.3	9 333.4	9 283.4	3 527.7	1 971.7
Singapore	9 303.0	13 532.5	7 594.3	13 245.4	12 463.8	10 949.4	7 654.6
Chinese Taipei	1 864.0	2 248.0	222.0	2 926.0	4 928.0	4 109.0	1 445.0
Indonesia	6 194.0	4 678.0	-356.0	-2 745.1	-4 550.0	-3 278.5	-1 523.0
Malaysia	7 297.0	6 323.0	2 714.0	3 895.1	3 787.6	554.0	3 203.4
Philippines	1 618.0	1 261.0	1 718.0	1 725.0	1 345.0	982.0	1 111.0
Thailand	2 337.7	3 881.8	7 491.2	6 090.8	3 350.3	3 813.5	1 067.8
East Asia total	81 579.2	90 373.7	83 312.3	99 369.2	133 319.4	91 278.2	81 348.4

ISBN 92-64-01442-X

Table 9.5. **East Asia: FDI Inflows and Outflows, 1980-2002**

Part B: Outflows

($ million)

	1980	1981	1982	1983	1984	1985	1986	1987
World	53 673.9	52 894.2	27 944.8	38 235.6	52 773.2	62 170.9	97 832.2	142 277.3
Developed countries	50 343.4	50 819.7	25 204.1	36 472.9	50 480.0	57 907.0	92 697.5	135 441.1
Developing countries	3 309.5	2 071.5	2 736.7	1 761.6	2 281.2	4 262.9	5 112.6	6 828.3
China	n.a.	n.a.	44.0	93.0	134.0	629.0	450.0	645.0
Hong Kong, China	82.0	31.0	52.0	566.0	1 076.0	961.0	1 372.0	2 318.0
Korea	26.1	47.5	151.3	129.9	52.1	591.0	1 226.8	514.9
Singapore	97.6	-14.7	304.2	49.2	92.4	237.7	181.4	206.1
Chinese Taipei	42.0	60.0	32.0	19.0	72.0	79.0	65.0	705.0
Indonesia	6.0	-1.0	-3.0	2.0	18.0	33.0	-11.0	-5.0
Malaysia	201.1	293.0	260.1	225.8	242.4	209.8	248.9	214.5
Philippines	1.0	5.0	25.0	14.0	5.0	-3.0	-5.0	9.0
Thailand	3.0	2.4	-0.3	1.4	0.6	0.9	1.1	168.4
East Asia total	458.9	423.1	821.3	1 007.3	1 558.5	2 109.3	3 079.2	4 130.9
	1988	1989	1990	1991	1992	1993	1994	1995
World	177 564.6	227 642.3	242 490.4	198 041.9	201 527.2	244 252.9	287 177.8	356 571.8
Developed countries	165 570.2	211 291.1	225 753.9	186 103.7	176 151.9	204 233.9	239 245.3	304 770.8
Developing countries	11 972.4	16 332.7	16 682.9	11 900.9	25 307.4	39 706.9	47 471.2	51 108.3
China	850.0	780.0	830.0	913.0	4 000.0	4 400.0	2 000.0	2 000.0
Hong Kong, China	2 533.0	2 740.0	2 448.0	2 825.0	8 254.0	17 713.0	21 437.0	25 000.0
Korea	642.9	597.8	1 051.6	1 488.6	1 161.5	1 340.0	2 461.1	3 552.0
Singapore	117.8	882.2	2 033.8	525.8	1 317.0	2 151.9	4 577.1	2 995.3
Chinese Taipei	4 121.0	6 951.0	5 243.0	2 055.0	1 967.0	2 611.0	2 640.0	2 983.0
Indonesia	26..0	32.0	-11.0	13.0	714.0	481.0	3 283.0	1 319.0
Malaysia	198.3	273.1	129.0	175.0	115.0	1 063.0	2 329.0	2 488.0
Philippines	13.0	6.0	22.0	27.0	101.0	374.0	302.0	98.0
Thailand	24.3	50.0	154.0	183.0	146.1	234.0	494.0	887.2
East Asia total	7 676.3	11 532.0	11 070.4	7 292.4	13 775.6	25 967.9	37 523.2	39 322.6

ISBN 92-64-01442-X © OECD 2005

Table 9.5. Part B (contd.)

	1996	1997	1998	1999	2000	2001	2002
World	395 727.7	476 934.5	683 211.5	1096 554.5	1200 782.8	711 445.5	647 362.6
Developed countries	333 330.4	396 057.4	630 890.9	1021 306.6	1097 795.6	660 558.4	600 062.9
Developing countries	61 137.0	76 662.1	49 837.0	72 785.6	99 051.7	47 382.0	43 094.5
China	2 114.0	2 563.0	2 634.0	1 775.0	916.0	6 884.0	2 850.0
Hong Kong, China	26 530.9	24 406.8	16 985.3	19 357.9	59 375.3	11 344.5	17 693.7
Korea	4 670.1	4 449.4	4 739.5	4 197.8	4 998.9	2 420.1	2 674.4
Singapore	6 233.9	8 955.4	380.0	5 396.7	6 061.2	9 547.8	4 081.6
Chinese Taipei	3 843.0	5 243.0	3 836.0	4 420.0	6 701.0	5 480.0	4 886.0
Indonesia	600.0	178.0	44.0	72.0	150.0	125.0	115.7
Malaysia	3 768.0	2 675.0	863.0	1 422.4	2 026.1	267.0	1 238.5
Philippines	182.0	136.0	160.0	-29.0	-108.0	-160.0	85.0
Thailand	932.0	584.0	132.0	349.0	-22.0	162.0	106.0
East Asia total	46 759.9	46 627.6	27 139.8	35 186.8	79 182.4	29 186.4	30 880.9

Note: n.a. = not available.

Source: UNIDO, Foreign Direct Investment Database.

Figure 9.2. **FDI Inflows to East Asian NIEs, ASEAN4 and China: 3-year moving average**

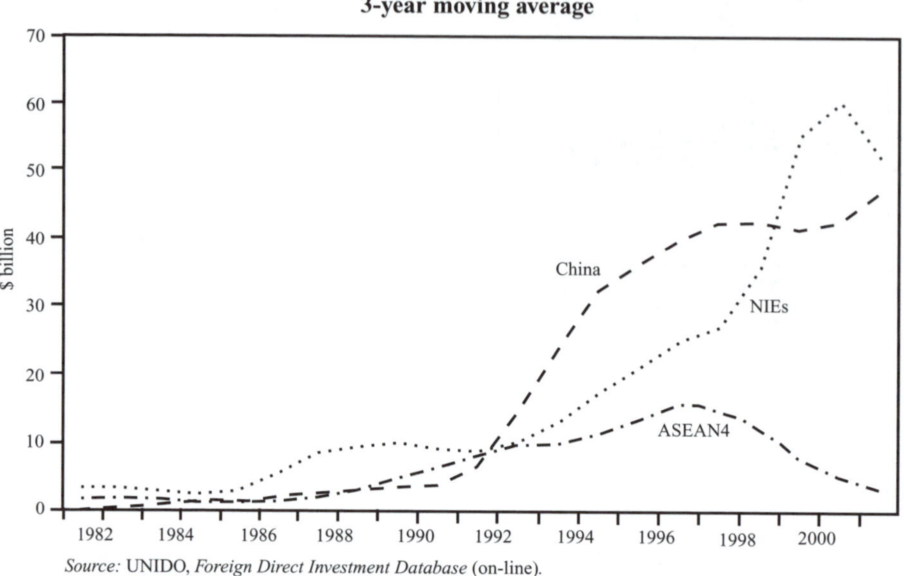

Source: UNIDO, *Foreign Direct Investment Database* (on-line).

The developed countries, as one would expect, have a dominant share in world FDI outflows. From 1980 to 2002, they accounted for 90 per cent of the total and the developing countries for only the remaining 10 per cent (Table 9.5). For FDI inflows developed countries had 70 per cent of the world total and the developing countries 30 per cent. The higher share of developed countries in FDI outflows than in inflows reflects their higher endowments of the capital, technology and management know-how required for undertaking FDI.

The East Asian countries have a dominant share (70 per cent) of FDI outflows from developing countries as a group. Among them, Hong Kong, China has been a very large supplier of FDI. Its figures are overstated, however, because they include not only FDI from local Hong Kong, China firms but also that from foreign firms; Hong Kong, China has played a role of intermediary for firms from other countries. Other than Hong Kong, China, Singapore, Chinese Taipei, Korea, China and Malaysia also have actively invested abroad. Although Table 9.5 does not show it, an increasingly large amount of FDI from developing East Asian countries, mainly the NIEs, has gone to other East Asian countries such as China and the ASEAN countries. Indeed, substantial increases in FDI among the East Asian countries contributed to the multi-layered development process.

 ISBN 92-64-01442-X © OECD 2005

Table 9.6. **The Importance of Foreign MNCs in East Asian Economies**

(percentages)

	1990	1991	1992	1993	1994	1995	1996	1997	1998	1999	2000	2001	2002
Employment shares (manufacturing)													
Hong Kong, China	12.9	13.4	13.2	14.2	16.9	19.3	20.3	22.5	--	--	--	--	--
Indonesia	--	--	3.3	--	--	--	4.7	--	--	--	--	--	--
Malaysia	--	--	43.2	45.6	45.9	43.2	43.7	38.5	--	--	--	--	--
Singapore	--	--	59.7	58.1	56.8	55.1	55.1	54.8	53.4	52.3	49.9	48.5	--
Chinese Taipei	--	--	12.8	11.9	9.9	10.6	--	--	--	--	--	--	--
Sales shares (manufacturing)													
China	2.3	5.3	7.1	9.1	11.3	14.3	15.1	18.6	24.3	27.7	31.3	--	--
Hong Kong, China	22.6	26.0	27.0	30.8	35.7	43.5	44.6	44.8	--	--	--	--	--
India	5.4	5.5	--	6.1	5.5	3.1	--	--	--	--	--	--	--
Malaysia	44.1	45.4	47.6	48.6	52.6	50.1	--	--	--	--	--	--	--
Singapore	76.9	75.4	74.7	74.8	75.1	75.6	75.9	75.8	76.0	81.1	--	--	--
Chinese Taipei	17.8	19.2	20.9	18.7	21.5	--	--	--	--	--	--	--	--
Value added share (whole economy)													
China	--	--	--	--	--	4.4	4.2	4.8	--	--	--	--	--
Malaysia	17.5	18.6	20.1	20.6	23.1	23.8	--	--	--	--	--	--	--
Capital formation (ratio of FDI inflows to gross domestic capital formation)													
China	3.5	3.9	7.4	12.2	17.3	14.8	14.3	14.6	13.1	11.3	10.4	10.5	--
Hong Kong, China	16.3	4.4	13.8	21.5	19.8	14.4	21.4	19.5	29.4	58.6	138.9	54.2	35.2
Chinese Taipei	3.7	3.2	1.8	1.6	2.3	2.4	3.0	3.4	0.4	4.4	6.8	7.8	2.9
Indonesia	3.4	4.1	4.7	4.8	4.3	7.6	9.2	7.7	-1.5	-9.7	-14.3	-10.8	--
Korea	0.8	1.0	0.6	0.5	0.6	1.0	1.2	1.7	5.7	8.3	7.1	3.1	1.6
Malaysia	18.0	22.6	23.7	22.1	15.3	15.0	17.0	14.7	14.0	22.2	16.5	2.5	--
Philippines	5.4	6.1	7.0	9.6	10.5	9.6	8.3	6.3	12.5	11.9	9.7	8.0	8.7
Singapore	46.8	33.6	12.5	23.1	36.1	40.8	26.6	37.0	24.7	47.6	45.6	43.8	--
Thailand	7.5	5.0	4.9	3.7	2.4	3.0	3.1	7.6	29.9	23.8	12.4	14.4	3.7

Note: The figures under employment, sales, and value added indicate the shares of overseas subsidiaries of foreign MNCs in these domestic economic activities.

Source: UN World Investment Report 2002, and UNCTAD website.

The Changing Patterns of Foreign Direct Investment

The changing patterns of FDI inflows to East Asian developing countries can be seen from four different perspectives — source countries, sectoral composition, sources of finance and types of FDI. Table 9.7 shows the changing patterns of FDI source countries for selected countries. Unlike the pattern of increasing intra-regional dependence through trade observed for many countries, the patterns of FDI sources as well as their changes do not appear to show any such feature. Indeed, the importance of intra-regional FDI in total FDI in East Asia declined in several countries from 1990 to 2002, largely reflecting a drop in FDI from Japan. One cannot detect in Table 9.7 a clear tendency towards the increasing importance of developing East Asian countries in FDI inflows to other developing East Asian countries. Nevertheless, such FDI is gaining importance in absolute terms because it has increased substantially[9].

In 2002 the United States was a major FDI source for Korea, Malaysia, Singapore and Chinese Taipei, while the EU was a large one for Malaysia and Singapore. Although Japan's share declined notably in the 1990s in many countries, reflecting Japan's falling FDI outflows, Japan still has 10-plus per cent of total FDI inflows for Korea, the Philippines, Singapore, Chinese Taipei and Thailand. The East Asian countries excluding Japan are important sources of FDI inflows for China, Indonesia and Thailand.

One common feature of the sectoral patterns of FDI inflows involves the high and increasing importance of the electronics industry in either overall FDI or manufacturing FDI in many East Asian developing countries (Table 9.8). Malaysia and Singapore record very high shares. In Malaysia the share of electronics in total manufacturing FDI inflows fluctuated between 20 per cent and 50 per cent in the 1990s, but since the end of the decade it has remained around 50 per cent. Electronics maintained consistently high shares of 40 per cent to 50 per cent of total FDI in Singapore. Korea and Chinese Taipei also witnessed rapid increases. The electronics share for China remains significantly lower than for others because FDI inflows to services such as real estate are very large. Chinese FDI statistics may contain a possible inconsistency, as a substantial part of FDI inflows are not registered in specific sectors but are included in "others".

 ISBN 92-64-01442-X © OECD 2005

Table 9.7. **Sources of Inward Foreign Direct Investment in East Asian Economies**
(percentages)

Sources	China (actualised value)			Indonesia (approved)			Korea (approved)			Malaysia (approved)		
	1990	1990	1995	1990	1995	2002	1990	1995	2002	1991	1995	2002
World	100.0	100.0	100.0	100.0	100.0	100.0	100.0	100.0	100.0	100.0	100.0	100.0
United States	13.1	8.2	10.3	1.8	6.9	4.8	39.6	33.2	49.4	10.5	19.7	23.5
East Asia	69.8	77.9	58.9	55.3	20.8	61.5	31.9	29.0	22.4	65.9	58.5	19.2
Japan	14.4	8.3	7.9	25.6	9.5	5.2	29.3	21.5	15.4	21.7	22.9	5.1
East Asia ex Japan	55.4	69.6	51.0	29.7	11.3	56.2	2.6	7.4	7.0	44.2	35.5	14.1
Korea	0.0	2.8	5.2	8.3	1.7	3.8	0.0	0.0	0.1	10.7	6.6	3.3
Chinese Taipei	0.0	8.4	7.5	7.1	1.4	0.4	0.5	0.5	0.0	21.1	15.8	2.0
Hong Kong, China	53.9	53.5	33.9	11.4	4.4	17.6	0.4	3.0	2.6	3.5	1.9	0.5
Singapore	1.4	4.9	4.4	3.0	3.7	34.2	1.7	3.4	1.6	6.5	11.0	7.9
China	0.0	0.0	0.0	0.0	0.0	0.3	0.0	0.6	2.7	2.3	0.2	0.4
European Union	3,4	5,2	6,0	8,1	21,4	13,0	20,8	17,5	10,6	4,7	5,6	52,3
Italy	0.1	0.7	0.3	0.0	0.1	0.0	0.2	0.2	0.0	0.2	0.2	0.2
UK	0.4	2.4	1.7	0.7	15.8	7.4	5.6	4.5	1.3	3.2	2.1	1.4
Netherlands	0.5	0.3	1.1	6.5	0.9	2.5	4.5	8.8	5.0	0.0	0.6	5.2
Germany	1.8	1.0	1.8	0.2	3.4	0.4	7.8	2.3	3.1	1.1	1.6	44.9
France	0.6	0.8	1.1	0.8	1.2	2.7	2.8	1.8	1.2	0.2	1.1	0.6

ISBN 92-64-01442-X

Table 9.7. (contd.)

Sources	Philippines(BOP)			Singapore (committed)			Chinese Taipei (approved)			Thailand (BOP)		
	1990	1990	1995	1990	1995	2002	1990	1995	2002	1900	1995	2002
World	100.0	100.0	100.0	100.0	100.0	100.0	100.0	100.0	100.0	100.0	100.0	100.0
United States	26.9	6.8	3.9	47.6	42.8	34.6	25.3	44.6	18.4	9.5	13.0	-30.4
East Asia	46.6	70.1	60.7	31.9	23.8	25.3	50.0	27.3	27.6	75.5	54.0	209.2
Japan	27.7	30.0	52.7	31.9	23.8	25.3	36.4	19.6	18.6	43.2	27.8	65.2
East Asia ex Japan	18.9	40.1	8.0	0.0	0.0	0.0	13.5	7.7	9.0	32.3	26.3	144.0
Korea	3.9	1.0	0.6	0.0	0.0	0.0	0.1	0.1	0.5	0.8	0.6	4.4
Chinese Taipei	3.9	0.9	0.0	0.0	0.0	0.0	0.0	0.0	0.0	11.1	4.8	8.0
Hong Kong, China	7.9	28.9	4.2	0.0	0.0	0.0	10.3	5.0	2.0	10.9	13.9	2.5
Singapore	3.2	9.3	3.1	0.0	0.0	0.0	3.2	2.6	6.5	9.5	6.8	127.1
China	0.0	0.0	0.0	0.0	0.0	0.0	0.0	0.0	0.0	0.2	0.1	2.0
European Union	7.7	12.9	12.0	17.5	30.9	29.7	8.4	104	17.5	5.7	12.3	-53.4
Italy	0.0	0.0	0.0	0.0	0.3	0.0	0.0	0.0	0.0	0.1	-0.3	0.2
UK	4.4	6.5	0.9	4.1	15.9	0.0	3.9	6.7	5.8	1.7	2.8	23.0
Netherlands	1.7	3.7	8.8	3.3	8.1	0.0	2.2	2.6	9.4	1.0	4.3	-76.7
Germany	1.1	2.0	0.3	7.5	3.8	0.0	1.6	0.8	1.7	1.8	1.9	1.0
France	0.5	0.8	2.0	2.7	2.9	0.0	0.8	0.4	0.6	1.1	3.6	-0.9

Source: Country data sources.

ISBN 92-64-01442-X © OECD 2005

Table 9.8. **Share of Electronics in Total FDI and/or Total Manufacturing FDI**
(percentages)

		1993	1994	1995	1996	1997	1998	1999	2000	2001	2002
China	Total FDI	n.a.	n.a.	n.a.	n.a.	5.9	n.a.	n.a.	11.3	n.a.	n.a.
	Manufacturing FDI	n.a.	n.a.	n.a.	n.a.	9.5	n.a.	n.a.	17.8	n.a.	n.a.
Korea	Total FDI	4.3	4.8	12.0	13.6	4.2	15.6	19.3	15.8	9.0	n.a.
	Manufacturing FDI	8.6	15.7	26.3	22.6	12.4	24.0	42.1	36.2	32.8	n.a.
Malaysia	Manufacturing FDI	n.a.	42.6	26.0	54.2	25.1	14.5	48.4	51.4	50.3	35.1
Singapore	Total FDI	34.2	28.4	39.1	43.1	46.4	41.0	42.3	49.3	50.3	51.6
Chinese Taipei	Total FDI	18.7	18.2	42.4	18.0	22.3	32.3	24.4	14.4	20.6	20.3
Thailand	Total FDI	8.2	4.5	11.7	10.6	16.7	5.1	11.9	10.6	17.6	n.a.
	Manufacturing FDI	31.4	11.7	41.3	34.0	33.2	12.0	33.5	16.4	30.7	n.a.

Note: Definitions of FDI data used in the table are as follows: Korea, Malaysia and Chinese Taipei, approved FDI; China, realised FDI; Singapore, committed FDI; and Thailand, BOP data.

Source: Country data sources.

A substantial part of FDI inflows to East Asia has taken the form of reinvestment financed by earnings from the operation of MNCs' overseas affiliates. According to information available from the IMF, the shares of reinvested earnings in FDI inflows for China; Hong Kong, China and the Philippines in recent years ranged from 30 per cent to 50 per cent[10]. High shares of reinvested earnings reflect two developments. One is the favourable performance of MNCs in these countries and the maturity of their investments, which yield profits for reinvestment. The other reflects the bright future business prospects of these countries that make them attractive for reinvestment.

Another notable development in recent years has been the rapid expansion of cross-border mergers and acquisitions (M&As), as has occurred in developed countries. M&A deals in East Asia increased sharply after the crisis in 1997; their value rose from $8.4 billion in 1996 to $16.7 billion in 1997, then continued upward to $31.7 billion in 2001[11]. The crisis countries, Korea, Indonesia, Malaysia, the Philippines and Thailand, recorded substantial amounts of M&A activity. Overall, the share of M&As in FDI inflows to the East Asian countries climbed from 10 per cent in 1996 to 18 per cent in 1997 and 34 per cent in 2001. At least two factors contributed to this expansion. First, a sharp decline in the foreign-currency value of equity owing to heavy depreciation of the currencies increased the attractiveness of M&As for foreign investors. Second, liberalisation of the regulations on M&As and other investment activities by foreign firms in the crisis countries facilitated cross-border M&As. One important implication of the increase in M&As is the increased importance of host countries' capability to assimilate technology and management know-how in order to reap benefits from FDI inflows. M&A does not expand physical capacity as does green-field investment, and therefore an improvement in technological capability through successful technology transfer is a major source of benefits. Also, in the aftermath of the crisis M&As played a crucial role in the survival of firms by injecting capital and introducing new management styles.

The Factors Leading to Rapid Expansion of Foreign Trade and FDI in East Asia

The factors behind the notable expansion in foreign trade and FDI inflows in East Asia fall into two groups, one domestic and the other external. The most important domestic factor was the liberalisation of both trade and FDI regimes. In addition, a favourable macroeconomic environment reflected in relatively stable price levels, a predictable and stable business environment and supporting institutions for private-sector activity and relatively well-developed infrastructures together with an abundant supply of well-educated, low-wage labour contributed to the expansion of exports and FDI inflows.

ISBN 92-64-01442-X © OECD 2005

Differences in the changes in wages among East Asian countries, which partly reflected differences in exchange-rate changes, led to the sequential pattern of FDI inflows noted above. Specifically, the sharp rise in wages in the NIEs resulted in FDI inflows to ASEAN from the NIEs as well as other countries, because the ASEAN countries could offer low-wage workers. Similar factors led to a shift of FDI from the ASEAN countries to China.

Among the external factors, the substantial realignment of exchange rates, particularly the yen-dollar rate in the mid-1980s, was crucial. The appreciation of the NIE currencies against the US dollar in the late 1980s promoted FDI outflows from the NIEs to other East Asian countries. Remarkable technical progress in information technology facilitated trade and FDI by reducing the cost of communications. Finally, increased competition among MNCs, which resulted partly from liberalisation and deregulation in many countries of the world, promoted their global activities and thereby expanded trade and FDI.

Liberalisation of Trade and FDI Regimes

In the 1980s and 1990s, as part of comprehensive structural reform policies, East Asian countries embarked on liberalisation of trade and FDI policies and on deregulation of domestic economic activities. Such policy changes were induced partly by their commitments to the World Bank and the IMF for obtaining economic assistance and largely by their own realisation that liberalisation and deregulation would promote economic growth. The liberalisation led to the expansion of exports and inward FDI because it shifted incentives from import-substituting production to export production and increased the attractiveness of these countries to foreign investors.

East Asian countries liberalised their import regimes by lowering tariff rates and non-tariff barriers (NTBs) from the early 1980s through the early 1990s (Table 9.9 on the following page). Hong Kong, China and Singapore had long since adopted virtually free trade regimes. Malaysia had relatively low tariff rates in the early 1980s, but they increased somewhat before coming down in the late 1990s. Indonesia and Thailand both maintained quite high tariffs, around 30 per cent, in the early 1980s. During the next 20 years, Indonesia reduced its rates dramatically, while Thailand's reduction was limited compared with Indonesia's. China had extremely high tariffs with an unweighted average rate of 50 per cent; it reduced them notably to an average 15 per cent. Despite this substantial reduction, China still has relatively high tariff rates in comparison with other East Asian countries. The incidence of NTBs declined in many East Asian countries except China. Most remarkably, Indonesia reduced the incidence of NTBs from 95 per cent in 1984-87 to less than 3 per cent in 1991-93. Korea reduced both tariffs and NTBs between 1988 and 1993.

Table 9.9. **Trade Liberalisation in Selected East Asian Economies**
(Average tariff rates and NTB incidence in per cent)

		Primary Products		Manufactured Products		All Products	
		Unweighted Averages	Import-weighted Averages	Unweighted Averages	Import-weighted Averages	Unweighted Averages	Import-weighted Averages
China							
Mean tariffs	1980-83	46.5	22.7	50.5	36.6	49.5	31.9
	1984-87	33.1	20.6	41.9	33.2	39.5	29.2
	1988-90	34.1	19.1	42.7	34.3	40.3	29.2
	1991-93	31.7	17.8	39.7	37.1	37.5	30.6
	2001	14.3	18.6	15.0	12.9	15.3	14.3
NTB incidence	1984-87	17.8	19.7	7.9	16.1	10.6	17.2
	1988-90	27.2	58.9	21.9	34.4	23.2	42.6
	1991-93	11.5	40.7	11.3	19.2	11.3	26.4
Hong Kong, China							
Mean tariffs	1984-87	0.0	0.0	0.0	0.0	0.0	0.0
	1988-90	0.0	0.0	0.0	0.0	0.0	0.0
	1991-93	0.0	0.0	0.0	0.0	0.0	0.0
	1998	0.0	0.0	0.0	0.0	0.0	0.0
NTB incidence	1984-87	6.9	38.7	2.1	3.3	3.4	14.3
	1988-90	0.8	1.9	0.3	0.3	0.5	0.9
	1991-93	0.8	1.9	0.3	0.3	0.5	0.9
Indonesia							
Mean tariffs	1980-83	23.0	13.6	31.3	28.5	29.0	23.5
	1984-87	14.7	10.4	19.4	21.7	18.1	18.2
	1988-90	14.8	9.1	22.5	22.6	20.3	18.0
	1991-93	13.6	8.5	18.3	14.7	17.0	12.6
	2000	5.4	2.8	8.9	6.6	8.4	5.4
NTB incidence	1984-87	98.9	98.4	93.1	89.8	94.7	92.5
	1988-90	15.7	14.9	7.0	10.8	9.4	12.1
	1991-93	4.6	11.2	2.0	5.3	2.7	7.3
Malaysia							
Mean tariffs	1980-83	4.3	2.0	12.7	13.0	10.6	9.7
	1984-87	8.6	6.4	15.4	17.7	13.6	14.7
	1988-90	7.7	5.4	14.8	14.5	13.0	11.5
	1991-93	7.3	5.3	14.7	14.1	12.8	11.2
	1997	5.8	10.0	10.2	5.5	9.2	5.8
NTB incidence	1984-87	4.5	6.3	3.2	9.1	3.7	8.2
	1988-90	1.6	1.6	3.0	8.0	2.8	6.0
	1991-93	1.2	1.6	2.4	7.0	2.1	5.1

ISBN 92-64-01442-X © OECD 2005

Table 9.9. (contd.)

		Primary Products		Manufactured Products		All Products	
		Unweighted Averages	Import-weighted Averages	Unweighted Averages	Import-weighted Averages	Unweighted Averages	Import-weighted Averages
Singapore							
Mean tariffs	1980-83	0.1	0.5	0.4	1.4	0.3	1.1
	1984-87	0.1	0.7	0.4	1.4	0.3	1.2
	1988-90	0.2	1.9	0.4	1.9	0.4	1.9
	1991-93	0.3	1.9	0.4	1.9	0.4	1.9
	2001	0.0	0.0	0.0	0.0	0.0	0.0
NTB incidence	1984-87	15.3	12.6	14.1	12.8	14.7	12.9
	1988-90	3.0	3.3	0.2	0.2	1.0	1.3
	1991-93	1.2	2.1	0.0	0.0	0.3	0.7
Thailand							
Mean tariffs	1980-83	26.3	13.7	34.6	28.7	32.3	24.8
	1984-87	28.0	16.5	32.5	30.4	31.2	26.9
	1988-90	33.4	31.5	43.7	40.9	40.8	38.0
	1991-93	26.2	26.4	41.8	41.6	37.8	36.9
	2000	9.7	7.7	15.9	10.1	17.0	9.7
NTB incidence	1984-87	24.4	28.6	7.8	16.3	12.4	20.2
	1988-90	7.9	12.1	8.8	3.7	8.5	6.5
	1991-93	8.8	12.0	4.2	6.2	5.5	8.2

Sources: Pacific Economic Cooperation Conference (1995). World Bank (2003).

In addition to trade liberalisation *per se*, several other policies adopted by East Asian countries had similar effects in promoting exports. One is the duty-drawback system, which rebates to producers tariffs paid on imported parts and components used for the production of exports. This system has virtually the same effect as free trade for export producers. Another is export-processing zones (EPZs) or free-trade zones (FTZs), in which exporters or producers of exports can take advantage of free trade on imported inputs. Many EPZs offer various incentives to foreign producers such as income tax holidays to attract export-oriented FDI. Many East Asian countries established EPZs and FTZs in the 1980s and 1990s after seeing the success of Chinese Taipei and Korea in the 1960s and 1970s[12]. Trade liberalisation itself promoted inflows of FDI with an export motive.

FDI policy liberalisation started in the mid-1980s and has continued as governments realised that FDI inflows would promote economic growth. Although it is difficult to quantify the restrictiveness of an FDI regime, it is clear that many East Asian countries have relaxed their policies toward FDI inflows since the mid-1980s[13]. FDI policy takes various forms, including restrictions on market access, most-favoured-nation (MFN) treatment and national treatment. Many East Asian countries lowered restrictions on market access by reducing the numbers of sectors and industries on "negative lists" and by relaxing limits on foreign equity ownership. Among them, Indonesia, Korea, Malaysia, the Philippines and Thailand adopted substantial FDI liberalisation measures in an effort to attract foreign investors. Furthermore, recognising the important contribution that FDI may make toward economic growth, a number of economies introduced incentives such as tax breaks to attract FDI. Indeed, keen competition has emerged among the countries in the region to attract FDI by reducing barriers and providing incentives.

Liberalisation of trade and FDI also progressed in bilateral, regional and global contexts. The ASEAN Free Trade Area (AFTA) process started in 1992. The agreement provided for liberalisation of tariff and non-tariff measures under Common Effective Preferential Tariffs. The target year for achieving liberalisation, originally set for 2008, was later moved forward to 2002. The AFTA has been in effect among the original five ASEAN members — Indonesia, Malaysia, Singapore, Thailand and the Philippines — since January 2002 when tariff rates were reduced to between zero and 5 per cent, although the exclusion list is long and individual country circumstances vary. Viet Nam was to comply with the same tariff standards by 2003, Laos and Myanmar by 2005 and Cambodia by 2007. By 2015, ASEAN expects to become a complete free trade area. FDI liberalisation has been underway since the creation of the ASEAN Investment Area (AIA) in 1998, which provides for co-ordinated investment co-operation and facilitation programmes, market access and national treatment of all industries[14].

Other than AFTA and AIA, the only major FTA in East Asia is the bilateral FTA between Japan and Singapore, which became effective in 2002. This comprehensive agreement includes not only trade liberalisation in goods and services but also FDI liberalisation, trade and FDI facilitation and economic co-operation[15]. Since the end of the 1990s many East Asian countries have become keenly interested in FTAs, and they are expected to establish various agreements in the near future[16].

Many East Asian countries have signed bilateral investment treaties (BITs) to promote FDI (Table 9.10). Typical BITs include liberalisation of FDI regimes and protection of FDI, although these measures apply to signatory

ISBN 92-64-01442-X © OECD 2005

countries. BITs may be discriminatory in that they promote FDI between BIT partners at the expense of non-partners. The cumulative number of BITs involving East Asian countries increased rapidly from 33 in 1980 to 418 in 2002. Among East Asian countries China had the most at 107 in 2002. Malaysia, Korea and Indonesia also have large numbers of BITs. Although increasing numbers of BITs may evidence liberalisation of FDI regimes, one has to examine the treaties to evaluate the openness of FDI regimes. Such study is beyond the scope of this chapter and remains for future research.

As a regional framework, APEC has contributed to the liberalisation and facilitation of trade and FDI for emerging East Asia. This trans-regional forum includes not only East Asian countries but also countries in North and South America and Oceania. Both China and Chinese Taipei are members. Indeed, APEC was the only international economic forum in which both pursued trade and investment liberalisation before they became the members of the World Trade Organization (WTO) in 2002[17]. Following the Bogor declaration in 1994, which called for full liberalisation of trade and FDI by 2010 for developed-country members and by 2020 for developing-country members, APEC members agreed to prepare and implement individual action plans specifying near-term and medium-term liberalisation measures. Peer pressure has played a crucial role in the implementation of these schemes. All APEC members have made significant progress toward freer trade and FDI regimes, and they helped both China and Chinese Taipei to join the WTO.

The Uruguay Round of multilateral trade negotiations under the former GATT started in 1986 and ended in 1994. Although they lasted eight years, twice as long as targeted, the Round made substantial progress toward liberalising trade and FDI. The achievements include reductions in tariff rates; framework agreements on trade in services, intellectual property rights and trade-related investment measures; a timetable for phasing out all quantitative restrictions on trade including those on textiles under the Multi-Fibre Arrangement (MFA); first steps toward bringing agriculture more firmly under multilateral discipline; a stronger dispute settlement mechanism; and the establishment of the WTO. Although it is difficult to estimate the impact of these achievements individually, there is no doubt that the GATT/WTO has promoted trade and FDI liberalisation in East Asia.

Table 9.10. **Cumulative Numbers of Bilateral Investment Treaties**

	1980	1990	1991	1992	1993	1994	1995	1996	1997	1998	1999	2000	2001	2002
World total	180	192	527	651	780	971	1 173	1 384	1 556	1 727	1 856	1 940	2 099	2 181
Developing countries	161	173	425	511	603	743	904	1 068	1 211	1 355	1 465	1 538	1 675	1 745
East Asia	33	34	111	151	175	215	252	290	324	354	373	392	405	418
China	0	0	31	46	57	66	71	80	87	92	94	96	104	107
Hong Kong, China	0	0	0	1	2	5	8	11	13	14	14	14	14	14
Chinese Taipei	0	0	1	6	8	9	10	13	14	15	16	17	17	17
Indonesia	7	7	12	17	17	24	28	34	41	46	52	53	55	56
Korea	8	8	24	28	32	35	41	49	52	57	60	60	62	62
Malaysia	6	7	17	22	25	36	43	49	53	61	63	65	65	67
Philippines	2	2	4	7	8	12	18	18	23	26	30	32	33	34
Singapore	7	7	10	11	12	12	15	16	19	20	21	24	24	24
Thailand	3	3	12	13	14	16	18	20	22	23	23	31	31	37

Source: UNCTAD, Foreign Direct Investment database online.

ISBN 92-64-01442-X © OECD 2005

External Factors behind Rapid FDI Inflows: FDI Promotion by Developed Countries

Developed countries contributed to export expansion and FDI inflows for East Asian countries by liberalising trade regimes through the series of multilateral GATT rounds and by providing assistance to FDI outflows. As Figure 9.3 shows, average tariff rates (ratios of tariff revenue to import value) of the major industrial countries are very low. Developed countries have used two types of measures to promote FDI inflows to East Asian countries. The first promoted FDI outflows from developed countries by reducing the cost of undertaking FDI. The second resulted in increasing attractiveness of East Asian countries as FDI hosts by improving their FDI environments through the provision of official development assistance (ODA).

Figure 9.3. **Average Tariff Rates (Tariff Revenue/Imports)**

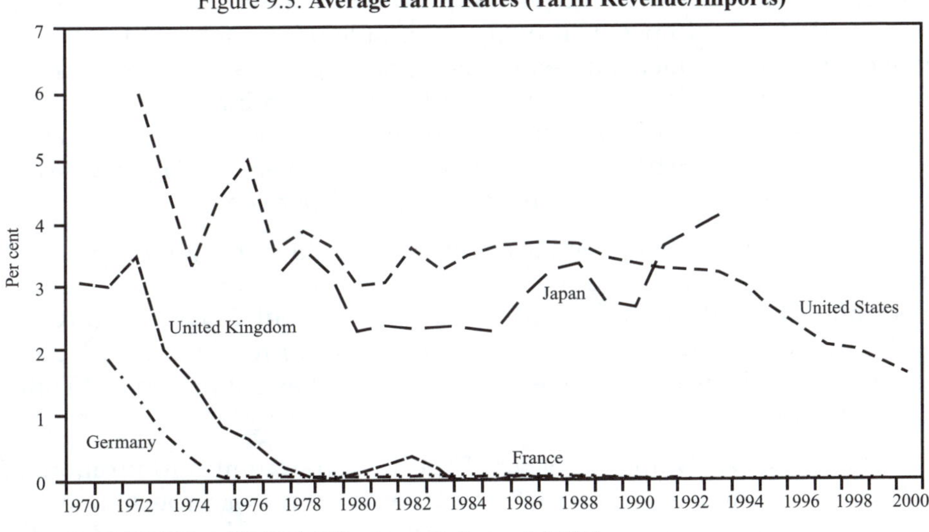

Source: World Bank (2001), *World Development Indicators*, CD-ROM.

The Japanese government has various financial and technical assistance programmes to promote FDI by Japanese firms. Several government agencies provide loans, loan guarantees and investment insurance. The Japan Bank for International Cooperation (JBIC) offers investment finance for Japanese firms of all sizes with preferential conditions for small and medium-sized

ISBN 92-64-01442-X

enterprises (SMEs). Many government and semi-government agencies provide financial assistance to SMEs. Major loan agencies include the Japanese Financial Corporation for Small Business (JFS) and the National Life Finance Corporation (NLFC). The National Federation of Credit Insurance Corporations makes loan guarantees. Multiple agencies also offer technical assistance, mainly information dissemination on investment opportunities and assistance in solving FDI-related problems. Major providers include the Japan External Trade Organization (JETRO) and the Japan Small and Medium Enterprise Corporation (JASMEC). Chambers of Commerce also provide various kinds of technical assistance such as information on potential investment markets to their member companies. All the forms of government assistance contribute to Japanese FDI by reducing its costs, especially for SMEs. Japanese SMEs have undertaken many FDI projects, particularly in East Asia[18]. Nevertheless, the effectiveness of the government's FDI-related technical assistance appears questionable. A survey by the Japan Small Business Research Institute of Japanese firms that have invested overseas[19] revealed that only 13 per cent of the respondents considered information received from government and semi-government agencies useful. Respondents thus ranked government help significantly lower than information provided by Japanese firms with investment experience (54 per cent), financial institutions with which they have business relationships (34 per cent) and other Japanese firms with such relationships (23 per cent).

The US government provides assistance to US firms, giving priority to small firms investing in developing countries. Financial assistance is important. Through the Overseas Private Investment Corporation (OPIC), the US government provides loans, loan guarantee and political-risk insurance[20]. Since its establishment in 1971 OPIC has supported $145 billion in investments.

The European Union has several specific programmes to promote FDI in Asia, recognising its relatively low level. Two major programmes[21] are Asia-Invest and the European Community Investment Partners (ECIP) scheme. Asia-Invest, implemented in 1996 in close collaboration with the private sector, disseminates information on FDI opportunities in Asia and provides financing for activities such as business exploration. ECIP, established in 1988, provides various types of support for FDI by SMEs. They include identification of potential joint-venture partners and feasibility-study loans. The European Investment Bank (EIB), an autonomous institution funded

 ISBN 92-64-01442-X © OECD 2005

by the EU members, provides investment finance. Its original mandate to finance projects in the EU later was extended to certain developing countries, including selected countries in Asia.

On the evidence of their operations, the importance of all the developed-country government programmes to promote FDI outflows in firms' decisions on FDI appears rather secondary. The major decision factors remain the economic ones, namely the costs and benefits of investing abroad *versus* investing at home. Although the effects of activist government policies may not be substantial, the very absence of official restraint or discouragement of FDI outflows has certainly helped to promote them.

The contribution of ODA to the promotion of FDI in East Asia appears undoubtedly substantial. ODA by both bilateral and multilateral donors played important roles in building and improving infrastructure in East Asia, which in turn helped increase the attractiveness of the region for foreign firms undertaking FDI. The Japanese government has long recognised the importance of the ODA-trade-FDI trinity for economic development, particularly in East Asia. Indeed, various government agencies involved in FDI and trade promotion such as JETRO and JBIC are routinely called upon to join in the formulation and implementation of ODA projects. Given the importance of infrastructure for attracting FDI, Japan's ODA contributed to FDI inflows to East Asia by providing financial and technical assistance for building infrastructure. For example, Japan's ODA loans financed 12 per cent and 16 per cent of the total costs to build the railroad system in Indonesia and electricity generation facilities in Thailand[22]. Many other cases show the contribution of ODA to FDI promotion by building infrastructure[23].

The Emergence of Trade-FDI Nexus in East Asia

The rapid expansion of foreign trade and FDI flows in East Asia since the mid-1980s suggests as only natural an assertion that they rose in tandem by forming virtuous spirals between them. The two are closely related in East Asia for several reasons. Realising that FDI brings benefits including the use of well-developed international sales/export networks of foreign firms and that export expansion would promote economic growth, many East Asian economies pursued policies simultaneously to attract FDI and promote exports. Faced with a growing opportunity to exploit comparative advantage

ISBN 92-64-01442-X © OECD 2005

in East Asian countries in favourable trade and FDI environments, cost-conscious foreign MNCs actively pursued FDI there. This resulted in successful expansion of shipments from the East Asian export bases. Countries that succeeded in expanding exports in turn attracted FDI, because they were seen as capable of providing environments conducive to efficient production. In this way, virtuous spirals of export growth and FDI expansion emerged, and the FDI-trade nexus was formed.

This section investigates the relationships between FDI and trade from three perspectives. One is the quantitative relationship at macro and industry levels. Another concerns the export activities of MNCs, and the third, which is related to the second, involves the formation of regional production networks by MNCs.

Close Relationships between FDI and Trade

Several studies have examined quantitatively the relationship between FDI inflows and the trade of host countries. Most did so by using the gravity-model framework, which tries to explain the factors determining bilateral trade flows. The standard gravity model of international trade, borrowed from physics, specifies bilateral trade flows as a positive function of trading partners' combined economic levels and as a negative function of the distance between them. To test the impact of FDI on trade, the standard model was extended to include FDI as one of the explanatory variables. To test the impact of trade on FDI flows, the gravity model of FDI uses bilateral FDI flows as a dependent variable and bilateral trade flows as well as the levels of economic activity in the FDI supplier and recipient countries and the distance between them as explanatory variables.

Kawai (1997) found positive relationships between Japan's foreign trade and FDI outflows by examining aggregated data. Kawai and Urata (1998) examined these relationships at sectoral levels for food, textiles, wood and pulp, chemical products, primary metals, general machinery, electric machinery and transport machinery for 1980-92. They found that Japan's outward FDI had positive and statistically significant impacts on Japan's exports of food, textiles, chemical products, general machinery and electric machinery, whereas it had positive and statistically significant impacts on Japan's imports for all the sectors. They also found similar patterns for the impacts of Japan's trade on Japan's outward FDI. Urata (2001*a*) applied basically the same model to

ISBN 92-64-01442-X © OECD 2005

explain the impact of FDI on trade for the APEC economies for 1980 and 1994 and found that bilateral FDI had a positive and statistically significant impact on bilateral trade.

One of the obstacles to the study of foreign direct investment is a shortage of data on bilateral FDI[24]. To overcome this problem, Lewer and Terry (2003) used information on capital-account and FDI policies as a proxy for FDI flows to test the impact of FDI on foreign trade. Using annual data from 1995 to 2000 for 74 countries, they found that open capital-account and FDI policies have positive impacts on trade, implying that FDI promotes trade.

Some studies, which examined the FDI-trade relationship at more detailed industry and product levels for regions other than East Asia, have found negative relationships, possibly indicating that macro or broad industry-level studies mask the variations among different firms and products. The following sections look at the relationship at more detailed industry levels in East Asia[25].

Trading Activities of Foreign Firms

An investigation of the trading activities of overseas affiliates of MNCs would reveal the relationship between FDI and trade. The analysis here uses two types of information. One is information on the activities of foreign firms in recipient countries based on data compiled by the recipient countries. This dataset enables a comparison of trading activities of foreign firms with those of local firms. The other is information on foreign firms based on data compiled by home countries. This dataset allows comparing foreign firms' activities in different recipient countries such as those in East Asia and those in other regions. This section uses these two sets of information to investigate the role of foreign firms in the trade of East Asian host countries. Unfortunately, the two types of data are available for only few countries, which limits the investigation to China and Singapore for the first set and Japan and the United States for the second.

The importance of foreign firms in China's trade has increased rapidly. Their shares in exports and imports increased from 29 per cent and 46 per cent respectively in 1994 to 55 per cent and 56 per cent in 2003 (Table 9.11). That large shares of China's exports and imports consist of various machinery products indicates that foreign firms in China operate regional production networks. The balance of trade for foreign firms changed from deficit to surplus

ISBN 92-64-01442-X © OECD 2005

during the 1990s. It was in continuously declining deficit from 1994 to 1997, turned positive in 1998 and showed a notably increasing surplus thereafter. These observations indicate that foreign firms have contributed to China's growing trade surplus since the late 1990s, as their operations have become successful and less dependent on foreign countries for the supply of imported intermediate goods such as parts, components and capital goods.

Table 9.11. **Exports of Foreign Firms in China**

($ billion, shares in per cent)

	1994	1995	1996	1997	1998	1999	2000	2001	2002	2003
Total exports	121.0	148.8	151.0	182.8	183.8	194.9	249.2	266.1	325.6	438.4
Exports by foreign firms	34.7	46.9	61.5	74.9	81.0	88.6	119.4	133.2	169.9	240.3
The share of foreign firms in total exports	28.7	31.5	40.7	41.0	44.0	45.5	47.9	50.1	52.2	54.8
Total imports	115.6	132.1	138.8	142.4	140.2	165.7	225.1	243.6	295.2	412.8
Imports by foreign firms	52.9	62.9	75.6	77.7	76.7	85.9	117.3	125.8	160.3	231.9
The share of foreign firms in total imports	45.8	47.7	54.5	54.6	54.7	51.8	52.1	51.7	54.3	56.2
Overall balance of trade	5.4	16.7	12.2	40.4	43.6	29.2	24.1	22.5	30.4	25.5
Balance of trade for foreign firms	-18.2	-16.1	-14.1	-2.8	4.3	2.7	2.2	7.4	9.7	8.4

Source: China's *Statistical Yearbook*, various issues.

Singapore also shows large contributions of foreign firms. Chia (2004) reports that the ratio of exports to output is significantly higher for foreign-owned firms than for local firms in Singapore. The ratios for wholly foreign-owned firms, majority-owned foreign firms, and minority-owned foreign firms were 71.9 per cent, 43.5 per cent and 49.6 per cent respectively in 2001, while the corresponding ratio for wholly local firms was significantly smaller at 29.8 per cent.

Turning to the second data set, one finds that for the Asian affiliates of Japanese manufacturing MNCs the shares of local sales in total sales and of local procurements in total procurements declined between 1992 and 1997, while the shares of exports in total sales and of imports in total procurements

ISBN 92-64-01442-X © OECD 2005

rose (Tables 9.12A and 9.12B). Specifically, the share of exports in total sales and the share of imports in total procurements rose from 34 per cent and 52 per cent respectively in 1992 to 50 per cent and 56 per cent in 1997. The corresponding figures for Japanese affiliates in North America changed from 8 per cent and 48 per cent to 12 per cent and 47 per cent, while the figures for Europe declined from 44 per cent and 71 per cent to 40 per cent and 59 per cent. These statistics indicate that Asian affiliates of Japanese firms pursued more trade-oriented strategies than did those in North America or Europe. They have achieved a remarkable increase in trade, particularly in exports. Wide variations occur in the importance of foreign trade among different sectors. The sectors with a strong export orientation include general machinery, electric machinery, precision instruments and coal and petroleum products. Those with a strong import orientation include iron and steel, electric machinery and coal and petroleum products.

The regional composition of foreign trade by Japanese affiliates reveals an increasingly important intra-regional trade in Asia. The share of the Asian affiliates' exports to Asia (including Japan and other Asia) in total sales increased from 27 per cent in 1992 to 42 per cent in 1997, and the corresponding share in total procurement increased from 47 per cent to 53 per cent. Different patterns of change in intra-regional trade occurred for sales and procurements. In sales, affiliates' dependence on both Japan and other Asia increased. In procurements, however, dependence on other Asia increased but that on Japan declined. These findings indicate that Japan has become a less important source of parts and components for the affiliates but a more important destination for their products, indicating a shift from Japan to other Asia as a source of imports. Furthermore, the importance of other Asian countries as both sources of supplies of parts and components and destinations of products rose in the 1990s.

The rapid expansion of foreign trade in Asia by Japanese MNCs came from the fast growth of intra-firm trade, both between parents and affiliates and between affiliates. Intra-firm trade accounts for a substantial share of foreign trade by the Asian affiliates in their total trade with Japan. In 1997 as much as 96 per cent of their exports to Japan were destined to their parents in Japan (Tables 9.13A and 9.13B). Although they depend less on intra-firm trade for their imports, some 83 per cent of their imports did come from their parents. Intra-firm trade is less important in trade between affiliates than in trade between parents and affiliates.

Table 9.12A. **Sales Patterns of Foreign Affiliates of Japanese Firms**

(per cent of sales in each regional category)

1992	WORLD					ASIA					NORTH AMERICA					EUROPE				
	Local	Exports to				Local	Exports to				Local	Exports to				Local	Exports to			
	Sales	Japan	North America	Asia	Europe	Sales	Japan	North America	Asia	Europe	Sales	Japan	North America	Asia	Europe	Sales	Japan	North America	Asia	Europe
Manufacturing total	76.7	6.3	2.7	3.6	9.9	66.1	15.8	3.7	11.2	2.0	91.9	2.8	2.2	0.6	1.9	55.7	1.2	2.1	0.5	39.7
Food	63.7	20.8	2.4	2.8	3.5	46.0	26.5	3.1	4.9	2.0	78.7	18.5	0.1	0.6	2.1	84.2	14.8	0.0	0.0	1.0
Textiles	58.5	11.3	6.6	10.4	9.9	56.1	14.2	7.2	12.3	6.7	99.0	1.0	0.0	0.0	0.0	53.4	3.0	6.9	5.0	31.4
Wood and pulp	47.7	32.5	11.1	2.4	4.1	50.2	47.2	2.4	0.3	0.0	49.0	33.9	10.2	2.8	1.3	72.2	0.0	1.5	0.0	26.3
Chemical products	64.5	4.9	3.0	10.1	15.4	64.7	4.9	0.4	28.6	0.2	80.1	5.4	3.5	1.9	7.6	45.3	1.4	4.7	0.1	47.6
Iron and steel	95.8	0.8	2.1	0.8	0.1	85.5	2.1	3.0	8.6	0.9	98.0	0.6	1.1	0.0	0.0	100.0	0.0	0.0	0.0	0.0
Non-metallic products	67.7	18.1	0.4	12.2	1.4	63.3	21.4	0.1	14.9	0.0	89.4	5.1	0.1	3.5	1.8	27.3	3.1	13.5	0.1	56.0
General machinery	72.3	4.2	5.1	2.1	15.3	53.0	23.6	2.1	11.3	9.8	86.1	0.8	7.5	0.4	4.0	57.2	0.5	1.7	0.0	40.5
Electric machinery	60.6	9.3	3.3	6.1	19.9	45.7	27.2	5.3	19.0	2.2	89.2	2.6	2.8	1.4	2.9	45.0	1.2	2.5	0.6	49.8
Transport machinery	94.1	1.4	1.8	0.4	1.9	92.6	1.7	3.9	1.0	0.5	96.4	1.1	1.0	0.2	0.9	82.3	0.5	0.2	0.0	16.3
Precision instruments	71.4	21.3	2.7	0.7	3.7	36.9	51.8	5.2	1.9	3.8	94.7	3.6	0.5	0.2	0.7	92.6	1.1	1.4	0.0	4.8
Coal and petroleum products	58.1	0.8	38.3	2.0	0.8	55.9	0.0	43.9	0.2	0.0	68.9	7.1	0.0	16.8	7.2	-	-	-	-	-
Other manufacturing	80.7	4.4	1.7	1.8	1.1	78.6	9.4	2.6	5.6	2.8	94.8	2.8	1.1	0.1	1.2	61.4	0.9	0.7	0.5	34.4

ISBN 92-64-01442-X © OECD 2005

Table 9.12A. (contd.)

1997	WORLD					ASIA					NORTH AMERICA					EUROPE				
	Local Sales	Exports to Japan	Exports to North America	Exports to Asia	Exports to Europe	Local Sales	Exports to Japan	Exports to North America	Exports to Asia	Exports to Europe	Local Sales	Exports to Japan	Exports to North America	Exports to Asia	Exports to Europe	Local Sales	Exports to Japan	Exports to North America	Exports to Asia	Exports to Europe
Manufacturing total	70.0	9.6	4.7	5.7	8.8	49.8	25.1	4.5	16.6	2.6	87.8	2.5	5.4	1.3	2.2	60.1	3.6	2.6	0.9	31.7
Food	76.7	11.6	1.4	2.5	7.0	69.1	16.1	3.3	6.4	3.5	90.1	8..0	0.2	0.7	0.7	54.5	8.1	0.0	0.9	36.5
Textiles	57.6	16.6	8.4	8.7	7.2	47.7	22.2	10.9	12.0	5.5	96.6		3.2	0.0	0.1	67.5	3.2	0.2	0.5	27.7
Wood and pulp	37.7	34.4	12.1	7.9	6.4	58.9	26.7	2.1	10.9	0.0	38.2	31.4	16.1	8.6	4.6	-	-	-	-	-
Chemical products	76.1	4.5	2.2	6.3	9.2	72.4	7.6	0.6	16.6	1.7	89.1	3.5	1.4	1.9	3.3	64.8	1.5	5.1	0.9	25.4
Iron and steel	91.7	1.3	2.2	2.2	0.7	85.3	3.0	2.7	6.6	0.1	95.4		2.5	0.3	0.1	59.8	-	0.0	0.0	40.2
Non-metallic products	63.0	14.6	2.8	9.5	9.9	55.9	15.6	0.9	26.3	1.0	82.3	6.3	0.6	0.6	10.1	29.4	27.7	4.1	0.0	38.8
General machinery	65.4	10.8	4.6	4.4	12.3	32.4	40.6	5.5	14.8	4.6	88.8	1.2	5.1	0.5	1.6	52.5	5.6	2.9	3.1	33.1
Electric machinery	57.9	15.4	4.0	11.5	10.0	32.3	33.0	5.3	24.8	2.9	84.6	2.8	3.5	3.6	4.8	60.4	4.0	1.3	1.1	32.0
Transport machinery	81.2	2.6	6.6	0.5	8.6	81.1	11.0	3.5	2.2	1.5	89.7	1.0	8.5	0.1	0.4	58.8	0.2	3.2	0.0	37.5
Precision instruments	46.5	27.6	5.9	13.1	5.2	27.2	46.0	1.5	23.0	2.0	67.6	8.4	15.3	1.1	4.5	66.1	5.6	7.1	3.9	15.8
Coal and petroleum products	18.9	63.3	0.1	1.6	15.0	21.2	65.7	0.0	2.9	10.2	88.5	6.9	1.2	3.2	0.2	-	-	-	-	-
Other manufacturing	81.3	7.2	3.0	2.3	5.0	59.8	24.9	4.1	8.9	1.8	94.0	2.1	2.3	0.3	0.9	76.6	1.7	2.5	0.5	18.0

Note: A hyphen "-" means that the data are not disclosed.

Source: Ministry of Economy. Trade and Industry. *Kaigai Jigyo Katsudo Kihon Chosa* (Comprehensive Survey of Overseas Activities of Japanese Firms). No. 5. (1994) and No. 7. (2001).

Table 9.12B. **Procurement Patterns of Foreign Affiliates of Japanese Firms**

(per cent of procurements within each regional category)

1992	WORLD					ASIA					NORTH AMERICA					EUROPE				
	Local	Imports from				Local	Imports from				Local	Imports from				Local	Imports from			
	Procure-ments	Japan	North America	Asia	Europe	Procure-ments	Japan	North America	Asia	Europe	Procure-ments	Japan	North America	Asia	Europe	Procure-ments	Japan	North America	Asia	Europe
Manufacturing total	46.5	40.9	1.3	5.2	5.0	48.5	37.9	1.8	8.9	0.5	51.5	41.7	1.3	4.0	0.6	28.8	44.6	0.8	3.8	21.9
Food	84.8	6.1	0.1	7.0	0.2	72.0	4.5	0.3	22.9	0.1	86.1	9.2	0.0	1.3	0.2	99.7	0.1	0.2	0.0	0.0
Textiles	44.4	20.8	4.0	9.8	6.1	40.7	22.4	4.7	12.1	1.4	81.7	18.3	0.0	0.0	0.0	11.1	27.0	0.0	0.0	61.9
Wood and pulp	89.1	7.8	1.8	0.1	1.2	83.7	13.2	0.9	0.3	1.9	93.0	5.9	1.0	0.1	0.0	58.8	23.1	8.2	0.0	9.9
Chemical products	64.9	26.2	2.5	1.5	3.2	71.4	16.9	3.7	3.5	1.3	70.3	28.1	0.5	0.0	1.0	41.8	46.0	2.7	0.0	9.1
Iron and steel	75.5	16.4	0.0	7.6	0.0	29.0	47.3	0.0	22.3	0.0	99.4	0.6	0.0	0.0	0.0	-	-	-	-	-
Non-metallic products	67.0	9.9	0.4	5.0	1.2	64.8	9.2	0.4	6.2	0.4	73.8	12.8	0.4	0.9	4.0	69.0	19.1	3.1	8.2	0.6
General machinery	43.4	47.6	2.1	1.7	5.1	49.0	47.8	1.7	1.1	0.4	48.6	44.1	2.6	2.3	2.4	32.1	52.3	1.2	0.9	13.5
Electric machinery	26.6	53.8	1.1	9.2	9.3	36.6	46.7	1.2	15.4	0.1	25.0	65.6	1.4	7.4	0.6	15.6	50.3	0.7	5.3	28.0
Transport machinery	55.1	39.3	1.3	2.5	1.1	52.9	43.8	1.8	1.1	0.4	57.3	36.3	1.4	3.8	0.1	45.0	41.8	0.3	0.2	12.7
Precision instruments	22.7	58.3	0.9	0.8	17.4	34.2	60.2	1.9	3.7	0.0	28.8	67.1	0.0	2.8	1.2	9.4	51.7	1.8	0.0	37.1
Coal and petroleum products	86.8	10.3	0.9	2.0	0.0	92.6	3.8	1.1	2.5	0.0	63.6	36.4	0.0	0.0	0.0	-	-	-	-	-
Other manufacturing	61.8	24.2	1.7	6.2	5.5	58.6	27.5	4.0	6.2	2.1	64.1	30.3	0.7	4.0	0.9	63.7	11.2	0.3	9.1	15.7

ISBN 92-64-01442-X © OECD 2005

Table 9.12B. (contd.)

1997	WORLD					ASIA					NORTH AMERICA					EUROPE				
	Local	Imports from				Local	Imports from				Local	Imports from				Local	Imports from			
	Procure-ments	Japan	North America	Asia	Europe	Procure -ments	Japan	North America	Asia	Europe	Procure -ments	Japan	North America	Asia	Europe	Procure -ments	Japan	North America	Asia	Europe
Manufacturing total	46.9	36.6	3.2	8.1	4.6	43.9	34.8	1.6	18.2	0.6	52.5	38.8	4.4	2.8	1.1	41.2	33.2	2.4	5.8	17.3
Food	81.7	4.1	1.8	10.0	0.3	78.8	6.6	0.4	8.0	0.5	90.6	1.6	4.0	3.4	0.2	51.9	7.6	0.0	40.4	0.0
Textiles	56.2	23.2	3.1	9.5	2.4	52.9	26.1	2.9	11.2	0.6	93.2	2.8	1.6	2.3	0.1	28.9	37.1	1.3	9.1	21.0
Wood and pulp	94.5	2.2	0.3	1.3	1.7	76.8	12.4	1.0	7.7	2.1	99.7	0.1	0.2	0.0	0.0	-	-	-	-	-
Chemical products	64.0	20.7	4.0	5.2	4.7	54.4	18.6	7.1	14.8	2.2	74.4	22.1	0.9	0.3	2.2	60.8	23.9	2.7	0.4	11.6
Iron and steel	63.2	29.9	1.9	3.7	0.2	19.2	70.0	0.0	10.4	0.2	92.7	5.0	0.0	0.7	0.0	56.4	41.9	0.0	1.8	0.0
Non metallic products	71.7	13.2	1.5	6.2	6.1	44.1	31.7	0.3	19.0	1.1	83.6	5.2	0.0	0.3	11.0	81.5	14.1	4.4	0.0	0.0
General machinery	38.6	44.1	2.6	2.8	11.3	57.7	32.2	0.8	8.8	0.4	35.6	54.8	4.7	0.7	2.9	30.8	37.6	0.5	1.6	29.5
Electric machinery	36.8	44.1	1.0	15.4	2.4	35.7	37.0	0.4	26.4	0.2	29.7	60.1	1.6	7.4	0.6	46.8	35.6	0.8	8.0	8.7
Transport machinery	50.2	35.8	6.1	2.0	5.6	53.7	37.0	2.5	6.0	0.7	59.2	31.8	8.0	0.1	0.7	34.9	35.1	5.2	3.6	21.2
Precision instruments	39.0	45.2	2.1	12.3	1.2	40.2	41.2	2.6	14.5	1.5	33.7	60.4	2.7	3.3	0.0	38.7	46.9	0.3	12.2	1.7
Coal and petroleum products	21.0	15.2	3.2	27.3	33.2	21.7	18.0	10.3	45.5	3.9	91.6	2.8	0.7	0.0	4.9	-	-	-	-	-
Other manufacturing	49.6	32.1	2.2	8.2	7.4	52.8	29.7	1.8	14.2	0.9	50.9	39.3	2.3	6.1	1.0	45.9	16.6	0.3	7.3	30.0

Note: A hyphen "-" means that the data are not disclosed.

Source: Ministry of Economy, Trade and Industry, *Kaigai Jigyo Katsudo Kihon Chosa* (Comprehensive Survey of Overseas Activities of Japanese Firms), No. 5 (1994) and No. 7 (2001).

Table 9.13A. **Intra-firm Transactions in Sales of Foreign Affiliates of Japanese Multinational Corporations**

(per cent of total sales in each cell category)

1992	WORLD					ASIA					NORTH AMERICA					EUROPE				
	Local Sales	Exports to				Local Sales	Exports to				Local Sales	Exports to				Local Sales	Exports to			
		Japan	North America	Asia	Europe		Japan	North America	Asia	Europe		Japan	North America	Asia	Europe		Japan	North America	Asia	Europe
Manufacturing total	17.4	78.3	47.5	43.9	37.8	6.3	84.2	62.4	44.4	47.6	24.4	73.5	39.0	60.7	39.6	15.0	48.5	30.0	18.2	3.,5
Food	5.2	84.6	27.2	17.2	18.6	7.6	85.4	51.9	26.3	50.1	5.7	91.6	0.0	2.2	29.9	0.0	39.3	0.0	0.0	0.0
Textiles	3.1	40.1	1.1	20.9	21.2	4.3	36.1	1.1	23.0	0.9	0.0	100.0	0.0	0.0	0.0	0.0	85.0	0.0	0.0	46.9
Wood and pulp	2.3	80.9	0.0	0.0	0.0	0.0	57.9	0.0	0.0	0.0	2.8	92.6	0.0	0.0	0.0	-	-	-	-	-
Chemical products	9.2	50.4	52.3	9.5	30.8	2.4	49.0	11.5	3.2	17.6	14.0	71.5	54.1	93.9	32.3	4.0	93.8	65.5	87.7	33.1
Iron and steel	0.0	16.2	3.2	0.0	0.0	0.0	29.0	23.3	0.0	0.0	0.0	5.0	0.0	0.0	0.0	0.0	0.0	0.0	0.0	0.0
Non-metallic products	7.8	82.6	73.5	53.0	18.9	0.8	82.6	0.0	55.1	0.0	29.8	93.0	37.6	19.9	70.4	0.0	100.0	100.0	0.0	1.6
General machinery	18.3	91.2	61.6	52.8	75.2	3.0	96.7	54.3	55.6	93.9	22.9	44.5	58.5	29.2	20.1	15.2	96.1	94.5	100.0	83.7
Electric machinery	17.2	86.2	49.5	52.7	34.8	8.0	90.0	82.6	53.7	58.0	21.5	79.3	18.8	64.5	34.5	15.6	30.6	12.6	108.0	34.0
Transport machinery	24.5	49.0	67.8	75.0	42.9	7.2	73.9	71.2	57.9	28.3	34.0	44.9	55.8	96.9	73.2	25.6	44.9	42.5	0.0	26.8
Precision instruments	7.5	95.1	39.2	74.1	42.2	32.4	96.5	51.1	77.9	50.8	3.4	68.2	0.0	0.0	21.6	0.2	79.7	9.8	83.3	38.2
Coal and petroleum products	0.0	100.0	0.0	90.1	100,0	0.0	0.0	0.0	0.0	0.0	0.0	100.0	0.0	100.0	100.0	-	-	-	-	-
Other manufacturing	5.5	62.0	28.3	51.4	28.6	6.3	67.0	25.3	49.8	18.4	4.7	41.7	37.8	19.7	13.0	7.1	87.4	61.9	84.8	28.0

ISBN 92-64-01442-X © OECD 2005

Table 9.13A. (contd.)

1997	WORLD					ASIA					NORTH AMERICA					EUROPE				
	Local	Exports to				Local	Exports to				Local	Exports to				Local	Exports to			
	Sales	Japan	North America	Asia	Europe	Sales	Japan	North America	Asia	Europe	Sales	Japan	North America	Asia	Europe	Sales	Japan	North America	Asia	Europe
Manufacturing total	20.4	94.6	50.6	56.7	40.5	16.1	95.7	66.4	58.9	66.1	21,8	88.0	26.7	29.9	27.5	23.5	95.8	65.6	40.2	40.3
Food	10.7	78.6	18.6	55.8	9.5	26.1	85.7	15.9	73.3	18.0	7.8	65.2	0.0	0.6	11.5	19.8	100.0	0.0	0.0	0.0
Textiles	5.8	84.2	62.0	52.6	48.0	11.2	83.4	60.0	52.2	66.5	0.2	0.0	100.0	0.0	0.0	3.9	99.9	44.8	91.8	35.4
Wood and pulp	4.2	87.3	35.3	20.5	0.0	16.3	76.6	30.4	42.4	0.0	0.3	95.6	28.0	0.0	0.0	-	-	-	-	-
Chemical products	16.5	92.1	37.5	27.2	23.1	12.0	91.3	42.5	25.4	38.3	18.4	91.9	0.0	32.0	33.3	19.8	95.1	59.2	42.1	17.5
Iron and steel	1.5	74.3	42.2	29.1	90.9	3.1	95.4	74.0	34.6	33.5	1.3	91.2	36.7	0.5	57.3	0.0	0.0	0.0	0.0	100.0
Non-metallic products	35.4	90.4	13.9	32.3	5.7	14.8	99.3	98.9	32.8	94.4	43.9	76.6	0.0	11.1	12.7	0.0	100.0	100.0	0.0	0.0
General machinery	11.3	98.1	90.8	81.5	69.8	10.8	98.5	95.0	94.4	99.2	11.5	91.9	89.5	61.2	76.0	10.0	94.8	80.6	33.4	65.7
Electric machinery	16.0	96.5	49.1	64.1	53.1	20.5	96.3	55.3	66.4	66.1	10.0	99.0	24.9	21.5	17.8	28.5	96.9	71.3	34.3	60.5
Transport machinery	33.8	94.0	45.6	59.9	21.4	11.5	96.9	98.6	56.7	94.7	41.6	84.2	15.0	87.1	35.3	29.5	89.0	1.9	86.7	19.0
Precision instruments	24.6	98.4	50.0	21.8	54.0	58.3	98.4	24.2	19.1	49.6	5.8	90.7	31.3	16.6	63.1	0.0	98.6	74.9	90.3	49.1
Coal and petroleum products	6.2	90.8	0.0	0.0	0.0	6.9	91.3	0.0	0.0	0.0	0.0	100.0	0.0	0.0	0.0	-	-	-	-	-
Other manufacturing	10.7	92.1	41.1	31.3	46.1	8.1	94.3	62.7	32.7	29.4	11.8	70.7	11.4	17.4	37.7	11.5	90.0	69.5	4.1	48.8

Note: A hyphen "-" means that the data are not disclosed.

Source: Ministry of Economy, Trade and Industry, *Kaigai Jigyo Katsudo Kihon Chosa* (Comprehensive Survey of Overseas Activities of Japanese Firms), No. 7 (2001).

Table 9.13B. **Intra-firm Transactions in Procurements of Foreign Affiliates of Japanese Multinational Corporations**

(per cent of total procurements in each cell category)

1992	WORLD					ASIA					NORTH AMERICA					EUROPE				
	Local	Imports from				Local	Imports from				Local	Imports from				Local	Imports from			
	Procurements	Japan	North America	Asia	Europe	Procurements	Japan	North America	Asia	Europe	Procurements	Japan	North America	Asia	Europe	Procurements	Japan	North America	Asia	Europe
Manufacturing total	9.0	84.3	52.6	58.9	68.6	4.2	78.0	47.7	50.2	35.8	12.6	86.4	52.9	74.8	38.1	9.6	92.1	79.0	56.4	72.7
Food	5.4	93.1	33.8	54.3	0.9	0.2	75.8	14.3	48.8	0.0	8.3	98.6	0.0	100.0	1.6	6.2	100.0	100.0	0.0	0.0
Textiles	15.1	37.1	3.2	31.5	2.7	19.5	34.2	3.3	31.5	14.3	0.0	7.6	0.0	0.0	0.0	69.6	100.0	0.0	0.0	0.0
Wood and pulp	6.3	30.1	0.0	0.0	0.0	0.1	79.4	0.0	0.0	0.0	8.2	36.1	0.0	0.0	0.0	0.0	0.0	0.0	0.0	0.0
Chemical products	13.5	81.7	31.8	4.6	50.8	18.0	57.5	7.7	4.3	17.1	11.7	84.7	10.4	100.0	36.2	10.5	95.4	91.7	0.0	64.4
Iron and steel	0.7	2.0	0.0	0.0	0.0	5.2	1.1	0.0	0.0	0.0	0.0	40.6	0.0	0.0	0.0	-	-	-	-	-
Non-metallic products	8.4	67.6	7.3	1.0	78.3	0.0	26.0	0.0	0.0	0.0	39.0	82.7	0.0	13.9	100.0	0.0	100.0	100.0	26.7	0.0
General machinery	28.7	90.8	32.5	78.7	60.1	4.5	93.9	80.3	84.8	23.9	45.0	87.6	24.2	75.9	7.6	10.9	93.1	33.7	89.0	79.7
Electric machinery	16.6	76.0	69.0	62.6	77.3	2.0	84.6	86.6	59.8	98.1	30.3	80.5	46.2	62.8	43.3	23.4	63.5	86.9	71.7	78.8
Transport machinery	3.3	98.6	72.2	90.3	19.0	0.6	81.7	76.2	34.6	86.2	4.8	92.9	76.4	98.3	66.5	1.0	100.0	100.0	100.0	10.7
Precision instruments	9.9	74.9	93.4	15.2	98.4	17.5	85.6	0.0	100.0	0.0	0.0	57.4	0.0	0.0	0.0	0.2	76.7	100.0	0.0	100.0
Coal and petroleum products	0.0	100.0	100.0	10.0	0.0	0.0	100.0	100.0	10.0	0.0	0.0	100.0	0.0	0.0	0.0	-	-	-	-	-
Other manufacturing	4.3	72.2	5.9	22.5	46.4	7.3	64.1	0.7	61.8	11.8	5.2	78.4	3.9	6.8	90.4	0.4	96.0	100.0	2.1	51.5

ISBN 92-64-01442-X © OECD 2005

Table 9.13B. (contd.)

1997	WORLD					ASIA					NORTH AMERICA					EUROPE				
	Local	Imports from				Local	Imports from				Local	Imports from				Local	Imports from			
	Procure-ments	Japan	North America	Asia	Europe	Procure-ments	Japan	North America	Asia	Europe	Procure-ments	Japan	North America	Asia	Europe	Procure-ments	Japan	North America	Asia	Europe
Manufacturing total	22.2	92.3	39.8	59.9	40.7	11.3	83.2	72.5	58.5	45.3	33.6	95.8	43.6	67.5	44.1	11.5	96.8	14.8	56.0	40.5
Food	13.6	93.3	56.1	44.0	9.1	3.9	94.4	48.8	71.7	15.1	13.2	100.0	55.6	63.3	0.0	0.0	86.6	0.0	20.3	0.0
Textiles	13.1	87.0	49.6	52.7	48.9	22.1	85.1	40.5	54.8	14.2	1.4	100.0	100.0	100.0	100.0	0.0	89.6	99.2	40.3	53.6
Wood and pulp	37.4	60.5	20.6	0.0	0.0	3.5	53.8	20.6	0.0	0.0	45.4	100.0	0.0	0.0	0.0	-	-	-	-	-
Chemical products	16.9	86.5	71.7	77.9	47.7	17.6	76.8	85.4	79.5	82.6	17.3	85.1	0.0	3.0	30.0	17.4	96.5	73.3	82.1	45.3
Iron and steel	13.6	85.6	0.0	100.0	0.0	42.6	85.3	0.0	39.9	0.0	8.6	82.0	0.0	41.3	0.0	0.0	100.0	0.0	100.0	0.0
Non-metallic products	29.3	83.2	10.4	39.5	16.0	20.3	78.9	58.1	37.9	1.4	0.0	100.0	0.0	96.4	100.0	0.0	100.0	100.0	0.0	0.0
General machinery	8.9	94.4	41.7	79.7	76.6	3.9	93.5	21.2	89.7	0.0	15.1	94.2	75.7	89.0	14.0	6.4	96.4	39.2	29.6	92.9
Electric machinery	19.2	91.2	39.1	59.6	51.4	8.6	80.8	32.8	58.8	10.8	40.9	99.1	32.1	68.5	92.6	14.1	93.8	74.1	46.5	52.4
Transport machinery	29.8	95.1	35.3	82.0	16.3	13.4	86.7	100.0	66.2	62.5	38.1	92.6	46.1	33.7	51.4	11.2	99.5	4.2	90.7	13.0
Precision instruments	28.9	95.7	13.3	34.3	94.4	39.1	95.5	0.0	28.3	99.5	10.6	99.9	0.0	96.4	25.0	0.9	91.1	100.0	81.0	75.6
Coal and petroleum products	59.5	2.0	0.0	9.4	0.0	74.6	1.7	0.0	9.4	0.0	0.0	0.0	0.0	0.0	0.0	-	-	-	-	-
Other manufacturing	13.7	90.6	38.3	35.3	77.6	6.1	81.2	48.0	57.3	34.2	28.8	95.7	9.2	41.8	90.0	1.1	98.2	93.6	2.4	7.4

Note: A hyphen "-" means that the data are not disclosed.

Source: Ministry of Economy, Trade and Industry, *Kaigai Jigyo Katsudo Kihon Chosa* (Comprehensive Survey of Overseas Activities of Japanese Firms), No. 7 (2001).

Similar highly export-oriented patterns appear for the Asian affiliates of US MNCs, compared with US affiliates in Europe and Latin America, with few exceptions (Table 9.14)[26]. One cannot, however, detect for US East Asian affiliates as clearly as for Japanese affiliates an increasing export bias in changes in sales orientation. For manufactures, export shares increased from 1989 to 1999 for US affiliates in China, Malaysia and the Philippines, while it declined for those in Singapore, Chinese Taipei and Thailand. Different patterns can be found in different sectors. An export bias is particularly strong for computers/electronics products and electrical equipment appliances/ components, similar to the pattern for the Asian affiliates of Japanese MNCs[27]. The share of exports in total sales is extremely high for US affiliates in computers/electronics products in Thailand (99.3 per cent), Malaysia (90.2 per cent) and the Philippines (90.1 per cent). Although a precise assessment cannot be made for lack of necessary information on the breakdown of export destinations under "others", an increasing portion of exports from US East Asian affiliates in manufacturing as a whole and electric and electronic equipment in particular appears to have been destined to East Asian countries, assuming that "others" mainly consist of East Asian countries[28]. On balance, the findings on US MNCs' activities in East Asia indicate that they do contribute similarly with Japanese MNCs to the expansion of intra-regional trade in East Asia, especially in computers and electronic products.

The Emergence of Regional Production Networks

An earlier observation of the sales and procurement patterns of Asian affiliates of Japanese and US MNCs suggests the formation of a regional production network in the electronics industry, within which parts and components are traded internationally for assembly into final products in East Asia[29]. East Asia has become a major global production site for electronics products since the 1980s[30]. As the discussions in the previous sections indicate, foreign companies undertake much of this production, although local producers have increased their output sharply in recent years.

Many foreign electronics companies have set up regional production systems in East Asia by adopting fragmentation strategies, which divide production processes into several sub-processes, each located *via* FDI in a country where it can be conducted most efficiently or at least cost. For example,

ISBN 92-64-01442-X © OECD 2005

the production of a personal computer (PC) is divided into design, parts production and assembly of the finished products[31]. A typical Japanese PC producer undertakes design in Japan, assigns production of various parts to different countries and assembles PCs in China with parts imported from different locations. Parts production, for example, may reflect the following assignments, depending on the suitability of locations for producing particular parts: HDDs in the Philippines, CPUs in the United States, memories in Korea and Liquid Crystal Displays in Chinese Taipei.

Foreign electronics producers have adopted fragmentation strategies for several reasons. One involves the standardisation of production processes, which requires only assembly of components without sophisticated technologies. Another reflects low tariff rates on components trade, partly because of EPZ arrangements. The Information Technology Agreement (ITA) under the WTO, in which developed and developing members agreed to remove tariffs on IT products by 2000 and 2005 respectively, has contributed to the reduction of tariffs on IT products. Table 9.15 shows the proportion of components in overall trade in electronics products. Note that trade in components accounts for a large share of the electronics trade of the East Asian countries — approximately 65 per cent of overall electronics exports and 75 per cent of electronics imports. The corresponding ratios for world trade are significantly lower at about 55 per cent. Moreover, the proportion of components trade is particularly high for intra-East Asian trade.

An examination of trade patterns alone does not provide accurate information on regional production systems. One can examine the East Asian system explicitly by using information available from international input-output (I-O) tables. The international I-O tables constructed by the Institute of Developing Economies in Tokyo link national I-O tables in order to document flows of goods between sectors in different countries. This analysis uses the tables for 1985 and 1995 to examine changes in the regional production system over time[32]. They cover nine East Asian countries (Indonesia, Malaysia, Philippines, Singapore, Thailand, China, Chinese Taipei, Korea and Japan) and the United States. Hong Kong, China is treated as a region involved only in trading, not production. The original tables adopted seven-sector and 24-sector aggregations; the latter is used here. Ideally, one would like to single out the electronics industry, but the closest classification available in the 24-sector aggregation is machinery.

ISBN 92-64-01442-X

Table 9.14. **Sales Patterns of Foreign Affiliates of US Firms, 1989 and 1999**

(per cent of total sales)

1989	China			Hong Kong, China			Indonesia			Korea			Malaysia			Philippines		
	Local Sales	Exports to USA	Exports to Others	Local Sales	Exports to USA	Exports to Others	Local Sales	Exports to USA	Exports to Others	Local Sales	Exports to USA	Exports to Others	Local Sales	Exports to USA	Exports to Others	Local Sales	Exports to USA	Exports to Others
Manufacturing	87.6	0.8	10.7	31.4	39.6	29.1	n.a.	n.a.	n.a.	61.5	30.4	8.2	25.3	45.8	28.9	66.3	15.4	18.3
Food	n.a.	n.a.	n.a.	n.a.	n.a.	n.a.	n.a.	n.a.	n.a.	99.0	0.0	1.0	n.a.	n.a.	n.a.	61.6	n.a.	n.a.
Chemicals	93.6	2.1	4.3	65.2	0.0	34.8	96.2	0.0	3.8	92.2	0.0	7.8	87.3	0.0	13.2	97.6	0.7	1.7
Primary and fabricated metals	100.0	0.0	0.0	n.a.	n.a.	n.a.	100.0	0.0	0.0	n.a.	n.a.	n.a.	n.a.	n.a.	n.a.	n.a.	n.a.	n.a.
Machinery	82.4	0.0	17.6	23.3	48.9	27.9	n.a.	n.a.	n.a.	n.a.	3.0	n.a.	n.a.	0.0	n.a.	n.a.	n.a.	n.a.
Electric and electronic equipment	n.a.	n.a.	n.a.	33.1	21.1	45.9	n.a.	n.a.	n.a.	20.2	69.3	10.6	13.8	57.3	29.0	22.0	39.9	38.1
Transportation equipment	n.a.	n.a.	n.a.	n.a.	n.a.	n.a.	n.a.	n.a.	n.a.	n.a.	n.a.	n.a.	n.a.	n.a.	n.a.	n.a.	n.a.	n.a.
Other manufacturing	88.9	0.0	11.1	20.2	69.2	10.5	n.a.	n.a.	n.a.	92.0	3.0	5.3	n.a.	n.a.	n.a.	n.a.	n.a.	n.a.
1989 (continued)	Singapore			Chinese Taipei			Thailand			Europe			Latin America					
Manufacturing	12.8	54.6	32.6	53.6	29.9	16.5	26.7	34.3	39.0	59.0	5.6	59.0	78.0	13.9	8.1			
Food	27.5	n.a.	n.a.	n.a.	0.0	n.a.	33.7	n.a.	n.a.	73.7	1.3	73.7	86.4	6.0	7.7			
Chemicals	22.8	n.a.	n.a.	85.2	0.4	14.2	98.5	0.0	1.5	56.4	2.8	56.4	92.3	n.a.	n.a.			
Primary and fabricated metals	34.8	21.3	42.7	n.a.	n.a.	n.a.	n.a.	n.a.	n.a.	61.8	2.5	61.8	69.7	n.a.	n.a.			
Machinery	4.5	70.5	25.0	n.a.	66.6	n.a.	n.a.	n.a.	n.a.	52.1	15.5	52.1	71.8	14.1	14.2			
Electric and electronic equipment	19.8	42.3	37.8	36.9	39.7	23.4	n.a.	61.0	n.a.	59.4	4.6	59.4	56.8	38.5	4.7			
Transportation equipment	n.a.	n.a.	n.a.	n.a.	n.a.	n.a.	n.a.	n.a.	n.a.	55.2	2.2	55.2	67.1	28.7	4.2			
Other manufacturing	n.a.	n.a.	n.a.	64.6	n.a.	n.a.	77.0	n.a.	n.a.	65.9	3.0	65.9	83.0	8.6	8.5			

ISBN 92-64-01442-X © OECD 2005

Table 9.14 (contd.)

1999	China			Hong Kong, China			Indonesia			Korea			Malaysia			Philippines		
	Local Sales	Exports to USA	Exports to Others	Local Sales	Exports to USA	Exports to Others	Local Sales	Exports to USA	Exports to Others	Local Sales	Exports to USA	Exports to Others	Local Sales	Exports to USA	Exports to Others	Local Sales	Exports to USA	Exports to Others
Manufacturing	63.1	16.3	20.6	31.8	25.8	42.4	75.2	3.7	21.3	n.a.	6.0	n.a.	20.0	38.2	41.8	43.7	19.3	37.1
Food	97.8	0.0	2.2	100.0	0,0	0.0	n.a.	0.0	n.a.	99.7	0.0	0.3	n.a.	0.4	n.a.	48.0	n.a.	n.a.
Chemicals	89.2	0.6	10.1	64.6	8.4	27.0	n.a.	5.7	n.a.	92.9	0.8	6.2	68.3	n.a.	n.a.	99.2	0.2	0.6
Primary and fabricated metals	96.9	1.0	2.1	99.5	0.0	0.5	n.a.	n.a.	n.a.	92.0	7.0	0.0	100.0	0.0	0.0	n.a.	n.a.	n.a.
Machinery	87.2	4.1	8.9	65.2	14.8	20.4	98.6	1.4	0.0	66.1	n.a.	n.a.	100.0	0.0	0.0	100.0	0.0	0.0
Computers and electronic products	44.5	22.8	32.7	18.0	27.0	55.1	n.a.	n.a.	n.a.	70.3	16.7	13.0	9.8	46.2	44.1	9.9	33.2	56.8
Electrical equipment appliances and components	36.3	43.4	20.2	n.a.	27.3	n.a.	n.a.	n.a.	n.a.	100.0	0.0	0.0	n.a.	n.a.	n.a.	n.a.	n.a.	n.a.
Transportation equipment	74.3	24.1	1.6	18.2	48.5	33.3	100.0	0.0	0.0	n.a.	1.7	n.a.	n.a.	n.a.	n.a.	n.a.	n.a.	n.a.
1999 (continued)	Singapore			Chinese Taipei			Thailand			Europe			Latin America					
Manufacturing	33.2	37.5	29.3	59.9	14.2	25.9	40.2	15.6	44.2	58.6	5.5	36.0	65.2	21.7	13.1			
Food	n.a.	n.a.	n.a.	n.a.	0.0	n.a.	49.5	n.a.	n.a.	74.4	1.1	24.5	74.3	7.7	18.0			
Chemicals	55.0	9.7	35.2	83.8	0.3	15.9	92.8	1.5	5.7	51.2	6.3	42.5	87.1	5.5	7.4			
Primary and fabricated metals	n.a.	20.7	n.a.	n.a.	n.a.	n.a.	89.9	6.4	3.7	70.0	3.7	26.3	57.9	11.0	31.2			
Machinery	40.0	20.5	39.5	n.a.	n.a.	0.9	20.0	n.a.	n.a.	54.3	9.9	35.8	67.8	22.0	10.2			
Computers and electronic products	25.2	46.3	28.5	38.1	24.1	37.8	0.7	29.5	69.8	46.5	9.6	44.0	43.7	30.0	26.4			
Electrical equipment appliances and components	14.5	15.4	70.1	n.a.	n.a.	0.0	100.0	0.0	0.0	46.8	6.4	46.8	72.8	19.4	7.8			
Transportation equipment	n.a.	56.4	n.a.	n.a.	n.a.	n.a.	47.6	n.a.	n.a.	51.5	6.5	42.0	51.9	40.9	7.2			

Note: "n.a." indicates that the figures are not disclosed.

Source: US Foreign Investment Benchmark Survey 1989 and 1999, Final Results, Tables III.E3, F.4, F7 and F8. See www.bea.gov/bea/uguide.htm.

Table 9.15. **Proportions of Electronics Components Trade in Total Electronics Trade**

(percentages)

	Year	Exports					Imports				
		East Asia	Japan	NAFTA	EU	World	East Asia	Japan	NAFTA	EU	World
China	1999	71	61	33	32	51	75	76	49	43	68
	2002	65	49	29	32	48	77	80	57	58	74
Hong Kong, China	1999	76	67	51	54	66	77	73	67	54	73
	2002	78	57	44	47	67	71	75	66	50	70
Korea	1999	86	67	59	52	66	83	77	74	61	76
	2002	71	74	42	43	57	81	74	66	62	73
Chinese Taipei	1999	88	59	56	57	67	83	73	69	56	75
	2002	85	62	49	50	66	78	71	70	68	74
Indonesia	1999	80	74	24	38	64	72	85	59	46	73
	2002	77	50	37	16	52	79	88	48	37	73
Malaysia	1999	86	61	65	67	72	91	87	88	84	89
	2002	86	57	40	59	65	87	88	84	82	86
Philippines	1999	93	72	79	77	83	89	90	92	76	89
	2002	88	66	63	73	76	82	89	94	79	87
Singapore	1999	80	53	46	55	62	86	78	71	68	80
	2002	80	69	0.52	55	67	82	81	69	74	79
Thailand	1999	94	68	57	69	75	89	83	83	64	84
	2002	91	69	46	56	68	81	81	78	49	76
East Asia	1999	82	63	55	57	66	82	78	74	60	78
	2002	78	61	43	48	62	78	79	72	64	76
Japan	1999	78	---	41	42	56	63	---	54	42	58
	2002	79	---	42	43	61	61	---	48	50	57
NAFTA	1999	74	54	51	47	54	55	41	51	49	51
	2002	72	48	45	48	52	43	42	45	49	44
EU	1999	60	42	49	39	42	57	42	47	39	44
	2002	64	50	49	41	44	48	43	48	41	43
World	1999	78	58	51	44	55	66	56	54	42	55
	2002	76	57	44	43	54	62	61	52	44	54

Source: Computed from ITI (Institute of International Trade and Investment) trade database.

ISBN 92-64-01442-X © OECD 2005

Table 9.16 shows the changing importance of different sources of machinery industry inputs for the East Asian countries in 1985 and 1995. The sources are divided into local and foreign, and the foreign sources are further divided into East Asia (including Japan), Japan and East Asia excluding Japan. For all of East Asia the importance of foreign sources increased, although wide variations appear in the patterns among different countries. Reliance on foreign sources is significantly high for developing countries compared with Japan. Among them, ASEAN registered stronger reliance than the NIEs or China. These findings are consistent with an observation that local component producers, a supporting industry, are underdeveloped in ASEAN countries.

The figures under East Asia excluding local sources show a substantial increase for many countries, indicating a deepening of intra-regional production relationships. This pattern is clear for the East Asian countries excluding Japan. Indeed, many countries including Malaysia, the Philippines, Singapore, Thailand and Chinese Taipei imported approximately half of their machinery inputs from other East Asian countries in 1995. East Asian developing countries still rely heavily on Japan for the supply of machinery industry inputs, but they have themselves become increasingly important sources of inputs for each other.

Table 9.16. **Intra-Regional Dependence in Machinery Production in East Asia**
(per cent of total inputs from different sources)

	Year	Indonesia	Malaysia	Philippines	Singapore	Thailand	China	Chinese Taipei	Korea	Japan	East Asia	East Asia ex.Japan
Foreign sources	1985	84.5	86.2	103.7	85.6	58.3	11.1	46.7	45.6	4.4	12.5	37.0
	1995	67.4	87.7	86.6	77.0	80.4	27.8	68.9	42.5	9.7	27.7	53.3
East Asia	1985	52.3	55.8	42.9	62.9	85.8	97.9	81.3	80.2	96.6	93.7	84.8
	1995	58.8	66.9	62.7	82.4	73.4	91.1	79.1	82.4	95.1	89.9	82.4
East Asia excluding local sources	1985	36.8	42.0	46.6	48.4	44.1	9.0	28.0	25.8	1.0	6.2	21.8
	1995	26.2	54.6	49.3	59.3	53.8	18.9	47.9	24.9	4.8	17.6	35.7
Japan	1985	24.4	19.3	13.6	24.3	33.6	6.2	25.2	21.9	95.6	75.6	15.3
	1995	15.0	26.5	24.1	26.9	25.0	9.5	28.0	17.4	90.3	60.8	18.8
East Asia excluding local sources and Japan	1985	12.3	22.7	33.0	24.1	10.5	2.8	2.8	3.9	1.0	1.6	6.5
	1995	11.2	28.1	25.2	32.5	27.9	9.4	19.9	7.6	4.8	7.0	16.9

Note: Machinery products include agricultural machinery and equipment, specialised industrial machinery, ordinary industrial machinery, heavy electric machinery, engines and turbines, electronics and electronic products and other electric machinery and appliances. The figure exceeding 100 for foreign sources in the Philippines in 1985 arises largely from a negative value for inputs from the Philippines recorded in the original table. This unusual observation should be investigated.

Source: Institute of Developing Economies, International Input-Output Tables, 1985 and 1995.

ISBN 92-64-01442-X © OECD 2005

Concluding Remarks

This chapter has analysed foreign trade and FDI in East Asia since the 1980s and identified the formation of the trade-FDI nexus that has contributed to rapid economic growth by initiating multi-layered regional development. In creating this nexus, East Asian countries have obtained the factors required for economic growth, such as financial resources, technology, management know-how and sales and procurement networks. East Asia's remarkable sequential development pattern has become the basis of multi-layered development, as the trade-FDI nexus has sequentially involved the NIEs, the ASEAN countries and China. The electronics industry has played a central role in the formation of the trade-FDI nexus, because it has special features, including production sub-processes that can be divided and situated in different locations *via* FDI to exploit opportunities for specialisation and international trade.

Developed countries have played important roles in the formation of the trade-FDI nexus in East Asia. They have been major sources of FDI, although FDI from East Asian developing countries has increased notably in recent years. Through FDI, developed countries have provided East Asian countries with technology and management know-how, sales and procurement networks and other benefits, including capital. Many developed countries have adopted measures to promote FDI to developing countries, such as provision of information on FDI environments and of FDI insurance. These measures have contributed to FDI outflows by reducing their costs. Moreover, developed countries have not restricted FDI outflows despite calls for such measures from labour unions and other interest groups. They have also contributed to the promotion of FDI by providing ODA for the construction of infrastructure in developing countries. Japan's ODA policy has emphasised its link with FDI and trade promotion.

Developed countries have provided not only markets for East Asian products, but also capital goods and intermediate goods used for production. They have liberalised import restrictions on many goods, especially electronics products, thus contributing to East Asia's export expansion. Yet they still restrict imports of products in which East Asian countries have a comparative advantage, such as agricultural and textile products. This indicates a need for further liberalisation on the part of the developed countries.

Developing countries in East Asia have successfully seized an opportunity by establishing business-friendly environments — including the availability of low-wage but well-disciplined labour, stable macroeconomic environments,

ISBN 92-64-01442-X © OECD 2005

sufficiently developed infrastructures and liberalised trade and FDI regimes. Their experience provides important lessons for other developing countries in pursuit of economic development.

Nevertheless, the East Asian countries face challenges to achieving further economic growth. One is the limited possibility of further expansion of export-oriented FDI. The remarkable growth of such FDI, which resulted in the formation of the trade-FDI nexus, was made possible by substantial realignments in exchange rates, particularly the large appreciation of the Japanese yen, and the liberalisation of FDI and trade regimes in East Asian countries. Although forecasting future exchange-rate developments is difficult, another major realignment of exchange rates in the near future may be unlikely, considering that the yen has appreciated substantially. As for FDI and trade liberalisation, the East Asian countries have more or less exhausted the relatively easy moves that did not require substantial industrial adjustment. This makes further liberalisation difficult. Given these conditions, East Asian countries cannot expect to repeat past experience of economic growth based on the trade-FDI nexus on a large scale.

This problem may not apply to all East Asian countries but only to some of them. Indeed, China has very successfully attracted FDI and expanded exports, while others including the ASEAN countries have not been so successful recently. This performance gap will likely widen as competition to attract FDI and expand exports intensifies as a result of multilateral liberalisation under the WTO or, more likely, bilateral and regional liberalisation under FTAs. To put it differently, a freer FDI and trade environment would benefit those countries endowed with the factors required for promoting economic growth, such as the availability of capable workers and well-developed, well-managed institutions, but it would impact negatively on countries without these necessary ingredients.

The East Asian countries also face the challenge of successful assimilation of foreign technology and management know-how. They have been able so far to achieve economic growth by taking advantage of the presence of foreign companies and their contribution to growth mainly through the expansion of output and exports. Yet this scenario sooner or later faces limits. To overcome them the East Asian countries must improve their technological capabilities, especially by assimilating foreign technologies owned by MNCs. Such assimilation *via* FDI has become difficult in recent years, as MNCs have changed their technology strategy from one based on codified technology to one based on uncodified tacit technology, in order to retain technology inside the MNCs and avoid technology spillover.

 ISBN 92-64-01442-X © OECD 2005

To surmount these challenges and to achieve further economic growth through increasing productive efficiency, the East Asian countries will be well advised to establish environments attractive to foreign companies and to improve their indigenous technological capabilities[33]. Further liberalisation of FDI regimes and improvements in hard and soft infrastructure must be achieved. Hard infrastructure includes transportation and communication facilities, while soft infrastructure includes well-functioning institutions such as legal, economic and educational systems. To achieve these objectives, the East Asian countries should use the various multilateral and regional frameworks such as the WTO, the World Bank, APEC and FTAs.

ISBN 92-64-01442-X

Notes

1. Prepared for "The Impact and Coherence of OECD-Country Policies on Asian Developing Economies" project organised by The Policy Research Institute of the Ministry of Finance, Japan and the OECD. The author benefited from discussions and comments from the participants at the workshops and especially those from Shahid Yusuf of the World Bank and Masahiro Kawai of the University of Tokyo.
2. World FDI inflows declined in 2001 and 2002.
3. See, for example, Perkins and Syrquin (1989)
4. This pattern has been detected by many studies including Urata (2001*a*) and Kawai and Urata (2004).
5. Fukao *et al.* (2003) found that vertical intra-industry trade in East Asia is closely related to FDI inflows.
6. The Business Risk Service lowered its political risk rating for Indonesia notably from 46 in 1997 to 39 in 1998 and to 36 in 2000, reflecting the political instability caused by the fall of President Suharto in 1998.
7. United Nations (2001), p. 25.
8. The share of FDI inflows in domestic capital formation does not accurately reflect the importance of MNCs' activities in host economies for several reasons. For example, MNCs procure investment funds not only from foreign countries but also from local sources; therefore FDI indicates only one part of MNC investment activities. Despite this deficiency, the indicator is used as a proxy because of its availability for many East Asian developing economies.
9. Substantial FDI was withdrawn from Thailand in 2002, which is reflected in the negative values shown for FDI inflows from the United States and the EU.
10. International Monetary Fund (2002).
11. UNCTAD FDI database on line.

ISBN 92-64-01442-X © OECD 2005

12. OECD (2002) points out the costs of EPZs such as loss of government revenue and discrimination against local firms, which it argues EPZ evaluations should take into account in assessing benefits such as export expansion.

13. Japan PECC (2002) examined the impediments to FDI in APEC economies and found that many East Asian economies reduced the number and the level of impediments by liberalising FDI policies.

14. AFTA is complemented by the ASEAN Industrial Complementation Scheme for investment liberalisation. This Scheme has moved more slowly than AFTA, putting its main focus on the rationalisation of the automotive industry.

15. The Japan-Singapore agreement is called the "Agreement between Japan and the Republic of Singapore for New-Age Economic Partnership" and goes beyond a conventional FTA.

16. Urata (2004) discusses the growing interest in FTAs in East Asia.

17. However, they are members of the Asian Development Bank.

18. On FDI by Japanese SMEs, see Urata (2002).

19. Reported in The Small and Medium Enterprise Agency of the Japanese Government (2004).

20. For OPIC, see http://www.opic.gov/.

21. For more information on the EU's initiative to promote FDI in Asia, see Urata (2001*b*).

22. JBIC. http://www.jbic.go.jp.

23. The author attempted to discern the impact of ODA on FDI promotion by conducting statistical analyses, but they did not reveal such an impact. Several problems appear to make such analysis difficult. One is the limited amount of ODA in the total cost of building infrastructure, which makes the statistical impact of ODA on FDI inflows small. Another is the causal relationship between ODA and FDI. The analysis hypothesises that ODA promotes FDI. Yet low-income countries with low levels of FDI may also receive FDI. These two contrasting causal relationships make the analysis difficult.

24. Not only bilateral FDI data are in shortage, but also FDI data in general. One problem concerning FDI data involves differences in the definitions of FDI adopted by different countries. Although the IMF defines FDI as equity investment of at least 10 per cent foreign ownership in the balance of payments statistics, many countries do not follow this definition. This problem often arises in the statistics on FDI by industry and by country, i.e. source and destination countries.

ISBN 92-64-01442-X © OECD 2005

25. OECD (2002) presents a good summary of previous studies on this subject.

26. The figures for East Asia or Asia totals cannot be obtained because of non-disclosure of the necessary figures.

27. Changes in sales orientation for computers/electronic products/electrical equipment appliances/components between 1989 and 1999 cannot be investigated because of changes in the industrial classification during the period.

28. This assumption is quite realistic in light of the behaviour of Asian affiliates of Japanese MNCs, a large portion of whose exports is destined to other Asian countries.

29. Kimura and Ando (2004) found that a large part of machinery trade in East Asia is composed of parts and components, providing evidence for the formation of regional production network.

30. Takeuchi (2004) analyses the development of the electronics industry in East Asia by focusing on trade and FDI.

31. For details, see Takeuchi (2004).

32. The tables have been constructed for 1975, 1985, 1990 and 1995.

33. Yusuf and Evenett (2002) provide useful discussions on the issues and problems that East Asian countries have to overcome to achieve further economic growth. In the discussions they emphasise the important role of innovation.

ISBN 92-64-01442-X © OECD 2005

Bibliography

CHIA, S.Y. (2004), "Inward FDI in Singapore: Policy Framework and Economic Impact", paper prepared for the World Bank Institute Project entitled "Foreign Direct Investment and Economic Development: Lessons from the East Asian Experience".

FUKAO, K., H.ISHIDO and K. ITO (2003), "Vertical Intra-Industry Trade and Foreign Direct Investment in East Asia", *Journal of the Japanese and International Economies,* Vol. 17, pp.468-506.

INTERNATIONAL MONETARY FUND (2002), *Balance of Payments Statistics Yearbook,* IMF, Washington, D.C.

JAPAN PECC (Pacific Economic Cooperation Conference) (2002), *An Assessment of Impediments to Foreign Direct Investment in APEC Member Economies,* Tokyo.

KAWAI, M. (1997), "Japan's Trade and Investment in East Asia", *in* D. ROBERTSON (ed.) *East Asian Trade after the Uruguay Round,* pp. 209-226, Cambridge University Press, Cambridge, UK.

KAWAI, M. and S. URATA (1998), "Are Trade and Direct Investment Substitutes or Complements? An Empirical Analysis of Japanese Manufacturing Industries", *in* H. LEE and D. ROLAND-HOLST (eds.), *Economic Development and Cooperation in the Pacific Basin: Trade, Investment and Environmental Issues,* pp. 251-293, Cambridge University Press, Cambridge, UK.

KAWAI, M. and S. URATA (2004). "Trade and Foreign Direct Investment in East Asia", *in* G. DE BROUWER and M. KAWAI (eds.), *Exchange Rate Regimes and East Asia,* pp. 15-102, Routledge Curzon, London.

KIMURA, F. and M. ANDO (2004), "Japanese Manufacturing FDI and International Production/Distribution Networks in East Asia", paper prepared for the World Bank Institute project entitled "Foreign Direct Investment and Economic Development: Lessons from East Asian Experience".

LEWER, J.J. and N. TERRY (2003). "Capital Account and Foreign Direct Investment Policies in the Late Nineties: What Effect on Trade?", *ASEAN Economic Bulletin,* Vol. 20, No. 3, pp. 256-271.

MINISTRY OF ECONOMY, TRADE AND INDUSTRY (1994), *Kaigai Jigyo Katsudo Kihon Chosa* (Comprehensive Survey of Overseas Activities of Japanese Firms), No. 5.

MINISTRY OF ECONOMY, TRADE AND INDUSTRY (2001), *Kaigai Jigyo Katsudo Kihon Chosa* (Comprehensive Survey of Overseas Activities of Japanese Firms), No. 7.

OECD (2002), *Foreign Direct Investment for Development: Maximising Benefits, Minimising Costs*, OECD, Paris.

PACIFIC ECONOMIC COOPERATION CONFERENCE (PECC) (1995). *1995 Survey of Impediments to Trade and Investment in the APEC Region*, Singapore, PECC.

PERKINS, D.H. and M. SYRQUIN (1989), "Large Countries: The Influence of Size", *in* H. CHENERY and T.N. SRINIVASAN (eds.), *Handbook of Development Economics*, Vol. 2, pp. 1691-1753, Elsevier Science Publishers, Amsterdam.

SMALL AND MEDIUM ENTERPRISE AGENCY OF THE JAPANESE GOVERNMENT (2004), *White Paper on Small and Medium Enterprises*, Government Printing Office, Tokyo, (in Japanese).

TAKEUCHI, J. (2004), "The Mechanism of Expanding Trade of Electronics Products in East Asia", *RIM*, Economics Department, Japan Research Institute, Vol. 4, No.13 (in Japanese), pp. 29-53.

UNITED NATIONS (2001), *World Investment Report 2001*, New York and Geneva.

UNITED NATIONS (2002), *World Investment Report 2002*, New York and Geneva.

URATA, S. (2001*a*), "Emergence of an FDI-Trade Nexus and Economic Growth in East Asia", *in* J. STIGLITZ and S. YUSUF (eds.), *Rethinking the East Asian Miracle*, pp. 409-459, World Bank, Washington, D.C., Oxford University Press, New York, NY.

URATA, S. (2001*b*), "Europe's Trade and Foreign Direct Investment in Asia", in V.K. AGGARWAL (ed.), *Winning in Asia, European Style: Market and Nonmarket Strategies for Success*, pp. 31-58, Palgrave, New York, NY.

URATA, S. (2002), "Engines of Globalization: Big and Small Multinational Enterprises in the Global Era", *in* KYUNG TAE LEE (ed.) *Globalization and the Asia Pacific Economy*, Routledge, London and New York, NY .

URATA, S. (2004) "Toward an East Asia Free Trade Area", *Policy Insight*, No.1, OECD, March, at http://www.oecd.org/dev/insights.

WORLD BANK (2003), *World Development Indicators*, World Bank, Washington, D.C .

WORLD BANK (2004), *World Development Indicators*, World Bank, Washington, D.C .

YUSUF, S. and S. EVENETT (2002), *Can East Asia Compete? Innovation for Global markets*, Oxford University Press, New York, NY.

ISBN 92-64-01442-X © OECD 2005

Chapter 10

Korea's Experience as an Asian Developing Economy and as a Newly Industrialised Asian Economy

Soogil Young

Abstract

Korea owes its economic success thus far to a strategy of export-led growth. It embarked on this strategy in a triangular trade with Japan and the United States. Over time, the industrial structure diversified rapidly and continuously toward higher-value-added heavy and chemical industries, and export markets expanded towards Europe, developing East Asia and, especially very recently, China. The strategy's success depended on the broadly liberal international economic order created by the developed countries after World War II. The GATT-sponsored multilateral trading system, the relatively liberal trade policies of the OECD countries, the international financial institutions and their support for developing countries' access to the international capital markets all made it possible. Encouraging FDI from the developed to the developing countries promotes industrial development in countries like Korea. Overseas direct investment (ODI) flows from Korea to developing East Asia relocated light manufacturing and facilitated diversification of Korea's exports to the region, contributing to industrialisation and export-led economic growth in the recipient countries. Structural adjustment in Korean industries prompted this ODI. In turn the liberalisation of trade and FDI policies as well as increases in production costs facilitated the adjustment.

The developed countries have not had entirely coherent policies in terms of their impact on Korea's economic development. The so-called new protectionism caused problems for Korea, and business and government responses to it contributed to changes in the economy. The international financial system stemming from developed-country financial policies has had structural flaws on the supply side of the capital markets, inducing institutional distortions and financial crises in countries like Korea. Korea has tried for some time to remove the resultant institutional distortions and structural vulnerabilities to crises through reforms and structural adjustment, groping for the right model. In its developmental process thus far, Korea has performed a "path explorer" role for other developing economies in East Asia. It will continue to do so as it goes through the rites of passage to become a newly developed country with mature institutions.

ISBN 92-64-01442-X

Introduction

The Republic of Korea joined the OECD as its 29th member in December 1996. This represented a remarkable accomplishment given that Korea was one of the least-developed countries even during the 1960s. In 1965, its GNP per capita barely reached $100, and it participated insignificantly in international trade. Politically, it lived under the authoritarian rule of Park Chung-Hee, a former general who took power by a coup in 1961. In contrast, by 1996 Korea had become a leading newly industrialised economy (NIE) with a GNP per capita of $11 000; it was the 13th largest economy and the 12th largest trader in the world. The economy had grown at an annual rate of 8 per cent on average during the preceding 35 years. It was emerging to join the global top players in many advanced industrial sectors such as steel, automobiles, shipbuilding, semi-conductors and electronics. Politically, democracy had been in full bloom since the late 1980s, and this too would not have been possible but for the rapid rise in living standards due to economic growth. Thus, within a single generation the growth of the economy, the transformation of industry and political and social development had been by any standard truly remarkable. In recognition of this achievement the members of the OECD invited Korea to join the Organisation as a full member and thus to contribute to the betterment of global economic governance.

It was then surprising, not to mention ironic, that in late 1997, barely a year after the country's accession to the OECD, Korea became engulfed in a currency crisis of unprecedented severity, as did Thailand and Indonesia a few months earlier. The country had to ask the IMF and the developed members of the OECD for a bailout. The contraction of the economy by 6.7 per cent in 1998 revealed the harshness of the crisis. Yet, equally surprising, economic recovery came quickly, in more or less three years from the onset of the crisis. By 2002, per capita GNP again surpassed $11 000 and the economy had regained its pre-crisis international relative size ranking. Moreover, the country had further strengthened its international competitiveness in many advanced industrial sectors including information technology (IT).

Korea has achieved rapid economic development through an active and sustained pursuit of export-led growth and industrialisation in an international economic environment broadly supportive of this strategy. It has needed open international markets for its manufactured products, open international capital markets for borrowing to finance expansion of productive capacity at home and foreign direct investment (FDI) from developed countries to promote rapid industrial development. All required Korea to integrate its

ISBN 92-64-01442-X © OECD 2005

economy continuously with those of the OECD countries. On the whole, the policies of the OECD countries have been favourable to these efforts, and Korea has made good use of them, albeit occasionally with what now appear to have been wrong policies.

In the pursuit of industrial development, Korea studied Japan's earlier and contemporary policy experiences carefully and copied many of them, sometimes to its own detriment. Korea regarded Japan as a *path explorer*, and Japan's policy experiences profoundly affected the evolution of Korea's development, trade and investment policies. East Asian developing countries on their part were eager to learn from Japan's *and* Korea's policy experience[1], watched and studied them carefully and drew lessons from them for their own economic and industrial development policies. These countries regarded the two as their most relevant path explorers, scrutinising Korea's policy successes and failures especially carefully because Korea was just ahead of them on the development path. Through its path-explorer role Korea has left deep impacts on the policies of Southeast Asia and China.

With continued industrial development, Korea needed to diversify its export markets toward the developing world. Moreover, in response to rises in production costs at home and in trade barriers in the advanced countries, an increasing number of Korean manufacturing firms had to move their plants to developing countries. For these reasons, and especially since the mid-1980s, Korea has increased exports to the developing world, especially to developing economies in East Asia, while also making overseas direct investment (ODI) in these economies. Through these actions Korea has joined the OECD countries in contributing to economic growth and industrialisation in the developing world, with the impact focused on East Asia.

This chapter first examines how Korea has integrated its economy with the OECD and developing worlds — and with developing economies in East Asia in particular — with a focus on the role of policies. It examines the aspects of Korea's experience that place the country in its path-explorer role for other developing economies of East Asia, i.e. those which seem to have influenced or to influence currently the development policies and paths of Southeast Asian countries and China. This examination reveals three important lessons from Korea's policy experience. The chapter then discusses the impact of OECD-country policies on Korea's economic growth and development performance under ten policy categories. Finally, it considers the impact of Korea's own policies on other East Asian economies, specifically its trade, investment and development assistance policies. A few broad observations conclude the study.

ISBN 92-64-01442-X

Three Lessons for Developing Economies from Korea's Development Experience

International Trade Is the Best Promoter of Economic Growth

That Korea did not participate actively in international trade until the early 1960s meant that it had remained by and large a closed economy. In 1962, its exports amounted to $55 million or 2.4 per cent of GNP and a minuscule percentage of world exports (Table 10.1). Owing to a large savings gap as well as chronic shortages of goods for domestic consumption, imports significantly exceeded exports, amounting to 18.5 per cent of GNP and 0.3 per cent of world imports and financed mostly by foreign aid. The small volume of exports reflected domestic production largely intended for sales in the narrow domestic market and for import substitution. Thus a vicious circle of low income and low production existed within the confines of the domestic market.

Table 10.1. **Korea's Merchandise Trade, 1962-2002**
($ million)

	Exports			Imports		
	Volume	Percentage of World Total	Percentage of GDP	Volume	Percentage of World Total	Percentage of GDP
1962	55	0.0	2.4	425	0.3	18.5
1972	1 624	0.4	15.3	2 522	0.6	23.8
1982	21 853	1.2	29.4	24 251	1.3	32.6
1992	76 632	2.0	24.4	81 775	2.1	26.0
2002	162 471	2.7	34.1	152 126	2.4	31.9

Source: Korea International Trade Association; IMF; Bank of Korea.

Under the new authoritarian leadership of President Park Chung-Hee, Korea shifted to a fresh economic strategy of export-led growth and launched an all-out effort to promote exports. It began a series of economic reforms, concentrated in the first several years of the 1960s, to develop and strengthen a system of incentives to export. The economy soon took off on a long-term path of high, export-led growth[2]. Various subsidies and assistance measures for exporters were created. During the 1960s virtually all economic reforms and the management of the economy were geared to export promotion. Exports began to increase rapidly. So did imports because export production required large imports of raw materials (natural resources) and intermediate goods, while sustained increases in exports required high levels of investment that in turn demanded heavy imports of capital goods. Korea's "export-led" growth

ISBN 92-64-01442-X © OECD 2005

has really been "trade-led" in this sense and, although the strategy has suffered occasional setbacks, Korea has been able to sustain its efficacy along the long-term growth trajectory.

During 1962-2002, the average annual rates of increase were 22 per cent for exports and 16 per cent for imports. By 2002, exports had grown to \$162 billion, 34 per cent of GNP and 2.7 per cent of the world total, while imports had climbed to \$152 billion, 32 per cent of GNP and 2.4 per cent of the world total. An average annual economic growth rate of 8 per cent over more than three decades testifies to the success of the strategy. The strategy has worked because it has allowed Korea to produce for the world market, thereby overcoming the limited size of the domestic market and reaping the economies of scale from mass production. It also has exploited the country's international comparative advantage by participating in international specialisation of production, making the most productive use of its only abundant resource, the labour force. Pursuit of these benefits put the country on the path of industrialisation, shifting the economy out of agriculture and fisheries into manufacturing and services, with light manufacturing as the leading sector. Producing for export has forced domestic producers to face international competition and try to learn and emulate global standards in manufacturing.

The rapid increase of exports has been led by manufactures (Table 10.2). Their share of total exports, 55 per cent in 1962, climbed to 88 per cent by 1972 and to 97 per cent by 2002. These numbers signify rapid industrialisation. Manufacturing output increased by 10 per cent annually on average and the share of the primary sector in GDP fell from 37 per cent in 1962 to 4 per cent in 2003. Thus, trade-led growth has been a process of trade-led industrialisation as well.

Table 10.2. **Composition of Korea's Exports, Imports and GDP, 1962-2002**
(percentages)

	Exports			Imports			GDP		
	Primary	Manufactures		Raw Materials	Capital Goods	Consumer Goods	Primary	Manu-facturing	Services
		Light	Heavy & Chemical						
1962	45.4	45.4	9.2				36.9	14.5	48.6
1972	12.1	66.6	21.3	51.5	29.9	18.6	27.0	22.3	50.8
1982	7.9	43.0	49.0	64.0	25.7	10.3	14.5	27.9	57.7
1992	4.2	32.9	62.9	52.5	37.9	9.2	7.4	28.7	63.8
2002	2.5	14.9	82.7	50.0	37.1	12.4	4.0	29.2	66.8

Source: Korea International Trade Association; Bank of Korea.

ISBN 92-64-01442-X © OECD 2005

Collectively, the OECD countries once were the main destination for Korea's exports. They accounted for 86 per cent of exports in 1971, but their combined share has decreased rather rapidly since the early 1990s, to below 50 per cent in recent years (Table 10.3). The export markets have diversified. The most important had been the United States and Japan until 2001, with the United States the largest by far. The two together took more than half of Korea's exports until the late 1980s. The European (EU) countries have come closely behind Japan since the early 1980s. In the late 1990s, Europe began to surpass Japan's falling share.

Table 10.3. **Direction of Korea's Trade, 1971-2002**

(per cent of total exports or imports)

Countries	Exports								
	1971	1980	1986	1989	1990	1997	1998	2000	2002
OECD countries	85.9	65.1	76.3	74.6	71.4	46.9	50.7	53.6	48.9
- USA	49.8	26.3	40.0	33.1	29.8	15.9	17.2	21.8	20.2
- Japan	24.5	17.4	15.6	21.6	19.4	10.8	9.2	11.9	9.3
- EU countries	8.1	16.7	13.4	13.2	15.4	12.4	13.7	13.6	13.4
Developing countries	14.1	34.9	23.7	25.4	28.6	53.1	49.3	46.4	51.1
- Middle East	0.9	14.6	6.5	3.7	4.0	3.7	5.0	4.4	4.6
- East Asia	7.8	12.5	10.1	14.7	16.7	35.7	32.8	33.3	36.3
Chinese Taipei	1.1	1.2	1.0	2.1	1.9	3.4	3.9	4.7	4.1
Hong Kong, China	3.8	4.7	4.9	5.4	5.8	8.6	7.0	6.2	6.2
China	0.0	0.1	0.4	0.7	0.9	8.8	10.3	10.7	14.6
ASEAN	2.8	6.5	3.9	6.5	8.0	15.0	11.6	11.7	11.3
- Other countries	5.4	7.8	7.1	7.0	7.9	13.6	11.5	8.8	10.3
Countries	**Imports**								
	1971	1980	1986	1989	1990	1997	1998	2000	2002
OECD countries	82.5	62.0	74.1	73.9	72.0	61.9	61.6	54.7	53.1
- USA	28.3	21.9	20.7	25.9	24.3	20.8	21.9	18.2	15.1
- Japan	39.8	26.3	34.4	28.4	26.6	19.3	18.1	19.8	19.6
- EU countries	10.7	7.6	11.4	11.5	13.0	13.1	11.7	9.8	11.2
Developing countries	17.5	38.0	25.9	26.1	28.0	38.1	38.4	45.3	46.9
- Middle East	6.4	26.0	7.9	7.5	8.9	11.9	12.2	16.1	13.7
- East Asia	9.5	8.6	11.2	12.7	13.5	18.0	19.1	23.0	26.7
Chinese Taipei	1.6	1.4	1.4	2.2	2.1	1.7	1.8	2.9	3.2
Hong Kong, China	0.8	0.4	1.3	0.9	0.9	0.6	0.6	0.8	1.1
China	0.0	0.1	2.0	2.3	3.2	7.0	7.0	8.0	11.4
ASEAN	7.0	6.7	6.6	6.8	7.3	8.7	9.8	11.3	11.0
- Other countries	1.6	3.3	6.7	5.9	5.6	8.2	7.1	6.2	6.4

Source: Korea International Trade Association.

ISBN 92-64-01442-X © OECD 2005

The combined share of the developing countries in Korea's exports has risen more or less steadily since the early 1970s. That of the non-Middle East developing countries increased rapidly from less than 10 per cent in the 1960s to more than 40 per cent in the mid-1990s. Most of this increase went to the East Asian economies — Hong Kong, China; China; Chinese Taipei and the ASEAN countries — where Korea's exports have increasingly concentrated. The combined share of developing East Asia climbed to 17 per cent by 1990, then increased sharply thereafter, because with normalisation of Korea-China relations in 1992 Korea's trade with China, especially its exports, began a steep rise. China's emergence as one of Korea's major export markets since the early 1990s has been remarkable. It became Korea's third-largest market after the United States and Japan in the late 1990s. In 2001 it overtook Japan in second place, and in 2003 it overtook the United States as Korea's largest market.

The composition of imports has not changed much since the early 1960s (Table 10.2). Raw materials (natural resources and intermediate goods) have always constituted the largest component, accounting for around half of the total. Capital goods accounted for less than 30 per cent, but since the early 1970s their share has remained between 30 per cent and 40 per cent. The share of consumer goods has held at around 10 per cent since the late 1970s. Thus huge industrial demand for raw materials and capital goods has kept the overall volume of imports large. The high propensity to export has required the importation of many raw materials. Trade statistics show that the average proportion of goods imported for export processing has risen steadily, from 30 per cent in the 1970s to 35 per cent in the 1980s and 1990s and to 43 per cent in the early 2000s.

In much the same way that the OECD countries provided Korea's main export markets during most of Korea's modern development history, they have also served as the main supplier of imports, especially capital goods for industrial investment and raw materials for export processing (Table 10.3). During the 1960s they collectively shipped more than 80 per cent of Korea's imports. Since then, that share has shown a decreasing trend, but it still stood at 53 per cent in 2002. Japan and the United States have been the two predominant import suppliers, with a combined share of more than 50 per cent until the early 1990s that decreased to 35 per cent by 2002. For most of the period, Japan has consistently remained the largest supplier of imports with the United States coming next, although in some years they exchanged places. The developing countries have increased their share in Korea's imports considerably. Developing East Asia has been a much larger supplier than the

ISBN 92-64-01442-X © OECD 2005

Middle East, and its import share has increased *pari passu* with its share in Korea's exports. China in particular has rapidly boosted its share. It caught up with the ASEAN countries in 2002.

Exports never exceeded imports in value until 1985. Reflecting a persistent savings gap at home, Korea ran deficits on the current account, which mostly reflected trade deficits, until 1986[3] (Appendix Table 10A.1). The Plaza Agreement in September 1985 led to a huge appreciation of the Japanese yen relative to the dollar and other currencies including the Korean won. Thanks largely to it as well as to the strengthening of the international competitiveness of domestic industries during the preceding few years, Korea began to record trade surpluses in 1986. This brought the current account into surplus too the next year, while the economic growth rate soared above 10 per cent. These surpluses were very large, close to 10 per cent of GDP during 1987-89. The trade deficit re-emerged in 1990 and continued until 1997, the year of the financial crisis, except in 1993. Since 1998 Korea has once again recorded trade surpluses. The shift of the trade account into surplus in the late 1980s while the economic growth rate remained high was a historic development. It signified that Korea had come to "graduate" from the status of a chronic trade-deficit country, considered both domestically and internationally as the mark of a "poor developing" country. For this reason, the trade-balance shift served to trigger a fundamental review of the broad range of the country's economic and social policies as well as its external economic policy stance. The analysis will elaborate this point later in the chapter.

Protection of Domestic Industries Can Be Costly

The evolution of the structure of Korea's exports also indicates that the industrial structure at home has grown rapidly in capital and technology intensity. As between light-industry and heavy and chemical industry products, the share of the latter in all exports has increased rapidly and steadily, from 9 per cent in 1962 to 21 per cent in 1972 and then to 49 per cent in 1982, and so on (Table 10.2). The share of light manufactures fell just as rapidly. These trends indicate a rapid shift toward heavy and chemical industries in the economy. Even more dramatically, while Korea was well known internationally in the late 1960s and 1970s as an exporter of plywood, shoes, textiles and clothing, it emerged in the 1990s as a leading exporter of steel, automobiles, ships, semi-conductors and electronic products, among others. This rapid industrial transformation would not likely have occurred to such

ISBN 92-64-01442-X © OECD 2005

a dramatic extent but for the so-called heavy and chemical industries (HCI) campaign that Korea undertook during the 1970s under President Park's relentless drive.

A distinct characteristic of Korea's export-promotion campaign in the 1960s was that it involved no sector-specific incentives. The HCI drive in the 1970s (1973-79) differed starkly in that it specifically targeted six strategic industries – petrochemicals, non-ferrous metals, steel, the electrical industries, industrial machinery and shipbuilding – collectively identified as "heavy and chemical industries"[4]. The HCI programme was the epitome of Korea's so-called compressed development efforts. It aimed to raise the share of the HCI sector in manufacturing value added from 36 per cent in 1970 to above 50 per cent by 1980 and to make those industries Korea's new export leaders. It offered highly selective subsidies and support, not only to the targeted industries but also to participating firms. The government in effect began nurturing national-champion firms. President Park personally directed and supervised this governmental campaign, supported by an inter-Ministerial Committee for Promotion of Heavy and Chemical Industries chaired by the Prime Minister. The programme offered a broad array of generous policy measures including virtually unlimited supplies of so-called directed financing, generous tax subsidies and protection from competing imports and foreign investors[5].

A number of concerns motivated the HCI campaign, chiefly worries over the prospects for continued economic growth led by exports of light manufactures[6]. First, these exports were encumbered by many trade barriers in the developed countries, such as MFAs on textiles and clothing, and the new protectionism was rising in the form of discriminatory barriers against light manufactures as the number of developing exporters kept growing. Second, the terms of trade for exports of light manufactures were deteriorating. With continuing growth in the global volume of such exports, their prices were falling relative to those for the intermediate and capital goods Korea imported. This pointed to the need to move up along the value chain in industrial production toward products with higher value added. Third, Korea depended heavily on Japan for the supply of high value-added intermediate and capital goods and as a result ran large and persistent trade deficits with Japan. These bilateral deficits were considered undesirable. All these concerns gave rise to the political determination to "upgrade" the industrial structure toward HCI. The strategy was to seek "dynamic" instead of "static" comparative advantage.

ISBN 92-64-01442-X

The HCI policies more or less achieved the targeted goal of raising the share of HCI to 50 per cent or above in both manufacturing and exports. In retrospect, the 1990s certainly would not have seen the emergence of some Korean firms of global ambition in several advanced industrial sectors if no such industry-promotion campaign had existed in the 1970s. Even to this day, however, Korea's HCI campaign of the 1970s remains controversial because it was very costly to the economy. For one thing, in confluence with other adverse developments, it was an important factor underlying the economic crisis Korea was driven into in the late 1970s and early 1980s.

The campaign resulted by the late 1970s in huge excess capacities in the targeted industries, and it failed to bring international competitiveness to them at least until the mid-1980s. The new HCI industries generally became non-performing. For example, the capacity-use ratio in the machinery and metal industries as a whole never exceeded 62 per cent during 1976-80. Given the high energy intensities of these industries as well as the heavy foreign indebtedness incurred under the HCI campaign, the combined impact on the economy of the second oil shock, the consequent global economic slowdown and a rise in international interest rates was especially severe and lasting. Affected as well by political turmoil consequent upon the assassination of President Park (1979) and a bad harvest of unprecedented severity (1980), the Korean economy went into a prolonged crisis[7].

Other than helping to bring this prolonged crisis to the Korean economy, the HCI policies had other, perhaps even costlier and lasting consequences. Most critically, the HCI campaign led to the institutionalisation of heavy government and bureaucratic intervention in the Korean market system. It stymied the development of Korea's financial system by institutionalising a government-directed banking system. The national-champions policy also led to the emergence of Korea's unique business conglomerates, the *chaebol*, as a dominant feature of the economy; they came to control Korea's major advanced industries. The consequent oligopolistic competition became fierce and encouraged excessive and risky investments. The growth of the *chaebol* suppressed that of small and medium enterprises (SMEs). On the whole, the HCI drive weakened rather than strengthened the foundations of the sound market system that the Korean economy was supposed to nurture along its development path. It made the problem of moral hazard prevalent throughout the economy, and it served as the hotbed for opaqueness in both policies and business practices as well as for corruption involving politicians and big businesses[8]. The authoritarian rule of the *chaebol* by their "owners", favouritism toward big businesses in the government's policies and practices (including labour policies) and a prevalent culture of opaqueness and

ISBN 92-64-01442-X © OECD 2005

corruption all took root. Resentment of workers over all this in turn contributed to the emergence of militant labour unions and an inflexible labour market in the late 1980s.

Subsequent administrations tried to grapple with various manifestations of all these institutional distortions of the market system, but some of them have persisted without being addressed effectively. They came to roost in the late 1990s as the underlying structural causes of Korea's financial crisis of 1997-98. They did so by creating the "too big to fail" myth under which the *chaebol* built sprawling empires of diverse and risky businesses on excessive debt, while the banking system subserviently financed them. Under adverse developments at home and abroad, including labour's excessive push for wage increases, a number of *chaebol* went bankrupt in 1997, eroding international lenders' confidence in the Korean economy and eventually triggering massive capital flight toward the end of the year[9].

Although Korea made a swift recovery from the crisis during 1999-2000 by undertaking many economic reforms and structural adjustments, a few serious legacies of the HCI drive still haunt the economy. Owing to incomplete structural adjustment the profitability of many big businesses continues to remain much too low to ensure their sustainability. Serious corporate-governance problems continue to persist in a number of conglomerates, causing under-valuation of corporate stocks and continuing to present risks of economic instability. The economy's dependence on conglomerates for exports and growth continues to grow while SMEs remain depressed. In response, the government struggles to strengthen its regulation of the conglomerates while their resistance intensifies. As a result, finding the appropriate market order remains an unresolved issue. The consequent frictions between the two have been politically divisive and create serious uncertainties for big business, discouraging investment. The militancy of the labour unions in the conglomerates also continues not much diminished, as does labour-market rigidity. Despite much progress in reforming and restructuring the banking sector, including the withdrawal of government intervention, restructuring of the non-bank financial sector has yet to take place, and there have been instances of major government bailouts.

On the whole, Korea's economic reforms remain incomplete as does economic restructuring, and this poses lingering uncertainties for the economy. The spectre of the HCI drive lurks in the background of the current economic fragility, and new factors also at work reinforce these uncertainties[10]. The future of the economy depends critically on how effectively Korea will address the persisting legacies of the HCI drive.

FDI and ODI by Comparative Advantage Hold the Key to Industrial Catch-up

FDI played a minor role in Korea's industrialisation until the mid-1990s. Very small inflows began to increase to substantial amounts only in the late 1990s (Appendix Table 10A.2). They also remained meagre relative to total fixed capital formation until the financial crisis (Table 10.4). At the end of 2001, the stock of FDI outstanding in Korea had risen to 9.5 per cent as large as the GDP[11], much higher than in Japan (1.1 per cent) but far lower than the world average (17 per cent).

Table 10.4. **FDI Inflows, Arrival Basis, 1962-2001**

(amounts in $ million; shares in per cent)

	FDI (A)	Loans (B)			Capital Formation (C)	Capital Inflow (D=A+B)	FDI as share of		
		Public	Commercial	Total	Gross		Total Loans (A/B)	Gross Capital Formation (A/C)	Capital Inflow (A/D)
1962-66	17	116	176	292	2 713	309	5.8	0.6	5.5
1967-71	96	811	1 355	2 166	9 069	2 262	4.4	1.3	4.2
1972-76	557	2 389	3 043	5 432	24 664	5 983	10.3	2.3	9.3
1977-81	1 666	5 751	7 381	13 132	88 872	14 798	12.7	1.9	11.3
1982-86	1 040	6 690	5 329	12 019	127 360	13 059	8.7	0.6	8.0
1987-91	4 404	3 319	3 436	6 755	379 308	11 159	65.2	1.2	39.5
1992-96	6 188	2 498	297	2 795	723 769	8 983	221.4	0.9	68.9
1997-2001	34 072	15 559	15 377	30 936	526 463	65 008	110.1	6.5	52.4
1962-86	3 376	15 757	17 284	33 041	252 678	36 411	10.9	0.6	9.3
1987-2001	44 664	21 376	19 110	40 486	1 629 540	85 150	135.2	17.7	52.5

Sources: SaKong (1993), Table 5,6, p.117; National Statistical Office, 1994, 1997, and 2002. *Major Statistics of Korean Economy.*

Of the total FDI realised during 1962-98, 59 per cent went to manufacturing and 39 per cent to services. FDI in agriculture, fishery and mining has been marginal (June-dong Kim, 1999). The average share of manufacturing in annual FDI inflows fell to 43 per cent during 1998-2002 while that of services rose to the same extent, reflecting increased FDI especially in financial services since the financial crisis.

The OECD countries have always been the main source of FDI in Korea (Table 10.5). Until the late 1980s, Japan was by far the largest source; it accounted for 50 per cent of all realised FDI. Next came the United States with 28 per cent of the total. The European countries' share was 13 per cent.

ISBN 92-64-01442-X © OECD 2005

Hong Kong, China's 3 per cent seems largely to have consisted of investments by the subsidiaries of multinational firms based in the OECD countries. Since the mid-1990s and especially after the financial crisis, however, the rankings have reversed dramatically. The European countries have become the largest source of FDI in Korea, claiming 46 per cent of the total over the entire period 1962-2004. The Netherlands, France and Germany lead in this group. The United States comes next with 24 per cent. It has overtaken Japan, whose share fell to 18 per cent for the whole period.

Table 10.5. **FDI[a] by Region and Country, 1962-2004[b]**

($ million; per cent of total)

	Amount		Percentage	
OECD countries	38 349	(4 760)	89.2	(91.7)
- USA	10 163	(1 467)	23.6	(28.3)
- Japan	7 582	(2 607)	17.6	(50.2)
- EU countries	19 590	(672)	45.6	(12.9)
- Others[c]	1 014	(14)	2.4	(0.3)
Developing countries	4 393	(332)	10.2	(6.4)
- Middle East	82	(42)	0.2	(0.8)
- East Asia	1 936	(177)	4.5	(3.4)
Hong Kong, China	692	(157)	1.6	(3.0)
Singapore	1 142	(17)	2.7	(0.4)
Chinese Taipei	102	(3)	0.2	(0.0)
- Others[d]	2 375	(113)	5.5	(2.2)
International organisations	256	(100)	0.6	(1.9)
- ADB	8	(8)	0.0	(0.2)
- IFC	248	(92)	0.6	(1.8)
Total	42 998	(5 192)	100.0	(100.0)

Notes: *a)* Inflows on the arrival basis.

b) Until May 2004. The figures in parentheses (…) are values for 1962-1990 (Feb.), taken from Won-Young Lee (1990).

c) Canada, Australia and New Zealand.

d) Mostly Panama, the Bahamas, Bermuda and Cayman Islands.

Source: Korean Ministry of Commerce, Industry and Energy.

The limited FDI inflows up to the early 1980s reflected the intended effect of the government's policy to restrict FDI. A major component of the HCI policies of the 1970s, this policy tried to protect would-be national champions in the technology-intensive industries from foreign competition. It went hand in hand with a restrictive trade policy toward imports of HCI products. FDI needed government approval, and that was given only when it would pose no competition for national firms and, subject to restrictions,

ISBN 92-64-01442-X © OECD 2005

would ensure transfer of advanced foreign technology[12]. The problematic consequences and legacies of the HCI drive already observed, however, demonstrate the inefficacy of such an FDI policy as well the protectionist import policy.

This is not to say that FDI played no role in Korea's industrial development. On the contrary, there was strategic inducement of FDI in the 1960s and 1970s, and much of the industrial catch-up at that time derived from it. Many foreign multinationals were brought in as partners for joint ventures or under technology-licensing agreements in the start-up phase of new strategic sectors such as electronics, automobiles, machinery and chemicals. They played the critical role of transferring the core technologies necessary for launching new industries (Lee, 1990). The problem was that foreign investors were not allowed to play the broader roles of putting competitive pressure on their domestic counterparts or of launching and developing new industries in Korea on their own to accelerate the diffusion of advanced technologies. FDI could have played a much larger role, which might have generated more effective and more efficient industrial catch-up.

As noted earlier, the Korean economy was driven into a major crisis in the late 1970s and the early 1980s in part as a result of the HCI drive. In response to this crisis, even taking advantage of it, the government tried to shift from its strategy of protecting domestic businesses from international competition to one of exposing them to it. The government undertook measures to nurture the market mechanism by focusing on macroeconomic stabilisation, encouraging science and technology and introducing competition policies. An important component of this policy shift was the adoption of new FDI and import policies in the 1980s. Together with specific measures to "rationalise" existing investments in HCI, the new competition strategy helped forcefully to promote restructuring in those industries as well as inefficiency-shedding managerial reforms, including greater focus on R&D within firms. Thanks in part to these reforms and in part to the large depreciation of the won in 1985 consequent upon the Plaza Agreement, many HCI products began to acquire competitiveness in the international market and make HCI viable. The key to this seems to have been exposure to competition from imports and foreign multinationals or the threat of it.

Korea thus began to liberalise both FDI and imports in the early 1980s. It pursued the reforms in steps over more than ten years. In quantitative terms, however, FDI did not much respond until the 1997-98 financial crisis. The domestic environment, such as wages and other production costs as well as various regulations including prohibitive restrictions on M&As,

ISBN 92-64-01442-X © OECD 2005

remained rather hostile to FDI. Government incentives to FDI had limited impact. A big spurt of FDI did not occur until Korea opened completely the domestic product, financial and capital markets, including liberalisation of hostile M&As, in response to the 1997-98 financial crisis and as part of the IMF-guided structural adjustment programme.

Korean overseas direct investment (ODI) began in 1968, but remained much smaller than FDI into Korea, indeed insignificant, until the mid-1980s (Appendix Table 10A.2). It increased rapidly thereafter, especially after 1987, the first year of current-account surplus, and during the 1990s until the crisis year 1997 it considerably exceeded FDI almost every year. As long as the current account remained chronically in deficit, ODI had been seen as a capital outflow draining scarce foreign reserves. The government discouraged and restricted it, except for two purposes[13] (Appendix Table 10A.3). One was to secure a stable supply of natural resources. ODI for forestry development in Southeast Asia and in petrochemical plants in the Middle East came under this category. The other was to facilitate exports by setting up trading subsidiaries, mostly in the United States and Japan. Korea also participated in the Middle Eastern construction boom of the 1970s. The exit from chronic trade deficits in the late 1980s removed the balance-of-payments constraint on ODI, and fundamental changes in the domestic and international environments prompted the government actively to encourage it.

First, the current-account improvement followed an export boom of unprecedented strength that triggered extraordinary growth dynamism in the economy. The boom also coincided with sudden political democratisation[14]. As a result, wages began to rise fast and industrial relations rather suddenly turned very unstable, while other production costs including land prices also began to rise steeply. In consequence, relatively labour-intensive manufacturing operations experienced sudden, large losses of international competitiveness, and many SMEs began relocating, or wanted to relocate, their production sites offshore to Southeast and South Asia, where labour and other resource costs were much lower. Second, the shift in the current account brought pressures from the United States and other OECD countries for Korea to relinquish its "developing country" policy legacies, to "graduate" from protecting domestic industries from foreign competition and to "adjust away" the current-account surplus by appreciating the currency. These pressures and Korea's resistance to them entailed many trade disputes. Korean exporters faced an increasing threat of protectionist measures in the industrial-country markets, in the form of anti-dumping actions and other retaliatory measures against their products of competitive strength[15].

Three new motives thus led the acceleration of ODI in the late 1980s and especially in the 1990s. A resource-seeking motive prompted the relocation of light industry to Southeast and South Asia in order to preserve competitive advantage based on low-cost local labour and land. A market-preservation motive pushed the establishment of production subsidiaries in sectors like electronics behind protectionist border barriers being set up against Korean products in the industrial countries. Still another new motive stimulated firms to seek strategic assets such as technological capability by investing in research-intensive operations in industrial clusters in the United States and other industrial countries. Government policy actively supported ODI of all three types with a strong push. Beginning in the late 1980s, the government took a series of measures to liberalise ODI over time, and it offered financial and tax incentives to Korean overseas investors.

The resource-seeking motive led Korean firms, mainly SMEs, to move their production plants to Asia, East Asia in particular. These investments facilitated structural adjustment in domestic industries losing competitive advantage. The host countries welcomed them, because most of these countries had adopted their own export-led growth strategies in the early 1980s, and the investments helped the host countries to embark on their own industrialisation.

A major characteristic of Korean ODI, especially in the late 1980s and early 1990s, involved heavy flows to the United States and other OECD countries (Table 10.6) relative to comparable newly industrialised economies such as Chinese Taipei (Nicolas, 2001). The *chaebol* led these outflows, and the government encouraged them. Market preservation and the search for strategic assets motivated them. Nicolas (2001) argues that in many cases Korean ODI in advanced countries cannot be seen as systematically based on any strong Korean ownership advantage. Sachwald (2001*b*) argues that in these cases a combination of protectionist threats abroad and oligopolistic rivalry at home has pushed the *chaebol* to venture into risky projects. As a result, they often have gone abroad prematurely, before building sufficiently strong advantages to cope with the intense competition in leading markets — although asset-seeking ODI aimed at creating stronger competitive advantages seems to have been quite successful in some cases. On the whole, however, the *chaebol* have tended towards over-ambition by attempting to diversify and upgrade simultaneously.

ISBN 92-64-01442-X © OECD 2005

Table 10.6. **Destination of Korean ODI by Region, 1968-97**
(percentages)

	1968-80	1981-90	1991-97
Asia	37.7	24.7	44.7
North America	23.9	44.8	27.5
Europe	4.1	4.3	15.6
Oceania	1.0	6.7	1.6
Middle East	14.3	10.7	2.3
Latin America	3.1	4.3	3.1
Africa	16.0	1.5	2.2
Total	100.0	100.0	100.0

Source: Nicolas (2001).

Sachwald (2001*b*) goes on to argue that Korea's large ODI flows to the OECD countries represented ambitious globalisation strategies and constituted an underlying cause of the 1997-98 financial crisis. The immediate cause of the crisis was financial, but the unsustainable indebtedness of the *chaebol* was rooted in their over-ambitious growth strategies. These strategies resulted in excessive investment both at home and abroad, in both equipment and R&D. The investments were often particularly risky. The financial crisis brought disruption to such *chaebol* globalisation strategies and has forced the restructuring of the *chaebol* themselves. Although it is still too early to foresee the ultimate outcome of this adjustment process, a new trend has emerged in a clear shift in the direction of ODI in the years since the crisis. East Asia, and China in particular, have emerged as the largest recipients of Korean ODI, with a rush of Korean firms both small and big to this region, apparently in search of both resources and markets.

Jacquet (2001) has had the insight that Korean ODI in the OECD countries and FDI at home have somehow acted as substitutes for each other in bringing technological and management capabilities. FDI brings in foreign competition, while ODI exposes domestic companies to foreign competition abroad and therefore provides a powerful learning mechanism likely to affect the way the domestic economy works. This limited the Korean approach. Despite its undeniable benefits, ODI had the shortcoming of preserving the oligopolistic structure of the *chaebol*-based domestic economy. It may have helped the *chaebol* to acquire technological and management assets, but the lack of domestic competition, compounded by restrictive policy toward FDI, acted as a barrier to diffusion of these benefits. By investing abroad, the *chaebol* became bigger rather than more efficient and innovative.

ISBN 92-64-01442-X © OECD 2005

This line of analysis implies that more technology transfer flowing into the country but outside the *chaebol* would be congruent with the necessary evolution of the national system of innovation. The system would be stronger if technological capabilities were more widely distributed among companies and institutions. This would depend both on stronger basic research capabilities and on a more competitive environment, including both foreign competitors and healthy smaller firms. In the quest for industrial catch-up, protection of national firms from foreign competition at home and promotion of their ODI into the industrial countries seems to have been a poor substitute for liberalisation and promotion of FDI. At the same time, the liberalisation and promotion of resource-seeking ODI in the face of shifts in comparative advantage is not something to be avoided, but an appropriate way of facilitating necessary industrial adjustment at home.

The Impact of OECD-Country Policies on Korea's Economic Development

Multilateral Trade Policies

Korea has achieved in one generation a remarkable transformation from a poor agrarian country to a leading newly industrialised one. Before it began this transformation it had virtually nothing but a relatively abundant labour force, but it has required not just the labour force but also capital, technology, and an open international market for Korea to launch and continue the transformation. Korea secured all these from the OECD countries through the international economic system, the most critical constituent of which, from Korea's standpoint, was the multilateral trading system.

This system, in turn, has been founded on the commitment of the developed countries to the GATT principles of non-discriminatory and liberal trade policies. These principles were not implemented in full by the developed countries. As will be argued below, many sectors and products remained subject to egregious and discriminatory trade barriers. Korean exporters were constantly concerned with threats of new trade barriers abroad. In retrospect, however, the trading system was sufficiently open to allow Korea relatively liberal access to the vast domestic markets of the United States and other OECD countries, which allowed the export-led growth strategy to work. The successive rounds of multilateral trade negotiations preserved the efficacy of this strategy.

ISBN 92-64-01442-X © OECD 2005

Japan's Trade and Investment Policies

After the normalisation of political relations between Korea and Japan in the early 1960s, their business communities rapidly developed close co-operation. Geographical and cultural proximity, together with mutual similarities and familiarities, facilitated this collaboration. Furthermore, Korea considered Japan, based on its economic success, as a model to benchmark as well as a rival to catch up with. Korea made persistent efforts to learn from and even imitate Japan, particularly in industrial and trade policies. Japan's trade and industrial policies left an indelible impact on Korea's own. Japan was the source of the inspiration for the export-led growth strategy. Many policies constituting the HCI drive in the 1970s were adaptations of what the Korean government thought had been Japan's trade and industrial policies. With some justification, many observers called Korea a "second Japan" during those years.

Whether the industrial and trade policies of the 1970s so heavily influenced by Japan's earlier policies have been beneficial to the Korean economy as a whole is a moot issue. Similar policies have not had the same outcomes. Korea certainly has not successfully caught up with Japan in terms of closing industrial technology gaps and eliminating the bilateral trade deficits. Japan's experience with the heavy and chemical industries spanned a much longer period, dating back as far as the Meiji era. Korea, however, very much compressed the whole industrialisation process in time, over 20 to 30 years at most depending on how the chronology is written.

More significantly, from Korea's perspective Japan was a moving target. Korea began the catching-up process at the stage of labour-intensive light manufacturing, subsequently moving into the downstream stage of HCI, replacing Japan as supplier of an increasing number of downstream products, and moving upstream along the industry chains over time. In the meantime, Japan moved further upward by advancing its product frontier in terms of technology and knowledge-intensity through R&D and innovation. As a result, Korea's dependence on Japan for the supply of upstream intermediate and capital goods has persisted, and so have Korea's trade deficits with Japan. The parallel industrial development of Korea and Japan, with Japan ahead, constituted part of the East Asia-wide development process described as the "flying-geese" model. An important component of the dynamic relationship between the two countries involved continuing transfers of technology and knowledge from Japan to Korea. They took place through imports from Japan, Japanese investment in Korea, business contacts and technical consulting. On the whole, then, Korea has benefited from Japan's industrial development.

ISBN 92-64-01442-X

Korea began to explore its own industrialisation path in the early 1980s, parting company with Japan by pursuing liberalisation as well as opening the domestic economy after the economic crisis in the late 1970s and the early 1980s. Progress in this direction has been steady but gradual. An even more decisive push arose from the crisis of 1997-98, which forced Korea to open thoroughly its domestic financial, capital and product markets, as well as the market for corporate control, while reforming the banking and the corporate sectors. This amounted to a major shift to the "neo-liberal" economic model, and one upshot has been the shedding of the old Japanese model in Korea.

Special and Differential Treatment of Developing Countries

In the earlier years, there was an important asymmetry in OECD countries' trade policies toward Korea and other developing countries. Especially until the mid-1980s, the developed members of the GATT maintained relatively open and non-discriminatory trade policies toward the developing countries but did not require the same of those countries, under the GATT Article XVIII provision for special and differential treatment (S&D) of the developing countries. Under this provision, the OECD countries essentially refrained from imposing the requirement of reciprocity on the developing countries and allowed them to maintain high import barriers, including quantitative restrictions. The developing countries thus enjoyed a considerable degree of trade-policy autonomy. One may argue that in this way S&D played the role of reinforcing the presumption that it was in the interest of the developing countries to maintain restrictive import policies. Korea joined the GATT in 1967 but did not have to participate actively in the GATT rounds of trade negotiations until the Uruguay Round. Under S&D, Korea could maintain a rather broad array of high import barriers, including various quantitative restrictions, while also enjoying access to the relatively open markets in the developed countries. Such barriers supported the HCI drive.

Korea's own experience[16] shows that a developing country may employ restrictive import policies to its own benefit during the early phase of its economic and industrial development, so there seems to be some economic justification for S&D from this perspective. Yet the S&D provision under Article XVIII failed to impose or spell out the conditions under which S&D should be applied — conditions such as transparency, limitation on the scope of its application, time-boundedness, etc. Without such qualifications, S&D tended to deprive the developing countries' trade policies of discipline and encouraged their abuse of trade barriers to their own detriment. Korea's import

ISBN 92-64-01442-X © OECD 2005

policies of the 1970s, in fact, suffered from such a problem, and in the end they came to undermine the international competitiveness of Korean industries (Young, 1982; Young and Yoo, 1982).

The New Protectionism: Discriminatory Trade Barriers

The developing countries did not in any case enjoy S&D treatment free of "costs" to them. It had the effect of weakening the discipline on developed countries' trade policies toward the developing countries, encouraging them to erect discriminatory informal trade barriers, outside the GATT system, against products from developing countries, especially the labour-intensive light manufactures in which they were competitive. This development earned the name, "new protectionism". Bilateral import restrictions such as the so-called voluntary export restraints (VERs) and other bilateral quota agreements sprang up. The new protectionism was already prevalent in the early 1970s, and it came to affect Korea's economic policies too. It was one of the factors that made the Korean government realise the limits of growth led by exports of light manufactured goods and pursue dynamic comparative advantage through the HCI policies[17].

The new protectionism or rather the need to attack it gave rise to a major case for launching a new GATT round of multilateral trade negotiations in the early 1980s. In the event, the Uruguay Round launched in 1986 produced a successful conclusion, including agreements to undo many of the developed-country trade measures associated with the new protectionism.

The Graduation Argument for NIEs and the US "Super 301"

The emergence of a group of developing countries that had successfully launched the industrialisation process by the late 1970s led the OECD to coin the phrase "Newly Industrialising Economies" (NIEs). Discussions of the NIEs' status in the international economic order produced the argument that they should graduate from S&D, both for their own economic good and for the health of the international trading system. This argument was formally incorporated into the so-called Enabling Clause, formally titled "Differential and More Favourable Treatment, Reciprocity and Fuller Participation of Developing Countries", that was adopted in 1979 by the GATT Contracting Parties.

ISBN 92-64-01442-X © OECD 2005

The developed countries used this argument so formalised as the basis for exerting political pressure on the NIEs to remove their restrictive trade practices unilaterally or reciprocally. Korea was, of course, a leading NIE. The United States in particular began in the early 1980s to press Korea to open its domestic markets to US products on the basis of this argument. This pressure created bilateral tensions as Korea tried to resist it. It became much more forceful once Korea's current account began to record surpluses in 1987. Armed with the so-called "Super 301", a trade law that mandates retaliation for "unfair" trade practices by trade partners, the US administration began to push Korea to take steps to remove all existing barriers against US products and to appreciate the Korean currency (Bayard and Young, 1989). A series of bilateral trade negotiations led to agreements under which Korea began to remove essentially all existing import barriers against US agricultural and industrial products as well as to "graduate" from the provisions of GATT Article XVIII under which, citing balance-of-payments needs, Korea had maintained various import restrictions on foreign agricultural products.

Thus under pressure from the United States Korea launched and implemented a series of broad import-liberalisation measures in the late 1980s and throughout the 1990s. This was unilateral action in the sense that Korea's trade partners undertook no reciprocal measures, and it was not Korea's first experience with unilateral trade liberalisation. As part of the economic reform implemented in response to the apparent failure of the HCI policies, Korea had undertaken pre-announced, multi-year programmes of removing import restrictions and cutting tariffs beginning in the early 1980s and lasting until the early 1990s[18]. These were major unilateral measures but exempted most agricultural products. The agreements with the United States addressed the remaining tariffs and non-tariff measures on many agricultural products of interest to the United States, with emphasis on non-tariff measures. All these unilateral trade liberalisation measures enabled Korea to take an active and forthcoming part in the Uruguay Round negotiations. Through the Uruguay Round, Korea completed its graduation from S&D, except in regard to a number of agricultural products (rice in particular) on which Korea has maintained relatively very high tariffs by claiming the status of a developing country.

The trade agreements with the United States were politically very controversial in Korea during their negotiation, and because the United States pushed them with threats of retaliatory measures they gave rise to much anti-American sentiment among the Korean public, especially farmers. To overcome domestic opposition to trade liberalisation and to dispel the undue anti-American sentiment, the Korean government undertook public education

ISBN 92-64-01442-X © OECD 2005

campaigns on the benefits of market opening, even establishing a Presidential Commission on Economic Restructuring[19] modelled after Japan's *Maekawa* Commission. In retrospect, as the Presidential Commission foresaw, the subsequent trade liberalisation measures made a forceful contribution to modernising the Korean economy, making it more efficient and resilient. Without them the Korean economy would not have become as modern and efficient as it is today. Korea would not enjoy as much access to foreign markets for its goods and services as it now has, and, deprived of much consumer surplus, Korean households' real income would not be as high as it now is.

It is often argued that governments should make use of foreign pressure or *gaiatsu* to overcome domestic interest groups' resistance to reforms. Korea's experience with US pressure for market opening shows that this approach can be costly, the cost in this case being the undermining of the domestic support for strong Korea-US relations. The public education campaign that the Korean government undertook on the benefits of market opening, including the launching of the Presidential Committee, attempted to internalise the *gaiatsu* and to minimise its political costs. It had considerable success.

Foreign Aid from the United States[20]

Korea received more than 70 per cent of its foreign aid between 1945 and 1960. This period consisted of three sub-periods: the period of political chaos that followed Korea's liberation (1945) from Japan's occupation, the Korean war period (1950-53) and the subsequent post-war reconstruction period. Foreign aid provided the main means of financing the balance of payments deficits and in fact was nearly the sole source of foreign capital throughout this period. Without the aid, Korea would not have been able to import many vitally needed commodities for basic livelihood and post-war reconstruction. Inflationary pressures would have been far more serious. Foreign aid kept Korea afloat economically and politically. The United States was by far its main source[21].

In the late 1950s, the flow of US aid began to diminish, and in 1961 the United States formally decided to shift to providing developmental loans rather than grants to help Korea economically. The diminishing volume of aid together with this policy change gave rise to the realisation by the Korean government and people that Korea could not go on indefinitely relying on foreign aid for its economic survival. Korea was thus compelled to find means of self-support, and it found them in exports. In fact, this was the only means available, so the Korean government shifted to the export-led growth strategy and began building export capacity vigorously. Politically, this involved transfer of political leadership from civilian governments to a military government through a military *coup d'état* in 1961. The civilian governments had not effectively coped with national poverty and with responding to the cessation of foreign aid. General Park Chung-Hee saw justification for his coup in the economic stalemate and committed his political leadership to economic development based on the outward-oriented development strategy. Dwindling foreign aid played a catalytic role in this transition to a new development regime.

The first five years, 1962-66, served as a transition period during which Korea shifted from dependence on grants to foreign borrowing to finance imports. Reform measures included among others the legislation of the Foreign Capital Inducement Law of 1966. Despite popular protests fired by the anti-Japanese sentiment that stemmed from the memory of Japan's colonial occupation of the country (1910-45), the military government also forced normalisation of diplomatic relations with Japan in 1965. It wished to make room for active capital inflows from Japan, including an inflow of reparation payments for the colonial occupation. In these ways, Korea transformed itself from a passive aid recipient to an active participant in the international financial markets.

The Plaza Agreement and Key Currency Alignment

The impact of the Plaza Agreement of September 1985 on the Korean economy shows dramatically how extensively the pattern of alignment of the G-3 currencies can affect a highly trade-dependent economy like Korea's. The Korean won fell with the US dollar against the Japanese yen, experiencing a real depreciation of 35 per cent in 1986-87 (Nam and Kim, 1995). Reinforced by concurrent declines in international interest rates and oil prices, this caused Korea's exports to jump by 31 per cent a year during 1986-88. The economy grew at a double-digit rate for three consecutive years, and the current account shifted from chronic deficits into large surpluses for the first time in Korea's modern history. Thanks to this boom, the economy emerged from the fragility that had plagued it since the late 1970s. Unemployment fell to a historic low of around 2.5 per cent. The economy finally reached essentially full employment.

The "three lows" (the currency, international interest rates and oil prices) thus quickly freed Korea from its long-held obsessions with unemployment, chronic payments deficits and international debt-service problems. The shift

ISBN 92-64-01442-X © OECD 2005

to current-account surpluses accompanied by a rapid rise of the income level above $5 000 brought about many profound, historic changes economically, politically, socially and internationally. The powerful international pressures for market opening and current-account adjustment, especially from the United States, have already been discussed. Even more significantly, a new political and socio-economic history began to unfold. The economic boom triggered largely by the Plaza Accord meant that Koreans' days of belt-tightening had passed, and consequently powerful popular demands erupted for democratisation and social equity. Ordinary citizens finally joined demonstrating students in demanding a popular and free vote for President. They won it in 1987, sparking a wave of democratisation of essentially all political and social institutions. That the country would come under close international scrutiny during the Seoul Olympiad in 1988 reinforced the pressure on the then-authoritarian government to yield to this popular demand for democratisation.

As one impact of democratisation, management of the economy became a highly complex task. The authority of the government weakened and so did the power of the bureaucracy. Most striking was the change in labour relations. Labour unions became fully liberalised, triggering a prolonged period of labour militancy. Korea began to look for and shift to "advanced" ways of seeing and addressing economic problems, finally finding the path toward becoming an advanced country — a path that led it to join the OECD as its 29th member in December 1996.

The magnitude and scope of the impact of a major realignment among key currencies became manifest once again with the depreciation of yen against the US dollar by nearly 50 per cent in 1995-96. This contributed to the onset of the Korean financial crisis in 1997. Korea's experience with international monetary shocks demonstrates the critical importance of exchange-rate stability among the key currencies as well as the importance of keeping national currencies appropriately valued for the stability and growth of emerging economies.

Assistance through International Financial Organisations: the IMF and World Bank[22]

Korea joined the IMF in 1955 under the transitional provision of Article XIV of the IMF Articles of Agreement, which allows a member to maintain existing restrictions on payments and transfers for current-account transactions. In November 1988 Korea formally accepted the full obligations of IMF Article VIII and eliminated all remaining restrictions on current-account transactions. As an IMF member Korea took full advantage of its surveillance mechanism, financial assistance, technical assistance and training services. The IMF's financial assistance in particular conferred important benefits on Korea whenever it drew on the arrangement. The government made good use of the discussions with the IMF that the programme entailed on its economic and financial policies.

Korea joined the World Bank in 1955 and the International Development Agency (IDA) in 1961. It graduated from the Bank's loan operations in 1995, but until then the Bank was the source of many public loans for social overhead capital, social development, agricultural development, etc. Korea also received structural-adjustment loans in the early 1980s and loans to support financial-sector liberalisation in 1983 and 1985. The Bank has also provided technical assistance through its project-lending operations. Meetings of the International Economic Consultative Organisation for Korea (IECOK) were held under the auspices of the World Bank. IECOK helped Korea by giving it an opportunity to persuade international lenders to extend loans and thereby improve the nation's credit standing. Korea also benefited from consultations with IECOK on its development strategies and policies.

Korea thus gained from its membership in the IMF and the World Bank through both loans for important projects and listening to their advice. These benefits had critical importance when Korea came under the IMF bailout programme during the 1997-98 financial crisis. With all their surveillance and policy advice, however, the Fund and the Bank could not have helped Korea prevent this crisis. This revealed the limits on the extent to which they can help their emerging member economies to identify and solve their domestic economic problems. The responsibility for this ultimately rests in the hands and depends on the *absorptive capacity* of national governments.

The International Financial Architecture[23]

The financial crisis of 1997-98 was a blunt reminder of the structural, institutional and policy weaknesses in the Korean economy. It also revealed the volatility of the international capital markets resulting from imperfect and asymmetric information, as well as how ill-equipped the international financial system is to help emerging market economies prevent financial crises and manage and resolve them should they arise. The Korean economy recovered from the crisis at a very rapid pace, and much of the recovery was

ISBN 92-64-01442-X © OECD 2005

due to the IMF emergency assistance programme made available in early December 1998. Yet many Koreans remain unhappy with the IMF's response to the crisis for the following reasons:

- The IMF's policy prescription is not considered to have been most appropriate, and it probably helped initially to deepen the crisis. Korea experienced a capital-account rather than a current-account crisis, which called for supportive fiscal policy and not the tight fiscal and monetary policies that the Fund imposed.
- Despite its surveillance function, the Fund failed both to see signs of the emerging crisis and to warn the Korean government about it. Immediately after the onset of the crisis, the Fund publicly expressed dismay over how the Korean and other crisis-hit Asian economies were fundamentally and structurally unsound. This deepened the crisis of confidence.
- Reforms prescribed by the Fund would certainly improve the long-term performance of the economy but some of them could not be implemented effectively or quickly in the limited time allowed by the IMF.

The Asian crisis of which the Korean crisis was a part also showed that the international capital market had not only demand-side problems but also supply-side problems that contributed to the crisis. Relatively small economies open to international capital flows are vulnerable to financial instability and crisis even if they have sound financial systems and good policies. Imperfect and asymmetric information, an inherent feature of capital markets, can give rise to overshooting, sharp corrections and in extreme cases financial crises. The crisis thus demonstrated the need to remedy flaws in the structure of international capital markets or the ways they are regulated by reforming the international financial architecture. Some of the necessary reforms include the following:

- There should be policy co-ordination to maintain stable exchange rates among the G-3 currencies;
- The G-7 governments should agree to regulate highly leveraged institutions such as hedge funds, especially to require timely disclosure of their uncovered positions;
- Measures are needed to address a serious bias toward short-term lending among major banks in the G-10 and other financial-centre countries, which is a major source of financial instability in the emerging markets;

ISBN 92-64-01442-X © OECD 2005

- There should be a well-defined framework for involving the private sector in the resolution of crises once they occur, including voluntary debt rollovers;
- Considering the huge magnitude of volatile capital flows, more resources should be made available to strengthen the role of the IMF as a quasi-lender of last resort; and
- The emerging markets and the Asian countries in particular should be better represented in the governance of the IMF.

Despite many reforms since the Asian financial crisis affecting how the IMF and the international capital markets function, these needs for the reform of the international financial architecture remain largely unaddressed. It seems that with the return of normalcy in the international capital markets complacency has set in to slow the momentum for reform. Meanwhile, the recognition of flaws in the international financial system as well as dissatisfaction with the IMF have led Korea to join other East Asian economies in launching the Chiang Mai Initiative (CMI) for financial co-operation in the region.

Policy Advice and Peer Pressure from the OECD Member Governments

The government's 1992 decision to apply for membership in the OECD was controversial in Korea from the beginning. The balance of public opinion in Korea held that accession would require Korea to accept the policy standards of the "rich developed" countries, which would be "too advanced" for the Korean economy. The economy was considered still too underdeveloped and financially fragile to accommodate accession without undermining the basis for continued catch-up with the developed countries and endangering economic stability. The government nonetheless pushed the accession process, arguing that Korea could more effectively address its institutional and structural problems by learning global policy standards and receiving the policy advice of OECD members as well as their peer pressure for its implementation. Korea's accession to the OECD became embarrassing when the financial crisis broke out one year after accession. Although the advocates of accession argued that the outbreak of the crisis indicated that Korea should have joined the OECD even earlier, the crisis strengthened the presumption in Korea and abroad that the accession had in fact contributed to the crisis and thus had been premature. The question of whether accession was premature still remains unresolved in Korea.

ISBN 92-64-01442-X © OECD 2005

Korea's experience at the OECD has been undoubtedly beneficial. Most important in this regard has been participation in discussions of member countries' policies. Korea has learned best policy practices and has benchmarked its own policies against them. Particularly important have been the country reviews on Korea in various policy areas, in which the Korean government subjects its own policy practices to evaluation, criticism and advice by other member governments and the secretariat. These reviews have enabled the Korean bureaucrats to assess their own standards and policies relative to the general practices of the OECD world and to learn where their policy weaknesses lie.

How beneficial these discussions and reviews can be to a member government depends on its absorptive capacity, specifically how willing and able it is to learn from them and to practice what has been learned. The Korean government has a mixed record in this regard. It has been rather receptive to evaluation, criticism and advice by other governments on domestically non-sensitive issues, but less than fully frank as well as strongly defensive and resistant on domestically sensitive ones. This attitude has constrained the scope of the benefit Korea can derive from the country reviews. A good and important example of this point lies in the Korean government's policy of a "big deal" on the *chaebol* in 1998. In the wake of the financial crisis, the government forced several *chaebol* to undertake M&As for consolidation among themselves in industries with excess capacity and non-competitive firms. This "big deal", actually a political decision led by the then-President Kim Dae-jung, received strong and wide criticism from other members and the secretariat of the OECD[24]. The Korean government at the time did not take this criticism well. It was less than fully frank at the country review on Korea on the governmental as well as political nature of the "big deal", which was ostensibly a deal among big businesses. The government subsequently drove a hard bargain with the secretariat to water down the policy critique printed in the country-review report. Yet actual developments thereafter have vindicated those criticisms.

More controversial were Korea's terms of accession to the OECD and their impact on its policies. Most contentious was the question whether the OECD forced Korea in the accession negotiations to liberalise the short-term capital account in preparation for accession and thus created the most proximate cause of Korea's 1997 financial crisis. Contrary to the general presumption in Korea and abroad, available evidence shows that this was not the case. In fact, the OECD member countries focused during the negotiation on persuading the Korean government to liberalise the long-

ISBN 92-64-01442-X © OECD 2005

term capital account but cautioned against the possibly destabilising cross-border movement of short-term capital in the context of Korea's fragile financial system[25]. Ironically, however, the Korean government "successfully" resisted the OECD pressure for liberalisation of the long-term capital account while it had already liberalised the cross-border movement of short-term capital by the mid-1990s.

Korea's own official investigation[26] of the causes of the financial crisis has revealed huge short-term capital inflows in the mid-1990s whose reversal in 1997 served as the most direct cause of the crisis. Many merchant banks mediated the inflows. Most of them had sprung up in the early 1990s, were created by *chaebol* and had remained largely free of governmental regulation. Accordingly, the controversy on the possible role of the OECD as a cause of Korea's financial crisis boils down to whether the OECD played any role in the deregulation of the merchant banks in the early 1990s. Three points apply here. First, the OECD played no formal role in the deregulation of merchant banking at that time. Second, the deregulation seems to have taken place under heavy lobbying by *chaebols* bitterly complaining of the shortage of financial capital at home and the consequent high interest costs of their funds. Third, it may still be possible to show that, in issuing licences to many new merchant banks, the government cited as a justification for the policy the need to deregulate the economy in general, and the financial sector in particular in preparation for accession to the OECD. It would thus have misused the authority or the philosophy of the Organisation for expediency.

This investigative analysis clears the OECD of the charge that in the accession process it was instrumental in causing Korea's financial crisis. It is also true, however, that while the OECD was aware of Korea's vulnerability to financial crisis, it did not go so far as to press the Korean government for specific preventive actions. This finding, once again, shows that the absorptive capacity of individual members basically determines the benefit of membership in the OECD[27]. In this sense, the OECD is a "soft" policy-advice organisation

Korea's accession to the OECD was premature in one specific respect, namely Korea's capability to accommodate the labour policy standards of the OECD countries. The member governments of the OECD requested as a condition for accession that Korea liberalise labour unions fully up to the OECD standards. Eager not to delay accession, the Korean government agreed to do so soon after it. This commitment later proved very problematic.

ISBN 92-64-01442-X © OECD 2005

During Korea's compressed economic and political development, industrial relations had not had sufficient time to mature, and with democratisation labour unions became both militant and violent. This concerned the business community, the public and the government. Accordingly, the government was trying to develop a labour-market order that it saw as best fitting Korea under prevailing circumstances, and it regulated aspects of the ways unions could organise and function. This varied far from OECD labour standards. As a result, at the time of accession the Korean business community and the public remained far from ready to support an immediate transition to OECD labour standards. They feared a one-sided empowerment of the labour unions, which they considered already far too militant, that would exacerbate the structural crisis of the economy then underway. This thinking reflected a view that Korea lacked the habit and culture of constructive dialogue and negotiation between unions and employers, which should constitute the infrastructure for OECD-style labour standards.

Immediately after accession, the government began the effort to bring Korea's labour standards into conformity with the OECD's through a series of sequential measures to deregulate labour unions. At the same time, also following the OECD's advice, it launched parallel efforts to promote labour-management co-operation and labour market flexibility[28]. These two goals were not quite compatible, at least in the short term, and the parallel efforts brought confusion to all the parties concerned — the government, business and the labour unions.

The effort to implement the commitment on labour laws has continued to this day under peer pressure from other members of the Organisation. Much progress has been made, and Korea has come very close to the full implementation of those labour standards. Yet turmoil continues to characterise industrial relations in Korea, and despite all the advice from the OECD Korea has not yet reconciled the OECD standards on the one hand and industrial peace and labour-market flexibility on the other. The members of the Organisation have accumulated much rich experience in this field that Korea can learn from. Their formal advice to Korea at the OECD on the subject has been rather restrained, however, and it has often sounded contradictory, perhaps because of the political sensitivity of the matter in their respective capitals. The tension between democracy and the market economy probably can be the most severe in labour relations. It appears that this field is the final testing ground for Korea's attainment of the capacity to promote parallel development of the two sets of values. Korea still gropes toward this goal largely on its own.

Impact of Korea's Economic Policies on Other East Asian Economies

Trade and Investment Policies

Korea entered the world economy in the early 1960s by seeking trading relationships nearly exclusively with what then was called the "first world", i.e. the OECD countries, mainly the United States and Japan, under its export-led growth strategy. It developed a "triangular pattern of trade, importing necessary raw materials and capital goods from the United States and (much more) Japan, and exporting most of the goods produced with these imports mainly to the vast, open domestic market of the United States, but increasingly to the European countries. This triangular trade was complemented by imports of natural resources from Southeast Asia, not to mention oil from the Middle East.

Changes in Korea's direction of trade over time (Table 10.3) show that Korea's trading pattern has changed dynamically since those earlier days. Korea's trade dependence on Japan, the United States and European countries has steadily decreased while its trading relationship with the developing countries, especially those in East Asia, has intensified. Korea's trading pattern has become increasingly diversified in terms of export markets and increasingly more East Asia-oriented — first toward Southeast Asia and subsequently also toward China. Import sources have also diversified in much the same ways.

Korea's trading relations in East Asia now are becoming increasingly China-centred. Until the early 1990s, Korea's main trade partners in developing East Asia were the Southeast Asian countries, which emerged as dynamic trade partners in the 1980s. As China's high economic growth continued and once Korea-China relations were normalised in 1991, China rose rapidly as Korea's newest and most dynamic trade partner in the 1990s. Since 2003 China has become Korea's most important trade partner in East Asia, even exceeding Japan. As suggested above, Korea's trade with both China and Southeast Asia are predominantly vertical. Korea exports mostly raw materials and capital goods to the region, which developing East Asian economies use to produce finished goods exported to the rest of the world.

The intensifying trading relationship with developing East Asia has formed part of a broader pattern of increasing intra-regional trade[29] and in fact has contributed importantly to this pattern. This contribution has come about naturally as Korea's industrialisation has progressed, with Korea beginning to shift from light industries to heavy and chemical industries as

ISBN 92-64-01442-X © OECD 2005

an exporter in the late 1980s. As Korea began to acquire international competitiveness in its HCI, developing East Asian economies embarked on their own export-led growth paths. Korea began to relocate its SMEs in light manufacturing to these economies as well as to export heavy and chemical products to them as capital goods and raw materials. Through this process, Korea has contributed to industrial development in developing East Asia and to its growing capacity to export light manufactures to the rest of the world, especially the United States and European countries, in increasing competition with Korea and other NIEs. Developing East Asia, in turn, has helped Korea further to upgrade its industrial structure and emerge as a new global player in the world market for HCI products by providing a rapidly growing new market in addition to the existing markets in the developed countries. The diversification of Korea's trading relationship with developing East Asia is part of a broader regional integration process that is giving rise to the emergence of a regional production network[30]. Increasing trade intensities in East Asia reflect its progress (Kim, 2002; Lee, 2002).

Korea's vertical trading relationship with developing East Asia more or less replicates Japan's vertical trading relationship with the rest of East Asia including Korea. Japan has played the leading role in the flying-geese pattern of regional industrial development in East Asia, with Korea emerging to share it. Korea's vertical trading relations with developing East Asia have generated surpluses on the bilateral trade accounts with the region's economies. These bilateral surpluses have the same nature as Japan's trade surpluses with Korea and reflect the same kind of trading relationship between Korea and developing East Asia.

ODI by Korean manufacturing firms, especially SMEs, has brought about Korea's trading relationship with developing East Asia. The intensification of ODI flows to the region is the composite result of a number of developments in Korea — the manifestation of sustained industrial development and the continued upgrading of the Korean industrial structure. Sustained industrial development, in turn, has been made possible by continued integration of the Korean economy with the global trading system through the liberalisation of trade, FDI and ODI.

Korea had restrictive policies toward trade, FDI and ODI during its early developmental years, and its trade-led industrialisation ran into a setback for a while as a result. The process resumed and accelerated when, in part from the effort to overcome this setback and in part under pressure from developed trade partners, Korea began steadily to liberalise trade, FDI and ODI. This process engendered spurts of painful structural adjustment in the

ISBN 92-64-01442-X © OECD 2005

economy, especially through the 1980s and in the late 1990s. Each major round of structural adjustment has been accompanied by accelerated investment and trade integration with developing East Asia.

Through integration with developing East Asia, Korea has both strengthened its own economic and industrial dynamism and contributed to economic growth and industrial development in the region. In other words, trade and investment integration has been mutually beneficial. The same applies to Japan's trade and investment relations with the rest of East Asia, including Korea. The mutuality of benefits from such engagement argues for the need to deepen the process of regional integration in East Asia.

In terms of specific Korean policies impacting economic relations with developing East Asia, the evolution of ODI policy and its impact on regional trade is clear, but the impact of FDI in Korea on the country's economic relations with developing East Asia may need emphasis. FDI in Korea promotes industrial upgrading, and through this channel it also contributes to further industrial development in developing East Asia, chiefly by accelerating Korea's ODI in the region. Korea once restricted FDI but more recently has begun to promote it aggressively.

It is well known that Korea has withheld concessions on agricultural trade policies at international trade negotiations. At the multilateral level, it has refused to abolish quantitative import restrictions on rice and to replace them with tariffs. It maintains very high tariffs on many agricultural products. These policies are being discussed with agricultural exporting countries in the current Doha Development Agenda (DDA) negotiations. The Korean government tries to minimise concessions on agricultural import barriers by insisting on maintaining its "developing country" status with respect to agricultural policies. For this reason it has not been able to take an aggressive stance on free-trade agreements (FTAs)[31]. The reason for Korea's agricultural trade policies is obvious. As a result of rapid industrialisation, agriculture as a productive industry has shrunk very rapidly, causing serious adjustment problems for farming households as well as the rural economy. All this indicates that Korea can continue to liberalise its agricultural imports only at a rather restrained speed.

Korea's restrictive agricultural policies undoubtedly have been detrimental to agricultural development in the developing countries, including those in East Asia. Time will tell the outcome of the DDA negotiations on Korea's agriculture, but domestically the Korean government is making serious efforts to prepare the farmers for substantial further agricultural

ISBN 92-64-01442-X © OECD 2005

liberalisation. It also has a plan to move towards FTAs with a number of agricultural exporters over time. In preparation for agricultural trade liberalisation to come, the government legislated a package of rural adjustment support measures worth 11.9 billion won (about $12 million) in 2003-04. This package goes a long way to prepare Korea for accelerated agricultural-market opening in the years to come. Over time, Korea's agricultural policies will grow increasingly more favourable to agricultural exporters in and outside East Asia.

Korea's restrictive agricultural trade policies do not mean that it is not an active importer of agricultural products. Korea imported $6.8 billion of agricultural products and $2.1 billion of forestry products in 2003. China was the largest import source for farm products, accounting for $1.8 billion or 27 per cent of the total. The United States, Australia, Brazil and the United Kingdom ranked next. The largest supplier of forestry-product imports was Indonesia, followed by Malaysia, New Zealand, China and Thailand. The four East Asian countries in the group together accounted for 52 per cent of the total. Korea's imports of agricultural and related products from East Asia and elsewhere are bound to grow as economic growth continues.

Development Assistance Policies

Given its recent and rapid rise as a newly industrialised economy, Korea has an understandably short history as a provider of official development assistance (ODA) to developing countries. It established the Economic Development Cooperation Fund (EDCF) under the Ministry of Finance[32] in 1987 in order to manage systematically concessional long-term loan programmes, which it had offered rather sporadically. It formed the Korea International Cooperation Agency (KOICA) in 1991 under the auspices of the Ministry of Foreign Affairs[33] in order to manage aid programmes more systematically while increasing total ODA over time. Korean ODA remains limited, although it has increased steadily. According to the government, it was $334 million in 2003 — $114 million (34 per cent) as contributions to multilateral agencies and $220 million (64 per cent) as bilateral assistance. The latter consisted of EDCF loans of S$100 million and aid programmes of $120 million. Relative to Gross Domestic Income, Korea's ODA amounted to 0.06 per cent in 2003. This represented a near doubling compared to the 0.034 per cent recorded in 1993.

ISBN 92-64-01442-X

The accumulated total of EDCF projects through February 2004 was 1.97 trillion won (about $2 billion). The main recipients were China, Indonesia, Viet Nam, Sri Lanka, Bangladesh, the Philippines, Uzbekistan, Cambodia, Romania and Myanmar. East Asia as a whole looms relatively large among these recipients. EDCF loans are extended mainly to modernise social infrastructures in developing countries, in such areas as communications, transportation, energy and public health.

Aid programmes have focused on projects to build or modernise social infrastructures in such areas as education and training, population and public health and public administration, as well as in specific sectors such as agriculture, forestry, fisheries, mining and construction. This focus has shifted over time to manpower co-operation in forms such as various trainee programmes and dispatching of professionals, in co-operation with development projects wherever possible. Most aid has gone to low-income developing countries, with more than half of the total extended to those in the Asia-Pacific region.

No study exists thus far on the impact of Korea's development assistance programmes on recipient countries. Their limited amounts indicate, however, that while undoubtedly beneficial the impact may not be measurable in any significant sense. Much influenced by the accession to the OECD, the Korean government intends to continue to strengthen its role and contribution as a provider of development assistance, most importantly by increasing its total scale. Given its relatively very low level of ODA, Korea is not yet a member of the Development Assistance Committee (DAC) of the OECD. It plans to join in the near future and is now preparing to raise its ODA/GNI ratio appreciably for this purpose. East Asian developing countries will be among main beneficiaries.

Concluding Remarks

Korea presents a unique case for studies on the impact and coherence of OECD-country policies on Asian developing economies. It began as one of the poorest Asian developing countries in the 1950s but rapidly developed into a leading Asian NIE. In about three and a half decades it joined the OECD by earning recognition as a newly industrialised as well as newly democratised country with a significant potential to contribute to global economic development. Through this process, Korea has emerged as a global

ISBN 92-64-01442-X © OECD 2005

player in a number of advanced-technology industries and joined the ranks of middle powers in global governance. It has also begun to impact on the development of other East Asian developing economies rather closely with its own policies.

Korea's modern development experience over the last four decades thus promises to be a success story of a country making the transition from the developing to the developed world. Such success has been rare. This chapter asks how Korea has achieved it, what the OECD countries have contributed to it and to what extent Korea's own policies have been and are conducive to development in East Asia. Korea owes its economic success thus far to its strategy of export-led economic growth. Its experiences along this trajectory demonstrate and confirm that international trade, especially exporting, is the best promoter of growth for a developing economy. Export-led growth has coincided with export-led industrialisation. This shows that, for an economy like Korea with a good labour force, export-led growth promotes industrialisation as well. Furthermore, FDI can bring advanced technologies and accelerate industrial development while domestic competition and import competition encourage industrial adjustment and innovation.

Prolonged and broad protection of domestic import-substituting firms, on the other hand — which Korea tried under the heavy and chemical industries (HCI) promotion drive — backfired. The HCI policies of the 1970s did indeed lay the foundation of the modern industrial structure that Korea boasts today, but it proved to be a costly investment. Undesirable effects included the institutionalisation of heavy government and bureaucratic intervention in the market system, particularly a government-directed banking system. The HCI policies created and strengthened the system of *chaebol* as Korea's unique kind of business conglomerates, with opaque corporate governance structures organised around "the owners" and insatiable appetites for excessive and risky investments backed by political relations. Through both effects, the HCI drive weakened the foundation for a sound market system and sowed the seeds of an economic crisis in the late 1970s and the early 1980s as well as the financial crisis of the late 1990s.

The earlier crisis prompted broad reform efforts aimed at domestic deregulation, strengthening domestic competition and liberalisation of trade and FDI policies, alongside measures to promote R&D. The later one prompted deep reforms focusing on banking, the opening of the domestic capital market, corporate restructuring and improvement of corporate governance. As a major lingering legacy of the HCI drive, however, the dominance of the economy by business conglomerates with their persistent corporate governance problems continues to pose a major policy challenge. It is plausible that the industrial catch-up could have occurred anyway but with less cost if the country had liberalised and welcomed FDI at the early stage of industrialisation, while the government focused on strengthening market competition, promotion of R&D and investment in human capital.

Korea started its export-led growth by engaging in a triangular trade with Japan, on which it depended for the supply of intermediate and capital goods, and with the United States, Korea's largest and main export market. With continued economic growth and industrial catch-up, the industrial structure as well as export markets diversified. Korea exported more and more heavy and chemical industry goods, and at the same time the developing economies became increasingly more important as export markets. Initially, mainly the economies of Southeast Asia took rising shares of Korea's exports. More recently, however, China has increased its share in Korea's exports rapidly; it became Korea's largest export market in 2003. Korea's increasing ODI to the region led these increases in Korea's exports to developing East Asia. These developments represent Korea's contribution to regional economic growth and industrial development as well as to the emergence of a regional production network.

Korea owes its economic success thus far both to its people's determination to overcome adversities and to the liberal international economic order created by the developed countries after World War II. This order had three main features. First, the GATT-sponsored multilateral trading system allowed access to the domestic markets of the OECD countries. Second, these countries have continued to pursue trade liberalisation. Third, access to the international capital markets was made possible with the support of international financial institutions such as the World Bank and the IMF. Under this order, increasing flows of FDI have moved from the developed to the emerging markets. Korea began relatively recently to rely on them for its continued industrial advancement and economic growth. Foreign aid was never important to Korea's economic development except during the early years when the export sector hardly existed.

During Korea's rise to newly industrialised status, OECD-country policies have not been entirely coherent in their impact on the developing countries. Most noteworthy, the developed countries responded with discriminatory trade barriers to the rise of the developing countries as exporters of industrial products, especially light manufactures. These

ISBN 92-64-01442-X © OECD 2005

responses, categorised as the "new protectionism" at the time, created uncertainties for the developing countries over the sustainability and reliability of the supposedly liberal international trading system. The new protectionism was one of the factors contributing to Korea's pursuit of HCI promotion.

The Asian financial crisis of which the Korean crisis was a part caused a major setback to Korea's progress toward becoming a high-income developed country. It highlighted both various institutional weaknesses at home, including Korea's underdeveloped financial system, and important structural flaws in the international financial architecture. The crisis served as the catalyst for a number of far-reaching domestic economic reforms, including those in the corporate and financial sectors. It also led Korea to join other East Asian economies in a joint effort to create a regional mechanism for emergency financial assistance under the Chiang Mai Initiative (CMI).

Throughout its development, Korea benefited greatly by listening to the policy surveillance and advice of the World Bank and the IMF. More recently it joined the OECD, primarily to benefit from peer advice and pressure from the developed members of the Organisation. There is a limit, however, to how much international organisations can do to help a member country improve and reform its policies and institutions. The limit is determined by the absorptive capacity of the member government. The same qualification applies to what a country may expect from the international financial institutions such as the IMF or an East Asian institution for financial co-operation that may emerge from the CMI.

A special issue related to the international financial architecture concerns the impact of the pattern of alignment of exchange rates among key currencies. A particular pattern can bring boom or bust to an emerging economy like Korea. This points to the need to keep exchange rates between key currencies stable.

The main conclusion that emerges from this analysis is that, over time, although with occasional deviations, Korea has adopted the broadly open and liberal policies of the OECD countries on competition, trade and investment. This has allowed Korea to continue its own economic growth and industrial development as well as to contribute to growth and development in developing East Asia. Korea's trade and investment interaction with OECD countries on the one hand and with developing countries on the other have contributed to economic integration in East Asia and to emergence of a regional production network in particular.

ISBN 92-64-01442-X © OECD 2005

Regional economic integration in East Asia and Korea's contribution to it have taken place neither as a result of special policies in Korea or other individual countries nor through formation of a trade bloc in the form of a regional economic community or a regional free-trade agreement. Rather, they continue through the market process, i.e. through trade and investment, under non-discriminatory trade and investment liberalisation by the regional economies. Korea can further contribute by opening its domestic markets for goods and services, including agricultural products.

One particular element at play to accelerate this process is the transfer of technology and knowledge from Japan to Korea and from Japan and Korea to other developing economies in East Asia. Such transfers have taken place through trade, investment and exchanges of information and people. One particular kind of knowledge thus transferred concerns economic growth and development policies. Much anecdotal evidence suggests that the developing economies in East Asia have learned much, including much about policy mistakes, from the experience of Japan and Korea in formulating and implementing their own economic policies. In this way both countries have played the role of path explorers for developing East Asia.

Another important lesson from Japan and Korea highlights the importance of investment in human capital. Based on it, Korea has begun to contribute to such investment in developing East Asia by focusing its development assistance programmes on education and training. This contribution will continue to increase.

The financial crisis in the late 1990s was a rite of passage for Korea in its transition from a developing to a newly developed country. Korea is still engaged in it, groping for the new order appropriate for an advanced and competitive economy in such areas as industrial relations or corporate governance. When Korea comes through this process and joins the ranks of developed countries with mature institutions, the country will indeed become a successful model of development for other developing economies in East Asia. For this to occur, Korea should continue to learn from the experience and policy advice of the developed OECD countries, at the same time enhancing its domestic absorptive capacity to benefit from what it learns.

ISBN 92-64-01442-X © OECD 2005

Table 10A.1. **Korea's Bilateral Trade Balances, 1971-2002**

($ million)

	1971	1975	1980	1985	1986	1989	1990	1995	1997	1998	2000	2002
OECD countries	-1 058	-1 246	-2 439	1 187	3 053	1 113	-3 893	-27 584	-25 582	9 654	4 507	-1 454
- USA.	-147	-348	-284	4 265	7 335	4 728	2 418	-6 272	-8 497	2 402	8 369	9 772
- Japan	-692	-1 141	-2 818	-3 017	-5 444	-3 992	-5 936	-15 557	-13 136	-4 603	-11 362	-14 713
- EU countries	-170	324	1 228	151	1 047	1 174	937	-1 890	-2 119	7 243	7 635	4 587
Developing countries	-269	-947	-2 348	-2 040	78	-201	-935	17 523	17 130	29 377	7 279	11 798
- Middle East	-144	-959	-3 259	-1 073	-259	-2 301	-3 569	-6 957	-12 174	-4 832	-18 206	-13 383
- East Asia	-143	-133	273	-666	-30	1 352	1 375	20 746	24 286	23 842	20 389	18 248
Chinese Taipei	-27	-99	-97	-137	-99	-20	-203	1 318	2 191	3 469	3 326	1 800
Hong Kong, China	22	162	725	1 073	1 290	2 793	3 166	9 844	10 822	8 720	9 447	8 450
China	-	-	-10	-438	-497	-1 267	-1 683	1 742	3 456	5 460	5 656	6 354
ASEAN	-138	-196	-345	-1 164	-724	-154	95	7 842	7 817	6 193	1 960	1 644
- Other countries	18	145	638	-301	367	748	1 259	3 734	5 018	10 367	5 096	6 933
World	-1 327	-2 193	-4 787	-853	3 131	912	-4 828	-10 061	-8 452	39 031	11 786	10 344

Source: Korea International Trade Association.

Table 10A.2. **Korea's FDI and ODI by Year**
($ million)

	FDI[a]	ODI[b]
1962-81	1 478	173
1982-86	1 158	556
1987-89	2 332	1 196
1990	895	959
1991	1 177	1 116
1992	803	1 219
1993	728	1 283
1994	992	2 303
1995	1 357	3 136
1996	2 308	4 415
1997	3 086	3 648
1998	5 156	4 730
1999	10 798	3 281
2000	10 173	4 980
2001	4 859	5 044
2002	3 679	3 055

Notes: *a)* Arrival basis. *b)* The amount invested.
Sources: Ministry of Commerce, Industry and Energy, *FDI Trends*; The Export-Import Bank of Korea, *Overseas Direct Investment Statistics Yearbook*.

Table 10A.3. **Distribution of Korean ODI by Sector and Region, 1968-1997**
(per cent of total)

	1968-80	1981-90	1991-97
Sectors:			
Mining	0.9	29.1	6.4
Forestry	17.2	3.1	0.2
Fishing	7.2	3.3	0.5
Manufacturing	22.8	41.8	53.9
Trade	20.9	15.2	19.1
Construction	18.1	1.8	2.1
Others	12.8	5.8	17.8
Regions:			
Asia	37.7	24.7	44.4
Middle East	14.3	10.7	2.3
North America	23.9	44.8	27.5
Latin America	3.1	4.3	3.1
Europe	4.1	4.3	15.6
Africa	16.0	1.5	2.2
Oceania	1.0	6.7	1.6

Source: Nicolas (2001), Tables 2.7a & 2.8.

ISBN 92-64-01442-X © OECD 2005

Notes

1. For example, Malaysia adopted the *Look East* policy for this purpose.
2. A huge volume of literature by both Korean and non-Korean authors documents and examines Korea's efforts to promote exports. See SaKong (1993), for example, for a succinct review and assessment of those efforts in English.
3. The term "trade account" used here refers to trade in goods. Trade in services is excluded. The current account, in addition, reports receipts and payments of income as well as current transfers. In 2003, the relative sizes of receipts on the services account, receipts on the income account and net receipts on the current transfers account, when measured against receipts on the goods account were 16.5 per cent, 3 per cent and -1.4 per cent, respectively. See the Bank of Korea's balance of payments statistics.
4. The review of the HCI policies here draws on Ahn and Kim (1995)
5. This aspect of the HCI campaign was the focus of analysis in Young and Yoo (1982) as well as the basis for their recommendation of an across-the-board removal of industrial protection.
6. See the later discussion of "new protectionism" for a more detailed analysis of this concern.
7. The growth rate of the economy in 1980 was minus 6 per cent.
8. For a journalistic but highly informative account of those dark sides of Korea's HCI drive, see Clifford (1997). For a critical analysis of the role of Korea's *chaebols* in the context of Korea's 1997-98 financial crisis, see Graham (2003).
9. For a comprehensive analysis of the Korean financial crisis, see Chopra *et al.* (2002).
10. The government of President Roh Moo-Hyun launched in early 2003 has attempted to reorient economic and non-economic policies in fundamental ways, creating what amounts to ideological confrontation between "conservatives" and "progressives" over a broad range of issues including the issue of business conglomerates. The consequent political tensions and economic uncertainties have been detrimental to the economy.

ISBN 92-64-01442-X © OECD 2005

11. According to the Ministry of Commerce, Industry and Energy.
12. See SaKong (1993) for a succinct review of the evolution of FDI policy up to the early 1990s. Nicolas (2001) offers a most in-depth and insightful analysis of Korea's FDI policy up to the late 1990s.
13. Sachwald (2001*a*) presents a body of collaborative and comprehensive studies on Korea's ODI. The discussion on the motivations for Korea's ODI in the text draws on Nicolas (2001).
14. On 29 June 1987, in response to widespread street demonstrations protesting against the system of indirect "election" of the President, the military elites' candidate for President, Roh Tae-Woo announced the decision to accept the popular voting system for the President at the forthcoming election. This so-called June 29 Declaration instantly sparked reforms for democratisation in all social institutions.
15. See Young (1989) for a review of such threats faced by Korean exporters in the US market. More on those threats later.
16. Kim (2001) traces the evolution of Korea's trade and industrial policies.
17. Another justification for the HCI drive was a national security argument for the development of defence-related heavy and chemical industries. The US administration began openly to mention the possibility of the withdrawal of its troops from Korea, and this made the Korean government realise that Korea should develop its own military security capability, or at least to argue this need.
18. The rationale and the model for these trade reforms were proposed by Young (1982) and Young and Yoo (1982). During 1984-93, the "import-liberalisation ratio" was raised to above 95 per cent and the average level of legal tariff rates on industrial products was lowered from above 20 per cent to 8 per cent under the principle of "8 per cent central rate".
19. See Presidential Commission on Economic Restructuring (1988).
20. This section draws heavily on SaKong (1993).
21. It goes without saying that even more important than material foreign aid was the military support the United States provided for Korea. It not only guaranteed the security of the country from the communists' aggression but also, by dint of this, maintained investors' confidence in the future of the economy.
22. This section is mostly also drawn from SaKong (1993).
23. This section draws on Young (2004*a*, 2004*b*)
24. See OECD (1998).

ISBN 92-64-01442-X © OECD 2005

25. See, for example, OECD (1996). There is also an internal memo of the OECD secretariat corroborating this point.

26. National Assembly (1999).

27. The appropriate analogy is offered by the proverb, "You can lead a horse to water but cannot force it to drink".

28. See OECD (2000).

29. See Urata (2005), a companion paper in the present volume, for a detailed analysis of the intensifying pattern of intra-regional trade in East Asia.

30. Urata (2005) defines and discusses this regional production network.

31. Early in 2004, Korea ratified its FTA with Chile, with many agricultural exceptions, after years of a domestic stalemate on it because of farmers' opposition. At the time of writing, Korea is on the verge of signing an FTA with Singapore.

32. Merged with the Economic Planning Board into the Ministry of Finance and Economy a few years ago.

33. Now called the Ministry of Foreign Affairs and Trade

ISBN 92-64-01442-X © OECD 2005

Bibliography

AHN, C.-Y. and J.-H. KIM (1995), "The Outward-oriented Trade Policy and Industrial Development", *in* D.-S. CHA and K.-S. KIM (eds.), *The Korean Economy over the Last Half Century* (in Korean), Korea Development Institute, Seoul.

BAYARD, T.O. and S. YOUNG (eds.) (1989), *Economic Relations between the United States and Korea: Conflict or Cooperation?*, Institute for International Economics and Korea Development Institute, Washington, D.C.

CHOPRA, A., K.KANG, M. KARASULU, H. LIANG, H. MA and A. RICHARDS (2002), "From Crisis to Recovery in Korea: Strategy, Achievements, and Lessons", *in* D.T. COE and S.-J. KIM (eds.), *Korean Crisis and Recovery*, International Monetary Fund and Korea Institute for International Economic Policy, Seoul.

CLIFFORD, M.L. (1997), *The Troubled Tiger, Rev.*, E. M. Sharpe, Armonk, NY, and London, U.K.

GRAHAM, E.M. (2003), *Reforming Korea's Industrial Conglomerates*, Institute for International Economics, Washington, D.C.

JACQUET, P. (2001), "Discussion: Macro- and Microeconomic Perspectives on Openness to International Investment", *in* F. SACHWALD (ed.), *Going Multinational: The Korean Experience of Direct Investment*, Routledge, London and New York, NY.

KIM, H. (2002), "Has Trade Intensity in ASEAN+3 Really Increased?", Working Paper 02-12, Korea Institute for International Economic Policy, Seoul.

KIM, J.-D. (1999), "Inward Foreign Direct Investment Regime and Some Evidences of Spillover Effects in Korea", Working Paper 99-09, Korea Institute for International Economic Policy, Seoul.

KIM, K.W.-S. (2001), *The Evolution of Korea's Industrial and Trade Policies*, Institute for Global Economics, Seoul.

LEE, C.-S. (2002), *A Study on the FDI-Trade Linkage* (in Korean), Korea Institute for International Economic Policy, Seoul.

ISBN 92-64-01442-X © OECD 2005

LEE, W.-Y. (1990), "FDI and Technology Transfer", Working Paper (in Korean), Korea Development Institute, Seoul.

NAM, S.-W. and J.-I. KIM (1995), "Macroeconomic Policies and Macroeconomic Changes", *in* D. -S. CHA and K.-S. KIM (eds.), *The Korean Economy over the Last Half Century* (in Korean), Korea Development Institute, Seoul.

NATIONAL ASSEMBLY (1999), *The Report of the Special Committee for Investigation of the Causes of the 1997 Financial Crisis*, Seoul.

NATIONAL STATISTICAL OFFICE, *Major Statistics of the Korean Economy*, various issues, Seoul.

NICOLAS, F. (2001), "A Case of Government-led Integration into the World Economy" *in* F. SACHWALD (ed.), *Going Multinational: The Korean Experience of Direct Investment*, Routledge, London and New York, NY.

OECD (1996), *Country Surveys: Korea*, OECD, Paris.

OECD (1998), *Country Surveys: Korea*, OECD, Paris.

OECD (2000), *Pushing Ahead with Reform in Korea: Labour Market and Social Safety-net Policies*, OECD, Paris.

PRESIDENTIAL COMMISSION ON ECONOMIC RESTRUCTURING (1988), *Reform Agenda for the Advancement of the Korean Economy* (in Korean and English), Korea Development Institute, Seoul.

SACHWALD, F. (ed.) (2001*a*), *Going Multinational: The Korean Experience of Direct Investment*, Routledge, London and New York, NY.

SACHWALD, F. (2001*b*), "Globalization and Korea's Development Trajectory: The Roles of Domestic and Foreign Multinationals", *in* F. SACHWALD (ed.), *Going Multinational: The Korean Experience of Direct Investment*, Routledge, London and New York, NY.

SAKONG, I. (1993), *Korea in the World Economy*, Institute for International Economics, Washington, D.C.

URATA, S. (2005), "East Asia's Multi-layered Development Pattern: Trade-FDI Nexus", in this volume.

YOUNG, S. (1982), "A Proposal for the Reform of the Tariff System", a Policy Symposium Paper (in Korean), Korea Development Institute, Seoul.

YOUNG, S. (1989), "Korean Trade Policy: Implications for Korean-US Cooperation", *in* T.O. BAYARD and S. YOUNG (eds.), *Economic Relations between the United States and Korea: Conflict or Cooperation?*, Institute for International Economics and Korea Development Institute, Washington D.C.

YOUNG, S. (2003), "The IMF, Economic Stabilization, and Democratic Politics: the Korean Case", a mimeograph presented at the Madrid Club General Assembly held in Madrid, Spain, on November 1-2.

YOUNG, S. (2004*a*), "Asia-Europe Co-operation on Global Financial Governance: An East Asian Perspective", *in* W. WALLACE and S. YOUNG (eds.), *Asia and Europe: Global Governance as a Challenge to Co-operation*, Council for Asia-Europe Cooperation, Japan Center for International Exchange, Tokyo.

YOUNG, S. (2004*b*), "Strengthening the International Financial Architecture: An Interim Assessment and Challenges to APEC", *Issues @PECC*, Pacific Economic Cooperation Council, Singapore.

YOUNG, S. and J.-H. YOO (1982), *The Basic Role of the Industrial Policy and Korea's Strategy for the Reform of Industrial Incentives* (in Korean), Korea Development Institute, Seoul.

ISBN 92-64-01442-X © OECD 2005

Chapter 11

China's Miracle: How Have OECD-Country Policies Contributed?

Justin Yifu Lin and Zhiyun Li

Abstract

Unlike most of the research seeking to explain the extraordinary results of China's economic reforms, this chapter moves away from internal factors to focus on how four major external ones have contributed to China's economic success. *International aid* — large but marginal given the size of the economy — has had its greatest impact through the demonstration effects of aid projects, drawing attention to key development issues, introducing new technologies, showing the way towards improved management and increasing Chinese awareness of international best practices. Its influence has shifted with the advancing stages of Chinese development. *International consultations*, not often mentioned explicitly in the literature as important, deserve credit for facilitating the spread of modern economics in China and for enhancing the government's capabilities in the design and implementation of economic policies. Even so, China has remained appropriately sceptical and selective in adopting and adapting policy suggestions from abroad. *Foreign Direct Investment* (FDI) has played the role expected of it, not only measurably supplementing domestic investment and enhancing growth, but also bringing advanced management and technology and impacting as a positive externality on domestic market and enterprise reform. Finally, fulfilment of the policy commitments embodied in China's *WTO Membership* spurs the completion of China's transition from a planned to a market economy.

ISBN 92-64-01442-X © OECD 2005

Introduction

China began far-reaching economic reform in its rural areas at the end of the 1970s. After 25 years of effort, nation-wide reforms have resulted in great economic strides. From 1979 to 2002, the average annual growth of real GDP reached 9.4 per cent, with real GDP per capita climbing by 8.1 per cent, rivalling the record of the four small East-Asian Dragons in their fastest development period. China's vividly and rapidly growing economy contrasts sharply with those of the former Soviet Union and Eastern European countries, most of which still face difficulties and have not recovered their former development levels. The great success of China's economic reforms has become recognised as a miracle in the history of human economic development. As the largest developing country in the world, China has provided invaluable experience and an example for other developing economies.

What motivated China's Reform and Open-door policies at the end of 1970s? Why has China chosen a gradual and piecemeal approach towards economic reform? What major internal and external factors have contributed to China's miracle? These important questions need proper, careful answers. Most of the literature on China's miracle concentrates mainly on the influences of internal factors, but little has been done on the external ones. This chapter systematically reviews and evaluates the impacts of major external factors on China's transition to a market economy. In begins in the next section with just a brief review of the major reform achievements, providing a consistent, logical framework to explain the origin and the choice of a gradual approach to economic reform. The third section launches an evaluation in the rest of the chapter of the influences of four major external elements on China's economic reform — international aid, international consultations, foreign direct investment (FDI) and China's entry to the World Trade Organization (WTO).

International aid is small-scale compared with China's GDP, and the impacts of aid on China's economic reform derive not from its volumes but from its exemplary effects. It has played different roles at different stages of China's economic development. After the mid-1990s, most aid to China shifted to supporting social development and poverty reduction, and the late 1990s witnessed a significant reduction in aid flows to China. Chinese policy makers are generally very cautious and selective in accepting policy suggestions proposed by western economists and international organisations, but international consultations nevertheless have significantly enhanced the government's capabilities in economic policy design and implementation and

 ISBN 92-64-01442-X © OECD 2005

have facilitated the spread of modern economic science in China. Because capital is extremely scarce in China, the influence of FDI on economic development is self-evident. Large FDI inflows not only make up for the scarcity of domestic capital, enhance the endowment structure and promote the upgrading of industrial structures, but also bring advanced management skills and technology. FDI also creates a positive externality for the reform of domestic markets and enterprises. The ultimate objective of China's economic reform is to establish a sound free-market system consistent with the requirements of the WTO Agreement. WTO membership will certainly facilitate China's transition from a planned to a modern market economy. The constraints and pressures resulting from the articles of WTO agreement require the Chinese government to expedite market-oriented reforms — in industrial policy, trade policy, regulation of the macro economy, the tax system and the legal infrastructure.

The Achievements and Logic of China's Economic Reforms

Achievements

Twenty-five years of reform have produced tremendous changes in almost every aspect of the Chinese economy and society. The economy certainly has achieved stunning growth. From 1979 to 2002, real GDP expanded by 9.4 per cent annually on average (Figure 11.1) while per capita real GDP increased by 8.1 per cent per year. At the end of 2002, GDP and GDP per capita reached 8.6 times and 6.4 times their 1978 pre-reform levels. With such fast development, living standards improved greatly. Rural net income per capita increased to 2 713.0 yuan in 2002 from 133.6 yuan in 1978, and urban per capita disposable income rose to 7 702.8 yuan from 343.4 yuan (Figure 11.2). Their growth rates were 7.6 per cent and 8.1 per cent a year, respectively, calculated using comparable prices. With the progress of reform, a market system has emerged from a traditional, highly centralised and planned economy. Inward-oriented before reform, China is an open economy today. In 2002, exports and imports reached $325.61 billion and $295.31 billion respectively, after average annual growth rates of 15.7 per cent and 14.7 per cent in 1978-2002. The ratio of total trade (imports and exports) to GDP jumped to 50.2 per cent in 2002 from 9.7 per cent in 1978. FDI leaped from $57 million in 1978 to $52.74 billion in 2002.

Figure 11.1. **GDP Trend and Structure**

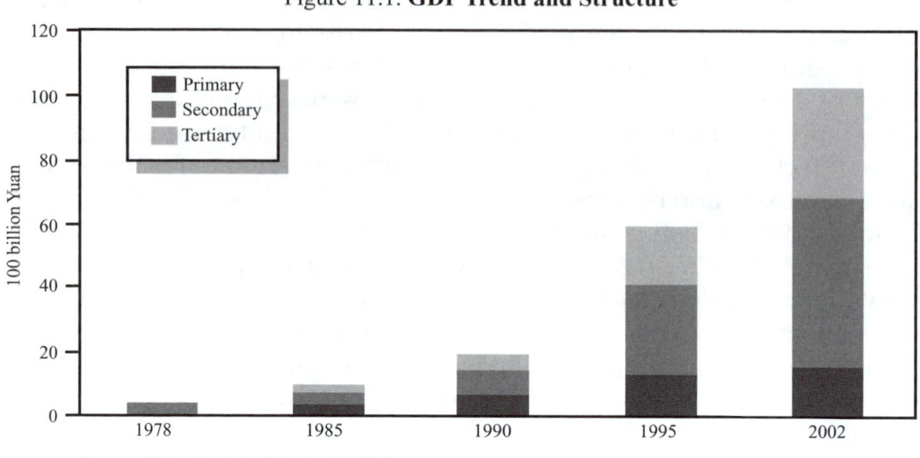

Source: China Statistical Yearbook (2003).

Figure 11.2. **Annual Net Income Per Capita**

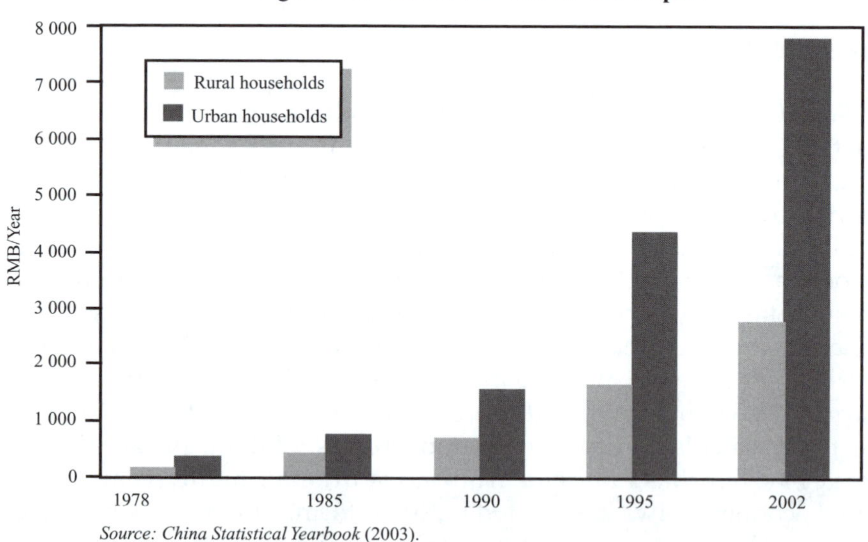

Source: China Statistical Yearbook (2003).

China is an important transition economy, and the success of its reforms has contrasted sharply with the performance of the former Soviet Union (FSU) and Eastern European countries, which adopted the big-bang reform approach. Figure 11.3 shows that after ten years of reform, the real GDP of Central and Southeastern Europe and the Baltics (CSB) merely recovered a

ISBN 92-64-01442-X © OECD 2005

level slightly higher than before reform. The real GDP of the Commonwealth of Independent States (CIS) in 2001 was less than 70 per cent of that in 1990. Poland, the best performer, increased its GDP by 44 per cent, while Russia's decreased by 36 per cent (World Bank, 2002, p. 5)

Figure 11.3. **CIS and CSB[a] Real GDP Trends, 1990-2001**

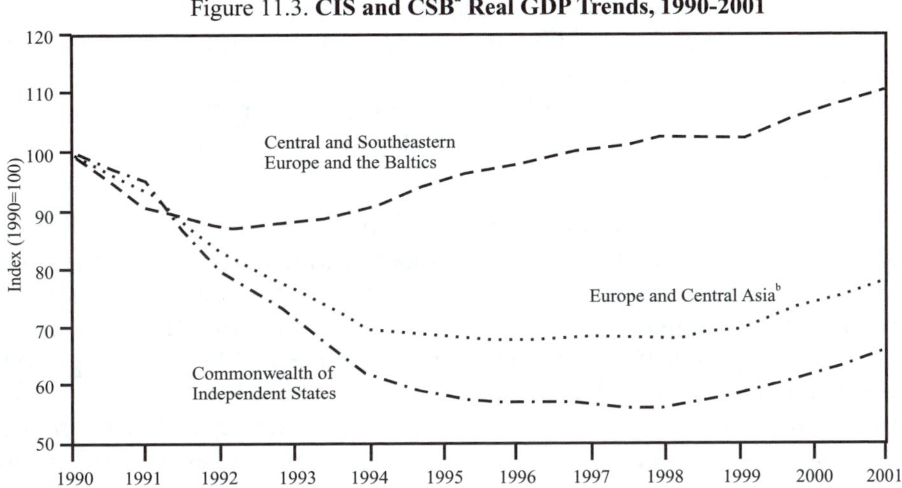

Notes: a) CSB countries: Central and Southeastern Europe and the Baltics.
b) Data for Europe and Central Asia are weighted averages for the CIS and CSB.
Source: World Bank (2002).

The Logic of a Piecemeal Approach to Economic Reform in China

Why did China choose its partial, piecemeal approach to economic reform in the late 1970s rather than the big-bang approach adopted later by the FSU and Eastern European countries? The choice in fact had its internal logic. After the foundation of the Peoples Republic in 1949, China, like many other developing economies, gave priority to the development of heavy industry under the government's "catching-up strategy". In an economy like China's, characterised by extreme capital scarcity, implementing such a strategy implies a highly distorted and centralised, planned-economy system (Lin *et al.*, 1999). Although China did achieve rapid GDP growth in some periods before 1978[1], this comparative-advantage-defying (CAD) strategy brought serious problems, such as distorted industrial and employment structures, low economic incentives and little improvement in people's living standards. The Great Cultural Revolution from 1966 to 1976 pushed the national economy to the edge of collapse.

Political leaders in authoritarian countries find it very difficult to change their strategies when still in power because it would endanger the legitimacy of their leadership. When Chairman Mao Zedong passed away in 1976, it became possible for the new leaders to implement new strategies. With the national economy at the edge of collapse, it was urgent for the new leaders, represented by Deng Xiaoping, to adopt new policies to restore the economy and improve living standards. Yet it remained difficult for them fully to abandon former policies because they had participated in the implementation of the "catching up strategy" and contributed to the formation of the centrally planned system. Therefore, they could choose only a piecemeal approach towards economic reform.

A distorted macro-policy environment, a plan-based resource allocation system and a low-incentive micro-management structure characterised the traditional planning system. China's reforms over the past 25 years started with micro-management reforms. They began in the rural areas. At the end of the 1970s, the household responsibility system (HRS) began to replace the collective farming system. The HRS links rural households' income with their output, generating great incentives to farmers. During 1978-84 when the HRS was widely introduced, the average annual growth of agricultural output calculated at comparable prices rose to 7.7 per cent from 2.9 per cent in the 26 years to 1978. About half of the output growth in 1978-84 came from the introduction of the HRS (Lin, 1992). With the success of rural reform, reform also started in the urban sector with a focus on state-owned enterprises (SOEs). It first attempted to improve economic incentives by giving autonomy to managers and allowing firms to share profits. Then came efforts to reform property-right arrangements by adopting the modern corporate governance system. These reforms still have not achieved significant success, however. Because SOEs still bear policy burdens, the problem of the soft budget constraint has not been eliminated (Lin and Tan, 1999). Yet the government has also loosened restrictions on the development of private enterprises, and the non-state-owned economy contributes significantly to China's rapid and sustainable economic growth.

China's reform path does not follow a neo-classical economic model. State-owned enterprises are not privatised and resources are allocated along dual tracks, both plan and market. Although China's strategy achieved miraculous growth in the 1980s, most economists remained pessimistic about its future, because they believed that the market economy should be based on private ownership, an approach that China did not take. Most economists

ISBN 92-64-01442-X © OECD 2005

believed that countries in the former Soviet Union and Eastern Europe would outperform China, because they adopted a shock therapy designed on the principles of modern economic theories.

Another ten years have passed and most economists' expectations at the beginning of 1990s failed to materialise. The Chinese economy continued to grow at 10.1 per cent per year and foreign trade by 15.2 per cent per year in the 1990s, while the FSU and Eastern European countries suffered serious inflation and recession (World Bank, 1996; Dabrowski, 2001)[2]. China's gradual, piecemeal, dual-track approach to transition is desirable because most SOEs operate in sectors inconsistent with China's comparative advantage and are nonviable in open, competitive markets. The government's distortions in market functions before the transition were endogenous to the needs of protecting these nonviable firms (Lin, 2003). China's approach gives the government the ability to support the SOEs continuously and encourages the growth of the non-state sectors that are consistent with China's comparative advantage but were suppressed previously. Therefore, China has achieved stability and dynamic growth simultaneously during the transition process. Nonetheless, completing the transition to a well-functioning market economy depends on success in addressing the SOEs' viability issues (Lin and Tan, 1999).

International Aid and Consultation

China's reform achievement results from interactions between internal and external factors. The existing literature has concentrated mostly on the internal factors. Here, the analysis turns to an evaluation of the impacts of major external factors on China's economic reform, beginning with an investigation of the effects of international aid and consultation.

International Aid

International aid takes three forms: Official Development Assistance (ODA) provided by the governments of the developed countries, multilateral aid provided by international organisations such as the World Bank and UNDP and the aid provided by non-government organisations (NGOs). Generally speaking, aid helps facilitate the GDP growth of the recipient

ISBN 92-64-01442-X

countries. According to research on the effects of aid on the economies of 56 countries during 1970-73 and 1990-93, international aid may have contributed some 0.08 per cent to 0.62 per cent to the GDP growth rates of the recipient countries. In general, small and medium-sized aid generated better results (World Bank, 1997, see p. 142).

For many large developing economies, the volume of international aid is quite small compared with their gross domestic incomes. The influence of aid on their economies results not from aid volume but from the exemplary effects of aid projects. By concentrating on specific projects and particular issues of economic development, the projects introduce advanced production technologies, improve management services and initiate innovative approaches to development and poverty reduction. For example, in the 1960s international aid made a major contribution to the spread of the Green Revolution in Asia by promoting investment in wheat and rice production, which greatly enhanced the ability of India and Indonesia to prevent famine.

After its opening at the end of the 1970s, China began to accept aid from international organisations and OECD countries. The official statistics show that it received about $6 billion in aid during 1978-2001. More than 2 000 aid projects have been completed or are continuing (Yi, 2002). Of total aid received in 1981-2002 (also about $6 billion) $670 million came from the Government of Germany and about $1 billion from Japan (Chinese Ministry of Commerce website). Although the volume of international aid was relatively small, it contributed to China's economic development by drawing the government's attention to key development issues, introducing advanced technologies, improving managerial levels and implementing international best practices. At different stages of China's economic and social development, international aid has played different roles in facilitating this development.

China's now more developed coastal regions were the major aid beneficiaries in the 1980s, largely for infrastructure improvements. Since the mid-1990s, most aid has flowed to China's poor and western regions. In 1998-2002, China received about $1.15 billion in aid, of which 70 per cent was invested in projects related to poverty reduction (Ministry of Commerce website). This became especially pronounced after China launched the Strategy of Developing the West in 2001. International aid to China has also fallen significantly since the mid-1990s, however. Figures 11.4 and 11.5 show the trends in the past two decades. Aid to China increased rapidly in 1979-95, but after that per capita aid dropped from $2.93 in 1995 to $1.15 in 2001.

ISBN 92-64-01442-X © OECD 2005

Figure 11.4. **Ratio of Aid to GNI and Gross Capital Formation**

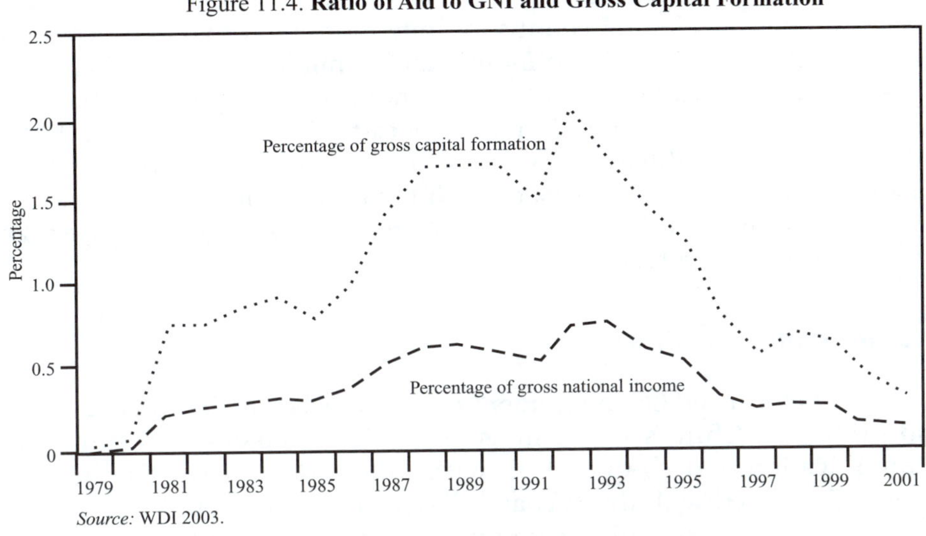

Source: WDI 2003.

Figure 11.5. **Trend of Per Capita Aid to China**

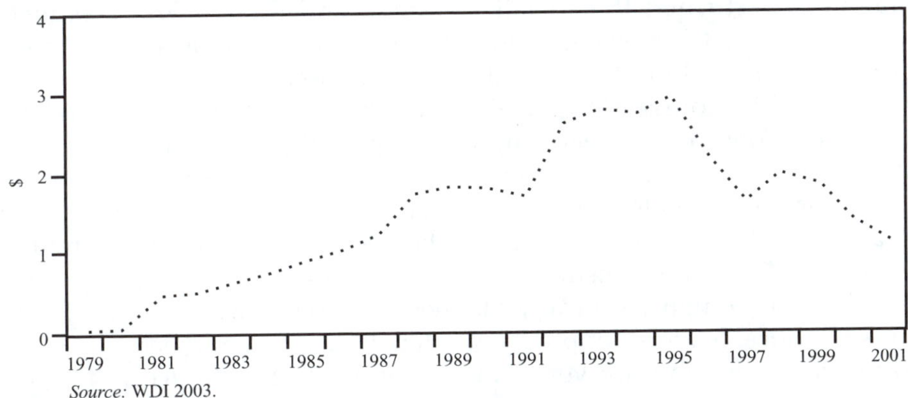

Source: WDI 2003.

Why did international aid flows to China fall significantly after 1995? First, the global aid environment changed. The United Nations targeted international aid provided by the developed OECD member countries at no less than 0.7 per cent of their GNP, but most donors have never reached this target. The ratio of aid to GNP of the OECD member countries decreased from 0.35 per cent in 1990 to 0.25 per cent in 1996 and then fell further to 0.22 per cent in 2001 (World Bank, 1997 and 2004). Second, subtle changes occurred in the political and economic relationships between China and the more developed countries. The governments of many OECD countries began to take for granted that China no longer needs international aid because

ISBN 92-64-01442-X © OECD 2005

rapid economic growth has greatly increased its economic strength. Yet China remains a poor developing country despite more than two decades of fast growth. In 1998, China still had more than 231 million people (18.5 per cent of the population) with consumption expenditure per day of less than $1.00 (World Bank, 2000/2001). In 2002 China's per capita income reached just $1 000, and great disparities still exist between urban and rural areas. In short, China remains entitled to receive reasonable international aid to complement its limited government budgets in better solving its pressing development and poverty-reduction problems.

International Consultation

The "Reform and Opening-door" policy launched at the end of the 1970s also prompted China's economists and policy makers to resume their communication and co-operation with international organisations and experts. Compared with the FSU and Eastern European countries, however, China has shown a quite different pattern in listening to and adopting policy suggestions proposed by foreign experts. The non-Chinese transition economies overturned the socialist system, and their newly established governments faced few obstacles in promoting market reforms. This made it easier for them to adopt the shock therapy proposed by mainstream western economists. The foundations of these reform schemes derived from the Washington Consensus, which emphasised privatisation, price liberalisation and macroeconomic stability. After more than ten years of reform, the shock therapy has not generated satisfactory outcomes (World Bank, 2002; Lin and Liu, 2003). Quite differently, China had launched its economic reform under existing socialist political institutions and ideology, and the economy evolved gradually from a highly centrally planned to a free-market system. Because Chinese political leaders adopted a gradual, tinkering approach to economic reform, they were and are very cautious and selective in accepting policy suggestions proposed by western economists and international organisations.

While international consultation does not play as pivotal a role in China as in other transition countries, it has significantly enhanced the Chinese government's capabilities in economic policy design and implementation and at the same time facilitated the spread of modern economics in China. Several important international conferences have had far-reaching influence on China's economic reform. In 1985, the Development Research Center of the State Council and the World Bank jointly organised the "International Conference on China's Macro-economic Reform", known as the *Bashanlun Conference* in the public media. Several world-renowned economists attended

ISBN 92-64-01442-X © OECD 2005

the conference, including James Tobin and Janos Kornai. The Chinese participants included senior government officials and major economists who participated in the design of China's reform policies. In the background lay the excessive expansion of bank credits in the fourth quarter of 1984 that had resulted in overheating of the economy and 10 per cent inflation in that quarter. China faced the risk of serious inflation. In the conference, the economists made many policy suggestions to government. Professor Tobin, especially, said that the government should simultaneously implement tight fiscal, monetary and income policies, rather than the conventional loose-tight combination policies applied in western countries in the face of inflationary risk. Besides discussing the inflation issues, the foreign participants systematically introduced modern macroeconomics to Chinese officials and economists, covering such topics as management of the macroeconomy and monetary policy. The *Bashanlun Conference* greatly improved the Chinese participants' understanding of modern macroeconomics and provided important theoretical preparation for the adoption of market-oriented reform policies in the national conference of Chinese Communist Party (CCP) in 1985.

In November 1993, the 14th CCP National Congress published the *Resolution of Establishing the Socialist Market Economy,* which was positively evaluated by Chinese and foreign economists and international organisations. International co-operation and consultation among economists in China and abroad had made theoretical contributions to the adoption of the *Resolution*. The reform measures taken in 1994 based on the *Resolution* were highly successful.

The reform of state-owned enterprises and the public sector has been a pivotal and extremely difficult issue, and international consultations have influenced reform schemes for the state sector. In 1987, the Commission of Economic System Reform of the State Council and the World Bank held the *International Conference on China's SOE Reform,* in which the participants systematically reviewed and evaluated international experience and lessons for public-enterprise reform. The topics discussed included ownership structure, the governance framework of modern corporations, pension mechanism design, etc. The Conference had an important influence on China's later ownership-oriented SOE reforms.

In August 1994, the State Commission of Economy and Trade, joined by other organisations, held the *International Conference on the Next Step of China's Economic Reform*. Foreign economists attending the conference included Oliver Hart, Paul Milgrom, Ronald Mckinnon, Lawrence Lau and Masahiko Aoki. The conference discussed several topics in modern microeconomics and firm theory, including governance of the modern corporation, the relationship between banks and enterprises, resolution of the non-performing loans problem and the bankruptcy process. The discussions and outcomes provided valuable insights for economic reform.

Policy suggestions proposed by western economists and international organisations are not always right, and they cannot be applied to China's particular economic environments without adaptation. The Chinese government remains very cautious and selective in accepting policy suggestions. Nonetheless, international consultation since the launch of China's Reform and Open-door policy has played an important role in improving Chinese policy makers' abilities to understand the issues, design reasonable economic reform schemes and facilitate the spread of modern economics in China.

The Impact of FDI on China's Economy

A capital-scarce country, China has taken various measures to attract foreign capital since the reform started in the 1970s. FDI is the principal form of foreign capital inflows; it accounted for 95.9 per cent of total inflows in 2002[3]. FDI increased rapidly from nearly zero in 1979 to $11.16 billion in 1992. Since 1992, China has become the largest recipient of FDI among all developing countries. Inflows reached $52.74 billion in 2002, exceeding those into the United States and ranking China in second place world-wide[4]. The ratio of FDI to GDP rose from nearly zero in 1980, peaked at 6.2 per cent in 1994 and stood at 4.3 per cent in 2002 (Figure 11.6).

Figure 11.6. **China's Use of FDI and the Ratio of FDI to GDP, 1980-2002**

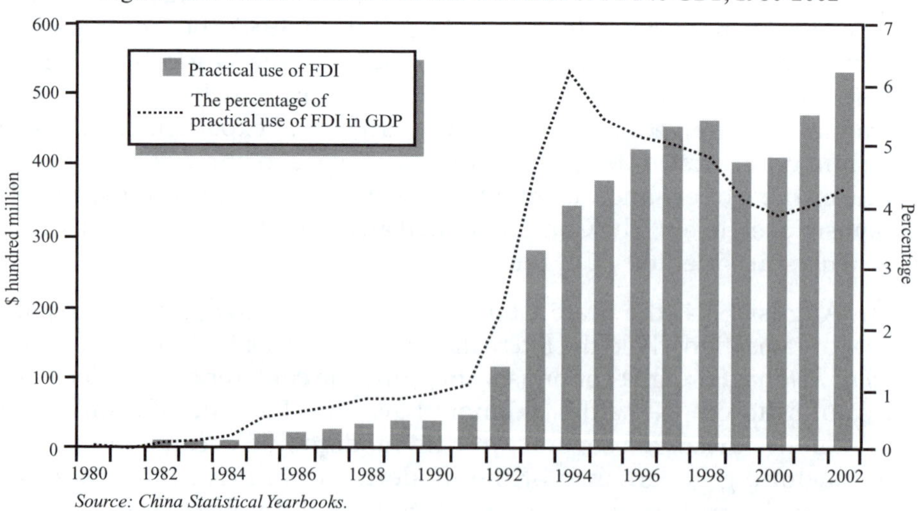

Source: China Statistical Yearbooks.

ISBN 92-64-01442-X © OECD 2005

The influence of FDI on the economic development of a capital-scarce and labour-abundant economy like China is self-evident. Large amounts of FDI can not only make up for the scarcity of domestic capital, improve the factor-endowment structure and promote industrial upgrading, but also bring in advanced management and technology. Given the effect of FDI on fixed capital formation and the export elasticity of FDI, the estimated contribution of FDI to GDP growth in China was about 0.6 per cent per year in 1990-2000 (Wang, 2001).

The Pattern of FDI in China

The geographical distribution of FDI is very uneven, with a large gap between the eastern region and the central and western regions. When the reforms started, FDI concentrated mainly on four special economic zones. Later on, with changing policy on attracting foreign investment, FDI gradually spread from the southern coastal region to the southeast, the eastern region and inland, but the eastern region still holds first place (Table 11.1). The vast central and western regions' GDP accounted for 38.5 per cent and their populations for 58.7 per cent of the national totals in 2002, but together they received only 12.7 per cent of the FDI inflow.

Table 11.1. **Distribution of FDI in the Eastern, Central, and Western regions of China**
(percentages)

	FDI 1984-1991	FDI 1992-2002	FDI 2002	Population 2002	GDP 2002
Eastern	90.7	87.7	87.3	41.3	61.5
Central	4.7	9.2	10.0	35.6	27.5
Western	4.6	3.1	2.7	23.1	11

Source: *China Statistical Yearbooks* for the years covered, authors' calculations.

China's National Bureau of Statistics classifies FDI by four types — joint ventures, co-operative operations, co-operative development and foreign enterprises[5]. From 1979 to 1985, co-operative operations were the main form. In 1986, joint ventures took the largest share (Zhang and Zheng, 1998), and in 2000 foreign enterprises moved into first place. Sole proprietorships reached 60.2 per cent of the total in 2002. FDI has concentrated mainly in manufacturing (Table 11.2) with the tertiary industries — chiefly real estate, social services and hotels[6] – next in importance. The proportion of FDI in manufacturing is increasing with the deepening of reform. In 2002, FDI agreements in manufacturing reached $61.13 billion, 73.9 per cent of the total.

Table 11.2. **Sector Distribution of FDI Agreements**[a]
(per cent of total agreements)

	Agriculture	Manufacturing	Construction	Trade, Transportation and Communication	Tertiary Industries	Others
1993-1998	1.7	60.7	3.5	6.3	24.3	3.6
1999-2002	2.6	72.1	2.0	4.3	15.9	3.1

Note: *a)* Differences may arise between the amounts of FDI specified in investment agreements and capital flows actually used in operations.

Source: *China Statistical Yearbooks* for the years covered, authors' calculations.

Hong Kong, China[7] has always been the most important source of FDI, followed by Japan, the United States and Chinese Taipei. From 1985 to 2002 the average proportions of FDI actually used from these four sources were 52.4 per cent, 9.7 per cent, 9.6 per cent and 5.8 per cent of the total, respectively. In 1985, the combined flow from Hong Kong, China; Japan; and the United States was 83.2 per cent. The sources of FDI gradually diversified in the 1990s as investment from Chinese Taipei, Korea, Singapore and European countries increased. In general, FDI in China still comes mainly from East Asia. Hong Kong, China and Chinese Taipei hold prominent positions both because China has a special policy to attract FDI and because they have close geographic and cultural affinity with the Mainland. In the later 1990s, an increase in FDI from the British Virgin Islands and the Cayman Islands revealed sources of capital available from the trend towards tax avoidance[8].

Because FDI comes from countries and regions that have different factor endowments, the associated enterprises have different comparative advantages and thus the purposes of FDI and the technologies used by foreign investors vary. Chen (1997), in a study of the 3 000 biggest FDIs in 1994, showed that FDI in China from Hong Kong, China; Chinese Taipei; Singapore; Korea and Asian countries other than Japan concentrated on labour-intensive industries and were mainly export-oriented[9]. This reflected development in the source countries. Their original comparative advantage had been in labour-intensive, export-oriented industries. With development, their labour costs increased, they lost this comparative advantage at home and they transferred these operations to China through FDI to take advantage of its cheap labour.

ISBN 92-64-01442-X © OECD 2005

In contrast, a significant part of other types of FDI, mainly from developed countries such as Japan, the United States and Western Europe seeks the penetration of China's domestic markets rather than cheap labour. This FDI comes mainly from the more capital-intensive economies, and the industries involved generally are capital-intensive too. For example, among the five manufacturing industries that received the most FDI from Chinese Taipei and Singapore, four are labour-intensive; from Hong Kong, China three are labour-intensive; from Japan the first two are capital-intensive; and from the United States the first three are capital-intensive.

The Functions and Economic Impacts of FDI

A country's factor endowment determines endogenously the level of development of its industrial structure. Therefore, an important development task involves upgrading the country's factor endowment, i.e. increasing the proportion of capital (Lin, 2003). The accumulation of capital depends on the scale of the country's economic surplus as well as its saving propensity. FDI contributes positively to both. First, it increases investment and the capital stock. Next, because FDI flows in pursuit of profits, the accompanying advanced technology and management help it to make full use of the opportunities in China's economy and to create large amounts of economic surplus. In addition, the competition and the spillover effects of the technology and knowledge brought by FDI also enhance the economic performance of domestically owned enterprises.

FDI and Capital Formation

Investment is a crucial determinant of economic growth. Most cross-country empirical studies show that a high growth rate is significantly related to a high rate of investment. The pattern of Chinese factor endowment indicates that China is scarce in capital at its current stage of development. Compared with other kinds of capital flows, FDI has high stability (Klein *et al.*, 2001). Large FDI inflows provide China with this comparatively stable source of capital, making a positive contribution to relieving capital scarcity and increasing the rates of investment and economic growth. Indeed, as reform proceeds, FDI plays an increasingly important role in Chinese capital formation. From 1992 to 2002, the average shares of FDI in China's fixed investment and net capital formation were 12.5 per cent and 18.2 per cent respectively. The latter is far above the average (under 10 per cent) in most OECD and developing countries (Herr and Priewe, 1999). Zhang and Zheng (1998) estimated that

ISBN 92-64-01442-X © OECD 2005

for a 1 per cent increase in the use of FDI, China's GDP growth increased by about 0.02 per cent. From 1992 to 2002, the average annual growth total FDI was 33.9 per cent. Therefore, FDI contributed about 0.68 per cent per year to China's average annual GDP growth in this period.

FDI and Foreign Trade

China's foreign trade has expanded rapidly since reform started in the late 1970s. Export gains benefit largely from the fast-rising exports of foreign-invested enterprises because these firms have good access to foreign markets. Most FDI in China is export-oriented, so the enterprises also have a higher propensity to export than domestic ones (Jiang, 2002). From 1992 to 2002, exports from foreign-invested enterprises took an increasing share of China's total exports. It averaged 39 per cent over the period and reached 52.2 per cent in 2002. Lin and Li (2001) found that the elasticity of GDP growth to the change in exports in the 1990s was 0.105 — a 10 per cent increase in exports resulted in a 1 per cent increase in GDP growth. Clearly, FDI contributes to GDP growth *via* exports. Exports rose by an average 15.2 per cent a year from 1992 to 2002. One thus can estimate the contribution of FDI to average annual GDP growth at 0.62 per cent, similar to the effect of FDI on growth through its impact on fixed capital formation estimated by Zhang and Zheng (1998).

FDI also enhances the export structure. International experience shows that exports of technology-intensive products usually grow faster than do other exports (United Nations, 1999). Large amounts of FDI have improved the pattern of China's exports. In 1980, primary products accounted for 50.3 per cent of total exports and industrial products for 49.7 per cent. By 2002, the share of industrial products had climbed to 91.2 per cent. FDI played a crucial role in the upgrading. For example, the share of electronic and mechanical products in total exports rose to 48.2 per cent in 2002 from 23 per cent in 1992. At the same time, foreign-invested enterprises in those industries had a much higher and faster-growing share of their exports. It rose to 66.9 per cent in 2002 from 31.2 per cent a decade earlier.

Spill-over Effects of Knowledge and Technology

Technology advancement can enhance factor productivity and hence improve enterprise performance and industrial efficiency. FDI has had a clear spillover effect from knowledge and technology on the development of China's economy. Foreign-invested enterprises, especially the large multinationals,

 ISBN 92-64-01442-X © OECD 2005

possess higher technology and better management than domestic enterprises. Both accompany FDI. In addition, foreign-invested enterprises will attune their technologies to levels consistent with China's comparative advantage, because only by doing so can they minimise their production costs. These kinds of technology are easy for domestic enterprises to imitate. Many empirical studies have shown that this spillover effect is significant. Graham and Wada (2001), Zhang (2001) and Liu (2002) all suggested that, with other factors controlled, total factor productivity (TFP) in the regions and sectors where FDI concentrated exceeded that of other regions and sectors. Liu also showed that in manufacturing the increase of foreign-owned stock not only benefited its industry, but also increased the TFP of related industries.

Improving the Quality of China's Capital Stock

Another important function of FDI is to improve industrial competitiveness and thus the quality of the existing capital stock[10]. New enterprises created by FDI generally are more competitive and have higher returns on investment than local private or state-owned enterprises. In 2002, the assets of foreign-invested enterprises in China accounted for 21.6 per cent of total industrial assets. They contributed 27.2 per cent of the gross value of industrial output, 23.7 per cent of total industrial value added, 26.6 per cent of industrial sales and 30.8 per cent of total profits (Jiang and Li, 2002). Obviously their efficiency is higher than the average level for domestic enterprises. Moreover, China's economy has a significant stock of low-quality assets. Foreign investments bring competitive pressure to bear on domestic enterprises, especially the SOEs, motivating their reform and facilitating the transformation of low-quality into higher-quality capital. Foreign-invested enterprises can also restructure domestic ones through changes in production and management. Some case studies show that foreign investors can transform loss-making enterprises simply by changing "software" like management, marketing and income distribution.

Other Impacts

FDI can also put pressures on the price formation mechanism by connecting domestic markets to international markets, facilitating the reform of distorted domestic factor prices, creating a factor-price structure that reflects relative factor scarcities and promoting the exploitation of comparative advantage. FDI also creates job opportunities, which has a multiplier effect just like other investment. FDI, especially investment by multinational enterprises, makes the distribution of intra- and inter-industry income more unequal (Zhang and Zheng, 1998).

The Impact of China's Entry into the WTO

China's entry into the WTO will challenge the Chinese government's longstanding authority to intervene in the economy. One can view the WTO rules as a mandatory legal instrument that will redefine the Chinese government's power. At the same time, WTO entry is consistent with the long-term objective of China's economic reform to establish a socialistic market economy, and WTO entry will accelerate the transition to such an economy.

The Economic Reform Background to WTO Entry

China has carried out a series of market-oriented reforms since 1978. They started with improvement of the micro incentive mechanisms and proceeded to resource allocation arrangements and the macro policy environment. Reform of the macro policy environment has proved difficult, however, for two reasons.

Reform of the political and administrative system lags far behind economic reform, making it hard to transform the legacy of the planned economy. When the government still unintentionally follows the "catching-up" strategy, it cannot avoid intervening extensively in running the national economy. Macro policy reform cannot proceed, especially the reform of factor prices, owing to the need to protect capital-intensive industries. Furthermore, government control of too many resources results in rent-seeking activities. The estimated annual losses arising from corruption and inefficiency in the second half of the 1990s amount to from 13.2 per cent to16.8 per cent of China's GDP[11].

· Second, the vested interest groups formed under the traditional planned economy may impede market-oriented reform. The public sector, especially the big SOEs that have benefited greatly from lower factor prices, is the potential opponent of market-oriented reform. The big SOEs employ large numbers of workers, and their managers have an intimate relationship with the government. Therefore, they have strong bargaining power in influencing the government's economic policies.

ISBN 92-64-01442-X © OECD 2005

The Impact of WTO Membership on the Chinese Economy

WTO entry will have a significant, positive effect on China's final resolution of problems linked to the macroeconomic policy environment. Theoretically, the first-best development path observes the comparative advantages of an economy. To make the whole society respond correctly to the economy's comparative advantages requires a market-based price mechanism that can reflect the relative scarcities of factor endowments. Achieving this demands a transparent macro policy environment and efficient markets. If factor prices can reflect relative factor scarcities, enterprises will make their product and technology decisions accordingly. The institutions for forming correct relative prices are consistent with those promoted by WTO principles, and WTO entry can help China overcome many problems affecting reform in the macro policy environment.

WTO membership will play a key role in facilitating China's change of development strategy. WTO agreements have many compulsory provisions on the relationship between governments and SOEs; they aim to prevent governments from giving the SOEs favourable positions in market competition through discriminatory policies. In an efficient market based on equal competition, industries consistent with China's comparative advantage will develop faster, and the upgrading of the factor endowment structure will accelerate.

Second, the WTO Agreement will press China to carry out reform of the administrative system. The transparency principle requires WTO members to make their economic management and policies stable and predictable. External pressure from the WTO will encourage the government to study and solve the problem of the "administrative black box" and reduce the opportunities for corruption, bureaucracy, administrative inefficiency, etc. WTO entry facilitates China's integration into the global economy. Government policies should conform to the principles of market competition, the rules of WTO and the characteristics of economic agents. In sum, the Chinese government needs to improve the efficiency and transparency of decision making according to WTO principles.

Finally, WTO membership offers a good opportunity for reforming the big SOEs. The problem of SOEs arises not from their state ownership but from their policy burdens, including their strategic and social responsibilities[12]. With these burdens gone, the profits of an SOE in a competitive market will reflect the performance of the SOE's management. The government will no longer be obliged to subsidise and protect SOEs. This would eliminate the remaining economic distortions and complete the transition from the planned to a market economy.

How China Faces the Challenges of WTO Membership

WTO membership brings more challenges to the Chinese government than to enterprises, because the WTO agreements stipulate restrictions on government intervention in economic activities rather than on enterprises. In this sense WTO entry provides a real basis for the transformation of the government's role. In the third year after China's WTO entry, China has been taking various measures to meet the requirements of WTO agreements. Great changes have taken place in many areas such as industrial policy, macroeconomic control, trade policy, the taxation system and the legal system.

Industrial Policy

WTO membership will greatly change China's industrial structure, which will have to adjust according to the principle of comparative advantage. Industrial policy must reflect the changes in China's comparative advantage, to facilitate enterprises' optimal choices of technologies and industries. As a WTO member, the government can no longer rely on direct controls and administrative measures. It will have to use indirect, market-based measures in order to realise its development and macroeconomic goals. The Chinese economy has experienced several cyclical fluctuations since the start of reform, and the. government has often relied directly on administrative measures to maintain economic growth within a certain range and to intervene in the daily operations of the SOEs. These direct government interventions into economic activities were reasonable in the former planned-economy system. To meet the current challenges of WTO membership, the government launched a new round of administrative reforms in 2003, and the approach towards macroeconomic regulation changed greatly, with the formerly powerful State Planning Commission replaced by the National Development and Reform Commission. This new Commission has simplified the process of business ratification and the responsibility for micro-management. Reforms of this kind, like separate financial regulation, have also been introduced in other government departments.

ISBN 92-64-01442-X © OECD 2005

Trade Policy

Adjustments consequent upon WTO entry affect four aspects of trade policy. First, the government has made policies more transparent with the assurance that they will be effectively implemented. According to the *Progress Report* of China's Working Group, it has followed the WTO's requirements, published its related trade policies on time and guaranteed their transparency. At the same time, the new Ministry of Commerce established in 2003 integrates the management of domestic and foreign trade to deepen trade system reform. Second, China has reduced its tariffs greatly, cancelled quantitative limitations on imports of industrial goods and adopted a tariff-quota system on staple agricultural products. China reduced its average tariff from 15.3 per cent to 12 per cent in 2002 and moved further to 11 per cent in 2003 (Figure 11.7). It thus fulfilled its commitments on tariff reduction ahead of schedule.

Figure 11.7. **Trend of China's Average Tariff**

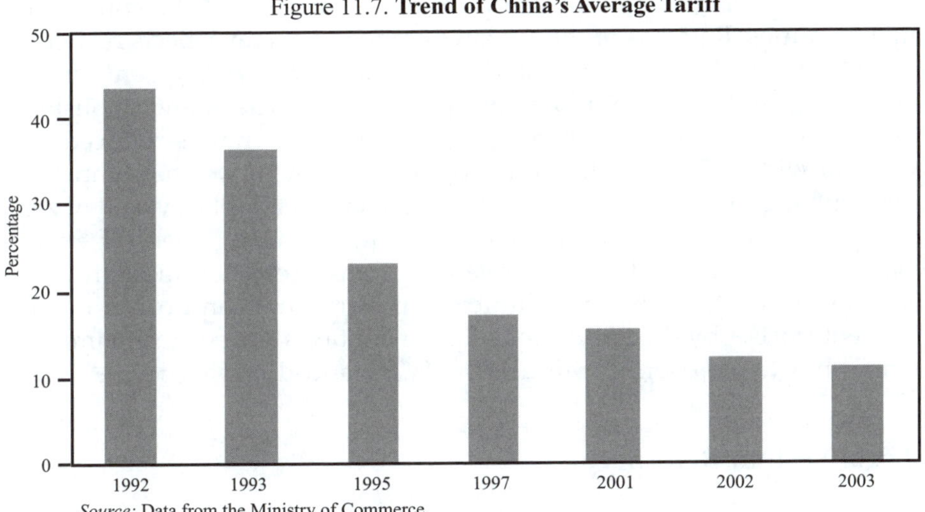

Source: Data from the Ministry of Commerce.

Third, an ongoing deregulation of import and export rights will finish in three years. At that time, China's foreign trade will change from the existing system dominated by state-owned companies to one that includes companies with all kinds of ownership structures, including state, joint venture, foreign capital, public, collective and private ownership. Fourth, trade disputes will be settled within the WTO framework. This change provides China with a favourable mechanism to deal with anti-dumping accusations. The OECD countries can no longer view China as a non-market economy and apply unfair alternative standards to it. Moreover, China can enjoy the favourable treatment for developing member countries in the WTO and improve its position in anti-dumping negotiations by using updated market information collected by the WTO.

Tax System Reform

WTO membership brings several challenges to China's tax system. In an era of globalisation, the ways to avoid or evade taxes become diversified, covert and broadened, so it becomes more difficult to fight against tax evasion. To regulate tax management, China enacted the *Outlines for Tax Collection Management Strategy: 2002 to 2006*[13], which laid out 13 reform items, including tax-collection institutions and laws, tax-source inspection and so on. This is a major achievement in settling China's taxation problems by combining international experience, opinions from foreign experts and the constraints of China's realities. Reforms of the tax laws embody several aspects related to foreign enterprises. First, the income tax of domestic and foreign enterprises will be unified, reducing domestic enterprises' tax burdens and abolishing the tax preference for foreign enterprises. While the tax rate is reduced, the tax base will widen. Second, the export drawback system will be completed. Together with the reform of value-added tax, China will adopt a system of zero tariffs for exports and gradually abolish the quota management of export drawback. Third, China will set up certain customs protection measures. For goods whose imports China must limit, the government can protect related domestic enterprises by specific duties, adjustment taxes and so on. For imports that China has to sanction, it can use the WTO anti-dumping rules.

Legal System Reform

To develop the economy according to China's comparative advantage and satisfy the requirements of the WTO, China needs to carry out major changes in its legal system, harmonising it with international practices and providing economic activities with a stable and transparent legal foundation and policy environment. The government has been amending related laws and regulations[14], but the influence of the previous system makes this part of reform the most difficult. Unsuitable laws and regulations have much to do with the old centrally planned system. WTO entry provides an impetus for

ISBN 92-64-01442-X © OECD 2005

cleaning up these remaining legacies of the planned system. It is predictable that the reconstruction of the legal system will be carried out successfully as the distortions in the macro policy environment are eliminated.

In short, WTO membership will become a catalyst for market-oriented reform because the ultimate goal of China's economic reform is to set up a mature market system consistent with what the WTO requires. Under the discipline of WTO's rules and the pressure from the schedule of liberalisation, the government must speed up the reforms and eliminate all obstacles to the development of a market economy. WTO entry will require it to accelerate reforms on industrial policy, macroeconomic management, trade policy, the taxation system and the legal system. Thus, while WTO membership brings serious challenges, it also brings huge development opportunities to the Chinese economy.

Concluding Remarks

China's economic reform has resulted in great achievements in the past 25 years. Many researchers have attempted to analyse various aspects of China's success. So far most research has focused on the internal factors in China's economy. This chapter describes the origins and logic of China's reform and reviews the impacts of major external factors on it.

It argues first that the passing away of Chairman Mao provided an opportunity for major policy change. The new leaders who returned to power after the Cultural Revolution required reform to improve people's living standards as a means to gain legitimacy. They were also veterans of socialist revolution, however. They had participated in the design and implementation of the traditional planned economy. Therefore it was natural for them to adopt a piecemeal, tinkering, gradual approach to reform.

The major external factors influencing China's economic reform included international aid, international consultations, FDI and WTO entry. The impacts of international aid on the reform did not come from the quantity of funds supplied but from the exemplary effects of aid projects, and aid has played different roles in different stages of China's reform. International consultations have enhanced the Chinese government's capabilities in economic policy design and implementation and have facilitated the spread of modern economics in China, although China's policy makers are generally very cautious and selective in accepting policy suggestions proposed by foreign economists and international organisations.

Large FDI inflows not only supplement China's domestic capital, but also bring in advanced management and technology. This creates a positive externality for reform of the domestic market and enterprises. According to empirical studies on the effects of FDI on the formation of fixed assets and on the export elasticity of FDI, FDI contributed an estimated 0.6 per cent annually to China's GDP growth in 1992-2002. Finally, WTO membership facilitates China's transition from a planned to a modern market economy. Under the WTO agreements, the Chinese government must expedite its market-oriented reform and clean up institutional arrangements inherited from the past that are not suitable for the market system.

ISBN 92-64-01442-X © OECD 2005

Notes

1. Average annual GDP growth was 9.1 per cent in the first five-year plan, 2.2 per cent in the second, 14.9 per cent in 1963-65, 6.9 per cent in the third plan and 5.5 per cent in the fourth. The average annual growth rate was 6 per cent during 1953-78.
2. The inflation and GDP indices of FSU and Eastern European countries are included in Lin *et al.* (1994, 1999), Figures 1.1 and 1.2.
3. Foreign capital inflows consist of three types: foreign loans, FDI and other foreign investment. Before 1992, foreign loans were the main form of foreign capital inflow. Since 1992, FDI has been the main form. The average percentage of FDI in total capital inflows during 1992- 2002 was 76.7 per cent. It reached 95.9 per cent in 2002.
4. Luxembourg received the most FDI in 2002, about $125.66 billion (UN *World Investment Report*, 2003). In UNCTAD world FDI data, Luxembourg and Belgium were counted together before 2002.
5. A new type named "foreign invested joint-stock enterprises" was added in 1997, and an "others" category was added in 1998, but both have little importance in FDI. In 2002, they accounted for 1.1 per cent and 0.1 per cent respectively.
6. Real estate, social services, hotels, finance and insurance are all included in the tertiary industries in Table 6.3; the finance and insurance share is very small.
7. Before 1991, FDI data from Hong Kong, China and Macao were calculated together.
8. The statistics on China's FDI are based on the geographic location of the source enterprise registry, which may differ from the country to which the enterprise actually belongs.
9. Because the capital intensity of large enterprises in general is higher than that of medium and small enterprises, the capital intensity reported in Chen's study, which is based on the 3 000 biggest foreign-invested companies, may be higher than the actual capital intensity of all foreign invested enterprises.

10. This section draws on Jiang (2001).

11. Guo and Hu (2002).

12. Many SOEs bear the strategic burden because they operate in sectors not consistent with China's comparative advantage. SOEs bear social burdens because they must employ many redundant workers and cover many old-age pensions for retired workers (Lin *et al.*, 1994).

13. The *Outlines for Tax Collection Management Strategy: 2002 to 2006* was a part of the UNDP's grant for China's tax system reform. The IMF implemented the research.

14. According to the WTO rules and for China's own benefit, about 40 laws and regulations needed to be amended or established. China has excellently fulfilled its obligations in this respect. For instance, in accordance with the WTO's prohibition of using foreign exchange balances to restrict imports, the 3rd clause of the 18th item in China's *Law of Foreign Investment,* which required foreign-invested companies to resolve foreign exchange problems by themselves, was deleted. According to the principle of non-discrimination, the 15th item in *Law of Foreign Investment* was also deleted. It had required companies to give priority to goods produced in China in their procurement.

ISBN 92-64-01442-X © OECD 2005

Bibliography

CHEN, C. (1997), "Comparison of Investment Behaviour of Source Countries in China", Working Paper No. 97/14, December, Chinese Economies Research Centre, University of Adelaide, Australia.

China Statistical Yearbook (multiple years), Beijing, China Statistical Press (in Chinese).

DABROWSKI, M. (2001), "Ten Years of Polish Economic Transition, 1989-1999" *in* M.I. BLEJER and M. SKREB (eds.) *Transition: The First Decade*. pp. 121-152, MIT Press, Cambridge, MA.

GRAHAM, E.M. and E. WADA (2001), "Foreign Direct Investment in China: Effects on Growth and Economic Performance" *in* P. DRYSDALE (ed.), *Achieving High Growth: Experience of Transitional Economies in East Asia*, Oxford University Press, Oxford.

GUO, Y. and A. HU (2002), "The Losses Caused by Administrative Monopoly Can Not Be Overlooked", *Chinese Economy Times* 15 July.

HERR, H. and J. PRIEWE (1999), "High Growth in China — Transition without a Transition Crisis?" *Intereconomics*, 34 (6), January, pp. 303-316. Also available at: http://www.macropolicies-berlin.de/download/HighGrowthinChina.pdf

JIANG, X. (2001), "Contribution of Foreign Economy of China to Growth, Updating of Structure and Competence" (in Chinese), China People's University Press, Beijing.

JIANG, X. (2002), *Foreign Capital in China*, (in Chinese) China People's University Press, Beijing.

JIANG, X. and R. LI (2002), "Contribution of FDI to China's Industry and Technology Progress", *China Industrial Economics 2002* (7), pp. 5-16 (in Chinese).

KLEIN, M., C. AARON and B. HADJIMICHAEL (2001), "Foreign Direct Investment and Poverty Reduction", Working Paper No. 2613, World Bank Policy Research, Washington, D.C.

LIN, J.Y. (1992), "Rural Reforms and Agricultural Growth in China", *American Economic Review*, Vol. 82, No.1, pp. 422-427.

LIN, J.Y. (2003), "Development Strategy, Viability, and Economic Convergence", *Economic Development and Cultural Change,* Vol. 51, No. 2, pp. 277-308.

LIN, J.Y. and Y. LI (2001), "A Second Review of the Relationship between International Trade and Economic Growth", Beijing University, CCER Working Paper Series, No.C2001008 (in Chinese).

LIN, J.Y. and P. LIU (2003), "Resolving Problem of Viability and Facilitating Economic Growth", CCER Working Paper Series, No. C2003019 (in Chinese), Peking University.

LIN, J.Y. and G. TAN (1999), "Policy Burdens: Accountability and Soft Budget Constraint", *American Economic Review,* Vol. 89, No. 2, pp. 426-31.

LIN, J.Y., F. CAI and Z. LI (1994), *China's Miracle: Development Strategy and Economic Growth,* (2nd version, 1999) (in Chinese), Shanghai People Press, Shanghai.

LIU, Z., (2002), "Foreign Direct Investment and Technology Spillover: Evidence from China", *Journal of Comparative Economics,* Vol. 30, No. 3, pp. 579-602.

UNITED NATIONS (1999), *World Investment Report,* United Nations, New York, NY.

UNITED NATIONS (2003), *World Investment Report — FDI Policies for Development: National and International Perspectives,* United Nations, New York, NY.

WANG, X. (2001), "Past and Future: Contribution of Investment to Growth", *Academic Journal of National Institute of Political Administration,* 2001 (4), pp. 56-61 (in Chinese).

WORLD BANK (1996), *World Development Report 1996: From Plan to Market,* Oxford University Press, New York, NY.

WORLD BANK (2002), *Transition: The First Ten Years — Analysis and Lessons for Eastern Europe and the Former Soviet Union,* World Bank, Washington, D.C.

WORLD BANK (1997, 2000/2001, 2004), *World Development Reports,* Oxford University Press, Oxford and New York, NY.

YI, X. (2002), "International Grant Aids and China", News Letter, Ministry of Commerce, Beijing, at http://www.mofcom.gov.cn/ (in Chinese).

ZHANG, F. and J. ZHENG (1998), "Impacts of Multinational Corporations on the Structure and Efficiency of China's Economy", CCER Working Paper No. C1998018 (in Chinese), Peking University.

ZHANG, K.H. (2001), "How Does Foreign Direct Investment Affect Economic Growth in China? *Economics of Transition,* 9 (3), pp. 679-693.

ISBN 92-64-01442-X © OECD 2005

Chapter 12

The Migration of Highly Skilled Asian Workers to OECD Member Countries and its Effects on Economic Development in East Asia

Yongyuth Chalamwong[1]

Abstract

This chapter seeks to review the highlights of major trends in international migration both from East Asia to OECD member countries and within East Asia, focusing on the movement of highly skilled workers. Large numbers of workers migrate from less-advanced East Asian countries to the more advanced economies of the region and to the OECD area. Movements of highly qualified foreign workers have become a focal point of the "brain-drain" *versus* "brain-circulation" debates in the international community. The study sheds light on these important debates. It examines the effects of migration of highly skilled workers on the sending and receiving countries. Different OECD policies concerning such migrants have led to various effects on economic development in East Asia. The chapter provides discussion of some "policy coherence" questions. It also compares measures used to cope with problems of illegal migration in the OECD countries and East Asia. Similarities and differences between policies on combating illegal entry into OECD and non-OECD countries are briefly examined. The paper recommends that it is in the interests of East Asian countries both to explore the usefulness of diaspora networks or communities as an alternative to reversing the "brain-drain" and to enhance the return options of overseas nationals. "Diaspora centres" could be established to seek co-operation from nationals abroad in exchanging talent or knowledge without uprooting them from the countries where they work.

ISBN 92-64-01442-X © OECD 2005

Introduction

This chapter measures the impact and coherence of OECD-country policies concerning labour migration on various Asian developing economies. The links among OECD member countries and the East Asian developing economies have been strong not only through flows of trade and services but also through inter-regional flows of capital, technology and labour[2].

The persistence of widespread unemployment worldwide suggests that strong migration pressures have been and will continue to be an important factor in the current decade (Abella, 2001). Most Asian countries with high unemployment rates are less developed than transition economies. East Asia had remarkable economic growth until the 1997/98 crises. Crisis-affected countries such as Korea, China, Malaysia and Thailand have recovered very quickly, and their labour markets have enjoyed full revival to pre-1997 levels. Yet the unemployment rate in China very unfortunately has remained high at around 9 per cent, despite China's enduring, impressively high growth rates. A key question is whether imbalances in the regional labour market and the global economy more generally have affected international migration, especially between East Asia[3] and the OECD countries.

A continuation of the economic upturn in most OECD member countries since the 1990s has created a "pull factor" that has a major impact on the labour market. The strong demand for unskilled labour and highly-skilled workers in some OECD member countries cannot be met by local nationals, which leads inevitably to higher wages and subsequently increased demand for immigrants. Garson's (2001)[4] assessment of the current demographic situation in OECD countries indicates that the labour shortages will be most severe over the next 25 years. To compensate for slow increases in population as a result of very low rates of natural population growth in most OECD countries, the promotion of immigration would seem an effective measure to increase the size of the economically active population and ease the labour shortage[5].

Since the mid-1990s, a gradual upturn has occurred in migration flows to most OECD countries for four main reasons: regional conflict, restrictions on other immigration channels, asylum seekers and family reunion. In recent years many OECD countries have increasingly adopted policies that promote the entry of skilled and highly skilled workers, especially in information and communication technology (ICT). This immigration of ICT workers has met market needs and will help to maintain or sustain the competitiveness of these countries in the world market (Garson, 2001).

ISBN 92-64-01442-X © OECD 2005

According to Abella (2001), among East Asian countries, especially the developing and transitional economies, the divergence in incomes with those of the OECD countries will likely become greater. Yet this has not been the case, at least in recent years, as ratios of per capita income between OECD and East Asian countries have gradually become smaller, although the gaps themselves remain large (Table 12.1). One still cannot conclude that the association with globalisation has led to further widening of income disparities. The traditional income differentials between OECD and East Asian countries may offer the only explanation for immigration into the OECD countries. In fact, past immigration policies have varied greatly across OECD countries, both historically and currently. Generally they have aimed to give preference to certain groups. Although there is free movement of people within the EU, laws differ across member countries in entry requirements for citizens of non-member countries (Bauer *et al.*, 2000). As the world shifts to a knowledge-based economy based on high-level skills and knowledge, the change is expected to exacerbate the movement of highly skilled workers from the East Asian countries to the West. Recent years have witnessed growing competition for highly skilled migrants as many OECD countries have opened their doors to ICT workers as well as other highly skilled professionals.

Table 12.1. **Comparison of Per Capita Income between Asian (10) and OECD Countries**

(dollars per person; ratios as multiples)

Country/Income	1998	2001	2002
(1) Asian (10)[a]	945.5	1 068.3	1 153.5
(2) OECD-East Asia (2)[b]	24 418.6	26 547.3	25 610.4
(3) OECD (30)	21 411.6	22 161.9	23 610.2
Ratio between (2) and (1)	25.8	24.8	22.2
Ratio between (3) and (1)	22.6	20.7	20.0

Notes: *a)* The ten study countries in Asia comprise Hong Kong, China; Singapore; Malaysia; Thailand; China; Indonesia; Philippines; Laos and Cambodia.

b) The two OECD members located in East Asia are Japan and Korea.

Source: *World Development Indicators* database, April 2004.

Since the second half of the 1990s, the movement of highly skilled workers, especially those in the ICT sector, from East Asia to the OECD countries has been remarkable. Different OECD-country policies concerning such migrants have led to various effects on economic development in East Asia. These are described in the fourth section of this chapter, after reviews of the broad patterns and trends regarding highly skilled East Asian workers in major OECD countries and of the relevant OECD-country policies. The final sections review how OECD members cope with the problems of illegal entry as compared with countries in East Asia, discuss policy coherence between the OECD countries and East Asia and offer conclusions and recommendations.

Patterns and Trends: Highly Skilled Asian Workers in Major OECD Countries

International migration from developing East Asia has become a significant feature of economic development in this region since the end of the 1980s when trade and investment started to play increasingly important roles. Among receiving countries, past immigration policies have led to different compositions of immigrants. Bauer *et al.* (2000) have sorted these countries into three types. The traditional immigration countries (e.g. the United States, Canada, Australia and New Zealand) considered immigrants essential for development and continued to accept immigration for permanent settlement. The second group includes post-colonial or other European countries actively recruiting labour (e.g. the United Kingdom, France, the Netherlands, Austria, Germany and Sweden) and the third includes nations just recently transformed from emigration to immigration countries (e.g. Ireland, Italy and Spain). Since the mid-1980s, immigration flows to the traditional immigration countries have concentrated on economic migrants, namely skilled workers or business immigrants. Flows to the second group did not shift until the late 1990s to economic migrants from east-west migration, inflows of asylum seekers, Commonwealth migrants and refugees. The third group accepts immigrants from both EU-countries and Non-EU-countries (Bauer *et al.*, 2000, pp. 7-9). Lucas (2001) identifies three principal streams of emigration from East Asia: to the Pacific-Rim OECD countries, to the Middle East and to other countries within the region. The analysis here focuses only on the first and third streams; the Middle East is not considered owing to data limitations.

Migration to OECD Countries

Carrington and Detragiache (1998) estimated the extent of migration by highly skilled workers from developing countries to OECD markets based on 1990 data. Their estimates showed that as a percentage of source populations people with tertiary education from Malaysia registered the

ISBN 92-64-01442-X © OECD 2005

highest migration rates to OECD countries, followed by those from Korea, the Philippines and Chinese Taipei (Table 12.2). The authors also concluded that the largest absolute flow of highly skilled migrants to OECD countries was from Asia and migration rates clearly increased with education levels.

Table 12.2. **Migration Rates to OECD Countries in 1990**
(migrants as percentages of home-country populations, by education level)

Home Country/ Area	Level of Schooling	
	Secondary	Tertiary
India	0.3	2.7
China	0.2	3.1
Indonesia	0.1	1.6
Korea	3.4	17.6
Malaysia	1.2	29.4
Philippines	6.4	9.9
Chinese Taipei	0.8	9.2
Thailand	1.8	1.6

Source: Carrington and Detragiache (1998) Table 3.

Adams (2003) estimated migration flows from 24 labour-exporting countries to OECD countries by using data on migration flows from OECD (2001) and applying the same strategy used by Carrington and Detragiache (1998) to estimate the educational distribution of migrants[6]. Table 12.3 shows that migrants with tertiary education from Indonesia, the Philippines and India accounted for more than 70 per cent of the total migrants from each country to the OECD, while tertiary-educated migrants from China produced only 54 per cent of all Chinese immigrants to the OECD.

Table 12.3. **Immigrants Aged 25 and Older from Selected Labour-Exporting Countries to the OECD Area, by Education Level, 2000**
(numbers of immigrants; per cent of total in parentheses)

Home Country	Total Number of Immigrants	Level of Schooling		
		Primary or Less	Secondary	Tertiary
India	375 283	18 471	57 199	299 613
		(4.9)	(15.3)	(79.8)
China	722 400	148 029	185 295	389 076
		(20.5)	(25.6)	(53.9)
Indonesia	142 540	3 910	32 347	106 283
		(2.7)	(22.7)	(74.6)
Philippines	356 134	27 604	70 079	258 451
		(7.7)	(19.7)	(72.6)

Source: Adams (2003) Table 6.

ISBN 92-64-01442-X © OECD 2005

Table 12.4 shows migration rates to the OECD by level of educational attainment using source data from selected countries in East Asia and measuring the rates as percentages of the total populations of the home countries. The estimates suggest that the rates are highest for migrants with a tertiary level of education, although those rates are not very large — 3.6 per cent and 2 per cent respectively for the Philippines and Indonesia, for example. These data confirm the importance for immigration of high-level education, which is in high demand in the OECD member countries.

Table 12.4. **Migration Rates to OECD, 2000**
(migrants as percentages of home-country populations, by education level)

Home Country	Total	Level of Schooling		
		Primary or Less	Secondary	Tertiary
India	0.1	0.1	0.1	1.3
China	0.1	0.1	0.1	1.9
Indonesia	0.1	0.1	0.2	2.0
Philippines	1.1	0.2	0.7	3.6

Source: Adams (2003) Table 7.

Migration to the United States

Table 12.5 shows the emigration of Asians to the United States since the second half of the 1990s. In 1998, Asians accounted for one-third of the immigrants to the United States; half of them received employment-based immigration visas. Many had been foreign students or foreign workers. In 2002, about 646 000 foreign students were in the United States on student visas, and more than half of them came from Asia. In addition, of an estimated 582 000 foreign temporary workers and trainees, about one-third were from Asia, according to the Bureau of Consular Affairs at the US Department of State (Carrington and Detragiache, 1998).

In 2002, the Asian-born population living in the United States accounted for a third of the total foreign population. About 32 per cent originated from East Asia, 25 per cent from South Asia and 35 per cent from Southeast Asia. The number of migrants from China, India and the Philippines is certainly large. More than 1.3 million of them were born in India, 1.4 million in the Philippines and about 960 000 in China. Emigrants from China reached between 300 000 and 400 000 by the early 1990s; their numbers have risen to over 700 000 since the mid-1990s. The number of migrants from India more than doubled from 540 000 in 1995 to 1.3 million in 2002. Filipinos living in the United States have exceeded 1.1 million for a decade. The Philippines has registered the highest level of out-migration of any country in Asia.

 ISBN 92-64-01442-X © OECD 2005

Table 12.5.**Stock of Foreign-Born Population in the United States, by Country of Birth, 1995-2002**
(thousands)

Country/Area of Birth	1995	1996	1997	1998	1999	2000	2001	2002
All countries	24 473	24 557	25 779	26 281	26 448	30 081	31 811	32 453
Asia (total)	6 143	6 620	6 874	7 042	7 187	8 029	8 573	8 352
Eastern Asia (total)	2 145	2 031	2 363	2 244	2 142	2 650	2 921	2 645
China	690	801	940	834	843	973	1,105	959
Hong Kong, China	146	124	166	188	142	217	239	196
Japan	358	286	305	268	235	306	356	439
Korea	710	550	591	589	611	787	907	756
Chinese Taipei	241	269	360	365	311	365	313	294
Southern Asia (total)	940	1 262	1 298	1 360	1 430	1 768	1 969	2 027
India	540	757	748	722	839	1 126	1 284	1 304
Southeast Asia (total)	2 647	2 607	2 511	2 763	2 972	2 876	2 885	2 900
Indonesia	39	64	61	52	56	56	98	104
Malaysia	19	40	51	44	33	47	54	56
Philippines	1 341	1 164	1 132	1 207	1 455	1 354	1 495	1 429
Thailand	187	163	136	157	117	164	160	131
Viet Nam	613	740	770	989	966	963	786	819

Source: Migration Information Source, "Migration Information Service", 2004. http://www.migrationinformation.org/GlobalData.

One important characteristic of the Asian-born population in the United States is that those aged 25 and older were likely to have higher education levels than either native or other foreign-born population groups. The share of the foreign-born from Asia with secondary or higher diplomas (86.8 per cent) was not statistically different from that of the native population (86.9 per cent). Among the foreign-born, the percentage of high school graduates from Asia was the highest (Table 12.6). The Asian-born population also was the most likely to have attained a bachelor's or higher degree (48.9 per cent), compared with the native (26.8 per cent) or total foreign-born (26.5 per cent) populations. According to Adams (2003), the majority of US immigrants from several countries in East Asia were well-educated (Table 12.7), i.e. more than half had tertiary education. Table 12.8 shows the migration rates of tertiary-educated migrants to the United States. The Philippines recorded the highest figure (11.7 per cent) and Indonesia the lowest (0.7 per cent). In other words, migration to the United States created enormous outflows of the best-educated persons from the Philippines, while it produced only a small movement of such people from other countries, ranging from 2.8 per cent for China to 0.7 per cent for Indonesia.

Table 12.6. **United States: Educational Attainment of the Native and Foreign-Born Populations: March 2002**
(per cent of each population)

Educational Attainment	Native	Foreign-Born	Europe	Asia	Latin America	Other Areas
High school diploma or better	86.9	67.2	84.0	86.8	49.1	82.0
Bachelor's degree or better	26.8	26.5	34.7	48.9	10.8	33.4

Notes: Most of those born in "Latin America" are from Mexico. Those born in "other areas" are from Africa, Oceania, Bermuda and Canada. The populations include persons aged 25 years and older. Education refers to years of school completed, not attended.

Source: United States Census Bureau, *Current Population Survey*, March 2002

Table 12.7. **Number of Immigrants (aged 25 and older) to the United States from Selected Labour-Exporting countries, by Education Level, 2000**
(per cent shares of each country total in parentheses)

Home Country	Total Number of Immigrants	Level of Schooling		
		Primary or Less	Secondary	Tertiary
India	836 780	41 185	127 540	668 055
		(4.9)	(15.3)	(79.8)
China	846 780	173 545	217 185	456 050
		(20.5)	(25.6)	(53.9)
Indonesia	53 170	1 460	12 065	39 645
		(2.7)	(22.7)	(74.6)
Philippines	1 163 555	90 200	228 955	844 400
		(7.7)	(19.7)	(72.6)

Source: Adams (2003) Table 4.

Table 12.8. **Migration Rates to the United States, 2000**
(migrants in per cent of home-country populations, by education level)

Home Country	Total	Level of Schooling		
		Primary or Less	Secondary	Tertiary
India	0.2	0.1	0.2	2.8
China	0.1	0.1	0.2	2.2
Indonesia	0.1	0.1	0.1	0.7
Philippines	3.6	0.6	2.2	11.7

Source: Adams (2003) Table 5.

ISBN 92-64-01442-X © OECD 2005

Of the employed Asian-born population in the United States aged 16 years or older, 40.4 per cent concentrated in managerial and professional occupations and 26.9 per cent had technical, sales and administrative-support jobs. Only 11.5 per cent were operators, fabricators and labourers, and 0.6 per cent worked in farming, forestry and fishing (see Table 12.9). In short, the United States admits foreign professionals and others as non-immigrants[7]. During the 1990s, the door opened much wider for non-immigrant professionals as the "dot.com" boom reached its height (Martin, 2002). The US government has made it easier for highly skilled workers to enter and fill jobs, but still makes it difficult to convert student or H-1B visas into immigrant visas.

Table 12.9. **Occupations of Employed Workers, by Origin in Various Regions of the World, March 2002**

(per cent of each population)

Occupation Group	Foreign-Born	Europe	Asia	Latin America	Other Areas
Managerial and professional	23.4	37.2	40.4	10.5	32.6
Technical, sales and admin. support	20.6	24.9	26.9	15.9	25
Service occupations	21.1	13.5	13.9	26.8	18.8
Precision production, craft and repair	12.7	12.9	6.7	16.1	8.9
Operators, fabricators, labourers	18.3	9.9	11.5	24.5	13.1
Farming, forestry, fishing	3.8	1.6	0.6	6.2	1.6

Notes: Most of those born in "Latin America" are from Mexico. Those born in "other areas" are from Africa, Bermuda and Canada. The populations include persons aged 16 years or older. Professional status refers to the reference week of the survey.

Source: United States Census Bureau, *Current Population Survey*, March 2002.

Migration within East Asia

The East Asian countries fall into two groups, namely the predominantly migrant-receiving or labour-importing economies (e.g. Japan, Korea and Chinese Taipei) and the predominantly migrant-sending or labour-exporting countries (e.g. China, the Philippines and Indonesia). Some higher-income East Asian countries have faced a transition from net emigration to net immigration (e.g. Thailand and Malaysia) based on growing numbers of unskilled immigrants and highly skilled emigrants (Lucas, 2001). Highly skilled migrants within the region move mostly within multinational enterprises, suggesting the importance of migration in East Asia for technology transfer and human resource development (Iguchi, 2002).

Among the net migrant-receiving countries, Japan hosts only small numbers of immigrants because government policy promotes job creation and technology transfer to developing countries. The government encourages industries to relocate their highly labour-intensive operations outside Japan, as in Thailand and Malaysia. It also motivates employers to offset manpower shortages not by using foreign labour but by focusing instead on optimum use of internal manpower resources (Hayase *et al.*, 2001). Nevertheless, the problem of Japan's declining and ageing population and the rapid increase in Japanese foreign direct investment (FDI) have caused a change in migration policy — from controlling the number of foreign workers to expanding the acceptance of skilled ones while confirming the policy of not accepting the unskilled. Table 12.10 shows that the stocks of foreign labour in Japan increased considerably from 85 500 in 1992 to 154 700 in 2000. The largest group comprised workers from the Philippines, who accounted for one-third of the total, followed by Chinese workers (23 per cent). Thus more than half the foreign labour in Japan comes from East Asia.

Table 12.10. **Japan, Stock of Foreign Labour by Nationality**
(thousands)

Country	1992	1995	2000
Philippines	21.3	13.7	45.6
China[a]	17.1	23.3	35.8
United States	18.3	17.5	17.6
Korea	5.5	6.4	10.7
United Kingdom	5.2	5.6	8.1
Canada	3.3	4.1	5.8
Australia	2.0	2.4	4.6
India	1.3	1.7	3.5
France	1.3	1.4	1.9
Germany	1.3	1.3	1.5
Others	8.8	10.6	19.6
Total	85.5	88.0	154.7

Note: The figures cover foreigners whose activity is restricted according to the Immigration Act (revised in 1990).
a) The figures for China include Chinese Taipei.
Source: OECD (2002).

Korea also has experience as a labour-importing country. This results from the Korean government's policy since 1991 to accept workers as technical trainees to solve the country's labour-shortage problems. Furthermore, the influx of Korean-Chinese migrants became prominent following the normalisation of diplomatic relations between Korea and China in 1987. During 1994-2000, the number of foreign labourers in Korea climbed

ISBN 92-64-01442-X © OECD 2005

significantly, from 30 500 to 122 500 (Table 12.11). China has been the largest source; Chinese workers comprise approximately 35 per cent of the total foreign labour force. Workers have also migrated to Korea from other East Asian countries such as the Philippines and Japan, but in smaller numbers.

Table 12.11. **Korea: Stock of Foreign Labour, by Nationality**
(thousands)

National Origin	1994	1995	2000
China	10.6	18.0	43.2
(Of which: Chinese with Korean ancestry)	4.4	6.7	20.4
Philippines	5.3	8.5	9.8
Uzbekistan	-	0.8	3.5
United States	2.7	4.2	3.4
Canada	0.4	1.1	2.5
Russian Federation	0.2	0.2	1.9
Japan	1.3	1.5	1.0
United Kingdom	0.2	0.3	0.5
Australia	0.1	0.2	0.4
New Zealand	-	-	0.4
India	0.1	0.1	0.3
France	0.1	0.1	0.2
Germany	0.1	0.2	0.2
South Africa	-	-	0.1
Other countries	9.3	17.0	55.1
Total	30.5	52.2	122.5

Source: OECD (2002).

Among the labour-exporting countries, outflows of Filipino workers have exceeded those of any other Asian country under the Philippine government's policy to promote overseas employment and the export of workers (Hayase, 2003*b*). Although the share of Filipino workers in the Middle East has declined, their share in East Asia, especially in Chinese Taipei, has increased. China played an important role as a labour exporter in the 1990s owing to rapid increases in foreign trade and economic co-operation (Hayase, 2003*a*). The share of Chinese working within Asia but outside China accounted for 65 per cent of total Chinese migration in 1999. An estimated 2.2 million Indonesians worked overseas in 2002, most of them unskilled (Hugo, 2002*a*). East Asian countries were their major destinations, accounting for 74 per cent of the total. Malaysia, the leader, accounted for about 1.4 million (63 per cent), followed by Saudi Arabia and Chinese Taipei. In contrast, the number of official temporary residents in Indonesia was very small in 1995 (100 000) compared with the outflows. Most foreign workers in Indonesia were highly skilled personnel from Australia, the Philippines, India and other Asian countries. This reflected the shortage of professional workers in Indonesia and the rapid increase in foreign investment there (Hugo, 2002*b*).

Economic growth in East and Southeast Asia has shifted the patterns of international migration from Thailand over the last quarter century, in three discernible principal streams — to Pacific-Rim OECD member countries, to the Middle East and to other countries within the region. Thailand has substantial in-migration as well as out-migration. Its transition from net emigration to net immigration has resulted from growing immigration of illegal unskilled workers and emigration of the highly skilled. As in Indonesia's case, the number of Thais moving to the OECD countries remains small, especially relative to Thailand's total population. By 1997, over 101 000 Thais worked in Chinese Taipei and 17 000 in the Middle East. Thailand developed a labour-contracting system much later than did the Philippines and Indonesia. It reported more than 180 000 workers living overseas in 1995 and over 200 000 by 1999. In the late 1980s, it sent significant numbers of workers to the Persian Gulf, especially to Saudi Arabia. Owing to a change in economic conditions in the Persian Gulf area and a diplomatic dispute with Saudi Arabia in 1991, the pattern of labour contracting shifted to Southeast Asia. The largest proportion of Thai workers went to Chinese Taipei in the 1990s, with smaller flows to Malaysia; Singapore; Hong Kong, China; and, outside the region, Israel. Thai workers abroad numbered about 200 000 in 2000, about 90 per cent of them in Asia. The stock of foreign residents in Thailand reached 300 000 in 2000 (Hayase, 2003*b*). Meanwhile, undocumented labourers illegally migrating into Thailand also evolved on a significant scale in the 1990s, with around 80 per cent of the approximately 1 million to 1.2 million of them coming from Myanmar (Chalamwong, 2001).

OECD Member Countries' Policies towards Highly-Skilled Foreign Workers

The policies of OECD members toward highly skilled foreign workers vary according to their philosophy and experience in managing migration (Mclaughlan and Salt, 2002). The most significant trend in recent years has involved the rise in temporary migration for employment as the consequence of the development of the ICT sector, which in some OECD countries has shortages of skilled and highly skilled workers. According to Garson (2003),

ISBN 92-64-01442-X © OECD 2005

a number of countries introduced new regulations. Examples include a new type of visa (UK and Norway), selected point-based systems (Canada and the United States) and quotas for computer specialists under the Green Card programme (Germany). These moves further encouraged the mobility of highly skilled workers, for which the upward trend in inflows is relatively clear in Italy and Spain. To some extent, the OECD countries have competed among themselves for these highly skilled Asian migrants (Iredale, 2000).

The United States

The United States has admitted foreigners with professional, technical and kindred skills as immigrants and non-immigrants for several decades. Immigrant visas entitle their holders to live and work anywhere in the United States, and after five years of residence they may seek to become naturalised US citizens (Martin, 2002). In the 1990s, the United States applied an employment-based system with the intention to permit the entry of skilled workers under the H-1B visa for professional workers. The H-1B visa was created under the Immigration Act of 1990 to allow US employers to admit highly skilled foreign workers with at least a bachelor's degree to fill US "specialty occupations". In 2002 there were 198 000 H-1B approvals, a big decrease compared with about 331 000 in 2001 (Table 12.12). More than half the H-1B petitions approved were those of Asians. Indian nationals held first place as H-1B visa holders, although their share decreased from 49 per cent in 2001 to 33 per cent in 2002, while H-1B beneficiaries from second-place China increased their share from 8 to 9 per cent. The highest number of H-1B petitions approved in 2002 went to workers in computer-related occupations, although the number fell significantly (by 61 per cent) to 75 100 from 191 400 in 2001. H-1B workers approved for initial employment in computer-related jobs dropped from 111 000 in 2001 to 26 000 in 2002 when the United States boosted security after "9/11" and owing to the high-tech recession in 2001-02. The number of H-1B visas issued annually was expected to drop from 195 000 in 2003 to 65 000 in 2004 (Martin, 2002). It is unlikely that the H-1B programme will be eliminated, but it is also not likely that US employers will ever again obtain the easy access to foreign professionals that they enjoyed in the late 1990s (Box 12.1).

Table 12.12. **H-1B Petitions Approved, by Country of Birth of Beneficiaries and Type of Petition, Fiscal Years 2001 and 2002**

Country or Area of Birth	All Beneficiaries		Initial Employment		Continuing Employment	
	FY 2001	FY2002	FY 2001	FY 2002	FY 2001	FY 2002
Total	331 206	197 537	201 079	103 584	130 127	93 953
Country or area of birth (known)	330 521	197 092	200 627	103 350	129 894	93 742
India	161 561	64 980	90 668	21 066	70 893	43 914
China	27 330	18 841	16 847	11 832	10 483	7 009
Canada	12 726	11 760	9 184	7 893	3 542	3 867
Philippines	10 389	9 295	7 294	6 648	3 095	2 647
United Kingdom	9 682	7 171	6 053	4 192	3 629	2 979
Republic of Korea	6 468	5 941	4 484	3 886	1 984	2 055
Japan	5 902	4 937	3 676	2 970	2 226	1 967
Chinese Taipei	5 808	4 025	3 406	2 366	2 403	1 659
Pakistan	6 313	3 810	3 904	1 955	2 409	1 855
Colombia	3 703	3 320	2 909	2 362	794	958
Other countries	80 639	63 012	52 202	38 180	28 436	24 832
Country of birth (unknown)	685	445	452	234	233	211

Notes: Countries of birth are ranked based on 2002 data.
Source: Immigration Statistics, USCIS.

Box 12.1. **H-1B Visa Will Be Reduced**

The guest-worker programme in the United States aims to fill a narrow range of labour-market vacancies. It gives US employers considerable latitude to determine their needs for highly skilled foreign workers. The migration infrastructure was developed especially to attract Asian professionals. Yet there is widespread dissatisfaction with the current system. It is likely that the future will see an effort to expand the fee or levy system under which employers prove that they made a good faith effort to recruit foreign workers by paying fees. The fees thus collected could be used to cover the cost of enforcement of labour laws in the industries affected, to train and retrain United States workers and to develop productivity-increasing technologies. Leading business groups, such as the Committee for Economic Development, have endorsed this approach, urging that the length of the H-1B visa be reduced from six to three years and that H-1B visas be auctioned to the highest bidders when the demand for them exceeds the supply.

ISBN 92-64-01442-X © OECD 2005

Australia

Immigration issues are important in Australia (Hugo, 2002*b*), which recognises the level and nature of skilled migration to Australia as an important component of the labour market and national society. The country has experienced a net gain of skilled people through permanent migration in recent years, even as the focus on skills has increased in the selection of permanent migrants. Significantly higher skills have been recorded among temporary business arrivals since a temporary business visa category was introduced in 1996. This type of visa has allowed employers to fill skill shortages from overseas and to assess new ideas, skills and technologies (Hugo, 2002*b*, pp. 74-78).

Australia uses a points-based selection system to ensure that migrants meet a minimum skills requirement or to identify foreign workers who have skills or outstanding abilities, especially in ICT and business. According to the Department of Immigration and Multicultural Affairs (DIMA), the number of settlers arriving under the skilled-migration category increased from 30 400 (39.7 per cent of the total programme) in 1994-95 to 60 700 (58 per cent) in 2002-03. The Skill Stream of the Australian Migration Programme granted 45 520 Skill visas in 2001-02. Of which 22.6 per cent (10 290) went to onshore applicants. The United Kingdom accounted for 15 per cent of the total, South Africa for 14 per cent, India for 10 per cent, Indonesia for 9 per cent and others for 8 per cent (Hugo, 2003). The number of long-term Asian visitors to Australia has increased significantly over the last ten years. Asian arrivals in 1999-2000 reached 70 100 or 53 per cent of all long-term arrivals, a more than tenfold increase over 1979-80 and almost threefold over 1989-90. This rapid growth resulted from the increasing number of Asians studying in Australia[8].

Overseas students from East Asia increased significantly from 20 496 in 1991 to 73 923 in 2001 and approximately 121 393 in 2002 (Table 12.13). Among the top ten countries with students enrolled in Australia in 2002, Singapore led with 16.2 per cent of all overseas students, followed by Hong Kong, China (14.6 per cent), Malaysia (12.8 per cent) and China (10.6 per cent). Students from East Asia made up 65.6 per cent of all overseas students. This significantly high number may be due partly to Australia's student-switching policy, which enables foreign students to switch their status and access a work permit on the basis of their skills. Previously, they had to leave the country after completing their studies.

Table 12.13. **Top Ten Countries with Overseas Students Enrolled in Australia, by Country of Permanent Residence, 1991-2002 (Selected Years)**

Country or Area	Overseas Students				
	1991	2000	2001	2002	
	Number	Number	Number	Number	Per Cent of Total
Singapore	3 542	16 652	18 277	29 956	16.2
Hong Kong, China	5 137	13 852	15 719	26 956	14.6
Malaysia	7 294	16 362	16 344	23 725	12.8
China	1 558	4 387	8 018	19 596	10.6
Indonesia	2 270	8 973	9 619	11 981	6.5
Thailand	695	2 807	3 259	5 202	2.8
Chinese Taipei	0	2 447	2 687	3 977	2.1
Subtotal (East Asia)	20 496	65 480	73 923	121 393	65.6
Other countries	13 912	30 127	38 449	63 665	34.4
Total	34 408	95 607	112 342	185 058	100.0

Source: Department of Education, Science and Training, Selected Higher Education Student Statistics <http://www.dest.gov.au>.

Effects of Migration Policies on Economic Development in East Asia

The effects of highly skilled workers from East Asia on the region's economic development have been studied for more than a decade. A considerable amount of research (Chang, 1992; Chang and Deng, 1992; Fields, 1994; Coe and Helpman, 1995 and Gaillard and Gaillard, 1997) concludes that the loss of highly skilled workers causes negative effects for the sending countries through the so-called brain-drain effect. Nevertheless, highly skilled emigration may in fact bring benefits to the countries of origin by stimulating the pursuit of higher education and providing a significant source of remittances and investment. Furthermore, mobility of the highly skilled may induce knowledge or technology transfer to their home countries through various networks of migrants (Lowell and Findlay, 2001; Lucas, 2001; OECD, 2002).

The Brain-Drain Effect

The concept of brain drain first emerged in the 1960s when it was used to describe the migration of British intellectuals and scientists to the United States (Gaillard and Gaillard, 1997). Traditionally, discussions concerning the brain drain have taken the perspective of the human capital approaches

ISBN 92-64-01442-X © OECD 2005

identified by Gary Becker in the 1960s (Fourie and Joubert, 1998). The human capital concept holds that the educational qualifications, abilities, skills and competencies that an individual possesses represent his or her human capital. Governments invest in this human capital through training and education and expect a return on their investment when the individual becomes economically active, starts paying taxes, etc. (Rosenbaum *et al.*, 1990). From this perspective, the migration of highly skilled human resources represents a "loss" to the sending country, which does not reap the returns on its investment in these people. ILO (2002) indicates that there is considerable evidence that the average level of human capital in a society has positive effects on productivity and growth. Conversely, low levels of education resulting from high levels of skilled emigration can slow the growth rate of the economy and adversely affect those who remain.

The brain-drain effect thus reduces economic growth by imposing costs on the source countries. The most obvious is the cost of education supported by the source-country government. For example, China fears the brain-drain effect because the high cost of educating large numbers of university students abroad each year creates no benefit for China. An idea of the magnitude of the loss is revealed in the relatively small proportion of Chinese students studying abroad who return home after graduation — less than 50 per cent of the total over more than ten years[9]. In contrast, India, a major supplier of ICT workers to the world market, has no great concern about this problem because many Indian ICT workers finance their own education (Gayathri, 2001).

Besides the cost of education, home countries also lose tax revenues from these highly skilled people. Desai *et al.* (2001) examined the direct fiscal losses associated with the brain drain to the United States by estimating the value of the potential earnings of highly skilled Indians had they stayed in India. They found that the net fiscal loss resulting from the migration of these highly skilled professionals, who account for only 0.1 per cent of India's population, ranged from 0.24 per cent to 0.5 per cent of India's GNP. Their aggregate income would have been equal to 10 per cent of India's national income.

The economic effects of the loss of skilled people should not be the only factor considered. There also are social ramifications. For example, the loss of a large number of Filipino nurses has almost certainly worsened health services in the Philippines[10]. In 1990, the number of Filipino nurses who had migrated to work abroad accounted for 61 per cent of the total number (174 202) of trained nurses currently working outside the Philippines (Ball, 2004). The great success of exporting nurses has created a major crisis

ISBN 92-64-01442-X © OECD 2005

in the delivery of health care in the Philippines. The nurses who have migrated to work overseas are the best educated and most experienced (Ball, 2004). In the mid-1990s, the country had an estimated 30 000 unfilled nursing positions, particularly in rural areas (Yukawa, 1996). The Bureau of Labor and Employment of the Philippines reported how critical the imbalance between demand for and supply of nurses had become at the turn of the century. The number of graduates and registered nurses had declined drastically since 1995, whereas the demand for Filipino nurses abroad had risen somewhat as the result of a global shortage of nurses or caregivers. This further depleted the already severely under-resourced health sector in the Philippines[11] (Tables 12.14 and 12.15). The movement of highly skilled workers can be classified into two types: permanent emigration, often referred to as the brain drain, and temporary or circular migration, also referred to as contract labour migration (Go, 2002). From 1988 to 2000, 12 300 Filipino nurses migrated permanently and in 2001 about 1 575 did so. The major destinations were the United States (83 per cent of the total), followed by Canada and Australia (Table 12.15).

Table 12.14. **Nursing Graduates and Registered Nurses in the Philippines, 1995-2000**

	1995	1996	1997	1998	1999	2000	Total
Nursing graduates	20 098	19 162	14 611	11 720	9 219	5 980	80 790
Registered nurses	27 272	15 701	11 693	9 441	8 419	5 784	78 310

Source: Bureau of Labor and Employment Statistics and Professional Regulation Commission, Philippines.

Table 12.15. **Permanently Emigrated Filipino Nurses, by Country of Destination, 1988-2001**

Year	No. of Professional Nurses who Emigrated Permanently	Country of Destination			
		United States	Canada	Australia	Rest of the world
1988-1990	3 860	3 266	262	235	97
1991-1995	5 577	4 574	606	186	211
1996-2000	2 863	2 290	341	115	117
2001	1 575	1 381	141	39	14
Total	13 875	11 511	1 350	575	439

Source: Bureau of Labor and Employment Statistics, Philippines.

ISBN 92-64-01442-X © OECD 2005

Table 12.16 shows that 83 394 Filipino nurses temporarily migrated abroad during 1992-2002. Their numbers have picked up significantly since 2000, suggesting that the demand for Filipino nurses in foreign markets has increased over time. This high demand from abroad results from increases in the demand for health care, due in part to ageing populations in developed countries such as the United States, Canada, the United Kingdom, Saudi Arabia and the United Arab Emirates. Moreover, in receiving countries the demand for suitably qualified staff exceeds the available supply, with resultant skill shortages in the nursing professions. Other "pull" factors for emigrants include their search for skill employment, better pay and mutual recognition of qualifications (Buchan *et al.*, 2003).

Table 12.16. **Temporarily Migrating Filipino Nurses, by Country of Destination, 1992-2002**

Year	No. of Professional Nursing Emigrants	Country of Destination						
		Saudi Arabia	United States	United Kingdom and Ireland	United Arab Emirates	Kuwait	Libya	Rest of the world
1992	6 078	3 279	1 767	0	271	320	269	172
1993	7 308	4 202	1 987	0	47	139	721	212
1994	7 171	3 332	2 853	0	270	455	15	246
1995	7 954	3 249	3 690	0	94	59	380	482
1996	5 477	3 071	270	0	137	269	809	921
1997	5 245	3 794	11	0	209	25	175	1 031
1998	5 399	4 098	5	63	279	143	89	722
1999	5 972	4 031	53	934	378	53	18	505
2000	8 341	4 386	91	2 755	305	133	17	654
2001	13 822	5 275	304	6 949	249	192	9	844
2002 (October)	10 627	5 083	295	3 633	367	104	345	800
Total	83 394	43 800	11 326	14 334	2 606	1 892	2 847	6 589

Source: Bureau of Labor and Employment Statistics, Philippines.

The argument described at the start of this section that skilled mobility may cause "brain circulation", or "brain exchange" rather than "brain waste" or "brain drain" will more likely hold for skilled mobility among developed countries and not among developing countries. Martin (2002) points out that a new era of "brain circulation" may have begun between Asian countries and the United States. Highly skilled migrants stay in United States for a time, then return to their homelands — either because of opportunities there or because they cannot obtain immigrant visas in the United States. Iguchi (2002), on the other hand, mentions that the highly skilled in Asia face more risk of becoming "brain waste" rather than entering into "brain exchange",

ISBN 92-64-01442-X © OECD 2005

because the intra-regional income gaps are much bigger in Asia. Many skilled emigrants from poor countries may buy one-way tickets to OECD countries in the expectation of receiving work visas. Once they fail to do so, they may become undocumented workers and continue to work in low-skilled occupations that do not make use of their higher skills.

Remittances and Capital Inflow

The positive side of migration is that remittances from migrants play a significant role in promoting economic growth. Worldwide, remittances are huge, an estimated $100 billion per year. About 60 per cent of them go to developing countries. Remittances to East Asia account for $11 billion. Some researchers argue that remittance income does not get converted into sustainable productive capacity, but is used for unproductive purposes such as direct consumption and the purchase of expensive household durable and non-durable goods. This may lead to increased inequality, growing consumption of imports and heavy dependency. Meyers (1998), for example, supports the view that relatives at home in the countries of emigrants' origin use remittance income mostly for daily expenses such as food, clothing and health care. Many more researchers, however, believe that remittances contribute significantly to improvement in the living standards of the people who receive them, although they may not constitute a full remedy for poverty. Lucas (1981) mentions that either skilled or unskilled emigrants may provide remittances to counter some of the potential negative impacts of emigrant departure, particularly in contexts where foreign exchange has a high social value. Yet this is likely to be true only in the Philippines; most countries in East Asia receive low levels of remittances.

Table 12.17 shows total remittances for selected East Asian countries by combining the gross inflow of workers' remittances and credited compensation of employees with other migrant transfers on capital account from 1990 to 2002. Only remittances from Filipino workers registered a significant proportion of GDP, about 9.6 per cent in 2002; total remittances to most countries in East Asia did not contribute such high proportions. The Philippines received by far the largest amount of remittances, ranging from $1.5 billion in 1990 to about $7.4 billion in 2002. China came next with $2.4 billion in 2002, although they had reached their highest level in 1997 at $4.6 billion. Remittance inflows to Indonesia increased gradually, growing from $200 million in 1990 to $1.3 billion in 2002. In contrast, remittances to Korea have shown a decreasing trend, dropping from $1 billion in 1990 to $600 million in 2002.

 ISBN 92-64-01442-X

Table 12.17. **Remittances Received by Selected East Asian Countries**

(total remittances in $ million; shares of GDP in per cent)

Country	1990	1991	1992	1993	1994	1995	1996	1997	1998	1999	2000	2001	2002
China	124	207	228	108	395	350	1 672	4 589	344	530	758	1 209	2 353
Share	*0.03*	*0.05*	*0.05*	*0.03*	*0.07*	*0.05*	*0.20*	*0.51*	*0.04*	*0.05*	*0.07*	*0.10*	*0.19*
Indonesia	166	130	229	346	449	651	796	725	959	1 109	1 190	1 046	1 250
Share	*0.15*	*0.10*	*0.16*	*0.22*	*0.25*	*0.32*	*0.35*	*0.34*	*1.00*	*0.79*	*0.79*	*0.74*	*0.72*
Japan	- - -	510	580	780	870	1 150	1 230	1 340	1 240	1 110	1 370	1 980	1 810
Share	- - -	*0.01*	*0.02*	*0.02*	*0.02*	*0.02*	*0.03*	*0.03*	*0.03*	*0.02*	*0.03*	*0.05*	*0.05*
Korea	1 037	1 172	1 114	1 112	1 038	1 080	947	852	542	666	735	652	581
Share	*0.41*	*0.40*	*0.35*	*0.32*	*0.26*	*0.22*	*0.18*	*0.18*	*0.17*	*0.16*	*0.16*	*0.15*	*0.12*
Malaysia	185	130	153	176	119	116	164	194	190	323	342	367	435
Share	*0.42*	*0.26*	*0.26*	*0.26*	*0.16*	*0.13*	*0.16*	*0.19*	*0.26*	*0.41*	*0.38*	*0.42*	*0.46*
Philippines	1 465	1 850	2 538	2 587	3 452	5 360	4 875	6 799	5 130	6 918	6 212	6 164	7 363
Share	*3.30*	*4.07*	*4.79*	*4.76*	*5.39*	*7.23*	*5.88*	*8.26*	*7.87*	*9.08*	*8.30*	*8.64*	*9.55*
Thailand	973	1 019	445	1 112	1 281	1 695	1 806	1 658	1 424	1 460	1 697	1 252	1 380
Share	*1.14*	*1.04*	*0.40*	*0.89*	*0.89*	*1.01*	*0.99*	*1.18*	*1.23*	*1.19*	*1.40*	*1.09*	*1.09*

Note: Total remittances are the sum of three IMF categories: workers' remittances, compensation to employees and migrants' transfers.

Sources: Remittance data: International Monetary Fund, *Balance of Payments Statistics Yearbook*, 1998 and 2003. GDP data: World Bank http://devdata.worldbank.org.

The international networks established by emigrants may provide capital flows in other ways. Lucas (2001) indicates that emigrants may be relatively likely to invest in their home countries because they are strongly positioned to evaluate investment opportunities and they possess contacts to facilitate investment. Saxenian (1999) points out that emigrants may encourage foreigners to make investments in the home countries. Successful direct investment frequently demands a local facilitating partner. Emigrants are well placed to identify trustworthy and competent partners. Moreover, returned migrants known to the foreign investor may even take on this local counterpart role.

Saxenian (1999) notes: "The scarce resource in this new environment is the ability to locate foreign partners quickly and to manage complex business relationships across cultural and linguistic boundaries. This is particularly a challenge in high-technology industries in which products, markets, and technologies are continually being redefined — and where product cycles are routinely shorter than nine months". Moreover, migrations of highly skilled workers may play a more critical role in trade expansion than other types of migration. Kapur (2001) mentions that exposure to nationals from a particular country may alter perceptions of doing business with those countries. Such migration together with "diaspora networks" may also help to promote capital flows. Highly skilled workers likely will invest in their own countries. For example, most investments in China by its emigrants come from highly skilled entrepreneurial emigrants and those dispersed in the Chinese diaspora (see Box 12.2).

Box 12.2. **The Chinese Diaspora**

The term "diaspora" implies some sort of commitment to one's homeland. For the Chinese, it also includes a "downside", as generations of ethnic Chinese abroad have faced discrimination and mistrust in their host countries. Chinese people have settled in communities all over the world. When they formed diaspora communities under the auspices of the Chinese government, they could return to China. The Chinese Diaspora has spread to many countries, particularly in Southeast Asia. Traditionally, the relationship with China in some communities did not carry a lot of influence, because these people were simply minorities in those societies and were even discriminated against. In recent times, host countries have accepted the Chinese Diaspora through assimilation. The overseas Chinese have even become important leaders, in positions that often give them power in determining foreign policy. The Chinese Diaspora has also influenced domestic politics; by lobbying and supporting politicians with their economic power, the Chinese have gained many advantages. The Chinese Diaspora, with its great economic strength, strongly influences host countries' GDP, particularly in Southeast Asia. Such assimilation is certainly true in Thailand and to some extent in the Philippines but may not be as strong in Malaysia, Indonesia and Brunei.

ISBN 92-64-01442-X © OECD 2005

Box 12.2 (contd.)

The Chinese Diaspora operates interconnected cultural and business networks around the world. It forms a major group in global society. Because China has joined the World Trade Organization, the diaspora network will become even more important if China becomes the biggest market in the world. If China and Chinese Taipei successfully reunite, the Asian region will become a more powerful economic and military power of increasing importance worldwide (Lim, 2000).

Stimulating Higher Educational Attainment; Inducing Knowledge or Technology Transfer

Skill mobility stimulates individuals in their home countries to pursue higher education, in the belief that it will give them better opportunities to emigrate to rich countries. Given the size of the outflows of such workers along with the expansion in global demand for them in some fields, educational systems in source countries may change. For example, the Philippines shows an upward trend in people graduating in business and related fields as well as mathematics and computer science. Data from the Philippine Commission on Higher Education indicate that during 1995-2000, graduates in business and related fields increased gradually from 85 781 (27 per cent of all tertiary graduates) in 1995 to 104 537 (29 per cent) in 2000. Graduates in mathematics and computer science also went up, from 21 338 (7 per cent of tertiary gradates) in 1995 to 34 015 (10 per cent) in 2002. China provides another example. After China expanded college enrolment rates in 1999 the number of college and university graduates climbed steeply from 1.15 million in 2001 to 1.45 million in 2002 and 2.12 million in 2003.

Most emigrants also still have connections and networks in their native countries, so they can bring back knowledge and new technology when they return, which contributes significantly to their countries' economic development. For example, the Chinese Institute of Engineers in the United States co-operates with its counterpart in Chinese Taipei to organise annual seminars and to provide useful advice to government officials (Lucas, 2001). Moreover, highly skilled migrants in the East Asian region easily transfer within multinational companies, suggesting an important role for them in the transfer of technology and the development of human resources in the region (Iguchi, 2002).

ISBN 92-64-01442-X

Such emigrants have credible backward linkages with their source countries, which can increase the availability of knowledge and technology vital to the improvement of productivity. Expatriates and/or members of the diaspora often organise networks that stimulate return flows of knowledge, sometimes leading to collaboration with local business entrepreneurs or researchers. In Thailand, the associations of Thai professionals in the United States, Europe, Canada and Japan exemplify highly skilled Thai expatriates who contribute to their home country without returning home permanently. Modern forms of communications such as the Internet have played a key role in this regard.

Issues Related to Illegal Migrants

OECD member countries have imported guest workers for decades, but because some of them often abandon their status and become illegal, the host countries have long tried to find ways to manage large numbers of such undocumented migrants. It would be useful to compare the OECD and East Asian developing countries' experience in this regard. While a large body of literature examines OECD member countries' policies on illegal immigration, not many studies investigate the policies of non-member countries. This section seeks to present similarities and differences in policies for combating illegal entry in both OECD and non-OECD countries, focusing on East Asia.

Measures to curb illegal immigration show several similarities. First, the most common sanction for foreigners engaged in illegal employment is forced departure. Some countries enforce other punishments, including fines and imprisonment. In Japan, for instance, foreign labourers working without work permits are forced to leave and face criminal sanctions involving fines up to 300 000 yen and/or imprisonment for up to three years. The United Kingdom expels illegal foreign workers and escorts them to their home countries, besides requiring fines of up to £5 000 or imprisonment for up to six months. In the United States, employers hiring illegal foreign workers face penalties, and foreign workers are removed to the border.

Similar approaches apply in East Asian countries. In Thailand, illegal foreign workers are expelled or face up to three years' imprisonment and fines of up to 60 000 baht. The Singapore government imposes the penalties of mandatory caning and up to six months' imprisonment for illegal entry.

 ISBN 92-64-01442-X © OECD 2005

Similarly, according to the Immigration Act 1959/63, penalties on illegal entry and overstaying in Malaysia involve a maximum fine of 10 000 ringits, imprisonment for up to five years and six lashes with the cane.

In both OECD and non-OECD countries, persons who employ illegal workers or assist or abet illegal employment or entry face fines and/or imprisonment. In Japan, employers who hire illegal workers and middlemen are liable to fines of up to 2 million yen and/or imprisonment for up to three years. The United Kingdom imposes sanctions for abetting illegal immigration or employment, but had no special penalties on employers of illegal workers until 1997, when it established fines of up to £5 000.

Other East Asian countries take similar measures. Singapore has tough laws to penalise employers who hire illegal workers; they are fined up to S$60 000 and/or imprisoned from six months to two years. Employers of more than five illegal foreign workers can also be caned. People who abet illegal entry or offer shelter to illegal offenders suffer the same penalties as employers. Malaysia, like Singapore, subjects people employing illegal workers and those protecting illegal migrants to a maximum fine of 50 000 ringits, five years in prison and six strokes with the cane. Malaysian officials aiding illegal migrants also face maximum fines of 60 000 ringits, jail terms of up to two years and six lashes with the cane. Unlike Singapore and Malaysia, Thailand imposes a greater penalty on persons abetting illegal entry than on those employing undocumented workers. While employers may receive no more than three years in prison and be fined not in excess of 60 000 baht, people abetting or assisting illegal entry can be imprisoned for as long as ten years and fined up to 100 000 baht.

Preventive measures to combat illegal entry in most OECD and non-OECD countries include information campaigns and toughened border controls. The United Kingdom has launched preventive steps by informing employers about the provisions of the 1996 Asylum and Immigration Act. The United States also has undertaken campaigns to notify employers of their obligation to verify the employment eligibility of their foreign employees. The Japanese government runs an information campaign through various media about the adverse effects of illegal employment.

As in most OECD countries, Southeast Asian countries such as Malaysia, the Philippines and Thailand have stepped up their anti-migrant campaigns by emphasising the serious threat to their internal security posed by illegal migration. Educational campaigns concern foreign-worker regulation, especially permission for employment of certain foreign workers

ISBN 92-64-01442-X

in specified sectors and areas. For instance, the Malaysian government has made it known that it authorises employers to hire foreign workers in only four sectors — plantations, construction, manufacturing and services — and that nationals from only five countries may be hired, namely Bangladesh, Indonesia, Pakistan, the Philippines and Thailand.

Border controls represent another common preventive strategy to curb illegal migration and employment. OECD countries, such as the United States and Japan, and most other countries in East Asia have used their military forces to toughen border controls to detect and deport illegal migrants.

Policies in OECD countries and East Asian countries on curbing illegal entry do differ on several minor points. First, some East and Southeast Asian countries, such as Japan, Malaysia, the Philippines and Thailand, apply amnesty programmes. Malaysia announced its first amnesty programme in 1991 to allow illegal migrants working in specific jobs, including housekeeping, construction, plantations, manufacturing and services, to register and legalise their positions. Similarly, a "*quasi*" amnesty programme in Thailand allows employers in some industries and some provinces to hire foreign migrants from Cambodia, the Laos and Myanmar to work in specified jobs that local workers generally do not want to do. Second, after the 1997/98 financial crises, several East Asian countries including Malaysia turned to new preventive measures by offering incentives to employers to hire few or no foreign workers. The Malaysian government imposes fines on employers who fire local workers and hire foreign ones. Third, to cope with the problem of foreign workers using forged documents, Singapore issues identity cards (with fingerprints) to foreign workers. Foreign workers, except for expatriates and professional workers, must have their fingerprints taken before getting or renewing their work permits, as is also the case in Italy and Japan.

In sum, the main measures to control illegal entry are similar in both OECD and East and Southeast Asian countries; they differ only on minor points. Nevertheless, Southeast Asian countries may face more difficulties in implementing them because their policies on foreign workers are non-transparent, inconsistent and difficult for employers to follow. Moreover, police and immigration officials are often corrupt and poorly trained.

ISBN 92-64-01442-X © OECD 2005

Policy Coherence between OECD and East Asia

Policy Coherence: Regional Co-operation

The OECD economies tend to be more homogeneous or less diverse than East Asian economies. Aside from Japan and Korea, Asia displays a great deal of heterogeneity in economic systems and labour markets. Levels of economic development can be measured by per capita incomes, levels of industrialisation, human resource development and institutional capacities. Table 12.18 compares the major development indicators of OECD countries and East Asian countries between 1998 and 2001. The disparities of per capita income, education and GDP between OECD and developing countries in Asia are clearly evident. The human-development indices of OECD member countries have gradually improved, but the human-development gap between them and East Asian countries has narrowed little.

Table 12.18. **Selected Development Indicators, 1998 and 2001**

	GDP per capita (PPP US$)	Education Index	GDP Index	Human-Development Index
		2001		
OECD	23 363	0.94	0.91	0.905
Developing countries	3 850	0.70	0.61	0.655
- East Asia & Pacific	4 233	0.80	0.63	0.772
- South Asia	2 730	0.56	0.55	0.582
		1998		
OECD	20 357	0.94	0.89	0.893
Developing countries	3 270	0.68	0.58	0.642
- East Asia & Pacific	3 564	0.80	0.60	0.716
- South Asia	2 112	0.54	0.51	0.560

Source: Human Development Report, 2000 and 2003.

Co-operation between OECD and East Asian developing countries should provide a means to reduce these disparities. So far, a certain degree of regional co-operation has emerged in trade, investment and finance, because the primary goal is to make all countries more prosperous and stable. The OECD countries can pursue their policy-coherence agendas by encouraging member countries to liberalise their trade and reduce restrictions on the movement of highly skilled people both among themselves and *vis à vis* developing Asian countries.

Japan (through the Japan Institute of Labour, Ministry of Health, Labour and Welfare), in co-operation with the OECD (through DELSA) and ILO (through its International Migration Branch), has taken the lead by financing and organising the Workshop on International Migration and the Labour Market in Asia for ten consecutive years. The workshop discusses international migration issues and provides a forum for exchanging opinions and sharing information on them. It has brought together both policy makers and country specialists from OECD countries, the ILO and up to 12 countries in Asia to share experience in managing national migration policies. Cross-country data have been compiled since the beginning of the workshop and the proceedings of the workshop have been edited and published by OECD for more than seven years. Box 12.3 indicates conclusions drawn in 2002 on "International Migration of the Highly Skilled" in 2002.

Box 12.3. **Lessons for Co-operation on Migration of the Highly Skilled, Drawn from the 2002 Meeting of the Workshop on International Migration and the Labour Market in Asia**

In Asia, intra-corporate transfers dominate the migration of the highly skilled. A policy option includes promoting research and development based on the use of the highly skilled. Each country should establish centres of excellence to attract the highly skilled *via* international co-operation. Each country should streamline intra-company transfers from the perspective of mitigating the risk of brain drain in Asia and finding ways of strengthening the migration of the highly skilled within the framework of regional economic integration. Since the effects of movements of the highly skilled differ among Asian countries, it is impossible to attempt to resolve in isolation the issues surrounding the highly skilled.

Policy Coherence: Regional Integration or Networks

Intra- and inter-regional economic integration or networks need continued promotion to seek another means for narrowing economic disparities between OECD and East Asia. Iguchi (2002) explores the possibility of regional economic integration in Asia as a measure to reduce the risks of globalisation, exploit opportunities for further economic development in the region and stimulate a common understanding of sustainable development. Such an approach might reduce labour movement because, according to traditional trade theory, the movement of goods, capital and labour are substitutes. Growing intra-regional foreign direct investment will also

 ISBN 92-64-01442-X © OECD 2005

establish networking and channels of highly skilled migration in both directions. Expanded international networks likely will arise in research and development (R&D) activities in Asia, as R&D centres move from developed to developing areas and establish branches within the region. In addition, positive measures, such as improvements in education, research and infrastructure, may improve economic conditions of Asian countries and eventually reduce the adverse (brain-drain) effects of outflows of highly skilled professionals.

Concluding Remarks and Recommendations

Most OECD and developed Asian countries have not introduced special measures to recruit highly skilled foreign workers. They continue to rely on their existing work-permit systems. The schemes that have been introduced invariably aim at ICT and health staff (especially care givers or nurses) and intra-company transfers for skilled workers. In Canada, Australia and the United States, policies have been perceived to benefit national economic growth through the permanent acquisition of high-level human expertise. Even in these countries, however, temporary migration is becoming increasingly important as a strategy to cope with labour shortages in some sectors, especially those requiring highly skilled professionals. In Europe, particularly the United Kingdom and Germany, temporary migration has been the norm, and schemes have been designed to deal with specific labour shortages that cannot be met by free movement within the EU region. The range of specific schemes and initiatives to attract the highly skilled has developed faster in the United Kingdom than in Germany, Australia and to a lesser extent Canada.

Most countries have managed to reduce the length of time for work permit approval; the United Kingdom provides a faster response rate than any other country. Student switching is not yet widespread, but several countries are exploring its possibilities, e.g. France and Germany for ICT graduates. Many countries have a range of criteria for measuring the success of their schemes; some are seen as part of broader training or migration policies. Australia, Germany and the United States have made systematic attempts to collect the necessary data on migrants or to carry out full evaluation and follow-up research. The schemes are employer-driven, sometimes resulting in over-estimation of the scale of shortages (McLaughlan and Salt, 2002). Despite reports of impeding shortages, their effects have been exaggerated.

McLaughlan and Salt (2002) suggest groupings of OECD countries according to their experience with different types of measures to attract foreign workers. They can be summarised as follows:

— countries with comprehensive schemes, such as the "green card" system in Germany and H-1B visas in the United States;

— countries that have made minor positive changes in their existing work-permit systems to facilitate quicker access to the labour market for highly skilled people, such as the fast-track work visas for ICT specialists in the Netherlands and the work authorisation system in Ireland;

— countries that have used exemptions from work permits or relaxation of work-permit regulations to enable employers and foreign workers to gain easier access to the labour market. Company transfers in Ireland are exempt from work-permit regulations and those in the Netherlands from a labour-market test;

— countries, particularly the Nordic countries, using tax incentives to reduce the tax burden for high-earning foreign workers; and

— countries (Ireland, notably) with policies to encourage return migration of the highly skilled.

Sending countries' strategies to counteract the brain drain can take two approaches. The first sees the brain drain as a loss. Strategies that have been recommended to counteract it include making migration more difficult, e.g. compulsory national service, and making emigration less attractive, e.g. offering highly skilled workers incentives to remain at home (Meyer *et al.*, 1997). The latter is not effective because developing countries cannot offer highly skilled professionals salaries and an infrastructure comparable to those in developed countries. Another recommendation involves taxing either the receiving country or the individual migrant to compensate the sending country for the loss of human capital (Bhagwatti, 1977), but its implementation proved difficult because of problems in measuring exactly in monetary terms the loss to the country of origin[13].

An alternative for East Asian developing countries, a return option, involves attempts to encourage highly skilled expatriates to return home. To make it work, developing countries like China or Thailand would have to offer the expatriates what they want — salaries and infrastructure comparable to those in the countries where they currently work. The Reverse Brain Drain Project encourages native professionals to return from abroad to assist in

ISBN 92-64-01442-X © OECD 2005

various development or technology-oriented projects. For example, the Association of Thai Professionals in America and Canada has actively involved itself in this programme, sending Thai professionals from universities and private agencies to carry out joint research studies, teach, provide advisory services and become involved in projects relating to higher education and quality assurance. The Association of Thai Professionals in Europe and the Association of Thai Professionals in Japan have rendered close co-operation. This approach has also worked in China, Australia, Ireland and Korea[14].

The second strategic approach to help to reduce the brain drain problem applies the diaspora option. The actual and potential contributions of diaspora communities were discussed extensively in an earlier section of this study. Unlike the return option, the diaspora option sees the brain drain not as a loss but as a potential gain to the sending country. It considers highly skilled expatriates as a pool of potentially useful human resources for the home country and challenges home countries to mobilise it without uprooting the expatriates from their countries of work.

This study has not fully investigated the question of migration policy coherence, which needs further research. Examination of both the theoretical and the empirical aspects of this question requires a more complete database to allow exploration of the full range of international lessons and best practices.

ISBN 92-64-01442-X

Notes

1. The author acknowledges with thanks the helpful comments and valuable suggestions of Jean-Pierre Garson, Ki Fukasaku, Louka Katseli, Alexandra Trzeciak-Duval, and Michael G. Plummer. Thanks also go to Saowaruj Rattanakhumfu and Sujittra Rodsomboon for their assistance in data and information gathering.

2. For more details, see Part I of this volume: Ki Fukasaku.

3. East Asia covers Northeast Asia and Southeast Asia and selected countries in South Asia, including India.

4. Garson (2001); Abella (2001).

5. It could be argued that the shortage is at least to some degree the result of over regulation of the OECD labour market.

6. The OECD countries do not report data on the educational distribution of migrants. To estimate educational attainment of migrants to OECD countries, the study assumes that their educational levels are the same as those for the United States.

7. The purpose of non-immigrant student and employment visas is to permit foreigners to enter the USA for specific purposes and time periods. There are generally no limits or quotas on the non-immigrant work visas available, except for H-1B workers.

8. For more details, see Australian Bureau of Statistics (2003) , *Year Book Australia.*

9. China Education and Research Network, <http://www.edu.cn>.

10. The Philippines has a deliberate policy to encourage the outflow of nurses and the inflow of remittances from them. In most other developing countries, outflow is the result of individual responses to push and pull factors.

11. Currently, doctors and specialists in the Philippines are training as nurses to take advantage of the rising demand for nurses in developed countries. It is estimated that about 2 000 doctors are switching professions (*The Lancet*, Vol. 361, 19 April 2003, available at: www.thelancet.com).

ISBN 92-64-01442-X © OECD 2005

12. EU member countries allow the free movement of workers under the Single European Act of 1986/7, especially highly skilled workers, and NAFTA and GATS have set the scope of movement of natural persons.

13. For more details see Mercy Brown. "Using the Intellectual Diaspora to Reverse the Brain Drain: Some Useful Examples", University of Cape Town, South Africa, p. 2, date unspecified.

14. Mercy Brown, *op. cit.*, p. 13 contains a comprehensive list of diaspora networks.

ISBN 92-64-01442-X © OECD 2005

Bibliography

ABELLA, M.I. (2001), "International Migration and Labour Market Development: A Survey of Trends and Major Issues", paper prepared for the Workshop on International Migration and Labour Market in Asia, 1-2 January 2001, organised by the Japan Institute of Labor, OECD and ILO, Japan Institute of Labor, Tokyo.

ADAMS, R. (2003), "International Migration, Remittances and the Brain Drain: A Study of 24 Labor-Exporting Countries", World Bank Policy Research Working Paper 3069, World Bank, Washington, D.C., June.

AUSTRALIAN BUREAU OF STATISTICS (ABS) (2003), *Year Book Australia*, ABS, Canberra.

BALL, R.E. (2004), "Divergent Development, Racialised Rights, Globalised Labor Markets and the Trade of Nurses – the Case of the Philippines", *Women's Studies International Forum*, 27, pp. 119-133.

BAUER, T., M. LOFSTROM and K.F. ZIMMERMANN (2000), "Immigration Policy, Assimilation of Immigrants and Natives' Sentiments towards Immigrants: Evidence from 12 OECD Countries", IZA, Bonn, March.

BHAGWATTI, J.N. (1977), "The Reverse Transfer of Technology (Brain Drain): International Resource Flow Accounting, Compensation, Taxation and Related Policy Proposals", United Nations Conference on Trade and Development, Geneva.

BUCHAN. J, T. PARKIN and J. SOCHALSKI (2003), "International Nurse Mobility: Trends and Policy Implication", World Health Organization, Geneva.

BUREAU OF LABOR AND EMPLOYMENT STATISTICS (Philippines) (2003), "Supply and Demand Situation for Nurses", *Labstat Updates*, 7(13).

CARRINGTON, W.J. and E. DETRAGIACHE (1998), "How Big Is the Brain Drain?", IMF Working Paper WP/98/102, International Monetary Fund, Washington, D.C., July.

CHALAMWONG, Y. (2001), "Recent Trends in Migration Flows and Policies in Thailand", *in* OECD, *International Migration in Asia: Trends and Policies*, OECD, Paris.

ISBN 92-64-01442-X © OECD 2005

Chang, S.L. (1992), "Causes of Brain Drain and Solutions: The Taiwan Experience", *Studies in Comparative International Development*, 27, 27-43, spring.

Chang, P. and Z. Deng (1992), "The Chinese Brain Drain and Policy Options", *Studies in Comparative International Development*, 27, 44-60, spring.

Coe, D.T. and E. Helpman (1995), "International R&D Spillovers", *European Economic Review*, 859-887, May.

Desai, M., D. Kapur and J. McHale (2001), "The Fiscal Impact of the Brain Drain: Indian Emigration to the United States", unpublished paper prepared for the Third Annual NBER-NCAER Conference, 17-18 December.

Fields, G.S. (1994), "The Migration Transition in Asia", *Asian and Pacific Migration Journal*, 3, 7-30.

Fourie, M.J. and R. Joubert (1998), *Emigration's Influence on South Africa: A Human Capital Theory Approach*, University of South Africa, Pretoria.

Gaillard, J. and A. Gaillard (1997), "Introduction: The International Mobility Of Brains: Exodus or Circulation", *Science, Technology and Society*, Vol. 2.

Garson, J.-P. (2001), "Main Trends in International Migration", a paper prepared for the Workshop on International Migration and Labour Market in Asia, organised by the Japan Institute of Labor, OECD and ILO, 1-2 January 2001, Japan Institute of Labor, Tokyo.

Garson, J.-P. (2003), "An Overview of Recent Trends in Migration Movement Policies in OECD Countries with a Special Focus on European Member Countries", a paper prepared for the Workshop on International Migration and Labour Market in Asia, organised by the Japan Institute of Labor, OECD and ILO, 6-7 February, Japan Institute of Labor, Tokyo.

Gayathri, V. (2001), "Rethinking High-Skilled International Migration: Research and Policy Issues for India's Information Economy", *in* OECD, *International Mobility of the Highly Skilled*, OECD, Paris.

Go, S.P. (2002), "Recent Trends in Migration Movements and Policies: the Movement of Filipino Professionals and Managers", a paper prepared for the Workshop on International Migration and Labour Market in Asia, organised by the Japan Institute of Labor, OECD and ILO, 4-5 February, Japan Institute of Labor, Tokyo.

Hayase, Y. (2003*a*), "International Migration in the Asia-Pacific Region: Its Linkages with Trade and Investment", *in* JETRO, *International Migration in APEC Member Economies: Its Relations with Trade, Investment and Economic Development*, JETRO, Tokyo.

Hayase, Y. (2003*b*), "Statistics of International Migration and Current Status of Migration in East Asia", a paper prepared for the United Nations Economic and Social Commission for Asia and the Pacific, August.

HAYASE, Y, H. NOGAMI and Y. NODA (2001), "Japanese Direct Investment to Asian Countries and Its Effects on International Migration", a paper prepared for the Workshop on International Migration and Structural Change in the APEC Member Economies, JETRO, Chiba.

HUGO, G.J. (2002*a*), "Indonesia's Labor Look Abroad", *Migration Information Source*, September.

HUGO, G.J. (2002*b*), "International Migration and Labour Market in Asia: Australia Country Paper 2002", a paper prepared for the Workshop on International Migration and Labour Market in Asia, organised by the Japan Institute of Labor, OECD and ILO, 4-5 February 2002, Japan Institute of Labor, Tokyo.

HUGO, G.J. (2003), "International Migration and Labour Market in Asia: Australia Country Paper 2003", a paper prepared for the Workshop on International Migration and Labour Market in Asia, organised by the Japan Institute of Labor, OECD and ILO, 6-7 February 2003, Japan Institute of Labor, Tokyo.

IGUCHI, Y. (2002), "Movement of the Highly Skilled in Asia: Present Situation and Future Prospect", *in* JAPAN INSTITUTE OF LABOR, *Migration and the Labour Market in Asia: Recent Trends and Policies*, Japan Institute of Labor, Tokyo.

INTERNATIONAL LABOUR ORGANIZATION (ILO) (2002), "Skilled Labour Mobilities: Review of Issues and Evidence", a paper prepared for the Workshop on International Migration of Highly Skilled Workers: Its Current Situation, Problems and Future Prospects in Asia, 4-5 February, Tokyo.

INTERNATIONAL MONETARY FUND (IMF) (1998, 2003 and 2004). *Balance of Payments Statistics Yearbook*, IMF, Washington, D.C.

IREDALE, R. (2000). "Migration Policies for the Highly Skilled in the Asia-Pacific Region", *International Migration Review*, 34, 882-906, Autumn.

KAPUR, D. (2001), "Diasporas and Technology Transfer", a background paper prepared for the *Human Development Report*, January.

The Lancet, 19 April 2003, Vol. 361, available at: www.thelancet.com.

LIM, S.P. (2000), "The Question of Diaspora in International Relations: A Case Study of Chinese Diaspora in Malaysia and Southeast Asia", unpublished dissertation, M.A. in International Relations, University of Sussex, Brighton.

LOWELL, L. and A. FINDLAY (2001), "Migration of Highly Skilled Persons from Developing Countries: Impact and Policy Responses", *International Migration Papers 44*, ILO, Geneva, December.

LUCAS, R.E.B. (1981), "International Migration: Economic Causes, Consequences and Evaluation", *in* M.M. KRITZ, C.B. KEELY, S.M. TOMASI (eds.), *Global Trends in Migration*, Center for Migration Studies, New York, NY.

ISBN 92-64-01442-X © OECD 2005

LUCAS, R.E.B. (2001), "Diaspora and Development: Highly Skilled Migrants from East Asia", a report prepared for the World Bank, November, World Bank, Washington, D.C.

MARTIN, P. (2002), "Highly Skilled Asian Workers in the US", a paper prepared for the Workshop on International Migration of Highly Skilled Workers: Its Current Situation, Problems and Future Prospects in Asia, Tokyo, 4-5 February.

MCLAUGHLAN, G. and J. SALT (2002), *Migration Policies Toward Highly Skilled Foreign Workers,* Migration Research Unit, Geography Department, University College London, London.

MEYER, J.B., J. CHARUM, D. BERNAL, J. GAILLARD, J. GRANÉS, J. LEON, A. MONTENEGRO, A. MORALES, C. MURCIA, N. NARVAEZ-BERTHELEMOT, L.S. PARRADO and B. SCHLEMMER (1997), "Turning Brain Drain into Brain Gain: The Colombian Experience of the Diaspora Option", *in Science, Technology and Society,* Vol. 2.

MEYERS, D.W. (1998), "Migrant Remittances to Latin America: Reviewing the Literature", a paper commissioned by the Inter-American Dialogue and the Tomas Rivera Policy Institute, Washington, D.C.

OECD (2001), *International Migration in Asia: Trends and Policies,* Paris, OECD, Paris.

OECD (2002), *Migration and the Labour Market in Asia: Trends and Policies,* Paris, OECD, Paris.

ROSENBAUM, J.E., T. KARIYA, R. SETTERSTEN and T. MAIER (1990), "Market and Network Theories of the Transition from High School to Work: Their Application to Industrial Societies", *Annual Review of Sociology,* Vol. 16.

SAXENIAN, A.-L. (1999), *Silicon Valley's New Immigrant Entrepreneurs,* Public Policy Institute of California, San Francisco.

YUKAWA, J. (1996), *Migration from the Philippines, 1975-1995: An Annotated Bibliography,* Scalabrini Migration Center, Quezon City.

ISBN 92-64-01442-X

Part Four

Development Lessons for Other Regions

Chapter 13

Integrating East Asia's Low-Income Countries into the Regional and Global Markets

Siow Yue Chia

Abstract

For decades the CLMV countries (Cambodia, Laos, Myanmar, Viet Nam) experienced the negative impacts of wrong economic ideologies and policies. Since the mid-1980s, they have engaged in economic transition from centrally planned to market-oriented economies, from inward-looking to outward-looking development strategies, and from close economic relations with the Soviet bloc to closer economic relations with the global and regional market economies. Despite considerable political obstacles along the way, these transition economies have achieved remarkable results in reforming their policies and institutions and in restructuring. The economic benefits are manifest in the buoyant economic growth rates of the 1990s and in recent years. After the outbreak of the Asian financial crisis, growth rates in the sub-region outpaced those in ASEAN-6. The CLMV economies have become increasingly integrated with ASEAN and the rest of East Asia and with the global economy, as witnessed by rising trade and investment flows.

The CLMV countries have experienced and continue to experience instances of political isolation, economic policy discrimination and policy incoherence on the part of OECD countries, which have impacted on their economic performance, particularly in trade and investment. While the OECD countries have advocated and pressured them for economic policy and institutional reforms, particularly more openness in trade and investment regimes, they have not always followed up with non-discriminatory or preferential market access.

Countries have the primary responsibility for their own economic and social development. As low-income and least-developed economies, the CLMV economies still face several development challenges and have to achieve greater policy coherence themselves. They need to pursue economic growth with social equity and environmental sustainability. They must develop human resources for economic efficiency and poverty alleviation. They should continue to liberalise and deregulate their economies to improve economic efficiency and competitiveness and to meet the commitments of WTO accession and ASEAN membership. Yet they also require enabling regional and global environments that provide open and preferential access to markets, access to investments, technology and know how and access to development and technical assistance.

ISBN 92-64-01442-X

Introduction

Cambodia, Laos, Myanmar and Viet Nam (CLMV) are low-income economies in East Asia and (except for Viet Nam) are designated as least-developed countries by the United Nations. With the end of the Cold War and the break-up of the Soviet bloc, Cambodia, Laos and Viet Nam sought integration into the global economy and applied for accession to the World Trade Organization (WTO). Cambodia became a member of the WTO on 13 October 2004, while Laos and Viet Nam are still negotiating their accessions. Myanmar became a member in 1995[1]. The CLMV economies have also sought regional integration through the Association of Southeast Asian Nations (ASEAN), with Viet Nam acceding in 1995, Laos and Myanmar in 1997, and Cambodia in 1999. Viet Nam joined the Asia Pacific Economic Co-operation (APEC) forum in November 1998, and the other three countries have applied for membership.

Since the mid-1980s, the CLMV countries have undergone economic transition — from centrally planned to market-based economies, from inward looking to outward-looking economic strategies and from economic relations with the Soviet bloc to economic relations with market economies. Initially they undertook policy and institutional reforms unilaterally, but as they seek membership in the WTO and ASEAN, they face pressures from these organisations to sustain and undertake further economic reforms.

In its economic transition, the CLMV sub-region benefits from a good geographical location. As noted in the Overview chapter of this volume, East Asia was, until the outbreak of the Asian financial crisis in 1997-98, an "economic miracle", with a string of success stories in economic performance. The East Asian pattern of economic development has often been characterised as the "flying geese" model. Japan was the first country to become developed, followed by the Asian newly industrialised economies (NIEs) of Hong Kong, China; Korea; Chinese Taipei and Singapore, followed in turn by the ASEAN economies of Indonesia, Malaysia, Philippines and Thailand and most recently by China. Two transmission mechanisms have been at work. The first is the transfer of development experiences and lessons from one tier to the next. Japan showed the way. The Asian NIEs adapted the Japanese model, focusing on high savings and investment, human-resource development, foreign direct investment and promotion of export manufacturing. The ASEAN economies made further adaptations to the "East Asian development model" with greater emphasis on natural-resource development and the role of foreign direct investment and less emphasis on industrial policy and industrial targeting

 ISBN 92-64-01442-X © OECD 2005

by the state. The second transmission mechanism is the flow of investment resources from Japan to the Asian NIEs and ASEAN and from Asian NIEs to ASEAN, resulting in the integration of national economies into regional production networks and supply chains. There have been reverse investments between the NIEs and ASEAN, but limited reverse flows to Japan.

The CLMV countries follow the ASEAN model of natural-resource development plus export-led and FDI-led manufacturing, although they are at the early stage of developing capabilities in exporting manufactures and produce mainly labour-intensive products such as clothing and footwear. East Asia also provides a large share of the investment resources for the CLMV countries, and Japan is the leading donor of bilateral development assistance.

Domestic economic reforms need an enabling international and regional environment to provide market access, investment, technological resources and development assistance. At the international level, the WTO is committed to improving market access for developing and least developed countries, but to take advantage of market-access opportunities, countries must be able to supply products that satisfy the price, quality and delivery-time requirements of the global market.

This chapter focuses on how domestic policies as well as external policies, particularly those of OECD countries, impact on the economic performance and economic prospects of Cambodia, Laos, Myanmar and Viet Nam, the low-income and least-developed economies of East Asia. It analyses how policy coherence, or rather the lack of it, adversely impacts on their economic performance. The chapter is divided into six sections. The next four discuss in turn the economic transition in the CLMV countries, their integration into ASEAN, global integration through trade and investment and WTO membership and the development and technical assistance provided under the Greater Mekong Sub-regional programme. The last section concludes.

Economic Transition

Background

In the mid-1980s the CLMV economies decided to abandon their Marxist socialist model of central planning and state ownership in favour of a market-orientation. ESCAP (1995) noted that they faced greater transition difficulties than the countries of Eastern Europe and the former Soviet Union. The CLMV countries had lower per capita income levels, had undergone war and insurgency with the resulting destruction of physical infrastructure and human resources and faced international discrimination and isolation.

Viet Nam embarked in 1986 on an economic reform known as "doi moi" (renovation), a transition from a centrally planned to a market-oriented economy with government continuing to play a leading role. Policy and institutional reforms included liberalisation and deregulation of trade and foreign direct investment and promotion of private enterprise. The reform suffered from the country's political and economic isolation when Vietnamese troops occupied Cambodia (until September 1989). Laos and Cambodia also initiated economic reforms around the same time as Viet Nam but theirs were less extensive, as civil war erupted in Cambodia while Laos was handicapped by being landlocked. Myanmar was also a command economy until the military coup in 1988, when the State Law and Order Restoration Council (SLORC) adopted a quasi-market economy as well as moving towards closer economic relations with China.

A number of developments in the CLMV sub-region in the 1990s affected the economic transition (ESCAP, 1995). First, political tensions in the sub-region eased following the withdrawal of Vietnamese troops from Cambodia in 1989 and the Paris peace accord on Cambodia in October 1991. Second, trade relations with members of the Council for Mutual Economic Assistance (CMEA) collapsed rapidly and unexpectedly in 1989-91, involving also the loss of substantial aid from the former Soviet Union and Eastern Europe. Third, the 1993 elections in Cambodia paved the way for further economic reforms[2]. Fourth, economic sanctions imposed by major trading nations against Viet Nam were gradually relaxed, culminating in removal of the US trade embargo in February 1994. Two other developments in the 1990s kept up the pressure and momentum for economic reform, namely when the CLMV countries acceded to ASEAN and when Cambodia, Laos and Viet Nam applied to join the WTO.

Reform of the Foreign Trade and Investment Regimes

The CLMV countries took crucial steps toward trade and investment liberalisation and deregulation, unilaterally as well as to meet the requirements of WTO accession (excluding Myanmar) and ASEAN membership. Viet Nam's trade regime before "doi moi" was characterised by complex, high import tariffs and non-tariff barriers and export restrictions. Trade-policy reform, the cornerstone of "doi moi", had two main objectives. The first was to liberalise domestic prices. The second was to promote export-oriented industrialisation, redressing the anti-export bias embodied in the earlier protectionist regime. Measures adopted included relaxing restrictions on the

ISBN 92-64-01442-X © OECD 2005

number of trading entities and progressive elimination of quotas and targets. The number of trading entities rose from about 30 in 1988 to 16 200 by 2001. All import quotas were abolished by 2003 except for sugar (to be kept until 2005) and petroleum products. Import tariffs were introduced in 1988, rationalised in 1992 and simplified in 1999 following Viet Nam's accession to the ASEAN Free Trade Area (AFTA) and in preparation for WTO accession. Duty exemptions and drawbacks for imports used in export production were introduced. Viet Nam's complex system of export restrictions has been substantially dismantled. To promote export development, several export-processing zones were established. In 1989 a unified exchange rate was achieved. The US-Viet Nam Bilateral Trade Agreement also gave impetus to reforms, particularly pertaining to services and intellectual property protection.

A World Bank study (Auffret, 2003) found the pace of implementation of trade reform impressive, but cautioned that fast trade liberalisation may conflict with the slow implementation of other reforms, including restructuring of state-owned enterprises and commercial banks. Problems with the banking system are reflected in the continuing high level of non-performing loans. Viet Nam has to undertake further policy, institutional and legislative reforms to meet WTO accession requirements. The WTO Working Party on Viet Nam's accession has held several meetings. The meeting in June 2004 found that Viet Nam had considerably improved its market-access offers for goods and services and its programme for applying WTO agreements, but concluded that "a lot of work still remains", which dashed Viet Nam's hope of joining WTO by 1 January 2005[3].

Cambodia has also undertaken substantial trade reforms since the mid-1980s and in recent years to meet the requirements of WTO accession. Until 1989, Cambodia maintained a government monopoly over external trade, and all imports and exports required licences. Since then, private-sector participation has been allowed, and in September 1993 the general obligation to obtain import and export licences was rescinded, with licences required only on some items. Tariff rates were rationalised and tariff levels brought down. In 1994 several export-promotion measures were introduced, including the establishment of special economic zones. Cambodia applied for WTO accession in October 1994 and embarked on fundamental economic reforms. In an August 2003 statement, the Cambodian government reported that implementation of WTO requirements was a "lengthy and difficult process" and asked for flexibility in negotiations on WTO commitments and for special and differential treatment as a least developed country[4]. In a subsequent September 2003 statement, the government said, "We managed to secure a package of commitments and concessions we feel was the most affordable and possible deal for Cambodia's accession, bearing in mind Cambodia's little political and economic weight and its current reliance on external assistance from the major donor countries who are also WTO members[5]." WTO accession approval was granted in September 2003 and the Cambodian national legislature ratified the accession agreement in September 2004.

The trade regime in Laos up to the mid-1980s was also characterised by complex and high import tariffs and export restrictions, but it was in practice less centralised and less transparent than that of Viet Nam. ESCAP (1995) reported on various reform measures underway, but noted that the incomplete nature of import liberalisation was manifest in the continuing large amount of regulated trade. Laos applied to join the WTO in July 1997 and has also to undertake further liberalisation and reforms, although it will be accorded special and differential treatment as a least-developed country. Negotiations on the terms of accession are ongoing[6].

The CLMV countries have also liberalised their foreign investment regimes to attract FDI inflows as part of their economic transition. FDI has played a very important role in the economic development of ASEAN-6. FDI is packaged, providing the host economy with financial resources as well as technology, management expertise and integration into global production and distribution networks. For FDI in export manufacturing, ease and availability of transport and logistics are an important consideration, in addition to abundant low-wage labour for labour-intensive industries and a skilled labour force, technological capability and available local suppliers for parts and components for high tech industries. FDI in natural-resource development and in manufacturing for the host market is more location-specific, with major determinants being the existence of abundant and marketable resources and the size and growth-potential of the national market or integrated regional market.

Many ASEAN countries have made extensive use of tax incentives to improve the overall investment climate and to induce FDI into desired sectors and projects. Critics of industrial policy and industrial targeting point to their negative effects on resource allocation, while critics of the tax incentives instrument also question their efficacy in determining investment decisions as well as the tax revenue foregone by host governments. In the past decade global and regional competition for FDI inflows has intensified. As prospective host countries liberalise their FDI regimes by removing investment restrictions and performance requirements, additional measures are used to attract FDI. The TRIMs Agreement did not include discipline on the use of investment incentives, and discussion of the investment issue in the ongoing Doha Round has stalled.

ISBN 92-64-01442-X © OECD 2005

The CLMV countries enacted foreign investment laws around 1987-88 to attract FDI, followed by amendments in later years. They adopted the ASEAN-6 FDI strategy of investment liberalisation, with the removal or relaxation of foreign ownership restrictions and performance requirements. They use an array of investment incentives including tax holidays, duty drawbacks and tax exemptions on inputs for export production and establishment of export-processing and special economic zones. Lower labour costs and abundant natural resources are the main attractions. Viet Nam also has a sizeable domestic market of 80 million consumers. Yet investors remain discouraged by a host of disincentives. The CLMV countries have to pay greater attention to improving the legal framework, the implementation of policy and regulatory commitments, improving administrative efficiency and probity, attending to infrastructure and human-resource bottlenecks and providing adequate protection of intellectual property and a transparent and impartial dispute-settlement mechanism.

GDP Growth, Structural Change and Poverty Alleviation

Chapter 1 of this volume shows that over a span of 50 years the average per capita GDP of East Asia has risen sevenfold, with wide variations in performance across countries and time periods. The NIEs led this growth (Hong Kong, China; Singapore; Korea and Chinese Taipei with a 17-fold increase), followed by Japan (11-fold), China (eightfold) and the ASEAN-4 (Indonesia, Malaysia, Philippines and Thailand, fourfold). The CLMV countries trailed with a threefold increase, ranging from a doubling in Cambodia and Laos, a tripling in Viet Nam and a quadrupling in Myanmar. By 2001 estimated per capita GDP (in 1990 dollars) stood at $1 124 for Cambodia, $1 204 for Laos, $1 408 for Myanmar and $1 850 for Viet Nam. The development gap as measured by per capita GDP between the NIEs and CLMV widened from a ratio of 1.8 in 1950 to 9.8 in 2001, and between ASEAN-4 and CLMV it widened from 1.7 to 2.4.

Table 13.1 shows that over 1990-2003, annual aggregate GDP growth averaged 6.6 per cent in Cambodia, 6.3 per cent in Laos and 7.5 per cent in Viet Nam (no data are available for Myanmar). The fruits of economic transition since the mid-1980s were becoming evident. Average annual GDP growth rates for the sub-region in 1992-96 ranged from 6.6 per cent to 8.4 per cent. The 1997-98 Asian financial crisis that afflicted much of East Asia did not directly undermine growth in the CLMV economies as they did not have fully open capital accounts and had minimal exposure to international short-term capital movements. Since 1997, GDP growth in the CLMV sub-region has outperformed the ASEAN-6.

Table 13.1. **ASEAN: Economic Indicators, 2003**

	Population	Land Area	GNI		GNI-PPP adjusted		GDP Growth	Merchandise Trade		
			Total	Per Capita	Total	Per Capita	1990-2003	Exports	Imports	Total
Brunei	0.4	6	5	15 000	n.a.	n.a.	n.a.	n.a.	n.a.	n.a.
Indonesia	214.5	1 905	173	810	689	3 210	3.5	60 650	32 390	93 040
Malaysia	24.8	330	94	3 780	222	8 940	5.9	100 726	81 067	181 793
Philippines	81.5	300	88	1 080	379	4 640	3.5	37 065	39 301	76 366
Singapore	4.3	1	90	21 230	103	24 180	6.3	144 134	127 898	272 032
Thailand	62.0	513	136	2 190	462	7 450	3.7	80 253	75 679	155 932
Cambodia	13.4	181	4	310	28	2 060	6.6	1 623	1 724	3 347
Laos	5.7	237	2	320	10	1 730	6.3	371	508	879
Myanmar	49.4	677	n.a.	n.a.	n.a.	n.a.	n.a.	2 802	2 515	5 317
Viet Nam	81.3	332	39	480	202	2 490	7.5	19 660	24 020	43 680
ASEAN-6	387.5		586	1 383				422 828	356 335	779 163
ASEAN-10	537.3		631	1 074				447 284	385 102	832 386

Notes: Population figures in millions; Land Area in thousands of square kilometres; GNI and GNI-PPP adjusted: totals in billions of US dollars and per capita figures in US dollars; GDP Growth in per cent per annum; Merchandise trade in millions of US dollars. n.a = not available.

Source: World Bank, *World Development Report*, 2005.

ISBN 92-64-01442-X © OECD 2005

Agriculture still dominates the economies of Cambodia, Laos and Myanmar, accounting for 40 per cent to 50 per cent of their GDP and providing employment for 70 to 80 per cent of their populations. In Cambodia and Viet Nam, the disruptions of war and agricultural collectivisation led to serious deterioration of the irrigation and drainage infrastructure. The sub-region has substantial inland and marine fishery resources, with good export potential. It also has substantial energy resources in the form of oil and gas and hydropower. Forestry resources have been over-exploited and continuing levels of recorded and unrecorded exports of timber are unsustainable. A challenge for the sub-region is to expand and improve processing facilities to add value to their natural resource exports. Tourism is a rapidly growing sector and has good potential.

The CLMV countries have been industrialising for economic growth, employment and poverty alleviation. By 2001, the share of manufacturing in GDP ranged from less than 20 per cent in Myanmar to a high of 37 per cent in Viet Nam. These economies have a comparative advantage in labour-intensive manufacturing and are increasingly dependent on the production and export of clothing. Viet Nam has the best prospects for industrialisation, as it has a large and well-educated labour force, low labour costs and a rapidly growing and sizeable domestic market.

Both trade and investment flows in the sub-region have increased markedly over the last decade. Their growing global integration is evident in sharply rising trade/GDP ratios since 1990, which reached over 90 per cent in Cambodia and Viet Nam and over 50 per cent in Laos in 2001. FDI/GDP ratios also have risen — to 4 per cent in Viet Nam, 3.3 per cent in Cambodia and 1.4 per cent in Laos (there are no figures available for Myanmar).

Notwithstanding its growth performance, the sub-region still has widespread poverty. Table 13.2 shows proportions of populations below national poverty lines at 39 per cent in Laos, 36 per cent in Cambodia, 29 per cent in Viet Nam and 23 per cent in Myanmar. The proportions below the international poverty line of $1.00 per day (ppp adjusted) were 39 per cent in Laos (1997), 34 per cent in Cambodia (1997) and 7 per cent for Viet Nam (no data on Myanmar). Poverty incidence thus measured in the CLMV is much higher than in the ASEAN-5, except for the Philippines. Cambodia, Laos and Viet Nam registered some improvement in their human development indices (HDI) in the 1990s, but the HDI rankings are worse than for ASEAN-5, except that Indonesia's is worse than Viet Nam's.

ISBN 92-64-01442-X © OECD 2005

Table 13.2. **ASEAN: Poverty and Human Development**

	Per Cent of Population Below National Poverty Line				Per Cent of Population below $1 Per Day		Human Development Index		2001 HDI Rank among 175 Countries
	Year	Total	Urban	Rural	Year	%	1990	2001	
Cambodia	1999	35.9	18.2	40.1	1997	34.1	0.512	0.556	130
Laos	1997	38.6	26.9	41.0	1997	39.0	0.449	0.525	135
Myanmar	1997	22.9	23.9	22.4		n.a.	n.a.	0.549	131
Viet Nam	2002	28.9	6.6	35.6	2002	13.1	0.603	0.688	109
Indonesia	2002	18.2	14.5	21.1	2002	7.5	0.619	0.682	112
Malaysia	1999	7.5	3.4	12.4		n.a.	0.721	0.790	58
Philippines	2000	34	20.4	47.4	2000	15.5	0.713	0.751	85
Singapore		n.a.	n.a.	n.a.	n.a.	n.a.	0.819	0.884	28
Thailand	2002	9.8	4	12.6	2000	1.9	0.705	0.768	74

Source: ADB Key Indicators 2004.

Table 13.3 shows the performance of CLMV in relation to the Millennium Development Goals (MDG). There have been improvements in poverty eradication, universal primary education and gender equality and empowerment. Infant, child and maternal mortality rates remain high, however. The prevalence of HIV/AIDS is also disturbing, though the proportions are very low compared with sub-Saharan Africa. There was continuing deforestation in 1990-2000, except in Viet Nam. All the CLMV countries have adopted national poverty-reduction strategies in recent years. The poverty-reduction targets require sustained economic growth as well as specific pro-poor policies. As these low-income countries face severe resource constraints, strategic policy choices have to be made to balance growth and poverty-reduction. UNCTAD's *The Least Developed Countries Report 2004* highlights the difficulties in ensuring that the benefits of trade liberalisation and export growth trickle down to the poor[7].

Table 13.3. **CLMV Countries: Millennium Development Goals**

	Cambodia	Laos	Myanmar	Viet Nam
Goal 1: Eradicate extreme poverty and hunger:				
Per cent of population below $1per day at 1993 ppp				
1990	48.3	53.0	n.a.	50.8
2000	35.5	34.6	n.a.	9.6
Per cent of poorest quintile in national consumption				
early 1990s	n.a.	9.6	n.a.	7.8
late 1990s	6.9	7.6	n.a.	8.0

ISBN 92-64-01442-X © OECD 2005

Table 13.3. (contd.)

	Cambodia	Laos	Myanmar	Viet Nam
Goal 2: Achieve universal primary education:				
Net enrolment ratio in primary education, per cent				
early 1990s	n.a.	61.4	n.a.	n.a.
late 1990s	102.6	76.2	n.a.	97.4
Literacy rate of 15-24 year olds, per cent				
1990	73.5	55.2	88.2	95.0
2002	80.1	73.3	91.4	97.3
Goal 3: Promote gender equality and empower women:				
Literate female/male ratio, 15-24 year olds, per cent				
1990	0.82	0.52	0.96	0.99
2000	0.93	0.74	1.00	1.01
Goal 4: Reduce child mortality:				
Under-5 mortality rate per 1000 live births				
1990	115	163	130	50
2001	138	100	109	38
Infant mortality rate per 1000 live births				
1990	80	120	91	36
2001	97	87	77	30
Goal 5: Improve maternal health:				
Maternal mortality rate per 100 000 live births, 1995	590	650	170	95
Goal 6: Combat HIV/AIDS, malaria, other diseases:				
Prevalence rate of HIV in 15-24 year olds, per cent, end-2001				
Female:				
low estimate, from	1.99	0.02	0.18	0.13
high estimate, from	2.98	0.03	0.38	0.20
Male:				
low estimate, from	0.77	0.03	0.17	0.25
high estimate, from	1.16	0.06	0.36	0.38
Prevalence rate of malaria per 100 000 population, 2000	476	759	224	95
Prevalence of tuberculosis per 100 000 population, 2000	474	148	132	101
Goal 7: Ensure environmental sustainability:				
% of land area covered by forest				
1990	56.1	56.7	60.2	28.6
2000	52.9	54.4	52.3	30.2
Urban water supply coverage, 2000, per cent	54	61	89	95
Rural water supply coverage, 2000, per cent	26	29	66	72
Urban sanitation coverage, 2000, per cent	58	84	65	86
Goal 8: Develop a global partnership for development:				
Debt service as per cent of exports of goods and services				
1990	4.1	8.9	19.1	n.a.
1999	3.0	7.9	5.4	n.a.

Note n.a. = not available.
Source: ESCAP (2003).

Regional Integration into ASEAN

ASEAN was formed in 1967 with Indonesia, Malaysia, the Philippines, Singapore and Thailand as founding members. They were joined by Brunei in 1984 (collectively the ASEAN-6) and Cambodia, Laos, Myanmar and Viet Nam in 1995-99. With the end of the Cold War and the break-up of the Soviet bloc, the CLMV countries were motivated to join ASEAN by both the political need to reorient their foreign policies and the economic need to restructure and reorient their economies. The newer members are at very much lower levels of economic development than the ASEAN-6, as Table 13.1 showed. While membership extension to CLMV increased the population of ASEAN by 39 per cent from 380 million to 530 million, it raised both the regional GNP and the volume of merchandise trade by only 7 per cent.

Regional economic co-operation and integration should help the CLMV economies modernise, diversify, specialise and respond more effectively to the challenges of globalisation, the technological revolution and the rise of China. CLMV membership has nevertheless slowed the pace of ASEAN economic integration, because the transitional economies need extra time to fulfil their trade and investment liberalisation commitments. The challenge of integration would lessen for the CLMV members if there were targeted technical assistance from the ASEAN-6. Such assistance did not materialise immediately after their ASEAN accession because the ASEAN-6 economies were still pulling themselves out of the Asian financial crisis.

Trade and Investment Integration

ASEAN agreed in 1992 to establish the ASEAN Free Trade Area (AFTA), with the objective of removing tariff and non-tariff barriers on intra-ASEAN trade in goods. It was the first regional trading arrangement (RTA) in East Asia and was motivated by the need to become more internationally competitive in the face of pressures from globalisation and the formation of RTAs in the Americas and Europe. (For further discussion of East Asian integration, see Chapter 8 in this volume.) AFTA originally had a time-frame of 15 years to reduce tariffs to the 0-5 per cent target, but the deadline was subsequently brought forward to 2002 for the ASEAN-6, 2006 for Viet Nam, 2008 for Laos and Myanmar, and 2010 for Cambodia. (Each of the CLMV countries was given a ten-year transitional period after AFTA accession). AFTA also agreed to achieve zero tariffs by 2010 for ASEAN-6 and 2015 for CLMV.

ISBN 92-64-01442-X © OECD 2005

Services-trade liberalisation comes under the 1995 ASEAN Framework Agreement on Services (AFAS) and investment liberalisation under the 1998 ASEAN Investment Area (AIA). Implementation of AFAS has been slow, as ASEAN members have been reluctant to liberalise their services sectors, although efficient services are essential for competitiveness in goods production and trade. The "impasse" led to two features of flexibility introduced in 2003. The first is the faster liberalisation for mode 1 (cross-border supply) and mode 2 (consumption abroad) and slower liberalisation for mode 3 (commercial presence) and mode 4 (presence of natural persons). Second, two or more ASEAN countries could go ahead to liberalise services trade between themselves under an "ASEAN minus X" formula, with other members choosing to join at a later date. The AIA aims at opening up economic sectors and granting national treatment to investment from ASEAN members and external sources. For intra-ASEAN investment, the ASEAN-6 as well as Myanmar (by self-election) phased out their temporary exclusion lists by 2003, while Cambodia, Laos and Viet Nam have until 2010 to do likewise.

Table 13.4 shows intra-ASEAN trade since the formation of AFTA. Singapore accounts for over 40 per cent of it, reflecting its regional trading-hub status[8]. Regional trade as a proportion of each country's total trade measures the extent of trade integration. For ASEAN-6, Brunei and Singapore record the highest ratios of over 25 per cent and the Philippines records the lowest (16 per cent). Data on the CLMV are available only for Cambodia and Myanmar[9]. Myanmar has the highest ratio of intra-ASEAN/total trade among the ASEAN countries (over 50 per cent in 2002)[10]. Its exports to ASEAN comprise largely mineral fuels (mostly crude oil), forestry products and vegetables, while its imports are mostly mineral fuels (refined petroleum), textiles and clothing, machinery and electrical appliances and plastics.

Table 13.4. **Intra-ASEAN Trade, 1993 and 2001-2002**

	Value in $ million			Per Cent of Intra-ASEAN trade			Per Cent of Country's Trade	
	1993	2001	2002	1993	2001	2002	2001	2002
Intra-ASEAN Exports by:								
Brunei	487	775	684	1.1	0.9	0.8	21.9	25.4
Indonesia	4 997	9 507	9 934	11.4	11.3	11.5	16.9	17.4
Malaysia	12 987	21 024	22 127	29.7	24.9	25.6	23.9	23.7
Philippines	795	4 986	5 530	1.8	5.9	6.4	15.5	15.7
Singapore	18 406	32 815	33 963	42.1	38.8	39.3	27.0	27.2
Thailand	6 008	14 357	12 840	13.8	17.0	14.9	22.0	19.4
ASEAN-6	43 681	83 464	85 077	99.9	98.8	98.5	22.5	22.2
Cambodia	n.a.	73	92	n.a.	0.1	0.1	4.9	4.8
Laos	n.a.	n.a.	n.a.	n.a.	n.a.	n.a.	n.a.	n.a.
Myanmar	n.a.	951	1 221	n.a.	1.1	1.4	42.9	49.8
Viet Nam	n.a.	n.a.	n.a.	n.a.	n.a.	n.a.	n.a.	n.a.
Total intra-ASEAN	43 681	84 488	86 391	100.0	100.0	100.0	22.8	22.5
As % of ASEAN total	21.1	22.8	22.5					
Intra-ASEAN Imports by:								
Brunei	886	545	599	2.3	0.8	0.8	41.6	37.4
Indonesia	2 659	5 727	6 932	6.9	8.5	9.6	18.5	22.2
Malaysia	8 904	15 254	17 245	23.0	22.6	23.9	20.9	21.9
Philippines	1 883	4 665	5 542	4.9	6.9	7.7	15.8	16.5
Singapore	18 761	28 991	30 441	48.4	42.9	42.1	25.0	26.2
Thailand	5 671	10 047	9 683	14.6	14.9	13.4	16.2	15.4
ASEAN-6	38 763	65 229	70 442	100.0	96.4	97.5	20.6	21.5
Cambodia	n.a.	1 092	598	n.a.	1.6	0.8	72.7	35.9
Laos	n.a.	n.a.	n.a.	n.a.	n.a.	n.a.	n.a.	n.a.
Myanmar	n.a.	1 319	1 191	n.a.	2.0	1.6	46.9	56.2
Viet Nam	n.a.	n.a.	n.a.	n.a.	n.a.	n.a.	n.a.	n.a.
Total intra-ASEAN	38 763	67 640	72 231	100.0	100.0	100.0	21.3	22.0
As % of ASEAN total	17.4	21.3	22.0					

ISBN 92-64-01442-X © OECD 2005

Table 13.4 (contd.)

	Value in $ million			Per Cent of Intra-ASEAN trade			Per Cent of Country's Trade	
	1993	2001	2002	1993	2001	2002	2001	2002
Intra-ASEAN Exports and Imports:								
Brunei Darussalam	1 374	1 320	1 283	1.7	0.9	0.8	27.3	29.9
Indonesia	7 656	15 234	16 865	9.3	10.0	10.6	17.5	19.1
Malaysia	21 891	36 279	39 372	26.6	23.8	24.8	22.5	22.9
Philippines	2 678	9 651	11 072	3.2	6.3	7.0	15.6	16.1
Singapore	37 167	61 806	64 404	45.1	40.6	40.6	26.0	26.7
Thailand	11 680	24 404	22 524	14.2	16.0	14.2	19.2	17.5
ASEAN-6	82 444	148 693	155 520	100.0	97.7	98.0	21.9	22.1
Cambodia	n.a.	1 164	690	n.a.	0.8	0.4	23.0	19.3
Laos	n.a.	n.a.	n.a.	n.a.	n.a.	n.a.	n.a.	n.a.
Myanmar	n.a.	2 271	2 412	n.a.	1.5	1.5	45.1	52.8
Viet Nam	n.a.	n.a.	n.a.	n.a.	n.a.	n.a.	n.a.	n.a.
Total intra-ASEAN	82 444	152 127	158 622	100.0	100.0	100.0	22.1	22.3
As % of ASEAN total	19.2	22.1	22.3					

Notes: Singapore's import and export figures include imports from ASEAN for re-export to ASEAN and exports to ASEAN of goods of ASEAN origin, so there is a large element of double-counting of intra-ASEAN trade. However, Singapore's trade figures exclude trade with Indonesia, which has not been reported by Singapore, so there is a significant element of under-reporting by Singapore of trade with ASEAN. Singapore-Indonesia trade has not been reported by Singapore since 1963. n.a. = not available.

Source : ASEAN Secretariat trade statistics.

Table 13.5 shows that investment from ASEAN accounted for 22.6 per cent of total CLMV FDI inflows in 1998-2001, ranging from highs of 49.4 per cent for Laos and 36.1 per cent for Cambodia to near 20 per cent for Viet Nam. Singapore is the leading investor in the CLMV sub-region, accounting for 57.8 per cent of ASEAN investments. Its investment concentrates in Viet Nam, followed by Myanmar and Cambodia. Thailand is the leading investor in Laos. FDI from the ASEAN-6 fell sharply after the Asian financial crisis erupted in mid-1997. Among the CLMV countries, Viet Nam is the largest recipient of FDI from ASEAN, overwhelmingly from Singapore, with Thailand and Malaysia ranking second and third.

ASEAN membership is expected to bring several economic benefits for the CLMV countries. First and foremost, they have preferential access to a larger regional market, enabling them to have greater market security, specialise according to comparative advantage, exploit scale economies and improve the prospects for attracting FDI into downstream and upstream industries. Joint development of tourist infrastructure and common marketing of ASEAN as a tourist destination have benefited CLMV tourism.

With their abundance of agricultural, marine and mineral resources as well as low-wage labour, the CLMV economies have comparative advantage in activities based on primary resources and in labour-intensive manufacturing. Their food exports compete with those from some ASEAN countries, but there is a ready demand from Singapore, which also helps CLMV suppliers with technical and sanitary and phytosanitary standards. The producing countries can move up the value chain from exporting unprocessed agriculture and aquaculture products to exporting processed food. They need technical assistance to raise sanitary and phytosanitary standards to meet regional and global market demand.

Relocation of labour-intensive manufacturing from the more advanced ASEAN economies experiencing higher and rising labour costs would enable the CLMV countries to become integrated into the regional value chains and industry clusters. ASEAN-5 has enjoyed rapid growth in the electronics industry and is part of the global and regional electronics supply chains and industry clusters. The CLMV countries, particularly the larger labour-abundant economies of Myanmar and Viet Nam, should have good prospects for the more labour-intensive end of the electronics value chain. The electronics industry in Viet Nam is already growing rapidly, in part from relocations from the more costly production centres in ASEAN and Asian NIEs. An integrated ASEAN electronics industry should provide a competitive response to the challenge of China. The low-wage advantage of CLMV could be negated,

 ISBN 92-64-01442-X © OECD 2005

Table 13.5. **CLMV: FDI Inflows from ASEAN Sources**
($ million; percentages as indicated)

	1995	1996	1997	1998	1999	2000	2001	1998-01
Cambodia:	150.7	293.7	168.1	271.9	232.0	148.8	148.3	801.0
ASEAN				96.9	84.2	71.1	37.2	289.4
Malaysia				24.2	32.3	45.9	10.9	113.3
Singapore				43.8	18.1	19.3	21.6	102.8
Thailand				27.6	32.3	12.0	3.3	75.2
ASEAN/World, %				35.6	36.3	47.8	25.1	36.1
Laos:	88.4	128.0	86.3	45.3	51.6	34.0	23.9	154.8
ASEAN	6.5	102.6	64.4	28.3	31.4	13.7	3.1	76.5
Malaysia	0.8	22.5	56.1	1.2	9.1	3.2	0.9	14.4
Singapore	0.0	1.3	1.7	0.2	1.7	0.5	0.1	2.5
Thailand	5.6	78.8	6.3	26.3	19.6	8.6	1.5	56.0
ASEAN/World, %	7.4	80.2	74.6	62.5	60.9	40.3	13.0	49.4
Myanmar:	317.6	580.7	878.8	683.6	304.2	208.0	192.0	1 387.8
ASEAN	96.7	228.6	323.3	153.9	41.2	74.0	67.4	336.5
Malaysia	5.7	10.6	5.1	12.0	15.5	5.9	2.2	35.6
Singapore	55.5	175.0	279.1	79.1	14.9	57.6	55.7	207.3
Thailand	32.4	42.6	32.0	58.0	9.6	3.0	6.0	76.6
ASEAN/World, %	30.4	39.4	36.8	22.5	13.5	35.6	35.1	24.2
Viet Nam:	1 780.4	1 803.0	2 587.3	1 700.0	1 483.9	1 289.0	1 300.3	5 773.2
ASEAN	387.3	328.7	547.2	398.7	289.3	202.4	241.5	1 131.9
Malaysia	83.2	36.8	53.4	19.0	96.5	84.0	27.2	226.7
Singapore	239.2	233.0	347.0	319.0	177.3	91.0	160.6	747.9
Thailand	55.0	37.0	105.4	51.0	10.6	13.2	45.2	120.0
ASEAN/World, %	21.8	18.2	21.1	23.5	19.5	15.7	18.6	19.6
CLMV:				2 700.8	2 071.7	1 679.8	1 664.5	8 116.8
ASEAN				677.8	446.1	361.2	349.2	1 834.3
Malaysia				56.4	153.4	139.0	41.2	390.0
Singapore				442.1	212.0	168.4	238.0	1 060.5
Thailand				162.9	72.1	36.8	56.0	327.8
ASEAN/World, %				25.1	21.5	21.5	21.0	22.6

Source : ASEAN *Statistical Yearbook* 2003.

however, by low productivity and poor transport infrastructure and logistics that raise transaction costs and impede "just-in-time" and "time-sensitive" manufacturing. For landlocked Laos, co-operation with Thailand is essential to minimise its transit costs for exports.

ASEAN membership will enable the CLMV countries to access more technical assistance, including customs harmonisation and procedures, technical, sanitary and phytosanitary standards and capacity-building measures such as training of bureaucrats, particularly trade and investment officials. The CLMV countries also learn from the economic development experience and economic management practices of ASEAN-5, as these countries have successfully gone through the development stages and processes that the CLMV countries undergo currently. In the transition from command to market economies and from economic isolation to economic opening, CLMV policy makers need to draw on the expertise and experience of the more advanced ASEAN countries and not rely primarily on the international and regional development and financial institutions.

Initiatives to Narrow the Development Gap

In recent years ASEAN has made special efforts to promote the development of CLMV, particularly under the ASEAN Integrated System of Preferences (AISP) implemented in January 2002 and the Initiative for ASEAN Integration (IAI) implemented in November 2002. The AISP provides preferential market access for exports from CLMV as they have been unable to benefit fully from the AFTA trade liberalisation of the ASEAN-6 because of their own delayed schedule of trade liberalisation. AISP is implemented on a voluntary and bilateral basis, with CLMV countries requesting that products be accorded preferential access[11].

IAI aims at enhancing productive capacity in CLMV countries through four component programmes and projects, namely infrastructure, information and communications technology (ICT), human resource development (HRD) and capacity building for regional economic integration. In most instances, the measures and projects in the IAI Work Plan, covering July 2002-June 2008, are part of region-wide programmes of ASEAN but specially focused on CLMV. Most of the proposals on infrastructure are segments of the Singapore-Kunming Rail Link, the ASEAN highway network, the ASEAN Power Grid and the Trans-ASEAN Gas Pipeline Network. The ICT component

ISBN 92-64-01442-X © OECD 2005

derives largely from the e-ASEAN programme and recommendations in the ASEAN e-readiness assessment. The HRD component runs through all the other components of IAI. Capacity building for regional economic integration is intended to help the CLMV countries take part in and benefit from all the economic integration schemes, particularly AFTA, AFAS and AIA. The Work Plan's 54 projects and programmes are at various stages of implementation and resource mobilisation.

The CLMV countries played the leading role in putting together the Work Plan and have committed themselves to take the necessary policy measures to make it work. The ASEAN-6 countries have taken the lead by making pledges and commitments to assist, and their contributions take various forms, including training, provision of technical experts and supply of equipment. ASEAN also seeks funding support from its dialogue and development partners. IAI activities are also carried out through various channels including the Mekong Basin Development Co-operation and bilateral technical assistance by ASEAN-6 countries and Dialogue Partners. For example, Japan has given active support, with several Japan-funded technical assistance projects, including capacity-building training for government officials. The role of the Asian Development Bank (ADB) in the Greater Mekong Sub-region (GMS) is discussed separately in a later section.

Global Integration through Trade and Investment

Trade Dependence and Integration

Official trade statistics do not fully reflect the extent of external trade of the CLMV economies. A large amount of unrecorded trade and smuggling occurs across the long and poorly patrolled borders of Cambodia, Laos, Myanmar and Viet Nam[12]. With this caveat, Table 13.6 shows the rapidly growing trade integration of CLMV countries. Viet Nam has the largest volume of trade, followed by Myanmar and Cambodia, while Laos has much less external trade. CLMV trade dependence, as measured by the trade/GDP ratio, is very high and rising. During 1990-2002, this ratio rose from 18 per cent to 101 per cent for Cambodia, from 6 per cent to 98 per cent for Myanmar, from 80 per cent to 98 per cent for Viet Nam and from 30 per cent to 46 per cent for Laos.

Table 13.6. **ASEAN External Trade**
(trade flows in $ million; shares and ratios in per cent)

	1990	1996	1997	1998	1999	2000	2001	2002
Merchandise imports:								
Cambodia	56	1 072	1 092	1 166	1 591	1 939	2 094	2 314
Laos	185	690	648	553	554	535	523	447
Myanmar	668	1 869	2 107	2 451	2 188	2 169	2 450	2 009
Viet Nam	2842	10 030	10 432	10 350	10 568	15 387	14 546	17 760
CLMV-4	3 751	13 661	14 279	14 520	14 901	20 030	19 613	22 530
Brunei	na	2 345	2 015	1 314	1 250	1 047	1 125	1 480
Indonesia	21 837	44 240	46 223	31 942	30 598	40 366	34 669	35 652
Malaysia	29 170	73 132	74 131	54 169	61 452	77 602	69 598	75 365
Philippines	13 042	31 885	36 355	29 524	29 252	33 481	31 986	33 975
Singapore	60 954	123 900	125 092	95 925	104 642	127 457	109 752	117 526
Thailand	33 408	70 815	61 349	40 643	47 529	62 423	60 576	63 353
ASEAN-6	158 411	346 317	345 165	253 517	274 723	342 376	307 706	327 351
ASEAN-10	162 162	359 977	359 444	268 037	289 625	362 407	327 319	349 880
CLMV/ASEAN share	2.31	3.79	3.97	5.42	5.14	5.53	5.99	6.44
Merchandise exports:								
Cambodia	42	644	862	800	1 129	1 401	1 571	1 750
Laos	79	317	313	337	302	330	310	301
Myanmar	409	938	975	1 065	1 140	1 644	2 529	2 404
Viet Nam	2 525	7 255	9 185	9 361	11 540	14 448	15 027	16 706
CLMV-4	3 055	9 154	11 335	11 563	14 111	17 823	19 437	21 161
Brunei	na	2 593	2 662	1 891	2 539	3 904	3 643	3 708
Indonesia	25 675	50 188	56 297	50 370	51 242	65 406	57 364	57 159
Malaysia	29 420	77 169	77 561	71 850	84 097	98 429	87 981	94 343
Philippines	8 180	20 543	25 228	29 496	34 210	37 295	31 243	34 376
Singapore	52 753	129 552	129 757	110 271	116 629	139 747	124 505	137 429
Thailand	23 572	54 667	56 725	52 878	56 801	67 889	63 070	66 092
ASEAN-6	139 600	334 712	348 230	316 756	345 518	412 670	367 806	393 107
ASEAN-10	142 655	343 866	359 565	328 319	359 629	430 493	387 243	414 268
CLMV/ASEAN share	2.14	2.66	3.15	3.52	3.92	4.14	5.02	5.11

ISBN 92-64-01442-X © OECD 2005

Table 13.6. (contd.)

	1990	1996	1997	1998	1999	2000	2001	2002
Imports + exports:								
Cambodia	98	1 716	1 954	1 966	2 720	3 340	3 665	4 064
Laos	264	1 007	961	890	856	865	833	748
Myanmar	1 077	2 807	3 082	3 516	3 328	3 813	4 979	4 413
Viet Nam	5 367	17 285	19 617	19 711	22 108	29 835	29 573	34 466
CLMV-4	6 806	22 815	25 614	26 083	29 012	37 853	39 050	43 691
Brunei	na	4 938	4 677	3 205	3 789	4 951	4 768	5 188
Indonesia	47 512	94 428	102 520	82 312	81 840	105 772	92 033	92 811
Malaysia	58 590	150 301	151 692	126 019	145 549	176 031	157 579	169 708
Philippines	21 222	52 428	61 583	59 020	63 462	70 776	63 229	68 351
Singapore	113 707	253 452	254 849	206 196	221 271	267 204	234 257	254 955
Thailand	56 980	125 482	118 074	93 521	104 330	130 312	123 646	129 445
ASEAN-6	298 011	681 029	693 395	570 273	620 241	755 046	675 512	720 458
ASEAN-10	304 817	703 843	719 009	596 356	649 254	792 900	714 562	764 148
CLMV/ASEAN share	2.23	3.24	3.56	4.37	4.47	4.77	5.46	5.72
Trade/GDP ratio:								
Cambodia	17.8	51.4	58.9	65.1	73.0	93.3	96.6	101.1
Laos	30.5	54.1	59.1	73.3	60.5	49.8	47.8	46.2
Myanmar	5.6	56.6	66.2	50.7	36.0	41.4	77.6	98.0
Viet Nam	79.7	70.1	73.1	72.4	77.1	95.3	89.9	98.2
CLMV	na	65.5	70.3	68.0	67.3	82.6	87.1	96.4
ASEAN-10	na	97.0	102.8	126.2	118.6	136.2	129.1	122.7

Source : 1990 data from ADB Key Indicators 2004; 1996-2002 data from ASEAN Secretariat website.

MFN, Trade Preferences, and Trade in Textiles and Clothing

WTO accession is expected to bring substantial benefits to Cambodia, Laos and Viet Nam. The first is MFN market access. Non-membership has subjected these countries to discriminatory treatment of their exports in various markets. Second, accession means that they can turn to the WTO dispute settlement mechanism to defend their trade interests. With falling tariffs and quantitative restrictions among WTO members, importing countries increasingly resort to the use of technical barriers to trade (particularly SPS) and antidumping measures to protect domestic interests. For example, Vietnamese exporters increasingly face these new trade barriers in their exports of shrimp and gas lighters to the EU, frozen fish fillets to the United States and garlic and waterproof footwear to Canada. Because Viet Nam is not yet a member of WTO and has no access to its dispute-settlement mechanism, it must use separate bilateral legal measures to resolve such disputes, which can be very costly. Third, WTO membership forces the CLMV countries to improve their legal frameworks and the transparency of rules, regulations and practices governing administration, trade and investment and state-owned enterprises. This should serve to lower business transaction costs and improve productivity in these economies.

As low-income developing countries and least-developed countries, the CLMV countries are beneficiaries and potential beneficiaries of the WTO's special and differential treatment (S&D) accorded to developing countries, particularly the least developed. These special provisions include imposition of fewer obligations on them; longer adjustment and transitional time frames for implementing WTO agreements and commitments; and technical assistance to help build their infrastructures for WTO work, handle disputes and implement technical standards. The WTO High Level Meeting on Integrated Initiatives for Least Developed Countries' Trade Development in October 1997 adopted initiatives to improve market access for the least developed countries[13]. In practice, S&D provisions have been considered inadequate by developing countries and there are various implementation problems. Various S&D issues are on the Doha Round agenda.

The Generalised System of Preferences (GSP) has been the main trade preference scheme for developing countries under the GATT/WTO. Developed countries offer unilateral and non-reciprocal preferential treatment (such as zero tariffs or tariff rates lower than MFN rates on imports) to products originating in developing countries. Over the years, some advanced developing countries have graduated from various GSP schemes, and

ISBN 92-64-01442-X © OECD 2005

currently there are 16 national GSP schemes. Among the OECD countries, Japan's GSP scheme grants duty-free entry for most industrial products and reduced-tariff rates for selected industrial, agricultural and fishery products. In April 2000 it added a new list of products enjoying duty-free and quota-free treatment for least-developed beneficiary countries. The EU GSP scheme covers most processed and semi-processed industrial goods and many agricultural products. In January 1998 the EU decided to extend the special treatment it has granted to the Lomé countries to all developing countries. Rules of origin were simplified by allowing derogations and by promoting cumulation. For example, the EU granted derogation from normal rules of origin to Cambodia and Laos (among others) to allow them to use neighbouring countries' raw materials to produce clothing for export to the EU duty-free under the GSP scheme. Further, the EU "Everything but Arms" (EBA) amendment grants unrestricted duty-free access to all products originating in least developed countries, except arms.

The US GSP scheme offers duty-free market access on nearly half of the products listed in the US HTS (Harmonised Tariff Schedule). In 1997, the US added 1 743 tariff lines for least-developed beneficiary countries, but lack of "normal trade relations" (NTR) penalises CLMV exports to the US market[14]. Instead of enjoying the US GSP as a developing country, Viet Nam saw its exports to the United States severely penalised until the lifting of the US trade embargo in 1994 and the implementation of the US-Viet Nam Bilateral Trade Agreement (BTA) in December 2001. Tariffs on Vietnamese goods fell from an average of 40 per cent to only 3 per cent, which boosted Vietnamese exports of textiles, shoes and seafood. Yet Vietnamese exports to the United States continue to face a huge disadvantage, because the United States still regards Viet Nam as a non-market economy. Under the BTA Viet Nam has to open its energy, financial services and telecommunications markets to US companies, and import-competing sectors face intensified competition.

Growth prospects for developing-country exports of textiles and clothing, a major export of developing countries, were constrained for two decades (1974-94) by the Multi-Fibre Arrangement (MFA). Under this, importing developed countries imposed country-specific export quotas on them through bilateral agreements. In 1995, the WTO Agreement on Textiles and Clothing (ATC) replaced the MFA. It provided for a ten-year transition period to phase out all bilateral quotas by 1 January 2005, which in fact occurred. The ATC also contained a safeguard mechanism permitting countries to establish transition-period quotas on articles not yet integrated into the GATT, if necessary to protect their domestic markets from import surges. It also required members to reduce trade barriers to textiles and clothing in their home markets and allowed countries to take action against quota circumvention. All WTO countries were subject to ATC disciplines, and only member countries were eligible for ATC benefits, with serious implications for non-member developing and least-developed countries, including Laos and Viet Nam.

Although the lifting of MFA quotas on 1 January 2005 finally enabled developing countries to benefit from participation in international trade in textiles and clothing, three concerns remain in the post-ATC world. First, developed countries could increasingly apply contingent protective measures on imports of textiles and clothing, which would nullify the liberalising effects of the quota removal. Second, the dismantling of quotas would level the playing field among developing countries and "penalise" preferred suppliers and high-cost suppliers protected by the former quota allocations. Third, many developing countries (including CLMV) have concerns over the rapid growth of exports from China. In 2001, China had already become the world's leading ATC supplier with exports of $53 billion[15]. Although China became eligible for quota-free market access under the ATC following its WTO accession in December 2001, exports to the United States will continue to be quota-restricted until December 2008 as part of China's WTO accession package. This has significance for other developing-country exporters of textiles and clothing to the United States; China overtook Mexico as the leading supplier to the US market in 2002. India, too, could follow the Chinese example and become a major textile and clothing exporter.

US imports of textiles and clothing from Viet Nam and Cambodia have grown rapidly in recent years following normalisation of trade relations. US clothing imports from Viet Nam jumped from $49 million in 2001 to $952 million in 2002, following implementation of the BTA, enabling Viet Nam's textile and clothing exports to the US market to enjoy much lower rates of duty than previously[16]. US imports from Cambodia rose from less than $1 million in 1995 (the year before the country received NTR status) to $1.1 billion in 2002. A US-Cambodia bilateral agreement that entered into force in January 1999 provides for quotas on imports of clothing from Cambodia and commits Cambodia to improve labour conditions in its textiles and clothing sector[17].

ISBN 92-64-01442-X © OECD 2005

CLMV Export Composition and Major Markets

Export growth in recent years has been very rapid for Cambodia, Myanmar and Viet Nam, but Laos has experienced slow and negative export growth, in part because of its heavy dependence on the Thai economy, which was adversely affected by the Asian financial crisis. Table 13.7 on the following page shows the major exports of CLMV countries in 2002. These data are culled by ITC from the import statistics of trade partners and could be incomplete in coverage. They show the transformation of Cambodia and Laos from exporters of primary commodities to exporters of clothing (HS61, HS62). Clothing accounted for 85.5 per cent of total Cambodian exports and 77.5 per cent of total Laotian exports, 39.5 per cent of Myanmar's and 15.1 per cent of Viet Nam's. As noted earlier, rapid growth of the clothing industry is due to preferential access to the US and European markets. With improved market access following the Bilateral Trade Agreement, Viet Nam's clothing shipments to the United States surged by 120 per cent in 2002 to over $2 billion, triggering the imposition of US quotas in 2003. There is concern that the exclusion of Laos and Viet Nam (as non-WTO members) from the quota-free, post-ATC world will penalise textiles and clothing exports from these countries as well as their ability to attract FDI[18].

Export performance and prospects for primary products are mixed. Up to the early 1990s, the CLMV countries depended heavily on such exports. Products of tropical agriculture are not seriously affected by the agricultural subsidies imposed by OECD countries, except for rice and sugar. Marine products have become key exports of Cambodia, Myanmar and Viet Nam. Improved market access being negotiated under the Doha Round should improve agricultural export prospects for the sub-region. Timber is a major export of Cambodia, Laos and Myanmar but such exports are unsustainable from the environmental perspective. Oil production and exports have grown rapidly for Viet Nam, and oil is also a key product of Myanmar. Hydroelectric power is a leading Laotian export with good potential for transmission to neighbouring countries, but sustained and increased exports depend crucially on investment in further hydroelectric projects. Tourism is growing rapidly, and the tourism potential in the sub-region will be better realised with improved transportation networks, particularly with direct flights to the tourist attraction of Angkor Wat in Siem Reap, and with greater and more effective regional co-operation in transportation development and tourism promotion. Much remains to be done in travel facilitation such as transportation, visa requirements and hotel facilities.

ISBN 92-64-01442-X

Table 13.7. **CLMV Countries: Major Exports in 2002**

(values in $ thousands; shares and growth rates in per cent)

HS	Product	Exports to World				Exports to OECD	
		Exports	Share in Country's Exports	Average Annual Growth 1998-2002	World Export Ranking	Exports	Share in Country's Exports
Cambodia:							
61	Articles of apparel, accessories, knit or crochet	820 702	43.4	24	27	776 077	94.6
62	Articles of apparel, accessories, not knit or crochet	796 300	42.1	32	31	764 432	96.0
64	Footwear, gaiters and the like, parts thereof	142 996	7.6	59	35	141 813	99.2
40	Rubber and articles thereof	23 226	1.2	-15	71	4 541	19.6
44	Wood and articles of wood, wood charcoal	19 835	1.0	-23	86	3 425	17.3
65	Headgear and parts thereof	17 552	0.9	136	27	17 538	99.9
63	Other made textile articles, sets, worn clothing etc.	12 936	0.7	70	73	12 516	96.8
71	Pearls, precious stones, metals, coins etc.	11 627	0.6	142	102	0	0.0
03	Fish, crustaceans, molluscs, aquatic invertebrates	7 792	0.4	-14	114	1 526	19.6
10	Cereals	4 550	0.2		76	1 474	32.4
	Total exports, top ten products above	1 857 516	98.3			1 723 342	92.8
	Total exports, all products	1 890 167	100.0		99	1 745 358	92.3
Laos:							
62	Articles of apparel, accessories, not knit or crochet	73 807	45.1	5	82	73 438	99.5
61	Articles of apparel, accessories, knit or crochet	52 946	32.4	1	78	52 408	99.0
44	Wood and articles of wood, wood charcoal	12 801	7.8	-19	94	6 097	47.6
09	Coffee, tea, mate & spices	11 920	7.3	-16	73	11 343	95.2
64	Footwear, gaiters and the like, parts thereof	4 341	2.7	38	84	4 341	100.0
12	Oilseed, oleagic fruits, grain, seed, fruit etc	1 581	1.0	5	114	141	8.9
71	Pearls, precious stones, metals, coins etc	1 502	0.9		135	1 454	96.8
40	Rubber and articles thereof	1 496	0.9		94	51	3.4
13	Lac, gums, resins, vegetable saps, extracts n.e.s.	650	0.4	23	72	549	84.5
94	Furniture, lighting, signs, prefab buildings	374	0.2	-16	136	165	44.1
	Total exports, top ten products above	161 418	98.7			149 987	92.9
	Total exports, all products	163 509	100.0		166	151 483	92.6

ISBN 92-64-01442-X © OECD 2005

Table 13.7 (contd.)

HS	Product	Exports to World			World Export Ranking	Exports to OECD	
		Exports	Share in Country's Exports	Average Annual Growth 1998-2002		Exports	Share in Country's Exports
Myanmar:							
61	Articles of apparel, accessories, knit or crochet	399 923	23.1	33	41	323 860	81.0
44	Wood and articles of wood, wood charcoal	309 000	17.9	11	39	75 766	24.5
07	Edible vegetables and certain roots, tubers	288 721	16.7	33	14	13 701	4.7
62	Articles of apparel, accessories, not knit or crochet	283 140	16.4	27	50	272 054	96.1
03	Fish, crustaceans, molluscs, aquatic invertebrates	158 802	9.2	3	46	114 879	72.3
10	Cereals	46 578	2.7	40	42	5 625	12.1
27	Mineral fuels, oils, distillation products etc.	28 901	1.7		118	28 883	99.9
71	Pearls, precious stones, metals, coins etc.	23 015	1.3	-18	91	10 465	45.5
64	Footwear, gaiters and the like, parts thereof	21 926	1.3	31	64	3 284	15.0
40	Rubber and articles thereof	15 237	0.9	-6	76	281	1.8
	Total exports, top ten products above	1 575 243	91.1			848 798	53.9
	Total exports, all products	1 729 308	100.0		107	986 230	57.0
Viet Nam:							
27	Mineral fuels, oils, distillation products etc.	3 243 958	20.8	26	39	1 554 835	47.9
64	Footwear, gaiters and the like, parts thereof	2 843 958	18.3	14	4	2 729 984	96.0
62	Articles of apparel, accessories, not knit or crochet	1 606 495	10.3	11	19	1 151 580	71.7
03	Fish, crustaceans, molluscs, aquatic invertebrates	1 294 846	8.3	20	11	1 186 929	91.7
85	Electrical, electronic equipment	783 824	5.0	29	50	388 020	49.5
61	Articles of apparel, accessories, knit or crochet	749 464	4.8	23	32	466 740	62.3
94	Furniture, lighting, signs, prefabricated buildings	597 676	3.8	28	26	156 550	26.2
09	Coffee, tea, mate & spices	520 357	3.3	-12	8	410 329	78.9
42	Articles of leather, gut, harness, travel goods	360 291	2.3	8	13	300 413	83.4
16	Meat, fish and seafood preparations n.e.s.	305 988	2.0	46	15	298 238	97.5
	Total exports, top ten products above	12 306 857	79.1			8 643 618	70.2
	Total exports, all products	15 559 984	100.0		53	12 027 080	77.3

Source: Extracted from ITC Trade Map Data based on COMTRADE statistics. The export data for CLMV countries are based on imports of partner countries.

The CLMV countries have yet to become plugged into the East Asian production networks for electronic products and components that have encompassed Japan, the Asian NIEs and the ASEAN-5. The larger economies of Myanmar and Viet Nam have begun to see FDI in this sector. Good prospects exist for relocating investment from the more advanced countries in the East Asian region, because Myanmar and Viet Nam have abundant low-wage labour, and investors seek to diversify dependence on China as a production centre. The electronics industry is extremely time-sensitive, however, with short product cycles and a need for reliable and quick supply responses to demands for products, parts and components. Myanmar and Viet Nam will need to improve their political climates and labour market flexibility to reduce risks of supply disruptions and to improve their transport and logistics infrastructures in order to become production and export nodes.

Before the 1990s, the CLMV sub-region traded largely with the CMEA (Council for Mutual Economic Assistance) group of the COMECON socialist countries. Table 13.8 shows the very sizeable changes in the direction of CLMV trade that occurred between 1990 and 2002 towards the US, EU and Japanese markets. The US share of Cambodia's exports leaped from zero to 60 per cent, while the EU's jumped from 5 to 24 per cent. The two markets combined accounted for 84 per cent of Cambodia's exports in 2002, with the exports dominated by clothing and footwear. For Viet Nam, the share of exports to the US surged from zero to 15 per cent and the EU's share climbed from 7 to 24 per cent. The US lifted its trade embargo on Viet Nam in February 1994. US imports from Viet Nam rose to $210 million in 1995 and reached $1.1 billion by 2001. After the BTA, they surged to $2.6 billion in 2002. For Laos, the US share remained low, but the EU's leaped from 9 to 29 per cent. Big gains also occurred in Myanmar's export shares to the United States and the EU. Japan remains a minor market for CLMV exports, and shares of exports to Japan declined, reflecting the diversion to the US and EU markets as trade-policy coherence improved. The experience of CLMV countries in the US and EU markets contrasts sharply with that of the ASEAN-5, where US and EU export shares have shrunk considerably.

 ISBN 92-64-01442-X

Table 13.8. **ASEAN: Direction of Trade, 1990 and 2002**
(per cent of total exports)

	Japan	United States	EU	Sum: Japan, USA and EU	Others
Cambodia					
1990	7.6	0.0	5.0	12.6	87.4
2002	3.9	59.9	23.9	87.7	12.3
Laos					
1990	7.1	0.1	9.4	16.6	83.4
2002	1.5	0.7	28.5	30.7	69.3
Myanmar					
1990	6.9	2.3	6.9	16.1	83.9
2002	3.8	13.2	13.8	30.8	69.2
Viet Nam					
1990	13.5	0.0	6.8	20.3	79.7
2002	14.6	14.9	24.2	53.7	46.3
Indonesia					
1990	42.5	13.1	12.0	67.6	32.4
2002	21.1	13.2	13.9	48.2	51.8
Malaysia					
1990	15.3	16.9	15.4	47.6	52.4
2002	11.3	20.2	12.4	43.9	56.1
Philippines					
1990	19.8	37.9	18.5	76.2	23.8
2002	15.0	24.7	18.1	57.8	42.2
Singapore					
1990	8.8	21.3	15.0	45.1	54.9
2002	7.1	15.3	12.5	34.9	65.1
Thailand					
1990	17.2	22.7	22.7	62.6	37.4
2002	14.5	19.6	14.8	48.9	51.1
ASEAN					
1990	18.3	19.6	15.8	53.7	46.3
2001	12.3	17.9	14.1	44.3	55.7

Source : *Asian Development Outlook 2004.*

There is much concern over the implications of China's rise and WTO accession for CLMV exports. Both the CLMV and China have comparative and competitive advantages in labour-intensive manufactures such as textiles and clothing, footwear and the labour-intensive segments of the electronics industry. While CLMV wage levels are competitive *vis-à-vis* China, these smaller economies cannot enjoy economies of scale unless ASEAN economic integration can quickly result in a unified ASEAN market. Partly in recognition of this concern, China has offered an economic co-operation and free trade agreement with ASEAN to provide preferential access to its large and dynamic market. The ASEAN-China FTA will be realised within ten years, with tariffs reduced or eliminated by 2010 for China and ASEAN-6 and by 2015 for the CLMV countries. Further, in recognition of ASEAN's interest in agricultural exports, China also offered an "early harvest" of liberalised two-way trade in a range of agricultural products with the phasing out of tariffs in 2003-06[19].

FDI Dependence and Integration

Table 13.9 shows inward FDI flows and stocks for all ASEAN countries since 1985. The ASEAN-6 group has attracted FDI to promote economic development, industrialisation and employment since the 1960s but more particularly since the mid-1980s. FDI inflows peaked at $30.4 billion in 1997 and since have fallen far below that level, to $13 billion in 2002 before some rebound in 2003. The downtrend reflects the fall-out from the Asian financial crisis, the global and regional economic slowdown, FDI competition from elsewhere (Latin America, Central and Eastern Europe and China), sizeable repayments of intra-company loans and the deteriorating economic and political environment in some ASEAN countries.

The CLMV sub-region has received considerably less FDI than the ASEAN-6. The sub-region opened to FDI only in the late 1980s and inflows reached $3.7 billion by 1997, accounting for 10.9 per cent of ASEAN's total FDI inflows. Apart from an investment climate less favourable than in the ASEAN-6, FDI inflows into Viet Nam and Myanmar were also dampened by political restrictions imposed by the United States and the EU. The sharp downtrend in FDI inflows reflected the after-effects of the Asian financial crisis. FDI dependence as measured by the FDI flow/gross investment ratio shows high dependence in Cambodia and Viet Nam and low dependence in Laos (no data are available for Myanmar). FDI dependence as measured by the FDI stock/GDP ratio, however, shows a rising trend, with the highest ratio in Viet Nam, followed by Cambodia and Laos. These stock ratios are higher than in some of the ASEAN-6 countries despite the more recent history of FDI in the sub-region.

 ISBN 92-64-01442-X © OECD 2005

Table 13.9. **ASEAN Countries: FDI Flows, Stocks and Ratios, 1985-2003**

(flows in $ million; ratios in per cent)

	1985-90 Average	1991-96 Average	1997	1998	1999	2000	2001	2002	2003
FDI inflows									
Cambodia	n.a.	120	168	243	230	149	149	145	87
Laos	2	53	86	45	52	34	24	25	19
Myanmar	28	256	879	684	304	208	192	191	128
Viet Nam	30	1 217	2 587	1 700	1 484	1 289	1 300	1 200	1 450
CLMV	60	1 646	3 720	2 672	2 070	1 680	1 665	1 561	1 684
Brunei	n.a.	210	702	573	748	549	526	1 035	2 009
Indonesia	551	2 985	4 678	-241	-1 866	-4 550	-2 977	145	-597
Malaysia	1 054	5 436	6 323	2 714	3 895	3 788	554	3 203	2 474
Philippines	413	1 226	1 261	2 212	1 725	1 345	982	1 792	319
Singapore	2 952	6 856	13 533	7 690	16 067	17 217	15 038	5 730	11 409
Thailand	1 017	1 964	3 882	7 491	6 091	3 350	3 813	1 068	1 802
ASEAN-6	5 987	18 677	30 379	20 439	26 660	21 699	17 936	12 973	17 416
ASEAN-10	6 047	20 323	34 099	23 111	28 730	23 379	19 601	14 534	19 100
CLMV/ASEAN-10 (%)	0.99	8.10	10.91	11.56	7.21	7.19	8.49	10.74	8.82
FDI inflows/GFCF									
Cambodia	n.a.	22.2	28.6	65.7	48.3	29.1	21.0	16.0	12.3
Laos	n.a.	21.4	18.2	14.4	15.7	9.1	6.2	6.9	5.2
Myanmar	n.a.	2.8	3.7	2.1	0.8	0.7	0.6	n.a.	n.a.
Viet Nam	n.a.	34.9	37.3	23.1	20.1	15.0	13.6	11.4	15.2
Brunei	n.a.	n.a.	n.a.	n.a.	n.a.	n.a.	n.a.	n.a.	n.a.
Indonesia	7.6	5.8	7.7	-1.0	-6.6	-13.9	-9.7	0.4	-1.8
Malaysia	43.7	19.3	14.7	14.0	22.5	16.4	2.5	14.5	10.8
Philippines	13.6	8.5	6.3	16.0	11.9	8.4	6.9	11.9	2.2
Singapore	59.3	28.8	37.0	25.0	57.8	62.8	60.1	25.6	45.7
Thailand	10.2	3.7	7.6	29.9	23.8	12.4	14.4	3.7	5.2

Table 13.9 (contd.)

	1985-90 Average	1991-96 Average	1997	1998	1999	2000	2001	2002	2003
		1980	1985	1990	1995	2000	2002	2003	
FDI stock									
Cambodia	n.a.	38	38	38	356	1 549	1 843	1 930	n.a.
Laos	n.a.	2	1	13	205	550	599	618	n.a.
Myanmar	n.a.	n.a.	n.a.	n.a.	649	3 865	4 248	4 376	n.a.
Viet Nam	n.a.	9	64	260	5 760	14 624	17 124	18 574	n.a.
CLMV	n.a.	49	103	311	6 970	20 588	23 814	25 498	n.a.
Brunei	n.a.	19	28	23	631	3 856	5 418	7 427	n.a.
Indonesia	n.a.	10 274	24 971	38 883	50 601	60 638	57 806	57 209	n.a.
Malaysia	n.a.	5 169	7 388	10 318	28 731	52 747	56 505	58 979	n.a.
Philippines	n.a.	1 281	2 601	3 268	6 086	12 810	11 148	11 467	n.a.
Singapore	n.a.	6 203	13 016	30 468	65 644	112 571	135 890	147 299	n.a.
Thailand	n.a.	981	1 999	8 209	17 452	30 106	35 108	36 910	n.a.
ASEAN-6	n.a.	23 927	50 003	91 169	169 145	272 728	301 875	319 291	n.a.
ASEAN-10	n.a.	23 976	50 106	91 480	176 115	293 316	325 689	344 789	n.a.
CLMV/ASEAN-10 (%)	n.a.	0.20	0.21	0.34	3.96	7.02	7.31	7.40	n.a.
FDI stock/GDP	n.a.								n.a.
Cambodia	n.a.	2.4	2.0	3.4	10.8	43.3	46.2	46.4	n.a.
Laos	n.a.	0.3		1.5	11.4	31.6	32.9	30.1	n.a.
Myanmar	n.a.	n.a.	n.a.	n.a.	n.a.	n.a.	n.a.	n.a.	n.a.
Viet Nam	n.a.	0.2	1.1	4.0	27.8	48.2	50.2	50.6	n.a.
Brunei	n.a.	0.4	0.8	0.7	12.1	89.4	126.6	156.0	n.a.
Indonesia	n.a.	13.2	28.2	34.0	25.0	40.4	33.3	27.5	n.a.
Malaysia	n.a.	20.7	23.3	23.4	32.3	58.5	59.5	57.2	n.a.
Philippines	n.a.	3.9	8.5	7.4	8.1	17.1	14.5	14.5	n.a.
Singapore	n.a.	52.9	73.6	83.1	78.2	121.5	153.9	161.3	n.a.
Thailand	n.a.	3.0	5.1	9.7	10.5	24.5	27.7	25.8	n.a.

Note: GFCF = Gross Fixed Capital Formation.
Source :UNCTAD, *World Investment Report*, 1997 and 2004.

ISBN 92-64-01442-X © OECD 2005

Table 13.10 (on the following page) shows the sectoral composition of FDI inflows into Laos, Myanmar and Viet Nam for 1999-2001 (no sectoral data are available for Cambodia). The sub-region has attracted FDI into the natural-resource sector, particularly oil and gas in Viet Nam and forestry and precious gems in Cambodia, Laos and Myanmar, as well as into aquaculture. No sizeable FDI in agriculture has occurred, largely because of host-government restrictions on foreign ownership of agricultural land. While such restrictions have protected rural farm households, they also have discouraged the introduction of agricultural technology and exploitation of scale economies. Laos attracted sizeable investments in the energy sector to harness the country's very substantial hydropower potential. Reflecting the sub-region's tourism attractions and potential, considerable FDI has gone into tourist infrastructure and services. In manufacturing, CLMV countries want FDI in export manufacturing and links with global and regional production networks and supply chains. While these countries have abundant low-wage labour, however, (especially Myanmar and Viet Nam), they remain handicapped by shortages of skills, lack of local suppliers of parts and components and transportation and logistics inefficiencies.

During 1998-2001, the bulk of FDI flows to CLMV (63 per cent) came from East Asia, including 26.8 per cent from the NIE-3 (Hong Kong, China; Korea and Chinese Taipei), 22.6 per cent from ASEAN and 13.6 per cent from Japan. The NIEs have invested heavily in the clothing and footwear industries. Cambodia, Laos and Viet Nam depend much more on East Asian investors than does Myanmar. The OECD countries (including Japan but excluding Korea) accounted for 45 per cent of FDI inflows into the sub-region, ranging from 19.3 per cent in Cambodia to 69.5 per cent in Myanmar (including substantial European investments in the oil sector). The main OECD investors in CLMV are the EU-15 ($1.58 billion in 1998-2001), followed by Japan ($1.1 billion) and the United States ($460.4 million). Viet Nam is the main recipient of OECD-country investment, which concentrates in agriculture, mining, manufacturing and services.

Viet Nam also accounts for most of the FDI flows to the sub-region, with investment flowing into natural resources and production for both the domestic and export markets. It has an abundance of resources including oil and gas, a sizeable domestic market of 80 million people with purchasing power growing at around 7 per cent annually and a large labour supply characterised by low wages, high levels of education and a strong work ethic. Earlier investments were in resource extraction and production serving the domestic market, but over time more FDI went into export production, particularly when bilateral restrictions on market access for Viet Nam's exports

Table 13.10. **CLMV Countries (Excluding Cambodia): FDI Inflows by Sector and Country Source, 1999-2001**

	Total	Japan	US	EU-15	J+US+EU	NIE-3	China	ASEAN	ROW	Total	J+US+EU	ASEAN
	Inflows in $ millions									Distribution (%)		
Laos:												
Agriculture, fisheries, forestry	12.48		0.0		0.0	0.0	0.0	1.0	11.5	11.4	0.0	32.3
Mining, quarrying	23.38				0.0	0.1		0.2	23.1	21.3	0.0	6.5
Manufacturing	31.29	0.4		1.1	1.5	0.4	11.3	0.7	17.4	28.6	53.6	22.6
Construction	4.16			0.4	0.4	0.1		0.1	3.6	3.8	14.3	3.2
Trade, commerce	2.23			0.0	0.0	0.2		0.2	1.8	2.0	0.0	6.5
Financial services	0			0.1	0.1	0.0		0.0	-0.1	0.0	3.6	0.0
Real estate	0	0.2			0.2	0.0		0.0	-0.5	0.0	7.1	0.0
Services	31.77		0.0	0.5	0.5	3.4			27.3	29.0	17.9	12.9
Others	4.2				0.0	0.0			3.6	3.8	0.0	19.4
Total	109.51	0.6	0.1	2.1	2.8	4.2	11.8		87.6	100.0	100.0	100.0
Myanmar:												
Agriculture, fisheries, forestry	14.23				0.0	0.0		0.5	13.7	2.0	0.0	0.3
Mining, quarrying	438.56		44.7	78.6	123.3	0.0	0.0	10.7	304.6	62.3	26.4	5.9
Manufacturing	104.68	32.5		15.0	47.5	25.7	0.5	27.6	3.4	14.9	10.2	15.1
Construction	0.04				0.0	0.0		0.0	0.0	0.0	0.0	0.0
Trade, commerce	35.59				0.0	0.0			35.6	5.1	0.0	0.0
Financial services	0				0.0	0.0			0.0	0.0	0.0	0.0
Real estate	60.85				0.0	4.1		60.9	-4.2	8.6	0.0	33.3
Services	39.35	7.6		3.6	11.2	1.2		62.5	-35.6	5.6	2.4	34.2
Others	10.55	2.6	37.2	245.0	284.8	12.5		20.4	-307.2	1.5	61.0	11.2
Total	704.21	42.8	81.9	342.1	466.8	43.5	0.5	182.7	10.7	100.0	100.0	100.0

ISBN 92-64-01442-X © OECD 2005

Table 13.10. (contd.)

	Total	Japan	US	EU-15	J+US+EU	NIE-3	China	ASEAN	ROW	Total	J+US+EU	ASEAN
	Inflows in $ millions									Distribution (%)		
Viet Nam												
Agriculture, fisheries, forestry	326.08	10.5	23.2	111.2	144.9	109.9	8.5	62.7	0.1	8.0	9.7	8.6
Mining, quarrying	874.37	85.1	78.5	207.5	371.1	22.1	0.0	120.4	360.8	21.5	24.8	16.4
Manufacturing	1 549.79	332.9	33.6	115.4	481.9	597.9	33.3	249.7	187.0	38.0	32.2	34.1
Construction	313.03	106.2	15.2	21.1	142.5	37.1	0.9	98.5	34.0	7.7	9.5	13.4
Trade, commerce	0.00	0.0	0.0	0.0	0.0	0.0	0.0	0.0	0.0	0.0	0.0	0.0
Financial services	45.81	2.2	1.5	31.4	35.1	10.8	0.0	0.0	-0.1	1.1	2.3	0.0
Real estate	0.00	0.0	0.0	0.0	0.0	0.0	0.0	0.0	0.0	0.0	0.0	0.0
Services	964.74	90.3	30.8	198.8	319.9	377.6	9.4	201.9	55.9	23.7	21.4	27.5
Others	0.00	0.0	0.0	0.0	0.0	0.0	0.0	0.0	0.0	0.0	0.0	0.0
Total	4 073.82	627.1	182.8	685.4	1 495.3	1155.3	52.1	733.1	638.0	100.0	100.0	100.0

Source : ASEAN (2002).

were progressively lifted and as the country nears WTO accession. By the end of the 1990s, foreign-invested-enterprises (FIEs), although they employed less than 1 per cent of the workforce, accounted for 35 per cent of industrial output, almost 13 per cent of GDP, 25 per cent of tax revenue and 27 per cent of non-oil exports (Freeman, 2002). That the top investors were East Asian in recent years explains why FDI inflows fell in the post-crisis years. ASEAN investments in Viet Nam come mainly from Singapore, Malaysia and Thailand. During 1995-2000, Singapore invested $1.4 billion, followed by Malaysia with $373 million and Thailand with $372 million.

Two factors impact on CLMV FDI prospects. First, facing competition for FDI from China, the CLMV countries will have to continue to improve their investment environments, removing policy barriers to FDI and improving project-approval procedures and transparency, property rights, physical infrastructure and skilled human resources. They must also hasten ASEAN economic integration towards a unified market and production network. Second, in the post-ATC world the CLMV countries may lose their competitiveness in attracting FDI into the textiles and clothing sector. Laos and Viet Nam need to hasten their WTO accession.

ODA and the Greater Mekong Sub-Region

Aid Dependence

For low-income countries, aid is critical to facilitate economic and social development and poverty alleviation, as it provides financial and technical resources, including development, managerial and skills training and introduces international best practices. Chapter 6 in this volume examines the aid issue in the broader context of OECD policy coherence.

Bilateral official development assistance (ODA) to the CLMV countries has responded to their low per capita incomes as well as political and economic relations. ODA is crucial to the economies of Cambodia and Laos, accounting in 2001-02 for over 12 per cent of national income, the bulk of gross capital formation and a large percentage of imports. Table 13.11 shows the net ODA receipts of CLMV countries for recent years. Members of the Development Assistance Committee (DAC) are the major sources, with Japan the largest bilateral donor. The Asian Development Bank is the major source of multilateral aid. Aid dependence as measured by net ODA received shows that Viet Nam has received the most, $1 billion per year, while Myanmar has received only something over $100 million a year. Aid dependence in per capita terms shows that Cambodia and Laos have received the most and Myanmar the least.

ISBN 92-64-01442-X © OECD 2005

Table 13.11. **CLMV Countries - Net ODA Receipts**

	Time Period	Cambodia	Laos	Myanmar	Vietnam
Net ODA receipts, $ million	1995	556	309	151	837
	1996	422	332	43	939
	2000	398	282	107	1 682
	2001	420	245	127	1 453
	2002	487	278	121	1 277
Net ODA from DAC, $ million	2001	265	150	89	822
Japan		120	76	70	460
US		22	5	3	9
France		21	11	1	62
Net ODA from multilaterals, $ million	2001	121	82	33	514
IFIs		95	74	0	492
United Nations		26	8	32	23
Bilateral share of gross ODA, %	2000	62	66	65	74
	2001	62	57	70	59
	2002	60	60	74	58
ODA per capita, $	1995	52	66	3	11
	1996	38	69	1	13
	2000	33	53	2	22
	2001	33	45	3	18
ODA/GNI, %	1995	19.1	17.6	na	4.2
	1996	13.6	17.8	na	3.9
	2000	12.6	16.8	na	5.5
	2001	12.8	14.7	na	4.4
	2002	13.8	17.3	na	3.6
ODA/GCF, %	1995	86.8	67.3	na	15.3
	1996	51.8	61.2	na	13.6
	2000	83.5	80.6	na	19.8
	2001	67.1	62.5	na	14.2
ODA/Imports, %	1995	38.6	40.5	7.0	8.4
	1996	30.5	42.5	1.8	7.3
	2000	21.5	41.5	3.7	9.4
	2001	20.1	40.6	4.1	7.7
ODA/Central government expenditure, %	1995	n.a.	n.a.	1.3	16.9
	1996	n.a.	n.a.	0.3	16.5
	2000	n.a.	n.a.	0.3	26.1
	2001	n.a.	n.a.	n.a.	18.0

Notes: GNI = Gross National Income. GCF = Gross Capital Formation.

Sources: *World Development Indicators, 2002 and 2003*; OECD, *The DAC Journal Development Cooperation* 2003 Report, Vol.5, No.2 (2004).

ISBN 92-64-01442-X © OECD 2005

Greater Mekong Sub-Region Programme

The Greater Mekong Sub-Region (GMS) Programme exemplifies development and technical assistance to the CLMV countries. GMS comprises all the areas bordering both the upper and lower reaches of the Mekong River, namely the CLMV countries, Thailand and Yunnan province in China[20]. The end of the Viet Nam War, withdrawal of Vietnamese troops from Cambodia and resolution of the Viet Nam-China conflict led to improved economic relations among GMS countries and the launching of the GMS Programme in 1992 with ADB assistance. It seeks to realise and enhance development opportunities, encourage trade and investment among GMS countries, resolve and mitigate cross-border problems, and meet common resource and policy needs.

The Programme covers co-operation in almost 100 projects in eight sectors — transportation, telecommunications, energy, environment and natural resource management, tourism, human resource development, investment and trade. It focused initially on infrastructure, with projects in transport and to a lesser extent energy and telecommunications. Transportation is necessary to facilitate flows of goods, investment, people (including labour and tourism) and ideas and knowledge. In energy, ADB completed the 210mw *Theun Hinboun* Hydropower Project, the first public-private joint venture in Laos, which has enabled Laos to increase revenues by selling hydropower to neighbouring countries, especially through a long-term agreement with Thailand. ADB also started a regional co-operation initiative in telecommunications in partnership with the private sector. Technical assistance projects are helping to create a reliable, high quality, low cost telecommunications service linking the GMS countries. The ASEAN Information Infrastructure (AII) which forges agreements among member countries on design, standardisation, interconnection and interoperability of information have yet to focus on the CLMV countries, and each country has been left to decide for itself on the priority and development of this sector.

ADB also has financed or co-financed several technical agreements in tourism, including promotion of GMS as a tourist destination; training the trainers in basic skills of tourism; training resource managers in conservation and tourism; a Mekong/Lancan River tourism planning study; village-based tourism projects; and a North-South tourism corridor project. GMS countries have also established the Agency for Co-ordinating Mekong Tourism Activities.

ISBN 92-64-01442-X © OECD 2005

An evaluation of the first decade of the GMS Programme (ADB, 2003) provided several lessons. First, infrastructure projects have long gestation periods and require long-term commitment, with time-consuming pre-feasibility and feasibility studies. The complexity of sub-regional projects and limited institutional capacity of GMS countries to co-ordinate, negotiate and implement such projects have slowed progress. Second, project initiatives should reflect the views of all stakeholders from project formulation to implementation and ensure equitable sharing of costs and benefits. Third, information, monitoring and co-ordination are critical for implementation and effective allocation of scarce resources. Fourth, the private sector should become more actively involved in the GMS programme. Finally, because the CLMV countries joined ASEAN during 1995-99, close co-ordination between the GMS Programme and ASEAN programmes is essential to avoid overlapping mandates and waste of scarce resources. With these lessons learned from the first decade of the GMS Programme and with changing priorities, the second decade (begun in 2002) has adopted a more multi-sectoral and holistic approach with five strategic thrusts:

— *Strengthen infrastructure linkages:* integration of the GMS Programme with national development plans; building physical infrastructure linkages; co-operation in the agriculture sector, recognising the role of infrastructure in reducing the cost of selling agricultural products in sub-regional markets.

— *Facilitate cross-border trade and investment*: cross-border trade facilitation initially focusing on simplifying customs procedures at selected border crossings and extending to transparency of customs procedures and adherence to the Kyoto Convention; harmonising banking regulations to remove the major impediment of a lack of a reliable payments system among commercial banks in GMS; establishment of economic corridors and other co-operation initiatives to exploit economies of scale in production and distribution and improve export performance; making technical, marketing, credit and management support more accessible; promoting joint tourism initiatives in the sub-region as a single tourist destination through simplifying visa issuance processes, improvement of tourist infrastructure and other activities in partnership with the private sector.

— *Enhance private-sector participation and improve competitiveness:* lowering production and distribution costs through efficient utilities and infrastructure services; improving skill competencies of the labour forces; training entrepreneurs for small and medium enterprise management, production and marketing; extending credit lines for provision of working capital; harmonising policy environments for private enterprise.

— *Develop human resources and skill competencies:* human-resource development (HRD) issues where sub-regional co-operation is logical include capacity building to address cross-border HRD and labour market issues; addressing health and social problems associated with mobile populations; and networking higher education and training institutions. Soft development, such as knowledge transfer and education are more difficult to implement because of different levels of human-capital absorption within GMS, but these are important measures for CLMV countries as they learn to cope with the development challenges existing within their own territories. Many of these programmes require FDI or ODA from multilateral agencies such as ADB.

— *Protect the environment and promote sustainable use of shared natural resources:* sub-regional monitoring of the cumulative environmental impacts of development; sound practices for sustainable use of shared resources.

Since the inception of the GMS Programme, the ADB has been a core partner, playing an active role in administering technical assistance and in soliciting potential investors to invest in GMS. The ADB and its partners have financed ten major infrastructure projects, representing investments of about $2 billion, with ADB providing $772 million in loans. ADB has also provided $56 million in technical assistance to support initiatives for human-resource development, tourism, environment, trade and investment. Such assistance has addressed social issues such as HIV/AIDS and drug trafficking. For the second decade, ADB has provided loan finance amounting to $887 million and mobilised about $303 million in co-financing for 15 priority GMS projects. ADB, co-financiers and the GMS governments have extended over $66 million in technical-assistance grants for project preparation as well as studies on various areas of GMS co-operation. Lack of financial resources and complications in financing have slowed down key projects. A more concerted approach with other development partners is needed to generate additional financing[21].

Concluding Remarks

For decades, the CLMV countries experienced the negative impacts of wrong economic ideologies and policies. Since the mid-1980s, they have engaged in economic transition from centrally planned to market-oriented economies, from inward-looking to outward-looking economic development strategies and policies, and from close economic relations with the Soviet

ISBN 92-64-01442-X © OECD 2005

bloc to closer economic relations with the global and regional market economies. They have encountered various political obstacles along the way, such as civil war in Viet Nam and Cambodia, Vietnamese occupation of Cambodia, and the military regime in Myanmar.

Still, these transition economies have achieved remarkable results in reforming their policies and institutions and in restructuring their economies. The economic benefits are manifest in the buoyant economic growth rates of the 1990s and in recent years. After the outbreak of the Asian financial crisis, growth rates in the sub-region outpaced those in ASEAN-6. The CLMV economies have become increasingly integrated with ASEAN and the rest of East Asia and with the global economy, as witnessed by rising trade and investment flows.

The CLMV countries have experienced and continue to experience instances of political isolation, economic policy discrimination and policy incoherence on the part of OECD countries, which have impacted on their economic performance, particularly in trade and investment. While the OECD countries have advocated and pressured them for economic policy and institutional reforms, particularly more openness in trade and investment regimes, they have not always followed up with non-discriminatory and preferential market access. The lifting of trade restrictions by the United States and the EU and S&D in the WTO as well as various GSP schemes have helped to boost their exports, particularly of textiles and clothing, and have served to attract FDI into their economies to produce for export. Development and technical assistance from the multilateral institutions (largely the ADB) as well as from DAC members (especially Japan) have helped improve supply capabilities with the development of transportation and telecommunication infrastructure, energy resources, tourism facilities and human-resource development.

As low-income and least-developed economies, the CLMV economies still face several development challenges and have to achieve greater policy coherence themselves. There are three main challenges:

— First, to pursue economic growth with social equity and environmental sustainability. While growth in the past decade has been satisfactorily high, widespread poverty remains a serious problem. The poverty reduction strategies as well as meeting the other Millennium Development Goals require access to more resources, more effective use of scarce resources through re-prioritisation, and improved efficiency and public-

ISBN 92-64-01442-X © OECD 2005

sector governance. Environmental sustainability is a serious issue given the overexploitation of forestry and aquatic resources, and it requires concerted efforts to conserve and renew resources.

- Second, to develop human resources for economic efficiency and poverty alleviation. In Cambodia, Laos, Myanmar and to a lesser extent Viet Nam, labour productivity is hindered by low literacy and schooling and in some cases by malnutrition and poor health. Economic development should be embedded in the continual development and upgrading of human resources.
- Third, continue to liberalise and deregulate the sub-region's economies to improve economic efficiency and competitiveness and to meet the commitments of WTO accession and ASEAN membership. WTO accession will entail heavy obligations to abide by WTO disciplines and rules and to open the markets of the sub-region to international competition.

Countries themselves have the primary responsibility for economic and social development. The CLMV countries must ensure the political will for development and coherence in policy implementation. As low-income and least-developed economies, however, they require enabling regional and global environments to provide open and preferential access to markets, access to investments, technology and know-how and access to development and technical assistance. OECD and East Asian countries' policies on trade and investment and their provision of development and technical assistance to the CLMV countries are critical for these economies to move forward. Their policy coherence for development is essential to ensure that the objectives are met.

ISBN 92-64-01442-X © OECD 2005

Notes

1. Myanmar's WTO membership has been under suspension.

2. Implementation of reform was interrupted by political uncertainty following withdrawal of Vietnamese troops in 1989, which continued up to the 1993 general election and beyond. With the formation of the new coalition government in October 1993 and adoption of the new Constitution, Cambodia reasserted its commitment to a market-oriented economy, pressed ahead with major trade and investment policy reforms and declared its intention to join GATT. Continuing political instability delayed Cambodia's admission into ASEAN until 1999. The two decades of armed conflict and genocide led to huge destruction of human resources and infrastructure.

3. Information on WTO web site, under "Accessions". The May 2003 meeting noted that a quantum jump in effort was needed if Viet Nam was to meet its goal of accession in 2005. The subsequent December 2003 meeting maintained that Viet Nam had started its "quantum jump" but still had some way to go. Viet Nam's latest offers included commitments to cut tariffs to an average of about 18 per cent and to provide some access to services in ten sectors with 92 sub-sectors. The June 2004 meeting noted that a lot of work remains in continuing to negotiate market access and other terms, further clarification of Viet Nam's regulations and policies, and putting into place the necessary laws and regulations.

4. WTO (2003).

5. WTO News, press release, 11 September 2003. Cambodia's terms of accession cover state ownership and privatisation; application of price controls; trading rights, customs duties and charges; tariff rate quotas and tariff exemptions; service fees and charges; application of internal taxes; quantitative import restrictions; customs valuation; rules of origin; pre-shipment inspection; antidumping, countervailing duties and safeguard regimes; export restrictions; export subsidies; industrial policy and subsidies; standards and certification; sanitary and phytosanitary measures; TRIMs; state trading; free zones and special economic areas; transit trade; agricultural policies; textiles regimes; TRIPS; transparency; and regional trading arrangements.

ISBN 92-64-01442-X © OECD 2005

6. According to the WTO web site, the Working party was established in February 1998, followed by the memorandum on the foreign trade regime in March 2001 and replies to questions from members in October 2003, but the Working Party has not yet met.

7. Most least-developed countries undertook deep trade liberalisation in the 1990s, received some preferential market access from developed and developing countries and enjoy higher rates of export growth than in the 1980s, but trade performance has not been reflected in poverty reduction in many of them. The Report argues for a more effective link between trade and poverty reduction through action on three fronts – a two-way mainstreaming of international financial and technical assistance for developing domestic production and trade capacities; an enabling international trade regime which includes phasing out of OECD agricultural support measures affecting least-developed countries, policies to reduce vulnerability to commodity price shocks, more effective market access preferences for the least developed countries, and enhanced South-South cooperation in trade and investment.

8. There is some double counting of intra-ASEAN trade because of Singapore's *entrepot* role. Nearly 50 per cent of its total exports comprise re-exports. In earlier days, Singapore imported western manufactures for re-export to Southeast Asia and imported Southeast Asian produce for re-export to Japan and the west. Increasingly, Singapore performs the *entrepot* function for Southeast Asian manufactures, particularly of electronic goods, parts and components that form part of the East Asian production network and supply chain. However, as Singapore's trade with Indonesia has not been published since the 1963-65 Indonesian economic confrontation against the formation of Malaysia, Singapore's intra-ASEAN trade is under-reported.

9. The ASEAN Secretariat web site maintains an ASEAN trade database, showing intra-ASEAN trade as well as ASEAN's trade with its major trading partners. Unfortunately the database has trade data for Cambodia and Myanmar only from the year 2000 onwards and has no data on the trade of Laos and Viet Nam. The incomplete database makes it difficult to draw meaningful conclusions on the trend and pattern of intra-ASEAN trade.

10. This high level of trade integration with ASEAN in part reflects its isolation by some OECD countries because of its human rights record. Myanmar has intensified efforts to integrate into ASEAN by accelerating its AFTA tariff-reduction schedule and removing constraints on intra-ASEAN investments under the AIA.

11. As of 2002, Malaysia had granted AISP treatment on 12 products for Laos, 345 products for Myanmar and 172 products for Viet Nam. The Philippines had granted it on 67 products for Myanmar, ten products for Viet Nam and two products for all CLMV countries. Thailand had granted it on 19 products for Viet Nam and is considering the list for Cambodia. Singapore

ISBN 92-64-01442-X © OECD 2005

imposes no tariffs on imports from all ASEAN countries except for alcoholic beverages, so there is no AISP list. At the meeting of the AFTA Council on 2 September 2004, it was noted that AISP suffered from low use, and CLMV countries were urged to request products highly traded in ASEAN, while the ASEAN-6 were urged to be more forthcoming in considering these requests.

12. For land-locked Laos, cross-border trade is often easier than internal trade among towns and provinces within the country because of geographical distance and a weak domestic transport system. With the existence of import and export restrictions and foreign exchange controls, smuggling is known to be sizeable.

13. Under this initiative, developed countries should, as soon as possible, provide tariff-free and quota-free market access on industrial products (including textiles and clothing) and should consider further market access measures on agricultural products. Developing countries should also provide preferential tariffs for the least-developed countries. The initiative also gives products from least-developed countries flexibility with regard to origin criteria. Developed countries could consider exemptions from origin requirements on a case-by-case basis, or introduce full cumulation of origin for least-developed country products.

14. The US has denied NTR or MFN tariff treatment to countries under Jackson-Vanik amendment to the US Trade Act of 1974. NTR tariff treatment is denied to any non-market economy in the 1974 Act and denies or seriously restricts or burdens its citizens' rights to emigrate. Since 1998, the United States has granted the Jackson-Vanik waiver annually for Viet Nam. Normal trade relations were finally achieved with the signing of the US-Viet Nam BTA in July 2000 after a four-year negotiation. With the BTA, NTR tariff treatment for Viet Nam became effective in December 2001, but also committed Viet Nam to sweeping economic reforms. The US granted NTR status to Cambodia in 1997. In 2004, the United States and Laos signed a bilateral trade agreement which will pave the way for NTR status for Laos.

15. Major ATC suppliers, in terms of the value of textiles and clothing exports and shares of countries' merchandise exports in 2001 were China ($53.3 billion, 20 per cent), followed by Korea ($15.2 billion, 10 per cent), Chinese Taipei ($12.3 billion, 10 per cent), India ($11.7 billion, 26 per cent), Turkey ($10.6 billion, 34 per cent), Hong Kong, China ($ 10.3 billion, 52 per cent), Mexico ($ 10.1 billion, 6 per cent), Indonesia ($ 7.8 billion, 14 per cent), Pakistan ($ 6.7 billion, 73 per cent), Bangladesh ($ 5.5 billion, 86 per cent), Thailand ($ 5.4 billion, 8 per cent), Malaysia ($ 3.1 billion, 4 per cent), and the Philippines ($2.7 billion, 8 per cent).

16. For example, the 2003 NTR duty rate on cotton shirts and blouses, a key clothing import from Viet Nam, was 19.8 per cent *ad valorem*, compared with a non-NTR rate of 45 per cent *ad valorem*. Exports to the United States rose

ISBN 92-64-01442-X © OECD 2005

sharply in 2003, as firms tried to maximise shipments ahead of the imposition of US quotas in September 2003. Exports to the US market in 2004 were capped by the quota at $1.7 billion.

17. Under the US-Cambodia Bilateral Textile Agreement, Cambodian factories are subject to annual US inspection to ensure that the labour-standard requirement is enforced. In December 2001, the Agreement was extended for another three years to December 2004. In the renewed agreement, the quota for most textile exports from Cambodia was raised. Cambodia was eligible for additional quota increases if working conditions in its garment industry complied with internationally recognised core labour standards.

18. There were cases of Thai firms shifting production to Laos in order to benefit from special privileges for least-developed countries, such as Japan's GSP scheme. Countries like Laos are not subject to the global ceilings that restrict exports under the GSP from other more developed countries.

19. The less developed members of ASEAN have yet to factor in the implications of a "rising India" as it continues with economic reforms and achieves high economic growth performance. Like China, India has offered ASEAN an economic partnership agreement with an FTA and an early-harvest arrangement.

20. The GMS covers an area of 2.3 million sq. km. with a wealth and variety of natural resources, including agriculture, fisheries, minerals, and energy (hydropower, coal, petroleum), which can be developed for economic growth and improved living standards. Presently the GMS has a population of about 250 million people with the majority living in rural areas and engaged in subsistence and semi-subsistence agriculture.

21. Member governments have tended to conserve concessional financing for national projects in the expectation that incremental funds would be available for sub-regional projects. Mechanisms are needed for better reconciling project financing with country-specific benefits. There is also a need to provide for maintenance, to ensure the realisation of expected returns from infrastructure projects. Some GMS countries also have limited absorptive capacities for ODA, while private-sector financiers think that projects in GMS require a high-risk premium.

ISBN 92-64-01442-X © OECD 2005

Bibliography

ASEAN Secretariat (2002), *Statistics of Foreign Investment in ASEAN*, ASEAN, Jakarta.

ASEAN Secretariat (2003), "Initiative for ASEAN Integration: Work plan for the CLMV countries", ASEAN Web site, www.aseansec.org, April.

ASEAN Secretariat (2004), *ASEAN Statistical Yearbook 2003*, Jakarta, ASEAN.

Asian Development Bank (2002), *Asian Development Outlook 2002*, ADB, Manila.

Asian Development Bank (2003), "GMS History and Background", "Institutional Arrangements", "ADB's Role", "Progress and Achievements", "10 Year Strategic Framework",), "Cambodia: Country Strategy and Program Update 2004-2006", "Myanmar: Country Assistance Plan 2001-2003", "Viet Nam: Strategy for Socio-Economic Development 2001-2010", "Building on Success: A Strategic Framework for the Next 10 Years of GMS", all available on the ADB website, www.adb.org.

Asian Development Bank (2004*a*), *Key Indicators 2004*, ADB, Manila.

Asian Development Bank (2004*b*), *Asian Development Outlook 2004*, ADB, Manila.

Auffret, P. (2003), "Trade Reform in Viet Nam: Opportunities with Emerging Challenges", *World Bank Policy Research Working Paper 3076*, World Bank, Washington, D.C, June.

Economic and Social Commission for Asia and the Pacific (ESCAP) (1995), "Strengthening Capacities in Trade, Investment and the Environment for the Comprehensive Development of Indo-China", *ESCAP Studies in Trade and Investment*, United Nations, New York, NY.

Economic and Social Commission for Asia and the Pacific (ESCAP) (2003), *Promoting the Millennium Development Goals in Asia and the Pacific*, United Nations, New York, NY.

Freeman, N.J. (2002), "Foreign Direct Investment in Viet Nam: An Overview", Paper prepared for the DFID Workshop on Globalisation and Poverty in Viet Nam, 23-24 September 2002, Hanoi.

UNITED NATIONS CONFERENCE ON TRADE AND DEVELOPMENT (UNCTAD) (2004), *The Least Developed Countries Report 2004*, UNCTAD, Geneva.

UNITED NATIONS CONFERENCE ON TRADE AND DEVELOPMENT (UNCTAD)(various years), *World Investment Report*, UNCTAD, Geneva.

WORLD BANK (2004), *World Development Indicators 2003*, World Bank, Washington, D.C.

WORLD BANK (2005), *World Development Report 2005*, World Bank, Washington, D.C.

WORLD TRADE ORGANIZATION (2003), "Report of the Working Party on the Accession of Cambodia", WTO web site, www.wto.org, 15 August.

WORLD TRADE ORGANIZATION, web site section on Accessions, www.wto.org.

ISBN 92-64-01442-X © OECD 2005

Chapter 14

OECD-Country Policies towards Developing Economies: Learning from East Asia, Lessons for South Asia

Mustafizur Rahman

Abstract

This chapter first sketches an economic and social profile of the South Asian region. It points out that this region of developing or least-developed economies is as profoundly affected by the forces of globalisation as any other part of the global economy but has only relatively recently begun to come to grips with the policy shifts that adapting to globalisation requires. The analysis then moves on to identify from a South Asian perspective the policy lessons to be drawn from the East Asian experience for the region's economies and especially for the broad lines of OECD-country policies that supported or contributed to East Asian economic expansion. These lessons generally confirm those drawn in the preceding chapters of this volume. The author stresses, however, that the "new reality" for South Asia in the global economy today differs from that faced decades ago by the East Asian economies and argues for the adaptations to OECD-country policies that these changed circumstances imply.

ISBN 92-64-01442-X © OECD 2005

South Asia in the Present Global Context

By the standards of the developing world South Asia is an important economic zone. Its combined GDP was about $605.3 billion in 2002, and its population is about 1 365 million (See Table 14.1 on the following page for some stylised facts about the region). The countries in South Asia have a common history and heritage but live under diverse economic and political realities. Among the region's seven countries, India is by far the largest economy with a population of 1 050 million (about 75 per cent of regional total) and a GDP of $480 billion (about four-fifths of the total). The two moderately large economies are Pakistan with 147 million people and a GDP of $58.7 billion and Bangladesh with 141 million and a GDP of $46.7 billion. In contrast, the combined population of the remaining four countries — Sri Lanka, Nepal, Maldives and Bhutan — is 45.5 million with a corresponding GDP of only $22.6 billion (2002). The region's systems of governance cover the entire spectrum from absolute monarchy to functioning parliamentary democracy. Three of the countries (India, Pakistan and Sri Lanka) are developing countries while the other four (Bangladesh, Nepal, Bhutan and Maldives) belong to the sub-stratum of least-developed countries (LDCs).

All the South Asian countries are now passing through a time of unprecedented changes and challenges. Over the past decade they have experienced crucial policy shifts, moving away from import-substitution strategies towards export orientation accompanied by trade liberalisation, privatisation of state-owned enterprises (SOEs) and deregulation of their financial sectors. Although Sri Lanka was an early liberaliser, most of the other countries saw accelerated liberalisation in the 1990s — India after the balance of payments shocks of the early 1990s and Bangladesh and Pakistan under the structural adjustment programmes of the late 1980s and early 1990s. South Asia now is connected with the global economy as never before. The openness of the region (measured by the ratio of the sum of exports and imports of goods and services to regional GDP) stands at about 0.31. South Asia's average GDP growth rate has attained a moderately impressive 5-plus per cent per annum in recent years, and the 2004 projections suggested 8-plus per cent growth for India.

ISBN 92-64-01442-X © OECD 2005

Table 14.1. **Salient Features of the South Asian Economies**

Indicators	Bangladesh	Bhutan	India	Maldives	Nepal	Pakistan	Sri Lanka	South Asia[a]
Population (million)	140.9	2.1	1 033.4	0.3	24.1	146.3	18.8	RT=1 365.9
GDP in $ billions	46.7	0.5	477.3	0.6	5.6	58.7	15.9	RT= 605.3
GDP per capita ($)	350	644	462	2 082	236	415	849	RWA= 447.0
GDP per capita (PPP, $)	1 610	1833	2840	4 798	1 310	1 890	3180	RWA=2 588.0
Life expectancy at birth (years)	60.5	62.5	63.3	66.8	59.1	60.4	72.3	RWA= 62.7
Adult literacy rate (%)	40.6	47.0	58.0	97.0	42.9	44.0	91.9	RWA= 54.9
HDI (human development index) value	0.5	0.5	0.6	0.8	0.5	0.5	0.7	
GDP rank	146	141	115	93	151	137	112	
HDI (human development index) rank	139	136	127	86	143	144	99	
Population below national poverty line 1990-2001 (%)	33.7	n.a.	28.6	n.a.	42.0	32.6	25.0	RWA= 29.7
Ratio of income: richest 20% to poorest 20%	4.6	n.a.	5.7	n.a.	5.9	4.8	5.3	RWA= 5.5
ODA disbursements received ($ million)	1 023.9	59.2	1 705.4	25.0	388.1	1 938.2	330.2	RT= 5 470.0
Exports of goods and services as (% of GDP)	15.0	30.0	14.0	93.0	22.0	18.0	37.0	RWA= 15.2
Degree of openness (%)	37.0	90.0	29.0	159.0	54.0	37.0	81.0	RWA= 31.0
Export of goods and services (as % of ODA)	684.1	253.4	3 918.2	2 232.0	317.4	545.1	1 781.6	RWA=1 685.8
Debt service as % of exports of goods and services	9.0	3.3	12.6	4.3	6.2	21.3	9.2	RWA= 12.9
Population below $1 a day (1990-2001)	36.0	n.a.	34.7	n.a.	37.7	13.4	6.6	RWA=32.3
FDI Inflow ($ million)	114.0	n.a.	3 449.0	12.0	10.0	823.0	242.0	RT= 4 650.0

Note: *a)* RT = Regional Total; RWA = Regional Weighted Average.
Source: UNDP, Regional *Human Development Report: South Asia,* 2003.

As Chapter 5 in this volume rightly points out, South Asia's growth in recent years has ranked among the highest in the developing world. The region has also achieved commendable success in terms of some human development indicators. At the same time, however, the countries of the region suffer from acute poverty, both absolute and relative. South Asia has the largest concentration of poor people in the world, and the disparity between the rich and the poor is increasing. About 30 per cent of the region's population (more than an astonishing 400 million) lives below the poverty line, and the richest 20 per cent of the population has an average income 5.5 times that of the poorest 20 per cent. The Gini coefficient of income inequality is on the rise in most of the countries.

Policies pursued by the OECD countries are both relevant and important for South Asian countries. Major South Asian countries connect closely to OECD members through the triad nexus of aid, trade and foreign direct investment (FDI). OECD countries are the major sources of earnings of the tourism sector for Nepal, Bhutan and the Maldives, where the industry is an important source of foreign exchange. Most of the $5 470 million in Official Development Assistance (ODA) that South Asian countries received in 2002 came from the OECD countries either through bilateral channels or from multilateral organisations in which OECD countries are the key players. OECD countries provide the major destinations for South Asian exports equivalent to $100 billion in 2002 – more than four-fifths of total exports for Bangladesh and about two-thirds for India. OECD countries also account for the largest part of the $4 650 million in investment that came to the region in 2002.

The relative importance of aid and trade in South Asian economies has undergone drastic changes in the recent past. Even countries predominantly dependent on aid have come to rely more on trade in recent years. Average tariff rates in Bangladesh have fallen from 85 per cent to 17 per cent since the early 1990s. Other countries have shown similar reductions. India, which long pursued a protectionist regime, has brought down its tariffs quite substantially to around 21 per cent. Sri Lanka, which started to liberalise its economy in the 1970s, has an effective protection rate of under 10 per cent.

This increasing global integration and the growing importance of trade (for example, *vis-à-vis* aid) is manifestly discernible in Bangladesh. As Table 14.2 shows, its exports of goods and services in the early 1990s about equalled aid received during that period, while in 2003 its exports reached four times the aid received. Exports of goods and services have become increasingly important for all the countries of South Asia. The region as a whole exports 17 times

 ISBN 92-64-01442-X © OECD 2005

what it receives as aid. This increasing dependence on trade and increasing global economic integration represent the new realities under which South Asian economies now function. On the other hand, the flow of FDI to South Asia, particularly trade-enhancing FDI, has stayed rather low. Poverty pervades South Asia and income inequality is widespread. A large part of whatever growth has been achieved has not become translated into equitable distribution. The pace of poverty reduction has been disturbingly slow — in countries such as Bangladesh it was about 1 per cent per year over the past decade. The Gini coefficient is rising nationally in both urban and rural areas.

Table 14.2. **The Growing Importance of the External Sector in the Bangladesh Economy**
($ million)

	1981	1991	2001	2003
1. Exports (X)	724.9	1 718.0	6 008.0	6 548.4
Primary Goods (%)	35.0	17.8	7.5	7.1
Manufactured Goods (%)	65.0	82.2	92.5	92.9
RMG Exports ($ million)	*3.4*	*866.8*	*4 859.8*	*4 912.1*
2. Imports (M)	1 954.1	3 472.0	9 335.0	9 141.3
3. Remittances (R)	379.0	764.0	1 882.1	3 062.0
4. ODA	1 146.0	1 733.0	1 369.0	1 442.0
5. FDI	n.a.	23.5	222.3	197.13
Total (1-5)	*4 204.0*	*7 710.5*	*18 816.4*	*20 390.8*
GDP	1 9811.6	3 0974.8	47 825.8	51 898.1
Extent of Globalisation (%)	21.2	24.9	39.3	39.3
X as % of ODA	63.3	99.2	378.3	454.1
RMG as % of X	*0.5*	*50.5*	*75.1*	*75.1*
RMG as % of MFD X	*0.7*	*61.4*	*81.2*	*80.8*
Knit RMG as % of RMG X	*3.3*	*15.1*	*30.8*	*33.7*
RMG X as % of ODA	*0.3*	*50.0*	*355.0*	*340.6*
X as % of M	37.1	49.5	64.2	71.6
RMG X as % of M	*0.2*	*25.0*	*52.1*	*53.7*

Note: "n.a." = not available. RMG = Ready-Made Garments.
Source: CPD-Trade Policy Database.

In one of the most important developments of recent times, South Asia is taking a number of important initiatives for regional co-operation. Table 14.3 shows clearly the emerging importance of trade alliances. Despite the historical ties and the heritage that bind South Asian countries, trade among them has been dismally low. Compared to the EU, NAFTA and ASEAN, where intra-regional trade as a share of global trade is significantly high (62 per cent,

ISBN 92-64-01442-X

46 per cent and 24 per cent, respectively), intra-regional trade among the countries of South Asia amounts to only 4 per cent of their global trade. However, the increasing trend towards greater regional co-operation has become visible in recent years because closer economic co-operation is perceived as necessary for strengthened global integration of the South Asian countries.

Table 14.3. **Current and On-Going Regional Trade Arrangements with South Asian Members**

South Asian Countries	Bilateral FTAs	SAPTA (est. 1993)	SAFTA (est. 2006)	BIMSTEC (est. 1997)	D-8 (est. 1997)	IOR-ARC (est. 1997)	Bangkok Agreement (est. 1975)	SAGQ (1998)
Bangladesh	India*, Pakistan*, Sri Lanka*	✓	✓	✓	✓	✓	✓	✓
Bhutan	India	✓	✓	✓				✓
India	Bangladesh*, Bhutan, Nepal, Sri Lanka	✓	✓	✓		✓	✓	✓
Nepal	India	✓	✓	✓				✓
Maldives		✓	✓					
Pakistan	Bangladesh*, Sri Lanka*	✓	✓		✓			
Sri Lanka	Bangladesh*, India, Pakistan*	✓	✓	✓		✓	✓	

Notes: * indicates ongoing negotiations.
SAPTA = SAARC Preferential Trading Arrangement.
SAFTA = South Asia Free Trade Area.
D-8 = Developing-8 (Bangladesh, Egypt, Indonesia, Iran, Malaysia, Nigeria, Pakistan and Turkey).
IOR-ARC = Indian Ocean Rim Association for Regional Co-operation.
SAGQ = South Asia Growth Quadrangle (Bangladesh, Bhutan, India and Nepal).

Under a decision of the 12th Summit of the SAARC (South Asian Association for Regional Co-operation) Heads of State, a South Asia Free Trade Area (SAFTA) will be established in 2006. An agreement to establish a BIMSTEC (Bangladesh, India, Myanmar, Sri Lanka, Thailand Economic Co-operation) Free Trade area has already been signed. There is talk of creating a South Asian customs union and, recently, the Prime Minister of India had floated the idea of a common currency for the region. All the South Asian countries belong to the WTO except Bhutan, which is an observer.

ISBN 92-64-01442-X © OECD 2005

There is a general recognition that South Asia stands at a critical threshold of enormous opportunities and challenges. The major challenges are:

— to attain a sustained high level of growth, with higher savings and investment and higher total factor productivity;

— to ensure that this growth is poverty-reducing, with better income distribution;

— to stimulate greater regional co-operation by creating a Free Trade Area; and

— to make the global trading system work for the development of South Asian economies.

In addressing these challenges OECD-country policies do matter for South Asia, for a number of reasons. The OECD countries are major markets for South Asia's $90 billion in exports. Most of the $4.6 billion in investment in South Asia comes from OECD investors. The OECD countries account for most of the $5.4 billion in ODA to the region. Thus policies pursued by the OECD countries in global institutions, regional forums and in their own domestic economies (e.g. those governing preferential access to domestic markets and those that impact on the competitiveness of South Asian products) have important implications for the South Asian economies. The transmission mechanisms through which OECD policies impact on the region include aid policies, aid volumes, OECD investment, OECD trade policies towards South Asia and the role OECD countries play in multilateral bodies and the various regional forums.

Many East Asian countries, now developed, passed through South Asia's current stage of development, with similar per capita incomes, income distributions and GDP structures. The interface between OECD policies and East Asian development practice could thus provide very useful insights into policies that could benefit South Asian countries as they seek to develop their economies and raise the standard of living of their people. This brief note tries first to identify some key OECD policies that contributed most to East Asian economic success and to examine their relevance for South Asia. Second, it attempts to articulate some of the distinctive features of the current global, regional and domestic scenarios that form South Asia's present development context, and to identify in this emerging reality new OECD-country policies that could help in promoting South Asian economic development. In this sense, the attempt is to learn from East Asia's experience and to look beyond it.

The first two parts of this volume provide fascinating and valuable insights into how various OECD policies have impacted on East Asian development and why particular policies were successful. This is not to say that there is consensus on the sources of the East Asian miracle. The intention here is not to enter that debate but to try to identify both OECD-country policies that have contributed to the East Asian success and the lessons that South Asia could draw from this experience.

OECD Policies in East Asia: Lessons for South Asia

OECD-country policies towards East Asia that would interest South Asia fall into three broad, interrelated groups. East Asia's experience shows that developing countries stand to benefit most when developed countries' policies work in tandem at all three levels:

- policies that stimulated growth and equity in the economies of East Asia;
- policies that promoted regional integration of East Asian countries; and
- policies that supported strengthened global integration of the East Asian economies.

Policies Stimulating Growth and Equity

Among the OECD-country activities that stimulated domestic economic growth and led to efficiency gains and structural changes in the East Asian economies, the impacts of aid, trade and FDI appear to have played critical roles. OECD-country development policies helped the East Asian economies to remove their anti-export bias through trade-policy reforms and by putting in place fiscal, financial and institutional incentives to promote the export orientation of domestic investors and entrepreneurs. The maintenance of appropriate exchange rates was crucial to ensuring competitive strength of East Asian producers in both national and global markets. East Asian policies of trade liberalisation followed careful sequencing and phasing with progressive liberalisation of inputs, intermediates and final goods, and selective support to strategic sectors. As the South Asian countries struggle to lock in their reforms and further liberalise their trade and exchange rate regimes it is pertinent to keep this aspect of trade and investment policies in mind.

ISBN 92-64-01442-X © OECD 2005

Managing inflation through prudent monetary policy supported by fiscal and credit policies, a hallmark of the East Asian experience, provides an important lesson for South Asia. Maintaining high growth with low inflation continues to remain a major challenge for South Asia. Before the financial crisis, the South Asian countries were able to sustain their growth momentum with low inflation. The financial crisis that some of the East Asian countries faced in the late 1990s also provides important lessons for South Asia. Financial-system and exchange-rate management have gained much more importance with the floating of many of the South Asian currencies in recent years (the Indian rupee and the Bangladeshi taka, for example). The East Asian experience also calls for a cautious approach towards capital-account liberalisation.

As East Asian experience shows, the creation of an efficient equity market with appropriate oversight institutions as an integral part of a professionally run financial system played a crucial role in mobilising domestic investment resources. Financial reforms promoted by OECD countries played a key role here. Most of the South Asian countries have opened their financial markets to encourage portfolio investors from abroad to invest in equity markets and to allow foreign banks to operate in domestic financial markets. Burdens of bad debt, high interest rates, weak prudential management, a lack of real central-bank autonomy and the absence of effective bankruptcy laws and professionally run, independent oversight institutions create an environment where investors' confidence is lost, savings are difficult to mobilise and funds cannot be channelled to productive investment. East Asia's experience draws attention to the critical importance of financial reforms for the growth of an economy and the role that institutions play in their successful implementation. In many of the South Asian countries, the first generation of reforms (fiscal reform and financial and banking liberalisation) failed to attain their objectives because the second-generation reforms of institutions and oversight bodies came only with a lag. East Asian experience shows that the sequencing of reforms is important.

Chapter 6 in this volume points to three phases of the aid relationship: the era of the engineers (support for large infrastructure), the era of neo-classical thinking (emphasis on market liberalisation) and the era of social scientists stressing the overriding importance of poverty alleviation. Poverty alleviation lies at the centre of macroeconomic policy making in all the countries of South Asia. For most of them the design of poverty reduction strategy papers (PRSPs) is a prerequisite for receiving ODA from their development partners. Much will depend on the availability of additional

ISBN 92-64-01442-X © OECD 2005

assistance from OECD countries to implement the targets set in the PRSPs. For the PRSP process to succeed, it is also crucially important to ensure that OECD-country support programmes do not undermine domestic ownership over the PRS agenda, a point stressed Chapter 6.

One of the distinctive features of the East Asian experience has been considerable reduction in both absolute and relative poverty, although the issue of equity remains a major concern. Given the current market-driven macroeconomic management in South Asian countries, the need for putting risk-reducing mechanisms in place can not be overemphasised. As Chapter 1 points out, there is a need for more formal mechanisms for managing risks and protecting the poor and the vulnerable. Moreover, emerging disparities and feelings of exclusion create a growing need for adequate social protection regimes in the South Asian countries. This is particularly important given the slow pace of reduction in poverty levels and increases in the Gini index of inequality observed in most of the South Asian countries. East Asian experience shows how important it is to invest in human capital and in education and training in order to ensure growth with equity. Targeted support to small and medium-scale enterprises (SMEs) is crucial in South Asia, and investment in human resources could be an important initiative in this respect. The emergence of the services sector as the major growth driver in the new economy, a sector that requires substantive investment in human resources, makes this even more important.

The ability to create an environment conducive to FDI and capacity to absorb foreign technology played a crucial role in East Asia. Chapter 9 analyses the trade-FDI nexus in East Asia. The nexus was created first by attracting capital to labour-intensive industries in the initial phase of development and later through spillover to knowledge-intensive industries. As a region with one of the lowest levels of FDI flows (total FDI was a mere $4.6 billion in 2002), it is important for South Asia to understand the East Asian experience from two perspectives. The first involves the incentives and institutions put in place to attract inflows of FDI. The second concerns how OECD-country policies and incentives towards their own potential investors encouraged and promoted flows of FDI from the OECD countries to East Asia. The promotion of regional production networks, particularly by Japan, played an important role in creating an attractive environment for flows of FDI to East Asia. More often than not, market-access initiatives by OECD countries (for example, Japan's revised GSP schemes of 2001 and 2003) fail to deliver the expected results because FDI that could translate potential opportunities into real results on the ground did not automatically follow

 ISBN 92-64-01442-X © OECD 2005

them. Domestic investment resources also are often limited. OECD-country policies should address this concern of South Asian countries, particularly that of the regional LDCs. It has now been proven that the creation of a conducive policy environment in the South Asian countries does not suffice to attract FDI to the region. Chapter 4 brings out this point quite convincingly.

ODA from OECD countries played an important role in implementing East Asian development plans. The important lesson for South Asia is that ODA-induced investment in East Asia did not crowd out private investment. Instead, through its role in infrastructure development and in soft areas such as education, skill upgrading and training, it played an important role in mobilising domestic investment and creating opportunities for income-generating and employment-creating activities. In South Asia, where there is more and more emphasis on the private sector's role, allocating ODA to attract more private investment has become a crucial factor in economic development.

Policies to Stimulate Regional Integration

One of the major successes of OECD-country policies in East Asia was to promote policies that encouraged closer economic co-operation among the countries of the region. It was understood early that there was a need to stimulate intra-regional flows of trade, that this could be enhanced by promoting both intra-regional as well as extra-regional flows of FDI and that trade and investment policies must be geared towards strengthened intra-regional co-operation. Chapters 1 and 8 rightly note that initially East Asian exports were mainly destined for OECD markets and that the issue of greater regional integration gained importance only later. South Asia's emerging interest in establishing bilateral and regional FTAs makes it very necessary that OECD-country policies support greater regional integration. It is widely perceived in the region that greater regional integration will enable strengthened global integration of the South Asian countries.

The intra-regional flow of trade in South Asia, at 4 per cent, is one of the lowest in the world. The flow of FDI, except for some Indian investment in Nepal, also is almost non-existent. The extra-regional FDI flow to South Asia also is low by any standard. Thus it becomes important that developed countries' policies, incentives and institutional support promote investment flows to the region and provide incentives to their own investors to go to regions such as South Asia. Japan's investment policy *vis-à-vis* East Asia is a case in point. Another is the recent 30 million euro credit from the European Investment Bank to establish the Lafarge Cement factory in Bangladesh, which will use clinker from Meghalaya State in India. Encouraging production and distribution networks in East Asia was also an important aspect of OECD-country policies, as Chapter 4 notes.

Policies to Strengthen Global Integration

Flow of resources to East Asia through multilateral agencies in which OECD countries are major players played an important role in East Asia's economic ascendancy. OECD countries also stimulated exports from East Asia by providing preferential market access to East Asian goods and services through their various GSP schemes. Cleverly crafted rules of origin and preferential access stimulated intra-regional co-operation in East Asia and created locational advantages that provided a competitive edge to East Asian goods in OECD markets. Preferential market access has become increasingly important for South Asia, particularly for its four LDCs. For example, the everything-but-arms (EBA) initiative of the EU is crucial for providing South Asian LDCs a competitive edge in developed-country markets. This type of initiative needs further extension. After Canada provided zero-tariff access in 2002 for exports of Bangladesh's apparel to the Canadian market, such exports shot up by 54 per cent in 2003. For the developing countries it matters what role the developed countries play at the global level in institutions such as the WTO, UNCTAD and in the multilateral organisations such as the World Bank and IMF.

The Need for a New Generation of OECD Policies for South Asia: Beyond the East Asian Experience

The global, regional and domestic contexts in which South Asia's development takes place today differ significantly from those of the 1970s and 1980s when East Asia started to undergo the rapid changes that produced its success. Future OECD-country policies will have to take cognisance of and build on today's realities. East Asia's experience of partnership with developed countries doubtless remains relevant for South Asia, but newly emerging realities demand new emphases, renewed effort in particular areas and different approaches to partnership. In some instances this will also require a new

ISBN 92-64-01442-X © OECD 2005

generation of policies, particularly for helping South Asia in general and LDCs in particular towards strengthened global integration of their economies and for ensuring that the gains from reforms reach the broad masses, particularly in the rural areas.

The new reality embraces the increasing openness of the South Asian economies and an unprecedented pace of globalisation with attendant challenges and opportunities, in the context of which South Asian economies have to exist and compete. It also involves a move towards greater regional integration and the rising importance of trade for employment, investment and macroeconomic performance. It reflects a growing felt need for greater roles for the private sector, civil society and non-governmental actors in economic governance, the increasing importance of non-economic factors such as the rule of law, independence of the judiciary, reduction of corruption and overall good governance and efficient functioning of institutions. The relative importance of these various factors has changed over time, and the new generation of developed-country policies must be sensitive to emerging new demands and become tailored to address the attendant interests and concerns of South Asian countries.

South Asia has the largest concentration of poor people in the world. OECD policies need more focus on this fact, and their priorities need appropriate redesign given the overriding importance of attaining the PRSP targets and MDG goals in the developing world in general and South Asia in particular. Developed countries as a community have pledged their support towards these two objectives and OECD-country policies must be informed by this pledge with, importantly, a positive response to the call for devoting 0.7 per cent of their GNP to aid for developing nations.

In view of the growing importance of trade in South Asian economies, the OECD support package needs more emphasis on trade-related technical assistance. This need covers many areas, such as enhancement of human resource capacities through skill upgrading, technology transfer, WTO compliance assurance (standardisation and quality-control compliance with SPS-TBT measures, trade facilitation), enhancement of trade-related negotiating capacities, trade-related knowledge management, strengthening of trade-related institutions and development of trade-related infrastructure.

Given the need for sound macroeconomic fundamentals that can promote higher growth rates, the role of non-economic factors in economic growth has reached critical importance for the countries of South Asia. OECD-country support in the areas of good governance, strengthening local governments and improving trade and investment climates have become crucial to realising potentials for faster growth that could ensure distributional justice.

Non-governmental organisations and civil-society groups play an important role in the South Asian economies today. They also likely will have the same importance for achieving national PRSP goals and the MDGs and ensuring good governance to deliver the outputs. The new generation of OECD-country policies must support, promote and strengthen these new actors. This message comes out strongly in Chapter 6 of this volume, and Chapter 1 rightly points out the need for more government-civil society partnerships to oversee and monitor social protection policies. OECD policies must promote these partnerships, particularly because in South Asia some governments remain rather reluctant to tolerate greater roles for civil-society organisations as service deliverers.

Policy Support for Regional Integration in South Asia

South Asia remains one of the least integrated regions in terms of trade, transport and communication connectivity and investment flows. Yet a new realisation of the need for closer economic co-operation in the region and efforts toward it has appeared. OECD-country policies towards South Asia should meet the growing requirements for enhancement of trade, transport and investment co-operation in the region, the exploitation of common natural resources and greater co-ordination of economic policies. OECD-country policies should also promote and support greater economic co-operation between East and South Asia through support of such initiatives as BIMSTEC and common exploitation of regional resources such as water, natural gas and energy.

Support for Strengthened Global Integration of South Asia

In the evolving global trading regime, OECD-country policies are important and relevant for the South Asian countries from a number of perspectives. The vast majority of people in South Asia realise that the existing multilateral trade regime has led, barring a few exceptions, to growing marginalisation of the developing countries. This requires a renewed effort by the OECD countries to take concrete actions in the WTO on the S&D provisions and implementation-related issues. Support through autonomous

ISBN 92-64-01442-X © OECD 2005

initiatives on market access is vital to ensure a competitive edge for South Asian goods in OECD markets. Global initiatives by the OECD countries in the WTO are required. Zero-tariff access for all LDC products to the markets of all OECD countries could be important in this regard. A stance more friendly to developing countries in ongoing negotiations in the WTO on agriculture, the Singapore issues, services, investment and other areas would allow South Asian and other developing countries better to exploit their comparative advantage and to safeguard their interests in the global trading system. Such a stance also is critically important given the January 2005 phase-out of the MFA and its potentially negative consequences for the RMG (Ready-made Garments) sectors of some South Asian countries such as Bangladesh and Nepal. Developed countries should help these countries to draw up plans to address the attendant concerns.

Another important issue relates to the opening of the labour markets in the developed countries (GATS Mode-4: Temporary Movement of Natural Persons). Flows of remittances remain a vital component of foreign-exchange earnings for almost all the countries of South Asia. They contribute significantly towards the absorption of new entrants to the labour market, poverty alleviation, replenishment of foreign exchange reserves and import payment capacity. In countries like Bangladesh, about 10 per cent of annual entrants to the labour market travel abroad for jobs. Their contribution is equivalent to annual net exports of RMG and twice that of the ODA disbursed annually. The Middle Eastern countries have hitherto absorbed most of this labour, and the developed countries have not had a very significant share. In the interests of the developing countries, renewed attention needs to go to opening a larger segment of the OECD labour market to labour from these countries under GATS Mode-4. In this context, OECD support for raising educational quality and skill upgrading becomes still more important, because as Chapter 12 points out many if not most of the potential openings for migrants in the OECD job market will be for skilled workers and professionals.

OECD-country support should also particularly target helping South Asian countries build the required supply-side capacities for strengthened global integration of their economies. It should also ensure more pro-active support for global initiatives such as the JITAP (Joint Integrated Technical Assistance Programme) in the WTO, and for helping South Asian LDCs to participate effectively in the Dispute Settlement Mechanisms in the WTO through legal aid support.

OECD countries must demonstrate more sensitivity to the implications of their policies towards some developing countries that work against the interests of other developing countries and LDCs. Their RTAs and trade initiatives such as NAFTA (North American Free Trade Agreement), the US-Viet Nam BTA, AGOA (Africa Growth and Opportunity Act), the Middle-East Trade and Engagement Act and CBI (Caribbean Basin Initiative) have excluded a number of developing countries and LDCs, many of them in South Asia. Preferential market access provided under these initiatives has tended to undermine the trade interests of South Asian countries. While it is the prerogative of developed countries to undertake such measures, they should be sensitive to growing concerns in this regard and take compensatory action to mitigate the adverse effects. A case in point involves the US initiative to provide zero-tariff access to apparel exported by African and Caribbean countries, which include most of the LDCs but exclude Asia-Pacific LDCs such as Bangladesh and Nepal. While in 2002 net US aid to Bangladesh was about $100 million, the duties imposed on exports from Bangladesh to the United States in the same year amounted to about $331 million. Some countries successful in debt servicing, like Bangladesh, were "penalised" for their success by exclusion from initiatives such as the HIPC. In some instances conflicting signals from developed countries also confuse South Asian countries. For example, the United States is asking the Bangladesh government to allow trade-union rights to workers in the EPZ and threatening to withdraw GSP privileges if this is not done. Yet Japan and Korea, fearing disruption of production in their factories, are not happy with this and are threatening to withdraw investment if it occurs. The region perceives such conflicting signals as a lack of coherence in OECD-country policies towards South Asia. As Chapter 6 points out, coherent policies must take a holistic approach that views aid, trade and FDI as an integral part of any strategic assistance package designed for the developing countries. South Asia can only benefit from such an approach.

ISBN 92-64-01442-X © OECD 2005

Chapter 15

The Impact of Coherence of OECD-Country Policies on Asian Developing Economies: Development Lessons for Central Asia

Richard Pomfret

Abstract

This chapter discusses what lessons the Central Asian countries can learn from the East Asian development experience and the coherence or incoherence of OECD-country policies. First, it focuses on the benefits — and the potential risk — of economic openness, as these countries have moved towards open economies since 1992. Second, it argues that, given the structure of the economies of the region, the only big links between OECD-country policies and the region's economic performance work through the markets for the small number of commodities exported from Central Asia. Cotton is the most significant in this respect, and OECD countries' textile trade and farm-support policies have been harmful for the region. The chapter concludes that the negative effects of these policies have been far greater than developmental benefits from international aid.

The Central Asian countries are all open economies in terms of trade/ GDP ratios, even though they were cut off from the global economy before 1992[1]. Their history is important because the countries do not have large diaspora or any other established links or networks outside the former Soviet Union. Isolation from the non-Soviet world also meant that they had unclear ideas about OECD policies or the Asian developing economies, although after independence they saw OECD countries as important markets and sources of capital and technology. Central Asian leaders were attracted to the Asian developing economies as models of economic growth with political stability, especially where they had been centrally planned (China) or were Islamic (Malaysia). Thus this exercise has resonance for Central Asia with respect to both coherence of OECD policies and lessons from East Asia

Major Development Challenges Facing Central Asia

Following the dissolution of the Soviet Union in December 1991, the immediate challenges facing the five new independent countries of Central Asia were nation building and the transition from central planning to market-based economies. The longer-term challenge was to ensure that the political and social institutions and the types of market economies that emerged from this unanticipated and tumultuous period would be appropriate for sustainable development. By the turn of the century the transition was essentially complete, although the five countries have distinctive systems and none has a well-functioning market economy. All remain heavily dependent on natural resource exports for their economic health (Table 15.1). The main challenge is to promote and manage resource-based income and, more importantly, to diversify their economies from their still narrow bases.

Table 15.1. **Basic Data, 2002**

	Population (million)	GDP per capita ($)	External Debt/GDP (%)	Major Exports
Kazakhstan	14.5	1 668	74	Oil, minerals, grain
Kyrgyz Rep.	4.8	334	135	Gold
Tajikistan	6.4	187	82	Aluminium
Turkmenistan	5.8	648	68	Natural gas
Uzbekistan	25.6	308	60	Cotton

Source: EBRD *Transition Report*, 2003.

ISBN 92-64-01442-X © OECD 2005

Lessons from East Asia: Openness and Trade

The strongest lesson from East Asia concerns the benefits of openness. Chapter 1 provides an excellent tour of the literature on openness and growth. It alludes to the significance of building institutional capacity, and one should underline the importance of this for Central Asia. This is consistent with results from cross-country growth regressions, where a much-improved fit in the growth/openness relationship is obtained when it is conditional on the degree of regulation[2].

Chapters 1 and 9 focus on the positive effects of foreign direct investment (FDI) in East Asia, especially their trade-creating influence. The record in this respect has been mixed in Central Asia. For much of the region FDI inflows since independence have been small, which is related primarily to institutional shortcomings as well as unattractive policy implementation. The big exception is in resource activities. The largest inward FDI by far has been into Kazakhstan, overwhelmingly in the oil sector. Exploitation of the oil depended critically on the expertise of the oil majors and only with their assistance could the fields be developed to their potential — or in the case of the offshore fields even be developed at all. Thus, FDI has been an indispensable prerequisite for the export boom Kazakhstan currently enjoys. The Kumtor goldmine in the Kyrgyz Republic also required the expertise of a foreign investor, and Kumtor's output accounted for as much as one-sixth of the country's GDP in the early 21st century. Institutions matter in facilitating such resource-based FDI, but the critical issue is how to share the risks and the resource rents. Central Asia has been conspicuous in its failure to attract the non-resource, export-oriented FDI that was so important in East Asia[3].

Chapters 1 and 8 both discuss the relative merits of multilateral and regional approaches to trade liberalisation, underlining that historically the East Asian countries relied on the global market and have only very recently turned to bilateral and regional arrangements. The experience of the Central Asian countries has also been one of *de facto* multilateralism. Despite great amounts of time spent in agreeing to an alphabet soup of overlapping regional trading arrangements, none of these has had any economic effect[4]. This has happened partly because the arrangements were politically driven and political alignments were so fluid that agreements have been overtaken by events. Yet it also occurred because when countries looked more closely at discriminatory trading arrangements they did not like what they saw. For economies exporting a narrow range of primary products (cotton, minerals and energy

ISBN 92-64-01442-X © OECD 2005

products) the potential was for much more trade diversion than trade creation so that, although the list of putative arrangements in Central Asia is even longer than that in Chapter 1's Table 1.4, they have been nugatory.

Chapter 1 treats the 1997 Asian Crisis as a consequence of openness on the capital account. The connection is valid, but for regions such as Central Asia to draw the lesson that the Asian crisis provides justification for not opening the capital account is false logic. Without underplaying the real hardships in 1997-98, especially for some of the poorer citizens of crisis-hit countries, one may argue that the crisis should be placed in the context of the stellar growth of the preceding years. Thailand was the fastest-growing economy in the world from the early 1980s until 1996, and institutional change failed to keep pace fully with economic change. In Korea and Malaysia the crisis enforced necessary institutional change, especially in the financial sector. To varying degrees these three countries regained their dynamism within a few years, and the crisis could be seen as a blip in the long-term trend. Indonesia's crisis had much harsher effects because the institutional deficiencies were larger[5]. An endnote in Chapter 1 states that China and Chinese Taipei avoided the crisis because of their closed capital accounts. A more important factor was the sustainability of their growth/institutional balance, in Chinese Taipei's case because there had been appropriate pre-1997 institutional changes and in China's case because the economy is still at a lower level of economic and institutional development than the other Tigers. The other Asian economies to avoid the crisis either had strong institutions (Singapore and Hong Kong, China) or had experienced anaemic growth (Philippines). In sum, the lesson should be that failure to maintain the pace of institutional change will lead to crises for countries pursuing outward-oriented development, rather than that a closed capital account can deliver sustainable growth without crisis[6].

Coherence of OECD Policies

Official development assistance flows to the Central Asian countries are smaller than the flows going to East Asia. The poorest countries, the Kyrgyz Republic and Tajikistan, receive less than similar-sized Laos. Small bilateral flows to every country suggest that the region is too unimportant to register on donor's screens to any significant degree. There were hopes after 11 September 2001 that the strategic importance of the region would become acknowledged, but the large aid flows went only into Afghanistan

ISBN 92-64-01442-X © OECD 2005

(Table 15.2). Military assistance from the United States did increase substantially, particularly to Uzbekistan and to a lesser extent to the Kyrgyz Republic, and Russian military spending remains important in Tajikistan and the Kyrgyz Republic.

Table 15.2. **Aid, 2002**

	Net ODA ($ million)	Bilateral (%)	Major Donors ($ million)	Population (million)
Kazakhstan	188	90	USA(65), Japan (38), Spain (12)	14.8
Kyrgyz Rep.	186	51	AsDF (43), USA (40), IDA (30)	5.0
Tajikistan	168	68	USA (59), IDA (22), EU (21)	6.3
Turkmenistan	41	86	Arab countries (18), Japan (14), USA (13)	5.5
Uzbekistan	189	89	USA (63), Japan (36), Germany (18)	25.4
Afghanistan	1 285	78	USA (188), EU (95), Germany (86)	28.0

Source: OECD website.

One striking feature of Table 15.1 is the high external debt ratios of the two poorest countries. Under the agreement by which Russia assumed all the external assets and liabilities of the Soviet Union, the other successor states started life with zero debt. Tajikistan accumulated its debt largely as a result of credit for military equipment purchased from Russia during the 1992-97 civil war; some of it has been written down and the status of the rest is unclear. The Kyrgyz Republic, however, owes its debt largely to the international financial institutions. During the 1990s the Kyrgyz were the poster boys for reform along Washington Consensus lines. They received substantial help from the World Bank and IMF, but the Kyrgyz authorities do not appear to have fully appreciated the extent to which this aid was in the form of loans that have to be repaid[7].

Chapter 5 makes a plea for a menu of assistance, and probably the most effective aid to Central Asia has been technical rather than financial. The multilateral institutions played an important training role, especially in the initial post-Soviet years through the joint Vienna Institute, for officials unaccustomed to market systems. Educational assistance through schemes such as the US Muskie Fellowships have enabled a rapid upgrading of human capital[8], Japan sent officials from the central bank to serve as in-country advisers and the EU's *Tacis* programme effectively got technical assistance beyond the capital cities. The impact of these programmes is difficult to measure. The general impression, however, is one of quantitatively small aid flows, mostly bilateral apart from those to the two smallest countries and with very little evidence of co-ordination.

Other explicit measures by OECD countries to promote economic development in Central Asia reinforce the impression of unimportance. The Central Asian countries receive GSP treatment but make little use of it[9]. They are mostly still classified by some OECD countries as non-market economies, which has adverse implications for anti-dumping determinations, but their exports are sufficiently innocuous that this has not mattered[10].

The most important way in which OECD countries' policies impact Central Asian countries' development is through the effects of sectoral policies rather than trade policies *per se* on the world prices of Central Asian exports. The most important sectoral issue concerns cotton. Uzbekistan is the world's fifth largest producer and second largest exporter. Cotton also has historically been an important export for Turkmenistan, Tajikistan, the Kyrgyz Republic and South Kazakhstan (one of the poorer regions of Kazakhstan). Throughout Central Asia the cotton sector under-performs because of inadequate maintenance of infrastructure and distorted incentive structures, but depressed world prices also affect it negatively. World cotton prices have fallen over the last half century[11], driven in part by technological change and in part by substitution to other fibres, reflecting artificially high prices to consumers of cotton clothing in the major markets as a result of trade barriers. The Multi-fibre Arrangement, and its successor, the Agreement on Textiles and Clothing (ATC) that terminated at the end of 2004, not only reduced demand for textiles and clothing and hence demand for all fibres covered by the ATC, but also discriminated against cotton relative to other fibres[12].

The world cotton price is volatile[13], but it also reflects structural aspects of the world cotton market in which government policies in many large producers encourage over-supply, depressing world prices to the detriment of more efficient poor-country producers, including Central Asia. Producer-price support has increased, especially since 1985 when the United States shifted from stockpiling to price supports. In the 2001/02 season US producer prices were 91 per cent higher than world prices. In Greece and Spain they were 144 per cent and 184 per cent above world prices. Direct assistance to cotton production amounted to $2.3 billion in the United States and $0.8 billion in the EU. Other OECD producers (Turkey and Mexico) provided much smaller amounts[14]. Estimates of the effects of removing these production and export subsidies go as high as a 71 per cent increase in cotton prices (using 2001/02 as the base year), and a 6 per cent increase in the volume of Uzbekistan's cotton exports[15].

ISBN 92-64-01442-X © OECD 2005

Other areas where OECD sectoral policies reduce world prices with negative consequences for Central Asian exports primarily concern Kazakhstan, whose non-oil economy is the most diversified in the region. Grains, coal and iron and steel are all export industries, although since the Soviet era they have declined both in absolute size and relative to the now-dominant energy sector. OECD environmental policies could harm Kazakhstan if conservation measures reduced energy demand, pulling down world oil and coal prices. The outcome of Russia's WTO accession negotiations in which natural gas pricing is a key issue also could have implications for the value of gas exports from Kazakhstan and Turkmenistan.

Dogs That Didn't Bark

This volume makes little mention of security or terrorism, but they are major issues in some OECD countries' dealings with Central Asia. There also is little mention of health, gender equity or environmental sustainability, perhaps because East Asian countries placed little emphasis on these goals, which have received greater prominence post-MDG. They are also ignored in practice in Central Asia, even though the Aral Sea is one of the world's great environmental catastrophes.

Concluding Remarks

The Central Asian countries can learn much from East Asia about economic development, most clearly the benefits of openness. They have less to learn about OECD policy coherence, mainly because they are minor players in the global economy and so distant from the OECD markets that the macroeconomic links described in Chapter 2 are far smaller than for East Asia. OECD policies towards Central Asia are similarly Lilliputian. Given the structure of the Central Asian economies the only big links between OECD policies and Central Asian countries' economic performance work through the markets for the small number of commodities exported from Central Asia. Cotton is the most significant, and OECD trade and farm-support policies are extremely harmful. The negative effects of restrictions on clothing imports into OECD markets and of cotton price supports for OECD producers far outweigh developmental benefits from aid or through any other channel[16].

ISBN 92-64-01442-X © OECD 2005

Notes

1. This chapter covers Kazakhstan, the Kyrgyz Republic, Tajikistan, Turkmenistan and Uzbekistan. Much of the analysis would also apply to the Caucasus countries, although they have differing economic structures, and to Afghanistan and Mongolia, although they have longer histories as independent nations. For background on the five countries, see Pomfret (2003).

2. Bolaky and Freund (2004) find that in heavily regulated economies the growth/openness relationship is insignificant, but in other economies it is significantly positive.

3. Manufacturing FDI has mainly involved production for domestic markets. There have been very few greenfield FDI projects; the largest is the Daewoo car factory in Uzbekistan. Claims have been made that Daewoo aims to sell in the wider regional market and even in South Asia, but is thwarted by trade barriers and lack of transit and trade facilitation in the neighbours of landlocked Uzbekistan; to date, sales have been almost entirely in the domestic market.

4. More details are in the paper prepared for the OECD Regional Trade Forum in Almaty on 3-4 June 2004, "Role of Multilateral and Regional Trade Disciplines in the Central Asian Countries" (CCNM/TD(2004)6).

5. Chapter 9 identifies a similar pattern with respect to FDI, which recovered immediately after the crisis in Thailand, plummeted in Indonesia and was constant in the Philippines.

6. Chapter 8 emphasises the importance of structural weaknesses in the crisis countries and draws as the two major lessons: *i)* the need to manage financial globalisation; and *ii)* "… emerging market economies need to strengthen their economic systems".

7. At a January 2003 conference on the seven poorest Soviet successor states (the CIS-7) organised by the Swiss government and the multilateral institutions, both sides accepted shared blame for the overexposure of the poor countries to official debt; see Shiells and Sattar (2004).

8. Apart from a one-off initial emigration of people with German blood, there has been little emigration from Central Asia to OECD countries like that described in Chapter 12 for East Asia. Permanent and temporary emigration has been important for Kazakhstan, the Kyrgyz Republic and Tajikistan, but it is overwhelmingly to Russia.

ISBN 92-64-01442-X © OECD 2005

9. GSP treatment is not universally granted. All five countries are excluded from the Australian System of Tariff Preferences, and Tajikistan and Turkmenistan are not in the US GSP scheme. None of the five countries is accorded the additional benefits granted to least-developed countries in the schemes of Canada, the EU, Japan and the United States. Their UN classification as landlocked developing countries rather than as least-developed countries reflects that, although they meet the first two conditions for least-developed country status (low per capita incomes and high economic vulnerability), none of them meets the third necessary condition (weak human assets).

10. China, however, did impose anti-dumping duties on steel from Kazakhstan in January 2004.

11. In January 1952 the price was $1.05 per kilo and in January 2002 96 US cents, an approximately 80 per cent decline in the real price (Baffes, 2004, Table F.5).

12. Will Martin estimated in 1996 that the MFA imposed an implicit tax of 20 per cent on cotton relative to other fibres, and that ending the MFA would increase the world price of cotton by 4 per cent (quoted in Baffes, 2004, p. 18).

13. The world price increased from US$1.31/kg in January 1992 to a peak of US$2.53 in May 1995 before falling to US$0.97 in December 1999, which had a dramatic impact on Uzbekistan. Helped by the buoyant cotton prices of the first half of the 1990s Uzbekistan weathered the transitional recession better than any other former Soviet republic, but when prices fell the government panicked and in October 1996 introduced exchange controls that became an obstacle to future long-term economic development.

14. The International Cotton Advisory Committee estimates that global support for cotton producers in 2001/2 was US$5.8 billion, including an estimated (but doubtful) US$1.3 billion in China (Baffes, 2004.). Australia is recorded as having little or no government intervention, although under pricing of irrigation water subsidises water-intensive crops like cotton.

15. Baffes (2004), pp. 18-19.

16. Using Baffes' (2004) upper-bound figure of a 71 per cent increase in the world price and a 6 per cent increase in the volume of Uzbekistan's cotton exports, removing OECD price supports would increase the value of Uzbekistan's merchandise exports by about a quarter and GDP by about five percentage points. In Tajikistan, although cotton output is only a tenth of Uzbekistan's, GDP would increase by six percentage points, and in Turkmenistan it would increase by three percentage points. Eliminating the MFA/ATC would increase Uzbekistan's export value by only 1 per cent, with much smaller GDP impact.

Bibliography

BAFFES, J. (2004), "Cotton: Market Setting, Trade Policies, and Issues", World Bank Policy Research Working Paper 3218, World Bank, Washington, D.C., February.

BOLAKY, B. and C. FREUND (2004), "Trade Regulation and Growth", World Bank Policy Research Working Paper No .3255, World Bank, Washington, D.C., March.

OECD (2004), Document CCNM/TD(2004)6, prepared for the OECD Regional Trade Forum in Almaty on 3-4 June on the "Role of Multilateral and Regional Trade Disciplines in the Central Asian Countries".

POMFRET, R. (2003), "Central Asia since 1991: The Experience of the New Independent States", OECD Development Centre Working Paper No. 212, Paris, OECD, July.

SHIELLS, C. and S. SATTAR (eds.) (2004), *The Low-Income Countries of the Commonwealth of Independent States: Progress and Challenges in Transition*, International Monetary Fund, Washington, D.C.

ISBN 92-64-01442-X © OECD 2005

Chapter 16

Latin America and the OECD: How Can Bilateral Support Help Improve Performance?

Barbara Stallings

Abstract

This chapter looks at the potential role of OECD countries in helping to improve Latin America's economic performance. It begins by stressing the fact that the Latin American countries have already left behind their days of closed economies and pervasive state intervention and turned themselves towards the market, following the structural reforms introduced in the 1980s and 1990s. Given this clear break, a key question to be asked here concerns the role of OECD countries in the context of the "new economic model" in the region. The chapter then examines the links between the Latin American economies and OECD-country policies from the economic, social and political points of view. It concludes that coherence could be improved in OECD-country policies *vis-à-vis* Latin America. Problems are of two types. Firstly, in the economic area, some OECD-country policies promote growth, investment, and exports, while others hinder them. Secondly, the lack of channels for OECD-country policy input causes missed opportunities to advance important social goals. It also undermines support for Latin America's new economic policies and for the democratic political system — a crucial component of development.

ISBN 92-64-01442-X

While East Asia has been an economic success story in the post-World War II period, Latin America has been much less so, especially in the last two decades. In the years between 1965 and 1980, Latin American countries grew rapidly (around 6 per cent per year), but their East Asian counterparts dideven better (over 7 per cent per year, although from a low starting point). Other variables also contributed to the performance gap. Latin America's exports grew slowly and tended to concentrate in natural resources with their well-documented price volatility. Saving and investment rates were substantially lower in Latin America than East Asia while inflation wasgenerally higher. Equally important, inequality has always been high in Latin America, and it did not improve much in the early post-war years. Closely related to inequality and poverty, insufficient attention was paid to human capital development in general and education in particular[1].

These differences notwithstanding, it was common in the early 1980s — when scholars began to take an interest in East Asia-Latin America comparisons — to focus on four so-called newly industrialising economies (NIEs) and their successful development trajectories. These were Korea and Chinese Taipei, Brazil and Mexico[2]. Soon, however, the picture changed dramatically. Latin America entered the "lost decade" of the debt crisis, and per capita GDP stagnated for nearly ten years, while East Asia raced ahead. Although things appeared to look up for Latin America in the first half of the 1990s, ironically the Asian crisis proved to be more long lasting in Latin America than in Asia itself, and a new "lost half decade" characterised the region from 1998 to 2003. (See the Appendix to this chapter for data comparing long-term economic trends in Latin America and East Asia.)

The typical explanation for the divergence between the East Asian and Latin American performance has been the latter's focus on import-substitution industrialisation, while the former emphasised export promotion. There is some truth to this story, but less than is commonly believed. On the one hand, import substitution provided a useful base for East Asia's later export drive. On the other hand, a number of Latin American countries combined import substitution and export promotion[3]. In any case, Latin America has now left behind its days of closed economies and pervasive, if inefficient, state intervention. The packages of structural reforms introduced in the 1980s and 1990s opened the economies and turned them toward the market[4]. Given this clear break, the rest of this brief chapter will concentrate on the role of OECD countries in the context of the "new economic model" in the region.

Before beginning the analysis, two introductory points need mention. First, much more than in East Asia, there has been a tendency to view foreign influence in Latin America as a negative factor. Indeed, a whole literature

ISBN 92-64-01442-X © OECD 2005

developed in the 1970s around the alleged evils of "dependency"[5]. At the same time, excessive attention has been devoted to foreign influence rather than to how Latin America could help itself. Second, before discussing how OECD countries might help the region to improve its performance, it is necessary to distinguish among OECD members. Far and away the main OECD influence in Latin America comes from the United States, which has a particular approach that may not characterise the rest of the OECD. Some European countries have also been influential, especially in the Southern Cone area (Brazil, Argentina, Chile, and Uruguay). Japan, while important in the past, especially in Brazil with its large population of Japanese descendants, retreated during the recession that began in 1990.

Table 16.1 provides a summary of three clusters of performance variables in Latin America — economic, social and political — and their relationship to the OECD countries. In the economic cluster (growth, exports, investment/savings), three types of OECD-country influence are important. They include macro/financial policies, foreign direct investment and market access; some of the impacts have been positive, others negative. In the social cluster (income distribution, poverty, human capital), the same economic variables have had an indirect impact, while official development assistance (ODA) might be expected to play a more direct role. In reality, few Latin American countries receive much ODA because of their relatively high per capita incomes. Finally, in the political cluster (governance, democracy, corruption), the main point is again the lack of channels for OECD-country policy intervention, despite their crucial importance for development and the potential for positive impact by OECD actors. The following pages focus on the economic variables, then turn to the need for greater social and political support.

Table 16.1. **Links between Latin American Performance and OECD Influence**

Performance Clusters	OECD Influence
Economic	Macro/financial policy
*Growth	Foreign investment
*Exports	Trade/market access
*Investment/savings	
Social	Economic policies (as above)
*Income distribution	Official development assistance (limited)
*Poverty	
*Human capital	
Political	Social outcomes (as above)
*Governance	Official development assistance (limited)
*Democracy	
*Corruption	

ISBN 92-64-01442-X © OECD 2005

One of the most controversial aspects of foreign influence in Latin America today concerns macroeconomic and financial policies, including the so-called new international financial architecture. Here all of the OECD countries are involved, as are the international financial institutions controlled by the OECD governments. The issue at stake is economic and financial volatility, which is harmful to all economies but especially to those in the developing world, since they tend to be smaller and more fragile. Research has shown that Latin America is even more prone to volatility than are Asia and other regions[6].

The volatility problem has two main aspects. One concerns spillover effects from world economic expansion, which affects Latin American economic growth through several channels. One works through the impact on exports, both volumes and prices. An important recent example was seen in Mexico in the last few years. Mexico sends nearly 90 per cent of its exports to the United States, and those exports had been growing over 16 per cent annually in the late 1990s. When the US economy went into recession, Mexico's exports contracted, helping to depress its growth rate from 5 per cent in 1997-2000 to 0.6 per cent in 2001-03. The cyclic downturn thus was much more severe in Mexico than in the United States. Another channel is interest rates. As international interest rates fall, Latin America — together with other emerging markets — becomes more attractive to foreign investors, but the opposite is also the case, which can produce very strong cyclical behaviour.

The other aspect of the volatility problem, which derives from policy rather than spillover, concerns capital flows. The United States in particular and other OECD governments to a lesser extent have insisted that Latin American countries open their capital accounts so that foreign investors can have access to their markets. The problem is that capital flows can be very large with respect to the size of local economies, and they can reverse at any hint of a problem in Latin America itself or in the international economy more generally. In addition, they tend to cause appreciation of the exchange rate and thus undermine export capacity — leading to the need for more capital inflows. In the worst cases, a "twin crisis" can result, which wreaks havoc on the banking sector, creates serious current-account problems, and slashes economic growth[7]. Given these difficulties that make it very hard to conduct sensible macroeconomic policy, some countries have tried to limit capital inflows, despite recognition that foreign capital can play a valuable role in development (especially for countries with low saving rates). Chile has taken the lead, although others have also moved in the same policy

ISBN 92-64-01442-X © OECD 2005

direction. While the IMF came to recognise the value of the capital controls, the United States insisted that Chile severely restrict use of the tool in the free trade agreement recently signed[8].

In response to the problem of capital flow volatility following the Asian crisis, there was a good deal of discussion about the need for a "new international financial architecture". Proposals were made to regulate international capital flows better and to establish new rules for crisis management (including the use of collective action clauses and international bankruptcy proceedings). As the Asian crisis came under control, however, the need for a new framework moved onto a back burner. None of the OECD countries has been willing to take the lead in looking for a solution, so the next crisis will again occur without policies in place to deal with it.

The capital-flow volatility problem centres mainly on portfolio flows, especially short-term flows. Foreign direct investment (FDI) has different characteristics and thus a different set of advantages and disadvantages. Latin American countries have dramatically changed their view on FDI. In the 1970s, it was considered the worst type of foreign capital, said to displace local firms from profitable investment opportunities and to undermine the power of local governments. As a consequence, many multinational corporation subsidiaries were nationalised in Latin America in that era. With the adoption of more open economies in the region in the last 15 years, however, FDI is now seen as the best kind of foreign capital — less volatile than portfolio flows, a good source of investment and accompanied by access to modern technology and markets in the multinationals' home countries or in third countries.

Data on capital flows to Latin America since the early 1990s show FDI as far and away the most positive type of flow. Other kinds of foreign capital became negative after the Asian crisis, but FDI continued to record large inflows, although they have shrunk in the last few years. Table 16.2 compares net capital inflows for Latin America and East Asia in 1991-2003[9]. During the period as a whole, total inflows were identical at an annual average of $75 billion; this amounted to 4.7 per cent of GDP in Latin America and 5 per cent in East Asia. Moreover, most of the components were also very similar, including FDI. FDI was 62 per cent of total capital flows in each case. Not surprisingly, the sub-periods varied more than the overall period. Latin America received less capital in the early 1990s, when the region was recovering from the 1980s debt crisis, while the same occurred for East Asia after its financial crisis in the second half of the 1990s. In the early years of the current decade, patterns were again quite similar.

Table 16.2. **Net Resource Flows to Latin America and East Asia, 1991-2003**
($ billion)

Region	1991-1995	1996-2000	2001-2003	1991-2003
Latin America	66.0	99.9	48.0	74.9
Long-term debt[a]	18.2	32.2	-0.4	19.3
Short-term debt	12.0	-9.0	-6.6	-0.4
FDI	20.2	69.6	50.4	46.2
Portfolio equity	12.5	4.2	1.7	6.8
Grants	3.1	2.9	2.9	3.0
Memo: GDP[b]	1 292	1 859	1 703	1 605
East Asia[c]	95.2	67.3	54.3	75.0
Long-term debt[a]	25.9	15.2	-11.1	13.2
Short-term debt	20.9	-8.7	6.8	6.3
FDI	34.5	54.7	53.3	46.6
Portfolio equity	11.5	3.6	3.1	6.5
Grants	2.4	2.5	2.2	3.4
Memo: GDP[b]	1 271	1 535	1 784	1 491

Notes: *a)* Public and private sources, excluding IMF.
b) GDP for 1991-1996, GNI for 1997-2003.
c) World Bank definition (excludes NIEs).
Source: Calculated from World Bank (1999, 2004*a*).

Despite the similarities in the volume of capital inflows, there were significant differences in the role that foreign capital played in the two regions. The most useful comparison for Latin America is with Southeast Asia and China, since — unlike Japan and the NIEs — all have a strong natural resource base in their factor endowments. Following the readjustment of international exchange rates in 1985, Japan (and later the Asian NIEs) began shifting capital to Southeast Asia both to provide cheaper goods for their own home markets and to export to third markets. As a consequence, Southeast Asia became integrated into the production networks directed by its northern neighbours and substantially increased its manufactured exports, although it continued to sell natural-resource based products as well.

In Latin America and especially in South America the situation has been very different. The main trade-FDI nexus involves natural resources, but even there the link is weak because the largest natural resource exporters are state-owned. Traditionally, foreign capital came to the region to produce for the domestic market, given the high tariff barriers. After the new economic model was implemented, the rising volume of FDI came in to buy out existing

ISBN 92-64-01442-X © OECD 2005

firms, either through privatisation of former public-sector enterprises or to purchase locally owned private firms[10]. In addition, much of the new investment has been in natural resources (thus continuing the region's specialisation in export products that lack dynamism) or in non-tradeables (especially utilities, including telecoms and electricity). Less has gone into the industrial sector, and a special lack has been investment in high-technology export industries.

A different situation exists in Mexico and to a lesser extent in Central America. US firms have been eager to incorporate Mexico into northern production chains, just as Japanese firms have done in Southeast Asia. In addition, Japanese and European corporations have set up subsidiaries in Mexico to gain access to the US market, particularly in electronics and automobiles. As a result, Mexico now accounts for more than half of all the exports of Latin America, with a high proportion in manufactured products. With the exception of Costa Rica, where the Intel Corporation undertook investments that have incorporated the country into several high-value production networks, most of the Central American cases involve garments and other low value-added products. Nonetheless, manufactured exports are much more prominent in Central America than in South America.

A third source of OECD influence on Latin American economies comes through trade more generally, beyond the trade-FDI relationship. Trade has increased substantially in Latin America since the new economic model was adopted. Two important aspects of the new model focused on trade: liberalisation of imports and promotion of exports. In 1990, for example, exports were 13 per cent of GDP, and they rose to 22 per cent by 2002. Imports were 11 per cent and 21 per cent, respectively. Nearly three quarters of these goods (and, increasingly, services) are sold in OECD markets, implying an important contribution to Latin American development[11].

Nonetheless, two types of market access problems are significant. One is access to the markets of OECD countries for both agricultural and industrial goods. The other involves export subsidies for particular OECD agricultural products. OECD countries have behaved somewhat differently in using these barriers, with different implications for Latin American economies. In Japan, Latin American exporters have had tremendous difficulty breaking into markets for anything except raw materials, typically exported to their home country by Japanese firms. Europe has had barriers against both industrial and agricultural products, in addition to the well-known agricultural subsidies. The United States has accepted large amounts of Latin American industrial exports as well as raw materials. In the US case, the problems for Latin American exporters come through subsidies for US agriculture and high tariffs on particular items heavily backed by special interests (e.g. steel, textiles, sugar and orange juice). Together, these barriers limit the expansion of Latin American exports and in turn limit economic growth.

Part of Latin America's recent export growth has come about through free trade agreements (FTAs). Chile and Mexico have been especially active in signing such agreements, and both now have FTAs with the United States and the European Union. The EU is also negotiating a trade agreement with Mercosur (Brazil, Argentina, Uruguay, and Paraguay), and Japan has completed an agreement with Mexico. In addition, the United States has provided special access to groups of countries that have political relevance, such as the Caribbean Basin Initiative (to seek allies during the period of civil wars in Central America) and the Andean Trade Preference Act (closely tied to the fight against drugs). It now seeks an agreement with the entire region through a Free Trade Area of the Americas (FTAA). It is important to note that trade integration in Latin America differs substantially from that in Asia. On the one hand, it is based on formal agreements among governments rather than market processes. On the other hand, many of the main agreements are between developed and developing countries, meaning that the power imbalances are significant. Latin Americans are especially wary of negotiations with the United States, considering them to be very one-sided. The United States wants to open Latin American markets to service exports and obtain protection for intellectual property, but without ceding to Latin American demands, especially with respect to agriculture, and without any special support for the less developed partner(s) in the agreements. As a consequence, trade negotiations have become increasingly contentious, and the FTAA seems unlikely to be signed in anything like its original form, again limiting Latin America's export potential.

Has there been coherence across these policy areas in individual OECD countries and/or across OECD countries? To answer this question, it is necessary to start by noting that OECD countries were firm backers of the move toward more stable, open, market-oriented economies in the Latin American region[12]. In this context, at least two types of capacity have utmost importance. One is the ability to manage macroeconomic balances in a given economy. The lack of follow-through toward the creation of a new international financial architecture is detrimental to macroeconomic stability in Latin America and developing economies more generally. At the national level, the opposition of OECD governments, especially the United States, to

 ISBN 92-64-01442-X

market-based controls on capital inflows — which, in times of capital surges, have proved helpful in supplementing other policies geared toward promoting macroeconomic stability — is not helpful to the new economic model. The other type of capacity that countries need to function in an open economy involves exports. In this respect, the picture is mixed. In some cases, FDI has been quite helpful in the drive to expand exports (as well as to support growth through investment), and OECD markets have generally been open. Yet agricultural subsidies and high tariffs on certain important export products certainly are not consistent with the new model.

At the same time, it is important to acknowledge that many of Latin America's economic problems do not come from the outside. Latin American countries themselves — public and private sectors alike — need to do more to make the region more competitive. They have taken some important steps. Inflation and deficits are much lower than they were in earlier years, major structural reforms have been undertaken and exports have increased. At least three areas need improvement in coming years. First, saving and investment rates must be raised; the current low levels of investment will not support sustained higher growth rates, and low saving rates increase the need for foreign capital. Second, institutions must be strengthened, including the rule of law as well as court systems, regulatory agencies, financial systems and so on. Third, skills must be developed, through the education system but also through training programmes. Without these prerequisites, Latin America will never become able to compete with Asia[13].

Another type of inconsistency goes beyond the economic sphere to the social and political aspects of development. Slow and volatile economic growth in Latin America — partially attributable to the behaviour of OECD actors — has contributed to the creation of serious social problems in the region. While East Asian countries before the crisis could get by with low levels of social expenditure because of high growth rates and the willingness of families to provide resources when necessary, neither has been present in Latin America. Moreover, inequality, generally acknowledged as higher in Latin America than in any other part of the world, has probably become worse under the new model[14]. On the one hand, large firms have been better able to take advantage of new opportunities than their smaller counterparts. On the other, skilled workers have been able to get higher salaries and better working conditions, while unskilled labour has seen its position eroded and its job security decline. Volatility and financial crises are also known to hit the poor especially hard[15].

Given these trends, Latin American governments had to expand their social spending greatly just to stay abreast of new problems. They did so between 1990 and 1997, and poverty fell as a result; social services also improved. The recession of 1998-2003, however, undermined these positive trends[16]. It would be highly desirable for OECD governments to help in this area. ODA might be thought a useful vehicle for doing so, but most Latin American countries receive only marginal amounts of it because of their relatively high per capita incomes. Table 16.3 provides data on the characteristics of ODA in the region; Panel A shows the top ten donors, while Panel B shows the top ten recipients. As can be seen, the United States provides almost one-quarter of all ODA, followed by Japan. On the recipient side, most of the leading countries are among the smaller, poorer ones; Peru and Colombia figure prominently because of US anti-drug programmes. That the small, poor countries should be the leading recipients is appropriate. In addition, it is also positive that Latin America has a larger share of ODA going to social uses than any other region[17]. Nonetheless, the lack of significant amounts of ODA going to most countries means that new mechanisms must be sought for OECD influence in the region. At least three elements are involved: greater financial assistance; technical advice to increase the efficiency of social spending; and pressure on Latin American governments to maintain social spending when budget cuts have to be made. Their absence means that social problems have festered and undermined support for the new economic model.

Table 16.3. **Official Development Assistance to Latin America, 2002**

Panel A. Top Ten Donors			Panel B. Top Ten Recipients		
Donor	Amount ($ million)	Share (%)	Recipient	Amount ($ million)	Share (%)
United States	1 225	23	Bolivia	681	13
Japan	592	11	Nicaragua	517	10
Spain	414	8	Peru	491	9
Germany	355	7	Colombia	441	8
European Union	315	6	Honduras	435	8
Netherlands	313	6	Brazil	376	7
United Kingdom	283	5	Guatemala	249	5
World Bank (IDA)	248	5	El Salvador	233	4
France	175	3	Ecuador	216	4
IDB Special Fund	167	3	Dom. Rep.	157	3
Other	1 131	22	Other	1 421	27
Total	5 218	100	Total	5 218	100

Source: DAC, "Net Aid by Region: Latin America."

ISBN 92-64-01442-X © OECD 2005

Moreover, social problems also undermine support for democracy as a system of government. A recent study by the United Nations Development Programme clearly demonstrates this. It reports that "... growing frustration — because of lack of opportunity and high levels of inequality, poverty and social exclusion — is resulting in loss of confidence in the political system, radical actions and crises of governability, which threaten the stability of the democratic system"[18]. More specifically, public opinion surveys conducted in 18 countries indicate that 55 per cent of Latin Americans would support authoritarian governments over democracies if this would "resolve" their economic problems[19]. These surveys are backed by political fact. Four presidents have been forced to resign before completing their terms in the last few years, and several others are under serious threat. While a decade ago it appeared that Latin America was ahead of East Asia on the political front, the balance is now uncertain.

The UNDP study also raises more specific issues of governance that need addressing in Latin America. The requirement for functioning institutions has been widely recognised even if it has proved difficult to upgrade them sufficiently. As mentioned earlier, they range from judicial systems to school systems to agencies to regulate newly privatised banks and utilities. At the same time, political institutions are under fire. Political parties in particular have decayed in most countries in the region, replaced by mass movements that have no way to channel demands into the executive, legislative, or judicial processes. Part of the problem is that parties and governing institutions are widely perceived as corrupt, which also undermines support for democracy. The OECD countries with their long history of functioning democracies and market economies could certainly provide help in strengthening political and economic institutions. As in the social area, a number of OECD countries include good governance as an element in their bilateral ODA programmes, but instruments to transmit these important policy concerns are missing in Latin America given the relative lack of ODA.

New channels need to be found. Given the long history of conflictual relations between Latin America and the United States — the region's biggest investor, trading partner and donor — such channels are perhaps best sought through regional and international organisations. Fortunately, several such organisations pursue both the social and political agendas. At the regional level, they include the Inter-American Development Bank, the Organization of American States, the UN Economic Commission for Latin America and the Caribbean, and the Latin American Division of the World Bank. OECD governments would be wise to work through them, providing both resources

ISBN 92-64-01442-X

and ideas based on their own experience. An example is a recent seminar co-sponsored by the European Commission and the IADB on "Social Cohesion in Latin America and the Caribbean"[20]. A complementary path would be to look for ways to reinforce steps taken by the Latin American governments themselves, such as the efforts of the "Rio Group" to strengthen democracy and reduce poverty.

In summary, coherence could be improved in OECD policies with respect to the Latin American region. Problems are of two types. In the economic area some OECD policies promote growth, investment, and exports while others hinder them. The lack of channels for OECD policy input causes missed opportunities to advance important social goals. It also undermines support for Latin America's new economic policies and for the democratic political system – a crucial component of development.

ISBN 92-64-01442-X © OECD 2005

ANNEX

Economic Indicators for Latin America and East Asia, 1965-2003

Indicator	Latin America	East Asia
GDP growth rates		
1965-1980	6.0	7.3
1980-1990	1.6	7.8
1990-2000	3.3	7.7
2000-2003	0.3	7.0
Export growth rate[a]		
1965-1980	-1.0	8.5
1980-1990	3.0	9.8
1990-2000	8.7	12.1
2000-2003	2.0	12.7
Savings rate[b]		
1965	22	22
1990	22	35
2000	20	35
2002	22	37
Inflation[c]		
1965-1980	31.4	9.3
1980-1990	192.1	6.0
1990-2000	84.1	7.7
2000-2002	7.8	2.6
Inequality[d]		
1960s	53.2	37.4
1970s	49.1	39.9
1980s	49.8	38.7
1990s	49.3	38.1

Notes: *a)* Merchandise exports only for 1965-1990, goods and services for 1990-2003.
b) Gross domestic savings as share of GDP.
c) Consumer price index.
d) Gini index (varies between 0 and 1, where higher is more unequal).

Sources: World Bank (1992) for GDP growth, export growth, savings, and inflation (1965-90); World Bank (2004*b*) for GDP growth, export growth, and savings (1990-2002/03); IMF (2003) for inflation (1990-2002); Deininger and Squire (1996) for inequality.

ISBN 92-64-01442-X

Notes

1. Like Asia, Latin America is a very diverse region — in size, per capita income, literacy, governance and so on. The points made in this chapter are most typical of the larger, more developed countries in the region (Mexico, Brazil, Argentina, Chile, Colombia, Peru, and Venezuela). Of particular note, only the smaller, poorer countries have received much ODA, which is an important issue in the last part of the chapter.

2. See, for example, Gereffi and Wyman (1990), one of the earliest and most influential of these comparative studies.

3. On Latin America's postwar experience with industrialisation, see Cárdenas *et al.* (2000).

4. On the reforms, see Stallings and Peres (2000).

5. The most influential work on dependency is Cardoso and Faletto (1979). Despite this intellectual background, Cardoso, a well-known sociologist, later went on to become President of Brazil and initiated many market-oriented policies.

6. See, for example, Inter-American Development Bank (1995).

7. See Kaminsky and Reinhart (1999) for a discussion of twin crises in Asia and Latin America. Ironically, capital account volatility problems seem to be more frequent in countries that have been most successful in their economic policy and growth performance; see Ffrench-Davis (2001).

8. For a critique, see Birdsall (2003). Some misunderstanding exists about the trajectory of Chile's capital controls. Since they focus specifically on capital inflows, they are redundant when capital flows are scarce. Thus, in September 1998, the rate was lowered to zero, but the instrument was maintained for future use, if necessary.

9. The data for East Asia exclude the NIEs, because the World Bank considers that they are no longer developing countries. Thus, the East Asian bloc is mainly Southeast Asia plus China. As will be explained below, this group is the most comparable to Latin America because of similar factor endowments.

ISBN 92-64-01442-X © OECD 2005

10. This type of transaction is investment from the point of view of the firm, but not of the host country. Calculations are difficult to make, but it is estimated that less than half of FDI has been of the "greenfield" type since the early 1990s. See ECLAC, *Foreign Investment in Latin America and the Caribbean* (various years).

11. ECLAC (2004*b*).

12. The existence of the "Washington Consensus", which many see as the blueprint for the reforms, was a clear indication of the support of the United States and the international financial institutions for the policy changes. See Williamson (1990).

13. Several regional organisations have been making similar proposals. See, for example, IADB (2001) and ECLAC (2002, 2004*a*).

14. Research on East Asia has changed the prevailing view on the relationship between growth and inequality. Whereas it was previously thought that growth required inequality (to provide savings and investment), it is now argued that inequality hinders growth (because of lack of skills). On the relationship between the two in Latin America and East Asia, see Stallings *et al.* (2000).

15. See Cline (2002).

16. For data and analysis of social spending, see ECLAC, *Social Panorama of Latin America* (various years).

17. DAC: "Net Aid by Region: Latin America".

18. UNDP (2004: 23); author's translation.

19. UNDP (2004: 137, table 46).

20. EC/IADB (2003).

ISBN 92-64-01442-X

Bibliography

BIRDSALL, N. (2003), "Chile FTA and Capital Flows: A Bad Precedent?", Center for Global Development, Washington, D.C.

CÁRDENAS, E., J.A. OCAMPO and R. THORP (2000), *An Economic History of Twentieth-Century Latin America, Vol. 3 (Industrialization and the State in Latin America: The Postwar Years)*, Palgrave, New York, NY.

CARDOSO, F.H. and E. FALETTO (1979), *Dependency and Development in Latin America*, University of California Press, Berkeley, CA.

CLINE, W. (2002), "Financial Crises and Poverty in Emerging Market Economies", Working Paper No. 8, Center for Global Development, Washington, D.C.

DEININGER, K. and L. SQUIRE (1996), "A New Data Set Measuring Income Inequality", *World Bank Economic Review*, 10:3.

DEVELOPMENT ASSISTANCE COMMITTEE (DAC), "Net Aid by Region: Latin America", OECD web site.

ECONOMIC COMMISSION FOR LATIN AMERICA AND THE CARIBBEAN (ECLAC) (2002), *Globalization and Development*, Santiago, ECLAC, Santiago, Chile.

ECONOMIC COMMISSION FOR LATIN AMERICA AND THE CARIBBEAN (ECLAC) (2004*a*), *Productive Development in Open Economies*, ECLAC, Santiago, Chile.

ECONOMIC COMMISSION FOR LATIN AMERICA AND THE CARIBBEAN (ECLAC) (2004*b*), *Statistical Yearbook for Latin America and the Caribbean*, ECLAC, Santiago, Chile, online version.

ECONOMIC COMMISSION FOR LATIN AMERICA AND THE CARIBBEAN (ECLAC) (annual), *Foreign Investment in Latin America and the Caribbean*, ECLAC, Santiago, Chile.

ECONOMIC COMMISSION FOR LATIN AMERICA AND THE CARIBBEAN (ECLAC) (annual) *Social Panorama of Latin America*, ECLAC, Santiago, Chile.

EUROPEAN COMMISSION/INTER-AMERICAN DEVELOPMENT BANK (2003), "EC/IADB Seminar on Social Cohesion in Latin America and the Caribbean", Brussels, June 5-6.

ISBN 92-64-01442-X © OECD 2005

FFRENCH-DAVIS, R. (ed.) (2001), *Financial Crises in "Successful" Emerging Economies*, Brookings Institution Press, Washington, D.C.

GEREFFI, G. and D. WYMAN (eds.) (1990), *Manufacturing Miracles: Patterns of Development in Latin America and East Asia*, Princeton University Press, Princeton, NJ.

INTERAMERICAN DEVELOPMENT BANK (IADB) (1995), *Economic and Social Progress, 1995 Report*, IADB, Washington, D.C.

INTERAMERICAN DEVELOPMENT BANK (IADB) (2001), *Economic and Social Progress, 2001 Report*, IADB, Washington, D.C.

INTERNATIONAL MONETARY FUND (2003), *International Financial Statistics*, IMF, Washington, D.C.

KAMINSKY, G. and C. REINHART (1999), "The Twin Crisis: The Causes of Banking and Balance-of-Payments Problems", *American Economic Review*, 89:3.

STALLINGS, B., N. BIRDSALL and J. CLUGAGE (2000), "Growth and Inequality: Do Regional Patterns Redeem Kuznets?", *in* A. SOLIMANO *et al.*, (eds.), *Distributive Justice and Economic Development*, University of Michigan Press, Ann Arbor.

STALLINGS, B. and W. PERES (2000), *Growth, Employment, and Equity: The Impact of the Economic Reforms in Latin America and the Caribbean*, Brookings Institution Press, Washington, D.C.

UNITED NATIONS DEVELOPMENT PROGRAMME (UNDP) (2004), *La democracia en América Latina: Hacia una democracia de cuidadanas y ciudadanos*, UNDP, New York, NY.

WILLIAMSON, J. (ed.) (1990), *Latin American Adjustment: How Much Has Happened?*, Washington DC, Institute for International Economics.

WORLD BANK (1992), *World Development Report*, World Bank, Washington, D.C.

WORLD BANK (1999), *Global Development Finance*, World Bank, Washington, D.C.

WORLD BANK (2004*a*), *Global Development Finance*, World Bank, Washington, D.C.

WORLD BANK (2004*b*), *World Development Indicators*, World Bank, Washington, D.C., online.

List of Contributors

The following list of contributors gives their affiliations at the time of the project.

Richard BARICHELLO	Professor, University of British Columbia, Vancouver.
Yongyuth CHALAMWONG	Research Director for Labor Development, Thailand Development Research Institute Foundation, Bangkok.
Siow Yue CHIA	Senior Research Fellow, Singapore Institute of International Affairs and Regional Coordinator, East Asian Development Network, Singapore.
Menzie D. CHINN	Professor of Public Affairs and Economics, University of Wisconsin, Madison, USA.
Peter DRYSDALE	Professor of Economics, Australian National University, Canberra.
Christopher FINDLAY	Professor of Economics, Australian National University, Canberra.
Kiichiro FUKASAKU	Counsellor, OECD Development Centre, Paris.
Masahiro KAWAI	Professor of Economics, University of Tokyo, Tokyo.
Fukunari KIMURA	Professor of Economics, Keio University, Tokyo.
Zhiyun LI	Ph.D. student, Centre d'Études et de Recherche sur le Développement International (CERDI), Clermont-Ferrand.
Justin Yifu LIN	Director, China Center for Economic Research, Peking University, Beijing.
David O'CONNOR	Chief, Policy Integration and Analysis Branch, United Nations, New York.

Michael PLUMMER	Professor of International Economics, Johns Hopkins University, Bologna.
Richard POMFRET	Professor of Economics, University of Adelaide, Adelaide.
Mustafizur RAHMAN	Research Director, Center for Policy Dialogue, Dhaka.
Hadi SOESASTRO	Executive Director, Centre for Strategic and International Studies, Jakarta.
Barbara STALLINGS	Professor, Brown University, Providence, USA.
Alexandra TRZECIAK-DUVAL	Special Advisor, Policy Coherence for Development, OECD, Paris.
Shujiro URATA	Professor of Economics, Waseda University, Tokyo.
Soogil YOUNG	Chairman, Korea National Strategy Forum, Seoul.

ISBN 92-64-01442-X © OECD 2005

OECD PUBLICATIONS, 2, rue André-Pascal, 75775 PARIS CEDEX 16
PRINTED IN FRANCE
(41 2005 04 1 P) ISBN 92-64-01442-X – No. 54457 2005